Mediated Interpersonal Communication

Mediated interpersonal communication is currently one of the most dynamic areas in communication studies, reflecting how individuals are utilizing technology more and more often in their personal interactions. Organizations also rely increasingly on mediated inter-action for their communication. Responding to this evolution in communication, this timely collection explores how existing and new personal communication technologies facilitate and change interpersonal interactions, establishing a theoretical and methodological foun-dation for future study by offering research on new topics from diverse disciplines.

Chapters offer in-depth examinations of mediated interpersonal communication in various contexts and applications. Contributions come from well-known scholars based around the world, reflecting the strong international interest and work in the area. The multidisciplinary approach bridges interpersonal communication, human–computer inter-action (HCI), human factors, organizational behavior, social psychology, and computer-mediated communication (CMC).

As the leading volume exploring how technology is affecting communication on an inter-personal level, this volume will appeal to scholars and researchers in communication – inter-personal, computer-mediated communication, language and social interaction. It also has much to offer to readers in HCI, organizational behavior, and social psychology. The volume lends itself to use in advanced courses addressing human communication and technology, interpersonal communication, and communication theory as well as computer-mediated communication; technology, media and society; and new communication technologies.

Elly A. Konijn is an associate professor in the Department of Communication Science, Faculty of Social Sciences at the VU University, Amsterdam, where she teaches Interper-sonal Communication and Media Psychology.

Sonja Utz is assistant professor at the Department of Communication Science, Faculty of Social Sciences at the VU University, Amsterdam, where she teaches Organizational Communication and Interpersonal Communication.

Martin Tanis is assistant professor at the Department of Communication Science, Faculty of Social Sciences at the VU University, Amsterdam, where he teaches Organizational Communication and Media Entertainment.

Susan B. Barnes is Director of the Lab for Social Computing and professor at Rochester Institute for Technology, , where she teaches graduate classes and courses in visual commu-nication, advertising, and the Internet.

LEA's Communication series
Jennings Bryant/Dolf Zillmann, General Editors

Selected titles in Journalism (Maxwell McCombs, Advisory Editor) include:

Real Feature Writing
Second edition
Abraham Aamidor

Communicating Uncertainty
Media coverage of new and controversial science
Sharon M. Friedman, Sharon Dunwoody, and Carol L. Rogers

Professional Feature Writing
Fourth edition
Bruce Garrison

The Troubles of Journalism
A critical look at what's right and wrong with the press
Third edition
William A. Hachten

Internet Newspapers
The making of a mainstream medium
Xigen Li

The Two W's of Journalism
The why and what of public affairs reporting
Davis Merritt and Maxwell E. McCombs

The American Journalist in the 21st Century
U.S. news people at the dawn of a new millennium
David H. Weaver, Randal A. Beam, Bonnie J. Brownlee,
Paul S. Voakes, and G. Cleveland Wilhoit

Mediated Interpersonal Communication
Edited by Elly A. Konijn, Sonja Utz, Martin Tanis, and Susan B. Barnes

Mediated Interpersonal Communication

Edited by
Elly A. Konijn, Sonja Utz,
Martin Tanis, and
Susan B. Barnes

Routledge
Taylor & Francis Group

NEW YORK AND LONDON

First published 2008
by Routledge
270 Madison Ave, New York, NY 10016

Simultaneously published in the UK
by Routledge
2 Park Square, Milton Park, Abingdon, Oxon OX14 4RN

Included in the ICA Handbook Series
Routledge is an imprint of the Taylor & Francis Group, an informa business

© 2008 Taylor & Francis

Typeset in Garamond by Bookcraft Ltd, Stroud, Gloucestershire
Printed and bound in the United States of America on acid-free paper by
Walsworth Publishing Company, Marceline, MO

Library of Congress Cataloging in Publication Data
Mediated interpersonal communication / edited by
Elly A. Konijn ... [*et al.*].
     p. cm.
     Includes bibliographical references.
     1. Interpersonal communication. 2. Telematics.
     3. Information technology–Social aspects.
     I. Konijn, Elly, 1959–
     HM1166.M43 2008
     303.48'33–dc22   2007037765

ISBN10: 0-805-86303-6 (hbk)
ISBN10: 0-805-86304-4 (pb)
ISBN10: 0-203-92686-2 (ebk)

ISBN13: 978-0-805-86303-1 (hbk)
ISBN13: 978-0-805-86304-8 (pb)
ISBN13: 978-0-203-92686-4 (ebk)

Contents

Figures

Tables

Contributors

Koos Anderson, Department of Communication Science, VU University, Amsterdam.

Jeremy N. Bailenson, Department of Communication, Stanford University.

Susan B. Barnes, Lab for Social Computing, Rochester Institute of Technology.

Gary Bente, Department of Psychology, University of Cologne.

Jim Blascovich, Department of Psychology, University of California, Santa Barbara.

Karen M. Douglas, Department of Psychology, University of Kent at Canterbury.

Felix Eschenburg, Department of Psychology, University of Cologne.

Rosanna E. Guadagno, Department of Psychology, University of California, Santa Barbara.

Tilo Hartmann, Department of Communication Science, VU University, Amsterdam.

SeungA Jin, Annenberg School for Communication, University of Southern California, Los Angeles.

Younbo Jung, Annenberg School for Communication, University of Southern California, Los Angeles.

Sriram Kalyanaraman, University of North Carolina, Chapel Hill.

Jan Kleinnijenhuis, Department of Communication Science, VU University, Amsterdam.

Christoph Klimmt, Department of Communication, The Johannes Gutenberg University of Mainz.

Elly A. Konijn, Department of Communication Science, VU University, Amsterdam.

Nicole C. Krämer, Department of Computer Science and Applied Cognitive Science, University Duisburg-Essen.

Louis Leung, School of Journalism and Communication, The Chinese University of Hong Kong.

Margaret McLaughlin, Annenberg School for Communication, University of Southern California, Los Angeles.

Dirk Oegema, Department of Communication Science, VU University, Amsterdam.

Wei Peng, Annenberg School for Communication, University of Southern California, Los Angeles.

Melanie D. Polkosky, IBM Media Effects Laboratory, South Florida.

S. Shyam Sundar, Media Effects Research Laboratory, Penn State University.

Martin Tanis, Department of Communication Science, VU University, Amsterdam.

Sonja Utz, Department of Communication Science, VU University, Amsterdam.

Anita van Hoof, Department of Communication Science, VU University, Amsterdam.

Henriette C. Van Vugt, Department of Communication Science, VU University, Amsterdam.

Joseph B. Walther, Department of Communication, Cornell University, Ithaca, New York.

Monica Whitty, School of Psychology, Queen's University, Belfast.

Nick Yee, Department of Communication, Stanford University.

Weirong Zhu, Annenberg School for Communication, University of Southern California, Los Angeles.

Acknowledgments

This book has in itself been an exciting endeavor in mediated interpersonal communication. Many of us, editors, authors, and reviewers, have never met in real life, yet productively worked together in developing the chapters for this volume. And, it must be said, with great pleasure, mutual understanding, and valuable bonding—communication qualities that have been regarded as impossible for mediated forms of interpersonal contact until very recently. We are very grateful to those authors who generously put their thoughts and most recent insights from their research on paper to be shared with us and the readers. Most authors also acted as reviewers for other chapters, as each chapter received at least two blind peer-reviews accompanied by an editorial letter. Thank you so much. In addition, other scholars shared their expertise in reviewing chapters for the present volume and several supportive colleagues contributed in other ways. We would very much like to express our gratitude toward them, among whom (alphabetically): Linda Bathgate, Piet Bakker, Elaine Chan, Jonathan Cohen, Johan Hoorn, Annette Linden, Heather Marshall, Roxanne O'Connell, Jochen Peter, Stacey Spiegel, Rebekah Tukachinsky, Peter Vorderer, and Kevin Wright. Thanks also to the students at the Seminar Mediated Interpersonal Communication 2006 at the VU University Amsterdam who enthusiastically reflected on and discussed earlier drafts of chapters in this volume, and strengthened our belief that this book is timely.

Part I

Bridging the disciplines

Chapter 1

Introduction

How technology affects human interaction

Elly A. Konijn, Sonja Utz, Martin Tanis, and Susan B. Barnes

Communicating with friends and family members via the (cell) phone or email, working in a virtual team, seeking a partner on an online dating site, looking for support in an online social support group, interacting with an automated speech system while booking a flight, getting help from an avatar while visiting an online store, watching "Sex and the City," and perceiving the girls as friends, or spending some time in Second Life—activities like these have become part of everyday life for many people.

A great deal of interpersonal communication is now mediated by technology, but computer-mediated technologies (e.g., sms, chat rooms, msn, email, virtual group work, weblogs, mobile social software) can sometimes facilitate or impede communication and can alter interpersonal interactions. The primary focus of this edited volume, *Mediated Interpersonal Communication*, is on the impact of communication media on interpersonal communication. The book covers a wide range of communication media as well as contexts. The chapters range from private contexts such as communication with family and friends via the cell phone or online dating via recreational contexts such as playing games and parasocial interactions with (new) media characters to professional contexts such as virtual collaboration practices. The chapters deal with more traditional media such as TV, newsgroups, and email, discuss newer trends such as mobile social media, and provide examples of technologies in development such as touch in computer-mediated communication.

Much attention is paid to how new technologies challenge the more traditional definitions of interpersonal communication. Recent trends in mass communication (such as the personalization of messages) and interpersonal communication (such as the increasing use of technical devices to communicate interpersonally) have blurred the boundaries between the two fields, forcing us to develop more sophisticated theories and models. New technologies can be seen as relationship enablers—they not only add new forms of interpersonal communication, but they fundamentally change how individuals interact (e.g. communication with avatars, parasocial interactions).

Despite the widespread everyday use of such media for interpersonal communication, the literature often falls short in discussing the interpersonal value of recent developments in communication technology. Moreover, theory building lags behind the rapid development and adoption of new technologies. Although empirical studies have been conducted in various disciplines, their results have not been integrated into a larger framework. For example, books on interpersonal communication often focus heavily on face-to-face communication, and many scholars in the field see new communication technology as a threat to the discipline of interpersonal communication. Books on computer-mediated communication and human-computer interaction seem to overlook the theories of interpersonal communication. Moreover, the shifting borders between mass communication and interpersonal communication are hardly ever addressed. Thus far, the disciplines of computer-mediated communication (CMC), human-computer interaction (HCI), traditional interpersonal communication, and mass communication have evolved separately. In this book, we aim to bridge the various disciplines that study mediated interpersonal interaction.

Our approach is explicitly multidisciplinary, demonstrating how the integration of disciplines can enrich our insights in the field and provide a solid basis for studying the newest trends. Authors included in the present volume have been selected on the basis of their specific expertise in one of the domains covered by mediated interpersonal communication. The book brings together authors from various disciplines such as communication sciences, (social) psychology, and computer sciences. Many of the authors work at the edges of disciplines, and are often transdisciplinary in their approach. We have included both established scholars and promising young scholars with a bright and innovative vision on their topic of interest, each bringing a unique view from his/her own background.

The goal of the book is to integrate these unique views. On a general theoretical level, it proposes a new definition of interpersonal communication and presents new understandings of the concepts of sender and receiver. As Polkosky (Chapter 3) convincingly shows, traditional definitions of interpersonal communication no longer encompass all instances of the field. For example, the assumption that both interaction partners have to be humans is challenged—by research on virtual humans, but also by research on parasocial interaction. The book covers new forms of mediated interpersonal communication on various levels. Overarching theoretical chapters provide a framework for studying mediated interpersonal communication or suggest new definitions and key concepts. Several chapters deal with more specific aspects, such as communication with avatars or parasocial interactions.

Overview

The book has 18 chapters, divided into three parts. Part I (*Bridging the disciplines*) deals with the general question of how internet and electronic communication devices challenge and change our definition and conception of interpersonal communication. Chapters in Part II (*Technology as relationship enabler*) emphasize how particular characteristics of technology may facilitate interpersonal communication in various forms. Many of these chapters deal with the role of nonverbal communication in interpersonal relationships—more specifically, with how nonverbal communication can be displayed or even transformed in mediated communication. The focus is on communication between two or more people as well as on communication between people and virtual humans. Another chapter focuses on a form of relationship only possible in mediated communication: the parasocial relationship. The last chapter in this section takes a look at the less desirable phenomena found in mediated communication: antisocial communication. Part III (*The appeal of communicating through technology*) further explores what motivates people to interact in a mediated environment and how this may lead users to new ways of interacting and creating social networks. The chapters cover a wide range of mediated environments, from online communities and online dating through multiplayer video games to cell phones.

Part I: Bridging the disciplines

After the introductory Chapter 1, Susan B. Barnes explains in Chapter 2, "Understanding social media from the media ecological perspective," how the media ecological perspective can be used to analyze the effects of social media. Social media are the latest craze on the internet and have become increasingly popular in recent years. The "umbrella concept" describes applications that enable people to interact with each other and build social networks that increase their social capital. Social media include photo sharing sites such as Flickr, social network sites such as meetup. com, collaborative writing as in Wikipedia, or weblogs. Media ecology examines how changes in media forms influence human behavior and cognition. Barnes focuses on the changed conditions of attendance and addresses directional, spatial, social, and political biases. Mediated interpersonal communication introduces new conditions of attendance. People no longer have to be in the same room to communicate. This characteristic of mediated communication influences issues such as presence or the development of trust. Mediated communication is also not bounded by national borders. This can affect politics, for example: people can now organize themselves around certain political topics. Barnes demonstrates, on the basis of several new technologies and a wide area of issues, how the media ecological perspective can aid in understanding the effects of the technological changes.

In Chapter 3, "Machines as mediators: the challenge of technology for interpersonal communication theory and research," Melanie D. Polkosky takes a different perspective. She emphasizes the fact that new technologies challenge our definition of interpersonal communication. The chapter identifies three applied, interdisciplinary fields (computer-mediated communication, augmentative and alternative communication, and speech user interface design) concerned with technology, communication, and social interaction. CMC is the field in which most empirical studies have been carried out. The relative lack of nonverbal cues has been a central issue in many of these studies; and how CMC affects self and other perception and relationships has been examined. Augmentative and alternative communication is a field that has received less attention. This transdisciplinary field uses technology to assist people with a range of disabilities that impair their communication abilities. Research on this topic has mainly focused on how technology improves the lives of these people, but also their relationships with a partner or other people in their social environment such as in school. Speech user interface systems on the other hand fully replace a human partner, mainly in business and customer service applications. In this field, the effects of technology on the relationship with customers have mainly been studied. Polkosky argues that these three fields have much in common, but that they also challenge traditional definitions of interpersonal communication such as the assumption that both partners have to be humans, that interpersonal communication can be clearly separated from other forms of communication (e.g. mass communication), and that the primary goal is relationship building or maintenance. In her chapter, Polkosky addresses these three assumptions and concludes that interpersonal communication should embrace a broader range of communicative partners, interaction types, theoretical approaches, and methodologies.

Shyam Sundar takes yet another perspective in Chapter 4. In his chapter "Self as source: agency and customization in interactive media" he offers a new vision for approaching new media from the point of view of the user. He criticizes the so-called face-to-face (ftf) fallacy—the assumption implicit in many studies that ftf communication is the gold standard against which CMC has to be compared and which it has to live up to. Instead, he argues that agency is the key variable that determines the efficacy. Agency means that the user feels relevant as an actor. Customization allows the individual user to feel unique and distinct. According to Sundar, customization is the most seductive aspect of modern online media because it is always related to an aspect of the self. Relating to the self makes users feel important and valued. The final level of customization is reached when the receiver is the source of communication. The theoretical implications of such a move towards "self as source" are explored from two perspectives— technological and psychological. Several studies are reviewed to assess the psychological impact of imbuing agency in the receiver. Positive as well as negative effects are discussed. Finally, an agency model of customization is presented and directions for future research are suggested.

Part II: Technology as relationship enabler

The chapters in part II focus on aspects of technology that facilitate or change relationships. The first three chapters are closely interrelated; they focus on avatar-mediated communication and discuss how the (trans- formed) display of nonverbal behavior and emotions influences commu- nication and relationships.

In their chapter "Transformed social interaction in mediated inter- personal communication" Jeremy Bailenson, Nick Yee, Jim Blascovich, and Rosanna E. Guadagno show how nonverbal communication and in turn social interaction can be transformed in avatar-mediated commu- nication. They present studies conducted in collaborative virtual envi- ronments (CVEs). CVEs are systems which track verbal and nonverbal signals of multiple interactants and render those signals onto avatars— three-dimensional, digital representations of people in a shared digital space. The authors explore the manners in which CVEs can qualitatively change the nature of remote communication. Interactants in CVEs have the ability to utilize Transformed Social Interaction, systematically filtering the physical appearance and behavioral actions of their avatars, amplifying or suppressing features and nonverbal signals in real time for strategic purposes. For example, a person in a CVE can look directly into the eyes of more than one person at once (augmented gaze), can change his avatar's facial structure to morph features of other interactants into his face (iden- tity capture), and can automatically mimic the nonverbal behaviors of other avatars (digital chameleons). Avatars cannot only transform the presenta- tion of the self but also the sensory abilities of the user. People can take multilateral perspectives, or behavior of communication partners can be displayed explicitly in behavioral flags. Moreover, avatar-mediated commu- nication transforms the situational context (e.g. transformed conformity). Up to now, transformations of the self have received the most attention in empirical studies. The authors describe several of these studies and show that these transformations can have a drastic impact on interactants' persuasive and instructional abilities.

Chapter 6, "Emotions in mediated interpersonal communication: toward modeling emotion in virtual humans" by Elly A. Konijn and Henriette C. Van Vugt, starts with a concise overview of contemporary views in emotion psychology, revealing the complexity of defining emotion. This complexity is partly due to the various perspectives on emotions (e.g., biological theories or cognitive appraisal theories). The authors discuss how emotions are exchanged in ftf interactions as well as in mediated environments, focusing specifically on how modern technologies increasingly allow people to communicate emotions in sophisticated ways through media. After having explained the functions of emotions from a broader emotion psychology framework, Konijn and Van Vugt focus on recent developments in the field of affective computing and virtual humans. In this field, more and more attempts are made to let human–computer interaction look more like interpersonal communication. Because emotions fulfill such an important role in interpersonal communication, modeling emotion in virtual humans has been chosen as a way to make the communication with virtual humans more realistic. The authors describe systems of virtual humans who can express emotions as well as systems which can detect emotions in users. They conclude that more theory-based interdisciplinary research is required to examine which kinds of emotion or emotional responses are especially important in different types of human–computer interactions.

In Chapter 7, "Is there anybody out there? Analyzing the effects of embodiment and nonverbal behavior in avatar-mediated communication," Gary Bente, Nicole C. Krämer, and Felix Eschenburg go into the deeper layers of analyzing the effects of embodiment and nonverbal behavior in avatar-mediated communication. The lack of nonverbal behavior has for a long time been considered as a characteristic of computer-mediated communication; avatar-mediated communication is not bounded to verbal communication. Bente *et al.* argue that the development of avatar-mediated communication has been mostly driven by a fascination with technical feasibility instead of a deeper knowledge about the social and psychological functions of embodiment and nonverbal behavior in net-based communications. The chapter elaborates on basic functional principles of embodiment and nonverbal behavior as established in face-to-face-interaction research and discusses the implications of this knowledge for the uses and effects of avatars. It shows that avatars cannot be regarded as mere extensions of communication channels. Situatedness and co-presence as well as anonymity and plasticity, i.e. the possibility to creatively shape appearance and behavior for strategic purposes (also addressed in the chapter by Bailenson *et al.*), are relevant properties of avatar communication. These properties make it qualitatively different from other communication media, such as video-conferencing. Against this theoretical background, recommendations for experimental research in this field are derived and a novel research platform is introduced.

Whereas avatar-mediated communication is relatively common in chats and games (although most of these venues do not yet systematically transform social interaction), Chapter 8 deals with a technology which is in its infancy and not yet widely implemented: In "Touch in computer-mediated communication," Margaret McLaughlin, Younbo Jung, Wei Peng, SeungA

Jin and Weirong Zhu point out why touch is so basic to interpersonal communication and should therefore also be implemented into mediated communication. Our understanding of social context and the character of our relationships with others is shaped by touch, but its implementation in computer-mediated communication is yet to be realized. The chapter describes ongoing research which seeks to make tactile communication a feature of mediated social interaction. The authors give an overview of the recent studies which enabled people to experience a sense of mutual touch over the internet, stroking the fingers of a remote partner. People were not only able to feel the touch of their remote partner, but they made attributions about the partner's personality based on the way in which they were touched. The authors discuss this and related work and speculate about the necessary conditions for the sense of touch to become an everyday component of computer-mediated communication.

Another intriguing field that challenges traditional definitions of interpersonal communication is that of parasocial interaction. In Chapter 9, "Parasocial interactions and paracommunication with new media characters," Tilo Hartmann provides the compelling argument that parasocial interaction with new media characters can be considered interpersonal communication despite the characters' lack of authenticity. However, in contrast to media characters on TV or the radio, avatars on the internet or nonplayer characters in online games often allow real give-and-take interactions. Therefore, the chapter is guided by the question of whether the user's social engagement with new media characters is still captured by the metaphor of parasocial interactions. A revision of the original concept is suggested. It is argued that parasocial processing is altered by the perceived authenticity of a character. If users feel addressed, parasocial communication sets in (as a simulacrum or an actual give-and-take). Instead of the traditionally highlighted lack of reciprocity, parasocial communication is thought to be affected by the perceived distance from a character: the smaller the distance, the less playful and the more committed the user's communicative behavior. Thus, the concept of parasocial interactions applies to various kinds of (new) media characters in both interactive and non-interactive settings.

In Chapter 10, "Antisocial communication on electronic mail and the internet," Karen M. Douglas addresses the dark side of electronic communication. Next to all the positive examples of relationship building in mediated communication, one should not forget that there are also negative examples. Douglas provides in this chapter an insightful overview of the current state of research concerning antisocial communication in electronic mail and on the internet. The chapter reviews various forms of antisocial communication and classifies them according to the underlying intention to harm. The review addresses flaming, cyberostracism, cyberhate, and online harassment. Cyberostracism is ignoring others in cyberspace, and research has shown that this has negative psychological consequences for the excluded person. Online extremists use the internet to express their hate towards other groups, mostly on ethnical or racial grounds. This phenomenon is called cyberhate. Online harassment is the intentional and overt act of aggression toward another person online that occurs particularly among youths who frequently visit chat rooms. After an overview of various forms of antisocial communication, the chapter discusses several theoretical explanations for cyberhate.

Part III: The appeal of communicating through technology

This part of the book opens with a broad perspective on various ways in which people present themselves in online formats, followed by several chapters describing in more detail the appeal of specific forms of mediated communication.

In Chapter 11, "Impression formation effects in online mediated communication," Sriram Kalyanaraman and S. Shyam Sundar present an overview of impression formation in online mediated communication. After a brief review of various theoretical models of impression formation and their similarities with attitude formation models, they focus on the importance of impression formation in new media environments. They introduce a distinction between mediated person impression formation (MPIF) and mediated technology impression formation (MTIF). The first relates to the ways individuals can present themselves on the internet and how these influence impression formation. The second refers to the fact that people also form impressions of websites or technologies; this is also described in Nass' "Computers as social actors" paradigm. An overview of the various online venues in which empirical research on impression formation has been conducted is followed by a focus on the variable-centered approach as a framework for the empirical examination of impression formation effects. Kalyanaraman and Sundar regard modality, interactivity, and customizability as crucial elements in self-presentation and impression formation and describe several empirical studies to strengthen their argument.

Monica Whitty escorts us into "The joys of online dating" in Chapter 12, and focuses on self-presentation in this specific setting. Not long ago, admitting to being registered on an online dating site was somewhat embarrassing. Nowadays, online dating is among the most popular ways to find a match. Whitty highlights the reasons why individuals choose to use online dating sites to locate a potential partner. She elaborates on the similarities and differences of online dating with dating via personal ads and video dating. Drawing from interview data, self-presentation strategies of online daters are discussed. Relationship theories, such as evolutionary theory, exchange and equity theories, and theories on self-presentation are considered. Online dating is also contrasted with other ways of meeting people online, such as in chat rooms or newsgroups. Based on the empirical findings, Whitty theorizes that the more successful approach to online dating is the "BAR approach" (balancing an attractive and a real self). Online daters have to solve the difficult task of creating a profile which presents themselves as attractive but is still perceived as realistic. The chapter ends with some thoughts on online compatibility tests—supposedly scientifically based tests which should be able to match compatible individuals.

From theories on self-presentation between dyadic encounters, we move on to the role of interpersonal communication in groups or communities. The next four chapters deal with virtual groups. In Chapter 13, "Social identification with virtual communities," Sonja Utz gives a general overview of virtual communities and the social processes underlying their formation and functioning, and then Chapters 14–16 focus on specific forms of virtual communities or groups. Chapter 13 starts with a definition of virtual communities which also covers new developments such as mobile communities. Utz gives an overview of the history of virtual settlements—from traditional ones such as newsgroups and chats to new ones such as social network sites or wikis. Utz argues that not every virtual settlement is a virtual community; social relationships are an essential prerequisite. She focuses on the role of social identification and argues that social identification is the glue that sticks individuals together in virtual communities. How social identification with virtual communities can develop is explained theoretically and demonstrated on the basis of several empirical studies. Next, the consequences of social identification of virtual communities within the community as well as outside the community (for the individual as well as society) are described. Finally, Utz presents an agenda for future research. While it is clear that virtual communities exist and that they do not lead to social isolation and the decay of community, the question remains open which of the new technologies have the potential to bind people. Moreover, researchers need to examine how people integrate various virtual communities into their everyday life.

The next three chapters deal with specific virtual groups. In Chapter 14, Joseph B. Walther's focus is on "Problems and interventions in computer-mediated virtual groups"—on groups in a professional context: virtual teams in educational or work settings. Walther reviews research on the interpersonal dynamics of virtual groups: groups that meet using computer-mediated communication and whose members may reside in different locations face challenges that ftf groups do not face or face them in a different way. Walther examines two questions: How do communication media change basic communication dynamics in groups, and how do virtual group members deal with unknown or less well-known group members in a different location? Attributions play a central role in mediated team work, especially attributions in conflict situations. In geographically dispersed teams, members tend to blame the distant group members. Group members who have ample time to solve the tasks and who trust each other adapt better to virtuality. Walther reviews theory-based interventions that repair faulty attribution and also participation-related issues common to distributed virtual groups. He concludes that new technologies and social engineering, developed on the basis of knowledge about the motivations of people to contribute, can help virtual groups to further tap their full potential.

The next chapter, "What makes the internet a place to seek social support?" by Martin Tanis, focuses on a different type of group: online social support groups. Social support plays an important role in everyday life and contributes to an individual's mental and physical well-being, whether offline or online. Tanis discusses why people seek support from online social support groups by looking at characteristics of CMC in general and online communities in particular. He illustrates various reasons why people go online to seek support, among them the relative anonymity that CMC affords, the text-based character, and the possibilities for extending social networks. These influence not only with whom one interacts, but also how one interacts.

After having discussed some of the more serious sides of mediated interpersonal communication, Christoph Klimmt and Tilo Hartmann turn their attention to a more recreational and playful context in Chapter 16, "Mediated interpersonal communication in multiplayer video games: implications for entertainment and relationship management." Video games have taken a key position in today's landscape of media entertainment and with the increase in broadband internet connections, more and more video games have adopted modes of interpersonal communication between users as a part of their "multiplayer gaming" functionality. Often research focuses on how far playing violent video games leads to aggressive behavior in real life and neglects the positive aspects of playing games. Given the growing popularity of multiplayer games, an in-depth discussion of the role of interpersonal (inter-player) communication in video game enjoyment and video game effects is relevant and identifies new directions for systematic research in this domain. The authors make a distinction between three types of communication: encounters with (mostly) unknown other human players, inner-group communication among members of relatively stable task-oriented teams (e.g. clans), and communication among members of social groups within the narrative virtual worlds (e.g. guilds). After characterizing these three forms of communication, they relate them to game enjoyment and social effects of frequent gaming. Thus, the chapter provides the systematics for analyzing communication in video games and focuses also on the positive aspects.

Dirk Oegema, Jan Kleinnijenhuis, Koos Anderson, and Anita van Hoof bring us back again to the darker sides of online communication. In Chapter 17, "Flaming and blaming: the influence of mass media content on interactions in online discussions," they study communication in online discussion forums. Political discussions in online forums are often viewed as unbiased articulation of public concerns. On the other hand, it is expected that mainly anti-status-quo extremists give their opinions in these forums. The authors compare the style and the content of discussion forums with those in the mass media. Conversational style characteristics that are associated with informal discussions are also found in discussion forums: namely the tendency to express personal emotions more frequently, and the tendency to *flame* by insulting other discussants and the authorities alike. The chapter also touches on the question of *agenda setting*. The authors contrast two questions: "Are issues in discussion forums a simple reflection of the agenda of the traditional media?" and "Do forums fulfill a bottom-up articulation function in the way that the traditional media respond to these forums?" The questions are answered through a large-scale content analysis of discussion forums and daily newspapers in the Netherlands on the highly controversial issue of Islamic immigration there. The results show that flaming is a unique stylistic feature of discussion forums, but that discussion groups still obtain their issues from mainstream mass media, either directly or mediated by other discussion groups on the web.

Whereas most chapters deal with computer-mediated communication, Louis Leung looks at another medium: the cell phone. Chapter 18 is titled "Leisure boredom, sensation seeking, self-esteem, and addiction: symptoms and patterns of cell phone use." As in early internet research, some worry whether people, especially adolescents, become addicted to the new communication medium. Leung identifies addiction symptoms that are uniquely associated with cell phone use and examines how demographics and psychological attributes of individuals are related to these addiction symptoms. Furthermore, he explores how these attributes, cell phone addiction symptoms and social capital, can predict various aspects of cell phone use (e.g. for interpersonal communication, entertainment). His arguments are based on a survey of 624 young adults (aged 14–28). About a quarter of this sample were classified as addicted to the cell phone. Results showed, among others, that respondents high on sensation seeking and leisure boredom were more likely to be addicted to the cell phone than others low on these traits. Conversely, respondents high on self-esteem demonstrated fewer addiction symptoms. Sensation seeking turned out to be the most powerful predictor of addiction; and addiction mediated the relationship between sensation seeking and phone use in number of minutes. The psychological variables also predicted cell phone use for entertainment. In all, future studies should focus on adaptive versus maladaptive patterns of adolescent cell phone use and provide some directions for intervention.

Chapter 2

Understanding social media from the media ecological perspective

Susan B. Barnes

In 1962, Marshall McLuhan envisioned a world in which electric media would extend the human embrace on a worldwide scale and create a new type of *global village*. Although his vision tends to be interpreted as a technological phenomenon, it is equally, if not more so, a human one. At a time when television and mass media messages dominated the media landscape, it was difficult to see the human communication aspect of media change—the use of media to facilitate human relationships. However, starting with the telegraph and telephone, media environments have gradually come to replace many face-to-face contexts in which interpersonal interactions occur. Utilizing a media ecological perspective, this chapter will describe how mediated contexts facilitate interpersonal human communication and how computers are now being used to initiate, support, and develop communication exchanges between people. Today, interpersonal communication takes place in mediated contexts and software developers are creating social computing tools to facilitate this process. The study of computer-mediated communication (CMC) explores how mediated environments support and extend the process of human communication and social computing examines the tools that facilitate this process.

The study of media is not only a technological endeavor. It also includes the human side of technological change (see Hickman, 1990; Postman, 1985 & 1992). Schroeder (1996) argued "technological and social change must be examined conjointly at several interrelated levels" (p. 137). On a basic level, understanding interpersonal communication in a mediated world requires awareness about how one person communicates with another using a communication medium. By focusing on how the interpersonal communication process is altered when moving from face-to-face to mediated contexts, the media ecological view can be utilized to study CMC and social media because it examines changes in communication patterns, such as the shift from broadcast mass media systems to interactive digital systems. What are the characteristic differences between these systems and how will the shift from one system to another alter the process of communication? In terms of interpersonal communication, what are the differences between communicating face-to-face and in a mediated context? How will these differences influence interpersonal communication and social activities? These are central questions asked in a basic media ecological analysis.

Interactivity is a key characteristic technological difference between mass media (television, radio) and digital media (computers, internet). With the introduction of digital communication, scholars are now developing interactive models to describe how human communication occurs in mediated space. An example is Rafaeli and Sudweeks' (1998) "One Way, Two Way, and Interactive Models of Communication." These models visualize the process of sending a one-way (mass) message, as well as interactive (interpersonal) exchanges between two people. Another visualization of this process is the one-to-one and many-to-many communication models, topics that were first discussed by computer scientists Licklider and Taylor (1968) (also see Barnes, 2003). Once a characteristic difference is discovered in a medium, the next question is how does the introduction of interactivity in mediated environments alter or change the process of communication? A simple answer is that interactivity enables two people to directly exchange personal messages in a mediated context.

A media ecological study of CMC also explores the similarities and differences between face-to-face and mediated communication contexts (Barnes, 2001; Rheingold, 1993; Turkle, 1995). For example, the primary form of communication in email is the exchange of written text instead of spoken language. Early CMC studies explored how this shift in linguistic codes influenced communication behaviors (Baym, 2000; Jones, 1995; Hiltz & Turoff, 1978; Murray, 1991; Rice & Love, 1987, Sproull & Kiesler, 1991; Walther, 1996; Zuboff, 1988). For example, textual exchanges led to the development of exaggerated behaviors between communicators. Researchers speculated that CMC would lead to the sharing of impersonal messages due to the lack of facial and tonal cues.

Moreover an underlying assumption of interpersonal communication research tends to be the notion that interpersonal communication must take place in a face-to-face context, but for a number of years media scholars have been challenging this idea (Gumpert & Cathcart, 1986; Horton & Wohl, 1956/1986; Meyrowitz, 1985; Reeves & Nass, 1996). Ironically, an early description of the human communication process was based on telephone communication systems (a mediated context), but the telephone as an interpersonal communication context is often ignored in basic texts (Adler *et al.*, 2005). In contrast, media ecologists (Barnes, Strate, Jacobs, Gibson) have been observing how mediated contexts have gradually been replacing face-to-face ones in the process of interpersonal communication.

The media ecological view

A number of writers have utilized the ecological metaphor to describe media in terms of perceptual and information space (Burnett, 2004; Davenport, 1997; Nardi & O'Day, 1999; Rennie & Mason, 2003). Although "ecology" is a popular metaphor for the study of information space, there is a theoretical perspective associated with the idea of *media ecology*. As a theoretical concept, the media ecological approach developed from the work of Marshall McLuhan (1964, 1962) and the Toronto School of Communication (Innis, 1951; Olson, 1994). Neil Postman and his various students (Barnes, 2001, 2003; Levinson, 1997, 1999; Meyrowitz, 1985; Strate, 1999) graduating from the Media Ecology Program at New York University further developed the concept in the United States. Media ecological principles include: all technological change is a Faustian bargain; technological change is not additive, it changes everything; the symbolic forms of technologies differ, leading to different *intellectual and emotional biases*; when the conditions in which we attend to media change, different media have *social biases*; and different technical and economic structures will contribute to media *content biases*. This is a systemic approach to communication that examines "the leading role that media play in influencing meanings and minds, ways of life and world views" (Barnes & Strate, 1996: 182). Media biases include space/time, sensory, intellectual, social, emotional, political, symbolic, and content biases.

From a media ecological point of view, introducing a new technology into a culture will alter the culture because the communication ecology of the social system will change. How that change will occur is dependent upon the culture. For example, television in American culture tends to take the form of entertainment because the United States is a capitalist country (Postman, 1985). Advertising is a central component of American television programming and entertainment programming attracts viewers who will be exposed to the commercial messages. Thus, commercial television in the United States tends to have a bias toward entertainment content. In contrast, Singapore is a dictatorship and the government edits and censors entertainment content to better conform to social ideals. Additionally, the government will often broadcast messages to further its political and social agendas. It is technology and society together that shape our communication environments.

Media ecologists contend that one change in a communication system will alter the entire environment. This reflects a systemic position and media ecology can ideologically be related to systems theory and cybernetics. Norbert Wiener (1954) created the concept of cybernetics, the science of communication and control. During World War II, feedback and control were applied to technology to foster the relationship between human and machine integration. Today, these ideas are applied to human-computer interaction (HCI), which describes human interaction with technology. A central idea of cybernetics and HCI is to help enable humans to be more efficient machine operators. In contrast, CMC tends to study the ways in which people exchange messages between themselves.

According to Postman (1979: 4), "Cybernetics is merely a synonym for ecology" because both examine how systems alter when a new element or change is introduced into the process. A media ecological view considers human–machine interactions to be included in the ecology of CMC environments because both humans and machines are part of the message system. The symbolic methods used in technology interaction can influence the interpersonal communication process. For instance, people need to have a computer and know how to use it before they have access to internet interpersonal communication.

Both the media ecological perspective and the transactional view of human communication examine systems and how systems alter interpersonal communication behaviors (see Greller & Barnes, 1993). In media ecology, the direction in which messages can flow or be exchanged is an important characteristic to be examined. Ong (1982: 176) states: "Human communication is never one-way. Always, it not only calls for a response but is shaped in its very form and content by anticipated response." The transactional or systems approach is a circular model that can include the communication environment along with personal and cultural experiences (see Adler *et al.*, 2005). The media ecological approach looks at the total communication process. For example, mass media supports a one-directional message flow and the internet is multidirectional (interactive), which includes one-to-one (interpersonal communication); one-to-many (human and mass communication); and many-to-many (organizational communication). Media ecological writings about internet interpersonal communication include the works of Strate *et al.* (1996, 2003), Gibson and Oviedo (2000), and Barnes (2001).

In addition to a directional bias, media also have a sensory bias. According to McLuhan (1964), global networks extend the human nervous system. Making social connections through the internet exposes individuals to a wider variety of ideas and worldviews. Thus, people are exposed to many more ideas than they would be when situated in a single geographic location. The internet's sensory bias is one that extends the human nervous system and fosters the formation of a global village. Thus, an intellectual worldview shift can occur as people become more aware of global issues. McLuhan (1964: 19) says:

> Today, after more than a century of electric technology, we have extended our central nervous system itself in a global embrace, abolishing both space and time as far as our planet is concerned. Rapidly, we approach the final phase of the extension of man—technological

simulation of consciousness, when the creative process of knowing will be collectively and corporately extended to the whole of human society, much as we have already extended our senses and our nerves by the various media.

The sensory bias of the internet extends human communication across time and space. This sensory extension fosters a new type of social bias—using technology to connect people together. Postman (1995: 193) stated: "Because of the conditions in which we attend to them, different technologies have different social biases." For instance, online or wireless communication does not require communicators to be co-present in the same physical location. Thus, conditions of attendance are different in face-to-face and online conversations because online communicators do not see the people they are talking to.

Additionally, online communicators can be dispersed spatially and temporally, which creates a time/space bias. The idea of a time/space bias in media is a key characteristic in any media ecological examination of communication technologies. Harold Innis (1951) argued that a communication medium tends to create a bias that emphasizes the idea of time or space. Carey (1989: 134) described Innis's idea in the following way:

> Innis divided communication and social control into two major types. Space-binding media, such as print and electricity, were connected with expansion and control over territory and favored the establishment of commercialism, empire and eventually technocracy. On the other hand, time-binding media, such as manuscript and human speech, favored relatively close communities, metaphysical speculation, and traditional authority.

The term "cyberspace" refers to the perceptual space created by computer networks, suggesting that networks have a spatial bias. However, computer networks also alter concepts of time, a characteristic that James Gleick (1999/2000) describes in *Faster: the Acceleration of Just About Everything*. For instance, email creates a situation in which there is no shared physical space or sense of time. Email correspondents can be dispersed spatially and temporally. Time speeds up as we quickly send messages through the network and space dissolves.

In interpersonal communication, a central media ecological question facing researchers utilizing this perspective is: How does the geographic separation of interpersonal correspondents influence the ways in which people communicate? When conditions of attendance change, how do communication messages change? One change is the lack of facial and tonal information, which can contribute to exaggerated communication, such as rude behavior and flaming.

Additionally the symbolic shift from face-to-face spoken to textual messages can blur the boundaries between reality and virtuality. For some correspondents, the virtual experience is believed to be more socially desirable than in-person encounters (see Walther, 1996). Instead of seeing physical objects and contexts, people now experience virtual objects and perceptual spaces that are constructed in mediated environments. Thus, our symbolic notions of abstraction and representation are altered as virtual experiences begin to replace actual ones. For example, pilots learn to fly in simulators before they fly physical planes and doctors can practice medical procedures on virtual, rather than actual, patients. In online dating, individuals tend to add fantasy elements to online communication (see Barnes, 2003).

Although, CMC creates new types of communication environments for interaction to occur, communicating in a mediated context is different from sharing face-to-face experiences. The media environment alters the ways in which people attend to the communication. First, conditions of attendance in face-to-face communication require physical co-presence. In contrast, online communicators generally interact while being physically removed from each other. Second, the separation of people from their words, has numerous implications for the communication exchange and internet behavior patterns. Initially, researchers hypothesized that the lack of physical co-presence would lead to the exchange of impersonal and hostile messages, but, the opposite was discovered to be true. It has been observed that people will type their most intimate thoughts into the computer (Whittle, 1997). Sitting at home alone typing on a keyboard creates the illusion of privacy. In contrast, the words can be distributed around the globe. Once a message is sent out over the internet, the author loses control over his or her message. Digital text does not evaporate like the sounds of words in the air. We can share private thoughts, but the media environment is not a private place. Therefore, ideas of privacy change as private words can become public; this is the situation with teenagers posting private information on blogs (Kornblum, 2005).

Observations of a virtual community (Barnes, 2001) revealed four reasons why conditions of attendance in internet communities are conducive to personal relationship development. First, people can choose when to disclose information about their age, sex, and race. Second, people voluntarily communicate with each other and conversations can easily be terminated. Third, people can put their best foot forward by carefully editing their replies. Finally, people have the ability to hide defects, including physical handicaps and shyness. For instance, email is a wonderful communication tool for deaf teachers and students because hearing is not a requirement for CMC correspondence to occur.

However, conditions of attendance can also lead to misbehavior. Postman (1995: 192) reminds us "all technological change is a Faustian Bargain. For every advantage a new technology offers, there is always a corresponding disadvantage". Separating the physical body from the human communication process allows people to separate themselves from their actions (see Barnes, 1999). Its easier for people to write deceptive messages, flame each other, and act in socially unacceptable ways, such as spam, and identity theft. How can we protect ourselves from harmful remarks and actions when the identity of the perpetrator is unknown? This is one of the many ethical questions facing societies today. By focusing on symbolic shifts, time/space relationships, interactivity, sensory biases, and conditions of attendance, media ecology provides a framework for understanding how interpersonal communication is shifted from face-to-face to mediated contexts.

Historical overview of the socialization of media

A number of scholars have applied a media ecological framework to historical studies of communication technologies and their influences on culture. For example, Eisenstein (1979) examined the influence of the printing press on early-modern Europe and Ong (1982) studied the technologizing of the word in terms of a shift from oral to literate cultures.

A media ecological critique of social media would begin with a historical overview of how mass media have gradually been replacing interpersonal communication as a socializing force. Beniger (1987: 353) says, "Although intimate group relations remained important, increased attention to mass media ultimately came—because the individual's time and energy were limited—at the expense of interpersonal communication." Moreover, mass media themselves have increasingly become more personalized. Direct marketing addresses people by individual name and database marketing enables marketers to pinpoint individuals to target for products and services. Beniger called this social change the development of *pseudo-community*, a trend in mass media to speak in a more personal voice. Today, web programs can directly address the consumer and websites can be personalized for every user. Thus, mass and computer generated messages appear to be personal ones directed at individuals rather than groups.

In 1956, Horton and Wohl (1956/1986) observed that mass media—radio, television, and the movies—create the illusion of a face-to-face relationship with a performer. They called this new type of relationship a *para-social* one. The idea of media creating a sense of interpersonal communication was the subject of Gumpert and Cathcart's (1986: 24) book *Inter/Media*. They state: "A systems theory of human communication assumes that all message inputs—verbal, nonverbal, firsthand or mediated, and purposeful or accidental—affect the internal states of the individual and help shape the message outputs from the individual to others (interpersonal behaviors) as well as the messages one sends to oneself (intrapersonal behaviors)." Building on concepts presented in *Inter/Media*,

Meyrowitz (1985) further examined television usage in terms of Goffman's (1959) dramaturgical model of social behavior. He argued that viewers consider television characters to be their *media friends*. Thus, Meyrowitz asserted that people develop a sense of having an interpersonal relationship with media content.

Presently, the internet has replaced the sense of an interpersonal relationship with a performer with the ability to conduct interpersonal relationships with other people. Digital media have now evolved to the point in which human-to-human exchanges are completely interactive. Senders and receivers exchange positions as if they were together in a face-to-face encounter. Early research on CMC speculated that textual exchanges with cues filtered out would create a hostile communication environment (Hiltz & Turoff, 1978). However, contrary to this view, observations and studies of online exchanges later revealed that people form virtual or electronic communities when they regularly exchanged messages through the internet (Baym, 2000; Jones, 1995; Rheingold, 1993). Although some writers remain skeptical about the relationships built through cyberspace (Doheny-Farina, 1996; Slouka, 1995; Stoll, 1995), others have begun to embrace the idea that CMC is a new form of interpersonal communication (Barnes, 2001, 2003; Baym, 2000).

People need to connect with others and this is the driving force behind online relationships. For this reason, email and Instant Messenger are two very popular software applications that support the creation of interpersonal media environments. Communication technologies are transformed into media environments when people begin using the tools to support social practices, such as chatting with friends or co-workers in Instant Messenger. According to Postman (1985: 86), while "a technology ... is merely a machine," it "becomes a medium as it employs a symbolic code, as it finds its place in a particular social setting." Thus, "a medium is the social and intellectual environment a machine creates." A new generation of software tools is emerging that are specifically designed to support social practices. This new technology sector is called "social media" or "social computing." Today, mediated contexts have developed from pseudo relationships to actual ones as people exchange messages through social software.

Social media

Social media is an umbrella concept that describes social software and social networking. "Social software refers to various, loosely connected types of applications that allow individuals to communicate with one another, and to track discussions across the Web as they happen" (Tepper, 2003: 19). Simply stated, social media is software that enables people to interact with each other and build social networks that increase social capital. The term "social media" may be new; however, the idea of using media environments for socializing practices goes back to the telegraph and telephone. Since the early twentieth century, communication technologies have been used to create media environments that facilitate interpersonal communication (see Marvin, 1988).

In the pioneering stages of the internet, computer scientists transformed the technology into a media environment when they started exchanging email messages with each other. Interpersonal message exchange is a central aspect of the internet. The social bias of the computer enables anyone with access to an internet connection to connect with others. This social aspect of the computer's transformation into a media environment has been demonstrated through the formation of discussion groups, forums, bulletin boards, and newsgroups. Today's social media environments include: chat, instant messages, online role-play games, collaborative work tools, online education, and cell phones with internet access. Many of these environments are used to share interpersonal messages.

The idea of social media is a new organizing concept that has come to the public's attention through activities such as music and photo sharing, the social networking site meetup.com, the collaborative writing of Wikipedia, and numerous blogs available on the internet. Social software is already starting to change political, social, and personal communication patterns between individuals and organizations in the U.S.A. (see Crumlish, 2004). For instance, online learning environments provide distance education to people in remote regions. Computer-supported collaborative work environments support collaborative teams and the building of research communities. Examples include the concept of "outsourcing"American technical support jobs to India and data entry positions to Cambodia (see Friedman, 2005). Websites such as meetup.com and Match.com are altering the ways in which members of political parties organize and couples meet each other. From politics to romance, social media is influencing how people meet and make contact with each other. According to Friedman (2005), the use of social media tools has already had a profound influence on social, professional, and political life around the world.

Today, these tools are influencing the political process. In the United States, cyber-politics are a new type of political communication that is being used by many political candidates. Whillock (1997: 1208) states: "cyber-politics involve information dissemination, communication exchange, and the formation of electronic political coalitions across the internet." For instance, Sakkas (1993) provides a description of the use of discussion lists during the 1992 presidential campaign. A political bias associated with computer networks is the ability to organize people around a political or social cause. Similarly, Rheingold (2002) describes how people around the world are using cell phones to organize themselves to promote activism.

Social media is interpersonal media. It supports the sharing of personal exchanges in new and unique ways. It is not the relationship between humans and machines that makes social media powerful. In contrast, it is the relationship facilitated between people through the use of machines to foster the building of social networks and a new network society. Castells (1996/2000) describes the network society as a culture that is virtually constructed "by pervasive, interconnected, and diversified media system[s]." He continues by saying "this new form of social organization, in its pervasive globality, is diffusing throughout the world" (pp. 1–2). The network society is based on the idea of using CMC to build *social capital*, which is an informal social norm that promotes cooperation between two or more individuals. The norms can range from the reciprocity between two friends to the use of social networks to support community involvement and work activities.

Research in the area of social media includes the visual mapping of social networks (Turner *et al.*, 2005); social networking in organizations (Quan-Haase, *et al.*, 2005; Garton *et al.*, 1997); distributed computing (Friedman, 2005; Holohan & Garg, 2005); peer-to-peer networks (Adar & Huberman 2000; Svensson & Bannister, 2004; Xu *et al.*, 2005); mobile communications (cell phones and personal digital assistants) (Ito *et al.*, 2005; Rheingold, 2002) and blogs (Crumlish, 2004; Hewitt, 2005; Kline & Burstein, 2005). Distributed computing primarily has economic and technological goals. "In Distributed Computing, a large computing problem is divided into small tasks that are assigned over the internet to be processed by individual users on their own computers" (Holohan & Garg, 2005: 1) An example of the use of distributed computing was the development of Linux, a current alternative to the Microsoft operating system (see Raymond, 1999/2001). It is a homegrown system that was constructed by thousands of programmers around the world, organizing themselves through the internet.

The geographic reach (space) and multidirectional (interactive) flow of message exchange available through the internet enabled programmers around the world to band together and create a computer program. By examining how the internet changes the way people interactively communicate (direction) across space, we can understand how the internet changes our notions of work and social collaboration. It was a networked group of thousands of programmers that began to challenge the hegemony of Microsoft's operating systems. This is an example of the potential social bias associated with social media. Individuals can organize themselves outside a corporate or government structure and their activities could challenge the hegemony of corporate and political systems. Friedman (2005) refers to this as the "flattening of the world," or the ability of individuals to easily communicate with each other across the globe to work, collaborate, and socialize with each other.

Social media analysis

Media ecology provides a framework in which to examine how social media tends to be used and how its media characteristics create new types of social challenge. The media characteristics being utilized in the following analysis are conditions of attendance, direction, time/space, social, and political biases. As previously stated, CMC introduces new conditions of attendance for communication partners—people no longer have to be physically co-present for communication to occur. Two issues introduced by this change are the issues of presence and trust.

People can now sit alone in their bedrooms and be part of a global conversation. According to Hillis (1999: 64): "When mediation inserts a 'psychic' distance, even among spatially proximate individuals, co-presence is superseded by telepresence." The idea of telepresence (Wood & Smith, 2001; Woolley, 1992) has evolved into presence research. Telepresence, a term created in the mid-1980s by NASA, originally referred to people controlling robots. A number of researchers have been examining how a sense of presence is created in electronic space (Biocca, 1997; Giese, 1998; Liu, 1999; Lombard & Ditton, 1997; Lombard *et al.*, 2000; Riva *et al.*, 2003; Short *et al.*, 1976).

Today's presence research conceptualizes the representation of self in mediated environments in a variety of ways. According to Lombard and Ditton (1997), there are six different conceptualizations of presence: presence as social richness (channels of communication) (Short *et al.*, 1976); presence as visual realism (computer graphics) (Heeter, 1995); presence as transportation (traveling across space) (Biocca & Levy, 1995); presence as immersion (perceptual space) (Mantovani & Castelnuovo, 2003); presence as a social actor within a medium (avatars and actions) (Laurel, 1993); and presence as medium as social actor (anthropomorphism of technology) (Reeves and Nass, 1996). A number of different theories and approaches are emerging to describe the sense of self and others in perceptually mediated space.

Perceptual space is an amalgamation of the visual space created by the computer screen, the information space established through the network, and the social space experienced as people interact with each other (see Strate, 1999). Because communicators are separated by geographic space, establishing a sense of presence for the other to perceive oneself is a central issue in CMC. Presence replaces visual "first impressions" and compensates for the lack of visual information. Although, presence can compensate for visual information, it cannot verify identity and build trust because people are separated from their words and actions.

Trust is an issue that people need to establish between themselves, and programmers need to consider how to integrate trust in their software designs. For e-business and online dating, people need to be able to trust the person that they are corresponding with. Friedman *et al.* (2000: 40) state: "Perhaps the greatest difference between trust online and in other contexts is that when online, we have more difficulty (sometimes to the point of futility) of reasonably assessing the potential harm and good will of others." To address the issue of online trust, multidisciplinary researchers want to create technology that accounts for human values in the design process. A number of interface researchers have been addressing the issue of trust in the online experience (Cassell and Bickmore, 2000; Shneiderman, 2000). From the social perspective, Uslaner (2000: 63–64) observed:

> People who mistrust others fear the Net as much as they accept all sorts of other conspiracy theories we might see on the *X Files*. They worry about their privacy generally and about the security of their medical records and the risk of downloading viruses in particular. Trusters view the Internet as more benign. Trusting people believe they can control the world and have faith that science will solve their problems and the Net is another tool giving them leverage over their world.

His research revealed that the internet is very much like the physical world. "Children develop trust in others by learning from and emulating their parents, not from what they (don't) see on television or online" (Uslaner, 2000: 64). The idea of trust that we develop as children tends to determine how much we trust people in later life. People need to be able to connect with others and establish a feeling of trust before a reciprocal and meaningful relationship can be established. In mediated contexts, establishing methods for developing trust in relationships is both a technological and social concern.

The many directions in which messages flow in social media can support the building of meaningful relationships and collaboration. The multidirectional flow of messages contributes to collaborative work between people around the globe, such as the development of Linux and the outsourcing of global services. In addition to connecting people together around the world, various social computing tools focus on aspects of conditions of attendance in terms of local geographic space. Services, such as Facebook, Friendster, and MySpace enable people to connect locally or across distances. For instance, some college students use Facebook to organize parties on their campus, while others use it as a way to meet students on different campuses. "Students can also add their course schedules to their profiles, allowing them to browse the people in their classes" (Majmudar, 2005: E4). Thus, Facebook can be used to facilitate meeting people in a specific geographic location, which is why it is so popular with students on campuses. It is the one-to-one communication between people that is most appealing to individuals because that communication can be with someone next door or thousands of miles away.

Time and space biases are characteristics to be examined in social media contexts. Geographic location is a factor in social media design. For instance, technologies are being developed that place geographic locators in cell phones. When you are in the close proximity of a cell phone buddy, the phone will beep you and you can arrange to meet. Dodgeball and England's Playtxt are mobile social-networking services (called MoSoSos) that connect nearby people who have subscribed to the service. Playtxt connects people together based on similar interests. Dodgeball enables users to find old friends and meet new ones. Social media is not just computing; it includes cell phones, personal digital assistants, the development of peer-to-peer networking, and file sharing (see Ito *et al.*, 2005; Rheingold, 2002).

The peer-to-peer sharing of information and mobilization of people illustrates a subversive aspect that is inherent in network design. The ability to easily share and distribute files and information is a new technological feature that could have profound political and social influences. For example, music file sharing impacts on the copyright laws in the United States. On a business level, peer-to-peer activities could alter social business practices (see Friedman, 2005). Eric Raymond (1999: 29) suggested that "Linux is subversive. Who would have thought even five years ago [1991] that a world-class operating system could coalesce as if by magic out of the part-time hacking of several thousand developers scattered all over the planet, connected only by the tenuous strands of the Internet?" Linux is an example of how distributed computing can be used to solve a problem. While participating in the project, social capital was also gained as people developed business contacts and interpersonal friendships with each other.

Peer-to-peer (P2P) networks enable people to communicate in multiple directions across time and space. In P2P networks, "the computer of each end user only connects to the computers of nearby peers, which themselves are connected to other computers, and so on, to form a dynamic, truly centreless network" (Svensson & Bannister, 2004: 2). P2P networking tends to foster the development of groups of individuals and the formation of online communities. Burnett (2004: 148) states:

> Wireless P2P devices, such as PDAs and cellphones, are part of a growing movement that involves everything from text messaging to the transfer of photographs and video images. These devices will enhance another characteristic of P2P communities, which is the spontaneous desire to meet like-minded people and build communities while moving from one location to another.

Peer-to-peer networks help to build social capital and online communities in new and unique ways. "Much of what happens in the P2P world is unpredictable, which is part of its allure. The technology that comes close to the duplication of P2P networks is the telephone. Unlike telephones, P2P communications can spread, grow and redefine the meaning of community. In fact, I would make the claim the P2P is a disruptive technology" because it alters common assumptions about how technology is used (Burnett, 2004: 164). For instance a number of researchers (Adar & Huberman, 2000; Carmichael, 2003; Svensson & Bannister, 2004) have examined P2P networks and deviant behavior, such as illegal file sharing and network virus attacks. A political bias embedded in the technology is its ability to directly connect individuals together across national boundaries. This is a shift from controlling individual behavior through mass media messages to the self-organizing of individuals through interpersonal communication. As described by Beniger (1987), the impact of mass media on behavior could be reversed by the interpersonal sharing of messages between people in CMC contexts.

The interpersonal sharing of resources and ideas contributes to the building of social capital. Social capital is a research focus for some CMC researchers (Hampton & Wellman, 2001; Kavanaugh & Patterson, 2001; Wellman *et al.*, 2001). Hampton and Wellman (2001: 477) argue that "community is best seen as a network—not as a local group. We are not members of a society that operates in little boxes, dealing only with fellow members of the few groups to which we belong: at home, in our neighborhood, in our workplaces, in cyberspace." An individual's social network includes kinship, friendship, neighbors, and work ties. People maintain these social ties through multiple mediated options, including telephone, mail, fax, email, discussion groups, and instant messaging.

According to Wellman *et al.* (2001), social capital includes three aspects: the building of network capital or the relations with family, friends, and co-workers; participatory capital or the involvement in voluntary organizations and politics; and community commitment, a strong attitude toward community and the willingness to mobilize their social capital. Building and mobilizing social capital is both local and global. A number of authors have examined how networks can be used to organize members of local communities into face-to-face interaction (see Horn, 1998; Rheingold, 1993; Schuler, 1996). Or people can globally share their personal thoughts through blogs.

Probably the most well-known social media tool is the weblog. A weblog (also known as a blog) is a personal website that offers frequently updated observations, news headlines, commentary, recommended links and/or diary entries, generally organized chronologically (Werbach, 2001: 21). Blogs change media content by doing two things. First, they enable individuals to have a voice in the media. Blogs can be a form of participatory journalism that is shared on a global level. As a result, mass media news is no longer the only type of authorial voice that is commenting on current events. Second, blogs are connected together through social networks. Social networks foster the formation of new types of electronic communities that share information together.

A goal of blogs is to present a personal point of view in a global village. Bloggers with similar interests will link their sites together into blogging communities. Blogging tools bring people together across time and space. On the opposite side of the spectrum, adding buddy lists and location tools to cell phones enables cell phone users to meet up and physically interact with friends in face-to-face contexts. For example, Ito *et al.* (2005) explore the social use of cell phones in Japanese life. Thus, social computing directly deals with changing notions of conditions of attendance and how people can communicate and interact across distances and in face-to-face interpersonal relationships.

The sensory bias of computer networks, which extend our nervous system into a global embrace, contributes to our changing notions about real and perceptual space. Because people can now communicate across distances, conditions of attendance in mediated contexts are different from face-to-face situations. Symbolically, people now interact in a perceptual space, often referred to as "cyberspace," instead of a physical one. Thus, the CMC context is abstract and open to interpretation or misinterpretation. This possibility adds a new level of abstraction to the process of understanding messages in mediated contexts, also raising issues about self-presentation and trust. Interpersonal communicators need to envision mental models of their communication contexts to better understand the words being exchanged (see Licklider & Taylor, 1968).

Changing conditions of attendance also alter social behaviors and this is a Faustian Bargain. Separation of people from words leads to the building of social capital as well as socially destructive deviant behavior, such as identity theft and flaming. On a social level, someone can flame another party without having to physically face the wrath of the other person. However, separating people from their actions also contributes to the technology's political bias. National borders no longer bind individuals. Networking technologies reach beyond national borders to enable people to self-organize around local or global political interests and issues. Thus, by examining the directional, spatial, social, and political biases embedded in social media, interpersonal communication scholars can better understand how the shift from face-to-face to mediated communication environments can influence the ways in which people interact. Moreover, this shift raises new technological factors and social issues that need to be considered when conducting interpersonal research.

Conclusion

A basic media ecological analysis of CMC and social networking reveals that embedded in the technology is a political bias of self-organization and self-expression, which is not possible with mass media. This bias is illustrated with the phenomenon of blogging and the application of

P2P networking in the solving of problems. The ability of individuals to express themselves on the internet changes the nature of media content. Much of the content shared through the internet is interpersonal rather than mass messages. Socially, networks bring people together who are geographically dispersed. New types of relationships are formed, while older relationships can be maintained by using social media tools. Thus, the internet supports the maintenance of established relationships and the development of new ones.

Symbolically, computer networks introduce a new level of abstraction and representation to the interpersonal communication process. People must now perceive the contexts and spaces in which they communicate instead of seeing the physical location. Our extension of the nervous system into a global embrace is a perceptual rather than a physical one, raising issues of identity and trust. We bridge space with our minds rather than with our bodies. And changes in conditions of attendance are probably the most profound influence of CMC media environments on people and culture.

As new types of social media environments emerge, interpersonal scholars are going to need to think about incorporating these contexts into their research agendas. Now, with the introduction of social software tools and the widespread use of the internet to support the exchange of human interactions, interpersonal research is needed to better understand how CMC contexts and social media technologies can be integrated into the traditional study of interpersonal communication.

One way to understand these profound technological changes is to apply a media ecological framework to the study of CMC and social media. As previously stated, the internet as a communication technology changes media content from mass to individual messages. Its political bias enables people to individually connect outside the control of organizations and national borders. The ways in which CMC changes conditions of attendance can be used to build social capital or enable people to engage in deviant behavior. Although, this is a result of a social bias in CMC and social media that is facilitated by the technologies, the bias does not determine our future. How new social media tools are used in socializing and the support of interpersonal communication will depend upon the societies in which they are developed and utilized. Or the social bias embedded in these tools could lead to the formation of a new global culture that crosses all national and geographic boundaries where internet access is available.

References

Adar, E., & Huberman, B. A. (2000) "Free riding on Gnutella," *First Monday 5* (10). Available at www.firstmonday.org. (last viewed September 15, 2005).

Adler, R. B., Proctor, R. F., & Towne, N. (2005) *Looking Out, Looking In*. Belmont, CA: Wadsworth.

Barnes, S. (1999) "Ethical issues for a virtual self." In S. J. Drucker & G. Gumpert (eds.), *Real Law @ Virtual Space*. Cresskill, NJ: Hampton Press.

Barnes, S. B. (2001) *Online connections: Internet Interpersonal Relationships*. Cresskill, NJ: Hampton Press.

Barnes, S. B. (2003) *Computer-Mediated Communication: Human-to-Human Communication Across the Internet*. Boston, MA: Allyn & Bacon.

Barnes, S., & Strate, L. (1996) "The educational implications of the computer: A media ecology critique." *New Jersey Journal of Communication, 4*(2), 180–208.

Baym, N. K. (2000) *Tune in, Log On*. Thousand Oaks, CA: Sage Publications.

Beniger, J. R. (1987) "Personalization of mass media and the growth of pseudo-community." *Communication Research, 14*(3), 52–371.

Biocca, F. (1997) "The cyborg's dilemma: Progressive embodiment in virtual environments." *Journal of Computer-Mediated Communication, 3*(2). Available at www.ascusc.org/jcmc/vol3. (last viewed May 13, 2003).

Biocca, F., & Levy, M. R. (1995) *Communication in the Age of Virtual Reality*. Hillsdale, NJ: Lawrence Erlbaum Associates.

Burnett, R. (2004) *How Images Think*. Cambridge, MA: The MIT Press.

Carey, J. W. (1989) *Communication as culture*. New York: Routledge.

Carmichael, P. (2003) "The Internet, information architecture and community memory." *Journal of Computer-Mediated Communication, 8*(2). Available at www.jcmc.Indiana.edu. (last viewed September 19, 2005).

Cassell, J., & Bickmore, T. (2000) "External manifestations of trustworthiness in the interface." *Communications of the ACM, 43*(12), 50–56.

Castells, M. (1996/2000) *The Rise of the Networked Society,* second edition. Boston: Blackwell.

Crumlish, C. (2004) *The Power of Many*. San Francisco, Sybex.

Davenport, T. H. (1997) *Information Ecology*. New York: Oxford University Press.

DeVito, J. A. (2004) *The Interpersonal Communication Book,* tenth edition. Boston: Allyn & Bacon.

Doheny-Farina, S. (1996) *The Wired Neighborhood*. New Haven, CT: Yale University Press.

Donath, J. (1999) "Visualizing conversation." *Journal of Computer-Mediated Communication, 4*(4). Available at www.jcmc.Indiana.edu. (last viewed September 16, 2005).

Dominick, J. R. (2002) *The Dynamics of Mass Communication,* seventh edition. New York: McGraw Hill.

Eisenstein, E. L. (1979) *The Printing Press As an Agent of Change*. New York: Cambridge University Press.

Forester, T. (1989) *Computers in the Human Context*. Cambridge, MA: The MIT Press.

Friedman, B., Kahn, Jr., P. H., & Howe, D. C. (2000) "Trust online." *Communications of the ACM, 43*(12), 34–40.

Friedman, T. L. (2005) *The World is Flat*. New York: Farrar, Straus and Giroux.

Garton, L., Haythornthwaite, C., & Wellman, B. (1997) "Studying on-line social networks." *Journal of Computer-Mediated Communication, 3*(1). Available at www.jcmc.Indiana.edu. (last viewed September 15, 2005).

Gibson, S. B., & Oviedo, O. O. (2000) *The Emerging Cyberculture: Literacy, Paradigm, and Paradox*. Cresskill, NJ: Hampton Press.

Giese, M. (1998) "Self without body: Textual self-representation in an electronic community." *First Monday, 3*(4). Available at www.firstmonday.dk/issues/issue3_4/giese. (last viewed April 14, 2000).

Gleick, J. (1999/2000) *Faster: the Acceleration of Just About Everything*. New York: Vintage Books.

Goffman, E. (1959) *The Presentation of Self in Everyday Life*. Garden City, N.Y.: Doubleday.

Greller, L., & Barnes, S. (1993) "Groupware and interpersonal text: The computer as a medium of communication." *Interpersonal Computing and Technology, 1*(2). Available at www.Helsinki.fi/science/optek. (last viewed April 15, 2001).

Gumpert, G., & Cathcart, R. (1986) *Inter/Media: Interpersonal Communication in a Media World*, third edition. New York: Oxford University Press.

Hampton, K., & Wellman, B. (2001) "Long distance community in the network society." *American Behavioral Scientist, 45*(3), 476–95.

Heeter, C. (1995) "Communication research on consumer VR." In F. Biocca & M. R. Levy (eds.), *Communication in the Age of Virtual Reality*, Hillsdale, NJ: Lawrence Erlbaum Associates, pp.191–218.

Hewitt, H. (2005) *Blog: Understanding the Information Reformation That's Changing Your World*. Nashville, TN: Thomas Nelson, Inc.

Hickman, L. A. (1990) *Technology As a Human Affair*. New York: McGraw-Hill.

Hillis, K. (1999) *Digital sensations*. Minneapolis, MN: University of Minnesota Press.

Hiltz, S. R., & Turoff, M. (1978) *The Network Nation: Human Communication Via Computer*. Reading, MA: Addison-Wesley.

Holohan, A., & Garg, A. (2005) "Collaboration online: The example of distributed computing." *Journal of Computer-Mediated Communication, 10*(4). Available at www.jcmc. Indiana.edu. (last viewed September 15, 2005).

Horn, S. (1998) *Cyberville*. New York: Warner Books.

Horton, D., & Wohl, R. R. (1956/1986) "Mass communication and para-social interaction: Observation on intimacy at a distance." In G. Gumpert & R. Cathcart (eds.), *Inter/Media: Interpersonal Communication in a Media World,* third edition. New York: Oxford University Press, pp.185–206.

Innis, H. A. (1951) *The Bias of Communication*. Toronto, Canada: University of Toronto Press.

Ito, M., Okabe, D., & Matsuda, M. (2005) *Mobile Phones in Japanese Life*. Cambridge, MA: The MIT Press.

Jones, S. G. (1995) *Cybersociety: Computer-mediated communication and community*. Thousand Oaks, CA: Sage Publications.

Kavanaugh, A. L., & Patterson, S. J. (2001) "The impact of community computer networks on social capital and community involvement." *American Behavioral Scientist, 45*(3), 496–509.

Kline, D., & Burstein, D. (2005) *Blog!* New York: CDS Books.

Kornblum, J. (2005) "Teens wear their hearts on their blogs." *USA Today* October 30. Available: at www.usatoday.com/tech/news/techinnovations/2005-10-30-teen-blogs_x.htm?POE=click-refer. (last viewed November 1, 2005).

Laurel, B. (1993) *Computers as Theatre*. Reading, MA: Addison Wesley.

Levinson, P. (1997) *The Soft Edge*. New York: Routledge.

Levinson, P. (1999) *Digital McLuhan*. New York: Routledge.

Licklider, J. C. R., & Taylor, R. (1968) "The computer as a communication device." *International Science and Technology,* April.

Liu, G. Z. (1999) "Virtual community presence in internet relay chat." *Journal of Computer-Mediated Communication, 5*(1). Available at www.ascusc.org/jcmc/vol5/issue1/liu.html. (last viewed May 13, 2003).

Lombard, M., & Ditton, T. (1997) "At the heart of it all: The concept of presence." *Journal of Computer-Mediated Communication, 3*(2). Available at www.ascusc.org/jcmc/vol3/issue2/lombard.html. (last viewed January 18, 2005).

Lombard, M., Reich, R. D., Grabe, M. E., Bracken, C. C., & Ditton, T. B. (2000) "Presence and television: The role of screen size." *Human Communication Research, 26*(1), 75–98.

McLuhan, M. (1962) *The Gutenberg Galaxy*. Toronto: The University of Toronto Press.

McLuhan, M. (1964) *Understanding Media: The Extensions of Man*. New York: Signet.

Majmudar, N. (2005) "College networking puts on a new face." *Democrat and Chronicle,* August 28, pp. 1E, 4E.

Mantovani, F., & Castelnuovo, G. (2003) "Sense of presence in virtual training: Enhancing skills acquisition and transfer of knowledge through learning experience in virtual environments." In G. Riva, F. Davide & W. A. Ijsselsteijn (eds.), *Being There: Concepts, Effects and Measurements of User Presence in Synthetic Environments.* Amsterdam: IOS Press, pp. 167–181.

Marvin, C. (1988) *When Old Technologies Were New.* New York: Oxford University Press.

Meyrowitz, J. (1985) *No Sense of Place.* New York: Oxford University Press.

Murray, D. E. (1991) *Conversation for Action: the Computer Terminal as Medium of Communication.* Amsterdam/Philadelphia: John Benjamins.

Nardi, B., & O'Day, V. (1999) *Information Ecologies: Using Technology with Heart.* Cambridge, MA: MIT Press.

Olson, D. R. (1994) *The World on Paper.* New York: Cambridge University Press.

Ong, W. J. (1982) *Orality and Literacy.* New York: Methuen & Co.

Postman, N. (1979) *Teaching as a conserving activity.* New York: Dell Books.

Postman, N. (1985) *Amusing Ourselves to Death.* New York: Penguin Books.

Postman, N. (1992) *Technopoly: the Surrender of Culture to Technology.* New York: Alfred A. Knopf.

Postman, N. (1995) *The End of Education.* New York: Alfred A. Knopf.

Quan-Haase, A., Cothrel, J., & Wellman, B. (2005) "Instant messaging for collaboration: A case study of a high-tech firm." *Journal of Computer-Mediated Communication, 10*(4). Available at www.jcmc. Indiana.edu. (last viewed September 15, 2005).

Rafaeli, S., & Sudweeks, F. (1998) "Networked interactivity." In F. Sudweeks, M. McLaughlin, & S. Rafaeli (eds.), *Network and Netplay: Virtual Groups on the Internet,* Cambridge, MA: The MIT Press, pp. 173–189.

Raymond, E. S. (1999, 2001) *The Cathedral and the Bazaar.* Sebastopol, CA: O'Reilly & Associates.

Reeves, B., & Nass, C. (1996) *The Media Equation.* New York: Cambridge University Press.

Rennie, F., & Mason, R. (2003) "The ecology of connection." *First Monday, 8*(8). Available at www.firstmonday.org. (Last viewed September 10, 2005).

Rheingold, H. (1993) *The Virtual Community.* Reading, MA: Addison-Wesley.

Rheingold, H. (2002) *SmartMobs.* New York: Basic Books.

Rice, R. E., & Love, G. (1987) "Electronic emotion: Socioemotional content in a computer-mediated communication network." *Communication Research, 14*(1), 85–108.

Sakkas, L. (1993) "Politics on the net." *Interpersonal Computing and Technology, 2*(1). Available: at www.Helsinki.fi/science/optek (last viewed: January 8, 2001).

Schroeder, R. (1996) *Possible worlds.* Boulder, CO: Westview Press.

Schuler, D. (1996) *New Community Networks.* Reading, MA: Addison-Wesley Publishing.

Short, J. Williams, E., & Christie, B. (1976) *The Social Dynamics of Telecommunications.* New York: John Wiley & Sons.

Shneiderman, B. (2000) "Designing trust into online experiences." *Communications of the ACM,. 43*(12), 57–59.

Sloan, N. J. A., & Wyner, A. D. (1992) *Claude Elwood Shannon: Collected Papers.* New York: IEEE Press.

Slouka, M. (1995) *War of the Worlds.* New York: Basic Books.

Sproull, L., & Kiesler, S. (1991) *Connections: New Ways of Working in the Networked Organizat ion.* Cambridge, MA: The MIT Press.

Stoll, C. (1995) *Silicon Snake Oil.* New York: Doubleday.

Strate, L. (1999) "The varieties of cyberspace: problems in definition and delimitation." *Western Journal of Communication, 63*(3), 382–412.

Strate, L., Jacobson, R., & Gibson, S. (1996) *Communication and Cyberspace.* Cresskill, NJ: Hampton Press.

Strate, L., Jacobson, R., & Gibson, S. (2003) *Communication and Cyberspace,* second edition.

Cresskill, NJ: Hampton Press.

Svensson, J. S., & Bannister, F. (2004) "Pirates, sharks and moral crusaders: Social control in peer-to-peer networks." *First Monday, 9*(6). Available: at www.firstmonday.org. (last viewed September 15, 2005).

Tepper, M. (2003) "The rise of social software." *Net Worker,* September, 19–23.

Turkle, S. (1995) *Life on the Screen.* New York: Simon & Schuster.

Turner, T. C., Smith, M. A., Fisher, D., & Welser, H. T. (2005) "Picturing usenet: Mapping computer-mediated collective action." *Journal of Computer-Mediated Communication, 10*(4). Available www.jcmc.Indiana.edu. (last viewed September 15, 2005).

Uslaner, E. M. (2000) "Social capital and the net." *Communications of the ACM, 43*(12), 60–64.

Walther, J. B. (1996) "Computer-mediated communication: Impersonal, interpersonal, and hyperpersonal interaction." *Communication Research, 23*(1), 3–43.

Wellman, B., Haase, A. Q., Witte, J., & Hampton, K. (2001) "Does the internet increase, decrease, or supplement social capital?" *American Behavioral Scientist, 45*(3), 436–455.

Werbach, K. (2001, May 29) "Triumph of the weblogs." *Release, 1,* 21–25.

Whillock, R. K. (1997) "Cyber-politics: The online strategies of 96." *American Behavioral Scientist, 40*(8), 1208–1225.

Whittle, D. B. (1997) *Cyberspace: The Human Dimension.* New York: Freeman.

Wiener, N. (1954) *The Human Use of Human Beings: Cybernetics and Society.* Garden City, NY: Doubleday Books.

Wiener, N. (1948/1961) *Cybernetics: or Control and Communication in the Animal and the Machine.* Cambridge, MA: The MIT Press.

Wood, A. F., & Smith, M. J. (2001) *Online Communication: Linking Technology, Identity & Culture.* Mahwah, NJ: Lawrence Erlbaum Associates.

Woolley, B. (1992) *Virtual Worlds.* Cambridge, MA: Blackwell Publishers.

Xu, H., Wang, H., & Teo, H. (2005) "Predicting the usage of P2P sharing software: The role of trust and perceived risk." *Proceedings of the 38th Hawaii Internation Conference on System Sciences.* New York: IEEE Publications [online] Number: 0-7695-2268-8/05.

Zuboff, S. (1988). *In the Age of the Smart Machine.* New York: Basic Books.

Chapter 3

Machines as mediators

The challenge of technology for interpersonal communication theory and research

Melanie D. Polkosky

In the past several years, we have become inundated with sleek, futuristic technologies that allow us to communicate more often from our places of work, homes, and everywhere in between. Communication technologies have become an important and prevalent means of social interaction that may be difficult, impossible, unavailable, or perhaps just more cumbersome through more traditional means. These technologies have impacted on our daily interactions with others and promise to do so for years to come.

Consider a recent business trip: I searched for and found my tickets on an internet webpage. A few days later when I called the airline, I spoke to an automated speech system, which confirmed my flight time and gate number. On the day of my flight, I received a text message on my cell phone alerting me that my flight was on time; when I arrived at the airport, I checked in and printed my boarding pass at a touch screen kiosk. After clearing security, I distractedly waited at the crowded gate, listening to the cacophony of people talking on their cell phones or fidgeting with their personal digital assistants (PDAs). Disturbing my hope of quiet contemplation, one man conspicuously and repeatedly yelled into his cell phone that his brother should definitely meet him at the apartment, not at the house, later that evening. Upon settling into my cramped seat on the plane, I heard about the safety features of my airline from a series of attendants shown on a small television screen. Aside from a couple of anonymous strangers who smiled at or briefly greeted me, my entire travel experience could have included no direct, face-to-face conversation with another human until I mentioned my beverage choice to a flight attendant.

Previous mediated interpersonal communication research

Despite its ubiquitous presence in our everyday lives, technology as a whole has had relatively limited attention in the interpersonal communication field. A brief review of journals for the period 1985 to 2004 suggests that communication research has had minimal penetration by technology-based studies. The broad keywords "technology" and "computer" retrieved only 6 percent of total articles published in *Human Communication Research, Communication Theory, Communication Research, Journal of Communication,* and *Journal of Language and Social Psychology* during the past two decades. A search of *Personality and Social Psychology Review, Personality and Social Psychology Bulletin,* and *Journal of Personality and Social Psychology* showed a similar limited retrieval of articles, although behavioral science publications generally increased their inclusion of computer-mediated communication in the late 1990s. Nonetheless, communication researchers do show interest in these areas, as evidenced by a number of recent journal publications (Bonito, 2003; Cornelius & Boos, 2003; Lee, 2004; Lee & Nass, 2002; Lin, 2003; Ramirez *et al.*, 2002; Tidwell & Walther, 2002).

The inconsistency between our daily communication experiences and communication as reflected in academic scholarship may make us pause to consider the future of interpersonal communication. Communication technology hasn't been a significant part of the field's past and is only modestly represented in our present. Why is technology an important focus for future interpersonal communication researchers? What might it teach us that our past research has not yet illuminated? How do we know if our current constructs and assumptions will adapt to the changes brought by increasingly sophisticated and subdiscipline-straddling forms of communication? By considering the emerging and ubiquitous area of communication technology, interpersonal communication may embrace new lines of future research, application, and practice.

Why study communication technology?

A review of issues in communication technology suggests it is an important topic of study that could complement, inform, utilize, and even lead interpersonal communication research in the coming years. Current definitions and theoretical models of interpersonal communication, typically developed long before the advent of chat, talking machines, cell phones, and intelligent bots, are not adequate to encompass the central concerns of applied research and practice with various technologies. However, the challenge to communication researchers is that these technologies further complicate an already complex subject. As in other experimental behavioral sciences, the goal of the researcher is to advance our understanding of communication behavior and its general laws through empirical research (Wickens & Hollands, 2000). In contrast, the applied researcher or practitioner has a problem-focused goal: to engineer working communication systems that take advantage of users' communication, social, and emotional abilities and accommodate their limitations (Hassenzahl, 2001; Norman, 2003; Wickens *et al.*, 1998). Research and applied work have a symbiotic relationship: The research literature offers a rationale for practical design decisions and applied problems offer the next generation of research questions.

To the unacquainted, engineering communicative systems may seem to be primarily a technological endeavor, concerned with networks, wires, hardware, algorithms, and programmer's code. However, because such systems are designed for and used by people, applied work is also grounded in human behavior. Successful usage of these systems requires a sophisticated understanding of how they impinge on the dynamic process of interpersonal interaction. In addition to a deep understanding of cognitive and mental functions (Hollnagel & Woods, 1999: 222), applied practitioners are modeling and designing for interpersonal interaction, using technology as a partner or as a medium of communication. Brennen (1998) argues that "transporting models from social and cognitive psychology to electronic communication and embodying such models in software has the potential to bring additional clarity and pragmatism to these fields."

The present review introduces three specialized disciplines that are concerned with interpersonal communication and technology. However, these forms of communication technology complicate an already complex topic and challenge the construct of interpersonal communication itself. I address three major challenges technology poses for interpersonal research, then turn to consideration of several ways that technology may be embraced within our scholarship to support and expand the relevance of our field for the future.

What is communication technology?

Communication technology encompasses a broad, diverse set of hardware and software products that resist simple categorization. However, applied behavioral researchers and practitioners have defined three highly specialized disciplines that, like interpersonal communication itself, are concerned with meaning exchange and relationship management between two (or more) partners (Beebe *et al.*, 2002; DeVito, 2004). Each discipline brings unique applied problems but the three areas are also bound to each other and more traditional areas of interpersonal research by their common interests in social interaction and communication.

The majority of empirical work has been conducted with communication technologies that serve as the medium of communication: These types of technology enable human partners to converse. Known collectively as *computer-mediated communication* (CMC) or *telecommunication* (Fussell & Benimoff, 1995; Spears *et al.*, 2001), technologies that allow human-human communication include the now familiar forms of email, chat, video conferencing, instant messaging, telephone, and cellular phone (Barnes, 2003; Fussell & Benimoff, 1995; Storck & Sproull, 1995; Walther,

1996, 1997). These technologies may disrupt or obscure nonverbal and extralinguistic communication, an issue that has been the focus of applied research and social-psychological theory development to date (for a review, see Barnes, 2003, or Spears *et al.*, 2001).

CMC has broad applicability to relationship management (Rabby & Walther, 2003). Researchers have explored a variety of relationships facilitated through CMC, including teacher-student (McComb, 1994), student-student (Lipponen *et al.*, 2003; Smith *et al.*, 2003), therapist-client (Peterson & Beck, 2003), as well as relationships between co-workers (Coovert & Thompson, 2001; Thompson & Coovert, 2002), and romantic partners (Nice & Katzev, 1998). In general, the findings have indicated that self- and other-perception are impacted by CMC (Spears *et al.*, 2001). Despite recognition of this technology as a relationship enabler, the concern that CMC may have negative affective and social outcomes on users has been an undercurrent in the literature (Bargh & McKenna, 2004; Caplan, 2003; Kraut *et al.*, 1998).

Augmentative and alternative communication (AAC) is "the transdisciplinary field that uses a variety of symbols, strategies, and techniques to assist people who are unable to meet their communication needs through natural speech and/or writing" (Lloyd *et al.*, 1997). AAC strategies often include various technologies, including forms of telecommunication and computer-mediated communication, as well as non-technology-based interventions including sign language, facial expression, and gesturing (Lloyd *et al.*, 1997). Like CMC, AAC interventions provide a means of communication between the user and his or her partners. This field is concerned with the application of interventions to improve the quality of life and social access for individuals with a range of complex disabilities, including cerebral palsy, amyotrophic lateral sclerosis, mental retardation, autism, and traumatic brain injury. AAC interventions often provide a system of communication that depends on the specific skills and needs of the individual: for example, a communication system may consist of natural speech, gestures, facial expression, and vocalization in the home environment, and use of other developed communication strategies (e.g., synthetic speech output device, communication board) in less familiar environments. Additional instruction and support is usually provided to teach the user and his or her partners how to adapt to the effects of their mediated interaction.

Also similar to CMC, AAC research has explored how the technology affects its users' relationships, such as those among co-workers (McNaughton *et al.*, 2003) and peers (Clarke & Kirton, 2003). However, a larger focus has been on the inclusion and participation of individuals who use AAC in social environments such as school (Kent-Walsh & Light, 2003; Trudeau *et al.*, 2003). AAC research is focused largely on empirically validating its outcomes for users, having emerged from anecdotal clinical findings that these interventions were successful with individuals who had not benefited from traditional speech therapy (Lloyd *et al.*, 1997).

In contrast to these technologies, speech user interface (SUI) systems *replace* a human partner in conversational exchanges. In business applications, when speech interfaces are used to provide customer service, they generally replace a human customer service representative or operator. Like some technology-based AAC systems, speech interfaces may use *speech recognition* to understand a human user's utterances and *synthetic speech* to respond. Alternatively, SUIs may use speech recognition for comprehension and the recorded utterances of a professional human voice to respond back to the user (Balentine & Morgan, 1999; Kotelly, 2003). An important aspect of SUI design is the persona of an interface, or its social cues conveyed through voice and linguistic characteristics (Kotelly, 2003). At the present time, most commercially deployed speech interfaces generally do not provide significant visual input to the user, but they do allow unlimited access between business and its customers via the common telephone or other wireless technologies, such as cellular phone (Balentine & Morgan, 1999; Rust & Kannan, 2002). In their broadest sense, speech interfaces may be combined with robotics, talking faces, and other visual interfaces (Bailly *et al.*, 2003; Severinson-Eklundh *et al.*, 2003; Watanabe *et al.*, 2004). Functions that are currently handled by speech user interfaces include banking and financial transactions, information retrieval, airline reservations, stock and mutual fund inquiries, directory assistance, and other relatively simple, predictable, or constrained customer service interactions (Balentine & Morgan, 1999).

SUIs are part of the burgeoning trend toward technological forms of service delivery known as e-service (Rust & Kannan, 2002). Speech interfaces are specifically thought to improve customer-business relationships, specifically increasing customer satisfaction and loyalty, over other types of self-service technologies, such as webpage or touch-tone applications (Kotelly, 2001). Although the relationships addressed by SUI systems are more specific and less intimate than those typically targeted by CMC and AAC systems, the businesses that implement SUI systems view them as a mechanism of customer relationship management and an extension of their corporate brand.

These three fields, despite apparent differences, have much in common with each other and with interpersonal communication. They are each grounded in a common concern with user-technology interaction, specifically aspects of social-communicative interaction. They each are concerned with the characteristics of a communicative interaction that build a relationship and cause it to be viewed favorably, as well as those user and interaction characteristics that lead to communicative breakdown or failure, thereby preventing a relationship from being formed or causing it to deteriorate. All three fields recognize that although technology is included in communication, at least one human partner is needed in a communicative system. From the needs, abilities, and limitations of the human partner(s) flow the requirements of the technology component of the communicative system. Each discipline views technology as an enabler, not the point, of social interaction with others. As such, communicative system design is derived from *human* cognitive, communicative, motor, and social skills and limitations, with additional constraints imposed by the technology itself. The central concern of these disciplines is the optimization of social-communicative dialogue for the human user, regardless of the specific technology involved in the interaction.

There are also several differences among the fields. While CMC and SUI systems have been primarily involved with individuals who make up the largest proportion of the distribution of human skills, AAC is concerned with a more specialized population. Thus, deriving general laws of communication may be more challenging in AAC because individual manifestations of impairment may make the resulting communicative system and its technology component unique to its user. However, AAC interventions may be generalized within specific disorder populations (e.g., autism, aphasia) or age groups (e.g., preschoolers) (Beukelman & Mirenda, 1998; Lloyd *et al.*, 1997). Another difference in these forms of technology use concerns the apparent "repeatability" of dialogue: Because ACC and SUI systems may use a constricted set of messages, dialogues involving these systems may be somewhat inflexible or restricted in their ability to span topics and use a somewhat stilted linguistic style. For this reason, communication breakdowns may be more cumbersome to resolve. The greatest apparent contrast occurs between SUI systems and the other two fields. However, in terms of a communicative system, an SUI simply replaces a different subcomponent of a communication system than CMC or AAC technology. The general process and laws of interaction are similar to any form of interpersonal communication, regardless of which system subcomponent technology occupies. SUI systems also seem different from CMC or AAC because interaction with a machine may not appear to be "interpersonal" at all, unlike mediated human-human interaction. In this assumption lies one of the primary challenges of technology for interpersonal communication.

Challenges to interpersonal communication

Technology opposes existing notions of interpersonal communication in several ways. Many existing definitions of the construct imply: (1) both interactants are human (persons); (2) interpersonal is a separable form of communication, distinct from other types (e.g., mass, impersonal, intrapersonal); and (3) the primary goal of communication is relationship building or maintenance (Barnes, 2003; Beebe *et al.*, 2002; Buber, 1970; DeVito,

2004; Krauss & Fussell, 1996; Stamp, 1999). However, consideration of communication technology suggests that it is these assumptions that may prevent cross-pollination of traditional interpersonal communication research and applied theory and practice in technology.

The personhood of the communicator

The first requirement of interpersonal interaction is the "personhood" of both communicators. Although this issue is less problematic for human interlocutors mediated by CMC and AAC systems, SUI systems may be rejected as a form of interpersonal communication specifically because they are not human. However, research is beginning to demonstrate that humans do respond to speech technology in a humanlike fashion (Brennen, 1998; Lee & Nass, 2004; Nass & Lee, 2001; Sundar & Nass, 2000). A parallel "lack of personhood" controversy has also occurred in non-human animal research: Despite empirical demonstration of animal comprehension of symbolic language approaching that of human children (Kaminski et al., 2004) and human perception of animals' language comprehension (Pongracz et al., 2001; Sims & Chin, 2002), the attribution of humanlike mental states to animals remains a controversial and frequently rejected explanation of findings (Schilhab, 2002; Wynne, 2004).

The notion that human users might perceive social characteristics in a conversational computer is not new: Turing (1950: 442) proposed an imitation test in which human interrogators question an obscured respondent as an evaluative method for the "humanness" of computers. He stated: "I believe that in about fifty years' time it will be possible to programme computers ... to make them play the imitation game so well that an average interrogator will not have more than 70 per cent chance of making the right identification after five minutes of questioning. The original question 'Can machines think?' I believe to be too meaningless to deserve discussion." The Turing Test has promoted significant progress and controversy in the field of artificial intelligence, yet has remained a gauge by which technological progress is still measured (Korukonda, 2003; Saygin et al., 2000), even though its implications are controversial (Adam & Hershberg, 2004; Dresner, 2003; Hopgood, 2003; Kugel, 2004, Pinker, 2005). For Turing, the essential question was not how specific behaviors were implemented but *what capabilities a machine must exhibit to reliably fool human perception.*

Turing's argument suggests that a minimum set of behaviors will result in a perception of humanness. Speech and language cues are well known to causally influence partner perceptions of both the traits (e.g., intelligence, attractiveness, trustworthiness, friendliness) and mood of the speaker (Apple & Hecht, 1982; Aronovitch, 1976; Berry et al., 1997; Clark, 1996; Cosmides, 1983; DePaulo, 1992; Fussell & Krauss, 1992; Holtgraves, 2002; Kappas et al., 1991; Krauss & Fussell, 1991; Krauss et al., 1996;

Murray & Arnot, 1993; Patterson, 2001; Wyer *et al.*, 1995). Thus, humanlike trait perception is the interpersonal effect of speech and language cues. Research has indicated these judgments occur extremely rapidly (within 250 milliseconds), without willful control, and perceivers may be unaware of the source of their judgments (Bargh & Ferguson, 2000). Taking these findings a step farther, vocal cues may even causally induce a speaker's emotional state in a communicative partner, also without awareness by the partner (Neumann & Strack, 2000).

Another strain of research suggests that behavior can have trait implications, suggesting that the mere presence of trait-relevant behavior like speech and language elicits personality judgments in perceivers. This literature has shown that individuals spontaneously infer traits from behavior (Carlston & Skowronski, 1994; Ham & Vonk, 2003; Winter & Uleman, 1984) and transfer these inferred traits to interaction partners (Skowronski *et al.*, 1998) or even to inanimate objects (Brown & Bassili, 2002). This rapid, automatic (heuristic) processing of incoming social information is thought to improve cognitive efficiency in humans by focusing attention on some subset of the constant barrage of social cues with which we must contend (Bargh & Ferguson, 2000; Fiske & Taylor, 1991; Wickens & Hollands, 2000). In communication, the use of this type of heuristic processing (i.e., judgments about a partner's characteristics) also is thought to assist with rapid, effective message formulation and exchange (Bavelas *et al.*, 2000; Clark, 1996; Fussell & Krauss, 1992; Krauss & Fussell, 1991).

Thus, assumptions of "personhood" (i.e., speaker personality and cognitive status) are elicited by the mere presence of speech and language behavior. In many ways, social attributions of personhood are more a testament to our cognitive capacity for social pattern recognition than an overt statement on the "personhood" of non-human communicators. In turn, it is these attributions that prevent social perception and judgment from exceeding our cognitive capacity and result in more efficient and effective interactions. As Turing implied, the question of whether a communicator is actually human becomes irrelevant, because he, she, or it demonstrates communicative behavior that holds trait-implying properties.

Distinguishing interpersonal interaction as a unique communication subtype

Almost two decades ago, Berger and Chaffee (1988) expressed consternation at the gulf between mass and interpersonal communication scholarship and encouraged greater collaboration between these subdisciplines. In 1991 (p. 112), Charles Berger lamented the state of theory-building in communication as well as the continued fragmentation of its subdisciplines. He predicted that "those who eagerly watch and wait for an Einstein-like figure to appear on the scene, complete with The General Theory of

Human Communication in hand, are very likely to be disappointed." By the end of the 1990s, O'Sullivan (1999) was describing the various ways communication technology research was facilitating the synthesis of mass and interpersonal communication, suggesting a significant improvement in the state of the discipline. However, even in our most recent publications, observers such Daryl Slack (2005: 6) still mourn the field's fragmentation by subdiscipline, "persistent loyalty overall to a model of transmission", and the existence of theoretical limitations.

Communication technologies do challenge arbitrary divisions among subfields, especially when SUI systems are considered. Interaction with SUI systems seems to have much in common with parasocial interaction (Barnes, 2003; Giles, 2002), in that the behavior of both an SUI system and media figure is typically scripted, often recorded for later playback, and intended to appeal to a mass audience. However, in both cases, the inter-actant's behavior is largely spontaneous. He or she reacts to the behavioral characteristics of the media figure or SUI system using an overlearned repertoire of social-communicative cognitions and behaviors. In addi-tion, the believability of the media figure and SUI system depends on the sophistication of the writer/designer's understanding of the character to be created, the needs and values of the audience, and the skillful rendering of behavior. SUI systems may also be considered very similar to inter-personal interactions mediated by AAC or CMC, in that the interaction is dynamic, ephemeral, unique to each pair of interlocutors, and involves turntaking, contingent behavior, and cooperation to achieve a social goal (Clark, 1996). Thus, SUI systems seem to occupy a unique space on a continuum bounded by mass communication on one side and interpersonal communication on the other. O'Sullivan (1999: 580) alluded to the poor fit of a categorical distinction between mass and interpersonal communica-tion, asserting "in light of developments in communication technologies, using criteria such as one-way versus two-way and large undifferentiated audiences versus small numbers of familiar interactants … are becoming a less useful distinction."

Interpersonal communication has also been contrasted with impersonal communication (Beebe *et al.*, 2002), based on differential categorization of the nature or quality of an interlocutor's intention toward a partner that is markedly different from that of an interpersonal one (Buber, 1970). Not only does this distinction require unobservable insight into the cognitions of a human communicator but it also does not account for recent findings that suggest communicators may be largely unaware of their cognitions and may have little or no insight into the causes of their own judgments about their partner (Bargh & Ferguson, 2000; Brown & Bassili, 2002). Both of these issues suggest that we cannot validly and reliably measure whether communication is impersonal or interpersonal, which presents a decided problem for empirical research to support this distinction. Interpersonal communication is also currently contrasted with *intra*personal communication, defined as "communication with yourself" or thinking (Beebe *et al.*, 2002). However, technological advancements may also obscure this apparent distinction as they provide direct access to brain functions (brain-computer interfaces) for communication with others (Neuper *et al.*, 2003) and other intrapersonal tasks (Curran *et al.*, 2004; Scherer *et al.*, 2004).

Non-relationship building social goals of communicative interaction

Finally, technology confronts the notion that relationship building and maintenance is the singular goal of interpersonal interaction. Other theoretical approaches to conversation assert that any communication is a form of goal-directed social behavior:

> language can also be viewed as a tool, a tool that is used for accomplishing particular ends. To use language is to perform an action, and it is a meaningful action, with consequences for the speaker, hearer, and the conversation of which it is a part. This is a very different view of language. To understand meaning there must be a speaker. And context is critical. What a speaker means with an utterance (what he intends to accomplish) can only be derived with some reference to a context.
>
> Holtgraves, 2002: 5

In this sense, language is the interpersonal means for accomplishing a particular goal in a defined social context. Language use necessarily implies social intent (Austin, 1962; Grice, 1975; Searle, 1969; Holtgraves, 2002).

Some researchers have suggested that communication is a means to any social goal, not just those concerned with relationships. As a framework for designing effective AAC systems, Light (1988) proposed four purposes of communication: transfer of information, communication of needs and wants, social closeness, and social etiquette. However, other social goals such as power and self-esteem maintenance may be based on a fundamental need for belongingness (Baumeister & Leary, 1995).

Regardless of the specific goals of communicators, it seems that any communication with another entity is interpersonal, even mundane interactions undertaken in the course of daily life. Along this line of reasoning, Mohr and Bitner (1991) argued that individual differences including background similarity, interaction frequency, script strength, number of subscripts, experience with a complementary role, and goal compatibility are independent variables that impact the roles and outcomes of interactions. Accordingly, brief, ritualized, task-based interactions like customer service interaction (Mohr & Bitner, 1991; Solomon *et al.*, 1985) are likely to be markedly different than those in which intimacy, longevity, and deep mutual knowledge are central characteristics. Snyder and Haugen (1994) found that priming communicators to acquire a stable social impression, ensure a smooth and pleasant interaction, or simply hold a conversation caused them to elicit different behaviors from a partner during conversation. In brief interactions in which getting to know a partner accurately is not a goal at all or would interfere with the primary goal of the interaction, it seems intuitively reasonable that the cognitive, affective, and behavioral outcomes of interaction would differ from interactions that enable a relationship. Walther (1997) found that expectation of future interaction did influence affective outcomes and effort in student groups communicating via CMC. This data may be interpreted as suggesting that when individuals view partners as integral to completing a task (similar goals), more positive interaction outcomes occur. Conversely, when goal achievement is thought not to require partners, more negative outcomes result (Wicklund & Steins, 1996). If utilitarian, short duration, task-based interactions between two humans are not a mainstay of interpersonal communication research, the replacement of one partner by a speaking technology will further challenge the bounds of interactivity deemed interpersonal.

Embracing technology in mediated interpersonal communication

Some researchers might assert that inclusion of technology in interpersonal communication research threatens the very foundation of the field. In contrast, technology has the potential to open our definitions and expand our research so that it becomes even more relevant and representative of the broad range of interactions we participate in every day. Pausing again on the vignette at the opening of this chapter, the commonality across my travel interactions, whether they took place with another person, with a technology, or via technology, is that they all made use of my social-communicative cognitions and behaviors. For interpersonal communication research to include the most modern and emerging forms of communication, researchers must embrace new communicative partners, interaction types, theories, and methods. In this section, I offer a preliminary view of a future for interpersonal communication that will encompass communication technologies.

Expanding the sample of interpersonal interaction participants

A vitally important step toward increasing applied research is the adoption of a broader definition of the potential range of interactants involved in interpersonal communication. Instead of specifically requiring people, a new definition may be based on the *coordinating communicative roles of interlocutors*. If we begin to highlight the use of observable communicative behavior (both behavior that is conventionally interpreted as communicative as well as idiosyncratic behaviors interpreted by at least one partner as communicative) instead of an abstract notion of personhood, our research samples will be broadened to include not only communicative partners with conventional symbolic communication but those with developing, non-human, and non-conventional skills (e.g., presymbolic, impaired). By defining interpersonal communication as consisting of two interactants in coordinating speaking and listening roles, researchers will have greater flexibility to study meaning exchange in a broader variety of ways than just between two similarly skilled humans. Instead, we will facilitate research with communicative pairs composed of two equivalently skilled partners, partners with similar but non-equivalent skills (e.g., individuals who use AAC-typical speakers, adult-child), and partners with very dissimilar communicative skills (e.g., SUI system-user, animal-human). Ultimately, this strategy for defining partners will give our empirical findings greater generalizability, eliminating the range restriction inherent in studies that only utilize individuals employing "typical" communication.

In addition to improved generalization of findings, we will be able to understand the skill and competence thresholds that make interpersonal interaction possible, satisfying, and successful. The interaction between a communicator's skills and the mode of communication also may be systematically explored. Light (1989) suggested mediated communication may require new forms of communicative competence beyond those types necessary for traditional forms of human-human interaction. She argued that competence:

> is predicated on knowledge, judgment, and skill in four areas: linguistic competence, operational competence, social competence, and strategic competence. The former two competencies (linguistic and operational) reflect knowledge and skills in tool use, while the latter two competencies (social and strategic) reflect functional knowledge and judgment in interaction. These four areas are interrelated and attainment of communicative competence is dependent on the mastery and integration of skills in each of them.
>
> Light, 1989

Strategic competence includes efforts by technology users to compensate for the limited or conflicting social cues created by a specific communication mode and partner, as well as the ability of interlocutors to adapt to novel communicative situations. Light (1989: 141) argued that strategically competent communicators "make the best of what they do know and can do" (within restrictions), but there is very little empirical data to illuminate the mechanisms that underlie such abilities. Thus, our research may not illuminate the extent to which such variables as adaptation, coping, social perception, and dialogue characteristics (e.g., turn exchange, pacing, number of communicative breakdowns) play a role in the success and affective outcomes of interpersonal exchanges.

A stream of research does support the use of a role-based definition of communicative behavior, which is part of schema theory. A role schema "is the cognitive structure that organizes one's knowledge about ... [appropriate] behaviors expected of a person in a particular social position" (Fiske & Taylor, 1991: 119). Within a communicative interaction, partners adopt both listener and speaker roles which may be influenced by their social standing, power, and other more specific context-based variables (Baldwin, 1992; Glover, 1995). Bavelas *et al.* (2000) examined the listener role in conversation and found that listeners are actively involved in co-constructing messages with speakers instead of passively attending to the message presented. In the case of technologies, role-appropriate behaviors may be impacted by increased difficulty to provide feedback and rapidly respond. Anecdotal information also suggests that when a service-based SUI system uses an imperative or directive linguistic style, users respond more negatively than when they utilize a polite style with more passive voice constructions; a possible (but not empirically validated) explanation may be that the system has violated the role expectation of customer service providers (Baydoun *et al.*, 2001; Cran, 1994; Holland & Baird, 1968; Humphreys, 1996). Yagil (2001: 350) argued that:

> a service provider's assertive behavior might be interpreted by the customer as reflecting a lack of respect; it may convey a degradation of the customer's status and thus lead to a general sense of dissatisfaction with the service. On the other hand, the ingratiatory behavior of the service provider, which is deliberately designed to please the customer, grants the customer a respectable status, enhances his or her self-esteem, and consequently results in satisfaction.

Thus, variations in use of role-appropriate behaviors may causally influence both the success of mediated social-communicative tasks and affective responses to the interaction.

Enhancing the range of interaction types

In addition to a broader range of interactants, our research should also include more mundane, everyday communicative encounters in addition to those interactions in which participants have an expectation of long-term intimacy. Human service encounters have been studied as a basis for interactions with service-based SUI systems (Polkosky, 2005). The outcomes of these types of brief, ritualized encounter may be influenced more heavily by our internal expectations about how the encounter should proceed and the partner's adherence to a prescribed role than other types of interpersonal events. These simple interactions are also likely to be candidates for automation with intelligent and speaking technologies or mediated with CMC because they help reduce the costs associated with communication. If we identify the variables that enable efficient or expect-ancy-consistent communication, it is likely we may also more effectively design technologies that are easier and more pleasurable to use.

Schema theory also offers a theoretical rationale for including more mundane interactions in our literature. Abelson (1981) defined a script as a set of expectations that influence and organize information processing during common events; simultaneously, it is also a sequenced set of behav-iors with specific eliciting contexts and entry criteria. The most familiar example of a script is the restaurant script, which includes expectations about the sequence of events that occur during a meal in a restaurant (e.g., ordering, obtaining food, paying, and leaving), role expectations for the waiter, and sequence rules specifying the order of behaviors (e.g., order before paying) (Fiske & Taylor, 1991). However, conversation itself is also a script (Glover, 1995), with roles for the participants and a set of sequenced behaviors such as greeting, turntaking, closing, mutual coop-eration to participate in message exchange (contributions), and repair of communicative breakdowns (Berger, 2001; Clark & Shaefer, 1989; Sacks *et al.*, 1974; Schegloff, 1968; Schegloff *et al.*, 1977; Schegloff & Sacks, 1973).Two examples of expectation-based design of SUI systems exist in the literature: Bernsen, *et al.* (1996) developed guidelines for designing a prototype conversational system that they observed were similar to Grice's (1975) maxims of conversational expectations and Saygin and Cicekli (2002) found that conversational violation of the Gricean maxims revealed a human versus computer partner.

Applying constructs of interpersonal communication

New theoretical and empirical theories are also an important means of expanding the boundaries of the field to encompass new forms of social interaction. To adequately describe the complex processes of commu-nication, especially those that involve technology, we must continue to develop new theoretical frameworks and apply existing findings to new, technology-related problems.

As an example of a new approach to technology systems, Polkosky (2005) recently developed a framework for service quality provided by SUI systems, based on previous literature concerned with conversational expectations (Grice, 1975; Holtgraves, 2002), the role of speech in social impression formation (Kappas *et al.*, 1991; Murray & Arnot, 1993), the usability of speech technology (Bernsen *et al.*, 1996; Saygin & Cicekli, 2002), and the social behavior of human customer service (Solomon *et al.*, 1985). Using principal components analysis, Polkosky (2005) showed that four factors are involved in perceptions of SUI systems: (1) User Goal Orientation, or the extent to which a system caters to the user's needs efficiently and promotes a sense of affiliation; (2) Speech Characteristics, or the pleasantness and naturalness of the system's voice; (3) Verbosity, or the talkativeness of the system; and (4) Customer Service Behavior, or the extent to which the system's behavior is similar to the expectations of human service providers (see Table 3.1).

In addition, the four factors were each significantly correlated with customer satisfaction (User Goal Orientation, $r = 0.71$; Speech Characteristics, $r = 0.43$; Customer Service Behavior, $r = 0.40$; Verbosity, $r = -0.26$; all ps<0.01), a major cognitive-affective outcome of such systems, although

Table 3.1 Four-factor framework of SUI service quality

User goal orientation
1	The system made me feel like I was in control.
2	The system gave me a good feeling about being a customer of this business.
3	I could find what I needed without any difficulty.
4	The system would help me be productive.
5	I could trust this system to work correctly.
6	I would be likely to use this system again.
7	I felt confident using this system.
8	The quality of this system made me want to remain a customer of this business.

Speech characteristics
1	The system's voice was pleasant.
2	The system's voice sounded like people I hear on the radio or television.
3	The system's voice sounded like a regular person.
4	The system's voice sounded natural.
5	The system's voice sounded enthusiastic or full of energy.

Customer service behavior
1	The system used terms I am familiar with.
2	The system used everyday words.
3	The system was organized and logical.
4	The system spoke at a pace that was easy to follow.
5	The system seemed polite.
6	The system seemed courteous.
7	The system seemed friendly.
8	The system seemed professional in its speaking style.

Verbosity
1	The messages were repetitive.
2	The system gave me more details than I needed.
3	The system was too talkative.
4	I felt like I have to wait too long for the system to stop talking so I could say something.

User Goal Orientation alone best predicted satisfaction. This research indicated the relevance of social-communicative theory and research to technology and further suggested that expectations associated with conversation, customer service, interpersonal interaction, and other media forms (e.g., television, radio) have a role to play in judgments of SUI systems. The four-factor framework has subsequently been applied in industrial settings as both an operationalized definition of speech technology service quality and usability, as well as an empirical measure for these systems.

Mediational causal modeling and theories of interpersonal communication

Another way of developing new models of interpersonal communication involves mediational causal modeling, a means of graphically depicting explanatory theories and testing them using statistical techniques like meta-analysis (Shadish, 1996). A number of linear, interactive, and transactional explanatory models of interpersonal communication have been described (Beebe *et al.*, 2002; DeVito, 2004; Wood, 2004), but the limitation of these models for applied technology research is that they are not concerned with the variables of specific interest for designing these technologies or understanding how to improve their usage.

Figure 3.1 depicts an example of a mediational causal model that is suggested by the previous literature and may provide a graphic representation of at least some of the issues of central concern in applied communication technology. In this model, two communication partners' individual difference (e.g., gender, pitch range, loudness, communication/social/cognitive skills, needs, expectations, etc.) and role variables are the independent variables. If an SUI or other intelligent technology system occupies one of the communicative roles, these variables might include gender of the system voice, linguistic variables related to the script, and use of synthetic speech or recorded human speech. The independent variables result in dialogue variables (a mediator) that, in turn, result in the various outcomes of the interaction such as task success, partner perception, and affective responses. The model also shows communication mode as a moderator (Chapanis *et al.*, 1972), assuming that the mode (e.g., chat, telephone, email, face-to-face conversation, or auditory only, visual only, or multiple sensory modes) causes a statistical interaction (Shadish, 1996). Stated differently, the model assumes that the relationship between individual differences of the partners and their dialogue is dependent on the mode of communication.

This model suggests interrelationships among variables that have been implied in the literature but not systematically explored. In many previous empirical studies and theoretical models, individual difference variables have often been assumed to have a direct causal relationship to commu-

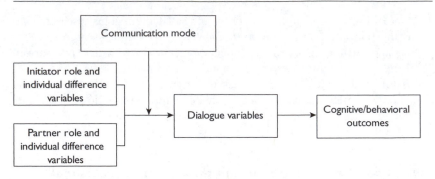

Figure 3.1 Causal mediation model of communication

nication outcomes, such as partner perception, impression management, and communicative success or efficiency (Bradac *et al.*, 2001; Cargile *et al.*, 1994; Lloyd *et al.*, 1997; Patterson, 1996, 2001). The problem with this approach for applied technology is that it ignores the critical linkage between a communicator and the dialogue; thus, we are unable to ascertain the skills required for dialogue, a critical issue in designing effective CMC, AAC, and SUI technologies. This issue recalls Turing's (1951) thought-provoking question about the minimum essential skills required for humanlike communication. In addition, the model also suggests that various dialogue variables cause the outcomes of communication. Identification of the dialogue variables that are critical to a specific outcome (e.g., a positively perceived and successful interaction) is another critical linkage of specific relevance for applied technology design that requires further empirical investigation.

Communication technology as a methodology

The final way that interpersonal communication might embrace technology is as a methodology. Because technology provides a method for building and controlling interactions, it provides a new approach to executing research in interpersonal communication. Kappas *et al.* (1991: 220) observed that synthetic speech has been utilized extensively in research on vocal emotion, because it allows "complete control over every acoustic parameter" and provides better internal validity than human speech. SUI systems are especially relevant as a methodological approach to interpersonal communication because variables of interest such as the system voice, message length and style, use of pausing, and metacommunication can be systematically varied among different user interfaces while the technology itself provides experimental control for other nuisance variables. Similarly, varying types of CMC or AAC may allow the applied researcher to compare dialogue and outcome variables. Anecdotal (and personal) information suggests that building such systems provides designers with a profound new appreciation of the complexity and sophistication of interpersonal communication. James Bradac provided a communication researcher's glimpse into the reality of his own aided communication:

> conversation is a series of short monologues in which the user expresses ideas and emotions through semantic and syntactic aspects of language exclusively…. expression is relatively impoverished as a result of the inability to control phonology and temporal aspects of discourse. I now really appreciate the flexibility and efficiency of typical conversations. Still, using this computer system is almost infinitely better than remaining inevitably and constantly silent, a situation that must have been forced on some 17th-century counterpart of mine unable to benefit from 20th-century technology.
>
> 1998: 5

The future of communication is already a significant presence in our everyday lives. It exists in the form of ultra thin, gleaming cell phones, machines that talk to us, video-conferencing and chat interfaces that make physical distance seem like a thing of the past. Over the next horizon, technology will bring us robot companions, direct access to our brain impulses, and a host of incredible innovations that we cannot even imagine in the early twenty-first century. Communication technologies hold the promise of uniting people. For researchers and practitioners, they give us a means of modeling human communication, critically examining our scholarship, and examining variable relationships in new ways. As O'Sullivan (1999) suggested, communication technology may well be the innovation that unifies and broadens our discipline as well.

References

Abelson, R. (1981) "Psychological status of the script concept." *American Psychologist, 36* (7), 715–729.

Adam, R., & Hershberg, U. (2004) "Testing the Turing test: Do men pass it?" *International Journal of Modern Physics, 15*(8), 1041–1047.

Apple, W., & Hecht, K. (1982) "Speaking emotionally: The relation between verbal and vocal communication of affect." *Journal of Personality and Social Psychology, 42*, 864–875.

Aronovitch, C. (1976) "The voice of personality: Stereotyped judgments and their relation to voice quality and sex of speaker." *The Journal of Social Psychology, 99*, 207–220.

Austin, J. (1962) *How to Do Things with Words.* Oxford: Clarendon Press.

Bailly, G., Berar, M., Elisei, F., & Odisio, M. (2003) "Audiovisual speech synthesis." *International Journal of Speech Technology, 6*, 331–346.

Baldwin, M. (1992) "Relational schemas and the processing of social information." *Psychological Bulletin, 112*(3), 461–499.

Balentine, B., & Morgan, D.P. (1999). *How to Build a Speech Recognition Application: A Style Guide for Telephony Dialogues.* San Ramon, CA: Enterprise Integration Group.

Bargh, J., & Ferguson, M. (2000) "Beyond behaviorism: On the automaticity of higher mental processes." *Psychological Bulletin, 126*(6), 925–945.

Bargh, J., & McKenna, K. (2004) "The internet and social life." *Annual Review of Psychology, 55*, 573–590.

Barnes, S. (2003) *Computer-Mediated Communication: Human-to-Human Communication Across the Internet.* Boston: Pearson.

Baumeister, R., & Leary, M. (1995) "The need to belong: Desire for interpersonal attachments as a fundamental human motivation." *Psychological Bulletin, 117*(3), 497–529.

Bavelas, J., Coates, L., & Johnson, T. (2000). "Listeners as co-narrators." *Journal of Personality and Social Psychology, 79*(6), 941–952.

Baydoun, R., Rose, D., & Emperado, T. (2001). "Measuring customer service orientation: An examination of the validity of the customer service profile." *Journal of Business and Psychology, 15*(4), 605–620.

Beebe, S.A., Beebe, S.J., & Redmond, M. (2002) *Interpersonal Communication: Relating to Others,* third edition. Boston: Allyn and Bacon.

Berger, C. (1991) "Chautauqua: Why are there so few communication theories? Communication theories and other curios." *Communication Monographs, 58*, 101–113.

Berger, C. (2001) "Miscommunication and communication failure." In W. P. Robinson & H. Giles (eds.), *The New Handbook of Language and Social Psychology.* New York: John Wiley & Sons, pp. 177–192.

Berger, C., & Chaffee, S. (1988) "On bridging the communication gap." *Human Communication Research, 15*(2), 311–318.

Bernsen, N., Dybkjaer, H., & Dybkjaer, H. (1996) "Cooperativity in human-machine and human-human spoken dialogue." *Discourse Processes, 21*, 213–236.

Berry, D., Pennebaker, J., Mueller, J., & Hiller, W. (1997) "Linguistic bases of social perception." *Personality and Social Psychology Bulletin, 23*, 526–537.

Beukelman, D., & Mirenda, P. (1998). *Augmentative and Alternative Communication: Management of Severe Communication Disorders in Children and Adults,* second edition. Baltimore: Paul H. Brookes.

Bonito, J. (2003) "Information processing and exchange in mediated groups: Interdependence and interaction." *Human Communication Research, 29*, 533–559.

Bradac, J. (1998) "It's all in your head." *ICA News, 27*(9), 4–5.

Bradac, J., Cargile, A., & Hallett, J. (2001). "Language attitudes: retrospect, conspect, and prospect." In W. Robinson & H. Giles (eds.), *The New Handbook of Language and Social Psychology* (pp. 601–623). New York: John Wiley & Sons.

Brennen, S. (1998) "The grounding problem in conversations with and through computers." In S. Fussell & R. Kreuz (eds.), *Social and Cognitive Approaches to Interpersonal Communication.* Mahwah, NJ: Lawrence Erlbaum, pp. 201–225.

Brown, R., & Bassili, J. (2002) "Spontaneous trait associations and the case of the superstitious banana." *Journal of Experimental Social Psychology, 38*, 87–92.

Buber, M. (1970) *I and Thou* (W. Kaufmann, Trans.). New York: Simon & Schuster. (Original work published 1923.)

Caplan, S. (2003) "Preference for online social interaction: A theory of problematic internet use and psychosocial well-being." *Communication Research, 30*(6), 625–648.

Cargile, A., Giles, H., Ryan, E., & Bradac, J. (1994) "Language attitudes as a social process: A conceptual model and new directions." *Language and Communication, 14*, 211–236.

Carlston, E., & Skowronski, J. (1994) "Savings in relearning of trait information as evidence for spontaneous inference generation." *Journal of Personality and Social Psychology, 66*, 840–856.

Chapanis, A, Ochsman, R., Parrish, R., & Weeks, G. (1972) "Studies in interactive communication I: The effects of four communication modes on the behavior of teams during cooperative problem-solving." *Human Factors, 14*(6), 487–509.

Clark, H. H. (1996) *Using Language.* Cambridge: Cambridge University Press.

Clark, M., & Kirton, A. (2003) "Patterns of interaction between children with physical disabilities using augmentative and alternative communication systems and their peers." *Child Language Teaching and Therapy, 19*(2), 135–148.

Clark, H., & Schaefer, E. (1989) "Contributing to discourse." *Cognitive Science, 13,* 259–294.

Coovert, M., & Thompson, L. (2001) *Computer Supported Cooperative Work: Issues and Implications for Workers, Organizations, and Human Resource Management.* Thousand Oaks: Sage.

Cornelius, C., & Boos, M. (2003) "Enhancing mutual understanding in synchronous computer-mediated communication by training." *Communication Research, 30*(2), 147–177.

Cosmides, L. (1983) "Invariances in the acoustic expression of emotion in speech." *Journal of Experimental Psychology: Perception and performance, 9,* 864–881.

Cran, D. (1994) "Towards validation of the service orientation construct." *The Service Industries Journal, 14,* 34–44.

Curran, E., Sykacek, P., Stokes, M., Roberts, S., Penny, W., Johnsrude, I., & Owen, A. (2004) "Cognitive tasks for driving a brain-computer interfacing system: A pilot study." *IEEE Transactions on Neural Systems and Rehabilitation Engineering, 12*(1), 48–54.

Daryl Slack, J. (2005) "Why the biotechnological body matters: Introduction to the special issue." *Communication Theory, 15*(1), 5–9.

DePaulo, B. (1992) "Nonverbal behavior and self-presentation." *Psychological Bulletin, 111,* 203–243.

DeVito, J. (2004) *The Interpersonal Communication Book,* tenth edition. Boston: Pearson.

Dresner, E. (2003) "'Effective memory' and Turing's model of mind." *Journal of Experimental and Theoretical Artificial Intelligence, 15*(1), 113–123.

Fiske, S. T., & Taylor, S. E. (1991) *Social Cognition.* New York: McGraw-Hill, Inc.

Fussell, S. R., & Benimoff, I. (1995) "Social and cognitive processes in interpersonal communication: implications for advanced telecommunication technologies." *Human Factors, 37*(2), 228–250.

Fussell, S., & Krauss, R. (1992) "Coordination of knowledge in communication: Effects of speakers' assumptions about what others know." *Journal of Personality and Social Psychology, 62,* 378–391.

Giles, D. (2002) "Parasocial interaction: A review of the literature and a model for future research." *Media Psychology, 4,* 279–305.

Glover, K. (1995) "A prototype view of context and linguistic behavior: Context prototypes and talk." *Journal of Pragmatics, 23,* 137–156.

Grice, H. (1975) "Logic and conversation." In P. Cole and J. Morgan (eds.), *Syntax and Semantics: Speech Act,* third edition. New York: Academic, pp. 41–58.

Ham, J., & Vonk, R. (2003) "Smart and easy: Co-occurring activation of spontaneous trait inferences and spontaneous situational inferences." *Journal of Experimental Social Psychology, 39*(5), 434–447.

Hassenzahl, M. (2001) "The effect of perceived hedonic quality on product appealingness." *International Journal of Human-Computer Interaction, 13*(4), 481–499.

Holland, J., & Baird, L. (1968) "An interpersonal competency scale." *Educational and Psychological Measurement, 28,* 503–510.

Hollnagel, E., & Woods, D. (1999) "Cognitive engineering: New wine in new bottles." *International Journal of Human-Computer Interaction, 17*(1), 43–60.

Holtgraves, T. (2002) *Language As Social Action: A Social Psychology of Language Use.* Hillsdale, NJ: Erlbaum.

Hopgood, A. (2003) "Artificial intelligence: Hype or reality?" *Computer, 36*(5), 24–28.

Humphreys, M. (1996) "Exploring the relative effects of salesperson interpersonal process attributes and technical product attributes on customer satisfaction." *Journal of Personal Selling and Sales Management, 16,* 47–57.

Kaminski, J., Call, J., & Fischer, J. (2004) "Word learning in a domestic dog: Evidence for 'fast mapping.'" *Science, 304,* 1682–1683.

Kappas, A., Hess, U., & Scherer, K. (1991) "Voice and emotion." In R. Feldman & B. Rime (eds.), *Fundamentals of Nonverbal Behavior: Studies in Emotion and Social Interaction,*. New York: Cambridge University Press, pp. 200–238.

Kent-Walsh, J., & Light, J. (2003) "General education teachers' experiences with inclusion of students who use augmentative and alternative communication." *AAC: Augmentative and Alternative Communication, 19*(2), 104–124.

Korukonda, A. (2003) "Taking stock of Turing test: a review, analysis, and appraisal of issues surrounding thinking machines." *International Journal of Human Computer Studies, 58,* 240–257.

Kotelly, B. (2003) *The Art and Business of Speech Recognition: Creating the Noble Voice.* Boston: Addison Wesley.

Krauss, R. M., Chen, Y., & Chawla, P. (1996) "Nonverbal behavior and nonverbal communication: What do conversational hand gestures tell us?" In M. Zanna (ed.), *Advances in Experimental Social Psychology.* San Diego, CA: Academic Press, pp. 389-450.

Krauss, R., & Fussell, S. (1991) "Perspective-taking in communication: Representations of others' knowledge in reference." *Social Cognition, 9*(1), 2–24.

Krauss, R. M., & Fussell, S. R. (1996) "Social psychological models of interpersonal communication." In E. T. Higgins & A. Kruglanski (eds.), *Social Psychology: a Handbook of Basic Principles* (pp. 655–701). New York: Guilford.

Kraut, R., Lundmark, V., Patterson, M., Kiesler, S., Mukopadhyay, T., Scherlis, W. (1998) "Internet paradox: A social technology that reduces social involvement and psychological well-being?" *American Psychologist, 53,* 1017–1031.

Kugel, P. (2004) "Toward a theory of intelligence." *Theoretical Computer Science, 317*(1–2), 13–30.

Lee, E. (2004) "Effects of visual representation on social influence in computer-mediated communication: Experimental tests of the social identity model of deindividuation effects." *Human Communication Research, 30*(2), 234–259.

Lee, E., & Nass, C. (2002) "Experimental tests of normative group influence and representations effects in computer-mediated communication: When interacting via computers differs from interacting with computers." *Human Communication Research, 28*(3), 349–381.

Lee, K., & Nass, C. (2004) "The multiple source effect and synthesized speech." *Human Communication Research, 30*(2), 182–207.

Light, J. (1988) "Interactions involving individuals using augmentative and alternative communication systems." *Augmentative and Alternative Communication, 5,* 137

Light, J. (1989) "Toward a definition of communicative competence for individuals using augmentative and alternative communication systems." *AAC: Augmentative and Alternative Communication, 5,* 137–143.

Lin, C. (2003) "An interactive communication technology adoption model." *Communication Theory, 13,* 345–365.

Lipponen, L., Rahikainen, M., Lallimo, J., Hakkarainen, K. (2003) "Patterns of participation and discourse in elementary students' computer-supported collaborative learning." *Learning & Instruction, 13*(5), 487–509.

Lloyd, L., Fuller, D., & Arvidson, H. (1997) *Augmentative and Alternative Communication: a Handbook of Principles and Practices.* Boston: Allyn and Bacon.

McComb, M. (1994) "Benefits of computer-mediated communication in college courses." *Communication Education, 43*(2), 159–170.

McNaughton, D., Light, J., & Gulla, S. (2003) "Opening up a 'whole new world': Employer and co-worker perspectives on working with individuals who use augmentative and alternative communication." *AAC: Augmentative and Alternative Communication, 19*(4), 235–253.

Mohr, L., & Bitner, M. (1991) "Mutual understanding between customers and employees in service encounters." *Advances in Consumer Research, 18,* 611–617.

Murray, I., & Arnott, J. (1993) "Toward the simulation of emotion in synthetic speech: A review of the literature on human vocal emotion." *Journal of the Acoustical Society of America, 93*, 1097–1108.

Nass, C., & Lee, K.M. (2001) "Does computer-synthesized speech manifest personality? Experimental tests of recognition, similarity-attraction, and consistency-attraction." *Journal of Experimental Psychology: Applied, 7*(3), 171–181.

Neumann, R., & Strack, F. (2000) "Mood contagion: The automatic transfer of mood between persons." *Journal of Personality and Social Psychology, 79*(2), 211–223.

Neuper, C., Muller, G., Kubler, A., Birbaumer, N., Pfurtscheller, G. (2003) "Clinical application of an EEG-based brain-computer interface: A case study in a patient with severe motor impairment." *Clinical Neurophysiology, 114*(3), 399–409.

Nice, M., Katzev, R. (1998) "Internet romances: the frequency and nature of romantic on-line relationships." *Cyberpsychology & Behavior, 1*(3), 217–223.

Norman, D. (2003) *Emotional Design: Why We Love (or Hate) Everyday Things*. New York: Basic.

O'Sullivan, P. (1999) "Bridging the mass-interpersonal divide: Synthesis scholarship in HCR." *Human Communication Research, 25*(4), 569–588.

Patterson, M. (1996) "Social behavior and social cognition: A parallel process approach." In J. L. Nye & A. M. Brower (eds.), *What's Social About Social Cognition? Research on Socially Shared Cognition In Small Groups*. Thousand Oaks, CA: Sage, pp. 87–105.

Patterson, M. L. (2001) "Toward a comprehensive model of non-verbal communication." In W. P. Robinson & H. Giles (eds.), *The New Handbook of Language and Social Psychology*. New York: Wiley, pp. 159–176.

Peterson, M., & Beck, R. (2003) "E-mail as an adjunctive tool in psychotherapy: Response and responsibility." *American Journal of Psychotherapy 57*(2), 167–181.

Pinker, S. (2005) "So how does the mind work?" *Mind and Language, 20*, 1–24.

Polkosky, M. (2005) Toward a social-cognitive psychology of speech technology: Affective responses to speech-based e-service. Unpublished doctoral dissertation, University of South Florida, Tampa.

Pongracz, P., Miklosi, A., & Csanyi, V. (2001) "Owner's beliefs on the ability of their pet dogs to understand human verbal communication: A case of social understanding." *Current Psychology of Cognition, 20*, 87–107.

Rabby, M., & Walther, J. (2003) "Computer-mediated communication effects on relationship formation and maintenance." In D. Canary & M. Dainton (eds.), *Maintaining Relationships through Communication: Relational, Contextual, and Cultural Variations*. Mahwah, NJ: Lawrence Erlbaum, pp. 141–162.

Ramirez, A., Walther, J., Burgoon, J., & Sunnafrank, M. (2002) "Information-seeking strategies, uncertainty, and computer-mediated communication: toward a conceptual model." *Human Communication Research, 28*(2), 213–228.

Rust, R., & Kannan, P.K. (2002) "The era of e-service." In R. Rust & P. Kannan (eds.), *e-service: New Directions in Theory and Practice*. Armonk, NY: M.E. Sharpe, pp. 3–21.

Sacks, H., Schegloff, E., & Jefferson, G. (1974) "A simplest systematics for the organization of turntaking in conversation." *Language, 4*, 696–735.

Saygin, A., & Cicekli, I. (2002) "Pragmatics in human-computer conversations." *Journal of Pragmatics, 34*, 227–258.

Saygin, A., Cicekli, I., & Ackman, V. (2000) "Turing test: 50 years later." *Minds and Machines, 10*(4), 463–518.

Schegloff, E. A. (1968) "Sequencing in conversational openings." *American Anthropologist, 70*, 1075–1095.

Schegloff, E. A., & Sacks, H. (1973) "Opening up closings." *Semiotica, 8*, 289–327.

Schegloff, E. A., Jefferson, G., & Sacks, H. (1977) "The preference for self-correction in the organization of repair in conversation." *Language, 53*, 361–382.

Scherer, R., Muller, G., Neuper, C., Graimann, B., & Pfurtscheller, G. (2004) "Anasynchronously controlled EEG-based virtual keyboard: Improvement of the spelling rate." *IEEE Transactions on Biomedical Engineering, 51*(6), 979–984.

Schilhab, T. (2002) "Anthropomorphism and mental state attribution." *Animal Behavior, 63*, 1021–1026.

Searle, J. (1969) *Speech Acts*. Cambridge: Cambridge University Press.

Severinson-Eklundh, K., Green, A., Huttenrauch, H. (2003) "Social and collaborative aspects of interaction with a service robot." *Robotics and Autonomous Systems, 42*(3–4): 223–234.

Shadish, W. (1996) "Meta-analysis and the exploration of causal mediating processes: A primer of examples, methods, and issues." *Psychological Methods, 1*(1), 47–65.

Sims, V., & Chin, M. (2002) "Responsiveness and perceived intelligence as predictors of speech addressed to cats." *Anthrozoos, 15*(2), 166–177.

Skowronski, J., Carlston, D., Mae, L., & Crawford, M. (1998) "Spontaneous trait transference: Communicators take on the qualities they describe in others." *Journal of Personality and Social Psychology, 74*(4), 837–848.

Smith, B., Alvarez-Torres, M., & Zhao, Y. (2003) "Features of CMC technologies and their impact on language learners' online interaction." *Computers in Human Behavior, 19*(6), 703–729.

Snyder, M., & Haugen, J. (1994) "Why does behavioral confirmation occur? A functional perspective on the role of the perceiver." *Journal of Experimental Social Psychology, 30*, 218–246.

Solomon, M., Surprenant, C., Czepeil, J., & Gutman, G. (1985) "A role theory perspective on dyadic interactions : The service encounter." *Journal of Marketing*, 49, 99–111.

Spears, R., Lea., M., & Postmes, T. (2001) "Social psychological theories of computer-mediated communication: Social pain or social gain." In W. Robinson & H. Giles (eds.), *The New Handbook of Language and Social Psychology*. New York: John Wiley & Sons, pp. 601–623.

Stamp, G. (1999) "A qualitatively constructed interpersonal communication model: A grounded theory analysis." *Human Communication Research, 25*(4), 531–547.

Storck, J., & Sproull, J. (1995) "Through a glass darkly: What do people learn in videoconferences?" *Human Communication Research, 22*(2), 179–219.

Sundar, S., & Nass, C. (2000) "Source orientation in human-computer interaction— Programmer, networker, or independent social actor?" *Communication Research, 27*(6), 683–703.

Thompson, L., & Coovert, M. (2002) "Stepping up to the challenge: A critical examination of face-to-face and computer-mediated team decision making." *Group Dynamics: Theory, Research, & Practice, 6*(1), 52–64.

Tidwell, L., & Walter, J. (2002) "Computer-mediated communication effects on disclosure, impressions, and interpersonal evaluations: Getting to know one another a bit at a time." *Human Communication Research, 28*(3), 317–348.

Trudeau, N., Cleave, P., & Woelk, E. (2003) "Using augmentative and alternative communication approaches to promote participation of preschoolers during book reading: A pilot study." *Child Language Teaching and Therapy, 19*(2), 181–203.

Turing, A. (1950) "Computing machinery and intelligence." *Mind, 59*, 433–460.

Walther, J. (1996) "Computer-mediated communication: Impersonal, interpersonal, and hyperpersonal interaction." *Communication Research, 23*(1), 3–43.

Walther, J. (1997) "Group and interpersonal effect in international computer-mediated collaboration." *Human Communication Research, 23*(2), 342–369.

Watanabe, T., Okubo, M., Nakashige, M., & Danbara, R. (2004) "InterActor: Speech-driven embodied interactive actor." *International Journal of Human-Computer Interaction, 17*(1), 43–60.

Wickens, C., Gordon, S., & Liu, Y. (1998) *An Introduction to Human Factors Engineering.* NY: Addison Wesley Longman.

Wickens, C., & Hollands, J. (2000) *Engineering Psychology and Human Performance,* third edition. Upper Saddle River, NJ: Prentice Hall.

Wicklund, R., & Stein, G. (1996) "Person perception under pressure: When motivation brings about egocentrism." In P. Gollwitzer & J. Bargh (eds.), *The Psychology of Action: Linking Cognition and Motivation to Behavior.* New York: Guilford, pp. 511–528.

Winter, L., & Uleman, J. (1984) "When are social judgments made? Evidence for the spontaneousness of trait inferences." *Journal of Personality and Social Psychology, 47,* 237–252.

Wood, J. (2004) *Interpersonal Communication: Everyday Encounters,* fourth edition. Belmont, CA: Wadsworth/Thomson.

Wyer, R., Swan, S., & Gruenfeld, D. (1995) "Impression formation in informal conversations." *Social Cognition, 13,* 243–272.

Wynne, C. (2004) "The perils of anthropomorphism: Consciousness should be ascribed to animals only with extreme caution." *Nature, 428,* 606.

Yagil, D. (2001) "Ingratiation and assertiveness in the service provider-customer dyad." *Journal of Service Research, 3*(4), 345–353.

Chapter 4

Self as source

Agency and customization in interactive media

S. Shyam Sundar

In a world of iPod and myYahoo, it appears as though communication technologies exist primarily to celebrate the individual rather than to bridge geographical distances or overcome physical barriers. What do new and emergent media technologies really add to the world of human communication? Are they simply meeting human need for information, entertainment, and social contact in a mediated setting or are they extending, as McLuhan (1964) claimed, our communicative abilities in space and time? In the brief history of computers and the internet, technology has advanced so rapidly that they have called into question fundamental assumptions about the nature of both interpersonal and mass communication.

Traditional forms of computer-mediated communication (CMC) such as chatrooms have given way to newer technologies such as blogs, which challenge once-sacred distinctions between interpersonal, group, and mass communication. Blogs are at once deeply personal in that they are one's diary or journal, often catering to a small group of commenters and lurkers, but they are shared, without access restrictions for the most part, with the rest of the world, making them, in principle, an example of mass communication on the web. Electronic mail, one of the oldest CMC devices, has undergone several modifications over the years, including the addition of synchronicity with the arrival of instant messaging (IM) and the ability to expand interpersonal to group communication with the aid of listserv and even to mass communication, as in spam. The ever-changing functionality of communication technologies persuades us, as scholars, to move away from an object-centered approach to the study of technology to a variable-centered one (Nass & Mason, 1990). It is less meaningful to study the uses and effects of any one particular CMC technology than to study variables that are embedded in—and cut across—several CMC technologies because technologies themselves die or metamorphose by incorporating newer features and affordances. Variables, on the other hand, exist to a lesser or greater degree across different technologies, thus allowing us to systematically assess their contribution to human communication. Moreover, their effects may be studied in their own terms without need to compare them to an ideal that would exist independent of the technology.

The ftf fallacy

A paradigmatic orthodoxy pervades the study of mediated interpersonal communication, particularly CMC, and that is the preoccupation with face-to-face (ftf) communication. Short *et al.* (1976) set the agenda and Kiesler *et al.* (1984) framed it for us: Ftf is the gold standard, and all CMC innovations, situations, and devices are to be measured against this standard. While this has provided an ideal toward which designers can strive, it has curtailed the development of criterion variables for measuring similarities and differences across different CMC scenarios. The degree to which a given CMC scenario approximates ftf is a monolithic measure, and a strong reliance on it runs the dual danger of: (1) subsuming important variables that might contribute in complex ways to achieving the approximation; and (2) overlooking other indicators of CMC efficacy.

For example, let's say the addition of audiovisual modalities to CMC vastly enhances its ability to approximate ftf, but modality as a variable is unlikely to be studied on its own, in all its richness. Instead, it will most probably be investigated for the degree to which it does or does not filter out cues in keeping with the cues-filtered-out perspective (Culnan & Markus, 1987) or the rate at which it can convey task-related and social information (Walther, 1992). Such a perspective is primarily concerned with modality as an affordance that results in certain communicative processes and outcomes (Burgoon *et al.*, 2002), but not as an independent technological artifact in and of itself. To illustrate, this is like approaching the study of television by carefully examining how the variables embedded in television technology (audiovisual modality, screen size, etc.) serve to enhance or diminish mediated experience of a real-life event as compared to experiencing it live. As we know, mass communication scholars seldom worry about the communicative difference between watching a sporting event in a stadium and a live broadcast of that event on TV. Instead, they treat television as a distinct symbol system whose structural features have certain effects on viewers' thoughts, emotions, and behaviors (e.g., Reeves & Anderson, 1991). The degree to which these features helps make the televised content similar to its real-life equivalent is largely irrelevant to the study of its effects. Being unmindful of this consideration enables media-effects researchers to examine all technological variables that have effects rather than only those that serve to enhance the medium's approximation of real life. More importantly, while examining any single variable such as modality, the emphasis is on attempting a comprehensive understanding of the psychological effects of each value of that variable (text, text+audio, etc.) regardless of its contribution to the transparency of the mediated experience. Furthermore, new values of that variable unique to the technology are fair game for exploration. For example, in studying web-based CMC interfaces, modality may include new values such as animation, pop-ups, download speed, and emoticons, which may not have any real-life equivalents or traditional media counterparts. Studying these solely to examine their contribution to the approximation of CMC to ftf is both limiting and somewhat inappropriate.

In this day and age of hyperpersonal communication (Walther, 1996), given the ability of technologies to facilitate communications which are far richer when mediated than in person, Ftf may no longer be the ideal for CMC. Indeed, studies have shown CMC outstripping ftf on performance-related measures (e.g., Burgoon *et al.*, 2002). The efficacy of CMC obviously depends on the functional motives of the interactants. Based on the purpose of the CMC interaction, users may expect a wide variety of outcomes, ranging from task efficiency (e.g., Burgoon *et al.*, 2002) to affective intimacy (Hu *et al.*, 2004), but these outcomes could be successfully achieved without necessarily approximating ftf. In fact, in certain situations, it would be detrimental to aspire for ftf likeness, as in the case of scheduling a meeting with a geographically dispersed group of people. Sometimes, in order to achieve greater telepresence, such meetings are arranged in a special video-conferencing facility with large displays and voice-sensitive cameras. While this may give participants a greater sense of being co-present with their distant partners during the course of the meeting, the expense and the effort involved in going to the special facility are likely to diminish the overall efficiency of such virtual meetings. If task efficiency is the crucial criterion variable, then that could be achieved by all participants staying in their respective offices and conducting the meeting via computers, using webcams if need be. While this would certainly diminish the sense of "being there," it most likely will enhance the overall efficiency of the CMC transaction. The real gains achieved here pertain to cost and time savings from cutting down on travel arrangements, efficiencies obtained by minimizing disruption of office routine, and so on. These have nothing to do with approximating ftf; indeed they have something to gain by minimizing likeness to ftf. Often, simple text-based CMC is far more effective than visually resplendent CMC, not just for task efficiency but also for promoting sociability and trust among other social judgments (Burgoon *et al.*, 2002). Even in the media equation literature, which catalogs the human tendency to treat computers and televisions as real people, Nass and colleagues have long argued that media richness is unnecessary for eliciting social attributions to communication technologies (Reeves & Nass, 1996; Nass & Moon, 2000).

All this raises the question: If approximating ftf is not the key, what then are the indicators of CMC efficacy? Let's consider the example of two classic CMC devices for interpersonal interaction—email and instant messaging. How do these two differ? Email is asynchronous while IM is real time. That is the primary difference. Does this mean IM is more inter-active, based on Steuer's (1992) definition? Is interactivity the key indicator of CMC efficacy? Let's consider two examples of CMC devices for group communication—chatrooms and blogs. Chatrooms allow for greater real time or interactive communication, but blogs are clearly far more satisfying to bloggers, given their recent dramatic proliferation. Blogs are indexed by search engines (Slavinsky & Glass, 2004), do not require formal member-ships or logins, provide for private as well as public posting of messages, maintain a searchable database archiving all the posts, feature a variety of options for threading of messages, act as repositories of references to news stories and other online sources, and offer a communal atmosphere for sharing of information and experiences (e.g., Scott, 2004). Are any of these relevant variables? Do these features all serve to make blogs more attractive? If so, then what is the underlying concept? Is it navigability? Do blogs offer greater navigation potential than chatrooms, is that it? But navigability does not vary much between email and IM (in that users do not typically engage in a whole lot of browsing while transacting via email or IM), so it's unlikely to be the crucial determinant of CMC efficacy.

Agency is key

If it's not modality, interactivity or navigability, then what is it that makes one CMC transaction "better" than another? The one variable that comes closest to a litmus test is agency. Agency is the degree to which the self feels that he/she is a relevant actor in the CMC situation. This means that it is the extent of manipulability afforded by the interface to assert one's influence over the nature and course of the interaction. IM certainly offers a more immediate sense of control to the user, an amplified version of the phenomenon of "caller hegemony" (Hopper, 1992) discussed in the telephone literature. And blogs, by serving as a public showcase for one's private thoughts and experiences, offer far greater agency to blog-gers than any chatroom ever can. Indeed, the history of mass communi-cation technology is one of increasing personalization of media, wherein the user is made to feel less and less like a passive receiver and more like a participant. Narrowcasting of messages and targeting audience members have been theorized as leading to a greater sense of community, even if somewhat disingenuously (Beniger, 1987). On the flip side, depersonaliza-tion in group CMC settings has been associated with deindividuation and a decreased sense of personal accountability (Spears et al., 2002).

When mass media resort to tailoring messages, they essentially imitate—or spuriously create the feel of—interpersonal communication. Conceptually, this means making each audience member feel like they are an audience of one, that the message is directed specifically at them.

Recent technological developments have vastly advanced the scope of such personalization of otherwise mass-produced messages by allowing receivers to make a priori specifications of the kinds of message they would like to receive. "Customization," as it's called, is now rampant in all domains of computer-based activities, from specifying the color of one's desktop to altering the nature of bells and whistles on one's IM interface to specifying what kinds of information one receives on a regular basis through their portal website. In explicating the concept of customization, Kalyanaraman and Sundar (2006) stress the importance of the individual user as opposed to a well-defined database of homogenous users. Customization allows each and every user to be unique and distinct.

Psychologically, what does customization mean for the user? Petty *et al.* (2002) suggest that the real appeal of a customized message lies in its reference to some aspect of one's self, be it the specificity of message content, the consonance between its emotional tone and one's personality, or its ability to cater to specific cognitive needs and processing styles. They base user preference for customization on the general principle of ego-defensiveness and egocentric construal of the interaction (see also Petty *et al.*, 2000). Given this, it's easy to understand the appeal of interactive media. Whether it is a medium devoted to mass communication (e.g., web portals) or interpersonal communication (e.g., instant messaging) or group communication (e.g., bulletin boards), greater interactivity allows for greater assertion of one's presence, by being able to steer the communication around one's felt needs and wants, likes and dislikes.

When self becomes the source

The crux of the individualization in customized messages lies not so much in the importance of the self as receiver (because that is merely targeting, which has been around for a long time in traditional media), but the self as sender or source. When the system allows the self to serve as the source of messages, the communication becomes truly interpersonal. A simple example: Imagine a speaker addressing a roomful of receivers, as in a classroom lecture. This ftf interaction becomes richly interpersonal only when an individual receiver raises his/her hand, asks a question, and receives a unique response customized to his/her need (articulated by way of the question). At this point, the receiver in question is engaged in interpersonal communication with the speaker where previously he/she was merely a recipient of mass communication by the speaker. Such a facility to obtain an individualized piece of information in an otherwise mass-mediated flow of messages lies at the heart of customization. The key aspect is the specification by the user of the exact nature of individualization desired. This is where the receiver becomes the source of communication.

In their typology of online sources, Sundar and Nass (2001) argued that, in addition to the traditional sender of communication ("visible sources"), the medium ("technological source") and the recipients ("receiver sources") can also be construed as sources in the online realm. The last mentioned was classified further, based on the level of analysis, as "audience as source" and "self as source," referring respectively to receivers as a collective and as individual users.

It must be noted that the sense in which the concept of "source" is used here is consistent with the use of the term by source credibility researchers from the early days of social-psychological work on persuasion and attitude change. (It is however different from the journalistic conception of source, which refers to the actual person originating a piece of information, often the person quoted in a news story, for example.) In investigating attitude change as a function of source credibility, social psychologists operationalized high and low credibility sources at the level of gatekeepers—newspaper, magazine, columnist, and so on.

It is heuristically appealing to consider gatekeepers as sources, especially in the context of web portals. For portals, and indeed all interfaces that offer customization, involve opening and closing gates, so to speak. In rudimentary terms, customization simply means choosing from among a set of options. The layout of most web portals features a set of square boxes on the screen, and the user can: (1) determine what a given box is about (e.g., horoscopes, football news, weather); and (2) specify *a priori* certain aspects of that content category that are of personal interest (e.g., horoscope information only for certain star signs, news only about certain favorite football teams or leagues, and weather information for only certain geographic locations of personal significance). The greater the freedom afforded by the interface to specify the gates, the greater the customization. For example, the beta version of Google News features an option to customize the page by allowing the user to choose an edition (U.S., U.K., India, and so on) and one or more sections from a given edition (e.g., Business, Sci/Tech, Sports). Both the edition and the section are chosen from pull-down menus, which means the universe of selection is limited and preset by Google News. For that reason, this is somewhat lower in customization compared to the feature that allows users to add a "custom section" by punching in keywords of their own. This Google feature allows the user to bypass traditional newspaper sections such as Sports, Business, Entertainment and World News, and enter their own idiosyncratic news category (say, "Beauty Contests" or "Libel Lawsuits" if you are interested in following news stories about beauty pageants and lawsuits pertaining to defamation). This is truly individualized news consumption, and therefore represents the height of customization. If one were to simply visit the Google News site and read the news of the day (or the moment, as it were), then the source is a technological one—the algorithm that scans news leads and assembles the page based on criteria such as recency and number of news outlets reporting the story. But once the user begins to specify news categories and sections, the site becomes a veritable portal and transfers the onus of gatekeeping to the individual receiver, thus making him or her the source.

Self-as-source has powerful psychological appeal it seems, given: (1) the marketplace success of customizable products; and (2) the widespread diffusion of technologies (e.g., blogs) and sites (e.g., Wikipedia) that allow—indeed depend on—users to provide information. Clearly, there is something seductive about serving as a source, be it as a gatekeeper or as information provider.

The theoretical implications of such a move towards "self as source" may be explored from two perspectives—technological and psychological. The source is a fundamental element in any conception of human communication (Sundar & Nass, 2000, 2001), but the ability to imbue sourcing to users is an artifact of recent technological developments in the area of customization. In particular, it is a direct consequence of inter-activity afforded by the interface. As Kalyanaraman and Sundar (2006) demonstrated, perceived interactivity significantly mediated the relationship between customization level and attitudes towards web portals.

Technological implications of self as source

Although the locus of interactivity is the message, with the level of contingency or interdependence between message exchanges being the key determinant (Sundar et al., 2003; Burgoon et al., 2002), it is more useful to conceptualize interactivity as a source, rather than message, feature for the purpose of understanding customization. As a source feature, interactivity is the degree to which the user can assert his or her agency in the interaction (Sundar, 2007). In an HCI (human-computer interaction) setting, it is the degree to which the system or interface allows the user to modify or create content. In a CMC setting, it is the degree to which the forum allows the user to influence the course and content of the interaction. The full potential of interactivity is reached when the user perceives himself or herself as the source of mediated content, although this is no guarantee of positive content evaluations.

Sundar and Nass (2001) experimentally created one such condition in the context of online news by providing participants with an interface that ostensibly allowed them to choose their own news stories for consumption from a menu of headlines. However, they liked the news stories less and rated them as being of lower quality and newsworthiness than participants in another condition who read the same stories but were told that other users of the online news service had collectively chosen the news stories. Clearly, this condition offers lesser agency to the individual user than the self-as-source condition, yet the content evaluations were more positive. How can we reconcile such a finding with the generally monotonic associations between level of customization and attitudes toward site, i.e., the greater customization, the more positive the attitudes toward the portals (Kalyanaraman & Sundar, 2006)? Sundar (2007) contends that greater interactivity simply breeds more involvement, focusing greater user attention on content. This means a more rigorous appraisal of content, which explains the somewhat negative content evaluations in the self-as-source condition in the Sundar and Nass (2001) experiment because the stories chosen were generally mediocre, meant not to evoke any strong emotions. We may interpret this also as providing greater agency to the user: Heightened interactivity not only affords higher potential for customization vis-à-vis content selection but also offers more intimate contact with content, thus resulting in closer scrutiny. This serves to imbue the user with a higher sense of authority and control over the communication.

The me-ness fostered by interactivity as a source feature is also evident in CMC situations. For example, blogging has rapidly surpassed message boards and other, more egalitarian forums of group-level and interpersonal communication because blogs represent the epitome of self-as-source. Instant messaging is often preferred over email because of its ability to allow the user to initiate immediate contact and obtain an instantaneous response from one's communication partner. More broadly, interactivity allows for a heightened assertion of self, both to oneself as well as communicating to others the core identity of oneself. The ability to use emoticons in an IM exchange, for example, allows for an enhanced assertion of one's identity.

Mediated content at all levels can be "sourced" at the individual user level with the aid of interactive devices for customization. Even the iPod phenomenon is an example of "self-as-source" because interactive features pertaining to music downloading have virtually eliminated gatekeepers (like radio DJs or even record store displays for that matter) from the decision-making cycle of purchasing songs. The customization available is so powerful that users can choose specific songs or tracks and create their own albums of songs without regard for how the artists recorded or packaged them.

At an extreme point, interactivity as a source feature eschews the need for gatekeeping and essentially reduces the massness of mass communication by creating unique individual experiences of mediated content. Communication receivers (be it oneself or collectively as a community) assume the role of "sources" thus turning an otherwise mass-mediated communication into group-level or interpersonal communication. For example, many newspapers showcase the most emailed stories of the day, thus letting the users as a collective determine the newsworthiness of stories. On e-commerce sites, it's common to see other users' opinions and experiences with a particular product, thus setting the stage for direct communications between and among users with little or no gatekeeping from the site itself. Even though the venue is one of mass communication, the interactive features allow for rich dialogues at the group and interpersonal levels. In some ways, we may think of interactivity as an HCI affordance that allows for CMC in its ideal form. After making a purchase, when I go to the e-commerce site and fill out a comment field, it is still HCI. But the moment my comment is published on the site and viewed by others, with room for others to add to it, then it becomes CMC. Ontologically then, the "self-as-source" conceptualization turns many sacred technological distinctions (such as HCI vs. CMC, Interpersonal vs. Mass Communication, and Sender vs. Receiver) on their heads because interactivity in the form of customization has largely rendered these distinctions meaningless.

Psychological implications of self as source

The psychological significance of "self as source" is evident in almost every facet of human communication research, particularly extant work on the effects of online interactive agents. Let's consider papers presented at a CAT (Communication and Technology) session entitled "Avatars and Embodied Agents" at the 2005 ICA (International Communication Association) conference. As the title suggests, all four papers in the session addressed, at some level, the broad notion of agency, along the way demonstrating the psychological appeal of self as source, even though none of the authors articulated its importance in so many words or drew implications for the concept of agency as such.

In their experiments about human-robot interaction, Jung and Lee (2005) showed that physical embodiment, combined with tactile interaction, is key to inducing positive evaluations of interaction with an agent. So, the crux of agency here is not simply a question of embodiment or imitation of human form but the ability of the user to interact with the agent. Therefore, interactivity is key, but interactivity as a source feature, not as a message attribute, underscoring the need for self to be in control of the interaction. The fact that lonely people in their experiment showed more positive social responses than nonlonely people implies even more agency in the hands of the user. Otherwise, we would not find individual differences making a difference in this study.

In Bailenson and Yee's (2005) study about immersive virtual reality, each participant interacted with an embodied artificial intelligent agent that either mimicked the participant's head movements at a four-second delay or utilized prerecorded movements of another participant as it presented an argument. The experiment found that mimicking agents were more persuasive and liked more than nonmimickers even though participants were unable to explicitly detect the mimic. The authors claimed that this is the first time that social influence effects have been documented with a nonhuman, nonverbal mimicker. Such a "digital chameleon" effect implies psychological assignment of agency to intelligent agents by study participants, but more importantly, highlights the importance of the self in interpreting the quality of user-agent interaction. For, it is the self that is being mimicked. As a study limitation, the authors point out that mimicry is confounded with contingency and wonder which one is a better explanation for the agent's positive social influence. Given that contingency is a necessary condition for mimicry, we may never be able to satisfactorily parse out their relative influence on the dependent variables, but they both underscore the importance of self in determining the course of the interaction. Therefore, the most parsimonious explanation pertains to the psychological importance of self as source. While mimicry is the system imitating the self, contingency refers to the system obeying the self.

In investigating the influence of anthropomorphic agents on attitudes toward websites, Nan *et al.* (2005) found that the positive impact of agents was mediated by viewers' emotional responses, but not the perceived credibility of the website. So, the key is in how the agent makes the user feel, not the halo effect surrounding the agent. This is yet another demonstration of the locus of the effect residing in the user, not the agent. As a user, your emotional responses to the agent dictate your attitudes toward the site, not the reputation of the site. Therefore, self is the real source in this example of human-website interaction.

Chung (2005) took a step back from interaction considerations and attempted to predict the purchasing behavior of avatar-related products. He found that the Technology Acceptance Model was superior to the Theory of Reasoned Action and the Theory of Planned Behavior in explaining undergraduate students' purchase of avatar-related products. As expected, typical usability and diffusion-of-innovations variables such as perceived usefulness and perceived ease of use were most predictive of avatar purchase. (Note that both these are extremely self-centered variables.) Contrary to the researcher's expectation however, peer group's subjective norm did not predict avatar use intention. This is probably unique to avatar adoption. One's avatar is so intimately connected to one's own self-image that peer group is probably not even remotely psychologically relevant. Avatar is all about self-representation and self-presentation. Its adoption is in effect a formal declaration of the self as source of communication.

All of these different strands of evidence from different programs of research, and increasingly most other technology work presented in the HCI and CMC literature, lead us to believe that customization (or the ability for the user to be a source in the chain of communication) is indeed the most seductive aspect of digital media. It's not simply interactivity, navigability, or modality, but the realization of one's agency in the generation and dissemination of mediated content. To the extent the user is able to see his or her own self in the interface and/or the content generated via that interface, it leads to a satisfying interaction.

Ultimately, self-as-source is psychologically powerful for three reasons:

1   It offers a vehicle for the user to assert his/her identity, via content and/or one's role in the interaction, signifying the superiority of the user, which can be ego-gratifying
2   Related to this is the cognizance of the receiver (or, more generally, the "audience") for the user's content (either "published" as on a personal homepage or posted as in the case of a bulletin board), with larger audiences imbuing a greater sense of the importance of one's agency
3   The creation of new content underlies the "sourceness" implied by the self-as-source conceptualization. In some venues on the web, the most that a user can do is serve as a gatekeeper (e.g., portals), but in others (e.g., blogs), there's a true opportunity to create new content based on original accumulation of related content obtained from different parts of the web. Likewise, in CMC, the degree to which the user is enabled to generate new content is the degree to which personal agency is evident in the interaction.

These psychological benefits form the core of our conceptualization of "self as source." They are made possible (or amplified) by developments in communication technologies in the areas of interactivity, modality, and navigability. The principle of contingency (Rafaeli, 1988) that characterizes the variable of interactivity emphasizes the importance of system responsiveness to user input. The sensory richness offered by various values of the modality variable (especially video and audio) offers a richer manifestation of agency for the user. And the promise of an idiosyncratic experience makes the navigability variable an ideal vehicle for asserting one's agency.

Agency model of customization

From the preceding discussion, an Agency Model of Customization might be proposed, featuring technological variables such as Interactivity, Modality, and Navigability as antecedents, which, via vastly different theoretical mechanisms, contribute to the key mediator of perceived agency or "self as source," en route to predicting psychological outcomes such as cognitive, affective, and behavioral responses (see Figure 4.1).

As Sundar et al. (2003) have elaborated, interactivity may be conceptualized under the functional view as a set of affordances facilitating a rich dialogue between the user and the system either for the sake of interacting with the system (HCI) or for conducting an interaction with another

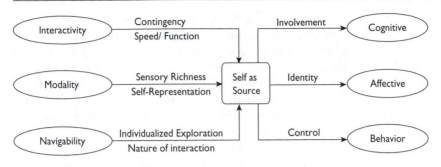

Figure 4.1 Agency model of customization

person (CMC). It may also be conceptualized under the contingency view as contributing to a series of interdependent messages threaded together in a sequence. Both types of interactivity serve to imbue the user with greater "sourceness," thus leading to greater engagement with the content of the interaction. Modality may contribute to the feeling of "self as source" by sensorially enriching the environment (thereby heightening the sense of "being there") as in virtual reality systems and/or by allowing differential levels of richness in self presentation and self representation through the system (for example, web users these days have a choice of modalities such as text, graphic, picture, animation, audio, and video by which to present themselves in cyberspace). Likewise, navigability of the interface also promotes the notion of "self as source" by allowing for individualized exploration of the system and/or its functions (as in the case of customized portals) as well as affording a variety of interaction modalities, ranging from textual to spatial to tactile. All these mechanisms are applicable both to HCI and CMC and, unlike traditional CMC research, they do not focus on limitations imposed by the technology (e.g., cuelessness) but rather on affordances offered by it. By encouraging the feeling of self as source, technological variables such as interactivity, modality, and navigability serve to inculcate a greater sense of agency in the user that can have direct effects on his or her cognitive, affective, and behavioral responses. In addition, the content of the interaction itself can have direct psychological effects, but the more interesting consideration would be the interactive effect of agency and content upon user cognitions, affect, and behaviors. However, that requires an advanced understanding of the main effects of agency and content upon the psychological outcome variables in the first place. Fifty years of media-effects research has already documented a wide array of content effects, but the psychological impact of agency is yet to be systematically addressed.

   To begin with, we could safely propose that a sense of agency will focus greater attentional effort on content, thereby amplifying one's experience of the content and its effects. Sundar (2007) demonstrates that interactivity as a source feature eventually results in greater engagement with message content. The involvement with content generated as a result of the sense of agency felt by the user in the interaction is likely to have psychological consequences, particularly in the area of cognitive activity. User involvement in the message has long been recognized by dual-process theorists (e.g., Chaiken, 1987) as a key determinant of the nature and depth of information processing. When users are involved, they engage with the content effortfully, resulting in informed attitudes and decisions that are more stable than when they form judgments based on heuristics or mental shortcuts. The egocentric nature of "self as source" is more likely therefore to engender systematic, rather than heuristic, processing of the interaction, be it HCI or CMC.

To the extent the interface makes salient the idea that the user himself or herself is the source, it encourages cognitive involvement as discussed above. In addition, it also serves to shape users' affective responses and attitudes toward the interaction. Postmodernists have long argued that the internet fundamentally challenges the notion of a well-defined and inner-directed self by allowing internet users and dwellers to constantly experiment with their identities (e.g., Turkle, 1995). Studies on self-presentation via personal homepages on the web implicitly stress the ability of internet-based technologies to allow users the luxury of carefully creating and revising their public persona or identity (e.g., Dominick, 1999), and experimental evidence suggests that one's true-self concept is more accessible in memory during internet interactions while one's actual-self is more evident in face-to-face interactions (Bargh *et al.*, 2002), with the former being more effective in communicating one's true identity, leading to more accurate impression-formation, among other positive outcomes. Therefore, when self is the source, the ability to consciously project one's identity is particularly pronounced, resulting in a highly egocentric construal—and hence a positive appraisal—of one's role in online interactions. More generally, such a preoccupation with one's identity is more likely than not to have an influence on one's affect and attitudes during and after the interaction.

Given that personal agency is an integral aspect of American individualism (Markus & Kitayama, 1991), the notion of self-as-source is in itself intrinsically appealing to those who belong to individualistic rather than collectivistic cultures. Beyond that, a sense of agency can be a powerful motivator for action. Self-determination theorists, Ryan and Deci (2000), have noted that across dozens of studies for intrinsic motivation to be evident, it is not simply enough to have competence and self-efficacy but a real sense of autonomy or at least an attribution of causality to oneself. They have shown that when something is self-authored, it results in greater vitality, persistence, creativity, and overall performance than when the same thing is other-authored. Such intrinsic motivation deriving from (real or perceived) self-determination could be a function of the increased level of internal (as opposed to external) locus of control (Rotter, 1966). It may be recalled that the self-as-source conceptualization emerged in the first place because online media, particularly their interactive ability, provided users with an unprecedented range of choices. In fact, interactivity is often defined in terms of choice (e.g., Heeter, 1989). Choice in selection of content, nature, and interactive partners is likely to imbue the user with an enormous sense of control given that media have historically over the centuries never come this close to acknowledging that the receiver is active rather than passive. But personal choice is not always monotonically related to a sense of control. Sometimes too much choice can be demotivating because an overabundance of choices can lead to decision aversion. For example, Iyengar and Lepper (2000) found that when the choice set is limited rather than extensive, individuals are more likely to engage in purchasing behaviors and report greater satisfaction with their selections. Personal choice is also less likely to be utilized by individuals who belong to collectivistic cultures and hold an interdependent, rather than independent, notion of self. Such individuals would rather have others, usually relevant in-group members, exercise choice on their behalf "presumably because it provides a greater opportunity to promote harmony and fulfill the goal of belonging to the group" (Iyengar & Lepper, 1999: 363). Both these instances of negative effects of personal choice illustrate the need for individuals to be in control of the situation, even if it means giving up on choice. Too many choices can increase cognitive dissonance and undermine a sense of personal control (Schwartz, 2000). Likewise, exercising personal choice in an interdependent culture would be a risky proposition at best and therefore a surefire way of losing control over one's social networks. So, the relevant dimension of self-as-source as a motivator of behavior is not simply choice, but the feeling of being in control. In sum, greater personal agency afforded by self-as-source can impact behaviors by offering users a greater sense of control in the interaction.

The psychological effects of self-as-source outlined in the preceding three paragraphs are merely illustrative. Although Figure 4.1 visually depicts the mediators discussed above, the agency model of customization does not specify that cognitive effects are necessarily mediated by involvement or that affective and behavioral effects accrue only due to the invocation of identity and control respectively. There could be many additional theoretical mechanisms governing the ways in which self-as-source affects cognitions, affect, and behaviors. The model simply claims that imbuing the user with a sense of personal agency will have powerful psychological effects cutting across thoughts, emotions, and actions, but does not specify all those effects. The real focus of the model is on the technological end—ways in which aspects of communication technologies promote the sense of "self as source."

Even then, this is only a tentative technological model with vast potential to add interface-related variables as well as theoretical mechanisms and paths. In essence, a model that makes prominent the role of the self as source of communication is crucial for attempting an academic understanding not only of recent technological developments such as social networking, podcasting and blogging that thrive on showcasing/broadcasting the user's own self but also older communication technologies such as email and websites that allow for rich manifestation of one's agency.

Future research pertaining to this model should: (1) identify more technological variables in CMC technologies that explain a significant portion of the variance in the dependent variables; (2) explicate the conceptual core of these variables in order to understand the various ways in which they manifest themselves; (3) identify and specify theoretical mechanisms by which the various technological variables cause a sense of agency in the user; (4) delineate philosophical and psychological dimensions of "self as source," involving such related concepts as involvement, identity, and control; (5) identify and specify theoretical mechanisms by which these concepts help us understand the psychological importance of agency; and (6) specify and test interaction hypotheses that explain the combined effect of agency and content attributes upon the three classic species of psychological dependent variables.

The basic structure of the model represents an argument that roughly goes as follows: Technological variables embedded in media systems affect the nature and psychology of our interactions with content as well as other humans by essentially highlighting the importance of our own selves. How exactly each of the various technological features enables the self to dictate interactions is of course a key concern for future exploration, as is the increasing psychological importance of agency evidenced by a dramatic preference for customization in the marketplace. For the eventual, fully developed model to be useful, however, it would have to explain a good deal of the variance on the psychological outcomes of CMC and HCI. This is why it is necessary to study the role of customization in altering users' conception of—and interaction with—the nature and content of their communications.

References

Bailenson, J., & Yee, N. (2005) "Digital chameleons: Automatic assimilation of nonverbal gestures in immersive virtual environments." Paper presented at the annual conference of the International Communication Association, New York City, N.Y. (May).

Bargh, J. A., McKenna, K. Y. A., & Fitzsimons, G. M. (2002) "Can you see the real me? Activation and expression of the 'true self' on the Internet." *Journal of Social Issues, 58*(1), 33–48.

Beniger, J. R. (1987) "Personalization of mass media and the growth of pseudo-community." *Communication Research, 14*(3), 352–371.

Burgoon, J. K., Bonito, J. A., Ramirez, A., Jr., Dunbar, N. E., Kam, K., & Fischer, J. (2002) "Testing the interactivity principle: Effects of mediation, propinquity, and verbal and nonverbal modalities in interpersonal interaction." *Journal of Communication*, *52*(3), 657–677.

Chaiken, S. (1987) "The heuristic model of persuasion." In M. P. Zanna, J. M. Olson, & C. P. Herman (eds.), *Social Influence: the Ontario Symposium*, Vol. 5. Hillsdale, NJ: Erlbaum, pp. 3–39.

Chung, D. (2005) "A comparison of three models to understand purchasing behavior of avatar-related products." Paper presented at the annual conference of the International Communication Association, New York City, N.Y. (May).

Culnan, M. J., & Markus, M. L. (1987) "Information technologies." In F. M. Jablin, L. L. Putnam, K. H. Roberts, & L. W. Porter (eds.), *Handbook of Organization Communication: an Interdisciplinary Perspective*. Newsbury Park, CA: Sage, pp. 420–443.

Dominick, J. (1999) "Who do you think you are? Personal home pages and self presentation on the world wide web." *Journalism & Mass Communication Quarterly*, *76*, 646–658.

Heeter, C. (1989) "Implications of new interactive technologies for conceptualizing communication." In J. Salvaggio and J. Bryant (eds.), *Media in the Information Age: Emerging Patterns of Adoption and Consumer Use*. Hillsdale, NJ: Lawrence Erlbaum, pp. 217–235.

Hopper, R. (1992) *Telephone Conversation*. Bloomington, IN: Indiana University Press.

Hu, Y., Wood, F. J., Smith, V., & Westbrook, N. (2004) "Friendships through IM: Examining the relationship between instant messaging and intimacy." *Journal of Computer-Mediated Communication, 10*(1), article 6.

Iyengar, S. S., & Lepper, M. R. (1999) "Rethinking the value of choice: A cultural perspective on intrinsic motivation." *Journal of Personality and Social Psychology*, *76*(3), 349–366.

Iyengar, S. S., & Lepper, M. R. (2000) "When choice is demotivating: Can one desire too much of a good thing?" *Journal of Personality and Social Psychology*, *79*(6), 995–1006.

Jung, Y., & Lee, K. M. (2005) "Are physically embodied social agents better than disembodied social agents?: Effects of embodiment, tactile interaction, and people's loneliness in human-robot interaction." Paper presented at the annual conference of the International Communication Association, New York, N.Y. (May).

Kalyanaraman, S., & Sundar, S. S. (2006) "The psychological appeal of personalized content in Web portals: Does customization affect attitudes and behavior?" *Journal of Communication*, *56*(1).

Kiesler, S., Siegel, J., & McGuire, T. W. (1984) "Social psychological aspects of computer-mediated communication." *American Psychologist*, *39*(10), 1123–1134.

Markus, H. R., & Kitayama, S. (1991) "Culture and the self: Implications for cognition, emotion, and motivation." *Psychological Review*, *98*, 224–253.

McLuhan, M. (1964) *Understanding Media*. New York: Signet.

Nan, X., Angelcev, G., Myers, J. R., Sar, S., & Faber, R. (2005) "The influence of anthropomorphic agents on attitudes toward the website: A test of two mediating routes." Paper presented at the annual conference of the International Communication Association, New York, N.Y. (May).

Nass, C. I., & Mason, L. (1990) "On the study of technology and task: A variable-based approach." In J. Fulk & C. Steinfeld (eds.), *Organizations and Communication Technology*. Newbury Park, CA: Sage Publications, pp. 46–67.

Nass, C., & Moon, Y. (2000) "Machines and mindlessness: Social responses to computers." *Journal of Social Issues, 56*(1), 81–103.

Petty, R. E., Barden, J., & Wheeler, S. C. (2002) "The elaboration likelihood model of persuasion." In R. J. DiClemente, R. A. Crosby, & M. Kegler (eds.), *Emerging Theories in Health Promotion Practice and Research*. San Francisco: Jossey-Bass, pp. 71–99.

Petty, R. E., Wheeler, S. C., & Bizer, G. Y. (2000) "Attitude functions and persuasion: An elaboration likelihood approach to matched versus mismatched messages." In G. R. Maio & J. M. Olson (eds.), *Why we Evaluate: Functions of Attitudes*. Mahwah, NJ: Lawrence Erlbaum Associates, Inc, pp. 133–162.

Rafaeli, S. (1988) "Interactivity: From new media to communication." In R. Hawkins, J. Weimann & S. Pingree (eds.), *Advancing Communication Science: Merging Mass and Interpersonal Processes.* Newbury Park, CA: Sage Publications, pp. 124–181.

Reeves, B., & Anderson, D. R. (1991) "Media studies and psychology." *Communication Research, 18,* 597–600.

Reeves, B., & Nass, C. (1996) *The Media Equation: How People Treat Computers, Television, and New Media Like Real People and Places.* Stanford, CA: CSLI Publications and Cambridge University Press.

Rotter, J. B. (1966) "Generalized expectancies for internal versus external control of reinforcement." *Psychological Monographs, 80.*

Ryan, R. M., & Deci, E. L. (2000) "Self-determination theory and the facilitation of intrinsic motivation, social development, and well-being." *American Psychologist, 55*(1), 68–78.

Schwartz, B. (2000) "Self-determination: The tyranny of freedom." *American Psychologist, 55,* 79–88.

Scott, L. C. (2004) "Deliberative communities online: Towards a model of civic journalism based on the blog." Paper presented at the annual convention of the Association for Education in Journalism and Mass Communication, Toronto, Canada (August).

Short, J., Williams, E., & Christie, B. (1976) *The Social Psychology of Telecommunications.* London: John Wiley & Sons.

Slavinsky, G., & Glass, T. (2004) "So, what's a blog?" *Johns Hopkins Bloomberg School of Public Health.* Online at http://www.jhsph.edu/dept/bh?CFID=1281399&CFTOKEN=2675 3101 (Last viewed on March 14, 2005).

Spears, R., Postmes, T., Lea, M., & Wolbert, A. (2002) "When are net effects gross products? The power of influence and the influence of power in computer-mediated communication." *Journal of Social Issues, 5*(1), 91–107.

Steuer, J. (1992) "Defining virtual reality: Dimensions determining telepresence." *Journal of Communication, 42,* 73–93.

Sundar, S. S. (2007) "Social psychology of interactivity in human-website interaction." In A. N. Joinson, K. Y. A. McKenna, T. Postmes & U-D. Reips (eds.), *The Oxford Handbook of Internet Psychology.* Oxford, UK: Oxford University Press, pp. 89–104.

Sundar, S. S., & Nass, C. (2000) "Source orientation in human-computer interaction: Programmer, networker, or independent social actor?" *Communication Research, 27*(6), 683–703.

Sundar, S. S., & Nass, C. (2001) "Conceptualizing sources in online news." *Journal of Communication, 51*(1), 52–72.

Sundar, S. S., Kalyanaraman, S., & Brown, J. (2003) "Explicating website interactivity: Impression-formation effects in political campaign sites." *Communication Research,* 30(1), 30–59.

Turkle, S. (1995) *Life on the Screen: Identity in the Age of the Internet.* New York, N.Y.: Simon & Schuster.

Walther, J. B. (1992) "Interpersonal effects in computer-mediated interaction. A relational perspective." *Communication Research, 19,* 52–90.

Walther, J. B. (1996) "Computer-mediated communication: Impersonal, interpersonal, and hyperpersonal interaction." *Communication Research, 23,* 3–43.

Part II

Technology as relationship enabler

Chapter 5

Transformed social interaction in mediated interpersonal communication

Jeremy N. Bailenson, Nick Yee, Jim Blascovich, and Rosanna E. Guadagno

Over time, our mode of remote communication has evolved from written letters to telephones, email, internet chatrooms, and video-conferences. Similarly, virtual environments that utilize digital representations of humans promise to further change the nature of remote interaction. Virtual environments are systems which track verbal and nonverbal signals of multiple interactants and render those signals onto *avatars*, three-dimensional, digital representations of people in a shared digital space. Unlike telephone conversations and video-conferences, interactants in virtual environments have the ability to systematically filter the physical appearance and behavioral actions of their avatars in the eyes of their conversational partners, amplifying or suppressing features and nonverbal signals in real time for strategic purposes. These transformations can have a drastic impact on interactants' persuasive and instructional abilities. Furthermore, researchers can use this mismatch between actions performed by a speaker and actions perceived by an audience as a tool to examine complex patterns of nonverbal behavior which are difficult to isolate in face-to-face interaction.

We first discuss a framework for classifying digital human representations and the role they play in Computer-Mediated Communication (CMC). We then present a theory called Transformed Social Interaction (TSI) that explores how CMC allows people to interact in ways not possible face-to-face. We review a number of published studies examining TSI as well as summaries of new, unpublished data and work that is currently in progress. We conclude by relating CMC to theories of social influence, discussing the next step in digital human research and applications, and discussing potential ethical problems with TSI.

A framework for digital human representation

The study of digital human representation within CMC has progressed significantly over the past 15 years, including conceptual, design, and empirical issues. Currently, vast numbers of individuals interact with digital versions of each other on at least a daily basis. The digital human forms utilized during these interactions range from digital audio representations on cellular phones to icons within emails to graphical representations in video games and chatrooms. In this section, we describe research approaches that provide frameworks relating to virtual humans.

Traditionally, researchers have distinguished *embodied agents*, which are models driven by computer algorithms, from *avatars*, which are models driven by humans in real time. Most behavioral research examining social interaction between people and virtual humans has utilized embodied agents (as opposed to avatars—see Bailenson & Blascovich, 2004, for a discussion). One reason for this disparity is that readily available commercial technology allowing individuals to create digital avatars which can look like and behave in real time like the individual has emerged only recently. Previously, producing real-time avatars that captured the user's voice, visual features, and subtle movements was quite difficult. Consequently, understanding the implications of the visual and behavioral veridicality of an avatar on the quality of interaction is an important question that has received very little empirical attention (see Schroeder, 2002, for a review of the existing empirical work on avatars).

Avatars are digital models that may look or behave like the humans they represent. In virtual environments, avatars are often rendered dynamically, in real time, to reflect at least some user behavior or movements (e.g., Reidsma *et al.*, 2005). However, when applied to more traditional forms of CMC, the definition of an avatar is fuzzy. For example, the definition of avatar including "looking like a user" encompasses a digital photograph, such as one posted on an online dating website. Some would object because such an image has little or no potential for behavior or movements. However, others would argue that people utilize static (i.e., nonanimated) avatars in synchronous internet chat. While many discuss the concept of avatars in the CMC literature, a standard definition of avatars that researchers subscribe to has not emerged. Here, we believe it important to examine the suitability of different types of avatars for representing the user (Konijn & Hoorn, 2004).

Figure 5.1 provides a preliminary framework for considering representations of humans. The abscissa for each graph represents form similarity, how much the representation statically resembles features of a given person. The ordinate for each graph denotes behavioral similarity—how much the behaviors of the representation correspond to the behaviors of a given person. The graph on the left classifies representations that correspond to a given person's form or behavior synchronously or in real time. The graph on the right classifies representations that correspond to a person's form or behavior asynchronously.

Illustrating synchronous avatar behavior (left side of Figure 5.1), a

Representations of Human Beings (Avatars)

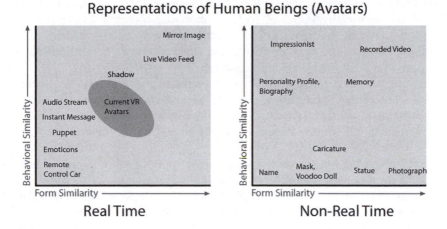

Figure 5.1 A framework for classifying representations of humans in physical and digital space

puppet is a representation of a person that has high behavioral similarity (the movements of the puppet's mouth are closely tied to the person controlling it) but low form similarity (a puppet does not look like the person controlling it). However, the controlling person's behaviors are expressed in real time. On the other hand, an impressionist (i.e., someone who can very closely reproduce or mimic the behaviors of a person who is not physically present) has high behavioral similarity by definition, but only high form similarity if the impressionist actually looks like the person being mimicked. Unlike the puppet, however, the impressionist is typically an asynchronous representation—the person being mimicked need not be present, aware of the impressionist's existence, or even still alive.

As Figure 5.1 demonstrates, representations of human beings can take many forms. The shaded oval denotes the space in which we typically discuss avatars—digital representations of humans that are utilized in virtual environments. Blascovich *et al.* (2002) provide a theoretical framework to determine the interplay of behavioral and form realism for the avatars that fall into this shaded region.

Digital humans today

Currently, digital humans are used in a number of CMC venues. For example, sound is transformed into digital information as it travels over fiber-optic cables and cellular networks; consequently, the audio representation we perceive over phone lines is actually an acoustic avatar of the speaker. This classification may seem trivial at first, but becomes less trivial when preset algorithms are applied to the audio stream to cause subtle changes in the acoustic avatar (e.g., Nass & Brave, 2005), such as cleaning and amplifying the signal or making phonetic assumptions concerning specific languages. In other words, because the voice is translated into digital information, it is an abstracted representation of the human, as opposed to raw perceptual input from the speaker.

The internet is filled with different forms of CMC employing digital representations. For example, as two people communicate via instant messaging (IM), they appear to each other as a series of text messages, emoticons, and pauses. Recent estimates show that 53 million people in the United States use IM (Project, 2004). Of those born after 1976, 62 percent use IM on a regular basis. Furthermore, there is ample use of video-conferencing technology; with digital video one can consider a human representation an avatar. Moreover, digital representations are also seen in video games. Currently, about 50 percent of the United States' population plays video games (ESA, 2005), men and women alike. On average, gamers spend about 7.5 hours per week playing (ESA, 2005).

Perhaps the best example of social interaction via graphical digital representation occurs in a genre of video games known as massively multiplayer online games (MMOGs). Millions of players spend on average 22 hours a week interacting, collaborating, and competing with each other via graphical avatars (Woodcock, 2005; Yee, in press). Users are often given a great degree of control over the appearance of their avatars. For example, in the game Star Wars Galaxies, users can alter their avatar's gender, age, height, weight, musculature, hair style and color, eye shape and color, lip fullness, cheek fullness, nose protrusion, freckles, baldness, and so on.

Human desire to transform representation

According to Goffman's approach to understanding identity, the presentation of the self must be understood as a constant performance in front of the social audience around us—that we choose our gestures, mannerisms, and actions to give off a desired impression of the self to others (Goffman, 1959). Of course, psychologists have also long noted that the primary function of self-presentation is instrumental. These forms of presentation involve making favorable impressions on others to gain social advantage, such as appearing pleasant or likeable (Jones, 1964; Jones & Pitman, 1982). In general, people want to present themselves positively and strike a balance between favorability and plausibility (Schlenker, 1980).

Alterations to self-presentation occur in many different forms and many different ways (see Figure 5.2). A wide range of cosmetic products and services provide short-term enhancements to our appearances. These include makeup, haircuts, and hair styling products among others. We also alter our nonverbal behaviors consciously and unconsciously for social advantage. For example, mimicking another person's gestures and behaviors

	Appearance	Nonverbal Behavior	Verbal Behavior
Short Term	Haircuts Makeup	Mimicking Ingratiating Gestures	Lying Word Choice
Long Term	Plastic Surgery Dieting	Habit Suppression Table Manners	Oratory Training Language Acquisition

Figure 5.2 Methods utilized to transform physical representations

for social rapport can occur both automatically and in a controlled fashion (Chartrand & Bargh, 1999).

It also occurs via verbal behavior, such as illustrated by speech accommodation theory—the process by which our accent, speech rate, and lexical choices come to converge with people we talk to (Giles & Claire, 1979).

Alterations to self-presentation can also be long-term or even permanent. For example, plastic surgery or weight training can provide more long-term effects on our appearances. Also, we learn a variety of nonverbal social rituals as children, such as table manners, and learning a new language can be viewed as a form of long-term alteration to our verbal behavior.

Transformed social interaction

In CMC, it is relatively trivial for a person to transform many aspects of their own avatar as well as the social world in which they interact. Consider the depiction of CMC depicted below in Figure 5.3.

The right panel indicates that the behaviors of three users in separate remote physical locations are tracked. Various technologies can be used to track various features of the users, such as voice, appearance, and movements (e.g., facial expressions, gestures). The left panel demonstrates a digital configuration in which the three users are rendered in the same virtual location where they can see and hear each other's avatar. Such virtual locations can be a teleconference, video-conference, chatroom, video game, or an immersive collaborative virtual environment.

In many CMC systems, each user has a digital image of the others' avatars stored locally on his or her system. The system receives digital

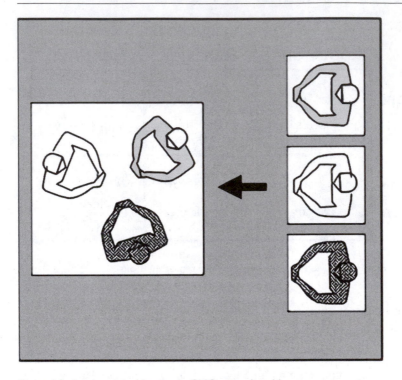

Figure 5.3 A schematic of a simple CMC using digital human avatars

tracking information regarding voice, movements, gestures, and other actions over a network, allowing the dynamics of the avatars stored in his or her system to be updated continuously and rendered more or less veridically. Given that CMC systems must render the world separately for each user simultaneously, it is possible to render the avatars differently for each user at the same time. In other words, for each CMC user, tracking devices transmit a stream of information that indicates his or her actions. However, that stream of information can be altered in real time for strategic purpose by system operators, who may or may not be the users themselves. The theory of Transformed Social Interaction (TSI, see Bailenson, 2006; Bailenson & Beall, 2006; Bailenson *et al.*, 2004) proposes that the possibilities that these real-time transformations raise can be classified into three categories or dimensions.

The first TSI dimension is *self-representation*. These transformations decouple the rendered appearance or behaviors of avatars from the actual appearance or behavior of the human driving it. That rendering can deviate from the actual state of the user. In a distance learning situation, it could be the case that some students learn better with teachers who utilize expressive gestures such as a smile, while some learn better with teachers with more stoic faces. In CMC, the teacher can be rendered differently to each student, with his facial gestures idiosyncratically depicted to each student in order to maximize that student's attention and learning style.

The second TSI dimension is *sensory abilities*. These transformations complement human perceptual abilities. One example is "invisible consultants," either algorithms or human avatars who can receive all sensory information from all interactants, but who are only visible (i.e., only rendered) to particular members of the CMC. These consultants can provide real-time summary information about the attentions and movements of other interactants (information which is automatically collected by tracking technology) or can scrutinize the actions of the user herself. For example, teachers using distance learning applications can utilize automatic registers that ensure that all students are looking in the direction of the teacher (a proxy for paying attention) to a sufficient degree.

The third TSI dimension is *situational context*. These transformations alter the spatial or temporal structure of a conversation. For example, the CMC can be optimally configured in terms of the geographical setup of a conference room. For example, every student in a class of 20 can sit directly in front of the virtual instructor, and perceive the rest of the students as sitting farther away. Furthermore, by altering the flow of rendered time in CMC, users can implement strategic uses of rewind and fast forward during a "real-time" interaction in an attempt to increase comprehension and efficiency.

Examples of TSI research

Here we review some previous findings relating to TSI, including published work as well as findings from some new work that has not yet been published.

Transforming the self

A majority of our work to date has centered upon examining transforming self-representation, largely because these are the types of transformation that are likely to occur across all types of CMC, compared to only media that involve very rich behavioral tracking and rendering such as immersive virtual reality.

Facial identity capture

Today, CMC involves the pervasive use of digital representations of people in video-conferences, static photographs accompanying emails and chats, as well as avatars used in online games. In a series of studies, we have demonstrated the effectiveness of algorithmic transformations that can be easily implemented in CMC which capitalize on human beings' disposition to prefer faces similar to their own (Bailenson, Garland, Iyengar, & Yee, 2006).

Similarity between two people instills altruism (Gaertner & Dovidio, 1977) and trust (DeBruine, 2002). Social explanations argue that people use physical similarity as a proxy for compatible interests and values (Zajonc et al., 1987). Currently, political candidates tailor the information content of their mailings and televised messages to targeted demographic groupings (Iyengar et al., 2001). Increasingly, they are in a position to vary salient attributes of their physical appearance, e.g. their weight, dress style, facial expression, or skin tone, depending on the audience in question. There is no reason to suspect that facial identity capture should be any different than clothing choice during digital campaigns.

In one study (Bailenson et al., 2006), researchers passively acquired digital photographs of a national random sample of voting aged citizens. One week before the 2004 presidential election, participants completed a survey of their attitudes concerning George Bush and John Kerry while viewing photographs of both candidates side by side (see Figure 5.4). For a random one-third of the subjects, their own faces were morphed with Kerry while unfamiliar faces were morphed with Bush. For a different one-third, their own faces were morphed with Bush while unfamiliar faces were morphed with Kerry. The remaining one-third of the sample viewed unmorphed pictures of the candidates.

Postexperimental interviews demonstrated that not a single person detected that his or her image had been morphed into the photograph of the candidate. Participants were more likely to vote for the candidate morphed with their own face than the candidate morphed with an unfamiliar face. The use of facial identity capture was sufficient to change the outcome of the presidential election by a double-digit margin, according to a national random sample. In conclusion, using digital photographs, video images, and digital avatars allows people to dynamically morph representations during CMC. And by doing so, new, unique patterns of social influence will emerge.

Augmented gaze

Another TSI tool is *augmented gaze*: directing mutual gaze at more than a single interactant in a CMC system at once. Previous research has demonstrated that eye gaze is an extremely powerful tool for communicators seeking to garner attention, be persuasive, and instruct (see Segrin, 1993, for a review on this topic). People who use mutual gaze increase their ability to engage an audience as well as to accomplish a number of conversational goals.

In face-to-face interaction, gaze is zero-sum. In other words, if Person A

Subject   Subject

George Bush   John Kerry

60:40 (Bush:Subject)   60:40 (Kerry:Subject)

Figure 5.4   Two subjects (top row), Bush and Kerry (2nd row), the morph of Subject 1 and Bush (3rd row left), the morph of Subject 2 and Kerry (3rd row right), and the vote intention score by condition (bottom row). The difference in vote intention for Bush and Kerry by condition was significant (p<.05).

looks directly at Person B for 85 percent of the time, it is not possible for Person A to look directly at other people in the interaction for more than a total of 15 percent of the time. However, interaction among avatars during CMC is not bound by this constraint. The virtual environment as well as the other avatars in CMC is individually rendered for each interactant locally. As a result, Person A can have his avatar rendered differently for each other interactant, and appear to maintain mutual gaze with many interactants for the majority of the conversation, as Figure 5.5 demonstrates.

Augmented gaze allows interactants to perpetuate the illusion that they are looking directly at each person in an entire roomful of inter-actants. Three separate projects (Bailenson *et al.*, 2004; Beall *et al.*, 2003; Guadagno *et al.*, 2005) have utilized a paradigm in which a single presenter read a passage to two listeners inside a collaborative virtual environment. All three interactants were of the same gender, wore stereoscopic, head-mounted displays, and had their head movements and mouth movements tracked and rendered, and the presenter's avatar either looked directly at each of the other two speakers simultaneously for 100 percent of the time (augmented gaze) or utilized normal, zero-sum gaze. Results across those three studies have produced and replicated three important findings: (1) participants never detected that the augmented gaze was not in fact backed by real gaze; (2) participants returned gaze to the presenter more often in the augmented condition than in the normal condition; and (3) partici-pants (females to a greater extent than males) were more persuaded by a

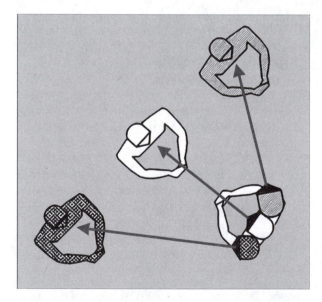

Figure 5.5 A schematic illustration of non-zero-sum gaze. Each interactant on the left perceives the speaker on the right gazing directly at him or her.

presenter implementing augmented gaze than a presenter implementing normal gaze. Augmented gaze will be a powerful tool in future computer-mediated communication. For applications such as distance learning, sales, online chatting and dating, utilizing computer guided gaze should have a high impact on social interaction.

The cyranoid

A *cyranoid* is an intermediary that communicates with a target person using the words or nonverbal behavior of another individual. Stanley Milgram described this concept and coined this term when he conducted a study in which participants interacted with an individual who, unbeknownst to them, was a cyranoid whose words were being controlled by a third party. In Milgram's words, cyranoids are: "People who do not speak thoughts originating in their own central nervous system: Rather, the words they speak originate in the mind of another person who transmits these words to the cyranoid by radio transmission" (Milgram *et al.*, 1992, p. 337).

In one study (Guadagno *et al.*, 2005), researchers examined whether a cyranoid (a virtual representation with verbal behavior controlled by one person and nonverbal behavior controlled by another) could be more persuasive than an avatar using augmented gaze (a virtual representation with verbal behavior controlled by one person and nonverbal behavior controlled by a computer algorithm). The cyranoid was instructed to engage or target a particular participant during the interaction by being persuasive with head movements. We expected that targeted nonverbal engagement by a third party (i.e., the cyranoid) would be more persuasive than a natural interaction, because a cyranoid can provide tailored nonverbal engagement without splitting attention between words and movements. Results indicated that as compared to control conditions, participants who interacted with the cyranoid remembered more details of the persuasive passage, engaged in more mutual gaze with the presenter, liked the presenter better, and perceived more eye contact.

The Proteus Effect

A great deal of social interaction occurs in virtual environments (Biocca & Levy, 1995; Parks & Floyd, 1995; Rheingold, 1993; Turkle, 1995; Walther, 1996; Walther *et al.*, 1994; Yee, 2006), but the impact of our flexible self-representation within these environments has seldom been explored quantitatively. But given that social interaction in virtual environments revolves around a digital representation that can be altered in dramatic ways, it is important to understand how our altered self-representations affect us—a process we term "the Proteus Effect." (Yee & Bailenson, 2006). We argue that just as men and women conform to gender roles (i.e., *social role theory*, Eagly &

Wood, 1999) and just as the elderly conform to expected age stereotypes (i.e., *self-stereotyping*, Levy, 1996), we might expect that people conform to stereotypical behaviors associated with their digital self-representations.

Two studies tested the Proteus Effect (Yee & Bailenson, 2006). The first explored the effect of attractiveness. Participants were immersed in a virtual room and saw their digital representation in a virtual mirror. Then they interacted with a confederate. In the *attractive* condition, participants were given an avatar of the same gender with an attractive face. In the *unattractive* condition, participants were given an avatar of the same gender with an unattractive face. These faces were chosen on the basis of a pretest and shown to differ significantly in terms of attractiveness ratings. Participants were then asked to perform an interpersonal distance task and a self-disclosure task. The results showed that participants in the attractive condition walked significantly closer and disclosed significantly more pieces of information than participants in the unattractive condition. In other words, the attractiveness of an avatar changes how friendly a person behaves towards other people in a virtual environment.

The second study explored the effect of height. The literature suggests that height is positively correlated with self-esteem (Judge & Cable, 2004). Thus, it was hypothesized that people given tall avatars would behave in a more confident way than those given short avatars, and three experimental conditions were developed. In the *tall* condition, participants had an avatar 15cm taller than the confederate's avatar. In the *short* condition, participants had an avatar 15cm shorter than the confederate's avatar. And in the *normal* condition, the participant's avatar was the same height as the confederate's avatar. These researchers employed a money-splitting negotiation task as a behavioral measure of confidence and found that participants in the tall condition were more willing to make unfair splits in their own favor, while participants in the short condition were more willing to accept unfair splits made by the confederate. Thus, this data again supported the Proteus Effect: Users given tall avatars became more confident than users given short avatars.

The Proteus Effect has broad implications for social interactions during CMC. We usually think of avatar creation as a one-way process, something of our own choosing, but the digital selves that we create in fact come to shape our behaviors in turn. Who we choose to be online changes how we behave.

Digital chameleons

Human behavioral researchers have long noted a synchronization and contagion of many verbal and nonverbal behaviors in social interactions, such as in speech patterns (Cappella & Panalp, 1981), posture (LaFrance, 1982), or mood (Neumann & Strack, 2000). More recently, researchers have found that automatic mimicry is a mechanism that increases social rapport in face-to-face interaction (Chartrand & Bargh, 1999; Chartrand & Jefferis, 2003). A subject who is mimicked by a confederate rates the confederate more positively after performing a task together, and subjects are more likely to mimic a confederate when there is a higher need for affiliation (Lakin & Chartrand, 2003). This line of evidence supports the claim that both unintentional (automatic) and intentional mimicry facilitates and expresses social affiliation and that the process is bi-directional— mimicry facilitates affiliation and prosocial behavior and affiliation goals increase mimicry (Lakin et al., 2003).

CMC systems are uniquely suited for employing automatic mimicry for social advantage. Given that the system is already tracking a wide variety of actions and movements of interactants precisely, it becomes easy to mimic a person's movements accurately. It also becomes possible to build "nonverbal profiles" of users based on their past behaviors and save that into a database. And this mimicry might also be applied to embodied agents as an easy-to-implement algorithm for gaining social rapport with a human user.

To test this "digital chameleon" hypothesis, Bailenson and Yee (2005) conducted an experimental study in which undergraduate students were immersed in a virtual environment. In the virtual environment, participants were seated opposite an agent who presented an argument for approximately four minutes. The participant's head movements (i.e., pitch, yaw, and roll) were tracked by the VR system. In the mimic condition, the agent played back the participant's head movements with a four-second delay. In the recorded condition, the agent played back the recording of a different participant from the mimic condition.

The results from the study showed that participants in the mimic condition were more likely to pay attention to the agent in terms of gaze and agree with the agent's argument than participants in the recorded condition. More importantly, fewer than 5 percent of the participants had detected the mimicry in the post-experiment questionnaire. These findings have substantial implications. Given the precision with which CMC systems can track an individual's nonverbal behavior, it allows avatars and agents to use automatic mimicry for social advantage. These findings also show that such an algorithm is easy to implement, requiring no preexisting library or syntax of nonverbal gestures to function. Thus, the interaction and the meaning of specific nonverbal gestures do not even need to be understood by the system for this transformation to be effective.

Transforming sensory abilities

Government funding agencies issued a major push in the late 1990s with a research agenda called Augmented Cognition (see Schmorrow & Kruse,

2004 for a detailed history), designing computer interfaces to extend the limitations of normal human cognition. One major rationale for this work was to provide digital wearable displays that could increase the working memory of people by allowing them to be able store cognitive information on displays as opposed to having to keep them actively stored in memory. Similarly, we have been conducting CMC research to provide augmentations of social sensory abilities. These transformations complement human abilities to draw inferences about the social world. In this section we discuss two examples of such augmentations.

Multilateral perspective taking

Many CMC systems, such as online games or video-conferences, use multiple viewpoints or virtual cameras to allow users to decouple their visual point of view from that of their avatars (i.e., the normal view from the eyes). In theory, in any digital communication system, it should be possible for an interactant to take a visual point of view from any single point in the virtual room. In other words, it is possible for Person B to disconnect the area of perception from the area in which Person A perceives her. Figure 5.6 illustrates this transformation.

In Figure 5.6, Person B is implementing a *multilateral perspective*. Specifically, she is choosing to adopt the sensory perspective of Person A during the conversation. In other words, she has left her own point of view and become a passenger to Person A, by viewing a digital world that is not contingent on her own movements, but instead a digital world that is

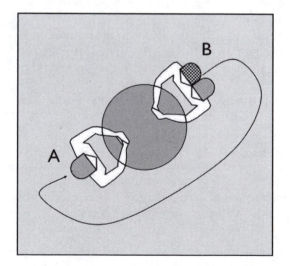

Figure 5.6 Person B takes on multilateral perspectives: she can experience the CVE from her own perspective and the perspective of Person A at the same time.

contingent on Person A's movements. As a result, she sees herself in real time from behind the eyes of her conversational partner. Either by shifting her entire field of view to the spatial location of other avatars in the interaction, or by popping up "field of view windows" in corners of the virtual display, an interactant can unobtrusively occupy the home space of any avatar in the CVE.

Research (Gehlbach *et al.*, 2005) is examining multilateral perspectives in a negotiation scenario inside a CVE. Previous work has used either role playing (Davis *et al.*, 1996) or observational seating arrangements (Taylor & Fiske, 1975) to cause subjects to take on the perspectives of others in a conversation, demonstrating more efficient and effective interactions. Equipping an interactant with the real-time ability to see one's avatar from another point of view should enhance these effects. In our work in progress, we are predicting more cooperative solutions in simulations in which negotiators can occupy the field of view of their opponents.

Behavioral flags

During any interaction, meaningful events occur that involve complex behaviors, verbal and nonverbal utterances. In order to render the actions of participants to one another in a CMC, it is necessary to capture all information about those actions. The current study examines how interactants benefit from receiving real-time, summary information about the social actions of themselves and others. We are planning to examine one-on-one scenarios such as tutoring, negotiation, and sales pitches, as well as one-on-many scenarios such as class lectures. Figure 5.7 illustrates a CMC system that displays information flags over the heads of three users. In these instances, one or more of the interactants in an immersive virtual environment CMC system will receive real-time information about the following behaviors:

1   *Nod/Head Shake Detection.* Using a simple device that tracks head orientation, it is possible to detect agreement nods or disagreement shakes using spectral analysis on the head orientation data. The ratio of these behaviors for a given user should be indicative of agreement and comprehension.
2   *Facial Expressions.* Using advanced software by Nevenvision which uses computer vision to automatically track facial features in real time (approximately 10 Hz), we have developed and tested a system that detects simple facial expressions, such as smiles and frowns. We will continue to attempt to isolate additional expressions.
3   *Gaze Behavior.* In previous work (Beall *et al.*, 2003), we have used head tracking equipment to determine when people look in each other's eyes (i.e. mutual gaze). This tool will help a user know how often he

has looked at all the other interactants as well as how often they have looked at him.

4   *Speaking Frequency*. Using a simple microphone that records the frequency of speech, we have previously automatically computed the percentage of time each person is speaking (Bailenson *et al.*, 2002).

Transforming situational context

This is the dimension of our theoretical framework which has received the least empirical attention as of yet. While technological development and empirical design is underway for multiple studies transforming a user's context, we discuss only one of these ongoing research studies in the current section, called *Transformed Conformity*.

Conformity is one of the most powerful forms of social influence (Asch, 1955; Festinger, 1954). Previous research in collaborative virtual environments (Blascovich *et al.*, 2002; Swinth & Blascovich, 2002) has demonstrated that participants conform to the behaviors of other people in immersive virtual reality, regardless of whether they are avatars (representations controlled by other people) or agents (representations controlled by the computer). In current work, we are examining the effect of overriding the behaviors of other group members in CMC. In other words, for

Figure 5.7 Three participants with the behavioral flags translucently displayed over their heads. Only the presenter (behind the podium) in this CVE can see the behavioral flags.

any given participant, instead of seeing the actual behaviors of his or her peers, participants can see transformed behaviors. The goal of this work is to examine the effectiveness of presenters who create a specific type of audience via transformed conformity.

We are currently designing and running studies in which participants are present in the same collaborative virtual environment, and manipulating the *types of transformed behaviors* that each participant perceives of his or her neighbors. Each participant either sees the actual behaviors (e.g., facial expressions, direction of eye gaze, nodding and head shaking behaviors) of the other group members or sees transformed behaviors that are created to induce participants to conform to a certain standard. For example, positive attention behaviors include overriding actual behaviors to make the surrounding students look at the presenter, nod, smile, and ask questions. On the other hand, negative attention behaviors include frowning, demonstrating boredom expressions, sitting with eyes closed and gaze aversion. In pilot studies, subjects learning in positive learning environments resulting from transformed conformity are demonstrating more learning, persuasion, and mutual gaze than subjects in control conditions.

TSI and social influence theory

In the previous section, we described a number of studies showing that TSI can be used for people to achieve social influence. Indeed, nearly every single example from above features interactants transforming their avatars, senses, or context in order to strategically accomplish some goal relating to teaching or persuasion (e.g., facial identity capture, digital chameleons, etc.). In order to provide a theoretical framework to guide research in TSI, we look to the model most relevant to this work. Blascovich and colleagues (Blascovich, 2002; Blascovich *et al.*, 2002) proposed a model of social influence during CMC in virtual environments. This model was primarily developed to understand social interaction inside immersive virtual environments, but it applies equally well to other types of CMC.

As Figure 5.8 depicts, there is a tradeoff between realism (the degree to which human representations look and behave as they would in the physical world) on the vertical axis and perceived agency (the extent to which the interactant thinks they are interacting with another actual human being) on the horizontal axis. The higher the realism, particularly communicative realism (e.g., facial expressions), then the less perceived agency needed to achieve social influence and vice versa. Hence, according to the model, social influence is likely to occur when either realism or agency are high, or both.

According to this model, individuals consciously respond differently to virtual representations that are computer controlled (agents) than they will to human-controlled virtual representations (avatars) at all but the highest levels of realism, as the threshold of social influence demonstrates in Figure 5.8. Specifically, embodied agents need to display more behavioral realism than avatars in order for conscious social influence to take place. However, the model specifies that the agent-avatar distinction is less important for unconsciously controlled low-level reflexive or automatic behaviors (e.g., maintaining appropriate interpersonal distance; facial mimicry).

According to Blascovich *et al.* (2002), the realism variable in the model is regarded as a latent variable, which can only be assessed or manipulated via manifest realism variables. The model specifies the latter in a hierarchical fashion such that communicative (i.e., social) realism is the most important manifest variable. Communicative realism involves movements (e.g., vocal chords to produce sounds; facial muscle and gestural muscle movements to produce nonverbal signals). Anthropometric realism (e.g., the shape or morphology of the virtual human representation) is important in its service of communicative realism (e.g., one cannot have a hand gesture or lip movements without an arm/hand or face, respectively). Photographic realism is less important dynamically but can be important in terms of social or group identity.

This model provides a general framework to make predictions of TSI manipulations as well as to interpret results, and suggests that photographic realism is much less important than realism associated with behaviors particularly communicative ones such as facial expressions, gestures, head movements, etc. Furthermore, it suggests that in terms of low-level or automatic behaviors, there should be no differences in terms of perceived agency. That is, both known agents and avatars should have the same effects on such unconsciously generated behaviors. For example, either

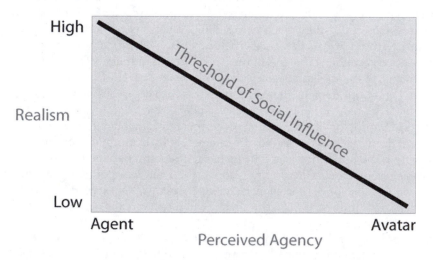

Figure 5.8 A model of social influence in CVEs

should be able to elicit a startle, defensive, or orientation response on the part of a user.

In the empirical section, we have discussed a number of manipulations in experiments which allow someone to achieve higher amounts of social influence via TSI. The question becomes, how do we apply these findings to a model of social influence? The answer is complicated: On the one hand, TSI should decrease realism, because the actual avatar projected is actually different from the person behind the avatar, and consequently less realistic objectively. On the other hand, the perception of the trans-formed avatar for the audience may in fact be perceived as more realistic because that avatar uses an optimal set of cues to achieve some conver-sational goal.

Walther's (1992; 1996) Social Information Processing Theory may provide guidance for this application. Walther argues that, in some instances, CMC can actually be "hyperpersonal," or more intimate than face-to-face settings, due to the fact that in CMC one can project an ideal self and redirect cognitive resources that would usually be applied to nonverbal behavior. Applying TSI may allow a user to become "hyper-realistic"—while the avatar is different from the actual self, it is idealized to become more real than would be possible in face-to-face settings. Of course, this is conjecture at this point, but future work should empirically examine the relationship between realism, hyperpersonal perceptions, TSI and social influence to shed light on these theoretical relations.

Ethics and implications

In sum, when people enter into new and novel types of CMC such as immersive virtual environments, some expectation of nonveridical rendering of others' behavior is most likely inevitable. However, when viewing more traditional types of CMC, such as two-dimensional video feeds, images on websites, voices enhanced by digital algorithms on cell phones, other players in online video games and text in chatrooms, we may not be so rigorous in our skepticism concerning the authenticity of form and behavior. The potential for using TSI for abuse in all forms of digital communication certainly warrants attention.

There is an underlying Orwellian theme behind TSI strategies such as identity capture, augmented gaze, and digital mimicry. Some might argue that these tools would be better left out of the hands of advertisers, poli-ticians, and anyone else who may seek to influence people. After all, TSI strategies allow them to gain advantages in persuasion and even in voting decisions that they would not have otherwise. On the other hand, "manip-ulative" strategies are nothing new to politicians. From sporting a sudden tan to selecting which video clips or photos to send to constituents, politi-cians have a great deal of control over how they present themselves to the public via different communication channels. And if it is inevitable that TSI strategies will be employed in the near future, then perhaps the most important thing is to make people aware of these manipulations—much as how people now widely assume that magazine cover models have been airbrushed.

Once TSI strategies become widely known however, another possible scenario might occur. People may begin to distrust interaction that occurs in virtual spaces. For example, we could imagine scenarios where the premium package from your local internet service provider is not related to access speeds, but access to sophisticated TSI suites. Widespread use of TSI might lead to an infinite regression, a complete distrust in the medium itself. However, this line of argument fails to take into account the prevalence and acceptance of nondigital TSIs in our everyday lives (see Figure 5.2). The claim that digital TSIs will cause distrust assumes that people want to see and interact with each other without any intentional alterations. A cursory glance at modern societies reveals otherwise. One main function of clothing is to conceal the naked body; deodorants (and the sheer diversity of bath and shower products) are used to suppress our natural scents. If anything, there are certain TSIs that our society demands that we perform.

There is also an assortment of nondigital TSIs that are not socially mandatory, and these typically fulfill a cosmetic role. For example, these include: hair coloring, teeth whitening, haircuts, and make-up. In most of these cases, instead of shunning a person for deliberately deceiving others, we in fact typically compliment them on the improvement in their appearance. This is also the case with weight loss and dieting programs. We do not distrust a person because they have "deceptively" tried to create a new appearance, but instead accept their new appearance as an improvement. Overall, it appears that alterations that improve one's social presentation are in fact encouraged by society.

Of course, like any new technology, it takes time for a culture to develop norms for the technology's use. As CMC becomes more advanced and prevalent, it will be fascinating to monitor the progress of TSI strategies as well as technology designed to detect and foil the nonveridical rendering of appearance and behaviors. In the meantime, TSI in CMC presents spectacular opportunities for social scientists studying communication and social interaction.

References

Asch, S. (1955) "Opinions and Social Pressure." *Scientific American, 193*, 5.
Bailenson, J. N. (2006) "Transformed social interaction in collaborative virtual environments." In P. Messaris. & L. Humphreys, (eds.), *Digital Media: Transformations in Human Communication*. New York: Peter Lang, pp. 255–264.

Bailenson, J. N., & Beall, A. C. (2006) "Transformed social interaction: Exploring the digital plasticity of avatars." In R. Schroeder, & A. Axelsson, (eds.), *Avatars at Work and Play: Collaboration and Interaction in Shared Virtual Environments*, Springer-Verlag, pp. 1–16.

Bailenson, J. N., & Blascovich, J. (2002) "Mutual gaze and task performance in shared virtual environments." *Journal of Visualization and Computer Animation, 13*, 1–8.

Bailenson, J., & Blascovich, J. (2004) "Avatars." In W. S. Bainbridge (ed.), *Encyclopedia of Human-Computer Interaction*. Great Barrington, MA: Berkshire Publishing Group.

Bailenson, J. N., & Yee, N. (2005) "Digital Chameleons: Automatic assimilation of nonverbal gestures in immersive virtual environments." *Psychological Science, 16*, 814–819.

Bailenson, J. N., Iyengar, S., & Yee, N. (2006) Facial Identity capture in the 2004 presidential election. Manuscript submitted for publication.

Bailenson, J.N., Garland, P., Iyengar, S., & Yee, N. (2006) "Transformed Facial Similarity as a Political Cue: A Preliminary Investigation." *Political Psychology, 27*, 373–386.

Bailenson, J., Beall, A., Loomis, J., Blascovich, J., & Turk, M. (2004) "Transformed social interaction: Decoupling representation from behavior and form in collaborative virtual environments." *PRESENCE: Teleoperators and Virtual Environments, 13*(4), 428–441.

Beall, A., Bailenson, J., Loomis, J., Blascovich, J., & Rex, C. (2003) "Non-Zero-Sum Mutual Gaze in Collaborative Virtual Environments." Paper presented at the Proceedings of HCI International, Crete.

Biocca, F., & Levy, M. R. (1995) *Communication in the Age of Virtual Reality*. Hillsdale, NJ: L. Erlbaum Associates.

Blascovich, J. (2002) "Social influence within immersive virtual environments." In R. Schroeder (ed.), *The Social Life of Avatars*. London: Springer-Verlag, pp. 127–145.

Blascovich, J., Loomis, J., Beall, A., Swinth, K., Hoyt, C., & Bailenson, J. (2002) "Immersive virtual environment technology as a methodological tool for social psychology." *Psychological Inquiry, 13*(2), 103–124.

Burgoon, J., Bonito, J., Bengtsson, B., Ramirez, A., Dunbar, N., & Miczo, N. (2000) "Testing the interactivity model: Communication processes, partner assessments, and the quality of collaborative work." *Journal of Management Information Systems, 16*, 33–56.

Cappella, J., & Panalp, A. (1981) "Talk and silence sequences in informal conversations. Interspeaker influence." *Human Communication Research, 7*, 117–132.

Chartrand, T. L., & Bargh, J. A. (1999) "The chameleon effect: The perception-behavior link and social interaction." *Journal of Personality & Social Psychology, 76*(6), 893–910.

Chartrand, T. L., & Jefferis, V. E. (2003) "Consequences of automatic goal pursuit and the case of nonconscious mimicry." In J. P. Forgas & K. D. Williams (eds.), *Social Judgments: Implicit and Explicit Processes*. New York: Cambridge University Press, pp. 290–305.

Davis, M., Conklin, L., Smith, A., & Luce, C. (1996) "Effect of perspective taking on the cognitive representations of persons: A merging of self and other." *Journal of Personality and Social Psychology, 70*, 713–726.

DeBruine, L. M. (2002) "Facial resemblance enhances trust." *Proceedings of the Royal Society of London B, 269*, 1307–1312.

Dion, K., Berscheid, E., & Walster, E. (1972) "What is beautiful is good." *Journal of Personality and Social Psychology, 24*, 285–290.

Eagly, A. H., & Wood, W. (1999) "The origins of sex differences in human behavior: Evolved dispositions versus social roles." *American Psychologist, 54*, 408–423.

ESA (2005) *Entertainment Software Association: Facts and Research*, from http://www.theesa.com/facts/gamer_data.php.

Festinger, L. (1954) "A theory of social comparison processes." *Human Relations, 7*, 117–140.

Gaertner, S. L., & Dovidio, J. F. (1977) "The subtlety of white racism, arousal and helping behavior." *Journal of Personality and Social Psychology, 35*, 691–707.

Gehlbach, H., Bailenson, J., Yee, N., & Beall, A. (2005) Perspective taking and negotiation in collaborative virtual environments. Unpublished manuscript.

Giles, H., & Claire, R. (1979) *Language and Social Psychology*. Oxford: Blackwell.

Goffman, E. (1959) *The Presentation of Self in Everyday Life*. New York: Anchor Books.

Guadagno, R. E., Bailenson, J. N., Beall, A. C., Dimov, A., & Blascovich, J. (2005) "Transformed social interaction and the cyranoid: The impact of non-verbal behavior on persuasion in an immersive virtual environment." Unpublished manuscript, University of California, Santa Barbara.

Higham, P. A., & Carment, W. D. (1992) "The rise and fall of politicians: The judged heights of Broadbent, Mulroney and Turner before and after the 1988 Canadian federal election." *Canadian Journal of Behavioral Science, 24*, 404–409.

Iyengar, S., Lowenstein, D. L., & Masket, S. (2001) "The stealth campaign: Experimental studies of slate mail in California." *The Journal of Law and Politics, 17*, 295–232.

Johnston, L. (2002) "Behavioral mimicry and stigmatization." *Social Cognition, 20*(1), 18–35.

Joinson, A. N. (2001) "Self-disclosure in computer-mediated communication: The role of self-awareness and visual anonymity." *European Journal of Social Psychology, 31*, 177–192.

Jones, E. E. (1964). *Ingratiation*. New York: Irvington.

Jones, E. E., & Pitman, T. S. (1982) "Toward a general theory of strategic self-presentation." In J. Suls (ed.), *Psychological Perspectives on the Self*, Vol. 1. Hillsdale, NJ: General Learning Press, pp. 231–262.

Judge, T. A., & Cable, D. M. (2004) "The effect of physical height on workplace success and income: Preliminary test of a theoretical model." *Journal of Applied Psychology, 89*, 428–441.

Konijn, E. A., & Hoorn, J. F. (2004) "Reality-based genre preferences do not direct personal involvement." *Discourse Processes, 38*, 219–246.

LaFrance, M. (1982) "Posture mirroring and rapport." In M. Davis (ed.), *Interaction Rhythms: Periodicity in Communicative Behavior*, New York: Human Sciences Press, pp. 279–298.

Lakin, J. L., & Chartrand, T. L. (2003). "Using nonconscious behavioral mimicry to create affiliation and rapport." *Psychological Science, 14*(4), 334–339.

Lakin, J. L., Jefferis, V. E., Cheng, C. M., & Chartrand, T. L. (2003) "The chameleon effect as social glue: Evidence for the evolutionary significance of nonconscious mimicry." *Journal of Nonverbal Behavior, 27*(3), 145–162.

Langlois, J., Kalakanis, L., Rubenstein, A., Larson, A., Hallam, M., & Smoot, M. (2000) "Maxims or myths of beauty?: A meta-analytic and theoretical review." *Psychological Bulletin, 126*, 390–423.

Levy, B. (1996) "Improving memory in old age through implicit self-stereotyping." *Journal of Personality and Social Psychology, 71*, 1092–1107.

Milgram, S., Sabini, J., & Silver, M. (1992) *The Individual in a Social World: Essays and Experiments*. New York: McGraw-Hill.

Nass, C., & Brave, S. (2005) *Wired for Speech: How Voice Activates and Advances the Human-Computer Relationship*. Cambridge, MA: MIT Press.

Neumann, R., & Strack, F. (2000) "Mood contagion: The automatic transfer of mood between persons." *Journal of Personality & Social Psychology, 79*, 211–223.

Parks, M. R., & Floyd, K. (1995) "Friends in cyberspace: Exploring personal relationships formed through the Internet." Paper presented at the International Communication Association, Albuquerque, NM.

Project, P. I. a. A. L. (2004) "*53 Million in US use IM*," from http://www.emarketer.com/Article.aspx?1003031.

Provine, R. (1986) "Yawning as a stereotyped action pattern and releasing stimulus." *Ethology, 72*, 109–122.

Provine, R. (1992) "Contagious Laughter: Laughter is sufficient stimulus for laughs and smiles." *Bulletin of the Psychonomic Society, 30*, 1–4.

Reidsma, D., Akker, R., Rienks, R., Poppe, R., Nijholt, A., Heylen, D., & Zwiers, J. (2005)

"Virtual meeting rooms: from observation to simulation." In *Proceedings of Social Intelligence Design, 2005.*

Rheingold, H. (1993) *The Virtual Community: Homesteading on the Electronic Frontier.* Reading, MA: Addison-Wesley.

Schlenker, B. R. (1980) *Impression Management: the Self-Concept, Social Identity, and Interpersonal Relationships.* Monterey, CA: Brooks/Cole.

Schmorrow, D. D., & Kruse, A. A. (2004) "Augmented Cognition." In W. S. Bainbridge (ed.), *Berkshire Encyclopedia of Human-Computer Interaction.* Great Barrington, MA: Berkshire Publishing Group, pp. 54–59.

Schroeder, R. (ed.), (2002) *The Social Life of Avatars.* London: Springer-Verlag.

Segrin, C. (1993) "The effects of nonverbal behavior on outcomes of compliance gaining attempts." *Communication Studies, 44,* 169–187.

Sproull, L., & Kiesler, S. (1986) "Reducing social context cues: Electronic mail in organizational communication." *Management Science, 32,* 1492–1512.

Sundar, S. S., Kalyanaraman, S., & Brown, J. (2003) "Explicating website interactivity: Impression-formation effects in political campaign sites." *Communication Research, 30,* 30–59.

Swinth, K., & Blascovich, J. (2002) "Perceiving and responding to others: Human-human and human-computer social interaction in collaborative virtual environments." Paper presented at the Proceedings of the 5th Annual International Workshop on PRESENCE. Porto, Portugal.

Taylor, S., & Fiske, S. (1975) "Point of view and perceptions of causality." *Journal of Personality and Social Psychology, 32,* 439–445.

Turk, D. J., Heatherton, T. F., Kelley, W. M., Funnell, M. G., Gazzaniga, M. S., & Macrae, C. N. (2002) "Mike or me? Self recognition in a split-brain patient." *Nature Neuroscience, 5,* 841–842.

Turkle, S. (1995) *Life on the Screen: Identity in the Age of the Internet.* New York: Simon and Schuster.

Walther, J. (1992) "Interpersonal effects in computer-mediated interaction: A relational perspective," *Communication Research, 19,* pp. 52–90.

Walther, J. B. (1996) "Computer-mediated communication: Impersonal, interpersonal, and hyperpersonal interaction." *Communication Research, 23*(1), 3–43.

Walther, J. B., Anderson, J. F., & Park, D. (1994) "Interpersonal effects in computer-mediated interaction: A meta-analysis of social and anti-social communication." *Communication Research, 21,* 460–487.

Woodcock, B. (2005) *MMOG Chart,* from http://www.mmogchart.com/

Yee, N. (2006, in press) "The demographics, motivations, and derived experiences of users of massively multi-user online graphical environments." *Presence: Teleoperators and Virtual Environments.*

Yee, N., & Bailenson, J. N. (2007) "The Proteus effect: Self transformations in virtual reality." *Human Communication Research, 33,* 271–290.

Young, T. J., & French, L. A. (1996) "Height and perceived competence of U. S. Presidents." *Perceptual and Motor Skills, 82,* 1002.

Zajonc, R. B., Adelmann, P. K., Murphy, S. T., & Niendenthal, P. M. (1987) "Convergence in the physical appearance of spouses." *Motivation and Emotion, 11,* 335–346.

Chapter 6

Emotions in mediated interpersonal communication

Toward modeling emotion in virtual humans

Elly A. Konijn and Henriette C. Van Vugt

Emotions are at the heart of interpersonal communication. That is, much of what is communicated in an interpersonal context is interpreted as or guided by emotions. In contemporary textbooks on interpersonal communication, the *interpersonal* of interpersonal communication is primarily defined by the quality of the interaction, being personal as opposed to impersonal (Beebe, *et al.*, 2002; DeVito, 2004; Wood, 2002). Hence, communication qualified as emotional is more likely to be included in the area of the interpersonal than communication without emotions. Perhaps because people believe that emotions reflect our most authentic selves (Bellman, 2003; Frijda, 1988). For example, intimacy, becoming friends, knowing one another, and resolving conflict goes hand in hand with personal affect and emotional experiences and these topics are typically included in interpersonal textbooks. Whether this stance is justified or not, emotions do play an important role in our daily communication. This does not necessarily mean that emotions are communicated explicitly or effectively. Sometimes, we even don't recognize our own emotions (e.g., nonidentified feelings of uneasiness) or express them differently (e.g., women are known for crying when actually being angry), making it difficult to correctly identify. Furthermore, emotions play an important role in guiding behavior, revealing what is important to one's goals, and have social communicative functions, among others.

Until recently, and in lay notions, interpersonal communication was commonly understood as occurring face-to-face and thought of as impossible to occur in mediated contexts (see debates on "media richness" and "cues filtered out" theories in Beninger, 1987; Polkosky, this volume; Walther, 1992). This is probably due to the fact that interlocutors often think that meeting face-to-face provides cues to the interlocutor's true emotions or feelings—they believe "you can just *see* it" (cf. Ekman, 1972). However, encoding and decoding emotions in everyday interpersonal communication is a matter of scientific debate. Basically, interlocutors always have to communicate their emotions in order to get them across. This can be done in various ways that will be described below, in face-to-face communication and mediated contexts alike. Modern technologies increasingly allow emotions to be communicated in sophisticated ways through electronic devices and screens, both between people being physically apart from each other (computer-mediated communication, CMC) and between people and computers (human-computer interaction, HCI). The role of emotions in mediated interpersonal communication is a salient one and covers an important area of research.

In the following, we will briefly describe the development of various emotion theories, because defining emotion seems largely dependent on the specific theory at hand. The first section provides a brief introduction to the main issues of emotion research and serves as a basis for understanding the remainder of the chapter. The next section describes how emotions are communicated and which functions they serve. The final section introduces the field of affective computing, including an overview of the existing research on designing virtual humans that can detect users' emotions and display "emotions" themselves.

Perspectives on emotions

Most people have an intuitive and inherent understanding of what emotions are. In naive psychology, emotions are placed opposite to cognition, or basically reflect physiological "disturbances" in which activated experiences are discerned from the deactivated. However, emotions as phenomena to be studied are so complex that even emotion theorists do not agree on a definition of emotion and the literature on emotion, including overviews of emotion theories, has proliferated widely. Recently, however, some consensus appears to have been put forward that emotions, cognitions, and physiology are intrinsically intertwined (e.g., Damasio, 1994; Frijda *et al.*, 2000; Lang, 1994; LeDoux, 1996; Panksepp, 1998; Rolls, 2003). Therefore, this section will not reiterate this work but merely provide some relevant insights into the scientific debate about emotions, outline some basic concepts and theories, and provide some basic understanding of what emotion research is about.

What do we mean when talking about emotions?

When talking about emotions, the complexity of defining emotion immediately becomes clear. First, the concept of emotion is used to indicate various aspects and forms of output of the emotion process. That is, emotion may refer to: (1) the subjective experience of having an emotion (e.g., I feel sad); (2) the physiological response accompanying most emotions (e.g., butterflies in the stomach, blushing, heartbeat); and (3) visible, audible, or behavioral expressions of emotions (e.g., tears, laughter, clenching fist). Sometimes, an individual might mean to say something about just one aspect, at other times, one may refer to the dynamics of an entire emotion process. In addition, issues of intensity and direction of emotions (valence) are addressed. Second, emotional experiences are referred to by various concepts, such as mood, feeling, passion, and affect, which are used interchangeably and represent not clearly separate classes of experience. Obviously, with the emerging field of affective computing, similar problems and confusions arise in studying emotions in human-computer and computer-human interaction that have been addressed in previous emotion research. Therefore, the following will briefly address the main issues as they pertain to emotion terminology (confusing concepts) and defining emotion within the context of emotion theories and current research. Thereafter, we will describe how emotions can be communicated in interpersonal (mediated) contexts.

Distinguishing emotion terminology

Lay persons and scholars alike use the concepts of emotion, mood, feeling, and affect interchangeably to indicate certain emotional states. *Affect* is sometimes used as an even broader concept than emotion, generally covering the various forms of emotional phenomena and often used to distinguish the affective state from cognition in research. A crucial difference between affect and emotions is that emotions have an object and relate to meaningful events, whereas affect is more free-floating and object-less (Russell & Barrett, 1999; Barrett, 2006a). Affect is usually reflected in varying degrees of pleasure-displeasure, or positive-negative affect, as well as (de)arousal or (de)activation. Furthermore, affect is conceptualized as a longer-lasting phenomenon than emotion. Thus, emotions are more clearly defined by a specific event, with a beginning and ending, and are more temporal than affects. *Mood* also is often applied to an enduring affective state, characterized by globality and not clearly elicited by an external event (i.e., not felt as motivated by situational meaning, Frijda, 1986; 1994). Furthermore, the term "mood" is often used to denote an experimental induction of an affective state in emotion research. Thus, a mood may also have a biochemical source (e.g., epinephrine), whereas emotions are characterized by increased activity in the sympathetic nervous system due to vital implications of threats and rewards for the human system (Damasio, 1994; LeDoux, 1996).

Prototypical emotions are what most people consider the clearest cases of emotion and are often conceptualized as fitting into discrete semantic categories of emotion types, like grief and happiness (Russell & Barrett, 1999). Prototypical emotions are close to so-called *basic emotions*. The "basic emotion" approach argues that certain emotions (e.g., described as anger, sadness, fear, happiness, disgust, and surprise) are universal, biologically basic, and "given by nature." Thus, this approach states that basic emotions are inherited, reflex-like modules that cause distinct and identifiable behavioral and physiological patterns (Barrett & Wager, 2006; Ekman, 1972; Ekman & Friesen, 1975; Panksepp, 1998). Other emotions are then considered blends or mixtures of basic emotions. However, the research distinguishing basic emotions is mainly based on the *recognition* of emotions through (facial) expression, or on interpretations of physiological indicators and neuroimaging data. Display rules and cultural differences, for example, limit conclusions regarding basic emotions from recognizing facial expressions (Hochschild, 1979; Manstead *et al.*, 1999; Wagner & Lee, 1999). Such conclusions from physiological and neuroimaging research are limited because of methodological constraints and, thus far, scholars have mainly focused on the most salient or distinctive features (e.g., specific brain areas) in the circuitry for a given emotion construct (Barrett & Wager, 2006). Hence, relations between facial expressions, emotion words, or aggravated brain circulatory and genuine emotional experiences is debated (e.g., Barrett, 2006b; Damasio, 1994; Ekman & Davidson, 1994; Zillmann, 2003). Therefore, substrates of emotional expression should not be taken for the emotional experience itself, as will be further discussed below.

Finally, *feelings* differ from emotions in that there is no action tendency truly pressing for action. Nevertheless, the word "feeling" is also used to express one's emotion, or to refer to the subjective experience of having an emotion, such as in "I feel angry." Feelings are often considered emotions of less intensity, although feelings can be strong and emotions weak. Thus, emotions, feelings, and affects are difficult to separate from one another. Notwithstanding theoretical attempts to do so, we will see in the remainder of this chapter that scholars may still use the various terms interchangeably and sometimes in ambiguous ways. For example, scholars discussing "emotional virtual humans" actually mean virtual humans that are able to display and respond to emotions, which is studied under the heading of "affective computing." As will become clear in the following, it is impossible for virtual humans to be emotional or to *have* emotions. The definition of emotion is inherently dependent on the focus in the specific discipline from which an emotion theory evolved. In the next section, theories of emotion are therefore addressed. This provides the background against which contemporary research guiding the design of "emotional computers" can be evaluated.

Definitions and theories of emotion

In trying to provide a clear definition of what an emotion actually is, one runs into the fact that emotions are studied from a wide variety of perspectives and have a long history as objects of scientific dispute. The simplified way of placing emotion opposite to cognition, for example, dates back to Descartes, who proposed a strict separation of body and soul—emotions residing in the soul and the soul driven by God. Thus, rationality and emotionality were clearly distinguished (Damasio, 1994). Although Diderot had previously rejected these ideas, by the end of the eighteenth century, Descartes' thinking had far-reaching consequences for twentieth-century scientific thinking and emotion theories in particular. For example, in the 1980s, leading scholars in the field of emotion psychology (Lazarus, 1982; Zajonc, 1984) debated forcefully about which factor actually defines the emotional experience: physiological (i.e. bodily) responses versus cognitive appraisals (i.e. the mind; see also Ekman & Davidson, 1994). Against this background, it is easy to understand how such different views on emotions may have evolved. Furthermore, defining emotion is inherently dependent on the focus in a particular theory. Therefore, instead of one clear defini-tion, we can only provide a brief overview in the following.

When psychology was established as a discipline on its own, at the turn of the eighteenth-to-nineteenth centuries, clearly identifiable emotion theories appeared. The now famous James-Lange theory (1884) stated that emotion stemmed from certain physical sensations. In this view, emotions are both the product and the expression of what happens in the body: First we respond physiologically, and then the emotion follows. There-fore, emotions were defined as interpretations of physiological arousal and beyond conscious control. The essence of James' theory is reflected in the example "I see a bear, I tremble and shake, I start running, therefore, I am afraid" (James, 1884: 188). Thus, the awareness of an emotion lies in the appraisal of peripheral cues of bodily sensations. A similar line of thought is found in the so-called facial feedback theories (Adelmann & Zajonc, 1989; Laird, 1974), stating that feedback from facial expressions was a primary source for attributing emotions.

In elaborating this view, Schachter (1959, 1964) stated that physiological activation ("arousal") alone is not sufficient to arouse an emotion. Physi-ological activation would motivate an individual to find an explanation in his/her surroundings or thoughts: "He will 'label' this state and describe his feelings in terms of the cognitions available to him. ... precisely the same state of physiological arousal could be labeled 'joy' or 'fury' or 'jealousy'" (Schachter & Singer, 1962: 381). Thus, in this view, an emotion is defined by, first, physiological arousal (or dearousal), and, second, cognitive attri-bution of that arousal to a source. Therefore, this theory is also called the *two-factor theory*. Well-known experiments tested this theory. Subjects were administered adrenaline ("epinephrine"), after which they were placed in a waiting room. An assistant in the waiting room behaved either cheerfully or maliciously. The subjects who were approached cheerfully described their (adrenaline-induced) agitated feelings as positive emotions. The subjects who were treated aggressively, on the other hand, described their arousal as malevolent emotions (Schachter & Singer, 1962). Of course, the two-factor theory was criticized extensively: for example, because the argument of the primacy of physiological feedback for an emotion to occur was questioned.

Another line of thought has simultaneously been developed. Beginning in 1927, Cannon opposed James' view when he stated that we experience the emotions first, and only thereafter we may experience the physiological changes such as trembling, muscular tension, heart beat, etc. Thus, in Cannon's view, emotions are only *displayed* in physiological phenomena, but the emotional experience is defined centrally in the brain. In Cannon's view, emotions are even possible without sensations of or from the body (Cannon, 1927). Nowadays, central theories on emotions are found among the neuroscientists aiming at delineating structures in the central nervous system that uniquely reflect specific emotion episodes (e.g., Crease, 1993; Damasio, 2001; LeDoux, 1996, 2000; Panksepp, 1998; Rolls, 1999). Basically, central theories state that perceptual input is screened for vital implications in the amygdala and related central brain areas prior to reaching the cortex. Thus, they argue that centrally located brain areas are activated (i.e. show elevated activity in the sympathetic nervous system) before perceptual input is cognitively processed or comprehended. New techniques for neurochemical analysis and brain imaging (e.g., functional magnetic resonance imaging, fMRI, and positron emission tomography, PET) have given research based on central theories a new impetus.

A common point of debate in the study of emotion today is whether the basic building blocks of emotional life are identifiable (Barrett & Wager, 2006). Although there is emerging evidence from a number of studies that seem to support such a view (e.g., Murphy et al., 2003; Phan et al, 2002; Wager et al., 2003), serious methodological problems still exist. That is, two criteria must be satisfied to indicate emotions as biologically defined, or as "a natural kind" (Barrett & Wager, 2006). First, patterns of neural activation must be *consistent* (i.e., show increased activation regardless of the induction method used) and, second, *specific* (e.g., a fear response should be separable from an anger response). However, many findings were *not* independent of the particular induction method used. In fact, induction methods accounted for a good deal of variability in the reported findings. For example, the amygdala seems particularly responsive to faces and other visual stimuli while the fear-amygdala correspondence is the most consistent finding (see meta-analyses in Phan et al., 2002, and Murphy et al., 2003). Furthermore, cognitive demand of particular emotional tasks (e.g., remembering a sad event) over others (e.g., viewing sad stimuli) confounds findings (Phan et al., 2002). Finally, evidence now emerges that the amygdala responds to simple perceptual cues (e.g., eyes in particular, see Adolphs et al., 2005) and is involved in detecting significant threats or rewards (Barrett, 2006a; Barrett & Wager, 2006). Thus, claims about the psychological meaning of activation in neuroimaging studies have to be reconsidered. Principally, it may be possible to map specific activity patterns in the brain as connected to emotions; however, thus far, most of the imaging research has focused on the most salient or distinctive feature (e.g., brain area) in the circuitry for a given emotion construct. The other way around (e.g., given amygdala activation, is there fear?) should also be tested. Thus, a biological definition of emotion is still the subject of sophisticated research.

In the 1980s and 1990s, a host of influential *cognitive appraisal theories* established another major theoretical perspective on emotions (Ekman & Davidson, 1994; Ellsworth & Scherer, 2003; Frijda, 1986; 2000; Lazarus, 1982, 1991; Oatley & Jenkins, 1996; Ortony *et al.*, 1988; Scherer, 2000). The appraisal perspective defined emotions as cognitively based in appraisal processes. In short, a certain *understanding* of the emotionalizing event or situation is deemed necessary for an emotion to occur. For example, when I see a bear, I will only experience fear if I understand its potential threat to my well-being. If I recognize an actor dressed as a bear, for example, I will not be fearful. In the appraisal view, emotions are defined as relationships between individual motives, needs, goals, and concerns relating to pleasure and pain, attraction and aversion, and one's physical and social environment. Events are appraised in view of individual goals and concerns. Most cognitive appraisal theorists nowadays see emotion as a process, which is completed in a fraction of a second, passing through different stages of appraisal in which potential threats and chances are assessed (Frijda, 1986, 2000; Gratch & Marsella, 2004; Izard, 1993; Kappas, 2002; Lazarus, 1991; Oatley & Jenkins, 1996; Scherer, 2000; Zillmann, 2003). Hence, when no relevant concerns are touched by an event, no emotion will occur. Appraisal definitions of emotion are challenged by how cognition is defined and because it deemphasizes the bodily sources and consequences of emotions (Damasio, 1994; Lang, 1994; Rolls, 1999; Sloman, 2003; Zillmann, 2003).

At first glance, the dominant emotion research domains nowadays, biological (mostly neuroimaging) and appraisal theories, may be hard to reconcile. However, much of the debate depends on how strictly cognition is defined—as purely rational thought and fully conscious or merely some basic understanding of the situational meaning in relation to personal concerns as necessary for an emotion to occur (Lang, 1994; Rolls, 1999; Sloman, 2003). Likewise, the brain structures as found through neuroimaging research do not seem that specific for basic emotions as they appeared to do at the turn of the nineteenth-to-twentieth centuries. However, some fundamental agreement may be found in the view that (basic) emotional experiences alert the organism to its well functioning and malfunctioning, to threats and dangers, and to rewards and punishments. While the appraisal theories emphasize the cognitive aspects of understanding the emotionalizing event, the brain-imaging scholars emphasize the biological basis and primary response to emotionalizing events.

Therefore, more elaborate information-processing models are currently being developed that try to integrate the various perspectives described above and include approaches from mental models, artificial intelligence, and neural networks (Barrett & Wager, 2006; Gratch & Marsella, 2004; Lang, 1994; Sloman, 2003; Rolls, 1999, 2003).

Communicating emotions in interpersonal (mediated) contexts

The following will provide a concise overview of how emotions are communicated; how the subjective experience should be distinguished from how an expression might be observed. Furthermore, a description of the functions of emotions is helpful in clarifying how emotions can be modeled for use in mediated communication, especially in virtual humans.

Communicating emotions through expression

An individual's inner emotional state, or "having an emotion," may become apparent in three ways: subjective experiences; physiological responses; and behavioral expressions. In communicating emotion, individuals (including scholars) often refer to just one salient aspect (e.g., "I feel sad" or "I tremble") and only rarely to the entire emotion process. Nevertheless, the various aspects of the entire emotion process may well be experienced— in all its complexities. The subjective experience of having an emotion is usually only arrived at through introspection, individuals claiming to undergo some experience that may be called an emotion. Because there is some agreement among emotion scholars that emotions alert the individual to their well functioning and malfunctioning, the *subjective experience* of an emotion will consist of the awareness of the situational meaning in terms of its threatening or beneficial potential and the *felt* need to act or not to act, to satisfy a concern or because one's concerns are in danger (Frijda, 1986). In analyses of emotion words, there is certain consensus on a dimensional view: for example, discerning emotion words denoting valence (pleasure/displeasure) and arousal (high activation/low activation; Russell & Barrett, 1999; Plutchik, 1997; Ortony *et al.*,1988); however, words denoting emotions may have nothing in common with the experience (Barrett & Wager, 2006). Furthermore, communicating the subjective experience of emotions is not restricted to the use of emotion words. People may use descriptions of any kind to convey their internal state. For example, the description "the mean fellow who brutally stole my beloved car, made my veins burst" may express one's anger. Humans are very creative in finding ways to express their emotional experiences without explicitly naming them (as is also evidenced in art).

Thus, it is obvious that there is no need to be in a face-to-face encounter in order to be able to communicate emotions. Indeed, subjective experiences of emotions can likewise be communicated through media such as computers, a phenomenon which is demonstrated in various chapters in this volume. For example, people express their love (Whitty, this volume) and hate (Douglas, this volume) and experience intimate relationships at a distance (Hartmann, this volume) in face-to-face and mediated contexts alike. In text-based mediated communication, paralanguage, such as capitals, italics, or bold face is used to underline meanings or attach emotional emphasis to the words (e.g., HATE; see Carey, 1980; Short *et al.*, 1976) and indeed, emoticons are widely used (e.g., Sanderson, 1994). However, to study the differences existing in expressing and reading subjective experiences of emotions in face-to-face as compared to mediated contexts can be an interesting endeavor.

A second mode through which emotions may express themselves is physiological change, such as arousal, accelerated heart beat, blushing, changes in blood pressure or hormone levels. Physiological references are often made in verbal expressions such as metaphors to denote emotional experiences (e.g., "Butterflies in the stomach"). For many, physiological change forms an integral part of the emotional experience and often is the "proof of the pudding" (Konijn, 2004; Sartre, 1934; Shields, 1984). Physiological cues are seen as strong, "objective" indicators of emotional experience, probably because physiological change is seen as hardly under voluntary control (Ekman *et al.*, 1983; Murphy *et al.*, 2003; Zajonc *et al.*, 1989). Notwithstanding its problematic scientific status, physiological methods are popular among HCI designers and scholars. Several virtual reality applications and video games provide the player with sensory feedback, which would enhance feelings of presence, as if the virtual encounters were real and as if the player were part of the virtual environment (cf. Hoorn, *et al.*, 2003). The physiological arousal seems easily (mis)attributed, just as if one were experiencing a "real' emotion (cf. Schachter's two-factor theory). How physiology is used to detect user emotions while interacting with computers will be discussed in the next section.

The third mode of communicating emotion is through *visible and audible behavior* such as tears, laughter, words, or clenching fists. Thus, emotional behavior covers a whole range of verbal and nonverbal behaviors that can be categorized in three groups. First, facial expressions may be considered a separate category, as the human face is fundamental in communicating emotions (Argyle & Cook, 1976; Ekman, 1972; Ekman & Friesen, 1969, 1975; Frijda, 1986). For example, surprise is characterized by widening of the eyes, brief suspension of breathing, general loss of muscle tone, and opening of the mouth (Ekman, 1972). Second, emotions can be expressed through language, both verbally using words, and nonverbally. Often, speakers do not explicitly verbalize their emotions but reveal them through other characteristics of speech. Frustrated speakers, for example, speak rapidly with high pitch levels and small pitch variations. Pleasantness is characterized by rapid speech with low pitch levels and large pitch variations, whereas boredom and sadness are characterized by slow speaking and low pitch levels (Scherer, 2003). Therefore, studying emotional language includes not only speech but also the emotional prosody of speech (the rhythmic and intonation aspects of speech), the speed of speaking, and the pitch of the voice. Third, emotion can be expressed through gesture, posture, and gaze. For example, a raised thumb may express praise, a fist may express anger, hanging shoulders fatigue, and a long gaze shows interest. Currently, emotional language analyses are widely used to design emotional language in virtual humans (see next section).

However, many behavioral expressions may be signifiers of *non*emotional states as well. Thus, one should realize that although an emotion may become visible or audible through behavior, the expressions do not necessarily indicate an emotion (Fridlund, 1991; Kappas, 2003; Manstead *et al.*, 1999). For example, a smile may just be put on for politeness and have no relation to any underlying emotion, tears may be the result of cultural customs, and the fist may express physical coldness. Nevertheless, in communicating emotions, facial expressions, language, and speech signifiers form strong vehicles to read one another's corresponding inner states. For example, while seeing a sad face, one is strongly inclined to infer a sad emotion—even when the sad face is just on a screen, or only indicated in a line drawing. Or, a smile is interpreted as the emotional experience itself, whereas it may only be a communicative act without an underlying corresponding emotion (Fridlund, 1991). Therefore, the emotional expression, which is accessible to others, should be clearly distinguished from the subjective experience of the emotion itself, which is not readily accessible to others. As said, humans are creative in communicating their emotions and, more importantly, in such a way as to make others believe the communicated cues refer to genuinely felt corresponding emotional states (e.g., Konijn, 2000). A look into the functions that expressing emotions may serve will further clarify why the expression of an emotion differs from a corresponding underlying emotion.

Functions of emotions

Emotions fulfill various functions for the human system, providing further insight into the nature of emotion (Rolls, 1999) and which are also used to model emotional virtual humans (e.g., Gratch & Marsella, 2005; Klesen, 2005). Leaving aside the more biological and adaptive functions that emotions serve (such as action preparation and guiding natural selection, LeDoux, 1996; Rolls, 1999), we will focus on their widely acknowledged social and communicative functions.

Darwin (2002 [1872]) already elaborated on the communicative potential of emotions and emotional expressions, most notably in drawing parallels between primates and human communication. In this respect, facial expressions are most often studied as communicating emotion. The supposed cross-cultural universality (e.g., Ekman, 1994; Izard, 1997) of facial expressions and the face-related sensitivity of the amygdala (e.g., Adolphs *et al.*, 2005; Phan, *et al.*, 2002) assume the biological connectedness of facial expression and emotional experience. However, as discussed above, such conclusions cannot yet be drawn from the current state of emotion research (Barrett & Wager, 2006). Nevertheless, communicating emotions clearly serves communicative and social functions.

Showing one's emotions helps to communicate what one needs. For example, babies cry to get the attention of their parents, because they need food, dry diapers, or some affection. It is therefore more functional to shed tears when in company than when alone. This led Fridlund (1991) to emphasize the social and communicative functions of emotional displays rather than being determined by emotional states. The human system seems hardwired to respond to such emotional displays—most find it difficult to suppress such responses (De Waal, 2003; Fridlund, 1997). Emotions may thus function as part of a system of social control to evoke particular responses from others (Fridlund, 1997). As such, the display of anger, for example, may be seen as an attempt to enforce social norms. Interestingly, also when confronted with a virtual human, people responded more politely and tended to make socially desirable choices (Krämer *et al.*, 2005), and responded more empathically (Paiva *et al.*, 2005).

Furthermore, to communicate one's emotional state helps to shape the social interaction; to inform the observer of a person's motives for action and the emotional significance of certain events; to allow the observer to derive assumptions about a person's personality; and to form a consistent pattern of beliefs and behaviors (Manstead *et al.*, 1999; Smith & Scott, 1997). The more one acquires such knowledge, the more one can predict the other person's behavior, which has important social and survival functions. Emotional displays are therefore strong vehicles for communicating personal information and for guiding interpersonal behavior. Emotional displays also regulate communication: for example a nod, a smile, and a wink may communicate one's pleasure in accepting a request and serve to turn the dialogue. Likewise, gaze, head position, and body posture serve an important function in turn-taking, showing interest or disinterest (Argyle & Cook, 1976; Bente *et al.*, 1998) as do specific speech characteristics (Scherer, 2003). Furthermore, mirroring the interlocutor's emotional state may positively influence the social interaction (Bernieri & Rosenthal, 1991) and confirmed in mediated communication contexts with virtual humans (Bailenson & Yee, 2005). Indeed, such emotional displays often occur through nonverbal cues (Fridlund, 1997; Bente *et al.*, this volume) and it is often not clear, and perhaps not necessary, to know the other's true underlying feelings (Fridlund, 1991).

In general, there is considerable social shaping of emotional expressions, for example under the constraints of feeling rules and display rules or cultural conventions (e.g., Hochschild, 1979; Manstead *et al.*, 1999). For example, one may put on a sad face to communicate one's regret or empathy, or to obey to certain cultural rules. Moreover, emotions can be deliberately manipulated to achieve certain ends. Pretense, deception, and masking one's true feelings, and even lying, are part of everyday interpersonal communication and people have difficulty detecting the deception (DePaulo *et al.*, 2003; Ekman & O'Sullivan, 1991; Kappas, 2003). Studies show that posed or feigned emotions are easier to recognize and more often correctly identified than spontaneous emotions from everyday life (Hess & Kleck, 1994; Wallbott & Scherer, 1986). In judging the genuineness of emotions, most people don't notice the right cues (Shields, 1984) and are not very accurate in detecting lies or in judging when someone is lying, even not "professional lie catchers"(Ekman & O'Sullivan, 1991).

This is not to say that it is always "bad" to communicate feelings other than what is actually felt. The capacity of people to play act offers the possibility to adjust to their environments and to behave socially. Thus, even if it doesn't reflect one's actual emotional state, one may communicate an emotion to achieve important goals or a social intention—in that sense, the function of communicating an "emotion" may be sincere. In the end, social behavior serves survival functions (Darwin, 2002; LeDoux, 1996; Rolls, 1999) and emotions do have a clear function in social bonding and social interaction (De Waal, 2003; Fridlund, 1997). In a recent study (Choi *et al.*, 2005) it is argued that the degree of automation of emotional displays (in this case, nonverbal behavior) is fairly high and occurs largely outside conscious awareness due to "the need to act quickly in social life." Furthermore, knowledge of the situational and verbal context in which the nonverbal behavior occurs, the visibility of its dynamic qualities, and consistency of (subtle) cues through various communication channels greatly improves the correct emotion attribution of nonverbal behavior in everyday life (see Bente, *et al.*, this volume).

Finally, emotions fulfill an important role in the notion of *emotional intelligence* (Salovey & Mayer, 1990) or emotional competence (Buck, 1999). Emotional intelligence includes the ability to recognize the emotions of another and to respond appropriately to these emotions (Barrett & Salovey, 2003). When such skills are lacking, interaction is more likely to be perceived as frustrating and not very intelligent. Therefore, to design virtual humans that are perceived as emotionally intelligent, one needs to model emotional competence into the application. Furthermore, virtual humans may be used to train such emotional competence. In all, virtual humans that are able to fulfill functions that emotions have in real life will be regarded as more emotionally competent (or intelligent) than those who do not, thereby possibly increasing their likeability and the user's intention to use the application in which they are employed.

Thus, to improve the interpersonal impression of human-computer interaction, it seems reasonable to design "emotional" virtual humans given the generally positive effects of emotions on human communication. However, in order to do so, computer scientists will be looking for the "right" emotion theory to design the "right" model to be implemented in an application. As may be clear from the above, there is not one right emotion theory and the multifaceted nature of the concept and of emotion research may easily confuse software engineers and obscure the academic debate as to what exactly should be modeled and which functions must be served on behalf of what is called "affective computing."

Affective computing

Although computers are extremely good at performing frequent, repetitive, and time-consuming tasks, designing computers that exhibit "creative, adaptive, social, and emotional" behavior demands more than just arithmetic power. Many research labs have been working on such systems in a field known under the heading of "affective computing." Affective computing is defined as "computing that relates to, arises from, or deliberately influences emotion" (Picard, 1997: 3). According to Rosalind Picard, the founder of the field of affective computing (http://affect.media. mit.edu/), research in affective computing may consider, among others: (1) designing ways for people to communicate their emotional states to computers; (2) creating new techniques to assess a user's mood, frustration, and stress indirectly, through natural interaction and conversation; and (3) showing how computers can look more emotionally intelligent— for example, by responding to a person's frustration such that it reduces negative feelings. The idea is that "emotional" computers that detect and "understand" user emotions and that react appropriately to the user's emotions (including portraying emotional expressions themselves, if necessary or appropriate), are less frustrating and more natural to interact with (Picard, 1997). In addition, virtual humans "showing emotions" may increase the user's likeability of a system. The positive effects of showing empathetic emotions is repeatedly demonstrated in human-human communication and is even seen as one of the functions of emotional display, as mentioned above. Such positive effects may also hold when communicating with a virtual human. A recent study (Brave *et al.*, 2005) showed that virtual humans in a blackjack computer game who showed empathic emotion were rated more positively, received greater likeability and trustworthiness, and were perceived with greater caring and support capabilities than virtual humans not showing empathy.

Why affective computing?

One of the first to address emotion in virtual humans was Bates (1994) and his research group. For them, a main reason for designing virtual humans with emotions was to enhance their believability (see also Paiva *et al.*, 2005). They argued that to clearly define emotional states in a virtual human, both goals and appraisals with respect to these goals are central issues. For example, a "Woggle" character creates "an analog of anger" (Bates, 1994: 124). It shows similar patterns to human anger in response to an important goal failure caused by another Woggle. Nowadays, virtual humans (e.g., Bates, 1994; Gratch & Marsella, 2004; Mateas & Stern, 2006) and robots (e.g., Brazeal, 2003) are increasingly used in various applications, ranging from e-learning environments, online banking sites, psychotherapy applications, to games and virtual reality worlds. Such humanlike creatures in computers are believed to be particularly appropriate because their faces and bodies can be used to exhibit emotions in ways similar to real humans. Their humanlike appearance may thus evoke a strong "interpersonal" feeling of communication in users.

The notion that human-computer interactions may improve by considering emotions is further facilitated by steady findings that humans, even experienced computer users, are inclined to treat their computers as largely natural and social and that they interact in affective ways with computers (Brave & Nass, 2002; Reeves & Nass, 1996). For example, people can feel pleased by the flattery of a computer, even though the flatterer is a piece of communication hardware. Furthermore, people are polite to computers, just as they are polite to humans. In contrast, people can also feel offended by an impolite computer, as is illustrated by a virtual human who suddenly disappears from the screen without saying or waving goodbye. This impolite behavior does not conform to the rules of leaving a social situation, and the virtual human is therefore seen as socially or emotionally incompetent, rather than as technologically deficient (Reeves & Nass, 1996). In addition, very elementary, simple forms of behavior representing emotional behavior in the emotionally expressive robot Kismet triggered sympathetic responses (Breazeal, 2003). Therefore, Picard (1997, 2000) argues that because humans are social beings that have emotions, computers designed to interact with humans have to deal with users that have emotions.

One may debate *how* computers should be designed for emotions so to satisfy users or improve interaction. In real life, the expression of an emotion is not necessarily causally related to a corresponding underlying emotion, and likewise, computers may communicate an emotional display without actually "having" the emotion. Thus, the benefits that are aimed for when implementing emotions into machines, such as less frustrated users, can also be achieved by other means. For example, Krämer *et al.* (2005) argue that a computer does not "have to be sad" when an error occurs; it just has to communicate the error in a way that the user does not return to the system angrily. They thus argue for a focus on the communicative functions of emotions instead of an intention to model emotions into computers. Emotion models may, however, serve the design of consistent and dynamic emotional behavior, as we will see later in this chapter.

Other opponents of designing emotional capable computers say that when people interact with such humanlike computers, they will construct an erroneous model of how computers work and what their capabilities are, and thus convey wrong expectations. Shneiderman (2002), for example, argues that the suggestion that computers can think, know, understand, or feel deceives computer users, especially children. He states that computers can never really think or feel like us, and thus, computers that suggest they have human characteristics that they actually do not have are lying and deceiving their users (e.g., Shneiderman, 2002; Shneiderman & Maes, 1997). In the end, deception may lead to frustrated users. However, computers pretending to have emotions that they actually do not have are actually much like ordinary humans. As we saw in the previous section, even in everyday human-human communication, pretense, deception, lying, and conforming to the social rules of emotion communication frequently take place. The expression of emotion serves a variety of social functions, and certainly does not always go hand in hand with actually felt emotions. Human are thus acquainted with the fact that expressed emotions may be different from the emotions actually felt (see also Bente *et al.*, this volume). Computer users will therefore probably also take for granted that computers may express emotions without actually feeling them.

Another issue concerns the input side of emotional computers: namely, the problem of privacy in the detection of user emotions. Relatively simple systems that detect and predict user emotions may be based on "common sense about prototypes of people" (Picard, 2003). However, emotion is not only the result of what happens right now; it is also dependent on the personality of the user, his or her goals, values, and expectations, and prior events. Ideally, thus, not just a prototypical, but a user-specific model is implemented in computers in order to understand user emotions. Storage of delicate user information, however, raises issues of privacy (Picard, 2003). In all, although the design of emotional capable computers is disputed in several ways, affective computing is a booming and interesting research area. Therefore, we will elaborate the various research undertakings in designing virtual humans that can "express" and "detect" emotions.

Examples of virtual human applications that consider emotion

Virtual humans that exhibit emotional behavior are used effectively in a range of applications, especially those in which human-human relationships are crucial, such as in health care, psychotherapy, and education. For example,

Bickmore *et al.* (2005) incorporated the virtual human Laura into a health care system. Laura motivated people to do their daily physical exercises. The patient's desire to continue working with Laura was highest when she showed relational, emotional behavior. The emotional and relational communication behaviors of patients were considered analogous to responses to real-life health providers. Emotional virtual humans may improve patient satisfaction and outcomes of health systems.

Virtual leaders may also have disastrous consequences, however. Virtual humans and online movements like ANA and "pro-ana" (promoting anorexia and self-starvation) can achieve cultlike appeal (http://www.msnbc.msn.com/id/8045047/; retrieved May 31, 2005). "Ana" is a very real presence in the lives of many adolescent girls, yet she exists only in a virtual world. Ana teaches the girls what to eat and mocks them when they don't lose weight. Finally, many girls suffer from the potentially fatal eating disorder. "Encouraging" words of "thinspiration" like "pain is temporary, but thin is forever" are posted on related websites and blogs. In 2005, experts estimated Ana influenced a few million girls.

Based on cognitive appraisal models of human emotion, Marsella *et al.* (2003) developed a virtual human psychotherapy application. The application aimed at improving the social problem-solving skills of parents of children with chronic diseases (e.g., cancer). In the application, the learner interacts with the emotional character Carmen, who has an ill child herself and wants to be a good mother. The learner makes decisions (for example, what problem to work on and how to cope with the stresses she is facing) and takes actions on behalf of Carmen, and sees the consequences of her decisions. A first evaluation of the Carmen application (Marsella *et al.*, 2003) revealed that it could improve the way mothers dealt with their own problems.

In an educational context, the "FearNot!" system was developed to teach children to deal with bullying behavior in schools (Aylett *et al.*, in press). In this system, one virtual human bullies the other virtual human: for example, he pushes him so that he falls down or takes his dinner money. The victim feels unhappy and might start crying. He asks the child users for help—should he avoid the bully, talk to the bully, or fight back? Or should he instead tell a friend or teacher about what happened? The child users may feel "empathetic engagement" with the bullied child, which hopefully makes them realize that bullying is a bad thing to do.

"Façade" (Mateas & Stern, 2003) is a system in which users can actively communicate with the virtual humans Grace and Trip, an attractive and materially successful couple in their early 30s who have marital problems. The user plays the character of a longtime friend of Grace and Trip who is unaware of these problems. Because their marriage is at stake, Trip and Grace become emotional. For example, Grace may become angry with the friend user and ask whose side he or she is on, Trip's or hers. The response of the user-friend might change the course of the conversation, and even the course of Grace and Trip's lives. Interestingly, the conversation the user-friend has with Trip and Grace is largely interactive, just as in real life.

In other contexts, users try to accomplish a certain goal or task in inter-action with a virtual human, which is often accompanied by emotional experiences (e.g., Van Vugt *et al.*, 2006): For instance, frustration at not finding the relevant information or happiness when a creative solution is found. The virtual human may calm the user down when angry, and react empathically when the user is frustrated (e.g., Hone, 2006; Klein *et al.*, 2001). For a successful understanding of the user's situation and to approach the illusion of human-to-human communication, both the detection of affec-tive states such as frustration, confusion, anger, joy, interest, and boredom as well as an "understanding" of why the user is feeling that way, are of importance (Picard, 2000). Imagine a face-to-face situation where a user is frustrated because of poor task performance due to a lack of skills. One would then be inclined to show empathy and offer some guidance through the task. However, a user who is frustrated because of bad equip-ment, just needs better equipment and will probably become even further annoyed when confronted with empathy: help cannot alter the bad equip-ment. When a virtual human is deemed useless and annoying, it should apologize and disappear. Clearly, a frustrated user with limited skills needs another kind of responding virtual human than the user with bad equip-ment. Thus, even if the emotion is similar, when the cause is different, users should be addressed differently.

To create virtual humans who respond appropriately in various situ-ations, sophisticated software is required that is not yet available, as it requires a deep understanding of the user's situation and characteristics. In the next sections, we therefore describe several techniques that are currently under study to design virtual humans that exhibit emotions and may detect the user's emotions.

Virtual humans that exhibit emotions

In real life, people have some idea of what a person normally behaves like, based on his or her (perceived) personality. For example: "She is a weak person—always crying" or "If my friend fears spiders today, I expect him to fear spiders tomorrow." Similarly, for users to get engaged in human-computer communications and to understand what is going on, the virtual human should show *consistent* emotional behavior (e.g., Nass *et al.*, 2006). That is, the various input and output channels of a certain emotion should act in accordance with each other as well as in accordance with the specifics of the situation and person at hand.

In order to design for consistency, rules or principles derived from emotion psychology can be used that determine which emotional behavior is expressed in what situation. The "Affective Reasoner" (Elliot, 1992) is an example of such a system that is based on some basic principles that determine the system's emotional behavior. For example, the principle "Students should attend to me as I am talking to them" has the system show annoyance when the student does not pay attention. The principle "I should be patient with the student" determines that after being annoyed with the student for not showing attention, the computer shows signs of shame or remorse. The Affective Reasoner cannot cope with interactive settings (Petta, 2003).

Several scholars have turned to psychological appraisal theories for *emotion modeling* (e.g., Gratch & Marcella, 2005) in order to design more sophisticated emotional consistent systems that are able to operate in interactive environments. Subtle emotion models allow the computer to appraise the emotional significance of events as they relate to its outer world (e.g., the user's behavior, or the student's plans and goals) and inner world (e.g., the previous "emotional state" of the computer, the computer's own plans and goals in view of its functionality). The model then predicts the emotional state of the user and the potential to cope with the particular situation, subsequently adjusting the system's behavior. The output of an emotion model is an emotional representation to be displayed by the virtual human. The thus selected "emotion" (output from the emotion model, e.g., sadness) is converted into appropriate behavioral components, such as facial expressions, head nods, gestures, gaze, body movement and/ or speech qualities such as utterances and prosody. In other words, the emotion model may specify how specific emotions may impact on the physical expressions of emotional states through suitable choices of gestures and body language in virtual humans (as implemented for example in the "Mission Rehearsal Exercise," Gratch & Marsella, 2001). Many programming and scripting languages and tools exist that function as movement generator and/or emotion converter, and some explicitly deal with affect and emotion expression. The Affective Presentation Markup Language, for example, is used to enrich the virtual human GRETA with multimodal emotional expressions using both face and gestures (De Rosis *et al.*, 2003). An overview of languages is provided by Pirker and Krenn (2002).

However, it is still a challenge to design believable emotional portrayals in virtual humans, to create the illusion of a virtual human itself having emotions, because emotion triggering and subsequent behavior activation are complex processes. As described in the above, not only the face and the body contribute in conveying emotional states but also their co-occurrences. For example, many observers judging a facial expression are also strongly influenced by emotional body language (e.g., Meeren *et al.*, 2005). Ideally, virtual humans will exhibit emotions using both face and body. For example, sadness can be specified in terms of depressed corners of the mouth and weeping and, in addition, in terms of hanging shoulders and the head hanging down. To ease the interpretation of the emotional state exhibited by the virtual human, it may be helpful to amplify significant features and signify only what is necessary for emotional expressions to be recognized, as is custom in the theater, art, and movies. In the same vein, and in contrast to what people in daily life tend (not) to do, virtual humans may also exhibit their emotions explicitly, using spoken utterances. For example, a virtual human may explicitly convey its emotional state by saying: "I sympathize with you," "I feel sad," or "I feel frustrated too." Whether the explication of emotions is preferred over other, more indirect/implicit types of emotion expressions (gestures, facial expressions, etc.), or which specific combinations of emotional cues are optimal for emotion recognition, are interesting research questions that, to our knowledge, have not yet been addressed. In addition, cultural differences for recognizing the emotional expressions of virtual humans need to be investigated in order to design virtual humans for a multicultural public (e.g., Kleinsmith *et al.*, 2006). In general, nonverbal cues act as strong signifiers of emotions, as discussed above. To arrive at optimal emotional displays, however, designers also need to take into account the situational demands, the verbal context in which the emotional nonverbal behavior occurs, the consistency of (subtle) cues through the various channels, and the dynamics of emotional display.

Virtual humans that detect user emotions

Various systems and devices are developed that can somehow detect the emotional state of the user in several ways. *Self-report systems* ask the user to show its emotional state to the computer or virtual human choosing from a list of emoticons, or via typed or spoken input (if natural language processing has been sufficiently advanced) (Picard, 2000). Furthermore, emotion recognizers can be based on haptic data that originate from *touching devices* such as keyboards, mice, and touch pads, because humans can express a range of emotions through touch. Bailenson *et al.*, 2006, for example, used button pressure as a measure of a game player's arousal. They found that button pressure was related to game difficulty. When playing a difficult game, video game players pressed the buttons harder, and hence were more emotionally aroused than with a simpler game. Furthermore, pressure patterns can discern gentle from rough handling, which is also used to indicate users' frustration, stress, or anger (e.g., Mentis & Gay, 2002)).

Sensors can be attached to the user to measure physiological signals to infer emotional states in real time (Picard, 2000). The Empathic Companion was used to accompany a user in preparing for a job interview (Prendinger & Ishizuka, 2005). Among other physiological indicators, the Empathic Companion uses skin conductance as a measure of arousal, and muscle activity as a measure of valence (positive versus negative). Increased arousal and positive valence is interpreted as "joy," whereas increased arousal and negative valence is interpreted as "'frustration." After interpreting the physiological signals as emotions, the Empathic Companion addresses the user's affective state in the form of empathic feedback. For example, it displays concern for a user in a negative emotional state by saying: "I am sorry that you seem to feel a bit bad about that question." The haptic or physiological methods for emotion detection are error prone, which reduces its reliability. Another disadvantage of such methods is that users are consciously aware of the computer sensing them (Picard, 2000); users either have to explicate their emotions themselves, or sensors are placed on their bodies making the measurement of emotions rather obvious, which may bias the results.

To *automatically* detect a user's emotional state without the need of self-reports or sensors, the expressions of humans that are associated with emotions are analyzed. General emotion research has already showed that human emotion influences verbal and nonverbal behavior, including gestures, gaze, and facial expressions. As said, facial expressions are fundamental in human emotion communication, although facial expressions are not always clear indicators of emotion. Nevertheless, facial expression analysis has become an active research area in the field of affective computing where facial expression classification suffers from a complex recognition problem. Facial expression cues first have to be *acquired* (e.g., the corners of the mouth face upward or downward), and can then be *recognized* in terms of facial expressions (e.g., smile ☺, or ☹) and *classified* or *interpreted* as emotions (e.g., happy or sad). Current systems are still far from achieving the capability of the human perception system (Zhao *et al.*, 2003). A simple example of emotion detection based on facial movement is provided in Bailenson (this volume). He used head nods and shakes as indicative of positive and negative attitudes. In addition, the *ratio* of head agreement nods and head disagreement shakes were indicative of agreement or comprehension.

Complex pattern recognition algorithms are also needed for the recognition of *gestures*. Although gesture analysis for emotion recognition is relatively unexplored in the field of affective computing, gestures are often indicative of emotion laden communication. In many societies, "thumbs up" means happiness, agreement, or satisfaction. Raising the middle finger indicates anger or frustration. Lifting arms in the air expresses joy. Both glove-based and vision-based gesture recognition systems have been developed to recognize gestures (e.g., Karpouzis *et al.*, 2004; Wu & Huang, 2001). Glove-based gesture recognition uses gloves with sensors to induce hand and finger positions. Vision-based gesture recognition requires one or more cameras to derive hand and finger positions. When hand and finger positions are derived using one of these methods, gesture *recognition* and *interpretation* as emotion need additional analysis. Several difficulties can be discerned for gesture recognition and interpretation as emotions. First, it is difficult to assess when the interpretation of gestures as emotional begins and ends. Second, there are difficulties with ambiguity. A salient characteristic of gestures (more so than of facial expressions) is that people often change the position of their hands without meaningfully gesturing. For example, they do so for grasping or manipulating objects such as the computer mouse and keyboard. Third, most gestures are culturally specific (cf. display rules). Despite these difficulties, automatic hand and body gesture recognition can be useful in virtual environments to improve the communication between virtual human and user. Furthermore, gesture recognition might be very useful in sign language applications in which virtual humans teach sign language, including expressions that are used to express emotions.

With the rise of adequate eye-tracking technology, *gaze* can now be analyzed in ways that were impossible before. As gaze is important in face-to-face interpersonal communication, it is also an important research tool in the area of affective computing. Gaze has a variety of communicative functions, such as the regulation of the flow of conversation and the provision of visual feedback (Argyle & Cook, 1976; Kendon, 1967) as well as the communication of emotions. For example, gaze serves as a signal for taking turns, to indicate that one is about to start speaking or listening (Kendon, 1967), or it may indicate (loss of) interest. Most gaze studies in a virtual human context that have focused on gaze behavior (of user and/ or virtual human) showed that it improved the quality of communication (e.g., Colbrun *et al.*, 2000; Vertegaal *et al.*, 2001).

Various approaches aim at recognizing emotions based on conversational *content*. One approach requires a database with emotion-tagged speech signals (words or other utterances). Speech signals may be classified into emotion categories, such as "sad," "enraged," and "happy." The Affective Reasoner (Elliot, 1992), for example, watches for such emotion words as well as intensity modifiers (e.g., extremely, somewhat, mildly) to recognize the emotional state of the computer user. Another approach is a statistical one, which is based on the idea that certain word combinations are more probable for the expression of certain emotions than others. Emotion-specific word choice information can be modeled by computing the probability of a certain word given the previous word and the speaker's expressed emotion (e.g., Polzin & Waibel, 2000). However, recognizing emotions based on speech signals is not easy, not least because speakers often do not explicitly verbalize their emotion or its intensity (e.g., "I feel very sad"). More specific emotional cues seem to be hidden in other, more implicit or nonverbal characteristics of speech. Therefore, most speech-based emotion recognizers make use of a variety of speech characteristics (such as pitch, prosody, durations of silence, speaking rate). For example,

Van den Broek (2004) used the prosody of speech to infer emotional states, and successfully discerned between stress/anxiety and relaxed states of speakers in psychotherapy. Another approach is proposed by Liu *et al.* (2003) that uses real-world knowledge to evaluate the affective qualities of the underlying semantic content of text. It allows for the recognition of emotions even when emotion words are absent.

Although such methods can often successfully be used to detect an affective state from a given set of affective states and some time after the actual speech, they do not allow for *real time* and *continuous* determination of a (changing) user's emotional state while speaking. Furthermore, methods are currently only capable of discerning between a *limited* set of predefined affective states (anxious versus relaxed). Although there have been attempts to build speech-based recognizers that distinguish between more than two emotions, this seems a difficult task. Correct classification levels go down while aiming at correctly recognizing a larger set of emotions. McGilloway *et al.* (2000) report a classification level of 55 percent for the automatic recognition of anger, fear, sadness, joy, and a neutral state. Higher classification levels seem hard to obtain. When sufficiently advanced, speech-based emotion recognition methods will greatly enrich the perceived "emotionality" of virtual humans and may increase the illusion of interpersonal communication because human emotion recognition is also often based on speech-signifiers (cf. Scherer, 2003).

In sum, verbal and nonverbal behaviors allow the researcher to unobtrusively detect the user's emotion through a computer in ways parallel to face-to-face communication. Although existing approaches mostly adopt methods based on *single* emotional cues, a problem in emotion detection based on individual cues is that each cue can be associated with *multiple* emotions. For example, lowered eyebrows may indicate anger as well as concentration, and fast speech may indicate frustration as well as pleasantness. Because of the ambiguity in interpreting individual cues of emotion expression, *multimodal automatic emotion recognition* (based on multiple cues) seems the most promising approach beause it reduces the uncertainty associated with using a single mode (e.g., Picard & Daily, 2005). For example, Zeng *et al.* (2004) combined audio and visual modalities and found that the emotion recognition accuracy was greatly improved from using single emotional cues (cf. consistency through communication channels). Future emotion recognizers are likely to need architectures that can handle the fusion of different modalities. For example, the neural network architecture of Fragopanagos and Taylor (2005) is able to combine signals from facial features, prosody, and content in speech to recognize emotions. In addition, environmental contexts and specific task demands further influence the way verbal and nonverbal behaviors should be interpreted. For instance, shouting could signify anger but it could also be necessary for communicating in a noisy environment. Intelligent fusion of all available modalities and contexts (cultural, environmental, and of users) seems a requirement for a reliable emotion detector, but is still an impending scenario. Therefore, Gratch and Marsella (2004) propose complex emotion modeling, mainly based on appraisal and coping theories of emotion, in order to arrive at appropriately functioning virtual humans that may resemble interpersonal communication or at least appear to be similarly powerful. Perhaps, future studies in affective computing may even benefit from the neuroimaging studies for emotion modeling of virtual humans, for example to detect basic approach-withdrawal functions.

Conclusion

Sophisticated attempts are being made in the field of affective computing to enrich virtual humans with emotional capabilities, thereby drawing on knowledge from emotion psychology. This chapter makes clear, however, that many studies in affective computing are based on naive psychology, taking the nonverbal cues for the emotions themselves. For example, many scholars in the field of affective computing use expressions such as "emotional virtual humans" and ascribe feelings and emotions to virtual humans. Clearly, this is not feasible—virtual humans cannot possess the subjective experience of emotions, they cannot feel, and cannot experience something of their own. They can only be designed in such a way that users may interpret certain cues as "emotional" or that they react in such a way to users' emotions that the virtual human is considered emotionally intelligent or competent (Buck, 1999; Salovey & Mayer, 1990). As a general trend, however, when it comes to communicating emotions, the expression of an emotion becomes easily blurred with the corresponding underlying emotion, whereas they are not necessarily causally related.

Despite the relatively simple theoretical approach of many studies in affective computing, positive results of implementing "emotions" in virtual humans are obtained. This is in line with the generally positive effects of human functions of emotions in the context of decision-making (LeDoux, 1996), memory storage and retrieval (Rolls, 1999), learning (Bower, 1991), social reasoning (Forgas, 2000), and their social and communicative functions (e.g., Manstead et al., 1999). Users may feel emotionally attached to virtual humans who portray emotions, and interacting with such "emotional" embodied computer systems may positively influence their perceptions of humanness, trustworthiness, and believability. In addition, user frustration may be reduced if the user's emotions are considered by computers. Clearly, such findings have motivated software engineers to implement the beneficial functions of emotions into various applications as described above. Therefore, affective computing is a promising field of research and, indeed, the field is rapidly growing.

Modern technologies increasingly allow for communicating emotions in sophisticated ways through "screens." In the near future, it will probably become increasingly difficult to tell whether a representation of a human in virtual space belongs to an existing person in real life (i.e. an avatar) or is construed by technical means (i.e. a bot). Even if it concerns a representation construed solely by technical means, observers will ascribe emotions to virtual humans due to their habit of deriving them from outer appearances (cf. Reeves & Nass, 1996). Furthermore, literal imitations of outward emotional expressions (i.e. photo-realistic images) are probably not necessary to trigger effects similar to human-to-human encounters; minimal cues, relevant signals, specific hints, symbols and icons can already result in the perception of humanness and lead observers to infer traits and moods.

Future research may show that simple models (e.g., mainly based on nonverbal cues and communication rules) are sufficient in certain cases to elicit the desired effects: for example, in mediated interpersonal communication situations with clear decision structures as in many commercial applications and first-aid medical applications. Others may need more complex modeling. What types of application will benefit most from virtual humans that may display emotions themselves and are able to detect and respond to users' emotions remains to be studied. In real life, one expects different emotional responses from teachers, bankers, and psychotherapists. Therefore computer systems should also be designed in accordance with their functions and users' expectations. For example, an e-learning environment might benefit from a virtual human who is sensitive to typical student emotions such as frustration or boredom, and provide attention triggering, enthusiastic, and motivating feedback (Elliott et al., 1999). Online banking sites, as another example, are more likely to benefit from virtual humans who are sensitive to relevant customer emotions such as trust and privacy. Psychotherapy applications, however, need to follow a more complex interaction pattern in dealing with their patients' emotions, such as listening to the patient's problems, analyzing the source of the patient's distress, and reacting appropriately—for example with advice on how to cope with the distressing situation.

Although emotion models and programming languages exist that have virtual humans "reason" about emotions and respond with emotional displays in similar ways to humans, it is hard to have virtual humans portray emotions while taking into account both the task at hand, the cultural context, and the user's emotional state. Not surprisingly, emotionally competent virtual humans are not yet on the market. Therefore, a next step could be to investigate which kind of human-computer interactions might benefit from which type of emotional response—to be exhibited by a virtual human, to be detected in users, and to respond to. In extending such research efforts, computer scientists, communication scholars, and emotion psychologists should work together.

References

Adelmann, P. K., & Zajonc, R. B. (1989) "Facial efference and the experience of emotion." *Annual Review of Psychology, 40*, 249–280.

Adolphs, R., Gosselin, F., Buchanan, T. W., Tranel, D., Schyns, P., & Damasio, A. R. (2005) "A mechanism for impaired fear recognition after amygdala damage." *Nature, 433*, January, 68–72.

Argyle, M., & Cook, M. (1976) *Gaze and Mutual Gaze*. London: Cambridge University Press.

Aylett, R., Paiva, A., Woods, S., Hall, L., & Zoll, C. (in press). In L. Canamero & R. Aylett (eds.), *Animating Expressive Characters for Social Interaction*, John Benjamins.

Bailenson, J. N., & Yee, N. (2005) "Digital chameleons: Automatic assimilation of nonverbal gestures in immersive virtual environments." *Psychological Science, 16*, 814–819.

Bailenson, J. N., Yee, N., Brave, S., Merget, D., & Koslow, D. (2007). "Virtual interpersonal touch: Expressing and recognizing emotions through haptic devices." *Human-Computer Interaction, 22*, 325–353

Barrett, L. F. (2006a) "Are emotions natural kinds?" *Perspectives on Psychological Science, 1*, 28–58.

Barrett, L. F. (2006b) "Solving the emotion paradox: categorization and the experience of emotion." *Personality and Social Psychology Review, 10*, 20–46.

Barrett, L. F., & Salovey, P. (eds.), (2003) *The Wisdom of Feelings: Processes Underlying Emotional Intelligence*. New York: Guilford Press.

Barrett, L. F., & Wager, T. (2006) "The structure of emotion: evidence from the neuroimaging of emotion." *Current Directions in Psychological Science, 15*, 79–85.

Bates, J. (1994) "The role of emotions in believable agents." *Communications of the ACM, 17*(7), 122–125.

Beebe, S. A., Beebe, S. J., & Redmond, M. V. (2002) *Interpersonal Communication: Relating to Others,* third edition, Needham Heights, MA: Allyn and Bacon.

Bellman, K. L. (2003) "Emotions. Meaningful mappings between the individual and its world." In R. Trappl, S. Petta, & P. Payr (eds.), *Emotions in Humans and Artifacts*. Cambridge, MA, USA: MIT Press, ch. 5.

Beninger, J. R. (1987) "Personalization of mass media and the growth of pseudo-community." *Communication Research, 14*, 352–371.

Bente, G., Donaghy, W. C., & Suwelack, D. (1998) "Sex differences in body movement and visual attention: An integrated analysis of movement and gaze in mixed-sex dyads." *Journal of Nonverbal Behavior, 22*, 31–58.

Bernieri, F. J., & Rosenthal, R. (1991) "Interpersonal coordination: behavior matching and interactional synchrony." In R. S. Feldman & B. Rimé (eds.), *Fundamentals of Nonverbal Behavior*. New York: Cambridge University Press, pp. 401–432.

Bickmore, T., Gruber, A., & Picard, R. W. (2005) "Establishing the computer-patient working alliance in automated health behavior change interventions." *Patient Educational Counseling, 59*(1), 21–30.

Bower, G. H. (1991) "Emotional mood and memory." *American Psychologist, 31*, 129–148.

Brave, S., & Nass, C. (2002) "Emotion in human-computer interaction." In J. Jacko, and A. Sears (eds.), *Handbook of Human-Computer Interaction*. Mahwah, NJ: Lawrence Erlbaum Associates, pp. 251–271.

Brave, S., Nass, C., & Hutchinson, K. (2005) "Computers that care: investigating the effects of orientation of emotion exhibited by an embodied computer agent." *International Journal of Human-Computer Studies, 62*(2), 161–178.

Breazeal, C. (2003) "Emotion and sociable humanoid robots." *International Journal of Human-Computer Studies, 59*(1–2), 119–155.

Buck, R. (1999) "The biological affects: a typology." *Psychological Review, 106*, 301–336.

Cannon, W. B. (1927) "The James-Lange theory of emotion: a critical examination and an alternative theory." *American Journal of Psychology, 39*, 106–124.

Carey, J. (1980) "Paralanguage in computer mediated communication." In N. K. Sondheimer (ed.), *Proceedings of the 18th Annual Meeting of the Association for Computational Liguistics and Parasession on Topics in Interactive Discourse: Conference*. Philadelphia: University of Pennsylvania, pp. 67–69.

Choi, V. S., Gray, H. M., & Ambady, N. (2005) "The glimpsed world: unintended communication and unintended perception." In R. R. Hassin, J. S. Uleman, & J. A. Bargh (eds.), *The New Unconscious*. New York: Oxford University Press, pp. 309–333.

Colbrun, R. A., Cohen, M., & Drucker, S. (2000) "The role of eye gaze in avatar mediated conversational interfaces." MSR-TR-2000-81, Microsoft.

Crease, R. P. (1993) "Biomedicine in the age of imaging." *Science, 261*, 554–561.

Damasio, A. R. (1994) *Descartes' Error: Emotion, Reason, and the Human Brain*. New York: Putnam Publishing.

Damasio, A. R. (2001) "Fundamental Feelings." *Nature, 413*, 781.

Darwin, C. (2002) *The Expression of the Emotions in Man and Animals*, third editon. Oxford: Oxford University Press.

DePaulo, B. M., Lindsay, J. J., Malone, B. E., Muhlenbruck, L., Charlton, K., & Cooper, H. (2003) "Cues to deception." *Psychological Bulletin, 129*(1), 74–118.

De Rosis, F., Pelachaud, C., & Poggi, I. (2003) "From Greta's mind to her face: modeling the dynamics of affective states in a conversational embodied agent." *International Journal of Human-Computer Studies, 59* (1–2), 81–118.

DeVito, J. A. (2004) *The Interpersonal Communication Book*, tenth edition. Boston: Pearson.

De Waal, F. B. M. (2003) "Darwin's legacy and the study of primate visual communication." In P. Ekman, J. J. Campos, R. J. Davidson, and F. B. M. de Waal (eds.), *Emotions Inside Out: 130 Years After Darwin's the Expression of the Emotions in Man and Animals*. New York: New York Academy of Sciences, pp. 7–31.

Ekman, P. (1972) "Universals and cultural differences in facial expressions of emotion." In J. Cole (ed.), *Nebraska Symposium on Motivation 1971*. Lincoln, NE: University of Nebraska Press, Vol. 19, pp. 207–283.

Ekman, P. (1994) "Strong evidence for universals in facial expressions: a reply to Russell's mistaken critique." *Psychological Bulletin, 115*, 268–287.

Ekman, P., & Davidson, R. J. (eds.), (1994) *The Nature of Emotions: Fundamental Questions*. New York: Oxford University Press.

Ekman, P., & Friesen, W. V. (1969) "A tool for the analysis of motion picture film or videotape." *American Psychologist, 24*, 240–243.

Ekman, P., & Friesen, W. V. (1975) *Unmasking the Face. A Guide to Recognizing Emotions from Facial Clues*. Englewood Cliffs, NJ: Prentice-Hall.

Ekman, P., & O'Sullivan, M. (1991) "Who can catch a liar?" *American Psychologist, 46*, 913–920.

Ekman, P., Levenson, R. W., & Friesen, W. V. (1983) "Autonomic nervous system activity distinguishes among emotions." *Science, 221*, 1208–1210.

Elliott, C. D. (1992) The affective reasoner: A process model of emotions in a multi-agent system. PhD thesis, Northwestern University, Illinois.

Elliott, C. D. (2003) "The role of elegance in emotion and personality: Reasoning for believable agents." In: R. Trappl, S. Petta, & P. Payr, (eds.), *Emotions in Humans and Artifacts*. Cambridge, MA, USA: MIT Press, ch. 8.

Elliott, C. D., Rickel, J., & Lester, J. (1999) "Lifelike pedagogical agents and affective computing: An exploratory synthesis." In M. Wooldridge and M. Veloso (eds.), *Artificial Intelligence Today* [number 1600 in *Lecture Notes in Computer Science*]. Springer Verlag, pp. 195–212.

Ellsworth, P. C., & Scherer, K. R. (2003) "Appraisal processes in emotion." In R.J. Davidson,

H. H. Goldsmith, & K. R. Scherer (eds.), *Handbook of the Affective Sciences*. New York: Oxford University Press, pp. 572–595.

Forgas, J. P. (ed.), (2000) *Feeling and Thinking. The Role of Affect in Social Cognition*. Cambridge: Cambridge University Press.

Fragopanagos, N., & Taylor, J. G. (2005) "Emotion recognition in human-computer interaction." *Neural Networks, 18(4)*, 389–405.

Fridlund, A. J. (1991) "Evolution and facial action in reflex, social motive, and paralanguage." *Biological Psychology, 32* (1), 3–100.

Fridlund, A. J. (1997) "The new ethology of human facial expressions." In J. A. Russell, and J. M. Fernández-Dols (eds.), *The Psychology of Facial Expression*. Cambridge, MA: Cambridge University Press, pp. 103–129.

Frijda, N. H. (1986) *The Emotions*. Cambridge: Cambridge University Press.

Frijda, N. H. (1988) "The laws of emotion." *American Psychologist, 43*, 349–358.

Frijda, N. H. (1994) "Varieties of affect: emotions and episodes, moods, and sentiments." In P. Ekman & R. J. Davidson (eds.), *The Nature of Emotions: Fundamental Questions*. New York: Oxford University Press.

Frijda, N. H., Manstead, A. S. R., & Sacha Bem, S. (eds.), (2000) *Emotions and Beliefs: How Feelings Influence Thoughts*. Cambridge: Cambridge University Press.

Gratch, J., & Marsella, S. (2001) "Tears and Fears: modeling emotions and emotional behaviors in synthetic agents." In *Proceedings of the 5th International Conference on Autonomous Agents,* Montreal, Canada, June 2001.

Gratch, J., & Marsella, S. (2004) "A domain-independent framework for modeling emotion." *Journal of Cognitive Systems Research, 5(4)*, 269–306.

Gratch, J., & Marsella, S. (2005) "Some lessons from emotion psychology for the design of lifelike characters." *Journal of Applied Artificial Intelligence* (special issue on Educational Agents – Beyond Virtual Tutors), *19(3–4)*, 215–233.

Hess, U., & Kleck, R. E. (1994) "The cues decoders use in attempting to differentiate emotion-elicited and posed facial expressions." *European Journal of Social Psychology, 24*, 367–381.

Hochschild, A. R. (1979) "Emotion work, feeling rules and social structure." *American Journal of Sociology, 85*, 551–575.

Hone, K. (2006) "Empathic agents to reduce user frustration: the effects of varying agent characteristics." *Interacting With Computers, 18(2)*, 227–245.

Hoorn, J. F., Konijn, E. A., & Van der Veer, G. C. (2003) "Virtual reality: do not augment realism, augment relevance." *Upgrade—Human-Computer Interaction: Overcoming Barriers,* 4(1), 18–26.

Izard, C. E. (1993) "Four systems for emotion activation: cognitive and non-cognitive processes." *Psychological Review, 100*(1), 68–90.

Izard, C. E. (ed.), (1997) *Human Emotions*. New York: Plenum Press.

James, W. (1884) "What is an emotion?" *Mind, 9*(34), 188–205.

Kappas, A. (2002) "The science of emotion as a multidisciplinary research paradigm."*Behavioural Processes, 60*, 85–98.

Kappas, A. (2003) "What facial activity can and cannot tell us about emotions." In M. Katsikitis (ed.). *The Human Face: Measurement and Meaning,* pp. 215–234. Dordrecht: Kluwer Academic Publishers.

Karpouzis, K., Raouzaiou, A., Drosopoulos, A., Ioannou, S., Balomenos, T., Tsapatsoulis, N., & Kollias, S. (2004) "Facial expression and gesture analysis for emotionally-rich man-machine interaction." In N. Sarris & M. Strintzis (eds.), *3D Modeling and Animation: Synthesis and Analysis Techniques*. Idea Group Publ., pp. 175–200. Idea Group Publ., http://manolito.image.ece.ntua.gr/papers/236.pdf.

Katsikitis, M. (ed.). *The Human Face: Measurement and Meaning*. Dordrecht: Kluwer Academic Publishers, pp. 215–234.

Kendon, A. (1967) "Some functions of gaze direction in social interaction." *Acta Psychologica, 32*, 1–25.

Klein, J., Moon, Y., & Picard, R. W. (2001) "This computer responds to user frustration: theory, design, and results." *Interacting with Computers, 14*(2), 119–140.

Kleinsmith, A., Ravindra De Silva, P., & Bianchi-Berthouze, N. (2006) "Cross cultural differences in recognizing affect from body posture." *Interacting with Computers, 18*(6) (Special Issue: Symbiotic Performance between Humans and Intelligent Systems), 1371–1389.

Klesen, M. (2005) "Using theatrical concepts for role-plays with educational agents." *Applied Artificial Intelligence, 19*(3), 413–431.

Konijn, E. A. (2000) *Acting Emotions; Shaping Emotions on Stage.* Amsterdam: Amsterdam University Press.

Konijn, E. A. (2004). "The heart of the actor: Let it all out or keep a healthy distance?" In I. Nykliek, L. R. Temoshok & A. J. J. M. Vingerhoets (eds.), *Emotional Expression and Health. Advances In Theory, Assessment and Clinical Applications.* London: Brunner-Routledge, pp. 303–320.

Krämer, N. C., Iurgel, I. A., Bente, G. (2005) "Emotion and motivation in embodied conversational agents." In L. Canamero (ed.), *Proceedings of the Symposium "Agents that Want and Like", Artificial Intelligence and the Simulation of Behavior (AISB) 2005.* Hatfield: SSAISB, pp. 55–61.

Laird, J. D. (1974) "Self-attribution of emotion: the effects of expressive behavior on the quality of emotional experience." *Journal of Personality and Social Psychology, 29*, 475–486.

Lang, P. J. (1994) "The varieties of emotional experience: a meditation on James-Lange theory." *Psychological Review, 101*, 211–221.

Lazarus, R.S. (1982) "Thoughts on the relations between emotion and cognition." *American Psychologist, 37*, 1019–1024.

Lazarus, R. S. (1991) *Emotion and Adaptation.* New York: Oxford University Press.

LeDoux, J. E. (1996) *The Emotional Brain.* New York: Simon & Schuster.

LeDoux, J. E. (2000) "Emotion circuits in the brain." *Annual Review of Neuroscience, 23*, 155–184.

Liu, H., Lieberman, H., & Selker, T. (2003) "A model of textual affect sensing using real-world knowledge." In *Proceedings of IUI 2003.* Miami, FL.

Manstead, A. S. R., Fischer, A., & Jacobs, E. B. (1999) "The social and emotional functions of facial displays". In P. Phillipot, R. S. Feldman, & E. J. Coats (eds.), *The Social Context of Nonverbal Behavior.* Cambridge: Cambridge University Press, pp. 287–316.

Marsella, S. C., Johnson, W.L., & LaBore, C. M. (2003) "Interactive pedagogical drama for health interventions." In U. Hoppe *et al.* (eds.), *Artificial Intelligence in Education: Shaping the Future of Learning through Intelligent Technologies,* Amsterdam: IOS Press, pp. 341–348.

Mateas, M., & Stern, A. (2003) "Façade: an experiment in building a fully-realized interactive drama. "In *Game Developer's Conference: Game Design Track,* San Jose, California, March 2003, http://interactivestory.net/.

McGilloway, S., Cowie, R., Douglas-Cowie, E., Gielen, S., Westerdijk, M., & Stroeve, S. (2000) "Approaching automatic recognition of emotion from voice: a rough benchmark," *Proceedings of the ISCA Workshop on Speech and Emotion,* Belfast, 2000, pp. 200–205.

Meeren, H. K., Van Heijnsbergen, C. C., & De Gelder, B. (2005) "Rapid perceptual integration of facial expression and emotional body language." *Proceedings National Academy of Science USA 2005 102*(45), 16518–16523, Nov. 8.

Mentis, H. M., & Gay, G. (2002) "Using touchpad pressure to detect negative affect." *ICMI 2002,* 406–410.

Murphy, F. C., Nimmo-Smith, I., & Lawrence, A. D. (2003) "Functional neuroanatomy of emotion: A meta-analysis." *Cognitive, Affective, & Behavioral Neuroscience, 3*, 207–233.

Nass, C., Brave, S., & Takayama, L. (2006) "Socializing consistency: from technical homogeneity to human epitome." In P. Zhang & D. Galletta (eds.), *Human-Computer Interaction in Management Information Systems: Foundations*. Armonk, NY: M. E. Sharpe.

Oatley, K., & Jenkins, J. (1996) *Understanding Emotions*. Oxford: Blackwell.

Ortony, A., Clore, G. L., & Collins, A. (1988) *The Cognitive Structure of Emotions*. New York: Cambridge University Press.

Paiva, A., Dias, J., & Aylett, R. S. (2005) "Learning by feeling: evoking empathy with synthetic characters." *Applied Artificial Intelligence, 19*(3–4), 235–266.

Panksepp, J. (1998) *Affective Neuroscience: The Foundations of Human and Animal Emotions*. New York: Oxford University Press.

Petta, P. (2003) "The role of emotions in a tractable architecture for situated cognizers." In R. Trappl, P. Petta, & S. Payr (eds.), *Emotions in Humans and Artifacts*. Cambridge, MA: MIT Press, pp. 251–288.

Phan, K. L., Wager, T. D., Taylor, S. F., & Liberzon, I. (2002) "Functional neuroanatomy of emotion: a meta-analysis of emotion activation studies in PET and fMRI." *Neuroimage, 16*, 331–348.

Picard, R. W. (1997) *Affective Computing*. Cambridge, MA: MIT Press.

Picard, R. W. (2000) "Toward computers that recognize and respond to user emotions" *IBM Systems Journal, 39*(3&4), 705–719.

Picard, R.W. (2003) "What does it mean for a computer to 'have' emotions?" In R. Trappl, P. Petta, & S. Payr (eds.) *Emotions in Humans and Artifacts*. Cambridge, MA: MIT Press, Ch.7.

Picard, R. W., & Daily, S. B. (2005) "Evaluating affective interactions: alternatives to asking what users feel." *CHI Workshop on Evaluating Affective Interfaces: Innovative Approaches*, April 2005, Portland, OR.

Pirker, H., & Krenn, B. (2002) "Assessment of markup languages for avatars, multimedia and multimodal systems." *NECA-project, May 2002*. Retrieved from http://www.oefai.at/NECA/publications/publications.html.

Plutchik, R. (1997) "The circumplex as a general model of the structure of emotions and personality." In R. Plutchik & H. R. Conte (eds.), *Circumplex Models of Personality and Emotions*. Washington, D.C.: American Psychological Association, pp. 17–46.

Polzin, T. S., & Waibel, A. (2000) "Emotion-sensitive human-computer interfaces". *Proceedings of the ISCA Workshop on Speech and Emotion*, Belfast 2000.

Prendinger, H., & Ishizuka, M. (2005) "The Empathic Companion: a character-based interface that addresses users' affective states." *International Journal of Applied Artificial Intelligence, 19*(3), 267–285.

Reeves, B., & Nass, C. (1996) *The Media Equation: How People Treat Computers, Television, and New Media Like Real People and Places*. New York: Cambridge University Press.

Rolls, E. T. (1999) *The Brain and Emotion*. Oxford: Oxford University Press.

Rolls, E. T. (2003) "A theory of emotion, its functions, and its adaptive value." In R. Trappl, P. Petta, & S. Payr (eds.), *Emotions in Humans and Artifacts*. Cambridge, MA: MIT Press.

Russell, J. A., & Barrett, L. F. (1999) "Core affect, prototypical emotional episodes, and other things called emotion: dissecting the elephant." *Journal of Personality and Social Psychology, 76*, 805–819.

Salovey, P., & Mayer, J. D. (1990) "Emotional intelligence." *Imagination, Cognition, and Personality, 9*, 185–211.

Sanderson, D. (1994) *Smileys*. Sebastopol, CA: O'Reilly & Associates.

Sartre, J. P. (1934) *Esquisse d'une théorie phénoménologique des émotions*. Paris: Hermann [*The Emotions*, New York: Philosophical Library, 1948].

Schachter, S. (1959) *The Psychology of Affiliation*. Stanford, CA: Stanford University Press.

Schachter, S. (1964) "The interaction of cognitive and physiological determinants of emotional state." In L. Berkowitz (ed.), *Advances in Experimental Social Psychology*, Vol. 1 New York: Academic Press, pp. 49–80.

Schachter, S., & Singer, J. E. (1962) "Cognitive, social and physiological determinants of emotional states." *Psychological Review*, *69*, 379–399.

Scherer, K. R. (2000) "Psychological models of emotion." In J. Borod (ed.), *The Neuropsychology of Emotion*. Oxford/New York: Oxford University Press, pp. 137–162.

Scherer, K. R. (2003) "Vocal communication of emotion: a review of research paradigms." *Speech Communication*, *40*, 227–256.

Shields, S. A. (1984) "Distinguishing between emotion and nonemotion: judgments about experience." *Motivation and Emotion*, *8*(4), 355–369.

Shneiderman, B. (2002): *Leonardo's Laptop: Human Needs and the New Computing Technologies*. MIT Press.

Shneiderman, B., & Maes, P. (1997) "Direct manipulation vs. interface agents." *Interactions*, *4*(6), 42–61.

Short, J., Williams, E., & Christie, B. (1976) *The Social Psychology of Telecommunications*. London: Wiley.

Sloman, A. (2003) "How many separately evolved emotional beasties live within us?" In R. Trappl, P. Petta, & S. Payr (eds.), *Emotions in Humans and Artifacts*. Cambridge, MA: MIT Press, Ch. 3.

Smith, C. A., & Scott, H. S. (1997) "A componential approach to the meaning of facial Expressions." In J. A. Russell, & J. M. Fernandez-Dolls (eds.), *The Psychology of Facial expression*. Cambridge UK: Cambridge University Press, pp. 229–254.

Sykes, J., & Brown, S. (2003) "Affective gaming: measuring emotion through the gamepad." In *CHI '03 Extended Abstracts on Human Factors in Computing Systems* CHI '03: New York, NY: ACM Press.

Trappl, R., Petta, P., & Payr, S. (eds.), (2003) *Emotions in Humans and Artifacts*. Cambridge, MA: MIT Press.

Van den Broek, E. L. (2004) "Emotional prosody measurement (EPM): a voice-based evaluation method for psychological therapy effectiveness." *Medical and Care Compunetics*, *1*, 118–125.

Van Vugt, H. C., Hoorn, J. F., Konijn, E. A., & de Bie Dimitriadou, A. (2006) "Affective affordances: improving interface character engagement through interaction." *International Journal of Human-Computer Studies*, *64*(9), 874–888.

Vertegaal, R., Slagter, R., Van der Veer, G., & Nijholt, A. (2001) "Eye gaze patterns in conversations: there is more to conversational agents than meets the eyes". In *Proceedings of CHI '01: ACM Conference on Human Factors in Computing Systems* (Seattle, WA, 2001), 301–307.

Wager, T. D., Phan, K. L., Liberzon, I., & Taylor, S. F. (2003) "Valence, gender, and lateralization of functional brain anatomy in emotion: a meta-analysis of findings from neuroimaging." *Neuroimage*, *19*, 513–531.

Wagner, H., & Lee, V. (1999) "Facial behaviour alone and in the presence of others." In P. Phillipot, R. S. Feldman, & E. J. Coats (eds.), *The Social Context of Nonverbal Behavior*. Cambridge: Cambridge University Press. pp. 262–287.

Wallbott, H. G., & Scherer, K. R. (1986) "Cues and channels in emotion recognition." *Journal of Personality and Social Psychology*, *51*, 690–699.

Walther, J. B. (1992) "Interpersonal effects in computer-mediated interaction: a relational perspective." *Communication Research*, *19*, 52–90.

Wood, J. T. (2002). *Interpersonal Communication: Everyday Encounters*. Belmont, CA: Thomson Wadsworth.

Wu, Y., & Huang, T. S. (2001) "Hand modeling, analysis, and recognition for vision-based human computer interaction." *IEEE Signal Processing Magazine*, *18*(3), 51–60.

Zajonc, R. B. (1984) "On the primacy of affect." *American Psychologist*, *39*(2), 117–123.

Zajonc, R. B., Murphy, S. T., & Inglehart, M. (1989) "Feeling and facial efference: implications of the vascular theory of emotion." *Psychological Review,* 96(3), 395–416.

Zeng, Z., Tu, J., Liu, M., Zhang, T., Rizzolo, N., Zhang, Z., Huang, T. S., Roth, D., & Levinson, S. (2004) "Bimodal HCI-related affect recognition." In *Proceedings of the 6th International Conference on Multimodal Interfaces* (State College, PA, USA, October 13–15, 2004). ICMI '04. ACM Press: New York, pp.137–143. DOI=http://doi.acm.org/10.1145/1027933.1027958.

Zhao, W., Chellappa, R., Phillips, P. J., & Rosenfeld, A. (2003) "Face recognition: a literature survey." *ACM Computer Survey, 35*(4), 399–458.

Zillmann, D. (2003) "Theory of affective dynamics: Emotions and moods." In J. Bryant, D. Roskos-Ewoldson, & J. Cantor (eds.), *Communication and Emotion. Essays in Honor of Dolf Zillmann.* Mahwah, NJ: Lawrence Erlbaum Associates.

Chapter 7

Is there anybody out there?

Analyzing the effects of embodiment and nonverbal behavior in avatar-mediated communication

Gary Bente, Nicole C. Krämer, and Felix Eschenburg

Embodiment in the broadest sense can be defined as the existence and/or the visibility of humanlike physical properties that enable the transmission of nonverbal signals (see Ruttkay *et al.*, 2002). Embodiment is a given fact in all face-to-face encounters but can be minimized or even absent in mediated communication. Avatars, i.e. virtual representations of real human beings, are a means of embodiment within computer-mediated communication (CMC). Avatars are increasingly populating the net, appearing in a wide range of applications from social gaming to net-based knowledge communication. The mere technical feasibility of realistic virtual characters with real-time behavior capabilities and transformable appearance is certainly one relevant motor for the rapid development of this field. This development also seems to be driven by the particular interest humans devote to the visual communication channel and the exceptional sensitivity they have developed towards nonverbal cues, such as gestures, postures, movements, and facial displays (Depaulo & Friedman, 1998; Fridlund, 1991; Krämer, 2006).

The social relevance of this sensitivity is underpinned by exhaustive psychological research that provides ample evidence that embodiment and nonverbal communication serve a number of conversational and socio-emotional functions in human encounters and—given the technical prerequisites—can also be influential in mediated communication as well (Bente & Krämer, in press; Biocca & Nowak, 1999, 2001; Blascovich *et al.*, 2002; Burgoon *et al.*, 1989; Petersen *et al.*, 2002; Slater & Steed, 2002). The question whether mediated communication in general and CMC in particular might suffer from disembodiment and the loss of nonverbal channels, however, has generated a series of diverging answers (see Walther & Parks, 2002, for an inspiring discussion of the relevant telecommunication and CMC theories). It has to be pointed out, however, that despite pronounced differences all CMC theories share the view that nonverbal channels account for socio-emotional variance in human interaction and that reduced bandwidth in this respect can principally cause an increase in interpersonal uncertainty. Whether we assume such a deficit to be deterministic for the course and outcome of CMC, as cues-filtered-out and social presence theory do (Culnan & Markus, 1987; Kiesler *et al.*, 1984; Rawlins, 1989; Rice & Love, 1987; Short *et al.*, 1976; Sproull & Kiesler, 1986); or we claim the dependency of nonverbal behavior effects on task type and complexity, as media richness theory would (Daft & Lengel, 1984 and 1986); or we rely on the creative potential in CMC users to compensate for channel reduction as Social Information Processing Theory state (Walther, 1992; Walther *et al.*, 1994; Walther & Burgoon, 1992), does not really make a difference with respect to this fundamental assumption. Tanis and Postmes (2007: 957) sum up: "The key point here is not that all these theories are the same, the point is that despite their differences they subscribe to the same meta-theory that the social effects of communication technology are caused by the disembodiment of interpersonal communication." Barring some face validity this position challenges our knowledge about the role of embodiment and nonverbal behavior in human communication, and queries which production and reception rules it follows and which particular functions it serves. In particular, it remains unclear what the differential effects of avatar-mediated communication (AMC) are as compared to face-to-face communication and other CMC modes, under which conditions they occur, and which basic psychological mechanisms these effects rely on.

These questions have guided our recent research and development efforts, aiming at the provision of a unified conceptual framework as well as of standardized tools for the analysis of embodiment and nonverbal behavior (NVB) in mediated encounters. Although our background is in nonverbal communication research and media psychology, the work presented here draws heavily upon concepts and paradigms as formulated in the areas of CMC, computer-supported collaborative work, and communication within shared virtual environments (SVEs). To review the broad literature in these fields, however, is beyond the scope of this chapter. Instead, we will focus on the unique properties of avatar-mediated communications. Since it can be assumed that the effects of mediated embodiment and nonverbal behavior cannot be understood without referencing their role in non-mediated face-to-face encounters. We will further summarize relevant knowledge gained from nonverbal communication research. Against this background we will discuss various features of current avatar platforms where relevant to the functions of nonverbal behavior, and introduce a desktop setup for avatar-mediated communication developed in our laboratory. The potential of this setup will be demonstrated by a recent study designed to provide basic insights into the interpersonal effects of simulated gaze behavior in avatar-mediated interactions.

What's special about avatar-mediated communication?

While some structural particularities of avatar-mediated communication (AMC) concerning nonverbal channels are obvious, their functional implications are not always as clear. For example, in contrast to text-based CMC, avatar-mediated communication as well as VoIP and web-based video-conferencing systems show similarities in providing immediate, though mediated, analogous communication channels, i.e. ears and eyes are directly addressed by "uncoded" voices and/or images of the communication partner. No symbolic transcription is involved. In addition to the paraverbal cues in the audio mode (prosodic aspects of speech, tone, pitch) video-conferencing systems and avatar-mediated communication offer additional visual bandwidth for nonverbal cues (such as gestures, movement, gaze, facial displays). Although principally involving the same channels (given highly sophisticated real-time AMC), there are still essential differences between avatar-mediated communication and video-based communication devices. These are: (1) *anonymity and plasticity*—avatars permit the possibility of hiding identity and transforming behavior—and (2) *situatedness and co-presence*—using avatars we can "meet" in shared virtual environments.

Plasticity and anonymity

Plasticity can be defined as the possibility of masking or transforming aspects of appearance and identity, as well as aspects of communicative behavior, independently from each other. The basis for this possibility is the resolution of the naturally existing confusion between visual appearance and nonverbal behavior that is present in face-to-face (FtF) encounters and in video-conferences but which is overcome in AMC. This confusion can be resolved in AMC because bodily features as well as behavior protocols are independently stored in a digital, i.e. editable, format (Bente *et al.*, 2001). Just as in a 3D animation tool, the modeler and the animator in an avatar system are in principle separate modules referring to independent data sets. Two types of plasticity emerge from this feature.

First, avatar-mediated communication is characterized by a unique *plasticity* regarding static features of appearance. The free choice of a virtual body implies that, in contrast to FtF and video, AMC can include visual behavior without necessarily disclosing the interlocutor's real visual appearance, i.e. their identity. The interlocutors can thus stay anonymous, although they engage in nonverbal communication. Beside the general social psychological implications of anonymity as discussed in the

CMC literature (Dyer *et al.*, 1995; Joinson, 1997, 1998; Karau & Williams, 1995), the lack of identity-related visual cues has further consequences for mutual impression formation. In particular, category-based inferences and stereotypical judgments, referring to gender, ethnicity, age, or attractiveness are "practically impossible" (see Loomis *et al.*, 1999). The embodiment via an avatar not only obscures the true identity of the interlocutor, it also creates the visual basis for new, and possibly identity-divergent, social perceptions (Castronova, 2004; Cheng *et al.*, 2002; Nowak, 2004; T. L. Taylor, 2002). Although aware of the avatars' artificial nature, users seem to respond to their appearance very much in the same way as they do to humans in real-life encounters (Nowak & Biocca, 1999). In this sense stereotyped judgments are not at all "impossible" but even most likely and can be even pronounced in AMC (Axelsson, 2002). Given these effects in person perception and impression formation on the receiver's side, it is also important to consider the possibilities for impression management and strategic communication on the sender's side. In this sense Bailenson and Blascovich (2004: 9) classify AMC as

> qualitatively different from other forms of communication, including face-to-face interaction, telephone conversation, and video-conferencing as well. Via avatar interactants possess the ability to systematically filter their physical appearance and behavioral actions in the eyes of their conversational partners, amplifying or suppressing features and nonverbal signals in real-time for strategic purpose.

The authors here also point out the second aspect of plasticity—with respect to dynamic features of nonverbal behavior—which might be called *behavioral plasticity*. Beyond the selection and transformation of visual appearance, avatar-mediated communication also allows for the unique control over the behavioral cues which are transmitted through the medium. For example frequency, and duration of emotional facial displays, particular gestures or eye contact can be modified according to specific rules. The implications of behavioral plasticity have already been explored in a series of studies, many of which are described in Chapter 6 of this book. As a basic feature of avatar-mediated communication, behavioral plasticity raises ethical questions on the one hand but also opens completely new research perspectives particularly relevant to the investigation of mediated nonverbal behavior (see Blascovich *et al.*, 2002). This aspect has been central to our own studies and will be exemplified later on.

Situatedness and co-presence

The second distinctive property of avatar systems is their potential to *situate* or *embed* communication and to generate an experience of *co-presence* in a shared virtual environment (Nowak & Biocca, 2003; Prasolova-Forland, 2002). In contrast to audio and video-communication, avatars allow people to "get together" in a shared virtual world, i.e. make use of location, spatial relations, and movement information, experience interpersonal distance, and share tools and artifacts (Benford, *et al.*, 2001; Garau, 2003; Hindmarsh *et al.*, 1998; Slater & Steed, 2002; M. J. Taylor & Rowe, 2000; T. L. Taylor, 2002). In this property Redfern and Naughton (2002: 207) see the most crucial difference between avatar-based CVEs and other communication media:

> If these things are not provided, then the CVE is merely a graph-ically-rich communication tool – not unlike teleconferencing and videoconferencing – which will lose out on the ability to act as a place, foster community, and enable important collaborative work principles such as work artifact collaboration, chance meetings, and peripheral awareness.

Again many authors would agree with this statement. However, the question still remains unanswered as to whether these media specifications really matter for CMC, and to what degree the illusion of a shared space fosters the effects of AMC. In fact, there are particular nonverbal subsystems such as proxemics and touch (Burgoon, 1994; Wallbott, 1994) which directly refer to spatial information. Thus, the creation of a virtual space in which avatars meet, can be essential for the socio-emotional impact of the avatars' behavior (for first implementations see Basdogan *et al.*, 2000).

What's special about nonverbal communication?

Everyday psychology as well as scientific theory hold that nonverbal cues, such as facial expressions, gaze, gestures, postures, and body movements have a deep impact on the process and outcome of our communicative efforts (Argyle *et al.*, 1970; Mehrabian & Wiener, 1967; Schneider *et al.*, 1979). Summarizing findings from different studies, Burgoon (1994) suggests that approximately 60–65 percent of social meaning is derived from nonverbal behaviors (see also Mehrabian & Ferris, 1967). Although important for an overall estimation of the impact of nonverbal behavior, such global estimations do not reflect the complexity and subtlety of the phenomena under investigation. The term "nonverbal communication" describes neither a structurally nor functionally homogenous behavioral category. Instead, it represents a multifaceted assembly of channels, cues, and behavioral qualities which serve a large variety of interpersonal functions. In fact, there are a number of specifics in nonverbal behavior that make it qualitatively different from verbal communication. We want to focus on three of these particularities that we consider most relevant to the use of nonverbal behavior in computer-mediated communication. These are (1) context dependency, (2) implicitness and dynamic qualities, and (3) automaticity and unconsciousness.

Context dependency

There is consensus that the effects of nonverbal behavior are largely dependent on the situation in which they are embedded and on other concomitant behaviors. The so-called Kuleshov effect demonstrates the influence of situational context (Pudowkin, 1961; Wallbott, 1988). Showing a short movie sequence of an actor's neutral face with either a dead woman's body, a little girl playing, or a pot of soup, Lev Kuleshov (a Russian film director) could induce distinct attributions in the audience such as terror, joy, or contentment (see also the replication of Goldberg, 1951, in a controlled study). Chovil (1991) could show that the interpretation of facial displays (more specifically, eyebrow movements) is also dependent on the verbal context, leading to such different interpretations of eyebrow movements as emphasis, marked questions, offers, surprise, or disbelief depending on the simultaneous speech activity. One of the most influential contexts for nonverbal behavior, however, is nonverbal behavior (Bente & Krämer, 2003). There are many empirical examples of situations in which an activity in one nonverbal channel affects the interpretation of other simultaneously occurring cues (Krämer, 2001). For example, Grammer (1990) showed that the function of laughter is modulated by additional nonverbal signals such as posture and bodily movements. In an intriguing study Frey and his colleagues (Frey *et al.*, 1983) demonstrated that even the evaluation of Mona Lisa's smile is dependent on another subtle cue, that is, the lateral head tilt.

Implicit behavioral qualities

Nonverbal behavior cannot readily be understood as a collection of well-defined cues, with clear-cut spatio-temporal characteristics. On the contrary, the effects of nonverbal behavior most often emerge from dynamic qualities that are implicit in the ongoing behavior and can hardly be identified with the naked eye. Riggio and Friedman (1986) conclude that these dynamic aspects of nonverbal behavior even determine perception and evaluation in the first place. Recent studies confirm this view, showing that dynamic qualities, such as speed, acceleration, complexity, and symmetry of body movements and facial expressions, may have a stronger impact on the observers' impressions than so-called semantic aspects, although they might not be identified as a possible cause (Grammer *et al.*, 1999). For instance, Grammer *et al.* (1997) could demonstrate that very subtle changes in women's movements were provoking attributions of interest and contact readiness in male observers. Also, it could be shown that the complexity level and speed of movements is dependent on levels of estrogen. Male observers do not consciously notice these subtle changes, but they nevertheless respond in a predictable manner. Similarly, Krumhuber and Kappas (2005) show that movement quality is equally important when observing facial behavior. Against this background, Grammer *et al.* (1997) even suggest a new conceptualization of (nonverbal) communication that radically differs from category-oriented or semiotic "body language" approaches and which stresses a more immediate coupling between movement production, movement perception, and sensory experience. Recent discoveries in neuroscience, pointing to the existence of so-called mirror neurons—which fire in the same way when producing or when only observing a motor behavior—seem to confirm this position (Gallese *et al.*, 1996; Gallese & Goldman, 1998; Iacoboni *et al.*, 1999; Rizzolatti *et al.*, 1996).

Automaticity and unconsciousness

Closely related to the aspect just discussed is the fact that production as well as perception of nonverbal behavior largely happen automatically and without awareness. Choi and his colleagues (Choi *et al.*, 2005: 327) concluded from numerous studies on encoding and decoding of emotional displays that "because of the need to act quickly in social life" the degree of automatization for both encoding and decoding of nonverbal behavior is fairly high. Consistent with the definition of automaticity given by Bargh (1994), nonverbal communication thus can be labeled as: unaware, unintentional, uncontrollable (i.e. it cannot be stopped), and most efficient. Burgoon *et al.* (2000) underline that unconscious processing—or in their terminology *mindlessness*—is ubiquitous in nonverbal communication. Similar conclusions have also been drawn by Grammer *et al.* (Grammer *et al.*, 1997; Grammer *et al.*, 1999). Frey (1999) used the term *inferential communication* to account for the overwhelming suggestive force of nonverbal behavior. Referring to Helmholtz's concept of *unconscious conclusions*, he argues that the effects of visual stimuli are not subject to cognitive control but leave us defenseless while at the same time affecting us both directly and deeply. In sum, it might be stated that nonverbal behavior can hardly be understood as a second language with a set of explicit conventionalized signs. On the contrary, it seems to owe its enormous interpersonal impact to its subtle and transient nature and the seemingly "hardwired" mechanisms that govern cue production and reception as well.

Communicative and relational functions of nonverbal behavior

The matter of understanding nonverbal behavior is complex even when taking a functionalistic perspective. Opening the visual channel in mediated communications can hardly be understood as adding a particular functionality. On the contrary, the transmission of nonverbal cues will inevitably and simultaneously affect different levels of social information processing. Even when concentrating on specific cues and a particular dialog function (e.g. raising a hand to get the turn), the mere visibility of a body will induce inferences which can go far beyond the intended range (a lack of a smile could be interpreted as cold and aloof). Recently, we have distinguished three major functional levels of nonverbal behavior which are blended in human interactions and which we consider of major relevance for the implementations of avatars as well. These are (1) discourse functions, (2) dialog functions, and (3) socio-emotional functions (see Bente & Krämer, 2003; Bente, *et al.*, 2001).

Discourse functions

Discourse functions of nonverbal behavior are closely related to speech production and understanding. So-called emblems, pointing gestures, illustrative gestures, and beat gestures belong to this functional category (Efron, 1941; Ekman & Friesen, 1969). Emblems are conventionalized gestures, which can replace a word or a phrase, often used when the audio channel is locked (e.g. while diving) or social settings do not allow the use of the voice (e.g. raising the hand to get a turn in the classroom). Emblems only cover a small range of nonverbal behavior. They have clear physical properties and a lexical meaning (at least within a culture), and thus can easily be implemented. It is interesting to notice that early avatar systems as developed by computer scientists mostly referred to this functionality (see Müller *et al.*, 2003).

Illustrators complement and clarify verbal exchange (Efron, 1941; Ekman & Friesen, 1969): They are frequently used to establish an object reference, e.g. by finger-drawing an object in the air (iconic gestures) or by pointing at it (deictic gestures), and can thus be of particular relevance for co-navigating a CVE and sharing virtual artifacts.

So-called *beat gestures* are used to underline speech rhythms and accentuate parts of an utterance (see McNeill, 1992, for his distinction between iconic, metaphoric, and beat gestures). They are thus relevant to improving the understanding and persuasiveness of the spoken words, which could be most important when, for example, extending VoIP by means of avatars. Successful implementations of beat gestures have also been demonstrated by Cassell *et al.* with embodied conversational agents (Cassell, 1998; Cassell *et al.*, 1994).

As evident from the literature, hand gestures are the predominant nonverbal subsystem when it comes to discourse functions of nonverbal behavior—which attaches great importance to the display of hands and fingers in avatar-mediated communication. But it has also been shown that facial movements can serve discourse functions: Chovil (1991) empirically identified various *facial illustrators*, such as eyebrow raising or lowering, widening of the eyes, as serving a series of syntactic and semantic functions. However, the detection and transmission of facial dynamics within avatar-mediated communication still poses some technical problems. Here, further endeavors have to be taken to realize appropriate features (see the development of an infra-red-based nonobtrusive system for the 3D tracking and rendering of human faces in real time within the Integrated Project PASION (Psychologically Augmented Social Interaction over Networks) funded by the European Commission in the 6th Framework Program (IST Project no. 27654).

Dialog functions

Dialog functions include so-called turn-taking signals (e.g. eye contact) and back-channel signals (e.g. head nods), which serve the smooth flow of interaction when exchanging speaker and listener roles (Duncan, 1972). As far back as the 1980s, Duncan and his colleagues presented an impressive research program, identifying a series of nonverbal (primarily visual) turn-taking signals (Duncan, 1972, 1974; Duncan *et al.*, 1979; Duncan & Niederehe, 1974). *Turn-yielding signals* are often a conglomerate of verbal (e.g. sociocentric sentences as "you know"), paraverbal (intonation or prolongation of the last syllable) and nonverbal cues (termination of gestures, head movements). The more cues a speaker shows, the smoother the turn-taking should be. This in fact makes a strong argument for higher bandwidth in CMC, especially when voice is involved. Kendon (1967) further identified changes in head position (raising, rotating towards the listener) as crucial: If the speaker does not look up at the end of his utterance, an expected reply is frequently delayed or missing (71 percent as compared to 29 percent when looking up). Other cues are used to prevent the listener from taking the turn. Increased gestural activity is signaling the speaker's intention to go on. *Backchannel signals*, such as head nodding, confirm the listener status and motivate the speaker to go on (see Yngve, 1970). If the listener wants to take the turn, he/she indicates this via a so-called *speaker state signal* that might consist of head rotations away from the interlocutor, starting gestural activity and body movement, and averted gaze (70 percent of utterances are started by looking away from the partner).

Despite these results the importance of visual cues within the turn-taking process has been doubted (see Rime, 1983), given the observation that interlocutors still are able to lead well-organized conversations when they do not see each other—e.g. during a telephone chat. Rutter and Stephenson (1977), however, demonstrated that this channel loss is coming at an expense, causing particular changes in the structure of the communication processes (see also Rutter *et al.*, 1978). For example, in audio communications fewer interruptions and fewer simultaneous speech activities (overlaps) can be observed. According to the authors this might be due to the fact that the socio-emotional effects of an interruption (e.g. displeasure) as potentially inferable from nonverbal cues cannot be observed directly and as a consequence communicative repair strategies cannot be launched in time (see also Donaghy & Goldberg, 1991).

Socio-emotional functions

Socio-emotional or relational functions of nonverbal behavior include its influence on person perception and impression formation, as well as the communication of emotions and interpersonal attitudes. Socio-emotional functions are not completely independent from dialog and discourse functions of nonverbal behavior. A smooth flow of the conversation will be likely to influence mutual person perception and the interpersonal climate in a positive way. On the other hand, a conceptual restriction of avatar-mediated communication to discourse and dialog functions (e.g. by merely transferring gestures) and a neglect of socio-emotional aspects could lead to undesirable effects. A lack of nonverbal variations, which do not directly pursue discourse and dialog functions, will most likely be interpreted as a negative social attitude, instead of being recognized as a consequence of media limitations (e.g. reduced bandwidth).

In an attempt to systematize nonverbal cues according to their socio-emotional functions, Mehrabian (1972) identified three basic effect dimensions and associated signal categories: the *evaluation* dimension (liking), the *activity* dimension, and the *potency* dimension (power).

Evaluation

According to Mehrabian (1972) the evaluation dimension (liking) is affected by so-called immediacy or "involvement" (Patterson, 1982) cues such as smiling, leaning forward, close proximity, touch, relaxed postures, and interpersonal distance (proxemics) etc. (see Haase & Tepper, 1972; LaCrosse, 1975; Mehrabian, 1969; Patterson, 1982; Rosenfeld, 1966; Schlenker, 1980). Although smiling has been discussed as a submissiveness cue (appeasement pattern, Henley, 1977; Keating *et al.*, 1979; Patterson, 1994), most studies prove its evaluative effects, documented as friendliness and affiliation (Brunner, 1979; Carli *et al.*, 1993; Carli *et al.*, 1995; Deutsch *et al.*, 1988; Graham & Argyle, 1976; Halberstadt & Saitta, 1987; Page, 1980). Further, it was demonstrated that head movements and specific head orientations can carry relevant social information (Frey, 1983; Frey *et al.*, 1983; Montagner, 1978; Signer, 1975).

The literature further reveals evidence that similarities in the nonverbal behavior of interlocutors are correlated with positive evaluation—being a cause and an effect of mutual liking (Bernieri & Rosenthal, 1991; Tickle, Degnen & Rosenthal, 1987; Wallbott, 1995). This class of nonverbal phenomena has been addressed in the literature using different terms, such as *reciprocity* and *compensation* (Argyle & Cook, 1976), *mirroring* (Bernieri & Rosenthal, 1991), *conversational adaptation* (Burgoon *et al.*, 1993), *simulation patterning* (Cappella, 1991), *synchrony* (Condon & Ogston, 1966), *congruence* (Scheflen, 1964), *motor mimicry* (Bavelas *et al.*, 1987; Lipps, 1907), and *accommodation* (Giles *et al.*, 1987). Initial experiments in avatar-mediated communication have confirmed the enormous impact of motor mimicry (Bailenson & Yee, 2005; see also chapter 6 in this book).

Activity

The activity dimension is expressed by vivid and extensive use of gestures, frequent facial displays and pronounced movements, and is hypothesized to communicate responsiveness (Mehrabian, 1969). DePaulo und Friedman (1998) also conclude that expressiveness (as a synonym for responsiveness) is related to likeability, empathy, charisma, and influence. It can be questioned, though, to what extent activity represents a dimension of its own, since higher activity and responsiveness is correlated with positive evaluation (see Bentler, 1969). As the activity dimension does not consist of isolated well-described cues but is defined by general behavioral qualities, such as number and duration of movements, movement complexity, speed and acceleration, it cannot be assigned to a distinct interpersonal function (see above). Moreover, variations in the general activity level will often work as amplifiers of qualitatively unequivocal cues and their effects will be context dependent. Mehrabian and Williams (1969: 54) state: "In particular, when a relatively high level of activity is combined with other cues which communicate liking, ... then activity may be seen as a vehicle for the communication of the intensity of liking." With respect to the transmission of such intensity cues, avatar-mediated communication can hardly be reduced to singular nonverbal signals, but would have to include the full range of movement dynamics.

Potency

The potency dimension (mostly synonymously used with power, dominance, and status) is addressed by so-called relaxation cues such as asymmetry, sideward and backward lean, relaxed extremities, staring or averted gaze, and expansive gestures (DePaulo & Friedman, 1998; Mehrabian,

1969; Millar *et al.*, 1984; Siegel *et al.*, 1992). The results on the effects of relaxation cues are equivocal (Aguinis *et al.*, 1998; Henley, 1977; Schlenker, 1980), showing only consistent results with respect to a few cues, such as backward lean (Carli *et al.*, 1993) and touch (Henley, 1977; Patterson, 1994). An empirically well-established relation exists between dominance and gaze behavior. People are perceived to be dominant when they look at the interaction partner especially while speaking and less so when listening (Dovidio *et al.*, 1988; Exline, 1971; Exline *et al.*, 1975). DePaulo and Friedman (1998: 12) conclude that dominant people "can stare more but have to look less." Gaze as a very powerful and also clearly definable cue has already gained some attention in avatar-mediated communication research (Bailenson *et al.*, 2005; see also chapter 6 in this book; Bente *et al.*, in press). Dominance also is attributed when specific facial expressions such as lowered brows and other anger displays are shown (Camras, 1977, 1982; Edinger & Patterson, 1983; Friedman, 1979; Keating *et al.*, 1979; Schlenker, 1980).

Research implementations for avatar-mediated communication

It can be assumed that providing nonverbal channels in CMC is less a question of feasability than a matter of costs and benefits which are dependant on the technologies, the tasks, and the people involved. In the following we will point out some distinctions of current AMC approaches and exemplarily describe the concrete AMC setup in our laboratory. The technical functionalities of the setup as well as the research strategies that can be pursued with this instrumentation will be outlined referring to a recent study in avatar-mediated social gaze.

Distinctive properties of avatar platforms

Current avatar platforms differ in many respects and thus are are not readily comparable with regard to the communicative functions they serve (Axelsson, 2002; Garau, 2003; Murray, 1997; Nowak, 2004). Beside the immersiveness of display technologies (desktop vs. HMD or CAVE systems) and the graphical realisms of the virtual environments and their virtual inhabitants, there exists a particularly relevant difference with respect to the way avatar-mediated communication systems capture and represent the nonverbal behavior of the actors. Two types of avatar-mediated communication systems can be thus distinguished: (1) "cue-driven" or "top-down" systems and (2) "behavior-driven" or "bottom-up" systems.

Cue-driven systems make selective use of nonverbal cues which have distinct spatio-temporal characteristics and clearly defined interpersonal meanings or communicative functions, such as raising the hand to get a turn or pointing to an object of reference (see e.g. Müller *et al.*, 2002; Müller *et al.*, 2003). These systems imply a priori knowledge about the structure and semantics of particular nonverbal cues. These cues can be captured from the natural stream of behavior and selectively transferred, but it is also possible to launch a particular prefabricated nonverbal action by just clicking a mouse button or hitting a key. Since the set of relevant cues is known, and these cues are conventionalized, it is not necessary to produce that particular behavior and to capture and transmit the real individual variation. In this case, there is no direct coupling between type of motor action on the sender side and perceived motor action on the receiver side.

Behavior-driven or bottom-up systems typically are different in two respects: First, in contrast to cue-driven systems they are transmitting spontaneous movement activity as it occurs during interaction. Second, they do not require any conscious selection of cues or decision to transmit. All aspects of nonverbal behavior that are captured by the sensors can also be conveyed to the receiver (see Blascovich *et al.*, 2002). Being "non-semantic," this approach nevertheless allows for switching on (or off, respectively) particular nonverbal channels or modifying them. The approach thus provides the behavioral plasticity of avatar-mediated communication systems as described above.

The above classification is definitely questionable because it implies different criteria dimensions, such as the selectivity of cues, the direct mapping of motor action, or the existence of a conventionalized cue set. Instead of clear-cut categories, it illustrates two extreme poles of a scale along which various hybrid systems are conceivable. Nevertheless, this distinction demonstrates that basic technological decisions can have far-reaching implications with respect to the scope of psychological functions which avatar-mediated nonverbal behaviors might serve. In contrast to the "behavior-driven" approach, the "cue-driven" approach, for example, is widely restricted to basic discourse and dialog functions (or conventionalized socio-emotional cues such as smiling).

As discussed, however, it is most uncertain whether these functions can be beneficially implemented without transmitting any socio-emotional cues: A blank face and a frozen body will most likely be evaluated negatively, in particular when the realism of the avatars raises specific expectations about nonverbal variation. Also, the fact that the transmitted cues are deliberately chosen can have an impact on sender and receiver as well. First, the sender will be more self-aware when consciously choosing what to display. Second, the number of cues sent per time unit is limited by the cognitive resources of the sender. Third, the receiver can come to different conclusions about the message knowing that the sender had time to premeditate. Given our primary interest in the subtle dynamics of nonverbal behavior and the limited knowledge about specific effects of mediated nonverbal behavior on the one hand and the plasticity of the "bottom-up" approach on the other, we decided in favor of a behavior-driven avatar platform for the present.

The ABC-Desk: a behavior-driven avatar platform

The ABC-Desk (avatar-based collaborative desktop environment) developed at the University of Cologne is conceptualized as a low immersive desktop VR (2D screen projections of 3D animated avatars instead of stereoscopic views via shutter glasses or HMD), enabling high behavioral realism and maximum plasticity. A wide range of spontaneous nonverbal behavior (movements of head, upper body, arms, hands and fingers as well as eye movement and gaze direction) is captured and transmitted (Bente et al., 2005; Petersen et al., 2002). In addition, a basic lip-synch algorithm has been implemented, allowing a voice-controlled opening and closing of the mouth. In sum, the ABC-Desk contains the following functionalities: (1) real-time interaction of up to four interlocutors including verbal and nonverbal signals (2) experimental variation of the visual appearance of the interlocutors, (3) experimental control of behavioral cues, (4) recording of verbal and nonverbal behavior, (5) interactive and/or algorithmic modification of behavior protocols in offline mode, and (6) the offline rendering and replay of stored movement data.

Figure 7.1 shows the basic setup of ABC-Desk. As depicted, nonverbal behavior is detected by means of Cybergloves, Polhemus trackers, and a high-resolution eye-tracking system, which has been developed for this purpose in our laboratory. The eye-tracking system is integrated in a headset, to which the Polhemus tracker for head movement measurement is also attached. A special calibration routine allows for the individual adjustment of all measurement devices and the fitting of user anatomy and avatar body measures. Eye movement is calibrated to the virtual camera in the middle of the screen. Thus, gaze coordinates can be read out for later analysis, assigning gaze direction to particular display areas (e.g., the face or the eyes of the interaction partner). Data are transmitted via Intranet, using a TCP-IP protocol. Based on the movement protocols a special AVI-CODEC performs the avatar rendering using an in-built low-resolution avatar (see Figure 7.2a). High-resolution avatars can also be controlled using a special real-time data interface with a commercial 3D animation tool (Motion Builder 7.0).

Avatars can be chosen from a set of 3D models available within the ABC-Desk, thus allowing for systematic variations of physical appearance, including aspects of realism (Bente et al., in press), gender (Bente et al., 1996) and ethnicity (Bente et al., 2007). Figure 7.2a shows three different levels of elaboration and avatar realism, from a reduced cartoon-like character to a full body anthropomorphic figure with skin and clothes. It has to be mentioned that cartoonish avatars provide more degrees of freedom

Figure 7.1 Base version of the avatar-based collaborative desktop environment (screen shot during calibration mirroring the interlocutor's own behavior).

(a)

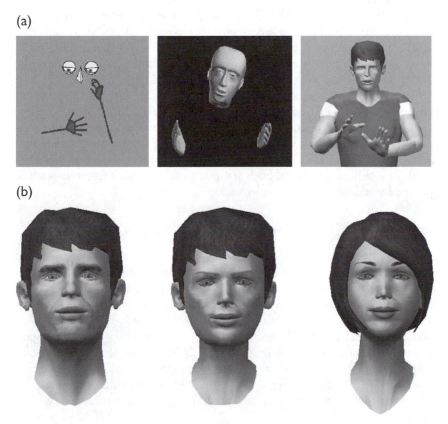

(b)

Figure 7.2 Variations of avatar appearance in ABC-Desk
(a: variations of realism; b: variations of gender typicality)

to accentuate singular morphological aspects (e.g. enlarging the eyes, see figure 7.2a) without interfering with aesthetic principles, as would be the case when showing a disproportional feature in a realistic face or body. Figure 7.2b exemplifies variations of gender, showing two extremes of male and female embodiment and an androgynous avatar as resulting from a morphing procedure.

Two different setups are currently used within the ABC-Desk. In the basic version the avatars are presented in full-screen mode (see Figure 7.1). The setup resembles a videophone conference where only the "talking heads" and upper body are visible and no contextual information as part of a shared environment is displayed. In the extended version the avatar window is integrated in a shared workbench (Cool Modes) developed by Hoppe and his colleagues (Bollen et al., 2002) for assisting net-based collaborations (see Figure 7.3). Although coupling the user's actions via the shared objects on the workbench, this setup is still low with regard to immersion since the avatars are not bodily represented within the SVE but displayed in a separate window. In this respect the ABC-Desk clearly differs from the two systems mentioned above (Blascovich et al., 2002; Müller et al., 2002), which both co-locate the avatars in the same 3D space. ABC-Desk in the current version thus abstains from fully situating or embedding the avatars, instead focusing on the subtle dynamics of nonverbal behavior. On the other hand, all setups allow for media comparisons, respectively channel comparisons, by replacing avatars by video transmissions or mere chat windows. Moreover, the ABC-Desk allows the masking of the participants' identity and also gives full experimental control (cue filtering and manipulation) over the behavioral data stream. Although originally configured for dyadic interactions, both setups can be extended to three or more people by adding windows or displays.

ABC-Desk in action: an exemplary study on social gaze

Plasticity has been identified as a major property of avatar-mediated communication allowing for systematic experimental control of static as well as dynamic visual cues relevant to interpersonal communication and impression formation. Given only limited space here, we will focus on the variation of dynamic cues and describe a recent study on gaze behavior and eye contact in virtual encounters. In fact, simulation studies on gaze behavior are not rare (see Bailenson et al., 2005; Garau, 2003; Garau et al., 2001). What is most important to note here is that ABC-Desk for the first time enabled a simulated gaze to be embedded into a natural stream of nonverbal behavior consisting of head and body movements as well as gestural activities.

Only female participants took part in this first pilot study in order to avoid specific cross-gender gaze phenomena as for example inherent in

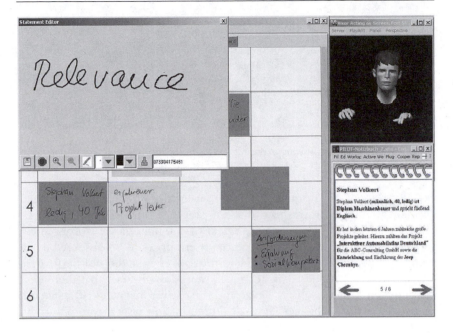

Figure 7.3 Integration of the avatar platform into a collaborative workbench (Source: Cool Modes, Bollen *et al.*, 2002).

flirting behavior. ABC-desk was used in the type 1 (full screen) version, with a low-resolution avatar, which permitted the eyes to be enlarged and make them more salient in the overall impression. Original eye movements were only transmitted for one of the interlocutors, while the eye movements of the partners were replaced by simulated data with different lengths of directed gaze (looking into the virtual camera). Based on previous research (Bente *et al.*, 1998), two conditions of gaze duration were chosen: normal gaze (4 seconds) and reduced gaze (2 seconds). In both simulated conditions the phases of averted gaze lasted 2 seconds. Figure 7.4 depicts three gaze directions as shown by the low-resolution avatar. Dynamics of the artificial eye movements, such as different angles of averted gaze as well as blinks, were simulated according to our knowledge of natural gaze behavior; this created a very realistic impression of the virtual eyes, as proved in the treatment check.

Consistent with the literature (e.g. Larsen & Shackelford, 1996) we found that longer phases of directed gaze, i.e. looking in direction of the partner (4 seconds), produced more favorable results than shorter gaze periods (2 seconds). As Figure 7.5 shows, the effects of social gaze mainly concerned the evaluation dimension of the socio-emotional measures taken. The longer gaze as compared to the short gaze and the natural gaze leads to significantly better evaluations of the partner. The activity and the

Figure 7.4 Screenshots showing experimental gaze variations: averted gaze (left, right) and directed gaze (middle) in a low-resolution avatar.

potency dimension (dominance/power) were not affected by the experimental variation. With respect to social presence only the factor co-presence showed a significant positive effect of a longer gaze. A pronounced tendency, also missing the significance criterion, could be observed in the factor behavioral contingencies. Here the longer gaze did not perform as well as the other modes. This might be caused by the fact that there were fewer dynamic changes in the gaze and thus fewer instances of accidental co-occurrence of changes in gaze direction and other communicative events, e.g. starting to speak or to move.

Interestingly, the remarkable quantitative differences in gaze duration, though leading to different evaluations of the partners, did not pass the threshold of conscious registration. Eye contact in both conditions was estimated as covering about 50 percent of the interaction time. It has to be mentioned that the relation between gaze duration and social evaluation

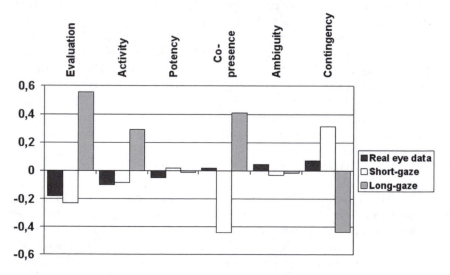

Figure 7.5 Effects of real and simulated gaze (2 seconds vs. 4 seconds) on social impressions and social presence scales.

is not linear. First results of further studies using even longer durations of directed gaze (16 seconds) show that the effect of prolonged gaze flips to the negative side somewhere between 8 and 16 seconds.

In sum, the results stress the most subtle and complex regulation mechanisms inherent in the nonverbal system, and underline the unique research possibilities for avatar-mediated communication. Regarding real-life applications, this example also points to the enormous potential of avatar-based CMC to "augment" social interactions by drawing on behavioral plasticity. These potentials are systematically explored in our current research projects.

Concluding remarks

It has been shown that the particularities of avatar-mediated communication not only make it a useful CMC tool but also a powerful research instrument for those interested in the functions of nonverbal behavior in more general terms. The exemplary study in particular demonstrated methodological advantages resulting from the plasticity of avatar-mediated communication: (1) avatars allow for the standardization, respectively, for the masking of physical appearance and thus help to establish direct causal relation between behavioral cues and person perception; (2) the relevant aspects of nonverbal behavior can be directly and reliably influenced, without risking a confusion with other aspects, as, for example, in studies using human actors or confederates; (3) other aspects of nonverbal behavior keep their dynamic properties and thus create a realistic overall impression; and (4) the experimental variation can be integrated in real-time interactions, thus placing the person perception and impression formation into an interactive process and not in a passive observer task.

As mentioned above it will be most relevant to further standardize technical setups as well as outcome and process measures relevant to avatar-mediated communication to make results more comparable and to allow for coherent knowledge aggregation. Basic knowledge from face-to-face communication research, in particular regarding the subtle dynamics and the functional levels of nonverbal communication should be used more systematically to design further research strategies and formulate directed hypotheses.

Acknowledgements

The research has been generously funded by the German Science Foundation (DFG) within the projects "Social presence in virtual teams" (BE 1745/4) and "Interaction, identity and subjective experience in virtual communication environments" (FK/SFB 427-B3) as well as by the European Commission as part of the Integrated Project "Psychologically augmented social interaction over networks" (PASION, IST Project no. 27654).

References

Aguinis, H., Simonsen, M. M., & Pierce, C. A. (1998) "Effects of nonverbal behavior on perceptions of power bases." *Journal of Social Psychology, 138*(4), 455–469.

Argyle, M., & Cook, M. (1976) *Gaze and Mutual Gaze.* New York: Cambridge University Press.

Argyle, M., Salter, V., Nicholson, H., Wiliams, M., & Burgess, P. (1970). "The communication of inferior and superior attitudes by verbal and non-verbal signals." *British Journal of Social and Clinical Psychology, 9*(3), 222–231.

Asting, T., Heim, J., Schliemann, T., Brundell, P., & Hestnes, B. (2001) *Medium Effects on Impression Formation.* Retrieved 5 February, 2007, from http://www.hft.org/HFT01/paper01/perception/12_01.pdf

Axelsson, A.-S. (2002) "The digital divide: status differences in virtual environments." In R. Schroeder (ed.), *The Social Life of Avatars.* London: Springer, pp. 188–204.

Bailenson, J. N., & Blascovich, J. (2004) "Avatars." In *Encyclopedia of Human-Compuer Interaction.* Berkshire Publishing Group, pp. 64–68

Bailenson, J. N., & Yee, N. (2005) "Digital chameleons. automatic assimilation of nonverbal gestures in immersive virtual environments." *Psychological Science, 16*(10), 814–819.

Bailenson, J. N., Beall, A. C., Loomis, J., Blascovich, J., & Turk, M. (2005) "Transformed social interaction, augmented gaze, and social influence in immersive virtual environments." *Human Communication Research, 31*(4), 511–537.

Bargh, J. A. (1994) "The four horsemen of automaticity: Awareness, intention, efficiency, and control in social cognition." In R. S. Wyer, Jr. (ed.), *Handbook of Social Cognition, Vol. 1: Basic Processes; Vol. 2: Applications, second edition.* Hillsdale, NJ: Lawrence Erlbaum Associates, Inc, pp. 1–40

Basdogan, C., Ho, C. H., Srinivasan, M. A., & Slater, M. (2000) "An experimental study on the role of touch in shared virtual environments." *ACM Transactions on Computer-Human Interactions, 7*(4), 443–460.

Bavelas, J. B., Black, A., Lemery, C. R., & Mullett, J. (1987) "Motor mimicry as primitive empathy." In N. Eisenberg & J. Strayer (eds.), *Empathy and Its Development.* New York: Cambridge University Press, pp. 317–338.

Benford, S., Greenhalgh, C., Rodden, T., & Pycock, J. (2001) "Collaborative virtual environments." *Communications of the ACM, 44*(7), 79–85.

Bente, G., & Krämer, N. C. (2003) "Integrierte Registrierung und Analyse verbaler und nonverbaler Kommunikation." In T. Herrmann & J. Grabowski (eds.), *Sprachproduktion (Enzyklopädie der Psychologie, Themenbereich C, Serie 3),* Vol. 1, Göttingen: Hogrefe, pp. 219–246.

Bente, G., & Krämer, N. C. (in press) "Virtual gestures. Embodiment and nonverbal behaviour in computer-mediated communication." In A. Kappas (ed.), *Emotion in the Internet.* Cambridge: Cambridge University Press.

Bente, G., Donaghy, W. C., & Suwelack, D. (1998) "Sex differences in body movement and visual attention: An integrated analysis of movement and gaze in mixed-sex dyads." *Journal of Nonverbal Behavior, 22*(1), 31–58.

Bente, G., Eschenburg, F., & Krämer, N. C. (in press) "Virtual gaze. A pilot study on the effects of computer simulated gaze in avatar-based conversations." In *Proceedings of the HCI International 2003 10th International Conference on Human-Computer Interaction:* Mahwah, NJ: Lawrence Erlbaum.

Bente, G., Feist, A., & Elder, S. (1996) "Person perception effects of computer simulated male and female head movement." *Journal of Nonverbal Behavior, 20,* 213–228.

Bente, G., Krämer, N. C., Trogemann, G., Piesk, J., & Fischer, O. (2001) "Conversing with electronic devices. An integrated approach towards the generation and evaluation of nonverbal behavior in face-to-face like interface agents." In A. Heuer & T. Kirste (eds.), *Intelligent Interaktive Assistence and Mobile Multimedia Computing.* Rostock: Neuer Hochschulschriftenverlag, pp. 67–76.

Bente, G., Rüggenberg, S., & Krämer, N. C. (2005) "Virtual encounters. Creating social presence in net-based collaborations." Paper presented at the Proceedings of the 8th International Workshop on Presence 2005, University College, London.

Bente, G., Rüggenberg, S., & Krämer, N. C. (in press) "Avatar-mediated net-working. increasing social presence and interpersonal trust in net-based collaborations." *Human Communication Research.*

Bente, G., Senokozlieva, M., Pennig, S., Al-Issa, A., & Fischer, O. (2007) "Explicating the implicit. A computer-based approach towards the cross-cultural analysis of nonverbal behavior." Paper presented at the Conference of the International Communication Association, San Francisco, CA, May 24–28.

Bentler, P. M. (1969) "Semantic space is (approximately) bipolar." *Journal of Psychology: Interdisciplinary and Applied, 71*(1), 33–40.

Bernieri, F. J., & Rosenthal, R. (1991) "Interpersonal coordination: Behavior matching and interactional synchrony." In R. S. Feldman & B. Rime (eds.), *Fundamentals of Nonverbal Behavior.* New York: Cambridge University Press, pp. 401–432.

Biocca, F., Harms, C., & Burgoon, J. K. (2001, May 21–23) "Criteria and scope conditions for a theory and measure of social presence." Paper presented at PRESENCE 2001, 4th Annual International Workshop, Philadelphia, PA.

Biocca, F., & Nowak, K. (1999). "'I feel as if I'm here, inside the computer' Toward a theory of presence in advanced virtual environments." Paper presented to the International Communication Association, San Francisco.

Biocca, F., & Nowak, K. (2001) "Plugging your body into the telecommunication system: mediated embodiment, media interfaces, and social virtual environments." In C. Lin & D. Atkin (eds.), *Communication Technology and Society.* Waverly Hill, VI: Hampton Press. pp. 407–447.

Blascovich, J., Loomis, J., Beall, A. C., Swinth, K. R., Hoyt, C. L., & Bailenson, J. N. (2002) "Immersive virtual environment technology as a methodological tool for social psychology." *Psychological Inquiry, 13*(2), 103–124.

Bollen, L., Hoppe, H. U., Milrad, M., & Pinkwart, N. (2002) "Collaborative modelling in group learning environments". Paper presented at the Proceedings of the XX International Conference of the System Dynamics Society, Palermo, Italy.

Brunner, L. J. (1979) "Smiles can be back channels." *Journal of Personality and Social Psychology, 37*(5), 728–34.

Burgoon, J. K. (1994) "Nonverbal signals." In M. L. Knapp & G. R. Miller (eds.), *Handbook of Interpersonal Communication.* Beverly Hills: Sage, pp. 229–285.

Burgoon, J. K., & Bacue, A. E. (2003) "Nonverbal communication skills." In J. O. Greene & B. R. Burleson (eds.), *Handbook of Communication and Social Interaction Skills.* Mahwah, NJ: Lawrence Erlbaum Associates Publishers, pp. 179–219.

Burgoon, J. K., Berger, C. R., & Waldron, V. R. (2000) "Mindfulness and interpersonal communication." *Journal of Social Issues, 56*(1), 105–127.

Burgoon, J. K., Buller, D. B., & Woodall, W. G. (1989) *Nonverbal Communication: the Unspoken Dialogue.* New York: Harper & Row.

Burgoon, J. K., Dillman, L., & Stern, L. A. (1993) "Adaptation in dyadic interaction: defining and operationalizing patterns of reciprocity and compensation." *Communication Theory, 3,* 196–215.

Camras, L. (1977) "Facial expressions used by children in a conflict situation." *Child Develop-*

ment, 48, 1431–1435.

Camras, L. (1982) "Ethological approaches to nonverbal communication." In R. Feldman (ed.), *Development of Nonverbal Behavior in Children*. New York: Springer, pp. 3–28

Cappella, J. N. (1991) "Mutual adaptation and relativity of measurement." In B. M. Montgomery & S. Duck (eds.), *Studying Interpersonal Interaction*. New York: Guilford Press, pp. 103–117.

Carli, L. L., LaFleur, S. J., & Loeber, C. C. (1995) "Nonverbal behavior, gender, and influence." *Journal of Personality and Social Psychology, 68*(6), 1030–1041.

Carli, L. L., Martin, C., Leatham, G., Lyons, K., & Tse, I. (1993) "Perceptions of nonverbal behavior." Paper presented at the the annual meeting of the American Psychological Association, Toronto, Ontario, Canada.

Cassell, J. (1998) "A framework for gesture generation and interpretation." In R. Cipolla & A. Pentland (eds.), *Computer Visions in Human-Machine Interaction*. Cambridge: Cambridge University Press.

Cassell, J., Steedman, M., Badler, N., Pelachaud, C., Stone, M., Douville, B., *et al.* (1994) "Modeling the interaction between speech and gesture." In A. Ram & K. Eiselt (eds.), *Proceedings on the Sixteenth Annual Conference of the Cognitive Science*. LEA.

Castronova, E. (2004) "The price of bodies: a hedonic pricing model of avatar attributes in a synthetic world." *KYKLOS, 57*(2), 173–196.

Cheng, L., Farnham, S., & Stone, L. (2002) "Lessons learned: building and deploying shared virtual environments." In R. Schroeder (ed.), *The Social Life of Avatars: Presence and Interaction in Shared Virtual Environments*. London: Springer.

Choi, V. S., Gray, H. M., & Ambady, N. (2005) "The glimpsed world: unintended communication and unintended perception." In R. R. Hassin, J. S. Uleman & J. A. Bargh (eds.), *The New Unconscious*. New York: Oxford University Press, pp. 309–333.

Chovil, N. (1991) "Social determinants of facial displays." *Journal of Nonverbal Behavior, 15*(3), 141–154.

Condon, W. S., & Ogston, W. D. (1966) "Sound film analysis of normal and pathological behavior patterns." *Journal of Nervous and Mental Disease, 143*(4), 338–347.

Culnan, M. J., & Markus, M. L. (1987) "Information technologies." In Fredric M. Jablin, Linda L. Putnam, Karlene H. Roberts, Lyman W. Porter, (eds.), (1987) *Handbook of Organizational Communication: an Interdisciplinary Perspective*. Thousand Oaks, CA: Sage Publications, pp. 420–443.

Daft, R. L., & Lengel, R. H. (1984) "Information richness: A new approach to managerial behavior and organizational design." *Research-in-Organizational-Behavior, 6*, 191–233.

Daft, R. L., & Lengel, R. H. (1986) "Organisational information requirements? Media richness and structural design." *Management Science, 32*(5), 554–571.

Depaulo, B. M., & Friedman, H. S. (1998). Nonverbal communication. In D. T. Gilbert, S. T. Fiske & G. Lindzey (eds.), *The Handbook of Ssocial Psychology,* Vol. 2, fourth edition New York: McGraw-Hill, pp. 3–40.

Deutsch, F. M., LeBaron, D., & Fryer, M. M. (1988) "What is in a smile?" *Psychology of Women Quarterly, 11*(3), 341–351.

Donaghy, W. C., & Goldberg, J. (1991) "Head movement and gender differences following the onset of simultaneous speech." *Southern Speech Communication Journal, 56*(2), 114–126.

Dovidio, J. F., Ellyson, S. L., Keating, C. F., Heltman, K., *et al.* (1988) "The relationship of social power to visual displays of dominance between men and women." *Journal of Personality and Social Psychology, 54*(2), 233–242.

Duncan, S. (1972) "Some signals and rules for taking speaking turns in conversations." *Journal of Personality and Social Psychology, 23*(2), 283–292.

Duncan, S. (1974) "On the structure of speaker-auditor interaction during speaking turns." *Language in Society, 3*(2), 161–180.

Duncan, S., Brunner, L. J., & Fiske, D. W. (1979) "Strategy signals in face-to-face interaction." *Journal of Personality and Social Psychology*, 37(2), 301–313.

Duncan, S., & Niederehe, G. (1974) "On signalling that it's your turn to speak." *Journal of Experimental Social Psychology*, 10(3), 234–247.

Dyer, R., Green, R., Pitts, M., & Millward, G. (1995) "What's the flaming problem? CMC—deindividuation or disinhibiting?" In M. A. R. Kirby, A. J. Dix & J. E. Finlay (eds.), *People and Computers X*. Cambridge: Cambridge University Press.

Edinger, J. A., & Patterson, M. L. (1983). "Nonverbal involvement and social control." *Psychological Bulletin*, 93(1), 30–56.

Efron, D. (1941). *Gesture and Environment*. Oxford: King's Crown Press.

Ekman, P., & Friesen, W. V. (1969) "Nonverbal leakage and clues to deception." *Journal for the Study of Interpersonal Processes*, 32(1), 88–106.

Exline, R. V. (1971) "Visual interaction: the glances of power and preference." In *Nebraska Symposium on Motivation*. Lincoln: University of Nebraska Press, pp. 163–206.

Exline, R. V., Ellyson, S. L., & Long, B. (1975) "Visual behavior as an aspect of power role relationships." In P. Pliner, L. Krames & T. Alloway (eds.), *Nonverbal Communication of Aggression* New York: Plenum, pp. 21–52.

Frey, S. (1983) "Unexplored dimensions of human communication." In *1983 Annual Report Standard Elektrik Lorenz AG* Stuttgart: Standard Elektrik Lorenz, pp. 63–66.

Frey, S. (1999) *Die Macht des Bildes*. Bern: Huber.

Frey, S., Hirsbrunner, H. P., Florin, A., Daw, W., & Crawford, R. (1983) "A unified approach to the investigation of nonverbal and verbal behavior in communication research." In W. Doise & S. Moscovici (eds.), *Current Issues in European Social Psychology*. Cambridge: Cambridge University Press, pp. 143–199.

Fridlund, A. J. (1991) "Sociality of solitary smiling: potentiation by an implicit audience." *Journal of Personality and Social Psychology*, 60(2), 229–240.

Friedman, H. S. (1979) "The interactive effects of facial expressions of emotion and verbal messages on perceptions of affective meaning." *Journal of Experimental Social Psychology*, 15(5), 453–469.

Gallese, V., Fadiga, L., Fogassi, L., & Rizzolatti, G. (1996) "Action recognition in the premotor cortex." *Brain*, 119, 593–609.

Gallese, V., & Goldman, A. (1998) "Mirror neurons and the simulation theory of mind-reading." *Trends in Cognitive Sciences*, 2(12), 493–501.

Garau, M. (2003) The Impact of Avatar Fidelity on Social Interaction in Virtual Environments. Unpublished PhD thesis, University College, London.

Garau, M., Slater, M., Bee, S., & Sasse, M. A. (2001) "The impact of eye gaze on communication using humanoid avatars." In *Proceedings of the SIGCHI Conference on Human Factors in Computing Systems*. Seattle, Washington, D.C.: ACM Press, pp. 309–316.

Giles, H., Mulac, A., Bradac, J. J., & Johnson, P. (1987) "Speech accommodation theory: the first decade and beyond." In *Communication Yearbook* (Vol. 10).

Goldberg, H. D. (1951) "The role of 'cutting' in the perception of the motion picture." *Journal of Applied Psychology*, 35(1), 70–71.

Graham, J. A., & Argyle, M. (1976) "The effects of different patterns of gaze combined with different facial expressions, on impression formation." *Journal of Human Movement Studies*, 1(4), 178–182.

Grammer, K. (1990) "Strangers meet: laughter and nonverbal signs of interest in opposite-sex encounters." *Journal of Nonverbal Behavior*, 14(4), 209–236.

Grammer, K., Fidova, V., & Fieder, M. (1997) "The communication paradox and a possible solution: toward a radical empiricism." In A. Schmitt, K. Atzwanger, K. Grammer & K. Schäfer (eds.), *New Aspects of Human Ethology*. New York: Plenum, pp. 91–120.

Grammer, K., Honda, M., Juette, A., & Schmitt, A. (1999) "Fuzziness of nonverbal courtship communication unblurred by motion energy detection." *Journal of Personality and Social Psychology*, 77(3), 487–508.

Haase, R. F., & Tepper, D. T. (1972) "Nonverbal components of empathic communication." *Journal of Counseling Psychology, 19*(5), 417–424.

Halberstadt, A. G., & Saitta, M. B. (1987) "Gender, nonverbal behavior, and perceived dominance: a test of the theory." *Journal of Personality and Social Psychology, 53*(2), 257–272.

Henley, N. M. (1977) *Body Politics: Power, Sex, and Nonverbal Communication.* Englewood Cliffs, NJ: Prentice Hall.

Hindmarsh, J., Fraser, M., Heath, C., Benford, S., & Greenhalgh, C. (1998) "Fragmented interaction: establishing mutual orientation in virtual environments." Paper presented at the ACM conference on Computer-Supported Cooperative Work (CSCW'98), November.

Iacoboni, M., Woods, R. P., Brass, M., Bekkering, H., Mazziotta, J. C., & Rizzolatti, G. (1999) "Cortical mechanisms of human imitation." *Science, 286*(5449), 2526–2528.

Joinson, A. N. (1997) "Anonymity, disinhibition, and social desirability on the internet." Paper presented at the The BPS Social Section Annual Conference, University of Sussex, England.

Joinson, A. N. (1998) "Causes and implications of disinhibited behavior on the Internet." In J. Gackenbach (ed.), *Psychology and the Internet: Intrapersonal, Interpersonal, and Transpersonal Implications.* San Diego, CA: Academic Press, pp. 43–60.

Kanawattanachai, P., & Yoo, Y. (2002) "Dynamic nature of trust in virtual teams." *The Journal of Strategic Information Systems, 11*(3–4), 187–213.

Karau, S. J., & Williams, K. D. (1995) "Social loafing: research findings, implications, and future directions." *Current Directions in Psychological Science, 4*(5), 134–140.

Keating, C. F., Mazur, A., & Segall, M. H. (1979) "Facial gestures which influence the perception of status." *Social Psychology Quarterly, 40*(4), 374–378.

Kendon, A. (1967) "Some functions of gaze-direction in social interaction." *Acta Psychologica, 26*, 22–63.

Kiesler, S., Siegel, J., & McGuire, T. W. (1984) "Social psychological aspects of computer-mediated communication." *American Psychologist, 39*(10), 1123–134.

Krämer, N. C. (2001) *Bewegende Bewegung. Sozio-emotionale Wirkungen nonverbalen Verhaltens und deren experimentelle Untersuchung mittels Computeranimation.* Legenrich: Pabst.

Krämer, N. C. (2006) "Nonverbal communication." Paper presented at the workshop for the Committee on Opportunities in Basic Research in the Behavioral and Social Sciences for the U.S. Military at the National Academies, Washington, D.C.

Krumhuber, E., & Kappas, A. (2005) "Moving smiles: the role of dynamic components for the perception of the genuineness of smiles." *Journal of Nonverbal Behavior, 29*(1), 3–24.

Kumar, N., & Benbasat, I. (2002) "Para-social presence: a re-conceptualization of 'social presence' to capture the emerging relationship between a web site and her visitors." Paper presented at the Proceedings of the 35th Annual Hawai'i International Conference on System Sciences, Los Alamitos, CA.

LaCrosse, M. B. (1975) "Nonverbal behavior and perceived counselor attractiveness and persuasiveness." *Journal of Counseling Psychology, 22*(6), 563–566.

Larsen, R. J., & Shackelford, T. K. (1996) "Gaze avoidance: personality and social judgments of people who avoid direct face-to-face contact." *Personality and Individual Differences, 21*(6), 907–917.

Lipps, T. (1907) "Das Wissen von fremden Ichen." *Psychologische Untersuchungen, 1*(4), 694–722.

Loomis, J. M., Blascovich, J. J., & Beall, A. C. (1999) "Immersive virtual environment technology as a basic research tool in psychology." *Behavior Research Methods, Instruments and Computers, 31*(4), 557–564.

McAllister, D. J. (1995) "Affect- and cognition-based trust as foundations for interpersonal cooperation in organizations." *Academy of Management Journal, 38*(1), 24–59.

McNeill, D. (1992). *Hand and Mind: What Gestures Reveal about Thought.* Chicago: University of Chicago Press.

Mehrabian, A. (1969) "Some referents and measures of nonverbal behavior."

Mehrabian, A. (1972) *Nonverbal Communication.* Oxford: Aldine-Atherton.

Mehrabian, A., & Ferris, S. R. (1967) "Inference of attitudes from nonverbal communication in two channels." *Journal of Consulting Psychology, 31*(3), 248–252.

Mehrabian, A., & Wiener, M. (1967) "Decoding of inconsistent communications." *Journal of Personality and Social Psychology, 6*(1), 109–114.

Mehrabian, A., & Williams, M. (1969)" Nonverbal concomitants of perceived and intended persuasiveness." *Journal of Personality and Social Psychology, 13*(1), 37–58.

Millar, F. E., Rogers, L. E., & Bavelas, J. B. (1984) "Identifying patterns of verbal conflict in interpersonal dynamics." *Western Journal of Speech Communication, 48*, 231–246.

Montagner, H. (1978) *L'Enfant et la communication.* Paris: Aubier.

Müller, K., Kempf, F., & Leukert, S. (2002) "Besser Kollaborieren durch VR? Evaluation einer VR-Umgebung für kollaboratives Lernen." In U. Beck & W. Sommer (eds.), *Learntec, 2002* .Vol. 2, Karlsruhe: Karlsruher Messe- und Kongress-GmbH, pp. 475–482.

Müller, K., Troitzsch, H., & Renkl, A. (2003) "Der Einfluss nonverbaler Signale auf den Kommunikationsprozess in einer kollaborativen virtuellen Umgebung." *Zeitschrift für Medienpsychologie, 15*(1), 24–33.

Murray, P. J. (1997) "A rose by any other name." Retrieved January 22, 2007, from http://www.december.com/cmc/mag/1997/jan/murray.html

Nowak, K. (2001) "Conceptualizing, differentiating and measuring copresence and social presence". Paper presented at the Fourth Annual International Workshop on Presence, Temple, PA., May.

Nowak, K. (2004) "The influence of anthropomorphism and agency on social judgment in virtual environments." *Journal of Computer Mediated Communication, 9*(2).

Nowak, K., & Biocca, F. (1999) "I think there is someone else here with me!: The role of the virtual body in the sensation of co-presence with other humans and artificial intelligences in advanced virtual environments." Paper presented at the Third International Cognitive Technology Conference, San Francisco, CA.

Nowak, K., & Biocca, F. (2003) "The effect of the agency and anthropomorphism on users' sense of telepresence, copresence, and social presence in virtual environments." *Presence: Teleoperators and Virtual Environments, 12*, 2–25.

Page, L. (1980) Perceived values of male and female smiling vs. not smiling. Unpublished manuscript.

Patterson, M. L. (1982) "A sequential functional model of nonverbal exchange." *Psychological Review, 89*(3), 231–249.

Patterson, M. L. (1994) "Strategic functions of nonverbal exchange." In J. A. Daly & J. M. Wiemann (eds.), *Strategic Interpersonal Communication.* Hillsdale, NJ,: Lawrence Erlbaum Associates, pp. 273–293.

Petersen, A. (2002) *Interpersonale Kommunikation im Medienvergleich.* Münster, Germany: Waxmann.

Petersen, A., Bente, G., & Krämer, N. C. (2002) "Virtuelle Stellvertreter: Analyse avatarvermittelter Kommunikationsprozesse." In G. Bente, N. C. Krämer & A. Petersen (eds.), *Virtuelle Realitäten.* Göttingen: Hogrefe, pp. 227–253.

Prasolova-Forland, E. (2002, August) "Supporting awareness in education: Overview and mechanisms." Paper presented at the International Conference on Engineering Education, Manchester, U.K.

Pudowkin, W. I. (1961) *Über die Filmtechnik.* Zürich: Arche.

Rawlins, C. (1989) "The impact of teleconferencing on the leadership of small decisionmaking groups." *Journal of Organizational Behavior Management, 10*(2), 37–52.

Redfern, S., & Naughton, N. (2002) "Collaborative virtual environments to support communication and community in Internet-based distance education." *Journal of Infor-*

mation Technology Education, 1(3), 201–209.

Rice, R. E., & Love, G. (1987) "Electronic emotion: socioemotional content in a computer-mediated communication network." *Communication Research, 14*(1), 85–108.

Riggio, R. E., & Friedman, H. S. (1986) "Impression formation: the role of expressive behavior." *Journal of Personality and Social Psychology, 50*(2), 421–427.

Rime, B. (1983) "Nonverbal communication or nonverbal behavior? towards a cognitive-motor theory of nonverbal behavior." *Current Issues in European Social Psychology, 1*, 85–141.

Rizzolatti, G., Fadiga, L., Matelli, M., Bettinardi, V., Paulesu, E., Perani, D., *et al.* (1996) "Localization of grasp representations in humans with PET. 1. Observation versus execution." *Experimental Brain Research, 11*, 246–252.

Rosenfeld, H. M. (1966) "Approval-seeking and approval-inducing functions of verbal and nonverbal responses in the dyad." *Journal of Personality and Social Psychology, 4*(6), 597–605.

Rutter, D. R., & Stephenson, G. M. (1977) "The role of visual communication in synchronising conversation." *European Journal of Social-Psychology, 7*(1), 29–37.

Rutter, D. R., Stephenson, G. M., Ayling, K., & White, P. A. (1978) "The timing of looks in dyadic conversation." *British Journal of Social and Clinical Psychology, 17*(1), 17–21.

Ruttkay, Z., Doorman, C., & Noot, H. (2002) "Evaluating ECAs—what and how?" Paper presented at the AAMAS02 Workshop on "Embodied conversational agents—let's specify and evaluate them!", Bologna, Italy.

Scheflen, A. E. (1964) "The significance of posture in communication systems." *Psychiatry, 27*, 316–321.

Schlenker, B. R. (1980) *Impression Management: the Self-Concept, Social Identity, and Interpersonal Relations.* Monterey, CA: Brooks/Cole Publishing.

Schneider, D. J., Hastorf, A. H., & Ellsworth, P. C. (1979) *Person Perception*, second edition. Menlo Park, California: Addison-Wesley.

Short, J., Williams, E., & Christie, B. (1976) *The Social Psychology of Telecommunications.* London: Wiley.

Siegel, S. M., Friedlander, M. L., & Heatherington, L. (1992) "Nonverbal relational control in family communication." *Journal of Nonverbal Behavior, 16*(2), 117–139.

Signer, M. (1975) Struktur und Funktion nichtverbaler Kommunikation. Manuskript geschrieben für (und Gewinner des) Lazarus Preis der Universität Bern. Unpublished manuscript.

Slater, M., & Steed, A. J. (2002) "Meeting people virtually: experiments in shared virtual environments." In R. Schroeder (ed.), *The Social Life of Avatars: Presence and Interaction in Shared Virtual Environments.* London: Springer, pp. 146–171.

Sproull, L., & Kiesler, S. (1986) "Reducing social context cues: electronic mail in organizational communication." *Management Science, 32*(11), 1492–1512.

Tanis, M., & Postmes, T. (2007) "Two faces of anonymity: paradoxical effects of cues to identity in CMC." *Computers in Human Behavior, 23*(2), 955–970.

Taylor, M. J., & Rowe, S. M. (2000) "Gaze communication using semantically consistent spaces." Paper presented at the CHI 2000, The Hague, The Netherlands.

Taylor, T. L. (2002) "Living digitally: embodiment in virtual worlds." In R. Schroeder (ed.), *The Social Life of Avatars: Presence and Interaction in Shared Virtual Environments.* London: Springer, pp. 40–62.

Tickle Degnen, L., & Rosenthal, R. (1987) "Group rapport and nonverbal behavior." In Clyde Hendrick (ed.), (1987) *Group Processes and Intergroup Relations.* Thousand Oaks, CA: Sage Publications, pp. 113–136.

Tu, C. H. (2002) "The measurement of social presence in an online learning environment." *International Journal on E Learning, 1*(2), 34–45.

Utz, S. (2000) "Social information processing in MUDs: the development of friendships in virtual worlds." *Journal of Online Behavior, 1*(1).

Wallbott, H. G. (1988) "Faces in context: the relative importance of facial expression and context information in determining emotion attributions." In K. R. Scherer (ed.), *Facets of Emotion: Recent Research*, Hillsdale, NJ: Lawrence Erlbaum Associates, pp. 139–160.

Wallbott, H. G. (1994) "Verhaltensbeobachtung." In R. D. Stieglitz & U. Baumann (eds.), *Psychodiagnostik psychischer Störungen*, Vol. 60, Stuttgart: Enke, pp. 95–106.

Wallbott, H. G. (1995) "Congruence, contagion, and motor mimicry: Mutualities in nonverbal exchange." In I. Markova, C. F. Graumann & K. Foppa (eds.), *Mutualities in Dialogue*. New York: Cambridge University Press, pp. 82–98.

Walther, J. B., Anderson, J. F., & Park, D. W. (1994) "Interpersonal effects in computer-mediated interaction: a meta-analysis of social and antisocial communication." *Communication Research, 21*(4), 460–487.

Walther, J. B., & Burgoon, J. K. (1992) "Relational communication in computer-mediated interaction." *Human Communication Research, 19*(1), 50–88.

Walther, J. B., & Parks, M. R. (2002) "Cues filtered out, cues filtered in: computer-mediated communication and relationships." In I. M. L. Knapp & J. A. Daly (eds.), *Handbook of Interpersonal Communication* third edition, Thousand Oaks, CA: Sage, pp. 529–563.

Walther, J. B., & Tidwell, L. C. (1995) "Nonverbal cues in computer-mediated communication, and the effect of chronemics on relational communication." *Journal of Organizational Computing, 5*(4), 355–378.

Witmer, D. F., & Katzman, S. L. (1997) "On-line smiles: does gender make a difference in the use of graphic accents?" *Journal of Computer Mediated Communication, 2*(4).

Yngve, V. H. (1970) "On getting a word in edgewise." *Proceedings of Chicago Linguistics Society, 6*, 567–577.

Chapter 8

Touch in computer-mediated communication

Margaret McLaughlin, Younbo Jung, Wei Peng, SeungA Jin, and Weirong Zhu

Overview

Touch is a sensory modality fundamental to interpersonal communication. From earliest infancy our experience of the world and our understanding of social context and the character of our relationships with others are shaped by touch. Tactile contact, and the occasions of its display, are governed by a complex, culturally variable set of rules and norms. In particular the impact of touch has been demonstrated to vary widely with relational intimacy and the relative status of interlocutors. Thus what may be welcome in the context of an intimate relationship or between equals may be perceived to be intrusive or patronizing between strangers or in pairs where there is a wide status discrepancy. Although touch is a critical component of the interpretation of interpersonal behavior, its implementation in computer-mediated communication is yet to be realized in any significant way. In this chapter we report on ongoing research, still largely in the laboratory, which seeks to make tactile communication a feature of social interaction over the network. This work, in a field generally referred to as "haptics," involves the sensation of shape and texture a computer user feels when virtually "touching" a digital object (for example, a 3D model of a friend's hand) with a force-feedback device such as a PHANToM stylus or an instrumented CyberGrasp glove. In our laboratory at USC's Integrated Media Systems Center, we have enabled people to experience a sense of mutual touch over the internet, stroking the fingers of a partner at a remote location. We have found that not only are people able to feel the touch of their remote partner, and feel co-present with the partner, but they sometimes make attributions about the partner's personality and character based on the way in which they are touched. We discuss this and related work and speculate about the necessary conditions for the sense of touch to become an everyday component of computer-mediated communication. First, however, we will review relevant literature on the impact of touch on interpersonal communication from its origins in parent–child interaction to its expression in adult relationships in social life and the workplace.

The origins of interpersonal touch: the parent–infant relationship

Touch is the earliest sensory system to develop embryologically (Montagu, 1986) and the most mature sensory system at birth, enabling infants to utilize tactile experience more systematically (Weiss *et al.*, 2004). Further, skin is the largest sensory organ used for sending and receiving touch stimulation (Muir, 2002). Having said that, it is little wonder that touch is one of the most fundamental means of interaction between a parent and a newborn infant. Studies have demonstrated the positive effects of touch on both the sender and receiver sides of parent-infant interaction for such factors as the regulation of arousal in infants (Kisilevsky *et al.*, 1991), their attention and affect (Stack & Muir, 1990, 1992), and their neurodevelopment (Ferber *et al.*, 2005; Weiss *et al.*, 2004), as well as on maternal depression (Ferber, 2004; Glover *et al.*, 2002), and paternal involvement (Cullen *et al.*, 2000).

Studies show both positive and negative effects of touch stimulation on the behavioral and psycho/sociological development of infants, depending on how touch is stimulated. Positive effects of touch include improvement in infants' early growth and development, less depression, and better performance on developmental assessments (Field *et al.*, 2004; Ottenbacher *et al.*, 1987). However, touch stimulation does not always have positive effects on development. Weiss and colleagues (2001) found that harsh touch is significantly related to more externalizing problems by the infants in spite of more frequent touch. In a similar vein, more frequent touch with less response to the caregivers from the infants was found to be related to the risk of infants' developing aggressive and destructive behavior. In spite of the well-known relationship between prematurity and neurodevelopmental handicaps (see Friedman & Sigman, 1992), the findings from various studies indicate that touch-based interaction can improve the neurodevelopment of low birth-weight infants up to the normative range (Ferber *et al.*, 2005; Weiss *et al.*, 2001), which highlights the importance of touch stimulation in early childhood development. These findings emphasize not only the importance of the quality dimension of touch stimulation for the infant's development, but also the communicative functions of touch, in that emotions and other specific information can be transmitted to infants (see Hertenstein, 2002, for a more detailed treatment of the communicative functions of touch).

Touch is reciprocal, and bidirectional stimulation can affect both administrator and receiver. Given the reciprocal characteristics of touch, studies have demonstrated a positive relationship between fathers who gave massages to their infants and their involvement, enjoyment, and feelings of warmth towards their babies (Cullen *et al.*, 2000), and the positive effects of touch-based mother-infant interaction on depressed mothers by increasing the mothers' self-esteem (Field, 1998). To sum up, the literature on touch in infant-caretakers' relationships clearly establishes that touch is one of the earliest and most basic forms of communication (Frank, 1957; Knapp, 1972; Montagu, 1986). As we grow and form additional relationships within and outside the family, touch continues to play an integral role in interpersonal communication (Guerrero & Andersen, 1994; McDaniel & Andersen, 1998). Some scholars, for example Thayer (1986: 12), even argue that "nothing comes closer than touch," acknowledging the considerable power of touch as a nonverbal communicative medium in social, intimate, and sometimes even in instrumental relationships.

Touch in personal relationships in adulthood

Nonverbal involvement is an indicator of the degree of an individual's activity and interest in social interaction (Cegala, 1981). Among the five components constituting nonverbal involvement proposed by Coker and Burgoon (1987), *immediacy* and *expressiveness* are the dimensions particularly relevant to touch. *Immediacy* cues, including close proxemic distancing, direct body orientation, touch, forward lean, and gaze (Guerrero, 1997; Patterson, 1983) indicate psychological and physical proximity, signal availability for communicative behaviors, and increase the level of sensory stimulation (Andersen, 1985). *Expressiveness* refers to the degree of both vocal and kinesic animation manifested by a communicator (Cappella, 1983; Coker & Burgoon, 1987; Guerrero, 1997). Thus, touch is associated with perceived *immediacy* and *expressiveness* in interpersonal communication.

Relatively stable communicator characteristics such as sex (e.g., Hall, 1985, 1990; Major *et al.*, 1990), personality (e.g., Burgoon & Koper, 1984) and relationship variables such as relationship type (e.g., Guerrero, 1997; Guerrero & Andersen, 1991) and relational stage (e.g., McDaniel & Andersen, 1998) have been considered to be important predictors that affect the way and the extent to which people display nonverbal involvement in interpersonal communication (Guerrero, 1997). For example, in an empirical study on nonverbal involvement behaviors of individuals across different types of close relationship (same-sex friend, opposite-sex friend, and romantic partners), Guerrero (1997) hypothesized that romantic relationships were characterized by significantly higher levels of touch and close proximity. Guerrero demonstrated that individuals touched their romantic partners an average of almost three times per 6-minute interaction, thus confirming that touch is an important nonverbal display within romantic dyads compared to other types of relationships. Heslin and Alper (1983) examined the affective response to touch as a function of the intimacy of the relationship between the toucher and the recipient, and the intimacy of the touch. If the relationship between the two persons is very close, as in the case of romantic relationships between lovers, intimate touch will cause no discomfort. On the other hand, for people in nonintimate relationships, such as strangers, the higher the level of intimacy of touch is, the higher the level of expected discomfort is.

Demographic factors, cultural differences (DiBiase & Gunnoe, 2004) and individual communicator characteristics also moderate the relationship stage to influence the display and interpretation of touch in adult romantic relationships. For example, taking both the effects of sex differences and relational stage on touch initiation into account, Guerrero and Andersen (1994) determined that men initiated touch significantly more in casual romantic relationships, yet women initiated touch more in married relationships. With respect to cultural variations in patterns of interpersonal touch, McDaniel & Andersen (1998: 66) confirmed that touch behavior among cross-sex couples varied as a function of nationality, showing that touch scores (number of body parts touched) for Northeast Asian couples were significantly lower than scores for dyads from Southeast Asian, Caribbean-Latin nations, Northern Europe, or the U.S.A. And individual difference factors such as touch avoidance (Andersen, 2005; Andersen & Sull, 1985; Guerrero & Andersen, 1994) may also inhibit or encourage both active touching and passive receipt of touch in couples at various stages of their relationship.

Adults touch in distinct ways when flirting, expressing power, or comforting (Eibl-Eibesfeldt, 1989; Hall et al., 2005). A recent study by Hertenstein et al. (2006) demonstrated that touch communicates distinct emotions: that is, people not only encode various emotions through specific touch behaviors but also decode distinct emotions by merely watching others communicate via touch. Hertenstein et al. concluded that the touch modality is a significant means by which people communicate distinct emotions. In addition to their theoretical contribution to emotional communication through tactile modality, Hertenstein et al. (2006) developed a systematic coding scheme and typology of tactile behavior as well as tools for measuring duration and intensity of tactile expressions that can eventually be applied and utilized for measuring touch in computer-mediated communication.

Touch in the workplace and public settings

Different forms of touch convey complex relational meanings in the organizational/social setting. In the workplace, touch could be interpreted as friendly, affectionate, dominant, condescending, flirtatious, inappropriate, or even harassing. The same type of touch might be perceived differently when it is initiated by people of different gender, age, and attractiveness; between the same or opposite genders; or when there is equality or inequality between actors (Burgoon & Hale, 1984; Lee & Guerrero, 2001). In addition, in actual observations of touch in public settings, gender,

gender asymmetry, age, the relationship between toucher and recipient, and culture also have been shown to moderate the frequency of touching (Dibiase & Gunnoe, 2004; Hall & Veccial, 1990; Major *et al.*, 1990; Remland *et al.*, 1995; Stier & Hall, 1984) and touch avoidance (Remland, 1988).

Burgoon (1991), basing her work on the social meaning model of nonverbal communication (Burgoon & Hale, 1984), investigated seven types of touch depicted in a picture of an organizational setting: a handshake, handholding, a touch to the forearm, an arm around the shoulder, an arm around the waist, a touch to the face, or no touch (control condition). Burgoon found that face touch and handholding were perceived to be the most intimate forms of touch, which implies the relational message themes of affection, immediacy, trust, similarity, equality, and depth. Handshaking conveyed the most formality but also receptivity and trust. In general, compared with nontouch, touch conveys more composure, immediacy, receptivity, trust, affection, similarity, depth, equality, dominance, and informality.

Lee and Guerrero (2001) added two additional touch behaviors—tapping the shoulder in a condescending manner and pushing against the shoulder—to extend Burgoon's (1991) study of types of touch behavior in the workplace. In addition, they used videotaped segments rather than still images. Lee and Guerrero confirmed Burgoon's (1991) finding that face touching is rated as the most affectionate and handshaking is evaluated as the most formal. They also found that face touching is perceived to be the most inappropriate and sexually harassing of the nine types of touch examined.

"Ambiguity of meaning is an inherent element of tactile communication" (Johnson & Edwards, 1991: 43) in the organizational/social setting. The same type of touch might be perceived differently when it is initiated by people of different gender, age, and attractiveness, between the same or opposite genders, or when there is equality or inequality between actors (Burgoon, 1984; Lee & Guerrero, 2001). In addition, in actual observations of touch in public settings, gender, gender asymmetry, age, the relationship between toucher and recipient, and culture also moderated the frequency of touching (Dibiase & Gunnoe, 2004; Hall & Veccial, 1990; Major *et al.*, 1990; Remland *et al.*, 1995; Stier & Hall, 1984) and touch avoidance (Remland, 1988).

Adding the sense of touch to computer-mediated communication

Many of the elements that could enable successful interpersonal communication by way of computer networks are already in place, including the ability to interact through the exchange of text, visual images, sounds, the virtual presence afforded by webcams, and through a host of applications such as email, instant messaging, blogging, newsgroups, online dating and social networking sites. Shared immersive environments with full visual and auditory sensory immersion are a staple of development in media labs around the world. Claims made in the 1980s that computer-mediated communication was too lean or lacking in richness to support formation, development (and even termination) of interpersonal relationships have been largely discredited. While only the most naive enthusiast would propose that the addition of tactile sensing and feedback would uniformly enhance computer-mediated communication or predictably impart "cues" to a medium presumably deficient in them—if in fact additional modalities such as the sense of touch were available to bolster the existing arsenal of digital tools for negotiating interpersonal relationships—certainly we could expect that there might be consequences. Clearly there might be some utility enabling people to collaborate in designing and making objects that require some sort of manual input. But will a robotically rendered handshake enhance a first-time meeting between business associates? If a newly expectant father stationed in Iraq can "stroke" a 3D model of his baby derived from an ultrasound, will that ultimately strengthen the parent-infant bond? What would the implementation of the ability to touch in CMC look like? And what should it look like?

Within the last ten years or so there has been a flurry of activity, first in university and then in commercial laboratories, in the area of so-called "machine haptics." What this term refers to is the use of robotic and other devices to simulate the sense of touch in computer-generated virtual reality or augmented reality environments, some of which are three-dimensional (McLaughlin *et al.*, 2002). You might think of a haptic interface as a sort of input device, like a mouse, which provides feedback to the user as to what objects on the computer display "feel like." A haptic device tracks the hand and finger movements of the user as she/he explores a digital object on a computer screen and detects the "collision" of the model of the user's hand with various digital objects represented in the environment. These devices can be as simple as a mouse which lets the user feel a "bump" when entering or exiting an application window or add greater "drag" to scroll bars and the like. One of the most widely used and researched (and much more costly) of these devices is called the "PHANToM", a stylus or pen-like device which communicates forces back to the user's fingertip which are similar to those that would be experienced if she or he were to touch a similar object in the real world. The sensation is something akin to probing an object with a stick; what the user feels is that his or her forward motion has been stopped by the encounter with the object, and by poking at it with the stick is able to feel its shapes, and contours, and gross textures. Some of the PHANToM devices reproduce the sense of torque at the wrist: that is, how hard you would have to push the object to make it rotate. The three-dimensional effect is enhanced when the user puts on stereoscopic goggles, a head-mounted display, or views the scene on an autostereoscopic display.

Another type of device which is being tested in some laboratories is the CyberGrasp, a unit which consists of an instrumented data glove which tracks the position of the five fingers in the virtual environment, a tracker for the position of the hand and wrist (sometimes built in, and sometimes wireless), and an exoskeletal "grasp" or set of tendons which provide force feedback. The CyberGrasp wearer might reach for a digital object such as a can of soda pop depicted on the computer display and will feel a sensation something like having a solid cylindrical object in his or her palm.

Both of these types of devices can be used to "feel" solid body objects, such as digital vases and teapots which do not yield to the user's touch, and deformable objects, such as soft tissue in surgical simulators or "clay" models in digital sculpture. And different characteristics of surface texture can be simulated. For example, a surface can be made to feel more or less viscous, or more or less slippery.

What the reader should understand about these devices and others like them is that in their current commercial incarnations they generally represent only one component of the sense of touch. They do not usually, for example, create any displacement of the fingertip skin such as would be experienced in exploring fine texture like the feel of velvet (although there are some "vibrotactile" displays which provide this sensation). Further, they do not generally have a thermal component with which to simulate the coolness of marble or the warmth of flesh, although there are some devices still in the laboratory stage which have incorporated thermal feedback.

Applications of haptics have been extensive within a few domains, most notably museum display, scientific visualization, and medical and surgical training. In our lab at USC, for example, we have used haptics to: (1) accompany an exhibition of nineteenth-century daguerreotype cases that we digitized using a 3-D scanner (Lazzari *et al.*, 2003; see also McLaughlin, 2002, McLaughlin *et al.*, 2002); (2) create a system for haptically rendering seismic information about earthquakes in the Los Angeles basin; and (3) create an exercise regimen for patients recovering from stroke (McLaughlin, 2005; McLaughlin, *et al.*, 2005). One of the areas that has received only a limited amount of attention is the use of haptics to reproduce the interpersonal aspects of touch in virtual environments. Where this has occurred the context at which the application ultimately aims has chiefly been one of collaboration, such as facilitating collaborative design of models for rapid prototyping by manufacturers. In the discussion that follows, we focus on efforts to enable hand-to-hand contact. (For an account of other varieties of computer-mediated touch, for example vibrotactile devices for exchanging mood states through a small set of predefined haptic "icons" or pulses, the reader is referred to the excellent review article by Haans and IJsselsteijn [2006].)

Work on collaborative haptics has involved having two users, sometimes at remote locations and sometimes co-located, simultaneously manipulate objects in a shared virtual environment. In an early study, designed with CSCW (computer-supported collaborative work) applications in mind, the in Touch system developed by Brave *et al.* (1998) employed the Synchronized Distributed Physical Objects concept to haptically couple sets of rollers so that persons separated by distance could manipulate the rollers collaboratively and passively feel each other's "touch." Later applications have used joysticks, haptic pens, or gloves. For example, Marsic *et al.* (2000) used the Rutgers force-feedback glove, a device similar to the CyberGrasp described above, to enable distributed navigation, manipulation, and sensing of objects in a simulation of military asset deployment. Basdogan *et al.* (2000) had partners at remote locations engage in cooperative tasks involving joint manipulation of digital objects, such as moving a ring back and forth across a wire without touching the wire. In one of the few studies in which the interpersonal aspects of shared, haptics-enhanced virtual environments were explicitly explored, Basdogan and colleagues measured feelings of co-presence or sense of togetherness of the collaborating partners, reporting that not only performance but also sense of co-presence was positively influenced by the inclusion of haptic as well as visual feedback. Similarly, Sallnas *et al.* (2001) found that haptic feedback improved both performance and sense of presence on a cube manipulation task. Brave *et al.* (2001) found that haptic feedback from a partner in a maze-navigating experiment increased feelings of efficacy and liking for the partner under a competitive but not under a cooperative task orientation. (The "partner" providing feedback was simulated and thus no mutual touch was involved, but we include the study by Brave *et al.* for its focus on the social impact of haptics-enhanced CMC.)

Where our work departs from the studies described above is that in the virtual computer-mediated environments we have designed, we are interested not just in collaborative navigation and object manipulation but in actual *hand-to-hand* physical contact. To that end we have developed an architecture for what we have called "heterogeneous haptic collaboration" (McLaughlin *et al.*, 2002, 2003) which assumes that there may be any number of users logged in to a server from various remote locations, with a variety of different types of haptic device, including the joystick, mouse, pen, and glove-based devices described above. Because the complexity both of haptic devices and the virtual environments and its objects influence the speed with which digital data can be sent over the network, our architecture is based on assigning people to "local groups" based on their connection speed. Leaving aside such technical issues, what may be of most interest about our work to social scientists is that we have been successful, in our early experimenting, in enabling people to touch each other's hands over the internet (McLaughlin *et al.*, 2003).

Figure 8.1(a and b) shows two users at remote locations participating in an experiment on mutual touch. The user in the picture at the top is employing a PHANToM haptic stylus to touch the fingers of the hand model of her fellow interactant, who is at a remote location and wearing a CyberGrasp haptic glove. That is, each computer screen contains two digital objects, one of which is a model of the whole hand of the Cyber-Grasp wearer and the other of which is a model of the fingertip of the PHANToM user (or more precisely, a single point of contact on the fingertip). Contact or collision between the two models results in a sensation of mutual touch. To the person holding the PHANToM, the contact feels as if he or she has encountered resistance from a solid object. To the person wearing the CyberGrasp, the contact can be felt at each individual finger and is experienced as having someone pressing down on the finger.

In our experiments, the paired participants have reported to separate labs and have been instructed in the use of the haptic equipment. They have been told that they will be asked to participate in a game in which one of them will have to guess what words the remote partner is trying to communicate to them through touch. As we explained to the participants, in the game, the letters of the alphabet have been mapped onto the five fingers:

> For example, when your press your partner's thumb once, you are transmitting the letter "A". When you press your partner's index finger four times, it means you are transmitting the letter "Q". The other 24 letters will be transmitted in the same way. You won't have to remember this code, as we will provide it for you on the keypad and also on a piece of paper. Just in case you are unsure, here are the thumb, index, middle, ring, and pinky fingers. (McLaughlin *et al.*, 2003).

In our studies the person wearing the CyberGrasp was the passive recipient of touch; it was his or her job to detect what the three-letter words were that the active partner, the PHANToM user, was trying to communicate through the pattern of taps. The CyberGrasp user's screen was blanked out so that the representation of the two hand/fingertip models was not visible. Thus success in identifying the communicated words was entirely dependent on haptic information. Each pair of participants worked their way through a word list that contained all 26 letters of the alphabet, sorted randomly into nine sets of three- and two-letter words. Participants were told that the words would not necessarily resemble words in English.

At the conclusion of the trials, participants completed a posttask evaluation with items adapted from the Basdogan *et al.* measure of co-presence.

(a)

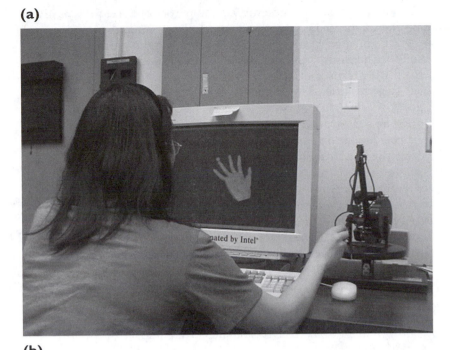

(b)

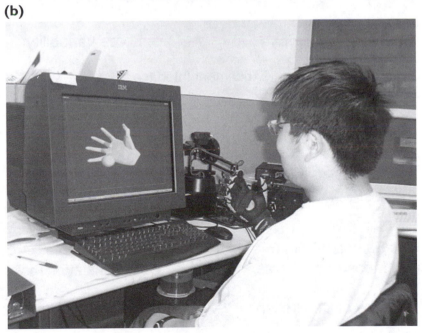

Figure 8.1 (a) User at location 1 uses a PHANToM haptic stylus to touch the fingers of the user at (b) location 2, who is wearing a CyberGrasp haptic glove.

Among the questions of interest: Did the participant feel present in the haptic environment? Did the participant feel co-present with the remote partner? Did the participant believe that the remote partner was a real person? Participants were also asked to make attributions about their partners with respect to standard dimensions of perception (unsocial-social; sensitive-insensitive; impersonal-personal; cold-warm) (Sallnas *et al.*, 2001).

In Figure 8.2 we attempt to summarize some of the relationships that we expected to see emerge between the passive partner's accuracy (success in identifying the location and number of touches) and certain characteristics of the active partner's performance in communicating the information over the network with the PHANToM device. For example, we thought that *greater mean applied force* and *less variability in the application of force* to the passive partner's fingertips would result in that partner's greater accuracy in detecting the location of touch and number of times she or he was touched than weakly applied or inconsistently applied force. And similarly, we thought that if it took the PHANToM user (the active partner) a long time to communicate the words, that is, if *task completion time were longer*, or if there were long "silences" (haptically speaking, this means that there would be *more frequent periods during the sampling of the user's movements when force was not being applied*), this would negatively impact on performance

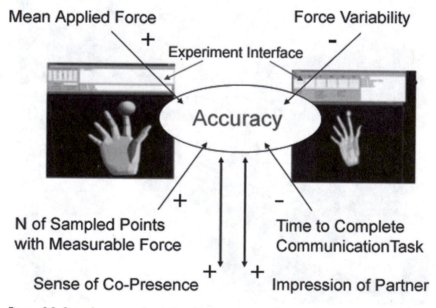

Figure 8.2 Set of proposed relationships among performance accuracy, mean force applied to the partner's fingers, variability in application of force to the partner's fingers (N sampled points measurable force), and task completion time.

accuracy, as the passive partner wearing the CyberGrasp would be left to his or her own devices to figure out what was happening.

With respect to the relationship between accuracy in detecting the location and number of touches and the passive participant's *sense of co-presence* and *impression of the partner*, the earlier literature indicates generally positive relationships, i.e., that greater feelings of co-presence and positivity toward one's partner are associated with higher quality performance, but the causal ordering of the relevant variables is unclear, and these relationships have not been tested in a mutual touch environment. If the person wearing the CyberGrasp is unable to keep his or her hand still, this complicates the task and could render the wearer unlikable to the passive partner while simultaneously increasing within the passive partner the sense of interacting with a real person rather than a computer, and thus increasing the feeling of co-presence. Similarly, firmly applied force on the part of the active partner might increase the sense of co-presence, but might cause the CyberGrasp wearer, the passive partner, to perceive the person applying the force as aggressive or inconsiderate.

Our experiments to date, because of their complexity and overhead, have involved a very small sample of pairs; we are still accumulating data. What we have determined so far is that the fidelity of mutual touch over the internet is still a work in progress. While our participants have been able in about 92 percent of cases to identify which of their fingers is being touched, and in what order, they have had greater difficulty in saying precisely how many times they have been touched, in part because of incidental vibration associated with the haptic glove; further, there is great variability among pairs in how successful they are at task performance. Total performance scores (identifying both the finger touched and the number of times it has been touched) in the study reported in Table 8.1 ranged from a low of 29 percent to a high of 69 percent. The reader can understand the extent to which machine haptics is still a science in its infancy when imagining how deficient a person's real-world haptic senses would be if she were only able to recognize where and how often she had been touched by a partner 29 percent of the time!

Table 8.1 presents performance values for six participant pairs for the number of points at which there was measurable force, mean force, force variability (standard deviation of sampled values), time to task completion, co-presence evaluation by the PHANToM user (active partner), co-presence evaluation by the CyberGrasp wearer (passive partner), and accuracy (percentage of correctly decoded letters). Pairs are presented in ascending order of accuracy. Comparison of the most accurate pair (Pair 6) and least accurate pair (Pair 1) indicates that the more accurate pair had greater mean force and took far less time to complete the task (although taken over all pairs these relationships are not monotonic with respect to task completion time). Comparison of the most and least accurate pairs (Pair 6, Pair 1)

Table 8.1 Performance variables and co-presence ratings for six participant pairs

Pair	N Points measurable force	Mean force	Force S.D.	Task time	Co-presence PHANToM user	Co-presence CyberGrasp user	Accuracy
1	494	0.2788	0.2623	27.40	3.80	3.60	0.269
2	6607	0.2278	0.2501	14.53	1.80	5.50	0.384
3	3688	0.1240	0.1699	19.19	4.60	5.70	0.423
4	467	0.2559	0.2840	15.79	5.00	5.60	0.423
5	693	0.3073	0.2907	23.59	5.10	3.60	0.423
6	458	0.3578	0.3054	12.41	4.90	4.10	0.692

indicated that perceived co-presence was rated higher by the more accurate subjects, by both members of the pair. However, taken over all pairs the relationship between co-presence and accuracy is not monotonic.

With respect to the issue of the relationship between task performance and sense of co-presence, our preliminary data indicate that there was in fact little relationship. The strongest obtained relationship was counterintuitive: as the number of points of measurable force increased (the number of sampled points at which the active partner using the PHANToM was touching the passive partner's hand), the active partner's sense of co-presence *decreased* ($r = -.818$, $p < .05$), but this effect is based on a very small number of cases and may be heavily influenced by one or two outliers. Many of our participants experienced a strong sense of co-presence, particularly the CyberGrasp wearers (the passive partner), and none expressed the belief when probed that his or her partner had been a "bot" or programmed computer as opposed to a real person.

The impression formation data showed little variability and in fact most users refrained from making attributions about the remote partner, although the anecdotal reports during debriefing indicated that partners who applied very strong force, couldn't hold their hands still, or who used inconsistent force with long periods of inactivity were disliked and complained about by their partners. This is consistent with the infant-parent literature on aversive affects associated with dysfunctional patterns of touch.

Given that it is in fact technically possible to create a sense of mutual touch in a network environment, albeit with a considerable lack of fidelity in some cases, what are the long-term prospects for integrating touch into computer-mediated communication?

The future of touch in computer-mediated environments

Currently there are a few computer and cell phone games commercially available that are enhanced with very low-level, two-dimensional haptics, implemented with inexpensive buzzers, vibrators, and joysticks. 2D devices have had a certain success in games, but efforts to promote them as alternative input devices to the standard mouse, for example, have not met with overwhelming success, despite the fact that they have retailed for less than $100.00 and sometimes quite a bit less. But what are the prospects for the eventual implementation of high-fidelity simulated touch in computer-mediated communication? At the present time, there are some significant barriers. The high-end devices, due to their cost (in the tens of thousands) and the need to invest many hours in learning how to use them, will remain largely in the hands of scientists and academics for the next dozen years or so, although there appear to be some early niche adoptions among designers and artists. One of the leading makers of these devices has recently offered a version of its flagship product at significantly reduced cost, but the high-fidelity 3D devices are out of reach for consumers at this time and it is unlikely that they will reach the point of mass adoption any time soon.

In addition to the cost of the high-end devices, and their limitations as discussed earlier, in particular the lack of integration of vibrotactile and thermal sensing into the commercially available force-feedback devices, there is the issue of bandwidth. Haptics-enhanced virtual environments generate a large amount of data owing to the constant demands of collision detection, force feedback generation, and continual refreshing of the visual display. Sampling rates must be very high to provide high-quality force feedback. Consequently, there can be serious lag or delay in networked haptic communication and its accompanying visuals. The effect can be something like seeing your hand reach for a coffee cup but not feeling it as a solid object in your palm at the same time that your eyes tell you that you have grasped it. One company, Handshake VR, currently makes a toolkit which enables development of mutual touch applications for the PHANToM device. The developers report that they have an effective solution for dealing with the latency problems that have been a major stumbling block. And we have described earlier our architecture which attempts to address such issues as latency and variations in the speed of users' network connections. But again, these are solutions that will continue to undergo testing and refinement in the laboratory for several years to come.

There are also barriers that are not technical but social or societal in nature. While many people can readily accept the idea of adding force-feedback haptics to first-person shooter games, for example, to add more realism to the simulated mayhem, they may balk at the idea that people could touch one another over the internet because of concerns that it might be used by purveyors of pornography or other even less savory pursuits to simulate intimate relations. Indeed at one time one of the device makers did create a whole-body haptic suit. But given the cumbersome and limited nature of the devices (most of us would prefer not to be poked at with a stick or have our fingers pressed backwards), not to speak of a general lack of will in the developer community to devote their resources to such applications, this outcome seems highly unlikely. Nonetheless it is a specter which may at some level have encouraged haptics developers to put their energies into museum display and surgical simulations rather than interpersonal touch.

Appropriate applications of machine haptics: Learning from the literature on human touch

As haptic devices continue to be refined, come down in price, and find a consumer user base through low-level interfaces to commercial games for PC and cell phone, some of the barriers noted above may become less formidable. If so, there are a number of lessons to be learned from the human touch literature which researchers and developers would be wise to consider. One of these is that not all touch is welcome, and not all touch is perceived in the same way. Studies of caregiver-infant interaction indicate that touch which is too forceful may be aversive, and touch which is inconsistent, infrequent, insufficiently firm, or unreciprocated may not have a positive emotional impact. Similarly, the extent to which touch is welcome is a function of relationship type, relational intimacy, relationship stage, and various demographic factors, and in both its utilization and interpretation is subject to a host of cultural differences which mitigate against its use in certain contexts or for certain applications. Of critical importance is the variable of relational symmetry and the appropriateness of touch in situations where partners differ with respect to power, control, and relational investment. And even in situations in which interlocutors are peers, for example in a distributed work group, there may be few occasions where virtual collaboratories would be enhanced by the addition of haptics for mutual touch, other than a perfunctory handshake, although it might be included for visualization of large data sets or enabling cooperative design. On the other hand, there are certain kinds of relationship in which there is a great deal of relational asymmetry, for example patient-provider interactions, in which the ability to touch, perhaps to offer hand-over-hand guidance in physical therapy, would be welcome and entirely appropriate.

Finally, it is useful to recall that touch takes a variety of forms, some of which (hand-holding, hand-shaking) may be comparatively less difficult to simulate and deploy in appropriate applications, and others of which (enclosure forms of touch such as arm around the shoulder, arm around the waist) are not likely to be effectively simulated in the near term owing to the complexity of the other senses involved including the pliancy of tissue, the scent and warmth of the other, and the large scale of the simulation area. Thus in the short term and for the foreseeable future long-distance sweethearts may have to content themselves with what our great-grandfathers once found so gratifying: holding hands.

Acknowledgments

The research reported here has been funded (or funded in part) by the Integrated Media Systems Center, a National Science Foundation Engineering Research Center, Cooperative Agreement No. EEC-9529152. Any opinions, findings and conclusions or recommendations expressed in this material are those of the author(s) and do not necessarily reflect those of the National Science Foundation.

References

Andersen, P. A. (1985) "*Nonverbal immediacy in interpersonal communication.*" In A. W. Siegman & S. Feldstein (eds.), *Multichannel Integration of Nonverbal Behavior.* Hillsdale, NJ: Erlbaum, pp.1–36.

Andersen., P. A. (2005) "The touch avoidance measure." In V. Manusov (eds.), *The Sourcebook of Nonverbal Measures: Going Beyond Words.* Mahwah, NJ: Lawrence Erlbaum, pp. 57–65.

Andersen, P. A., & Sull, K. K. (1985) "Out of touch, out of reach: Tactile predispositions as predictors of interpersonal distance." *Western Journal of Speech Communication, 49*(1), 57–72.

Basdogan, C., Ho, C., Srinivasan, M. A., & Slater, M. (2000) "An experimental study on the role of touch in shared virtual environments." *ACM Transactions on Computer Human Interaction, 7*(4), 443–460.

Brave, S., Ishii, H., & Dahley, A. (1998) "Tangible interface for remote collaboration and communication." *Proceedings of CSCW '98.*

Brave, S., Nass, C., & Sirninian, E. (2001) "Force-feedback in computer-mediated communication." In C. Stephanidis (ed.), *Universal Access in HCI: Towards an Information Society for All,* vol 3., Hillsdale, NJ: Lawrence Erlbaum.

Burgoon, J. K. (1991) "Relational message interpretations of touch, conversational distance, and posture." *Journal of Nonverbal Behavior, 15*, 233–259.

Burgoon, J. K., & Hale, J. L. (1984) "The fundamental topoi of relational communication." *Communication Monographs, 51*, 193–214.

Burgoon, J. K., & Koper, R. J. (1984) "Nonverbal and relational communication associated with reticence." *Human Communication Research, 10*, 601–626.

Cappella, J. N. (1983) "Conversational involvement: approaching and avoiding others." In J. M. Wiemann & R. P. Harrison (eds.), *Nonverbal interaction,* Beverly Hills, CA: Sage, pp. 39–68.

Cegala, D. J. (1981) "Interaction involvement: a cognitive dimension of communicative competence." *Communication Education, 30*, 109–121.

Coker, D. A., & Burgoon, J. K. (1987) "The nature of conversational involvement and nonverbal encoding patterns." *Human Communication Research, 13*, 463–494.

Cullen, C., Field, T., Escalona, A., & Hartshorn, K. (2000) "Father-infant interactions are enhanced by massage therapy." *Early Child Development and Care, 164*, 41–47.

Dibiase, R., & Gunnoe, J. (2004) "Gender and culture differences in touching behavior." *The Journal of Social Psychology, 144*, 49–62.

Eibl-Eibesfeldt, I. (1989) *Human Ethology.* Hawthorne, NY: Aldine de Gruyter.

Emmers, T. M., & Dindia, K. (1995) "The effect of relational stage and intimacy on touch:

An extension of Guerrero and Andersen." *Personal Relationships, 2,* 225–236.

Ferber, S. G. (2004) "The nature of touch in mothers experiencing maternity blues: The contribution of parity". *Early Hunan Development, 79,* 65–75.

Ferber, S. G., Feldman, R., Kohelet, D., Kuint, J., Dollberg, S., Arbel, E., *et al.* (2005) "Massage therapy facilitates mother-infant interaction in premature infants." *Infant Behavior and Development, 28,* 74–81.

Field, T. (1998) "Early interventions for infants of depressed mothers." *Pediatrics, 102,* 1305–1310.

Field, T., Hernandez-Reif, M., Vera, Y., Gil, K., Diego, M., Bendell, D., & Yando, R. (2004) "Anxiety and anger effects on depressed mother-infant interactions." *Infant Behavior and Development, 31,* 109–114.

Frank, L. K. (1957) "Tactile communication." *Genetic Psychology Monographs, 56,* 209–225.

Friedman, S., & Sigman, M. (1992) *The Psychological Development of Low Birth Weight Children.* Norwood, NJ: Ablex.

Glover, V., Onozawa, K., & Hodgkinson, A. (2002) "Benefits of infant massage for mothers with postnatal depression." *Semin Neonatol, 7,* 495–500.

Guerrero, L. K. (1997) "Nonverbal involvement across interactions with same-sex friends, opposite-sex friends, and romantic partners: Consistency or change?" *Journal of Social and Personal Relationships, 14*(1), 31–58.

Guerrero, L. K., & Andersen, P. A. (1991) "The waxing and waning of relational intimacy: Touch as a function of relational stage, gender, and touch avoidance." *Journal of Social and Personal Relationship, 8,* 147–165.

Guerrero, L. K., & Andersen, P. A. (1994) "Patterns of matching and initiation: Touch behavior and touch avoidance across romantic relationship stages." *Journal of Nonverbal Behavior, 18*(2), 137–153.

Haans, A., & IJisselsteijn, W. A., (2006) "Mediated social touch: A review of current research and future directions." *Virtual Reality 9,* 149–159.

Hall, J. A. (1985) "Male and female behavior." In A. W. Siegman & S. Feldstein (eds.), *Multichannel Integrations of Nonverbal Behavior.* Hillsdale, NJ: Erlbaum.

Hall, J. A., & Veccial, E. M. (1990) "More 'touching' observations: new insights on men, women, and interpersonal touch." *Journal of Personality and Social Psychology, 59,* 1155–1162.

Hall, J. A., Coats, E. J., & LeBeau, L. S. (2005) "Nonverbal behavior and the vertical dimension of social relations: a meta-analysis." *Psychological Bulletin, 131*(6), 898–924.

Henley, N. M. (1973) "Status and sex: some touching observations". *Bulletin of the Psychonomic Society, 2,* 91–93.

Henley, N. M. (1977) *Body Politics: Power, Sex and Nonverbal Communication.* Englewood Cliffs, NJ: Prentice-Hall.

Hertenstein, M. J. (2002) "Touch: Its communicative functions in infancy." *Human Development, 45,* 70–94.

Hertenstein, M. J., Keltner, D., App, B., Bulleit, B. A., & Jaskolka, A. R. (2006) "Touch communicates distinct emotions." *Emotion, 6*(3), 528–533.

Heslin, R., & Alper, T. (1983) "Touch: A bonding gesture." In J. M. Wiemann & R. P. Harrison (eds.), *Nonverbal interaction.* Beverly Hills: Sage, pp.47–75

Johnson, K. L., & Edwards, R. (1991) "The effects of gender and type of romantic touch." *Journal of Nonverbal Behavior, 15,* 43–55.

Kisilevsky, B. S., Stack, D. M.,& Muir, D.W. (1991) "Fetal and infant response to tactile stimulation." In M. J. Weiss & P. R. Zelazo (eds.), *Newborn Attention: Biological Constraints and the Influence of Experience.* Norwood, NJ: Ablex, pp. 63–98.

Knapp, M. L. (1972) *Nonverbal Communication in Human Interaction.* New York: Holt, Rinehart, and Winston.

Lazzari, M., Francois, A., McLaughlin, M. L., Jaskowiak, J., Wong, W. L., Akbarian, M., Peng, W., & Zhu, W. (2003) "Using haptics and a 'virtual mirror' to exhibit museum objects with reflective surfaces." *Proceedings of the 11th International Conference on Advanced Robotics*.

Lee, J. W., & Guerrero, L. K. (2001) "Types of touch in cross-sex relationships between coworkers: Perceptions of relational and emotional messages, inappropriateness, and sexual harassment." *Journal of Applied Communication Research, 29*(3), 197–220.

Major, B., Schmidlin, A. M., & Williams, L. (1990) "Gender patterns in social touch: The impact of setting and age." *Journal of Personality and Social Psychology, 58*(4), 634–643.

Marsic, I., Medl, A., & Flanagan, J. (2000) "Natural communication with information systems." *Proceedings of the IEEE, 88*(8), 1354–1366.

McDaniel, E., & Andersen, P. A. (1998) "International patterns of interpersonal tactile communication: A field study." *Journal of Nonverbal Behavior, 22*(1), 59–75.

McLaughlin, M. L. (2002) *Haptic museum*. National Science Foundation Project Report, Integrated Media Systems Center, University of Southern California, Los Angeles.

McLaughlin, M. L. (2005) "Simulating the sense of touch in virtual environments: Applications in the health sciences." In P. Messaris & L. Humphreys (eds.), *Digital Media: Transformations in Human Communication*. New York: Peter Lang Publishers.

McLaughlin, M. L., Hespanha, J., & Sukhatme, G. (2002) *Touch in Virtual Environments: Haptics and the Design of Interactive Systems*. Upper Saddle River, NJ: Prentice-Hall.

McLaughlin, M., Rizzo, A., Jung, Y., Peng, W., Yeh, S., Zhu, W., and the USC/UT Consortium for Interdisciplinary Research (2005) *Haptics-Enhanced Virtual Environments for Stroke Rehabilitation*. IPSI 2005, Cambridge, MA.

McLaughlin, M. L., Sukhatme, G., Hespanha, J., Shahabi, C., & Ortega, A. (2000) "Touch in immersive environments." *Proceedings of the EVA 2000 Conference on Electronic Imaging and the Visual Arts*, Edinburgh, Scotland.

McLaughlin, M. L., Sukhatme, G., Peng, W., Zhu, W., & Parks, J. (2002) "An experimental study of performance and presence in heterogeneous haptic collaboration: Some preliminary findings." *Proceedings of the Seventh Phantom User's Group Workshop*. Santa Fe, New Mexico.

McLaughlin, M. L, Sukhatme, G., Peng, W., Zhu, W., & Parks, J. (2003) "Performance and co-presence in heterogeneous haptic collaboration." *Proceedings of IEEE VR 2003*.

Montagu, A. (1986) *Touching: the Human Significance of the Skin*, third edition. New York: Harper and Row.

Muir, D. W. (2002) "Adult communications with infants through touch: The forgotten sense." *Human Development, 45*, 95–99.

Ottenbacher, K. J., Muller, L., Brandt, D., Heintzelman, A., Hojem, P., & Sharpe, P. (1987) "The effectiveness of tactile stimulation as a form of early intervention: A quantitative evaluation." *Journal of Developmental and Behavioral Pediatrics, 8*, 68–76.

Patterson, M. L. (1983) *Nonverbal Behavior: A Functional Perspective*. New York: Springer-Verlag.

Remland, M. S. (1988) "Cultural and sex differences in touch avoidance." *Perceptual and Motor Skills, 67*, 544–546.

Remland, M. S., Jones, T. S., & Brinkman, H. (1995) "Interpersonal distance, body orientation, and touch: Effects of culture, gender, and age." *The Journal of Social Psychology, 135*, 281–297.

Sallnas, E. L., Rassmus-Grohn, K., & Sjostrom, C. (2001) "Supporting presence in collaborative environments by haptic force feedback." *ACM Transactions on Computer-Human Interaction, 7*(4), 461–476.

Stack, D. M., & Muir, D. W. (1990). "Tactile simulation as a component of social interchange: New interpretations for the still-face effect." *British Journal of Developmental Psychology, 8*, 131–145.

Stack, D. M., & Muir, D. W. (1992). "Adult tactile simulation during face-to-face interactions modulates five-month-old's affect and attention." *Child Development, 63*(6), 1509–1525.

Stier, D. S., & Hall, J. A. (1984) "Gender differences in touch: an empirical and theoretical review." *Journal of Personality and Social Psychology, 47,* 440–459.

Thayer, S. (1986) "History and strategies of research on social touch." *Journal of Nonverbal Behavior, 10,* 12–27.

Tronick, E. Z. (1995) "Touch in mother–infant interaction." In T. M. Field (eds.), *Touch in Early Development.* Mahwah, NJ: Erlbaum, pp. 53–65.

Weiss, S. J., Wilson, P., & Morrison, D. (2004). "Maternal tactile simulation and the neurodevelopment of low birth weight infants." *Infancy, 5*(1), 85–101.

Weiss, S. J., Wilson, P., Seed, M., & Paul, S. M. (2001) "Early tactile experience of low birth weight children: links to later mental health and social adaptation." *Infant and Child Development, 10*(3), 93–115.

Chapter 9

Parasocial interactions and paracommunication with new media characters

Tilo Hartmann*

Contemporary research on mediated interpersonal communication is motivated by the spread of new media applications in the domain of human-human interaction (e.g., video chats or massive multiplayer online role-playing games, MMORPGs) and in human-computer interaction (e.g., communication to chatter bots or other intelligent agents; see Polkosky, this volume). While users are able to interact with numerous media characters in the emerging field of new media technologies, some types of conventional mass communication, especially television and radio, also display considerable similarities and affinity to already known interpersonal communications. The concept of parasocial interaction, introduced by Horton and Wohl (1956), belongs to the earliest theoretical approaches making connections between mass communication and interpersonal-social settings. Their foundational observation was that real people in the media direct their social and communicative behavior towards the anticipated audience, much as they would for actual interpersonal communication. They greet, wink, gaze, and direct communication acts toward the audience in many ways. The viewers, in turn, may respond to such social behavior "just like" they would if the media character was actually in their living room instead of merely appearing there on the TV screen or the radio. This seemingly "conversational give-and-take" (Horton & Wohl, 1956: 186) between a mass media performer and a user, which closely resembles interpersonal communication (Cathcart & Gumpert, 1983), has been termed "parasocial interaction" (e.g., Giles, 2002; Rubin et al., 1985; Klimmt et al., 2006; see next section).

The concept of parasocial interactions originated in the 1950s, ahead of ubiqituous interactive computer technology. Consequently, Horton and Wohl's (1956) account of parasocial interactions focused primarily on nonfictional mass media performers, such as newscasters, that were typical in this period. As psychological knowledge about the social perception of mediated characters was virtually non-existent, their concept, although of great analytical depth, necessarily built on vague assumptions. With the advent of new media technologies, a growing number of researchers started to analyze how users perceive and interact with mediated social entities. In addition, the variety of "available" media characters increased dramatically. Surprisingly, the concept of parasocial interactions was barely picked up and adapted to these trends.

Therefore, the purpose of the present chapter is to examine how parasocial interaction theory can be adapted for new types of mediated interpersonal communication. This task is promising because much knowledge from conventional research can then be used to describe and explain phenomena related to the newer modes of mediated interpersonal communication that involve digital social entities. However, the application of parasocial interaction theory is a challenge because new media characters (and, in turn, the way users interact with them) differ from the original mass media personalities in three related aspects:

1   Character perception vs. communication: While many would agree that new media characters allow for a form of interpersonal communication, it seems less intuitive that parasocial interactions with mass media personalities also resemble interpersonal communication. One could ask how an interaction should be possible at all in unidirectional mass media settings. Accordingly, one could rather think of parasocial interactions as simple perceptions of mass media characters that have little in common with interpersonal communication.

2   Nonreciprocity: Many new media characters are able to react to users' input. They often talk back. Traditional mass media characters, in contrast, provide no feedback. Accordingly, many regard parasocial interactions as a playful and carefree social involvement. It might be argued that, in contrast, the interactive conversation with new media characters is characterized by a stronger adherence to norms (cf., Reeves & Nass, 1996).

3   Authenticity: Whereas there is little doubt about the reality status of a newscaster or a radio host, computer engineers still work towards portraying sufficiently authentic digital characters, especially, when they are autonomous agents (cf. Bente *et al.*, 2001; Dehn & van Mulken, 2000; Polkosky, this volume). Mass media personalities may often appear to be more authentic than new media characters. Accordingly, one could argue that they allow for a different social involvement than many new media characters.

In sum, the original concept of parasocial interactions primarily relates to users' playful involvement with mass media characters that are both authentic and noninteractive. Therefore, to apply parasocial interaction theory to mediated interpersonal communication with new media characters, the three differences highlighted above need to be discussed. After a short review of parasocial interaction theory, I will first highlight that parasocial interactions with non-interactive mass media performers may sometimes resemble mediated interpersonal communication, what can be called "paracommunication." Second, I will argue that, in contrast to the original notion, playful paracommunication is not solely bound to noninteractive settings, but that the user's perceived distance from the character is key. Third, I suggest that mediated characters need to be perceived as authentic enough to foster paracommunication. Less authentic characters might only lead to simple (and often automatic) parasocial reactions.

A review of parasocial interaction theory

The term "parasocial interactions" was coined by Horton and Wohl (1956). They were puzzled that during media exposure characters like anchormen or show hosts adjusted their performance to an anticipated audience, so that the audience would feel directly addressed and integrated into a social situation. "Parasocial interaction resembles personal interaction in that one party [the media performer] appears to address the other(s) directly, adjusting his course of action to the latter's responses. Insofar as the other [the user] responds as suggested, he may experience the encounter as immediate, personal, and reciprocal, but these qualities are illusory and are presumably not shared by the speaker" (Horton & Strauss, 1957: 580). From a dyadic perspective, then, parasocial interactions are asymmetrical interactions (Jones & Gerard, 1967) that occur during an episode of media use. Originally, they were regarded as a specific illusion of conversational give-and-take between a user and a performer in the mass media. However, some of the later approaches broadened the concept to any kind of social interaction with mediated characters (Giles, 2002; Hartmann et al., 2004). Also, later approaches tried to highlight the psychological processes of the individual is perceiving a media character. From these perspectives, parasocial interactions are regarded as tantamount to any processes of character perception and elaboration that result in "inner" or behavioral reactions during media exposure (the term "interaction" might be misleading and could be replaced by the phrase "parasocial processing" cf. Giles, 2002; Gleich, 1997; Hartmann et al., 2004; Klimmt et al., 2006; see "impression and perception," Hoffner & Cantor, 1991: 63). Parasocial processes might remain as elusive automatic reactions. Depending on the style of the encountered character and the nature of the social situation, however, they might also involve more complex processes of interpersonal communication (e.g., role-taking, Kelley et al., 1974; see Polkosky, this volume).

Horton and Wohl (1956: 185) argue that by a user's "as if" interactions with media personalities *parasocial relationships* develop, which they characterize as a "seeming face-to-face relationship between spectator and performer." Since this original formulation, many researchers have used the terms "parasocial interaction" and "parasocial relationships" interchangeably (e.g., Rubin & McHugh, 1987: 280). From this view, parasocial relationships resemble a long-term involvement (or interaction) with a media character (e.g., Rosengren et al., 1976). Recent conceptualizations call for a clear analytical and empirical distinction of interactions with a character during an exposure situation on the one hand (i.e., parasocial interactions), and (positive or negative) cognitive and affective enduring bonds to a media character on the other (i.e., parasocial relationships; Giles, 2002; Klimmt et al., 2006; Krotz, 1996a; Schramm et al., 2002). Following this notion, many researchers have studied (positive) parasocial relationships instead of parasocial interactions in the past (e.g., Grant et al., 1991; Perse & Rubin, 1989; Rubin et al., 1985; Vorderer, 1996). Most of the measurements that exist so far also measure parasocial relationships (e.g., the popular "parasocial interaction scale" that assesses aspects of a positive relationship; Rubin et al.,1985; for exceptions see Auter & Palmgreen, 2000; Gleich, 1997). Related research has shown that parasocial relationships resemble real-world relationships in many ways. For example, they develop in a similar fashion (Cole & Leets, 1999; Perse & Rubin, 1989; Rubin & McHugh, 1987). Also, they seem to build on similar determinants. For example, a recent meta-analysis (Schiappa et al., 2007) shows that parasocial relationships gain intensity if users perceive a character similar to themselves. Although weaker, parasocial relationships may sometimes approximate real social relationships in their breadth of relational qualities (e.g., intimacy, trust, passion, etc.; Gleich, 1997). Consequently the break-up of parasocial relationships may be felt as a loss (Eyal & Cohen, 2006).

Research on parasocial relationships made important findings, but conceptualizations of how social entities in the media are perceived, or models of parasocial interactions as a psychological process during exposure, are still rare. Uses-and-gratification researchers, for example, simply considered parasocial interactions as gratification obtained by certain media formats (e.g., Palmgreen et al., 1980). Studies on parasocial interactions during an episode of exposure also barely exist (e.g., Auter, 1992; Auter & Palmgreen, 2000; Hartmann & Klimmt, 2005; Schiappa et al., 2005). A couple of researchers tried to shed more light on the psychology of parasocial interactions (cf., Hartmann et al., 2004; Wulff, 1996a; see for similar notions Cohen, 2001; Hoffner & Cantor, 1991). In addition, some scholars refer to the original ideas of Horton and Wohl (1956) by grounding their approaches on the asymmetrical nature of parasocial interactions (Cohen, 2001; Ellis et al., 1983; Hippel, 1993; Krotz, 1996a; Schramm et al., 2002; Vorderer & Knobloch, 1996). The following discussion refers to both perspectives in order to adapt parasocial interaction theory to new media characters.

Paracommunication

It might be argued that parasocial interactions have nothing in common with mediated interpersonal communication. If so, it could be a futile endeavour to try to adapt parasocial interaction theory. However, parasocial interactions, especially in their original definition (Horton & Wohl, 1956), share many similiarities with interpersonal communication (Krotz, 1996b).

Communication automatically arises if two social entities become aware of each other (Watzlawick *et al.*, 1967). An observer feels drawn into a communicational situation if the perceived behavioral expression of the other social entity is taken as a symbolic/meaningful and rather intentionally performed action (Hartley, 1999; Knapp & Miller, 1985; Littlejohn, 1999). "Symbolic/meaningful" implies the subjective assumption that the observed behavior was not solely carried out for "non-social, functional matters" (e.g., reaching out the hand to grab an object, Sperber & Wilson, 1995). "Intentional" implies that the observer assumes that the behavior was carried out voluntarily, consciously, and building on a free will (cf., Sperber & Wilson, 1995; "intentional stance", Mar & Macrae, 2006). In general, then, if users perceive a character to be authentic (i.e., autonomous, intelligent, etc.) enough to perform intended meaningful behaviour, they can feel addressed. If they believe that the other is more or less aware of—or at least anticipates—their reactions, users might react to the character in a specific way that resembles interpersonal communication. Parasocial encounters with an "authentic and aware" media character, then, can be regarded as a type of communication, as they build on mutual awareness and include symbolic behaviour (see Polkosky, this volume). In order to distinguish these more complex parasocial interactions from simple social reactions to media characters, I shall refer to them by the term "paracommunication" (Krotz, 1996b) throughout the remainder of the chapter. Paracommunication, then, is considered as a specific type of parasocial interaction. Paracommunication is likely if users think that the mediated character performs symbolic behaviour towards them and is aware of or at least anticipates their social reactions. If these requirements are not met, the parasocial interaction might take more simple forms, like (automatic or elaborate) processes known from person perception (Fiske *et al.*, 1999).

It can be argued that paracommunication can occur in new interactive environments, but also in traditional mass media settings. Artificially intelligent computer characters, for example, are able to establish eye contact with the user, to address him or her in many other ways, and to provide some feedback (Colburn *et al.*, 2000). Thus they potentially create an illusion of mutual awareness and symbolic behaviour. Traditional mass media characters, in turn, often address their anonymous audience directly by means of talk (e.g., "hello", "good evening, listeners") or gesture (i.e. body direction, gaze; Cummins & Bradford, 2005; Giles 2002: 294) as well. And even if characters do not talk to or look at an audience directly, users can still feel addressed. Mikos (1996) argues that media resembles a public stage. Characters that enter the stage are aware of their public presence. Media performers adapt their behavior "in front of the camera" to an anticipated audience (cf. reciprocal effects; Lang & Lang, 1953). Therefore, any behavior displayed on public media could inherently address people. If audience members know about this aspect, they could feel like being part of a communicational situation whenever they encounter a character in the media. Thus, even if a television character, for example, does not address the audience directly, but just talks to other characters on the screen, users could still feel like co-viewers or co-listeners that are joining a paracommunicational setting (cf. Bavelas *et al*, 2000; Horton & Wohl, 1957; Hippel, 1993; Wulff, 1996a).

In sum, it can be argued that both new media characters as well as traditional mass media performers hold the potential to establish paracommunication through modes of direct and indirect address and the display of symbolic behaviour. In this respect, parasocial interaction theory might share many similiarities with a general conceptualization of mediated interpersonal communication, including applications to new media characters.

Playful paracommunication

Traditionally, many researchers define paracommunications, respectively parasocial interactions, by their asymmetrical nature (Ellis *et al.*, 1983; Hippel, 1993; Horton & Wohl, 1956; Krotz, 1996a; Vorderer & Knobloch, 1996; Wulff, 1996a). As Horton and Wohl (1956: 215) state, "the crucial difference in experience obviously lies in the lack of effective reciprocity." The basic argument is that mass media characters can only anticipate the audience, but are actually not aware of it. Thus, they might create the illusion of a mutual awareness, while in fact they are blind to the users' reactions. For many, this aspect defines the nature of paracommunication (e.g., Cohen, 2001; Hippel, 1993; Horton & Strauss, 1957; Horton & Wohl, 1956; Vorderer & Knobloch, 1996; Wulff, 1996a). It enables users to freely dwell on or doubt the illusion of mutual awareness. Accordingly, for many, the prefix "para" in parasocial communication stands for the playful "as if" nature of the social encounter (Wulff, 1996b).

In general, communication involves expectations about how the other will react (Burgoon & Le Poire, 1993). Often, these expectations follow context-based rules or norms (Bennet & Bennet, 1970). Thus, reactions can be appropriate (according to a norm) or inappropriate (violating a norm). In a similar fashion, the symbolic behaviour of media characters comes with what Horton and Wohl (1956: 191) called an "appropriate answering role." A comedian, for example, who tells a joke to an anonymous audience expects an answering role of "finding the joke funny" or of "feeling entertained." Due to the playful "as if nature" of parasocial communication, users are absolutely free to accept the answering role or to reject it (playful "role-taking", Horton & Wohl, 1956: 193; Cohen, 2006). Thus, media characters might create a carefree "social playground" for users. With so many characters available in the media at any given time, users can select from an abundant choice of response roles that they can enact playfully. Some of the roles might match the self-image of the users, but move beyond the ones available in real life (e.g., to accompany a party of female heroes who save the world; Cohen, 2006). Some roles that are accepted could be "inappropriate" in real life (e.g., an emancipated female passionately admiring a male hero with a macho personality). Still other roles might be rejected, merely to enjoy the experience that follows from such a rejection (e.g., by beneficial social comparisons; see Vorderer, 1996).

One could argue, then, that paracommunication is genuinely distinct from "typical" interpersonal communication, since it provides addressees with an unusual freedom to react to a conversational offer without having to care about any consequences. Accordingly, one could argue, that parasocial interaction theory contributes little to describing interactive conversations with new media characters which do take into account the reaction of a user. It might have even less to say about mediated interpersonal communication with natural persons. For example, real interactions are more likely to call for a committed behavior that is obliged to follow norms (Rimal & Real, 2003), whereas paracommunication is inherently playful (cf. Hippel, 1993; see Hoorn & Konijn, 2003: 251; Oatley & Mar, 2005; Ohler & Nieding, 2006). Also, as distinct to real interactions, the rejection of "answering roles" or other expectations does not lead to any sanctions. While in face-to-face interaction people are sometimes urged to suppress emotions and other behavioral expressions (Richards & Gross, 1999), users would have fewer reasons to express emotions or thoughts throughout paracommunication (cf., Vorderer & Knobloch, 1996). In sum, if a "lack of reciprocity" and the resulting playful opportunities are considered as defining aspects (Horton & Wohl, 1956; Hippel, 1993; Vorderer & Knobloch, 1996), the applicability of parasocial interaction theory to conversations with new media characters could be questioned.

However, in the light of the differences addressed, paracommunication could just be considered as a specific type of mediated interpersonal communication. Instead of "nonreciprocity," I would suggest that it is actually the perceived inability of the character to monitor (and to react to) the user's behavior that allows for a playful interaction. Likewise, I would argue that paracommunication is not always playful and carefree, but could also take more serious and committed forms (Hippel, 1993) if an encountered character seems to respond to one's own behavior. I refer to this aspect in the following section as the "perceived distance" of a user from a media character.

Perceived distance

In general, I would argue that the *perceived distance* between individuals affects their adherence to norms in social situations (see also Horton & Strauss, 1957; "minimal social distance," Cohen, 2001: 254). Perceived distance, as it is understood here, results from an individual's interpretation of the social situation. It can be regarded as the degree of conviction the user has that his or her behavioral expressions do or do not have an impact on the symbolic behavior of the other (Berger & Luckman, 1967). Perceived distance, for example, relies on the user's assumption that the other character is not aware of their reactions. Consequently, any expressions would have no important consequences (e.g., defiance of norms; Lapinski & Rimal, 2005; see also Garau *et al.*, 2005). The higher the perceived distance, the more the user is convinced that their reactions do not have an impact on his or her life (Berger & Luckman, 1967).[1] In general, I think that perceived distance is closely linked to the degree the user regards another entity as an existing social being (Adoni & Mane, 1984; Mar & Macrae, 2006; see also processes of moral disengagement due to dehumanization; Bandura, 2002) who is "within reach" (Bilandzic, 2006; Burgoon & Jones, 1976) and "well informed" (i.e. aware of the situation and intelligent enough to construe it), and also effective (i.e., is able to affect the world; see Garau *et al.*, 2005). Only well-informed social beings are able to perceive symbolic behavior and are intelligent enough to comprehend it. Only effective beings are able to react to the behavioral expressions of an observer (e.g., to perform sanctions), especially if they share his or her personal space.

Determinants of perceived distance

Various factors might affect a perceived distance to a media character. For example, the mode of reception (Bilandzic, 2006; Liebes & Katz, 1986; Vorderer, 1992) might play a pivotal role. Users will frequently be involved during exposure and—at least momentarily—tend to believe in what they perceive (see Busselle *et al.*, 2006; Lee *et al.*, 2006). I assume that in general the perceived distance is smaller if users encounter a character in an involved mode rather than in an analytical mode (Vorderer, 1992). But even within an involved mode the perceived distance from a media character might differ, in a similar way to differences experienced in real life settings (cf. Horton & Strauss, 1957). For example, other characters might be perceived by the user as "within reach" and thus less distant, if they become aware of his or her presence (cf., Biocca *et al.*, 2003). Such a mutual awareness could be established, for example, if a character addresses and identifies a user directly or signals a "yes to social contact" by an eyebrow flash (Colburn *et al.*, 2000; Grammer *et al.*, 1988). Vice versa, perceived distance in a parasocial situation should be greater if the user feels like an unnoticed and unidentified observer (e.g., a video game character hiding behind bushes). Second, as research on proxemics shows, communicative behavior is affected by the perceived *physical* distance between the interactants (Burgoon & Jones, 1976). Meyrowitz (1986) argues that paraproxemics mediate a seemingly physical distance between a media user and a character, too (see also Lombard, 1995; Reeves & Nass: 1996: 37). Perceived distance should be greater, then, if a character is perceived to be remote from the user's personal space (cf., Lombard, 1995), because the character could be less "informed" and therefore would be less effective. Third, interactivity or reciprocity could be a determinant of perceived distance as well. A lack of reciprocity leads to "unaware" characters who can only "anticipate", but are not able to see the user directly. Perceived distance might be greater, then, if users construe a social situation as noninteractive (cf., Garau *et al.*, 2005). In a similar fashion, anonymity provides another facet of "unaware" social entities (McKenna & Bargh, 2000).

If a character or the whole media setting appears to be barely *authentic*, users are likely to switch to a critical and analytical mode of reception. For example, an interactive character (such as a speech user interface, Polkosky, this volume) lacking intelligence could be perceived as nonauthentic. Thus, it will foster "critical" elaborations. In an analytical mode, users are aware of the abstract and artificial nature of the perceived social entity (Bilandzic, 2006; Vorderer, 1992). The character may be perceived as an "illusion," and thus as "not effective" at all. From such a critical perspective, users should perceive a great distance from a character (cf. Bilandzic, 2006, who refers to Adoni & Mane, 1984: 334), because principally "elements that are [...] more general and abstract are categorized as remote." In addition, it might be argued that most of the factors that affect a perceived distance in an involved mode are relevant in an analytical mode, too. Users could become aware of a lack of reciprocity, for example, if they encounter a character in traditional mass media. A lack of reciprocity leads to anonymity and thus increases perceived distance. Interactive settings, for example a virtual environment like "Second Life," also allow users to hide in anonymity behind the masks of their avatars. In an analytical mode, users would become aware of the anonymity established by the media setting. They would realize that other characters are only able to perceive limited information about them. They would know that they can barely be identified. Therefore, they would perceive others to be not "well informed" and to lack "effectiveness." Accordingly, the perceived distance might be great (but see also Tanis & Postmes, 2007).

Perceived distance and paracommunication

In their original outline, parasocial interactions and paracommunication were thought to rest on a *nonreciprocal* symbolical exchange with a media performer (e.g., Horton & Wohl, 1956). Thus, they were thought to resemble illusions of conversational give-and-take that might be playfully "exploited" by the user. However, according to the revised theoretical body, paracommunication also occurs with *interactive* characters who establish a real give-and-take. Nonreciprocity is regarded as just one possible mediator of a perceived distance towards an encountered media character. The perceived distance, in turn, is thought to crucially determine whether a user will be able to playfully engage in paracommunication with a character (great distance) or rather stick to a committed behavior (less distance; see Hippel, 1993). From this perspective, most types of mediated interpersonal communication would reveal at least some parasocial nature. For example, a human-to-human conversation in a videochat allows for some anonymity. Also, the conversational partner is physically out of reach. Thus, the perceived distance might be greater than in physically close nonmediated conversations. In turn, the conversation would probably allow for some of the playful reactions that have been considered as parasocial. In sum, by replacing "a lack of reciprocity" with the more global construct of "perceived distance," parasocial interaction theory could be enhanced to cover interactive conversations as well, while it would still describe and explain the nature of parasocial interactions in traditional noninteractive settings.

Parasocial processing

Several researchers have tried to elaborate the psychological processes that underlie parasocial interactions (Hartmann *et al.*, 2002; Hartmann & Klimmt, 2005; Klimmt *et al.*, 2006; Six & Gleich, 2000; see for similar approaches Konijn & Hoorn, 2005; Hoffner & Cantor, 1991). A review shows that these approaches interpret parasocial interactions broadly. For example, they regard any mediated character as a starting point for parasocial processes, while originally the phenomenon was solely bound to certain nonfictional mass media performers. Also, in contrast to the original concept, they regard any processes of character perception as a parasocial interaction, no matter if the user is addressed and included into a communicational setting. However, one might argue that these approaches used the term "interaction" in a misleading way, as they actually only focused on processes of character perception (that do not necessarily have to take place in an interactive social situation). Therefore, it seems reasonable to refer to the addressed phenomena as a user's *parasocial processing* of media characters (see for similar terms "engagement" Konijn & Hoorn, 2005:

107; "parasocial involvement", Klimmt *et al.*, 2006: 295). The term includes all of the psychological processes related to media characters, from simple automatical perceptions and categorizations of a mediated character to more elaborate experiential and behavioral reactions (see Klimmt *et al.*, 2006: 297–300).

However, more simple automatic processes can be distinguished from rather complex, elaborate ones (see "spontaneous social perception versus controlled social judgments" Mar & Macrae, 2006: 110). Hartmann *et al.* (2004), for example, link parasocial processing to the dual-process model of person perception proposed by Fiske *et al.* (1999) (see also Klimmt *et al.*, 2006). They argue that characters can either be processed in a simple, stereotypical way or in a more deliberate, elaborate manner. Motivational aspects are thought to play a major role in the shift from simple automatic reations to more elaborate processing. Consequently, among the various factors that account for more elaborate processing (see Hartmann *et al.*, 2004; Hoffner & Cantor, 1991; Hoorn & Konijn, 2003; Konijn & Hoorn, 2005), the user's interest in engaging with a character is crucial. For example, a character that is similar to the user or displays desirable characteristics might trigger pleasurable interest (Konijn & Hoorn, 2005: 111). Thus, the user might be motivated to engage further in a broader range of parasocial processes. Konijn and Hoorn (2005) argue that characters with complex and possibly opposing esthetic, ethic, and epistemic characteristics might trigger a stronger interest than "flat characters" who are rather one-dimensional (cf., Silvia, 2005). Alternatively, very complex characters might be perceived as too difficult to comprehend, which might result in a limited parasocial engagement.

In addition, parasocial processes that resemble character perception (e.g., interpretation and evaluation) should be analytically distinguished from characteristic paracommunicational processes (like perspective-taking, encoding of symbolic behaviour, etc.). Certainly, paracommunication builds on a set of parasocial processes. Just as person perception is not the whole of communication, it can be argued, however, that paracommunication often includes specific and quite elaborate processes.

Perceived authenticity

Spontaneous parasocial processes of character perception automatically begin as soon as a mediated object is identified as "social." This is likely to occur frequently, as people in general engage in social behavior with artificial agents or objects easily (see Polkosky, this volume). "Such engagements do not appear to be cognitively taxing" (Mar & Macrae, 2006: 111). It is easy for children to perceive a puppet, such as the protagonist of a Punch and Judy show, as a social agent (Zillmann, 1996). Adults perceive many objects in a social and meaningful way, too (Mar & Macrae, in press).

For example, they tend to treat computers as social machines (Reeves & Nass, 1996). Media technology plays an important role in creating illusions of characters. Two simple geometric figures on a screen that follow one another are likely to be perceived as social entities chasing another (Heider & Simmel, 1944). A moving structure of light dots can powerfully evoke social perceptions (see "biological motion"; Ahlstrom *et al.*, 1997; Johansson, 1973). In general, human beings easily see faces or social entities in mediated objects or images (Mar & Macrae, in press). Accordingly, users will often perceive social entities in the media that in turn might trigger "simple" parasocial processing (Bente & Otto, 1996).

It can be argued that certain requirements must be met before users might switch from spontaneous reactions to a more elaborate processing of a character and eventually engage in paracommunication. Motivation has already been addressed. However, the establishment of paracommunication might not only depend on a user's interest and motivation. Similar to the notion proposed by others, it seems reasonable to assume that characters also have to be authentic or real enough ("epistemics") to facilitate the interpersonal processes that underlie paracommunication. For example, the parasocial processing of "Pac-Man," i.e., a simple two-dimensional video game figure who moves through an artificial maze, could differ from the perception of an authentic person in a realistic context such as Jerry Springer. Pac-Man might display some aspects of social behavior, like biological motion, which in turn could trigger a set of simple social reactions. However it seems unlikely that users would feel addressed by Pac-Man, consider it to be aware of them, and thus start to engage in more complex interpersonal processes. It can be argued that the epistemic qualities of the character do not allow for such processes.

Epistemic qualities of a character relate to the question of "whether [or not the observed character] might possibly exist in real life" (Giles, 2002: 291; Konijn & Hoorn, 2005: 115). By definition, media provides characters moderated or completely generated by technology. Real-life characters in the media are either recorded or imitated (e.g., by actors); many other characters have no real-life counterpart at all. Beyond simple social reactions (Reeves & Nass, 1996), users can check whether or not they should "trust" their perception of a character. Thus, users evaluate the *authenticity* of a character. In a rough sense, users' judgement of a character might vary between the attributes existent/authentic/real and fictional/artifical (Giles, 2002; Konijn & Hoorn, 2005; Lee, 2004). The less authentic a character appears to be, the more it's clear that it is produced by media technology. It could be argued that parasocial processing is affected by this judgement (cf., Giles, 2002; Lee, 2004). Processes of interpersonal behaviour that underlie paracommunication might be hindered if characters are perceived as too artificial.[2] Thus, given that the reality status of many new media characters can be doubted, parasocial interaction theory might not account for related social encounters.

Determinants of perceived authenticity

The user's authenticity judgement is likely to depend on numerous factors (e.g., Holtgraves, in press). First of all, the way a character carries out actions is important: that is, how it reacts to and engages in the environment ("agency"; Dehn & van Mulken, 2000: 6; see also Polkosky, this volume). Actions provide proof of the existence of a living entity and thus tell a lot about a character's authenticity. Most importantly, an "intentional stance" is perceived from a character's behavior (Mar & Macrae, in press; see also Garau et al., 2005). Also, intelligence is inferred from a character's (re)actions (Koda & Maes, 1996; Lester et al., 1997). Shapiro et al. (2006: 282) argue that a character can lack "personhood" if it has "no creativity or free will." Therefore, authenticity should strongly depend on whether or not users attribute a general intelligence and self-determination (i.e. an "intentional stance") to a character. For example, a Tamagotchi might be perceived as a quite authentic character, since the underlying media technology powerfully creates an illusion of an intentional stance.

Accordingly, a character's behavior seems to be more important than its outer appearance (Bente & Krämer, in press; Dehn & van Mulken, 2000; Hoorn et al., 2003). For example, Bente and colleagues (2001) find that the social perception of simply sketched avatars does not differ from that of sophisticated 3D-modeled figures as long as their bodily movement appears to be natural (see Bente, Krämer & Eschenburg, this volume). Accordingly, scripting the movements of, for example, a cartoon figure or a video game character in a natural way, probably helps to increase authenticity. As research on biological motion (Johansson, 1973; Scholl & Tremoulet, 2000) suggests, individuals sensitively perceive changes in their immediate environment that speak for a living entity (Mar & Macrae, in press). As noted above, even simple patterns of moving dots can create a figure sufficiently authentic to trigger social perception. The way a character moves, including the portrayal of muscle activities, is also important, as this reveals his or her emotional state (see, for facial muscle activities, for example, Ekman & Rosenberg, 1997). Research on believable characters suggests that a correct and sufficient display of emotions is, in turn, an important determinant of authenticity (cf., see Konijn & van Vugt, this volume; Dehn & van Mulken, 2000; Gratch & Marsella, 2004; Thórisson, 2005). A believable emotional nature of the character might not only rest on correct visual appearances but also on vocal cues. The computer HAL9000 in Kubrick's movie *2001: A Space Odyssey* has been regarded as an example of how a voice can produce a believable character (e.g., Lee & Nass, 2005; Olive, 1998).

Narratives provide a context that probably also affects a character's authenticity, (Cohen, 2006). Lee *et al.*, (2006) argue, for example, that narratives could become a major means for creating believable characters in video games (see also Lee *et al.*, 2006; Shapiro *et al.*, 2006). A narrative holds the potential to immerse (Green *et al.*, 2004) or to involve the user (Wirth, 2006). Research shows that involved users are more ready to believe in character presentations (Hartmann & Klimmt, 2005; cf. Slater & Rouner, 2002). Some studies show that strong parasocial bonds exist with cartoon figures (e.g., Vorderer, 1996). Again, a reason could be the appealing emotional behaviour and the dense narrative context in which these figures are placed. Thus, a narrative, if coherently scripted, should powerfully support a character's authenticity.

Perceived authenticity and paracommunication

If one considers most new media characters as inherently nonauthentic, it could be argued that parasocial interactions do not apply to how users engage with them, since the concept might be considered to refer only to "as if" conversations with "real people" in the media. However, taking into account the factors discussed above, some new media characters probably appear to be very authentic and almost real. In addition, if parasocial interaction theory is thought not to include only paracommunication, but all kinds of parasocial processes as well, it also accounts for more simple social reactions towards characters. Thus, it could also illuminate the social engagement with less authentic characters. Therefore, the link between parasocial processing, paracommunication, and perceived authenticity needs to be examined in more detail.

According to Konijn and Bushman (2007: 158) there is "no published research on the topic of whether real and fictional media characters are perceived differently." However, drawing on related research, some hypothetical arguments can be made about how perceived authenticity might alter the scope of parasocial processing. As stated above, characters that are too artificial might not be regarded as appropriate conversational partners. Paracommunication might require characters that are sufficiently authentic. Research conducted by Shechtman and Horowitz (2003) shows, for example, that individuals display fewer social responses during conversations with a computer program if they perceive it as artificial than if they believe they are conversing with a human. Likewise, Shapiro *et al.* (2006: 282) argue that "people seem to be more willing to engage in relational behaviors and to make attributions about characters they believe to be human." Related research shows that parasocial relationships to moderately authentic characters like "Lara Croft" indeed remain restricted to only a very few relational qualities as compared to relationships with more authentic characters (Gleich, 1997; Hartmann *et al.*, 2001). It might be assumed, then, that a character needs to be authentic enough to allow for the more elaborate processes that render paracommunication.[3]

One explanation for this assumed relationship is that a severe lack of authenticity might irritate the user and urge him to switch to a critical or analytical reception mode (Bilandzic, 2006; Busselle et al., 2006; Cohen, 2006; Konijn & Hoorn, 2005; Liebes & Katz, 1990; Vorderer, 1992; Wirth & Boecking, 2005). During such an analytical mode of reception, users approach characters, events, and storylines "from the outside," i.e., as aspects of a media production (see also "identification" vs. "specta-torship", Cohen, 2001; Oatley, 1999). In general, if users switch to an analytical perspective, the genuine "make-up" (i.e. the mediated nature) of characters becomes salient. It is plausible, that numerous socio-emotional and cognitive parasocial processes are "impeded" in an analytical recep-tion mode (Koriat et al., 1972). In fact, research on regulation of emotions during media exposure suggests that users actively switch to an analyt-ical mode in order to decrease authenticity if the emotional involvement becomes too intense (Wirth & Schramm, 2007).

Another argument is that users might need to believe in the existence of a character (i.e., that it exists as a living entity in the real world) before they engage in communicational processes (Giles, 2002: 295; Shapiro et al., 2006; Shechtman & Horowitz, 2003). Gleich (1997) compared paraso-cial relationships with fictional television characters to relationships with friends or "formal acquaintances" like neighbors. He found that parasocial relationship qualities (e.g., idealization, intimacy, passion) were both lower and more specific if compared to those of a real friendship. Giles (2002) assumes that the general possibility for contact with a character enhances social involvement with him or her (see also Hoffner & Cantor, 1991: 64). For many users, it might be inappropriate, for example, to fall in love with a fictional character, i.e. to accept processes of extensive passion, intimacy, and commitment (Sternberg, 1986; see also individual differences in the worship of celebrities, McCutcheon et al., 2003).

In sum, it seems likely that paracommunication can only begin if a char-acter is perceived to be authentic enough to conduct meaningful behavior and to perceive or anticipate the user. Otherwise, users would "only" engage in character perception and evaluation. Traditionally, parasocial interaction theory (Horton & Wohl, 1956) dealt with realistic mass media performers on television or the radio. Anchormen, for example, are real-istic portrayals of human beings. They always behave in a natural way, and they never lack the social cues necessary to create a believable character. For the audience, questions about their reality status probably do not enter the equation. Thus, it is reasonable to assume that the users' involve-ment with them can be defined as paracommunication (Krotz, 1996b). And even if parasocial interaction theory were discussed in the context of fictional mass media characters such as "puppets anthropomorphically transformed into 'personalities'" (Horton & Wohl, 1956: 216)—although this has seldom been done—one could argue that these figures are quite authentic, because their behavior is often scripted by skilled human writers in the context of dense narratives. Consequently, a cartoon figure, such as for example "Homer Simpson," probably allows for paracommunication as well.

New media characters, however, probably vary in their epistemic qualities to a greater degree. Some might be very authentic. For example, quite similar to the mass media, natural audio-visual recordings of real people exist in new media settings as well (e.g., in human-human communication, Polkosky, this volume). In a similar fashion, among the new media characters with no real-life counterparts, those might still be more authentic that simply "copy and paste" human behavior. Often, the production of convincing computer-rendered movie characters like Gollum in *Lord of the Rings* relies on motion capturing; other characters, like Shrek, are given celebrity voice narrators and their behaviour is scripted by human beings. In a similar fashion, many avatars or video game characters manipulated by real users might become authentic, because they just "translate" human behavior (e.g., Bailenson *et al.*, this volume; Bailenson *et al.*, 2003). However, computer engineers still struggle to create believable new media characters that are completely *autonomous*. Contemporary examples of such characters include video game figures (Shapiro *et al.*, 2006), and artificial agents, avatars, or chatter bots on the internet (Bente *et al.*, this volume). If a character's authenticity is indeed a necessary condition for paracommunication, some of the new media characters might not be able to provoke parasocial communications. Rather, they might only foster more "simple" parasocial processes of character perception and evaluation.

Conclusion

This chapter has proposed an adaptation of parasocial interaction theory that originated in the 1950s in the context of mass media performers to new modes of mediated interpersonal communication. To achieve this goal, the original concept was revised. Formerly, the notion of parasocial interactions was bound to the non-interactive (anonymous) social setting of the mass media, where a user encounters authentic characters, i.e., real people. Anchormen, for example, might display symbolic behavior that makes the users feel addressed and observed. As a result, paracommunication could be evoked as the illusion of a playful conversation at a distance (Horton & Wohl, 1956; Vorderer & Knobloch, 1996). Consequently, many researchers regarded the playful nature of parasocial interactions as their defining characteristic.

However, this chapter has suggested that parasocial interactions might also occur in interactive settings with less authentic characters. The nature of mediated social interactions is thought to depend primarily upon two factors, the perceived authenticity and the perceived social distance from the other character. Paracommunication requires quite authentic characters. Therefore, paracommunicational processes could be impeded if a character lacks authenticity. "Simple" parasocial processes, such as an interpretation of or judgement about the character, might still occur, however, even if the media character is perceived as not very realistic. Thus, parasocial interaction theory might account for communicational behavior towards real people in the mass media as well as less authentic characters in new media settings.

The perceived social distance, in turn, is thought to determine how serious or playful interactions with a character are. Playful paracommunication is regarded to be likely if users perceive themselves to be distant from the other character, as in the unidirectional context of mass communication. However, the revised conceptualization suggests that interactive media characters can also be perceived as distant: for example, if they are seen as *physically* distant or if users remain aware of their mediated nature.

In sum, the concept that has been defined as paracommunication or parasocial interaction (e.g, Horton & Wohl, 1956) should apply to many encounters with characters in new interactive media settings, but only if they are perceived as sufficiently authentic and distant.

Notes

* I would like to thank the reviewers, Christoph Klimmt and Susanne Baumgartner, for helpful comments on an earlier version of this chapter.

1 Please note that the term "perceived distance" is used in a different way than in the PeFIC model (Konijn & Hoorn, 2005). Hoorn and Konijn (2003: 259) define distance as "the tendency to avoid" a character (see also Konijn & Hoorn, 2005: 121). My notion also partly differs from the way that the term is understood by Bilandzic (2006: 336). Building on Schutz's (1970) spheres of distance, she argues that "a viewer may perceive television content as close [...] if the content pertains to actual experiences or concerns," that is, if it is relevant. I also argue that characters deemed as relevant are perceived as more authentic, and in turn decrease perceived distance and foster "committed" behavioral reactions. However, apart from relevance, I also regard other determinants of "perceived distance".

2 In addition, a character's epistemics might also account for the user's interest in becoming involved in more elaborate parasocial processes. Interest in a character is likely to depend on relevance checks (Smith et al., 2006). It can be argued that characters are only relevant if they inform the user about important circumstances in his or her real world (cf., Adoni & Mane, 1984; Smith et al., 2006; see Cohen, 2006; Konijn & Hoorn, 2005, for a similar notion). If characters consider issues in such an unrealistic way that nothing is related about the real world, interest in the character might be dimished.

3 A lack of authenticity might limit the breadth of parasocial processes, even beyond paracommunication. Very artificial characters, like Pac-Man, could just lack the display of sufficient "natural" social cues (e.g., facial motor activity) to trigger some basic social

responses (Bente & Kraemer, in press; Morrison & Ziemke, 2005). For example, spontaneously induced emotions (Gratch & Marsella, 2004; Wild *et al.*, 2001), which can be regarded as a simple affective parasocial process (Klimmt *et al.*, 2006), could be diminished.

References

Adoni, H., & Mane, S. (1984) "Media and the social construction of reality. Toward an Integration of theory and research." *Communication Research. 11*, 323–340.

Ahlstrom, V., Blake, R., & Ahlstrom, U. (1997) "Perception of biological motion." *Perception, 26*, 1539–1548.

Auter, P. J., & Palmgreen, P. (2000) "Development and validation of a parasocial interaction measure: The audience-persona interaction scale." *Communication Research Reports, 17*(1), 79–89.

Auter, P. J. (1992) "TV that talks back: An experimental validation of a parasocial interaction scale." *Journal of Broadcasting and Electronic Media, 36*, 173–181.

Bailenson, J. N., Blascovich, J., Beall, A. C., & Loomis, J. M. (2003) "Interpersonal distance in immersive virtual environments." *Personality and Social Psychology Bulletin, 29*, 1–15.

Bandura, A. (2002) "Selective moral disengagement in the exercise of moral agency." *Journal of Moral Education, 31*(2), 101–119.

Bavelas, J. B., Coates, L., & Johnson, T. (2000) "Listeners as co-narrators." *Journal of Personality and Social Psychology, 79*, 941–952.

Bennet, D. J., & Bennet, J. D. (1970) "Making the scene." In G. P. Stone & H. A. Farberman (eds.), *Social Psychology through Symbolic Interaction*. Waltham: Ginn-Blaisdell, pp. 190–196.

Bente, G., & Krämer, N. C. (in press) "Virtual gestures. Embodiment and nonverbal behaviour in computer-mediated communication." In A. Kappas (ed.), *Emotion in the Internet*. Cambridge: Cambridge University Press.

Bente, G., & Otto, I. (1996) "Virtuelle Realität und parasoziale Interaktion" [Virtual reality and parasocial interactions]. *Medienpsychologie, 8*(3), 217–242.

Bente, G., Krämer, N. C., Petersen, A., & de Ruiter, J. P. (2001) "Computer animated movement and person perception. Methodological advances in nonverbal behavior research". *Journal of Nonverbal Behavior, 25* (3), 151–166.

Berger, P. L., & Luckmann, T. (1967) *The Social Construction of Reality*. New York: Doubleday Anchor.

Bilandzic, H. (2006) "The perception of distance in the cultivation process: A theoretical consideration of the relationship between television content, processing experience, and perceived distance." *Communication Theory, 16*, 333–355.

Biocca, F. Harms, C., & Burgoon, J. K. (2003) "Towards a more robust theory and measure of social presence: Review and suggested criteria." *Presence, 12*(5), 456–480.

Burgoon, J. K., & Jones, S. B. (1976) "Toward a theory of personal space expectations and their violations." *Human Communication Research, 2*, 131–146.

Burgoon, J. K., & Le Poire, B. A. (1993) "Effects of communication expectancies, actual communication, and expectancy disconfirmation on evaluations of communicators and their communication behavior." *Human Communication Research, 20*(1), 67–96.

Busselle, R., Bilandzic, H., Zhang, L., DeLisle, J., Hmielowski, J., & Zhang, Y. (2006) "Inconsistency as un-realness in viewers' involvement in TV narrative." Paper presented to the Mass Communication Division of the International Communication Association Annual Conference, Dresden, June 18–26.

Cathcart, R., & Gumpert, G. (1983) "Mediated interpersonal communication: toward a new typology." *Quarterly Journal of Speech, 69*, 267–277.

Cohen, J. (2001) "Defining interaction: a theoretical look at the identification of audiences with media characters." *Mass Communication & Society, 4*(3), 245–264.

Cohen, J. (2006) "Audience identification with media characters." In J. Bryant & P. Vorderer (eds.), *The Psychology of Entertainment*. Mahwah, NJ: Lawrence Erlbaum, pp. 183–198.

Colburn, A., Cohen, M., & Drucker, S. (2000) *The Role of Eye Gaze in Avatar Mediated Conversational Interfaces*. Technical Report MSR-TR-2000-81, Microsoft Corporation, 2000.

Cole, T., & Leets, L. (1999) "Attachment styles and intimate television viewing: Insecurely forming relationships in a parasocial way." *Journal of Social and Personal Relationships, 16*(4), 495–511.

Cummins, R., & Bradford, M. B. (2005) "'Are you talking to me?' The effect of direct address on viewer attention and arousal." Paper presented at the annual meeting of the International Communication Association, New York City.

Dehn, D., & van Mulken, S. (2000) "The impact of animated interface agents: a review of empirical research." *International Journal of Human-Computer Studies, 52*, 1–22.

Ekman, P., & Rosenberg, E. (1997) *What the Face Reveals*. New York: Oxford University

Ellis, G. J., Streeter, S. K., & Engelbrecht, J. D. (1983) "Television characters as significant others and the process of vicarious role taking." *Journal Of Family Issues, 4*(2), 367–84.

Eyal, K., & Cohen, J. (2006) "When good friends say goodbye: a parasocial breakup study." *Journal of Broadcasting and Electronic Media, 50*(3), 502–523.

Fiske, S. T., Lin, M., & Neuberg, S. L. (1999) "The continuum model. Ten years later." In S. Chaiken & Y. Trope (eds.), *Dual-Process Theories in Social Psychology*. New York: Guilford, pp. 231–254.

Garau, M., Slater, M., Pertaub, D. P., & Razzaque, S. (2005) "The responses of people to virtual humans in an immersive virtual environment." *Presence, 14*(1), 104–116.

Giles, D. (2002) "Parasocial interaction: a review of the literature and a model for future research." *Media Psychology, 4*, 279–305.

Gleich, U. (1997) *Parasoziale Interaktionen und Beziehungen von Fernsehzuschauern mit Personen auf dem Bildschirm: ein theoretischer und empirischer Beitrag zum Konzept des aktiven Rezipienten*. [Parasocial interactions and relationships of television viewers] Landau: Verlag Empirische Paedagogik.

Grammer, K., Schiefenhövel, W., Schleidt, M., Lorenz, B., & Eibl-Eibesfeldt, I. (1988) "Patterns on the face: the eyebrow flash in crosscultural comparison." *Ethology, 77*, 279–299.

Grant, A. E., Guthrie, K. K., & Ball-Rokeach, S. J. (1991) "Television shopping: a media system dependency perspective." *Communication Research, 18*, 773–798.

Gratch, J., & Marsella, S. (2004) "A domain-independent framework for modeling emotion". *Journal of Cognitive Systems Research, 5*(4), 269–306.

Green, M. C., Brock, T. C., & Kaufman, G. F. (2004) "Understanding media enjoyment: The role of transportation into narrative worlds." *Communication Theory, 14*(4), 311–327.

HAL's Legacy. 2001's Computer as Dream and Reality (E-Book). Retrieved online at http://mitpress.mit.edu/e-books/Hal/ (April, 2007).

Hartley, P. (1999) *Interpersonal Communication*. London: Routledge.

Hartmann, T., & Klimmt, C. (2005) "Ursachen und Effekte Parasozialer Interaktionen im Rezeptionsprozess: Eine Fragebogenstudie auf der Basis des PSI-Zwei-Ebenen-Modells" [Causes and consequences of parasocial interactions]. *Zeitschrift für Medienpsychologie, 17*(3), 88–98.

Hartmann, T., Klimmt, C., & Vorderer, P. (2001) "Avatare: Parasoziale Beziehungen zu virtuellen Akteuren" [Avatars: Parasocial relationships to virtual social entities]. *Medien und Kommunikationswissenschaft, 3*, 350–368.

Hartmann, T., Schramm, H., & Klimmt, C. (2004) "Personenorientierte Medienrezeption: Ein Zwei-Ebenen-Modell parasozialer Interaktionen" [Person-oriented media exposure: a two-level model of parasocial interactions]. *Publizistik, 49*, 25–47.

Heider, F., & Simmel, M. (1944) "An experimental study of apparent behavior." *American Journal of Psychology, 57*, 243–249.

Hippel, K. (1993) "Parasoziale Interaktion als Spiel [Parasocial interactions as play]. Bemerkungen zu einer interaktionistischen Fernsehtheorie." *montage/av, 2*(2), 127–145.

Hoffner, C., & Cantor, J. (1991) "Perceiving and responding to mass media characters." In J. Bryant & D. Zillmann (eds.), *Responding to the Screen: Reception and Reaction Processes.* Hillsdale, NJ: Erlbaum, pp. 63–103.

Holtgraves, T. M., Ross, S. J., Weywadt, C.R., & Han, T.L. (in press). "Perceiving artificial social agents." *Computers in Human Behavior.*

Hoorn, J. F., & Konijn, E. (2003) "Perceiving and experiencing fictional characters: an integrative account." *Japanese Psychological Research, 45*(4), 250–268.

Hoorn, J. F., & Konijn. A., & van der Veer, G. C. (2003) "Virtual reality. Do not augment realism, augment relevance." *Upgrade, 4*(1).

Horton, D., & Strauss, A. (1957) "Interaction in audience participation shows." *The American Journal of Sociology, 62*(6), 579–587.

Horton, D., & Wohl, R. R. (1956) "Mass communication and para-social interaction: Observation on intimacy at a distance." *Psychiatry, 19*, 185–206.

Johansson, G. (1973) "Visual perception of biological motion and a model for its analysis." *Perception & Psychophysics, 14*, 201–211.

Jones, E. E., & Gerard, H. B. (1967) *Foundations of Social Psychology.* New York: John Wiley.

Kelley, R. L., Osborne, W. J., & Hendrick, C. (1974) "Role-taking and role-playing in human communication." *Human Communication Research, 1*, 62–74.

Klimmt, C., Hartmann, T., & Schramm, H. (2006) "Parasocial interactions and relationships." In J. Bryant & P. Vorderer (eds.), *Psychology of Entertainment.* Mahwah, NJ: Lawrence Erlbaum, pp. 291–313.

Knapp, M. L., & Miller, G. R. (eds.), (1985), *Handbook of Interpersonal Communication.* Beverly Hills: Sage.

Koda, T., & Maes, P. (1996) "Agents with faces: the effects of personification of agents." *Proceedings of HCI '96*, London, August 20–23, 98–103.

Konijn, E., & Bushman. B. (2007) "World leaders as movie characters? Perceptions of George W. Bush, Tony Blair, Osama bin Laden, and Saddam Hussein." *Media Psychology, 9*, 157–177.

Konijn, E. A., & Hoorn, J. F. (2005) "Some like it bad. Testing a model on perceiving and experiencing fictional characters." *Media Psychology, 7*(2), 107–144.

Koriat, A., Melkman, R., Averill, J. R., & Lazarus, R. S. (1972) "The self-control of emotional reactions to a stressful film." *Journal of Personality, 40*(4), 601–619.

Krotz, F. (1996a) "Parasoziale Interaktion und Identität im elektronisch mediatisierten Kommunikationsraum" [Parasocial interactions in a mediated communication space]. In P. Vorderer (eds.), *Fernsehen als "Beziehungskiste".* Opladen: Westdeutscher, pp. 73–90.

Lang, K., & Lang, G. E. (1953) "The unique perspective of television and its effect." *American Sociological Review, 18*(1), 3–12.

Lapinski, M. K., & Rimal, R. N. (2005) "An explication of social norms." *Communication Theory, 15*(2), 127–147.

Lee, K. M. (2004). "Presence, explicated." *Communication Theory, 14*, 27–50.

Lee, K. M., & Nass, C. (2005) "Social-psychological origins of feelings of presence: creating social presence with machine-generated voices." *Media Psychology, 7*, 31–45.

Lee, K. M., Park, N., & Seung-A, J. (2006) "Narrative and interactivity in computer games." In P. Vorderer & J. Bryant (eds.), *Playing Computer Games: Motives, Responses, and Consequences.* Mahwah, NJ: Erlbaum, pp. 259–275.

Lester, J., Converse, S., Kahler, S., Barlow, S., Stone, B., & Bhogal, R. (1997) "The persona effect: affective impact of animated pedagogical agents." In S. Pemberton (eds.), *CHI97*

Conference Proceedings. New York: ACM Press, pp. 359–366.

Littlejohn, S. W. (1999) *Theories of Human Communication*. Belmont, CA: Wadsworth.

Liebes, T., & Katz, E. (1986). "Patterns of involvement in television fiction: A comparative analysis." *European Journal of Communication, 1*, 151–171.

Lombard, M. (1995) "Direct responses to people on the screen: Television and personal space." *Communication Research, 22*(3), 288–324.

Mar, R. A., & Macrae, C. N. (2006) "Triggering the intentional stance." In G. Bock & J. Goode (ed.), *Empathy and Fairness*. Chichester, UK: John Wiley & Sons, pp. 110–119.

McCutcheon, L. E., Ashe, D. D., Houran, J., & Maltby, J. (2003) "A cognitive profile of individuals who tend to worship celebrities." *The Journal of Psychology, 137*, 309–322.

McKenna, K., & Bargh, J. A. (2000) "Plan 9 from Cyberspace: The implications of the Internet for personality and social psychology." *Personality and Social Psychology Review, 4*, 57–75.

Meyrowitz, J. (1986) "Television and interpersonal behavior: codes of perception and response." In G. Gumpert & R. Cathcart (eds.), *Inter/Media. Interpersonal Communication in a Media World*. New York: Oxford University Press, pp. 253–272.

Mikos, L. (1996) "Parasoziale Interaktion und indirekte Adressierung" [Parasocial interactions and indirect addressing]. In P. Vorderer (eds.), *Fernsehen als "Beziehungskiste"* (pp. 97–106). Opladen: Westdeutscher Verlag.

Morrison, I., & Ziemke, T. (2005) "Empathy with computer game characters: A cognitive neuroscience perspective." *Proceedings of the Joint Symposium on Virtual Social Agents*. Hatfield: AISB, pp. 73–79.

Nowak, K. L., & Rauh, C. (2005) "The influence of the avatar on online perceptions of anthropomorphism, androgyny, credibility, homophily, and attraction." *Journal of Computer-Mediated Communication, 11*(1), Article 8.

Oatley, K. (1999) "Meeting of minds: dialogue, sympathy, and identification in reading fiction." *Poetics, 26*, 439–454.

Oatley, K., & Mar, R. A. (2005) "Evolutionary pre-adaptation and the idea of character in fiction." *Culture and Evolutionary Psychology, 3*, 181–196.

Ohler, P., & Nieding, G. (2006) "An evolutionary perspective on entertainment." In J. Bryant & P. Vorderer (eds.), *Psychology of Entertainment*. Hillsdale, NJ: Lawrence Erlbaum, pp. 423–433.

Palmgreen, P., Wenner, L. A., & Rayburn, J. D. (1980) "Relations between gratifications sought and obtained. A study of television news." *Communication Research, 7*, 161–192.

Perse, E. M., & Rubin, R. B. (1989) "Attribution in social and parasocial relationships." *Communication Research, 16*, 59–77.

Reeves, B., & Nass, C. I. (1996). *The Media Equation: How People Treat Computers, Television, and New Media Like Real People and Places*. Stanford, CA: CSLI Publications.

Richards, J. M., & Gross, J. J. (1999) "Composure at any cost? The cognitive consequenses of emotion supression." *Personality and Social Psychology Bulletin, 25*, 1033–1044.

Rimal, R. N., & Real, K. (2003) "Understanding the influence of perceived norms on behaviors." *Communication Theory, 13*, 184–203.

Rosengren, K. E., Windahl, S., Hakansson, P. A., & Johnsson-Smaragdi, U. (1976) "Adolescents' TV relations. Three scales." *Communication Research, 3*, 347–366.

Rubin, A., Perse, E., & Powell, R. A. (1985) "Loneliness, parasocial interaction and local television news viewing." *Human Communication Research, 12*(2), 155–180.

Rubin, R. B., & Mc Hugh, M. P. (1987) "Development of parasocial interaction relationships." *Journal of Broadcasting and Electronic Media, 31*(3), 279–292.

Schiappa, E., Allen, M., & Gregg, P. B. (2007) "Parasocial relationships and television: A metaanalysis of the effects." In R. Preiss, B. Gayle, N. Burrell, M. Allen, & J. Bryant (eds.), *Mass Media Effects: Advances through Meta-Analysis*. Mahwah, NJ: Lawrence Erlbaum Associates, Inc, pp. 301–314.

Schiappa, E., Gregg, P. B., & Hewes, D. E. (2005) "The parasocial contact hypothesis." *Communication Monographs, 72,* 92–115.

Scholl, B. J., & Tremoulet, P.D. (2000) "Perceptual causality and animacy." *Trends in Cognitive Science, 4,* 299–309.

Schramm, H., Hartmann, T., & Klimmt, C. (2002) "Desiderata und Perspektiven der Forschung über parasoziale Interaktionen und Beziehungen zu Medienfiguren" [Desiderata of parasocial interaction research]. *Publizistik, 47,* 436–459.

Shapiro, M. A., Peña, J., & Hancock, J. T. (2006) "Realism, imagination, and narrative video games." In P. Vorderer & J. Bryant (eds.), *Playing Computer Games: Motives, Responses, and Consequences.* Mahwah, NJ: Erlbaum, pp. 275–289.

Shechtman, N., & Horowitz, L. M. (2003) "Media inequality in conversation: How people behave differently when interacting with computers and people." *Conference on Human Factors in Computing Systems,* Fort Lauderdale, FL.

Silvia, P. (2005) "What is interesting? exploring the appraisal structure of interest." *Emotion, 5*(1), 89–102.

Six, U., & Gleich, U. (2000) "Sozio-emotionale und kognitive Reaktionen auf Ereignisszenarien mit TV-Personen" [Socio-emotional and cognitive reactions to television characters]. In A. Schorr (eds.), *Publikums- und Wirkungsforschung.* Wiesbaden: Westdeutscher Verlag, pp. 363–383.

Slater, M. D., & Rouner, D. (2002) "Entertainment-education and elaboration-likelihood: Understanding the processing of narrative persuasion." *Communication Theory, 12,* 173–191 .

Smith, C. A., David, B., & Kirby, L. D. (2006) "Emotion-eliciting appraisals of social situations." In J. Forgas (ed.), *Affect in Social Thinking and Behavior.* New York: Psychology Press, pp. 85–101.

Sperber, D., & Wilson, D. (1995) *Relevance, Communication and Cognition.* Blackwell, Oxford.

Sternberg, R. J. (1986) "A triangular theory of love." *Psychological Review, 93,* 119–135.

Tanis, M., & Postmes, T. (2007) "Two faces of anonymity: paradoxical effects of cues to identity in CMC." *Computers in Human Behavior, 23,* 955–970.

Thórisson, K. R. (2005) "On the Nature of Presence." *Proceedings of the Joint Symposium on Virtual Social Agents.* Hatfield: AISB, pp. 15–21.

Vorderer, P., & Knobloch, S. (1996) "Parasoziale Beziehungen zu Serienfiguren. Ergänzung oder Ersatz?" [Are parasocial relationships a substitute or supplement?] *Medienpsychologie, 8,* 201–216.

Vorderer, P. (1992) *Fernsehen als Handlung* [Viewing TV as an action]. Berlin: Edition Sigma.

Vorderer, P. (1996) "Picard, Brinkmann und Co. als Freunde der Zuschauer" [Media personalities as friends of the television viewer]. In P. Vorderer (eds.), *Fernsehen als "Beziehungskiste". Parasoziale Beziehungen und Interaktionen mit TV-Personen.* Opladen: Westdeutscher Verlag. pp. 153–171.

Watzlawick, P., Beavin, J., & Jackson, D. (1967) *Pragmatics of Human Communication.* W. W. Norton: New York.

Wild, B., Erb, M., & Bartels, M. (2001) "Are emotions contagious? Evoked emotions while viewing emotionally expressive faces: quality, quantity, time course and gender differences." *Psychiatry Research, 102*(2), 109–124.

Wirth, W., & Boecking, S. (2005) "Towards conceptualizing suspension of disbelief for communication research." *Paper presented at the annual meeting of the International Communication Association,* Sheraton New York, New York City.

Wirth, W., & Schramm, H. (2007) "Emotionen, Metaemotionen und Regulationsstrategien bei der Medienrezeption. Ein integratives Modell" [A model of emotions, metaemotions, and regulation during media exposure]. In W. Wirth, H.-J. Stiehler & C. Wünsch (eds.), *Dynamisch-transaktional denken: Theorie und Empirie der Kommunikationswissenschaft.* Köln: Halem Verlag, pp. 153–184.

Wulff, H. J. (1996a) "Parasozialität und Fernsehkommunikation [Parasocial phenomena and TV-communication]. *Medienpsychologie, 8,* 163–181.

Wulff, H. J. (1996b) "Charaktersynthese und Paraperson: Das Rollenverhältnis der gespielten Fiktion" [Character synthesis of personae]. In P. Vorderer (eds.), *Fernsehen als "Beziehungskiste"*. Opladen: Westdeutscher, pp. 29–48.

Zillmann, D. (1996) "The psychology of suspense in dramatic exposition." In P. Vorderer, H.-J. Wulff & M. Friedrichsen (eds.), *Suspense: Conceptualizations, Theoretical Analyses, and Empirical Explanations.* Hillsdale, NJ: Lawrence Erlbaum, pp. 199–232.

Chapter 10

Antisocial communication on electronic mail and the internet

Karen M. Douglas

> Anti-social—"opposed to sociality, averse to society or companionship"
> *Oxford English Dictionary*

> The Internet is like alcohol in some sense. It accentuates what you would do anyway.
> Esther Dyson—Interview in *Time Magazine*, October 2005

Recently, I posed a question to a group of students in my final-year class on social psychology and communication. I asked half of the group to think about the positive aspects of computer-mediated communication (CMC) such as email and the internet, and I asked the other half to think about the negative aspects. We then spent some time discussing the students' responses. While everyone agreed that email and the internet made life much easier—indeed most of the students could not remember a time when they did not exist—everyone in the class agreed that there was a "dark side" to using the internet. Many students recalled colorful incidents of harassment, being ignored, being abused, having their financial details stolen, and were clearly upset at recalling these unsavory events. However, what intrigued me the most was that everyone had an interesting tale to tell, suggesting just how widespread these experiences are.

In this chapter, I will consider several phenomena which fall under the banner of antisocial communication on email and the internet. These phenomena vary in several important ways. Some are targeted at individuals, and some are aimed at groups. Some are active forms of aggression, yet others are more passive forms of antisocial behavior. However, perhaps the most obvious way in which the various forms of antisocial communication differ is in the degree of *intended harm* to, or *personal attack* on, the victim or victims. That is, while some negative aspects of CMC may be unintended consequences of the medium (e.g., losing email through network difficulties, therefore failing to respond), others may be direct intentions to cause harm or distress to the recipient or recipients (e.g., harassment and bullying). In my discussion, I will organize phenomena with respect to their intended harm. Specifically, I will begin my discussion with an examination of flaming, moving on to more intentional and prolonged behaviours such as ostracism. I will then discuss the most intentionally harmful aspects of antisocial behavior on the internet: cyberhate and online harassment. After outlining the phenomena, I will then attempt to provide an overall perspective, and consider if it is the case that when people behave negatively on the internet, they are just "doing what they would do anyway." Although it is not possible to high-light all aspects of online antisocial communication within the scope of this chapter, I will outline what are perhaps the most common behaviors in this regard.

Flaming

The most commonly studied and well-known example of antisocial online behavior is *flaming*. Flaming has been defined as the "practice of expressing oneself more strongly on the computer than one would in other communication settings" (Kiesler *et al.*, 1984: 1130). It has also been described as "hostile expression of strong emotions and feelings" over computer networks (Lea *et al.*, 1992: 89). Research on flaming dates back to the very beginnings of CMC in the 1980s. At that time, Kiesler and colleagues (e.g., Kiesler, 1986; Kiesler *et al.*, 1984; Siegel *et al.*, 1986) conducted a series of studies investigating problem-solving behavior in CMC, and to their surprise, they observed relatively high levels of disinhibited behavior among communicators. In particular, compared to Face-To-Face (FTF) communication and CMC settings where participants were asked to identify themselves by providing their name, anonymous CMC was associated with more swearing, insults, and name-calling.

At the time, this challenged the popular belief that CMC was a "cool" rather than an interpersonally or socially "warm" communication medium which encouraged swift and efficient information exchange rather than facilitating interpersonal communication. CMC was never supposed to be about social behavior, and features such as arguments and hostility, or indeed positive social behavior such as expressions of liking, were not supposed to happen in CMC as they did in more conventional commu-nication (Hiltz & Turoff, 1978). However, the observation of flaming led to the popular view that CMC was suitable for work-related tasks such as group problem solving, but not suitable for tasks requiring inter-personal feedback. This was not because CMC was considered "cool," but because it was now thought to encourage deviant antisocial behavior (e.g., Rice, 1987).

Early findings sparked much research interest into flaming, and indeed it was and still is widely assumed that anonymous CMC *promotes* flaming (Lea *et al.*, 1992). People can let loose with their hostility on CMC just like they can face-to-face, and perhaps even more so. However, it should be noted that although observations of flaming are common, research suggests that in absolute terms, flaming occurs infrequently and depends more on the context of the communication (Lea *et al.*, 1992). For example, communicators who are under time pressure may flame others more because they are frustrated about being unable to communicate effectively. People cannot type as quickly as they speak, which may be one cause of frustration when trying to get one's point across in CMC.

To examine the impact of identifiability on flaming, Douglas and McGarty (2001; 2002) investigated the online comments that people made about a racist target. Results revealed that participants' responses were much more likely to stereotype the target under conditions of identifiability (not anonymity) to a like-minded audience. Presumably therefore, the increased hostility toward the target was facilitated by the supportive context of communicating with others who also felt negative feelings towards the target. Other factors have been linked to flaming behavior. For example, males tend to flame more than females (Aiken & Waller, 2000), and those with an external locus of control are more likely to flame than those with an internal locus of control (Alonzo & Aiken, 2002). Further, anger and assertiveness have been linked with hostile behavior online (Alonzo & Aiken, 2002).

However, it is useful to consider that flaming is not necessarily always negative. It often serves a positive purpose. For example, people who flame might be attempting to protect others from being hurt, or trying to uphold the rules of a group when someone attempts to violate those rules (see Denegri-Knott & Taylor, 2005; Lea *et al.*, 1992; O'Sullivan & Flanagin, 2003). Flaming can therefore facilitate the maintenance of a group's norms and standards and of course will not always lead to an all out "flame war" among communicators. Nevertheless, being the object of even moderate flaming is enough to make people feel angry and experience negative affect. Sometimes when flames are defamatory or violent, this can even lead to lawsuits being brought against the perpetrator of the abuse (see Alonzo & Aiken, 2002).

However, in terms of the intention to harm a victim, flaming can perhaps be considered a relatively benign form of online abuse. Specific and isolated incidents of flaming might often happen in moments of frustration or anger, and may not be deliberately composed to harm the recipient. Rather, flaming may be a way for an individual to vent their temporary frustration. Also, flaming may have a purpose and be relatively harmless when conducted in a chat room or newsgroups. In conclusion, flaming is considered as one negative consequence of CMC, but other forms of antisocial communication may in fact be more harmful to internet users.

More specifically, intentional aspects of antisocial behavior exist that may present an immediate psychological threat to a participant. One such example of intentional antisocial behavior is ostracism.

Cyberostracism

Being ignored, or ostracized, has negative psychological consequences (Gruter & Masters, 1986; Williams, 1997). For example, ostracism has been associated with depressed mood, anxiety, loneliness, helplessness, invisibility, and frustration (see Williams *et al.*, 2000). Being ostracized threatens the basic human needs for belonging, self-esteem, control, and meaningful existence (Williams *et al.*, 2000). The study of *cyberostracism* examines the negative impact of being ignored in cyberspace. This work, pioneered by Kip Williams and colleagues (e.g., Williams *et al.*, 2000; Zadro *et al.*, 2004), defines cyberostracism as "any intended or perceived ostracism in communication modes other than face-to-face" (Williams *et al.*, 2000: 750). This can be anything like unanswered emails, or being consistently ignored in a chat room.

Williams *et al.* (2000) argue that cyberostracism has the potential to be more ambiguous than ostracism that takes place via face-to-face communication or other means. For example, a technological problem may mean that an email goes unanswered, or a post in a chat room is not responded to. Also, people may be away from their email on vacation, but nevertheless a lack of response to urgent messages can easily be perceived as a personal snub. Whether or not this ambiguity makes the target of ostracism feel better or worse about being ignored however, remained to be tested.

To examine the impact of cyberostracism, Williams and colleagues (2000) designed a virtual ball-tossing experiment called "Cyberball." Experimental participants were led to believe that they were playing a game with two other individuals and were asked to throw the ball to one of these individuals. Participants were assigned to one of four conditions: over-inclusion (participants were thrown the ball 67 percent of the time), inclusion (33 percent), partial ostracism (20 percent), or complete ostracism (0 percent). The game continued until participants chose to quit. Results revealed that participants indeed reported negative affect if they were ostracized. Also, this aversive impact was influenced by decreased feelings of belonging. Further results indicated that ostracized participants were more likely to attempt to "repair" their belonging by complying with the incorrect views of a new group. Therefore, even in the most minimal of settings when communicators are unable to see each other, or are subject to public embarrassment, ostracism has a strong negative impact on people's feelings. Zadro *et al.* (2004) have recently extended these findings to show that people still feel bad even when they are led to believe that they are interacting only with a computer. That is, being "ostracized" by a machine is enough to make people experience negative affect.

The need to avoid social exclusion is very powerful and the research on cyberostracism reveals that this need does not disappear when people communicate over the computer. People still feel the need to be wanted and included even when they cannot see their communication partner or partners. Perhaps the lack of social cues present in CMC makes this need for inclusion more or less salient. The internet also makes it easy for people to ostracize others. Email can be ignored or left for a long time without reply. Unanswered email may cause distress and may lead the sender to (rightly or wrongly) infer that the recipient is ignoring them. A recipient may do so unintentionally either due to carelessness, or simply being too busy, but might also do so intentionally to cause psychological distress to the sender. Therefore, ostracism can be viewed, especially if intentional, as a particularly poignant example of antisocial computer-mediated communication.

However, while potentially damaging to the target's self-esteem and psychological well-being, there are arguably more harmful aspects of intentional antisocial behavior than cyberostracism. One such example is the phenomenon of cyberhate. Cyberhate is a unique phenomenon because it does not necessarily involve negative one-to-one communication. Specifically, cyberhate is intentionally targeted at groups of people, especially social groups based on race, religion, and sexual orientation. Here, individuals intentionally attempt to reach a larger audience with messages of hate and prejudice.

Cyberhate

An examination of *The Hate Directory* (http://www.bcpl.net/~rfrankli/hatedir.pdf) shows that in April 2006, there were over 2,300 extremist websites on the internet. The general overarching feature of online extremist groups is that they express *hate* toward other groups, most commonly on racial or ethnic grounds (The Hate Directory, 2006). Online hate groups express their hate by presenting themselves in a variety of different ways, such as selling merchandise, presenting persuasive mission statements, organizing protests and rallies, and some advocating violence.

This phenomenon is now commonly referred to as *cyberhate* (e.g., Douglas, 2007; Douglas *et al.*, 2005). For scholars, the proliferation of cyberhate has brought two main questions into focus. First, can we regulate it, and should it be regulated? (Gerstenfeld *et al.*, 2003; Leets, 2001; Levin, 2002; Siegel, 1999; Zickmund, 1997). Second, what are the *effects* of hate expressed online, especially when they advocate violence? Understanding online hate groups therefore provides an important challenge for researchers. What is their purpose? What motivates the individuals and groups who author them? What action can be taken to combat them? Also, what is the impact, on *individuals*, of this kind of communication?

It is argued that online hate sites allow individuals to seek solidarity with other like-minded individuals who would not otherwise take action against other groups, or to express views that would otherwise be socially unacceptable (e.g., Gerstenfeld *et al.*, 2003; Lee & Leets, 2002; Levin, 2002; see also Schafer, 2002). Using the internet, hate groups can let others know that they are not alone in holding their views (Gerstenfeld, *et al.*, 2003). Along the same lines, the internet allows people running online hate sites to recruit new members, including children, giving them the opportunity to strengthen and grow as groups (e.g., Douglas, *et al.*, 2005; Levin, 2002).

To achieve their aims, hate groups have several strategies at their fingertips. McDonald's (1999) analysis of racist/nationalist hate groups revealed that most sites attempted to persuade their readers by stating their views in a neutral manner, without insults or advocated violence. Similarly, Douglas, *et al.* (2005) revealed little evidence of advocated violence in their analysis of White-power websites. Instead, these groups used more *socially creative* strategies that redefine the elements of the comparative situation without being overtly hostile. As McDonald (1999) notes, clever techniques such as these may not persuade many people to advocate the groups' viewpoints, or become racist themselves, but clearly do not dissuade people from doing so. They are also a means to maintain a positive image of the group.

So, what can we do about cyberhate? At least in the U.S.A., options for shutting down hate sites are limited because of the protection of freedom of expression provided by the First Amendment. However, many websites are rightly closed down because they explicitly encourage violence towards groups, while others are simply sabotaged by well-meaning individuals and groups (Leets, 2001). However, as an alternative to censorship or bans, a handful of antihate activists are using the internet to expose hate and discrimination online. An example of this is *The Hate Directory*. However, it is interesting to note that in comparison to over 2,300 sites advocating hate on the internet as listed on *The Hate Directory* in 2006, there are only 25 similar sites listed with an explicit aim to combat hate. Clearly therefore, combating hate on the internet presents a difficult challenge.

One very important question that remains relatively unanswered in the literature on cyberhate is the question of their direct consequences. That is, do these sites really meet their aims? One study by Turpin-Petrosino (2002) suggests that these strategies might not be as successful as desired, at least on youths. Instead, greater support for White-supremacist groups for a sample of adolescents was associated with more traditional media such as word-of-mouth and printed matter (see also Lee and Leets, 2002). However, taking a different perspective, Gerstenfeld *et al.* (2003) argued that youths visiting hate websites may simply not be aware that they are being influenced by the content they are viewing. We know from social

206 Karen M. Douglas

psychological research that people are often unaware of the influence that persuasive media have on themselves while predicting a substantial influence on others (see research on the *third-person effect*, e.g., Davison, 1983; Douglas & Sutton, 2004; Duck & Mullin, 1995). So internet hate sites may indeed be a more powerful influence on attitudes than self-report data may suggest.

To summarize so far, it is clear that negative aspects of communication on the internet differ in their degree of intentional harm to the recipient. Cyberhate, as just discussed, is an attack on a social group with an intentional effort to have wide-spread impact. Expressing hate presents a direct attack and threat to groups and individuals belonging to groups. Cyberhate has the potential to reach millions of internet users with messages of bigotry and hate, sometimes advocating violence and other forms of overt hostility. On the other hand, cyberostracism can be an intentional way of causing distress to another individual by actively avoiding their emails, posts, or not including them in a sustained conversation. It may have a negative psychological impact on the individual who is ostracized. Flaming is an example of a more immediate antisocial act. Communicators are "flamed," but this may be an act of frustration rather than the result of a chronic intention to harm someone. However, even flaming is considered particularly harmful when it invades one's email inbox, or continues over an extended period of time (Alonzo & Aiken, 2002). It is often the case that flaming and hostility extends beyond casual encounters to more frequent or menacing encounters. It is at this point that the flaming turns into intentional harassment, sometimes bullying, and potentially "cyberstalking." I argue that this is perhaps the most damaging *interpersonal* form of intentional antisocial communication on the internet.

Online harassment

Harassment that exists in conventional communication also occurs in online communication (Khoo & Senn, 2004). The dynamics and features of harassing communication are similar, but the harassment is achieved over electronic media rather than face-to-face, over the phone, or by letter. Email is the most popular mode of online harassment (Khoo & Senn, 2004). This includes forwarding offensive material and jokes (usually sexist or racist), chain letters, sexual requests, and pornography (see Moulton, 1998). It may also entail sending the target a file with a virus, using their email address to subscribe to listservs, and may even extend to harassment beyond email and the internet into the real world (Finn, 2004). Harassment is usually assumed to occur when the sender explicitly intends to cause the recipient stress (Ybarra & Mitchell, 2004), but can also occur when a hostile environment is created without the intention of the sender (Moulton, 1998). Of course, we should also consider that in sending pornographic material in particular, senders may cause harm to the person who is the subject of the material. However, concentrating this discussion on receivers, emails become classified as harassment when they fulfill the legal definition of harassment, in that they insult, degrade, embarrass, or create a hostile environment for the receiver (see Frazier *et al.*, 1995). The term *cyberstalking* is also used to describe online harassment. According to Finn (2004: 469), cyberstalking involves "(a) repeated threats and/or harassment (b) by the use of electronic mail or other computer-based communication (c) that would make a reasonable person afraid or concerned for their safety."

Email harassment and cyberstalking are relatively understudied phenomena (Khoo & Senn, 2002) which is also the case for some of the more "conventional" forms of harassment such as obscene phone calls, dirty jokes, racist jokes, and the display of pornographic material (Gruber, 1992). Through the technology of email, a harassing message can reach its target instantaneously, and can reach many other potential targets across the globe with the click of the "send" button. Strangers can harass strangers, people can be harassed by individuals that they know, and sometimes senders can harass people they know while only posing to be anonymous. It is a powerful medium by which to make a target or targets feel very uncomfortable and vulnerable.

Recent research also points to the increasing prevalence of bullying over email, particularly in an organizational context. One study by Baruch (2005) demonstrated that a "considerable level" of bullying was identified over email in a large multinational corporation, and that this was associated with anxiety. Some respondents also indicated an intention to leave the organization and were dissatisfied with their job and their performance.

Research suggests, perhaps not surprisingly, that women are more frequently the targets of email harassment than men, and they also judge the content of harassing email as more offensive than men (Khoo & Senn, 2002). This mirrors research outside the realm of the internet which suggests that women are more often the victims of sexual harassment than men (Reilly *et al.*, 1986). However, email harassment is also reported to be a problem among youths (Ybarra & Mitchell, 2004). One media report suggests that online harassment is a significant issue for young internet users with 7 percent of surveyed youths between the ages of 11 and 19 reporting having been harassed in chat rooms, and 4 percent having been bullied or harassed over email (BBC Online, 2002, 2006).

Further, the same reports reveal that youths are also being targeted through instant messaging (IM). Of survey respondents, 44 percent stated that they knew someone who had been bullied through IM services such as MSN and Yahoo. Also, approximately a third of respondents knew instances where bullies had hacked into others' email or IM accounts and sent embarrassing messages from them. The types of harassment uncovered in the surveys included threats of beatings, and death threats. A more benign yet still harmful type of bullying involves the spreading of malicious gossip.

In another survey of students on a university campus, Finn (2004) found that 10–15 percent of students reported receiving repeated emails or IMs that were threatening, harassing or insulting. Of these, more than half reported receiving unwanted pornography. Interestingly, only 7 percent of the harassed participants said that they had reported the harassment to authorities. Internet harassment has led to the development of programs such as New Zealand's "Netsafe" project (http://www.netsafe.org.nz/) for computer users and especially children to be safe from online harassment. It has also led to the development of organizations such as "Working to Halt Online Abuse" designed to combat internet harassment in general (http://www.haltabuse.org/).

Another emerging source of online harassment is unsolicited email, usually in the form of advertisements or pornography (Khoo & Senn, 2004). Also known as *spam*, this may not be classified as harassment per se, or an intentional act to harm someone, but it is nevertheless an unwanted and negative feature of being connected via computer. The content of spam may be particularly offensive or disturbing, meaning that the target is left feeling uncomfortable. It is often easy for people to obtain others' personal and work email addresses in order to flood them with unwanted email (Seddon, 2002). This type of unauthorized identity use is not uncommon and can have other, sometimes financially damaging consequences for the victim or target. Again, while rarely intended to harm a particular individual, the theft of someone's identity to purchase goods on the internet is becoming more commonplace (Milne *et al.*, 2004; Sovern, 2004, Stafford, 2004). It is often difficult to clear one's name after an occurrence of identity theft (Linnhoff & Langenderfer, 2004).

The "whys" of antisocial behavior on electronic mail and the internet

While placing different forms of antisocial online behavior in a framework of intended harm to recipients, it still remains difficult to provide an overall *explanation* for these behaviors. The phenomena I have discussed in this chapter are very different from each other and each has different consequences for individuals and groups. However, it is important to consider if something about CMC is conducive to antisocial communication in general. Is there a particular feature of CMC that allows people to behave differently than they would in conventional communication? Does the internet "do" something to people? Or, are people simply behaving in a more "extreme" way than they normally would?

Early observations of CMC focused on the influence of anonymity on behavior. Work on CMC focused on the prediction that communication via computers will be different than other modes of communication because it allows people to be anonymous when they communicate. This idea has been explored extensively in a variety of settings since CMC originated in the 1980s, such as work-related behavior, group productivity (e.g., Siegel et al., 1986; Sproull & Kiesler, 1986) and the development of online relationships (e.g., Lea & Spears, 1995; van Gelder, 1985). In this research, people show more "disinhibited" behavior via CMC such as self-disclosure (Joinson, 2001), and flaming, hostile communication towards others (e.g., Douglas & McGarty, 2001, 2002; Kiesler et al., 1984; Lea et al., 1992).

The widely accepted explanation for this is that communicating without specific social cues (e.g., nonverbal feedback) and accountability releases people from constraints that would normally motivate them to keep their behavior at a level that is socially acceptable. Derived from research on deindividuation (Diener, 1980; Zimbardo, 1969), this argument suggests that people are able to get away with antisocial behavior because they are not accountable for it. Although there is little support for the idea that anonymity on its own increases antisocial behavior, and flaming in particular (see Lea et al., 1992; Postmes & Spears, 1998; Walther et al., 1994), the belief that anonymity is responsible for uninhibited behavior is commonly expressed in the literature. It is therefore unsurprising that the internet is popularly perceived to be the ideal medium for people to express the darker sides of themselves, to insult, harass and abuse others, to be unduly ignorant towards each other, and to express extreme hateful views.

Another explanation relates to the specific norms of interacting over computer networks. According to this account, uninhibited behavior occurs because there are specific norms and accepted values, language, signs, and artefacts associated with CMC (Denegri-Knott & Taylor, 2005; Lea et al., 1992; O'Sullivan & Flanagin, 2003). People are often impolite, unconventional, and irreverent with each other when they communicate this way. While these features of CMC were originally thought to be exclusive to specific groups such as computing departments at universities and people working in the computer industry, it is argued that these norms now have had a wide influence over lay persons because computers are used so extensively in everyday work and social life. Perhaps an understanding of flaming and cyberostracism can be facilitated by this account. It may be typical to flame people in certain CMC contexts. Also, the medium may give people more license to ignore or ostracize others because it is more acceptable or normative in that context. However, what is normative in CMC may not necessarily also be normative in society.

Another explanation associates CMC with increased frustration due to technological difficulties (Denegri-Knott & Taylor, 2005; Lea et al., 1992). According to this account, because CMC is often inefficient, slow, and malfunctioning, people become frustrated and let their frustrations out on others. Again, flaming could be explained using this account. People

210 Karen M. Douglas

who become frustrated with the medium may take their aggression out on others in the form of abusive communication, when this is something they would not normally do in conversation.

While each of these explanations can partly aid in our understanding of phenomena such as flaming and ostracism, cyberhate and online harassment are more difficult to explain. Social psychological accounts of uninhibited behavior in CMC do not seem quite sufficient to explain these particularly damaging and/or criminal aspects of email and the internet. Indeed, the anonymity provided by CMC may make these antisocial acts easier for people to commit. In a similar fashion to flaming and cyberostracism, cyberhate and harassment can be facilitated by the anonymity of CMC and people's ability to conceal their identity from others. However, it would be difficult to argue that anonymity is *responsible* for this type of behavior. People do not commit criminal acts, or express extreme hate towards groups simply because they are anonymous. Some tendency or motivation to hate or harass others must precede the act.

The social identity model of deindividuation effects (SIDE; Reicher *et al.*, 1995; see also Spears & Lea, 1994) is useful to consider in this respect. SIDE proposes that anonymity can facilitate the enactment of salient aspects of one's social self. Rather than proposing that anonymity always leads to chaos and de-regulated behavior that is outside the boundaries of a person's typical behavioral repertoire, Spears and Lea (1994) proposed that anonymity of the self to others may liberate communicators to enact aspects of their identity that would normally be deemed unacceptable (Reicher & Levine, 1994 a,b). People therefore may choose to be anonymous to enact aspects of their self that are usually hidden. Indeed, the internet makes it possible for marginalized individuals to affiliate with each other (e.g., Back, 2002; McKenna & Bargh, 1998) so that they gain a sense of togetherness and solidarity. In this respect, therefore, the internet and email may simply exaggerate preexisting tendencies to behave in a certain way.

This explanation might facilitate our understanding of flaming and also cyberhate. When people flame others, particularly members of other groups, they may be expressing more extreme opinions of these groups because they cannot see who they are speaking about and therefore cannot individuate them (see Spears & Lea, 1994). The consequence of this may be that communicators express their preexisting stereotypes and beliefs more strongly. On the other hand, being able to openly express one's views in a visually anonymous environment may allow people to express stronger views about groups than would normally be the case in face-to-face interaction, even when their identity is known (see Douglas & McGarty, 2001, 2002). In the case of cyberhate, the far-reaching and visually anonymous medium of the internet allows individuals and groups to express their strongly held opinions without the need to answer for these views. So, online hate groups may find an outlet to enact aspects of their identity and express their opinions because it suits a specific purpose (e.g., to recruit new members) and not simply because it allows them to behave in a random and antisocial manner.

However, this broadly defined *social identity* explanation might also be useful in considering online harassment. One recent study by Maass *et al.* (2003) is particularly useful to consider in this respect. Maass and colleagues examined male participants' tendency to sexually harass a female communication partner in a computer-mediated paradigm. Participants underwent a gender identity threat manipulation (or no threat in a control condition), and were then given the opportunity to send pornography to a virtual female interaction partner. Results demonstrated that participants harassed the female more under conditions of identity threat than when there was no threat. However, more interestingly, this was primarily the case for high-identifying males—i.e., males for whom being "male" is very important. This finding suggests that, at least in this experimentally controlled setting, males who strongly identify as males are more likely to harass a female partner when they are threatened. This is not to say that high-identifying males are more likely to harass women in general, but once a threat to their masculinity is issued, a preexisting tendency to act in a gender-identified manner might be brought out. Relating this back to the explanation of online harassment, it may be the case that individuals with a preexisting tendency to harass others may do so given the right circumstances. So it is not anonymity per se that makes people do bad things on the internet, but a combination of identity, motivation, and the circumstances that allow them to do so.

Concluding remarks

In this chapter, I hope to have provided an overview of some of the negative or "darker" features of email and internet. Flaming, cyberostracism, cyberhate, and online harassment are all features of CMC that typical internet users would rather avoid. Explanations for these phenomena often implicate the medium's anonymity. According to this explanation, people are "freed" from normal constraints on their behavior which might include concealing extreme views or holding back hostile feelings towards individuals or groups. Although other explanations can aid in our understanding of antisocial communication on the internet, it seems plausible to conclude that people's behavior on CMC reflects "real life," but in a more exaggerated fashion that is permitted by the features of the medium. People might conceal their dislike for others when speaking to their face, but not need to do so in CMC. Likewise, communicators might be free to express views that would normally meet with repulsion in typical conversational encounters. More damaging aspects of antisocial CMC such as harassment can also somewhat be explained using this reasoning. Preexisting attitudes and motivations, which can sometimes be socially undesirable, may come out when the context permits. However, an understanding of these understudied phenomena can only be gained through further research. Also, understanding the underpinnings and the impact of negative online behavior will lead to an understanding of how these negative phenomena can be combated. This will indeed be a challenge for future research in this area.

References

Aiken, M., & Waller, B. (2000) "Flaming among first-time group support system users." *Information and Management, 37,* 95–100.

Alonzo, M., & Aiken, M. (2002) "Flaming in electronic communication." *Decision Support Systems, 36,* 205–213.

Back, L. (2002) "Aryans reading Adorno: Cyber-culture and twenty-first century racism." *Ethnic and Racial Studies, 25,* 628–651.

Baruch, Y. (2005) "Bullying on the net: Adverse behaviour on e-mail and its impact." *Information and Management, 42,* 361–371.

BBC Online (2002) "Youngsters targeted by digital bullies." Retrieved from http://news.bbc.co.uk/1/hi/uk/1929944.stm on 07/08/06.

BBC Online (2006) "Cyber bullies haunt youth online." Retrieved from http://news.bbc.co.uk/1/hi/technology/4805760.stm on 01/11/07.

Davison W. P. (1983) "The third-person effect in communication." *Public Opinion Quarterly 4,* 1–15.

Deiner, E. (1980) "Deindividuation: The absence of self-awareness and self regulation in group members." In P. Paulus (ed.), *The Psychology of Goup Influence.* Hillsdale, NJ: Erlbaum.

Denegri-Knott, J., & Taylor, J. (2005) "The labelling game: A conceptual exploration of deviance on the internet." *Social Science Computer Review, 23,* 93–107.

Douglas, K.M. (2007) "Psychology, discrimination and hate groups online." In A. Joinson, K. McKenna, U. Reips & T. Postmes (eds.), *Oxford Handbook of Internet Psychology.* (p.155–164), Oxford UK: Oxford University Press.

Douglas, K.M., & McGarty, C. (2001) "Identifiability and self-presentation: computer-mediated communication and intergroup interaction." *British Journal of Social Psychology, 40,* 399–416.

Douglas, K.M., & McGarty, C. (2002) "Internet identifiability and beyond: A model of the effects of identifiability on communicative behavior." *Group Dynamics, 6,* 17–26.

Douglas, K.M. McGarty, C., Bliuc, A.M., & Lala, G. (2005) "Understanding cyberhate: social competition and social creativity in online white supremacist groups." *Social Science Computer Review, 23,* 68–76.

Douglas, K.M., & Sutton, R.M. (2004) "Right about others, wrong about ourselves? Actual and perceived self-other differences in resistance to persuasion." *British Journal of Social Psychology, 43,* 585–603.

Duck J.M., & Mullin B.A. (1995) "The perceived impact of the mass media: Reconsidering the third person effect." *European Journal of Social Psychology, 25,* 77–93.

Finn, J. (2004) "A survey of online harassment at a university campus." *Journal of Interpersonal Violence, 19,* 468–483.

Frazier, P.A., Cochran, C.C., & Olson, A.M. (1995) "Social science research on lay definitions of sexual harassment." *Journal of Social Issues, 51,* 21–37.

Gerstenfeld, P.B., Grant, D.R., & Chiang, C.P. (2003) "Hate online: a content analysis of extremist internet sites." *Analyses of Social Issues and Public Policy, 3,* 29–44.

Gruber, J. E. (1992) "A typology of personal and environmental sexual harassment: research and policy implications for the 1990s." *Sex Roles, 26,* 447–464.

Gruter, M., & Masters, R.D. (1986) "Ostracism as a social and biological phenomenon: an introduction." *Ethology and Sociobiology, 7,* 147–158.

Hiltz, S. R., & Turoff, M. (1978) *The Network Nation: Human Communication Via Computer.* Reading, MA: Addison-Wesley.

Joinson, A. N. (2001). "Self-disclosure in computer-mediated communication: The role of self-awareness and visual anonymity." *European Journal of Social Psychology, 31, 177-192.*

Khoo, P.N., & Senn, C.Y. (2004) "Not wanted in the inbox! Evaluations of unsolicited and harassing e-mail." *Psychology of Women Quarterly, 28,* 204–214.

Kiesler, S. (1986) "The hidden messages in computer networks." *Harvard Business Review,* Jan/Feb, 46–58.

Kiesler, S., Siegel, J., & McGuire, T.W. (1984) "Social psychological aspects of computer-mediated communication." *American Psychologist, 39,* 1123–1134.

Kraut, R. Patterson, M., Lundmark, V., Kiesler, S., Mukopahdyay, T., & Scherlis, W. (1998) "Internet paradox: A social technology that reduces social involvement and psychological well-being?" *American Psychologist, 53,* 1017–1031.

Lea, M., O'Shea, T., Fung, P., & Spears, R. (1992) "'Flaming' in computer-mediated communication. Observations, explanations, implications." In M. Lea (ed.), *Contexts of Computer-Mediated Communication.* New York: Harvester Wheatsheaf.

Lea, M., & Spears, R. (1995) "Love at first byte? Building personal relationships over computer networks." In J.T. Wood & S. Duck (eds.), *Under-Studied Relationships: Off the Beaten Track. Understanding Relationship Processes:* Vol. 6. Thousand Oaks, CA: Sage.

Lee, E., & Leets, L. (2002) "Persuasive storytelling by hate groups online: Examining its effects on adolescents." *American Behavioral Scientist, 45,* 927–957.

Leets, L. (2001) "Response to Internet hate sites: Is speech too free in cyberspace?" *Communication and Law Policy, 6,* 287–317.

Levin, B. (2002). "Cyberhate: A legal and historical analysis of extremists' use of computer networks in America." *American Behavioral Scientist, 45,* 958–988.

Linnhoff, S., & Langenderfer, J. (2004) "Identity theft legislation. The fair and accurate credit transactions act of 2003 and the road not taken." *The Journal of Consumer Affairs, 38,* 204–216.

Maass, A., Cadinu, M., Guarnieri, G., & Grasselli, A. (2003) "Sexual harassment under social identity threat: The computer harassment paradigm." *Journal of Personality and Social Psychology, 85,* 853–870.

McDonald, M. (1999) "Cyberhate: extending persuasive techniques of low credibility sources to the World Wide Web." In E. Thorson, D.W. Schumann (eds.), *Advertising and the World Wide Web.* Mahwah, NJ, USA: Lawrence Erlbaum Associates, pp. 149–157.

McKenna, K.Y.A., & Bargh, J.A. (1998) "Coming out in the age of the Internet: Identity 'demarginalization' through virtual group participation." *Journal of Personality and Social Psychology, 75,* 681–694.

Milne, G.R., Rohm, A.J., & Bahl, S. (2004) "Consumers' protection of online privacy and identity." *The Journal of Consumer Affairs, 38,* 217–232.

Moulton, M. (1998) "Reducing charges of e-comm harassment." *Computer and Security, 17,* 137–142.

Netsafe (2006) Retrieved August 22, 2006, from http://www.netsafe.org.nz.

O'Sullivan, P.B., & Flanagin, A.J. (2003) "Reconceptualizing 'flaming' and other problematic messages." *New Media and Society, 5,* 69–94.

Postmes, T., & Spears, R. (1998) "Deindividuation, power relations between groups and the expression of social identity: the effects of visibility to the out-group." *British Journal of Social Psychology, 33,* 145–163.

Reicher, S., & Levine, M. (1994) "On the consequences of deindividuation manipulations for the strategic communication of self: identifiability and the presentation of social identity." *European Journal of Social Psychology, 24*, 511–542.

Reicher, S., Spears, R., & Postmes, T. (1995) "A social identity model of deindividuation phenomena." *European Review of Social Psychology, 6*, 161–197.

Reilly, M.E., Lott, B., & Gallogly, S.M. (1986) "Sexual harassment of university students." *Sex Roles, 15*, 333–358.

Rice, R.E. (1987) "Computer-mediated communication and organizational innovation." *Journal of Communication, 37*, 65–94.

Schafer, J.A. (2002) "Spinning the web of hate; web-based hate propagation by extremist organizations." *Journal of Criminal Justice and Popular Culture, 9*, 69–88.

Seddon, A.E. (2002) "Cyberterrorism: Are we under siege?" *American Behavioral Scientist, 45*, 1033–1043.

Siegel, J., Dubrovsky, V., Kiesler, S., & McGuire, T.W. (1986) "Group processes in computer-mediated communication." *Organizational Behaviour and Human Decision Processes, 37*, 157–187.

Siegel, M.L. (1999) "Hate speech, civil rights and the Internet: The jurisdictional and human rights nightmare." *Albany Journal of Science and Technology, 9*, 375–398.

Sovern, J. (2004) "Stopping identity theft." *The Journal of Consumer Affairs, 38*, 233–243.

Spears, R., & Lea, M. (1994) "Panacea or panopticon? The hidden power in computer-mediated communication." *Communication Research, 21*, 427–459.

Sproull, L., & Kiesler, S. (1986) "Reducing Social Context Cues: e.lectronic Mail in Organizational Communication." *Management Science, 32*, 1492–1512.

Stafford, M.R. (2004) "Identity theft: Laws, crimes and victims." *The Journal of Consumer Affairs, 38*, 201–203.

The Hate Directory (2006) Retrieved August 22, 2006, from http://www.bcpl.net/~rfrankli/hatedir.pdf.

Turpin-Petrosino, C. (2002) "Hateful sirens … who hears their song?: an examination of student attitudes towards hate groups and affiliation potential." *Journal of Social Issues, 58*, 281–301.

van Gelder, L. (1985) "The strange case of the electronic lover". *Ms Magazine*, October. Reprinted in C. Dunlop and R. Kling (eds.), *Computerization and Controversy: Value Conflicts and Social Choices*. San Diego, CA: Academic Press (1991).

Walther, J.B., Anderson, J.F., & Park, D. (1994) "Interpersonal effects in computer-mediated interaction: A meta-analysis of social and anti-social communication." *Communication Research, 21*, 460–487.

Williams, K.D. (1997) "Social ostracism." In R. Kowalski (ed.), *Aversive Interpersonal Behaviours*. New York: Plenum, pp. 133–170.

Williams, K.D., Cheung, K.T., & Choi, W. (2000) "Cyberostracism: Effects of being ignored over the Internet." *Journal of Personality and Social Psychology, 79*, 748–762.

Working to Halt Online Abuse (2006) Retrieved August 22 2006 from http://www.haltabuse.org.

Ybarra, M.L., & Mitchell, K.J. (2004) "Youth engaging in online harassment: Associations with caregiver-child relationships, Internet use, and personal characteristics." *Journal of Adolescence, 27*, 319–336.

Zadro, L., Williams, K.D., & Richardson, R. (2004) "How low can you go? Ostracism by a computer is sufficient to lower self-reported levels of belonging, control, self-esteem, and meaningful existence." *Journal of Experimental Social Psychology, 40*, 560–567.

Zickmund, S. (1997) "Approaching the radical other: the discursive culture of cyberhate." In S.G. Jones (ed.), *Virtual Culture: Identity and Communication in Cybersociety*. Thousand Oaks, CA: Sage Publications, pp. 185–205.

Zimbardo, P.G. (1969) "The human choice: individuation, reason, and order versus deindividuation, impulse, and chaos." In W.J. Arnold and D. Levine (eds.), *Nebraska Symposium on Motivation:* Vol. 17. Lincoln NE: University of Nebraska Press.

Part III

The appeal of communicating through technology

Chapter 11

Impression formation effects in online mediated communication

Sriram Kalyanaraman and S. Shyam Sundar

The web's capability to encompass such myriad activities as information seeking (e.g., search engines), information dissemination (e.g., blogs), interpersonal communication (e.g., chat rooms), mass communication (e.g., a political candidate's website), relationship formation (e.g., dating sites), and shopping (e.g., e-commerce), among others, makes it uniquely positioned for the study of impressions. That is, compared to "traditional" media environments, new media environments provide several different venues that facilitate the process of communication—both mass and interpersonal. In addition, these new technologies also offer several unique tools that enhance communication processes. Such tools can be content-based (e.g., sexual overtures in online dating sites; use of flattering pictures of oneself on a social networking site) or technology-based (e.g., personalized recommendations in customized portals, interactive elements in political websites, emoticons in online chat rooms). Not surprisingly, given the numerous types of venues as well as the various tools that can be employed in these venues, new media environments provide unprecedented options for self-presentation and self-expression, with profound implications for creation and formation of impressions.

The presentation of a person's attributes is fundamental to how that person is perceived and evaluated by others. Foundational work in impression formation by Asch (1946) suggests three routes for impression formation effects: first the perception of a person would be based on the individual personality attributes; second, a "general" impression—based on an affective valence dimension—would be combined with the sum of individual attributes; and third, the notion that individual attributes would be analyzed vis-à-vis each other, depending on the evaluation situation (see Leyens & Corneille, 1999). Clearly, a person's attributes constitute the crux of impression formation, as evidenced by subsequent theoretical work in the area. Anderson's (1968) information-processing model, for example, involves weighing the meaning associated with individual trait information and then forming a summary evaluation by integrating different bits of meaning together. Later, serial models of impression formation (Brewer,

1988; Fiske & Neuberg, 1990) proposed that impression formation effects are primarily dictated by stereotypes. These models downplay the importance of individual traits or attributes and invoke them only under situations when greater scrutiny is demanded or when stereotypical information is insufficient to arrive at judgmental inferences. In contrast, Kunda and Thagard's (1996) parallel constraint-satisfaction model of impression formation accounts for the role of stereotypes, attributes, and behaviors within the context of an associative network. Thus, all pieces of information are given equal weight, and impressions are formed based on the connection between—and among—information from these various sources.

In some respects, as Ottati *et al.* (2005) point out in their review, forming impressions is theoretically quite similar to forming attitudes. They draw parallels between Wyer's (1981) social information-processing model of impression formation and McGuire's (1968) information-processing model of attitude change in that both models include similar process-based stages such as comprehension, retention, and integration. They also argue that Bem's (1965) self-perception theory is conceptually similar to Wyer and Srull's (1989) framework in privileging cognitive accessibility, and that Anderson's (1981) information-processing model, with its emphasis on combining meaning from several sources of information, is consistent with those theories of attitude change that accentuate the relative valence of each persuasive element (e.g., Fishbein & Ajzen, 1981). As these examples from Ottati *et al.* (2005) illustrate, impression formation effects are, in many ways, analogous to attitudinal effects observed as a result of exposure to persuasive communications.

Online impression formation—MPIF vs. MTIF

If impression formation is indeed theoretically similar to persuasion, then all online activities that lead to changes in attitudes could be considered as impression formation activities. However, to keep things simple, we distinguish between two broad types of impression formation effects on the web. Clearly, as the earlier listing of different types of websites illustrates, the structure of the web provides abundant room for interpersonal interaction. Moreover, the architecture of the web—with its wide-ranging technological capabilities—also offers online interactants enhanced modes of presenting themselves, both qualitatively and quantitatively. By employing text-based tools (e.g., capital letters to convey anger) to creating a streaming video (e.g., promotion of a personality profile in various situations such as dating, employment, etc.), users can run the entire technological gamut from the simple to the sophisticated in conveying self-expression. As in interpersonal settings, the outcomes of such self-expression are likely to result in tangible impression formation effects (e.g., the recipient of a "flame" mail will, in all likelihood, perceive the sender's hostility, leading to an overall impression of the sender as "negative"). Such impressions are similar to those that have long been studied in both the interpersonal communication and social psychology literature, and we label them *mediated person impression formation* (hereafter referred to as MPIF). As is evident from the above discussion, MPIF effects are best studied in computer-mediated communication (CMC)—interaction between two or more humans in a technologically mediated venue. We form impressions of others with whom we interact online.

In addition to MPIF, the web also presents a quite singular opportunity to investigate another type of impression formation effect: namely, perceptions or impressions that we form of the website or technology itself. Here, the focus is on the interaction between a user (of the technology) and the technology itself. That is, impressions can be formed about a "thing" (technology/website) as opposed to a person (which is the norm underlying this body of research). We call this *mediated technology impression formation* (hereafter referred to as MTIF) wherein computer users form impressions about particular computer terminals and other interfaces, including websites. Empirical work in the "Computers Are Social Actors" (CASA) paradigm has shown that social rules apply to computers just as well as they do to humans, and that rules of personality psychology as well as social psychology are applicable to the study of computers and technology. Reeves and Nass (1996: 12) suggest that "our brains automatically respond socially and naturally because of the characteristics of media or the situations in which they are used." That is, individuals respond automatically or "mindlessly" when cues that elicit social responses are present in media messages and form impressions when responding to computers or other new technologies, just as they would in human-human interaction (Nass & Moon, 2000). This kind of impression formation is particularly relevant as technologies, rather than other humans, increasingly serve as sources of our information (Sundar & Nass, 2001) and command our psychological orientation during our online interaction (Sundar & Nass, 2000).

In sum, there are two types of impression formation online depending upon the object of one's impressions. While MPIF refers to impressions of other humans with whom we interact online, MTIF refers to impressions that we form about various technological interfaces, including particular computers and websites.

Self-presentation and impression formation

The notion of self-presentation is central to the study of impression formation in online environments. At its core, self-presentation inherently lies with the sender or source, while perceptions of displayed self-presentation are made by the receiver. Two important aspects accentuate the role of self-presentation in new media environments. One, individuals tend to form perceptions not only about the physical entity behind the technology but also tend to orient themselves to the technology itself as the source or provenance of information (Sundar & Nass, 2001), thus stimulating the generation of both MPIF and MTIF, irrespective of whether the nature of the interaction is restricted to CMC settings. Two, the strategies available for online self-presentation are diverse and manifold—now far more so than ever enabling conjecture in interpersonal communication situations. Individuals can call upon a bewildering array of techniques, or "affordances" (see Norman, 1999) to present their "best" or ideal self in an attempt to create desired impressions. Such techniques can be contingent both on technological bells and whistles (e.g., deployment of multimedia) as well as individual user characteristics (e.g., social situation).

In some ways, self-presentation online (and the resultant impression formation) can be characterized in terms of the bandwidth available (and utilized) for conveying cues. Theoretical perspectives in CMC suggest that the bandwidth nomenclature can be placed on a continuum ranging from "restrictive" to "enhanced." As an example of restrictive bandwidth, the cues-filtered-out (CFO) perspective suggests that the impoverishment of nonverbal cues in CMC fails to approximate the richness and personalization of face-to-face (FtF) scenarios (Culnan & Markus, 1987; Walther, 1996). Such bandwidth constraints would lead to resultant impressions being, at best, indeterminate. Later models, such as Lea and Spears' (1991) Social Identity model of Deindividuation Effects (SIDE) and Walther's (1993) social information-processing theory, accounted for the reduced bandwidth associated with the CFO perspective and demonstrated how social cues and temporal factors can enhance bandwidth and hence foster more structured and precise impressions. More recently, Walther's (1996) hyperpersonal model incorporated elements or constraints from both the SIDE model and social information-processing theory to argue that, in some CMC situations, online impressions can be punctuated to a greater degree than in FtF because communicators can employ characteristics of the medium to promote a self-presentation strategy premised on the "idealized" self—the representation of what individuals want or wish to be in order to be seen as endurable (see Cooper, 2003).

Promoting impressions online

An early attempt by CMC users to overcome the cuelessness of the medium pertains to the invention and use of emoticons, which are graphical, computer-enabled representations of human facial expressions such as smiles, frowns, etc. that can be incorporated within textual exchanges. A few studies that have examined communication processes in email exchanges have shown that the use of such nonverbal cues influences impression formation effects. For example, Thompson and Foulger

(1996) found that the use of emoticons reduced perceptions of hostility or "flaming" for a "tense" message but that they increased perceptions of hostility as the messages became more vitriolic. Walther and D'Addario (2001) observed somewhat limited effects of emoticons when employed in an email exchange since positive emoticons (e.g., smiling face) had no significant effects and negative emoticons (e.g., frown) only weakened the perception of positive email messages without affecting negative messages. While speculating on the influence of emoticons, Walther and D'Addario suggested that emoticons may be a useful device for self-presentation online strategies but that their propensity to evoke or elicit psychological insights may be somewhat subdued. More recently, Kruger *et al.* (2005) observed that people tend to overestimate their communication effectiveness via email—presumably, such overestimation may also lead email senders to incorrectly assess the level of impressions that they expect to generate with their messages.

Impression formation effects have also received attention in other online venues and applications with primarily communicative functions. For example, Utz (2000) discovered that emoticons were effective predictors of relationship growth in MUDs (multi-user dungeons). In the context of chat rooms, Kalyanaraman and Ivory (2006) explored impression formation effects in an experimental setting by manipulating the gender of a topic expert, the seriousness of the topic discussed in the chat room, and the presence of emoticons in the chat. These researchers found that the presence (absence) of emoticons was the most significant predictor of both cognitive and affective dimensions of impression formation effects. For instance, when topic experts used emoticons, study participants evinced more positive attitudes toward them. Also, when emoticons were present, the content of the chat transcript itself was rated more positively. In addition, participants exposed to the transcript with emoticons scored significantly higher on chat memory than did those participants exposed to the same transcript without emoticons.

While emoticons constitute a simple and common method of self-presentation in CMC, leading to MPIF, interfaces have to use several different "strategies" in order to generate positive MTIF. For example, search engines have to produce highly relevant results to users' queries (Kalyanaraman *et al.*, 2000) and virtual reality interfaces have to fake a personalized gaze (Bailenson *et al.*, 2005).

In addition to empirical findings in an assortment of venues, the phenomenal explosion of blogs, and especially social networking sites (e.g., Facebook, MySpace), renders the online world a fertile stomping ground for the study of impressions. The popularity of social networking sites—especially among the younger generation—is well established. While the reasons for featuring a profile on a social networking site may be varied, the essential idea behind every one of these sites is the same: that individuals use a range of technological affordances available at their command to project their selves online, which in turn can influence both the magnitude and valence of impressions. We speculate that, similar to most other online venues, the degree to which one is able to project the self will be dependent on the bandwidth of the web interface. In turn, the greater the use of available bandwidth, the greater the richness of self-presentation; subsequently, both the quality and quantity of impressions that can be formed should be enhanced. This raises the question of conceptualizing bandwidth. What variables of mediated online interaction would be implicated in our consideration of bandwidth?

Key bandwidth variables shaping impression formation effects

Nass and Mason's (1990) variable-centered perspective to technology suggests that new technologies can be best understood by studying those distinct elements or variables that define them. By isolating the different variables endemic to the technology and examining them in experimental contexts, the unique effects of each of those variables can be uncovered. It also bears noting that this approach places a formidable constraint on the importance of content. That is, with some exceptions, the essential content per se is more or less the same, but the way in which the content is presented via technological manipulation can be quite different (e.g., the same information is presented either interactively or noninteractively, either using animation or simply statically). Although there are several concepts that can be studied under the variable-centered standpoint, we propose the elements of modality, interactivity, and customizability as particularly germane to both the creation of self-presentation strategies as well as resultant impressions that may be generated as a consequence of exposure to such self-presentations. In addition to being grounded in extant theory, these elements are ubiquitous in present-day online applications.

Modality

Modality, or mode, is the communication equivalent of what psychologists refer to as "codes," and has generally been assumed to refer to the types of channels that are present in a communication scenario (e.g., text, audio, text+audio, etc.). Paivio's (1986) Dual Coding Theory (DCT) posits the existence of two cognitive systems. The verbal system deals with linguistic or textual information, while the image or nonverbal system deals with auditory, visual, and other sensory information. The essence of DCT is that when information is presented in more than one modality, it enhances cognitive abilities (recall or recognition) since the bits of information are processed independently and exert an additive effect. In CMC and human factors research on multimodal interfaces, the two dominant conceptual frameworks that have guided the examination of modality effects are social presence theory (Short *et al.*, 1976) and media richness theory (Daft & Lengel, 1984). Primarily, both these frameworks suggest that the social presence or richness of a medium encompasses the gamut of cues, ranging from verbal (e.g., text) to nonverbal (e.g., audio, video), with the capability to transmit nonverbal communication indicating the highest level of social presence or media richness. Of course, these frameworks are in contrast to the hyperpersonal perspective which would suggest impoverished media to be suitable for social interaction and generation of impressions due to actualization of the "idealized" self. That is, interactants may tend to rely on more stereotypical bits of information to compensate for the reduced interpersonal cues available in impression formation scenarios (see Hancock & Dunham, 2001).

Although the fundamental belief behind multimedia or multimodal interfaces is that infusing a system with more modalities leads to more positive impressions—whether cognitive or affective—being generated, this supposition has hardly received consistent empirical support. Drolet and Morris (2000) and Jensen *et al.* (2000) examined modality differences within the context of the "Prisoner's Dilemma" game. In addition to a control condition (no communication), Jensen *et al.* allowed dyads of participants to communicate during the course of the game using text only, voice only, or text and voice modalities and found that the voice-only condition resulted in the highest scores of cooperation. Furthermore, the voice condition also fostered greater perceptions of trustworthiness and likeability than did the control and text-only conditions. Drolet and Morris examined differences between dyads of participants who communicated via telephone or face-to-face to test the proposition that the latter would enhance the quality of communication since it provided for inclusion of nonverbal cues. Consistent with their expectations, participants in the face-to-face condition displayed significantly more positive affect toward their partners than did those participants in the audio condition. While findings from these studies suggest that richer media foster more positive perceptions of a communication partner, other empirical findings have failed to find a linear pattern of increasing positive impressions with increasing levels of modality. For instance, Asting *et al.* (2001) asked dyads of participants to rate their interaction partners based on their communication exchanges via one of four modalities (text only, audio only, audio and video, and face-to-face) during a problem-solving and conflict resolution task. In contrast to their hypotheses, Asting *et al.* found that participants rated each other more positively in the audio condition compared to the text condition, but failed to discern any other modality differences. Similarly, Burgoon *et al.* (2002) found that, broadly speaking, audio- and text-based information elicited more positive impressions of communication partners than did video-based content. Of course, as Burgoon *et al.* pointed out, their experimental context involved a simple decision task, and the results could well be different in tasks that necessitate a high degree of socio-emotional negotiation. Also, in their program of research on factors that underlie deception, Burgoon and colleagues have tested the principle that the ability to deceive in online environments would be moderated by communication modality (see Carlson *et al.*, 2004). For instance, Burgoon *et al.* (2003) examined perception differences between deceivers and truth-tellers in a communication scenario employing either FtF, audio, video, or text-based modalities, and found that participants perceived deceivers to be more honest than truthtellers in the text condition. Sundar (2000) examined modality effects in news websites and found that multimedia enhancements adversely affected experimental participants' impressions of the website.

It appears that increasing the number of modalities increases the user's or receiver's level of elaboration. This is primarily because some semblance of incongruency creeps in when information is presented in more than one modality (that is, even though different bits of information may not be appreciably incongruent, in practice it is somewhat difficult to achieve perfect congruence between different modes of information). Consequently, increased elaboration leads to more attention being paid to the multimodal information while also serving to decrease the evaluative component (see Russell, 2002). Thus, the inclusion or enhancement of multimedia features needs judicious consideration. Enhanced multimedia is also a double-edged sword in venues such as personal websites, blogs, and social networking sites because, on the one hand, a person can take full advantage of increased bandwidth and augment their self-presenta-tion strategies, but on the other hand, increased multimodality may also provide perceivers more manifest cues (and hence information). If such information violates or is inconsistent with the perceiver's frame of refer-ence, resultant impressions of the target are likely to be negative. One recent experiment found that modality enhancements to the output of a search engine query resulted in the search engine being evaluated more favorably, but only when the enhancement was perceived as congruent or relevant to the search output (Kalyanaraman & Ivory, 2007). When the information from the modality addition was inconsistent with that from the primary search result, modality did not affect participants' impressions of the search engine. Such preliminary findings prompt us to recommend new directions for scholars to undertake in the context of impression formation vis-à-vis modality effects: namely, to explore the possibility that depending on users' level of involvement, modality could function as a cue or heuristic (see Petty & Cacioppo, 1986; Eagly & Chaiken, 1993). Although research has investigated modality effects based on the type of task (e.g., simple, emotionally neutral decision tasks or tasks high in socio-emotional currency) and has also shown how increasing the number of modalities can increase elaboration, there is a dearth of research evidence in studying whether users tend to rely upon or discount modality under conditions of high or low personal involvement. Consistent with dual process accounts of persuasion, which generally posit that persuasion occurs through one of two routes—the central/systematic/conscious route under conditions of high involvement, motivation, and ability, or the peripheral/heuristic/automatic route under conditions of low involvement, motivation, and ability (see Chaiken & Trope, 1999, for a review), we speculate that modality effects would be negligible under conditions of high involvement, but would exert significant effects for low-involvement information processors. We also predict that modality effects would be more pronounced at the time of initial impressions, but that such effects would taper over time. These claims are, of course, untested, but ones that we believe are worthy of future exploration, especially in terms of traversing the conceptual thread between modality, impression formation, and persuasion research.

Interactivity

In one of the first conceptually organized explications of interactivity, Sundar *et al.* (2003) classified the concept into two species of definitions— the functional view and the contingency view. Under the functional view, interactivity can be realized by adding or incorporating various bells-and-whistles features that establish the provision of a meaningful dialogue between a user and the interface or between two or more users. Such functions could refer to feedback forms, message boards, and so on. Contingency-based interactivity arises from Rafaeli's (1988) distinction between noninteractive, reactive, and interactive communications, with the specific distinction residing at the level of a feedback mechanism that governs the relationship between present and future threads of communication. A noninteractive communication is easy enough to understand because it precludes the existence of a feedback loop, implying the absence of any dialogue between sender and receiver. The differentiation between reactive and interactive communications is more subtle. While reactive communication posits a dialogue between sender and receiver, a message thread has to go through three loops before it can be considered truly interactive. Thus, functional interactivity may be considered to be a feature of the medium, while contingency interactivity can be construed as a message feature.

While the dominant assumption has long been that higher levels of interactivity foster more positive perceptions, the available evidence suggests otherwise. In a study of impression formation effects based on exposure to a fictitious political candidate's website, Sundar *et al.* (2003) found an inverted-V relationship between level of contingency interactivity and impressions on measures of both MPIF and MTIF. Moderate levels of interactivity generated the most positive impressions, higher than both low- and high-interactivity sites. This pattern of findings is also evident in studies that have examined the psychological effects of interactivity from the functional perspective. Sundar *et al.* (1998) found that the inclusion of functional features produced the inverted-V pattern with politically involved voters, leading them to surmise that interactivity may potentially function as a cue or heuristic (see Sundar *et al.*, 2003). In a similar vein, Bucy (2004) examined functional elements in the context of a news site and found that highest levels of interactivity did not contribute to the most positive impressions. While findings such as these have prompted conjecture about "too much" interactivity resulting in negative impressions, we deem it rather preliminary to toll the death knell. For one, new media scholars, especially those studying technology from a media effects perspective, have generally confined the importance of content as a typical external validity limitation of experimental designs. But, the role of content cannot be negated—it is conceivable that only such content that is perceived as interesting and relevant to users may receive approbation when presented interactively. Essentially, interactivity affords a closer scrutiny of content (Sundar, 2007).

Another conceptualization of interactivity, one based on the principle of information control (e.g., Ariely, 2000; Kristof & Satran, 1995; Teo *et al.*, 2005) can be useful, particularly in the context of gauging impression formation effects. Under this conceptualization, interactivity is the degree to which the user has control over the information being consumed and exchanged. Such control can include the ability to manage the pace (e.g., clicking on a hyperlink to advance to another page), sequence (e.g., the ability to proceed anywhere at any time), media (e.g., playing, stopping, or pausing video), and so on (see Kristof & Satran, 1995, for other examples of user control). This conceptualization accounts for some of the potential drawbacks of the functional and contingency classifications by espousing both the principle of nonlinearity as well as transferring the locus of information control to the user. Experimental evidence operationalizing interactivity from the information control view has shown that increasing levels of interactivity generally lead to more positive impressions of the interface or task (e.g., Ariely, 2000; Kalyanaraman *et al.*, 2007; Teo *et al.*, 2005) thereby refuting, to some degree at least, other experimental findings that have proclaimed the inimicality of "too much interactivity." Of course, the benefits of information control are likely to be more substantial when information is complex (as opposed to simple) and also in those interactions that occur over time. We suggest that an ecumenical understanding of interactivity and its role in impression formation research can be best achieved by employing an experimental design presenting information of varying levels of interest or relevance and also varying levels of complexity, with each information module being operationalized according to principles of contingency, functionality, and information control. The evidence from such a design will help clarify the exact role of interactivity in either reducing or enhancing impressions.

Customizability

The final concept which we examine under the rubric of the variable-centered approach is that of customizability. The technological ability to provide content and information tailored to individualized user interests and to treat each user as an inimitable individual forms the crux of customization, and it is therefore not surprising that the facility to offer customized information has begun to attract sizable interest in both the academic and professional communities (see Kalyanaraman & Sundar, 2006). Although the concept of presenting individualized messages has been examined under different nomenclatures such as customization, personalization, and tailoring, the essential idea is one of matching messages to some aspect of the self (see Petty *et al.*, 2002). In this discussion, we adopt the term "customizability" to reflect not just those unique aspects of the individual that can be projected to display their identity but also in acknowledgement of the interface's ability to offer customizable features. Customizability has meaningful import for impression formation research in online environments. When individuals project their identity to resonate their unique self, they do so with the primary intention of being able to influence perceivers into forming positive impressions. In addition, those users who create their individualized profiles will disport either positive or negative perceptions depending on the interface's ability to achieve a high degree of customizability. The bottom line as far as customizability is concerned is the process and means of conveying facets of one's specific identity (see Sundar, this volume).

Identity has been conceptualized as "the subjective concept of oneself as a person, and is therefore, a form of representation" (Vignoles *et al.*, 2000: 340). A defining property of any representation involves identification of individual attributes that independently may not be useful but which, when considered as a whole, may lead to a complementary profile of a distinctive identity. For example, consider the hypothetical example of Mary with the following attributes: she is a statistics geek, fulfills her surveillance needs via NPR, enjoys Latin jazz, regularly cooks Indian cuisine, is passionate about geocaching, and loves traveling to Curaçao. While every one of these parameters can distinguish her from others who do not have these specific attributes (e.g., those who are not statistics geeks), they do not individually mark her out as a unique individual (she will still have something in common with other statistics geeks, others who are fans of Indian cuisine, others who pursue geocaching as a hobby, and so on). However, when taken together, these attributes produce or constitute a holistic representation of Mary as a unique person. This rationale permeates the essence of customizability: to identify such attributes of individuals that provide a unique representation of themselves. For instance, customized web portals implicitly recognize that they can create unique user representations by drawing on defining attributes of users' identities.

In some ways, this parallels the fundamental precepts of self-verification theory: that individuals want others to confirm their self-views (Swann et al., 2000). Self-verification theorists suggest that when a target acts in ways similar to a perceiver, the resulting experience of self-congruence may increase perceptions of consistency and improve social interaction between the perceiver and the target (Swann, 1983; Swann et al., 2000). The positive effects of congruence between perceivers and targets have been shown in several experiments (e.g., Swann, 1983; Swann et al., 1992; Swann et al., 1994). As Swann et al. (2000: 240) suggest, "receiving self-verifying evaluations from others may cause group members to feel as if they have 'personalized' the group by establishing a self-verifying niche." Swann et al. (2000) posit that establishing an environment favorable to self-verification (by creating "psychological niches") will promote effective social interaction and lead to a heightened appreciation of that environment. Although self-verification effects have generally been studied in group contexts, the basic rationale can be extended to inform the relationship between users (perceivers) of customized websites and the customized portal itself (target). A customized website adapts itself to reflect the preferences and desires of individual users. Doing so leads to an environment where an individual's self-views (or preferences) are represented and verified by the site (when it recognizes user expectations and displays the individual's preferences and interests on its site). This adaptation will likely create a sense of congruence between users and the web interface, leading to the establishment of a psychological niche, and promotion of effective human-website interaction due to generation of positive impressions.

Although MPIF effects of customizability in venues such as social networking sites and blogs certainly warrant scholarly attention, the existing experimental evidence has largely been confined to MTIF effects in customized portals. Kalyanaraman and Sundar (2006) found that offering higher levels of customized information in web portals (e.g., MyYahoo!) led to more positive perceptions toward the portal interface. Study participants also displayed behavioral effects of impression formation as observed from their browsing and navigational actions. The authors also found that the relationship between customizability and impressions was mediated by perceptions of interactivity, involvement, relevance, and novelty. Another recent experiment found results consistent with Kalyanaraman and Sundar. Kalyanaraman (2007) examined the link between customizability and need for cognition—an individual difference variable pertaining to an intrinsic need for cerebration and somewhat analogous to the concept of involvement. The findings appear to offer support to the multiple role hypothesis that a persuasive variable can function as a cue or argument in the same communication situation depending on situational and dispositional factors (see Petty *et al.*, 2002). Kalyanaraman found that customizability appeared to serve as an argument for high-involvement processors with resulting positive impressions consistent and stable over time, whereas it appeared to operate as a cue or heuristic for low-involvement processors with resulting positive impressions neither as robust nor as enduring. A fruitful endeavor for new media scholars to undertake in future is to examine impression formation effects as a consequence of the provenance of customizability—whether customized by the interface or by individual users themselves. Another promising direction for scholarship is to examine the effects of customizability over time and also explore how and whether the process-centered mechanisms unfold over time.

Conclusion

In this chapter, we have outlined the importance of impression formation effects in online environments. Unlike traditional impression formation research, we identified the importance of studying impression formation effects not only of online interactants or communicators but also of the technology itself. We showcased the mercurial nature of the internet and web by offering examples of impression formation research of diverse online locations, while also pinpointing the suitability of newer online venues like social networks and blogs for the study of impressions. Finally, we proposed the utility of the variable-centered approach to technology for studying impression formation effects, and, in the process, advanced the concepts of modality, interactivity, and customizability as eminently worthy of empirical attention in impression formation research. Beside suggesting how each of these concepts could be linked to established research traditions in persuasion, we offered examples of questions whose examination would further advance our conceptual understanding of impression formation effects in new media. In conclusion, we hope to have stimulated scholarly attention and invite other researchers to embark on an odyssey of programmatic empirical research on online impression formation effects.

References

Anderson, N. H. (1968) "A simple model for information integration." In R. P. Abelson, E. Aronson, W. J. McGuire, T. M. Newcomb, M. J. Rosenberg, & P. H. Tannenbaum (eds.), *Theories of Cognitive Consistency: A Sourcebook*. Chicago: Rand McNally, pp. 731–743.

Anderson, N. H. (1981) "Integration theory applied to cognitive responses and attitudes." In R. E. Petty, T. M. Ostrom & T. C. Brock (eds.), *Cognitive Responses in Persuasion*. Hillsdale, NJ: Lawrence Erlbaum Associates, pp. 361–397.

Ariely, D. (2000) "Controlling the information flow: Effects on consumers' decision making and preferences." *Journal of Consumer Research*, *27*, 233–248.

Asch, S. E. (1946) "Forming impressions of personality." *Journal of Abnormal and Social Psychology*, *41*, 258–290.

Asting, T., Heim, J., Schliemann, T., Brundell, P., & Hestness, B. (2001) "Medium effects on impression formation." *Proceedings of the 18th International Symposium on Human Factors in Telecommunication*. Bergen: Norway.

Bailenson, J. N., Beall, A. C., Blascovich, J., Loomis, J., & Turk, M. (2005) "Transformed social interaction, augmented gaze, and social influence in immersive virtual environments." *Human Communication Research, 31*, 511–537.

Bem, D. J. (1965) "An experimental analysis of self-perception." *Journal of Experimental Social Psychology*, *1*, 199–218.

Brewer, M. B. (1988) "A dual process model of impression formation." In T. K.Srull & R. S. Wyer (eds.), *Advances in Social Cognition*. Hillsdale, NJ: Erlbaum, pp. 1–36.

Bucy, E. P. (2004) "The interactivity paradox: closer to the news but confused." In E. P. Bucy & J. E. Newhagen (eds.), *Media Access: Social and Psychological Dimensions of New Technology Use*. Mahwah, NJ: Lawrence Erlbaum Associates, pp. 47–72.

Burgoon, J. K., Bonito, J., Ramirez, A., Kam, K., Dunbar, N., & Fischer, J. (2002) "Testing the interactivity principle: Effects of mediation, propinquity, and verbal and nonverbal modalities in interpersonal interaction." *Journal of Communication*, *52*, 657–677.

Burgoon, J. K., Stoner, G. M., Bonito, J., and Dunbar, N. E. (2003) "Trust and deception in mediated communication." *Proceedings of the annual meeting of the Hawaii International Conference on Computers and System Science*, Kona, HI.

Carlson, J. R., George, J. F., Burgoon, J. K., Adkins, M., & White, C. H. (2004) "Deception in computer-mediated communication." *Group Decision and Negotiation*, *13*, 5–28.

Chaiken, S., & Trope, Y. (eds.), (1999) *Dual-Process Theories in Social Psychology*. New York: Guilford.

Cooper, T. D. (2003) *Sin, Pride & Self-Acceptance: the Problem of Identity in Theology & Psychology*. Downers Grove, IL: InterVarsity Press.

Culnan, M. J., & Markus, M. L. (1987) "Information technologies." In F. Jablin, L. L. Putnam, K. Roberts & L. Porter (eds.), *Handbook of Organizational Communication*. Newbury Park, CA: Sage, pp. 420–443.

Daft, R., & Lengel, R. (1984) "Information richness: A new approach to managerial behavior and organization design." *Research in Organizational Behavior, 6*, 191–233.

Drolet, A. L., & Morris, M. W. (2000) "Rapport in conflict resolution: Accounting for how face-to-face contact fosters mutual cooperation in mixed-motive conflicts." *Journal of Experimental Social Psychology*, *36*, 26–50.

Eagly, A. H., & Chaiken, S. (1993) *The Psychology of Attitudes*. Fort Worth, TX: Harcourt.

Fishbein, M., & Ajzen, I. (1981) "Attitudes and voting behavior: An application of the theory of reasoned action." In G. M. Stephenson & J. M. Davis (eds.), *Progress in Applied Social Psychology*. Chichester, UK: Wiley, pp. 253–313.

Fiske, S. T., & Neuberg, S. L. (1990) "A continuum of impression formation, from category-based to individuating processes: Influences of information and motivation on attention and interpretation." In M. Zanna (ed.), *Advances in Experimental Social Psychology*. San Diego, CA: Academic Press, pp. 1–74.

Hancock, J. T., & Dunham, P. J. (2001) "Impression formation in computer-mediated communication revisited: An analysis of the breadth and intensity of impressions." *Communication Research*, *28*, 325–347.

Jensen, C., Farnham, S. D., Drucker, S. M., & Kollock, P. (2000) "The effect of communication modality on cooperation in online environments." *Proceedings of the SIGCHI Conference on Human Factors in Computing Systems*, Seattle, WA.

Kalyanaraman, S. (2007) The interplay between customization and cognition in web portals: the multiple role hypothesis explanation. Manuscript submitted for publication.

Kalyanaraman, S., & Ivory, J. (2006) "The face of online information processing: Effects of emoticons on impression formation, affect, and cognition in chat transcripts." Paper presented at the 56th annual convention of the International Communication Association (ICA), Dresden, Germany.

Kalyanaraman, S., & Ivory, J. (2007) "Enhanced scent or selective discounting: Informative versus persuasive information in search engines." Paper to be presented at the 57th annual convention of the International Communication Association (ICA), San Francisco, CA.

Kalyanaraman, S., & Sundar, S. S. (2006) "The psychological appeal of personalized content in Web portals: Does customization affect attitudes and behavior? "*Journal of Communication, 56*, 110–132.

Kalyanaraman, S., Ito, K., & Ferris, E. (2007) Control ergo cogito: the effects of interactive Websites on sexual health information. Manuscript submitted for publication.

Kalyanaraman, S., Mahood, C., Sundar, S. S., & Oliver, M. B. (2000) "Priming effects of accidental exposure to internet pornography: An experimental study of construct accessibility in search engine output." Paper presented at the 83rd annual convention of the Association for Education in Journalism and Mass Communication (AEJMC), Phoenix, AZ.

Kristof, R., & Satran, A. (1995) *Interactivity by Design: Creating and Communicating with New Media*. Adobe Press, CA.

Kruger, J., Epley, N., Parker, J., & Ng, Z. W. (2005) "Egocentrism over e-mail: Can we communicate as well as we think?" *Journal of Personality and Social Psychology, 81*, 925–936.

Kunda, Z., & Thagard, P. (1996) "Forming impressions from stereotypes, traits, and behaviors: A parallel constraint satisfaction theory." *Psychological Review, 103*, 284–308.

Lea, M., & Spears, R. (1991) "Computer-mediated communication, deindividuation, and group decision-making." *International Journal of Man-Machine Studies, 34*, 283–301.

Leyens, J. P., & Corneille, O. (1999) "Asch's social psychology: not as social as you may think." *Personality and Social Psychology Review, 4*, 345–357.

McGuire, W. J. (1968) "Personality and attitude change: An information-processing theory." In A. G. Greenwald, T. C. Brock, & T. M. Ostrom (eds.), *Psychological Foundations of Attitudes*. San Diego, CA: Academic Press, pp. 171–196.

Nass, C., & Mason, L. (1990) "On the study of technology and task: A variable-based approach." In J. Fulk & C. Steinfeld (eds.), *Organizations and Communication Technology*. Newbury Park, CA: Sage, pp. 46–67.

Nass, C., & Moon, Y. (2000) "Machines and mindlessness: social responses to computers." *Journal of Social Issues, 56(1)*, 81–103.

Norman, D. A. (1999) "Affordance, Conventions, and Design." *Interactions, 6*, 38–43.

Ottati, V., Edwards, J., & Krumdick, N. D. (2005) "Attitude theory and research: Intradisciplinary and interdisciplinary connections." In D. Albarracin, B. T. Johnson, & M. P. Zanna (eds.), *The Handbook of Attitudes*. Mahwah, NJ: Lawrence Erlbaum Associates, pp. 707–742.

Paivio, A. (1986) *Mental Representations: A Dual-Coding Approach*. New York: Oxford University Press.

Petty, R. E., Barden, J., & Wheeler, S. C. (2002) "The elaboration likelihood model of persuasion." In R. J. DiClemente, R. A. Crosby, & M. Kegler (eds.), *Emerging Theories in Health Promotion Practice and Research*. San Francisco: Jossey-Bass, pp. 71–99.

Petty, R .E., & Cacioppo, J. T. (1986) *Communication and Persuasion: Central and Peripheral Routes to Attitude Change*. New York: Springer-Verlag.

Rafaeli, S. (1988) "Interactivity: From new media to communication." In R. P. Hawkins, J. M. Wiemann, and S. Pingree (eds.), *Advancing Communication Science: Merging Mass and Interpersonal Processes*. Sage Annual Review of Communication Research, Vol. 16. Newbury Park, CA: Sage, pp. 110–134.

Reeves, B., & Nass, C. (1996) *The Media Equation: How People Treat Computers, Television, and New Media Like Real People and Places*. Stanford, CA: CSLI Publications and Cambridge University Press.

Russell, C. A. (2002) "Investigating the effectiveness of product placements in television shows: The role of modality and plot connection congruence on brand memory and attitude." *Journal of Consumer Research, 29*, 306–319.

Short, J., Williams, E., & Christie, B. (1976) *The Social Psychology of Telecommunication*. London: John Wiley.

Sundar, S. S. (2007) "Social psychology of interactivity in human-website interaction." In A. N. Joinson, K. Y. A. McKenna, T. Postmes & U-D. Reips (eds.), *The Oxford Handbook of Internet Psychology*. Oxford, U.K: Oxford University Press, pp. 89–104.

Sundar, S. S. (2000) "Multimedia effects on processing and perception of online news: A study of picture, audio, and video downloads." *Journalism and Mass Communication Quarterly, 77*, 480–499.

Sundar, S. S., Hesser, K., Kalyanaraman, S., & Brown, J. (1998) "The effect of Website interactivity on political persuasion." Paper presented at the 21st General Assembly & Scientific Conference of the International Association for Media and Communication Research, Glasgow, U.K., July.

Sundar, S. S., Kalyanaraman, S., & Brown, J. (2003) "Explicating web site interactivity: Impression formation effects in political campaign sites." *Communication Research, 30*, 30–59.

Sundar, S. S., & Nass, C. (2000) "Source orientation in human-computer interaction: Programmer, networker, or independent social actor?" *Communication Research, 27*(6), 683–703.

Sundar, S. S., & Nass, C. (2001) "Conceptualizing sources in online news." *Journal of Communication, 51*, 52–72.

Swann, W. B., Jr. (1983) "Self-verification: bringing social reality into harmony with the self." In J. Suls & A. G. Greenwald (eds.), *Social Psychological Perspectives on the Self*. Vol. 2. Hillsdale, NJ: Erlbaum, pp. 33–66.

Swann, W. B., Jr., De La Ronde, C., & Hixon, G. (1994) "Authenticity and positivity strivings in marriage and courtship." *Journal of Personality and Social Psychology, 66*, 857–869.

Swann, W, B., Jr., Stein-Seroussi, A., & Giesler, B. (1992) "Why people self-verify." *Journal of Personality and Social Psychology, 62*, 392–401.

Swann, W. B., Jr., Milton, L. P., & Polzer, J. T. (2000) "Should we create a niche or fall in line? Identity negotiation and small group effectiveness." *Journal of Personality and Social Psychology, 79*, 238–250.

Teo, H. H., Oh, L. B., Liu, C., & Wei, K. K. (2005) "An empirical study of the effects of interactivity on web user attitude." *International Journal of Human-Computer Studies, 58*, 281–305.

Thompson, P. A., & Foulger, D. A. (1996) "Effects of pictographs and quoting on flaming in electronic mail." *Computers in Human Behavior, 12*, 225–243.

Utz, S. (2000) "Social information processing in MUDs: the development of friendships in virtual worlds." *Journal of Online Behavior, 1*(1). Retrieved October 25, 2006, from http://behavior.net/JOB/v1n1/utz.html.

Vignoles, V. L., Chryssochoou, X., & Breakwell, G. M. (2000) "The distinctiveness principle: identity, meaning, and the bounds of cultural relativity." *Personality and Social Psychology Review, 4*(4), 337–354.

Walther, J. B. (1993) "Impression development in computer-mediated interaction." *Western Journal of Communication, 57*, 381–398.

Walther, J. B. (1996) "Computer-mediated communication: impersonal, interpersonal, and hyperpersonal interaction." *Communication Research, 23*, 3–43.

Walther, J. B., & D'Addario, K. P. (2001) "The impacts of emoticons on message interpretation in computer-mediated communication." *Social Science Computer Review, 19*(3) 324–347.

Wyer, R. S., Jr. (1981) *Cognitive Organization and Change: an Information-Processing Approach.* Hillsdale, NJ: Lawrence Erlbaum Associates.

Wyer, R. S., Jr., & Srull, T. K. (1989) *Memory and Cognition in Its Social Context.* Hillsdale, NJ: Lawrence Erlbaum Associates.

Chapter 12

The joys of online dating

Monica Whitty

Online dating has to some extent taken over from less traditional forms of dating, such as personal ads and video dating. As Whitty and Carr (2006) report in their book *Cyberspace Romance: The Psychology of Online Relationships*, online dating is increasingly becoming a popular way to find a match—so much so that they believe that online dating is here to stay (although the format will probably change). Houran *et al.* (2004) report that in 2004 web services accounted for approximately 43 percent of the $991 million United States dating service sector. They also report that Jupiter Research expects online dating sites to record over $640 million by 2007.

In this chapter the reasons why individuals choose to use online dating sites to locate a potential partner are initially highlighted. It then moves to consider how online dating is both similar to and different from personal ads and video dating. Drawing from interview data, self-presentation strategies of online daters are discussed. Relationship theories, such as evolutionary theory, exchange and equity theories, and theories on self-presentation are considered. It is theorized here that the more successful approach to online dating is the *BAR approach* (balancing an attractive and a real self). Finally, the appeal of online compatibility scales is considered.

The data mostly drawn on here comes from 60 interviews conducted with 30 men and 30 women Australian online daters (see Whitty & Carr, 2006; Whitty, 2007(a), for a more in-depth discussion of the sample and the findings). It is worthwhile mentioning that participants of the site investigated paid to use it. Participants were recruited by asking the manager of a large Australian online dating company to select a random sample and email an invitation for individuals to participate in a telephone interview. Individuals interested in participating contacted the researcher. She then organized a suitable time to call the participants. Interviews ran for approximately 50–60 minutes. The participants' ages ranged from 23–60 years, with an overall mean age of 43.40 years ($SD = 8.70$). Of the sample, 43 percent stated that their relationship status was single, 46 percent were divorced or separated, 8 percent had a girlfriend or a boyfriend, and 3 percent were married or in a cohabiting relationship. All of the participants were heterosexuals. Individuals had been using the online dating site for an average of 27.42 months ($SD = 16.36$).

For the study a structured interview schedule was designed that mainly consisted of open-ended questions. Participants were initially asked to report basic demographic details about themselves (e.g., age, relationships status, and socio-economic status). Next they were asked to explain their motivations for using the site. Participants were then asked to explain in detail how they went about using the site, including questions on how they constructed their own profiles, what sort of profiles they were attracted to, and how they went about contacting other individuals on the site. They were then asked to explain how the relationship progressed from online to offline, including questions on the pace of the relationship, how well others matched up to their profiles, as well as what kind of personal information they disclosed to their online potential date. They were asked to describe how their face-to-face dates were typically arranged and why they were set up in this way. They were finally asked to compare online dating with other forms of dating. This chapter will only report a subset of the findings (see Whitty & Carr, 2006, Whitty, 2007(a), for a more in-depth discussion of the results).

Definition of online dating

As Whitty and Carr (2006: 4) explain:

> Online dating sites began appearing in the 1980s and are still increasing in popularity as an alternative or addition to offline dating. Similar to newspaper personals (but with much more information), individuals construct a profile, describing themselves and often providing photographs of themselves and sometimes sound bites and video. Users typically have to pay to use this service and once they identify a person whose profile they like, online contact is made through the system to gauge whether the other individual might also be interested. From there, individuals typically organise to meet face-to-face.

As Whitty (2007 (b)) highlights, many online dating sites try to effectively match individuals using their service. These dating sites are continuing to work on refining tools to match the most suitable people together. Online daters are often expected to complete personality tests, as well as surveys on their interests and what qualities they are looking for in a partner. From there, matches are often given compatibility ratings.

In addition to the generic online dating sites that exist, such as, e-Harmony, True.com, and Match.com, there are also more specialized online dating sites which gather like-minded individuals together. For example, there are sites designed specifically for Christians, Jews, vegans,

Goths, or spiritual people. Sites like these are similar to social groups which one might join in the hope to find another who shares the same values or interests. Moreover, as Whitty (2007(b)) contends, it potentially cuts out some of the work involved with the search for the perfect other.

Motivations for using an online dating site

So why choose to find a partner via an online dating site? Research to date has reported social and personality reasons for choosing online dating as a way to find a match. For example, Brym and Lenton (2001) have hypothesized a number of reasons, including:

- given that career and time pressures are increasing, people are looking for more efficient ways of meeting others for intimate relationships;
- single people are more mobile due to demands of the job market, so it is more difficult for them to meet people face-to-face for dating; and
- workplace romance is on the decline due to growing sensitivity about sexual harassment—hence, alternative dating approaches are needed.

Albright (2007) argues that the appeal is the large pool of availables in an environment which enhances romantic projections. In my own research, participants reported a number of reasons for using an online dating site, including:

- it was an alternative to the pubs and clubs scene;
- because they were shy or reserved;
- they felt they had no other options;
- it was convenient; and
- because of the privacy it affords (Whitty & Carr, 2006).

Scharlott and Christ (1995) in 1990 surveyed 102 registered subscribers to the online dating site Matchmaker. They found that the majority of participants they sampled were very shy individuals. More recently, Whitty and Buchanan (in press) found that individuals who scored high on shyness were more likely to have tried online dating and were more likely to rate online dating as a form of dating they would like to use in the future. They argue that shy individuals might find online dating sites to be a safer and more enjoyable space in which to initiate relationships.

Newspaper personal ads and video dating

This chapter began by making the claim that online dating has taken the place of previous dating methods, such as newspaper ads and video dating. This next section considers how online dating compares to these other types of matchmaking methods. It is argued here that researchers often ignore some of the important similarities between online and offline relating. As this chapter will highlight, the way individuals present themselves in newspaper ads and video dating is in many ways quite similar to the way they currently present themselves on online dating sites. First, let us consider the research on newspaper personal ads.

Newspaper personal ads

Many newspapers have allowed and still do allow individuals (for a small cost) to compose a personal ad. In composing such an ad individuals are given the opportunity to describe in a few lines themselves and what they are looking for in a partner. Advertisers can remain anonymous in their ads and provide either a personal phone number or are given a number where individuals can leave a message if they are interested in meeting this person.

Psychologists have been interested in examining how individuals present themselves in such ads. Cameron *et al.* (1977: 27) found from their analysis of 347 heterosexual ads appearing in "Singles News Register" that the pattern of offers and requests was "reminiscent of a heterosexual stock market". In other words, the self is commodified. Individuals were much more likely to present self-descriptions that included favourable traits (e.g., warmth, friendliness, and sincerity). Of the personal ads, 85 percent described attractive traits, with just 3 percent of men and 6 per cent of women including negative qualities.

Distinct gender differences in self-presentation and qualities sought after by men and women have been identified in these personal ads. For example, Cameron *et al.* (1977) found that personality qualities were emphasized by women more than by men. Appearance was stressed by women (67 percent) more than men (35 percent). In contrast, 38 percent of men compared to 12 percent of women wrote that appearance characteristics were desirable in a potential partner. Occupation was mentioned by men (46 percent) more often than by women (20 percent). In contrast, women (24 percent) were more likely to specify the desired occupation of the prospective partner than men (3 percent). In Smith *et al.*'s, (1990) analysis of 514 singles ads, it was found that physical attractiveness was more frequently sought by men (57 percent) when compared to women (26 percent). Moreover, requests for a thin partner were made by a third of men compared to a mere 2 percent of women. Koestner and Wheeler (1988) found that men wrote that they had expressive traits (e.g., a good communicator) but sought instrumental traits (e.g., likes outdoor activities). In contrast, women offered instrument characteristics and sought expressive ones.

Interestingly, Gonzales and Meyers (1993) found in their analysis of personal ads that many of the advertisers described themselves as the "ideal" man or woman. At first glance this might seem a little "over the top"; however, it is arguably a sensible strategy for men and women to highlight certain traits over others. If one is to attract a potential partner in the first place, one needs to advertise attractive wares over ones that might seem unattractive or mediocre.

Theorizing about newspaper personal ads

Beyond simple descriptions of what traits individuals present in their personal ads, psychologists have tried to understand theoretically why men and women might employ certain presentation strategies. The following section will consider evolutionary theory, exchange/equity theories, and theories on self-presentation.

Evolutionary theory

According to evolutionary theory, through natural selection the human species has inherited certain traits and emotional reactions. We have evolved to value certain qualities in the opposite sex. Hence, when it comes to mating, the more an individual possesses certain characteristics the more likely they are to attract others of the opposite sex (Buss, 1987). According to this theory, women are more attracted to men who can provide for their offspring. Men, in contrast, are attracted to women who are fertile and reproductively valuable. In their analysis of personal ads, Greenless and McGrew (1994) found evidence to support evolutionary theory. They found that women sought men who were financially secure and older. Men, in contrast, sought women who were physically attractive and younger.

Exchange and equity theories

Exchange theory and equity theory have also been drawn upon to examine how individuals describe themselves and the type of partner they are seeking. Exchange theories explain relationships in terms of rewards and costs. Thibaut and Kelley (1959) developed the first of these theories and argued that whatever our feelings are for someone (no matter how pure and admirable our motives might seem), individuals pursue relationships with others only so long as they are satisfying in terms of the overall rewards and costs. Exchange theory contends that individuals try to maximize their profits; that is, rewards should outweigh the costs. Thibaut and Kelley (1959) also argued that in order to predict how satisfied an individual is likely to be with a given relationship it is necessary to take their expectations into account. For instance, individuals develop expectations about relationships based on their past relationships and observations of relationship outcomes with other people similar to themselves. Hence, to be satisfied with a relationship the outcomes must match or exceed one's comparison levels. Like exchange theory, equity theory argues that individuals in personal relationships are trying to maximize their outcomes. It argues that when individuals find themselves in inequitable relationships they experience distress, and the degree of distress increases in proportion to the perceived inequity. When individuals experience such distress they will attempt to restore equity.

In contrast to Thibaut and Kelley's (1959) theory, which says that information for generating comparison levels comes from one's past experiences and/or from observations of similar others, equity theory focuses on the relative contributions and outcomes of the partners. Therefore, the relevant information for deciding what is fair in the relationship comes from within the relationship. Those who make more of a contribution should expect to get more out of it; those who put in less should expect less from the relationship.

Harrison and Saeed (1977) performed a content analysis on 800 heterosexual personal ads. They found evidence to support exchange and equity theories; that is, they found complementary but gendered differences between what individuals offered of themselves and what they hoped for in a potential partner. In other words, they found that that individuals seek out others of about equal attractiveness as themselves and if they sought out someone more attractive they typically offered some other quality in return (e.g., social status and wealth) to balance out the difference.

Lies or selective truth telling

Researchers have also been interested in how honest daters are in their personal ads. Austrom and Hanel (1983, cited in Ahuvia & Adelman, 1992) found in their research that no outright lies were told in personal ads, but there was evidence of exaggeration and selective truth telling. Obviously this is more achievable than in face-to-face conditions where the truth, especially about one's physical appearance, is more difficult to hide. Lynn (1986, cited in Ahuvia & Adelman, 1992) found that some people were very selective in what information they provided. For instance, individuals only advertised their weight when it was of a socially desirable amount. Raskin and Hillman (1984, cited in Ahuvia & Adelman, 1992) found that single women with children tended to omit any mention of having children in their personal ads. Perhaps evolutionary theory might explain the types of lies reported here. For instance, woman might lie about attractiveness because this is a quality men are seeking in women. Moreover, evolutionary theory predicts that women are attracted to men for their resources. If women mention previous children, this factor is putting larger demands on the potential partner's resources.

Video dating

When it comes to video dating, clients are presented with written information and video clips of their potential dates. The video dating service typically selects potential partners they consider might be a good match for their client. The client is then presented with demographic information, self-descriptions, and photographs of prospective dates followed by a videotaped interview. The client then decides which of these potential dates they are interested in. The individuals they select are then contacted to decide, if in turn, they might be interested in meeting this individual.

Researchers have been interested in gender differences with video daters' presentation and choices. As with previous research on attraction, it was found that men were mostly attracted to good-looking women and that women desired men with high social status (Green *et al.*, 1984). Again, this is what evolutionary theory would predict. Riggio and Woll (1984), in contrast, found that the more popular male video daters were the ones who were physically attractive, good actors, and were, overall, expressive. Popular women were those who were physically attractive. Exchange theory might better explain the male daters here, in that they might be trying to maximize the qualities they have to offer.

Woll and Young (1989) were interested in the relationship and self-presentational goals of video dating clients, the strategies they employ in obtaining these goals, as well as the images they choose to present to others. These theorists suggest that the video daters hoped that by presenting a realistic picture of themselves they would, in turn, be successful in attracting the ideal partner they were looking for. Despite this apparent sensible strategy, Woll and Young (1989) point out that these same video daters are dissatisfied with the people who have been selecting them, perceiving a discrepancy between their ideal partner and the person who is realistically interested in their profile.

Comparing online dating with personal ads and video dating

Online dating, personal ads, and video dating are similar in many ways. One obvious similarity between each of these dating methods is that initial contact is made in text prior to meeting the potential romantic partner. This is very different from more traditional forms of dating where individuals typically meet face-to-face (e.g., in bars and clubs, at work). Moreover, with each of these forms of matchmaking a dater has more control over impression formation than they would face-to-face (Whitty, 2007(a)).

There are also some obvious differences that are worthwhile noting. With newspaper ads often the person contacting the advertiser is not someone who has constructed a personal ad themselves. Another clear difference is that more visual information is available for video daters and online daters. This chapter now turns to make more detailed comparisons between each of these forms of dating by drawing from my interview data with 60 Australian online daters (pseudonyms have been used to replace participants' real names).

Presenting oneself on an online dating site

As with individuals who construct personal ads, online daters interviewed for the study said they went to great efforts to construct an attractive profile. Some even expressed explicitly that they needed to "sell" themselves. For example, Wayne stated:

> The other thing for me personally is I'm great at writing trade manuals for someone, but when it comes to writing about yourself and trying to sell yourself it's a very different story. I don't know whether that's more of a male trait than a female trait. It depends how good you want to try selling yourself too, isn't it? … It's a fine line between over selling yourself and under selling yourself.

As with those who compare newspaper ads, this study demonstrated that online daters are driven to commodify the self—ensuring they were presenting a self that others would feel compelled to "buy" into. This view parallels nicely with Cameron *et al*'s (1977: 27) claim, mentioned earlier, that newspapers ads are "reminiscent of a heterosexual stock market".

Some of the characteristics online daters considered important to present included: their looks (typically through a photo), interests and activities, personality, sense of humor, occupation, intelligence, uniqueness, and hopes and dreams (see Whitty & Carr, 2006, for an exhaustive list and percentages). Many of the online daters presented numerous positive characteristics rather than just a few. If we revisit exchange theory, we will recall that this theory posits that individuals look to maximize rewards when it comes to deciding upon an appropriate relationship. Hence, it would seem a sensible strategy to outline as many positive characteristics as possible to appear to be a highly rewarding option. Moreover, one has to appear a more rewarding choice than the many other available profiles.

As with the previous research on personal ads and video dating, individuals were strategic in how they presented themselves. Online daters were savvy enough to know that simply presenting an attractive self was not enough. They understood the importance of offering an honest and "real" presentation of themselves (Whitty, 2004, 2005, 2007(a)). This is nicely explained by James:

J: I tried to be very accurate about what I've said about myself … but you've got to put it in a way that hopefully other people will be interested in seeing you.

I: Would you say you exaggerated anything in any way?

J: I've tried not to. I've tried to be pretty honest about it and I mean you're not going to say negative things are you? You're going to say positive things.

As mentioned earlier in this chapter, most individuals write personal ads which focus purely on their favorable traits (Cameron *et al.*, 1977). Again, considering exchange and equity theories, if one is to be a "good exchange," then presenting negative qualities will possibly push them out of the running. This was also evident with online daters. To give an example:

A: I put in what I thought were the most attractive or unique qualities about me that would differentiate me from the others.

(Andrew)

As also demonstrated in the quote above, many of the online daters were acutely aware of the multitude of profiles they were competing against. While there is some obvious competition for individuals constructing personal ads and video profiles, it would seem that for many online dating sites there are far more singles to compete with than in the other forms of dating. Given this, the online daters talked about the need to have their profiles stand out in the crowd. This point is illustrated in the following quote:

S: Well I guess it is because I come from the sort of Buddhist end of the spectrum thinking, and when you start making reference to sort of Buddhist, or rather peculiar spiritual concepts and ideas and alike, you know that it's a bit different.

I: And you have found by doing that you have been able to get more— generated more—interest, and it's also more accurate as well?

S: Well, that is right.

(Shane)

Also akin to the advertisers in personal ads and video dates, many online daters tried to include very specific details about themselves in order to attract the "ideal" partner. For example, Shane (quoted above) was hoping to attract someone with similar religious beliefs. Others wanted to attract people with similar hobbies or philosophies of life.

Unlike the individuals who construct personal ads and those who construct profiles for video dating, online daters are able to rewrite their profiles at no extra cost. Many took advantage of this as a way either to increase the number of potential dates or to achieve better success in attracting their "ideal" date. To give some examples:

I: Have you experimented with different profiles and were some more successful?

M: Oh yeah. … basically, my photos, I've left alone. I've changed them a couple of times you know. I've experimented with a few and I guess the one I've got in there at the moment has probably been the most successful, so that's been in there for probably nine months now I guess. I've probably found that I've got a better response from that and the type of people that have responded have been nicer people too.

I: What's the difference about that one?

M: Basically, I said you know what's wrong with you guys out there, what do you want? Do you want me to tabletop dance or something for you or … Here I am, a reasonably good looking guy and reasonably well off and so on, and I can't remember how I finished it off now. I haven't looked at it for a while. But just basically putting the challenge out to them, I guess. I don't know, I haven't got the gift of the gab some guys put in there….

(Martin)

T: I had changed my profile and my name on several occasions.

I: And why was that?

T: Well the reason I changed, the first time I put my profile up in September I had no idea what to write; I found it enormously diffi-cult. It took me ages to put anything together and I wasn't happy with it, so I changed it. And I didn't put a photo up and I got very little response, or the response wasn't good that I did get. Then I changed; I found a photo that I was happy with and put that on…

(Teresa)

A perfect match, or a numbers game?

As noted earlier, Woll and Young (1989) found in their study of video daters that these individuals hoped that by being realistic in their presenta-tions of self they would attract their ideal partner. In spite of this strategy, their participants were still very dissatisfied with the clientele they were attracting. A similar finding was revealed with the sample of online daters. Despite the opportunities to find one's perfect match, the online daters complained about not finding the partner they were seeking—although they often began using the site with great hopes that they would. For example, Andrew states:

A: It's one of the things that's frustrating about using the site as well is that you'd hopefully be meeting the same sort of people who go well. I don't like that either. Where else can I meet people? But most of the profiles you read all say the same things…

(Andrew)

It could be argued that online daters become fussier than they would be offline and raise their expectations about the sort of partner they are likely to attract—especially when they can see so many choices available to them. As stated earlier, most people only described their favorable traits, and consequently these sites consist of a sea of attractive availables (who, as Andrew explains, all start to look the same). Moreover, as explained later in this chapter, many of these available choices are exaggerations and distortions of the real thing—airbrushed versions that cannot be lived up to offline.

Exchange theory again might help explain these results. As explained earlier in this chapter, Thibaut and Kelley (1959) argued that individuals developed expectations about relationships based on their comparisons with their own relationships and other people's relationships. There is a greater pool of "hypothetical comparisons" that can be made by online daters. Perhaps unrealistic comparisons are being made, leaving online daters dissatisfied with what they are attracting.

Another explanation for this "mismatching" might be that different people use the site in different ways. Some online daters do indeed spend copious amounts of time constructing an appropriate profile and reading through others' profiles to find their ideal match, while others play a "numbers game" (see Whitty & Carr, 2006). Some of the online daters (10 percent) firmly believed that others were contacting them without having closely read their profiles. Women (9 percent) claimed this more than the men (1 percent). To give an example:

A: I have had a hell of a lot sent to me [emails sent to her]. I have a feeling they just look at the photo and they don't actually bother reading the actual profile …

(Alison)

The women's concern that men were not reading their profiles was perhaps not unfounded. Some of the participants admitted to playing a "numbers game"; that is, they contacted many individuals hoping that someone would respond. The online daters that took this strategy were not so interested in the details of another profile, and often the men choose profiles with women they felt looked physically attractive in their profile. As demonstrated in the following extract:

A: that is the smorgasbord approach. I guess it comes back to what I was saying before in that life is a numbers game. If you go to a dance, then a barn dance is a numbers game and the purpose of that is, of course, is for the girls to met a guy; but this is a similar thing [the online dating site] without the music in the sense that you can see, you can get an understanding of and get an appreciation of the individual before a move is made in a way that you can't do in a pub or a club or, for that matter, even at a dance. So the shotgun approach is a reasonably sophisticated manner …

(Alan)

The online daters who played the "numbers game" used this strategy as a way to recruit some responses—even if these were not the "ideal" partners they were looking for. Men (60 percent) were much more likely to play this game compared to women (43 percent).

Gender differences

As with personal ads and video dating, men and women engaging in online dating differed in the types of characteristics they presented in their profiles, as well as the characteristics they sought in the opposite sex (see Whitty & Carr, 2006a for a more detailed discussion). Both men and women were looking for partners who were physically attractive. However, more women than men included photographs of themselves— some of these women going as far as having a professional glamour photograph taken of themselves. That women would go to more trouble can, in part, be explained by evolutionary theory. As was argued earlier in this chapter, and supported by research on personal ads, men have evolved to be attracted to young, attractive, fertile women. Given this, constructing a physically attractive photo is likely to attract more potential mates.

Evolutionary theory predicts, and previous research has found, that women are typically more attracted than men are to earning potential, social dominance, prowess, personality, and men who are willing to invest in them (Buss & Barnes, 1986; Kendrick *et al.*, 1990; Townsend & Wasserman, 1997). This result was only partly supported in the study on online dating. Women did focus on looking for a man with specific personality characteristics more than men did; however, there were no significant differences in wanting a partner with higher social economic status (SES). Rather than this being downplayed by women, it appears that men are also considering SES to be an important attribute to seek in a woman. Arguably, with so many perceived choices, men are raising the goal post and adding to their dating shopping list.

It was reported earlier in this chapter that research on personal ads has found that individuals exaggerate details about themselves or were selective with the truth they revealed in their ads (Ahuvia & Adelman, 1992). Similarly, online daters exaggerated aspects about themselves, though, unlike the results in research on personal ads, online daters did admit to stating complete lies (perhaps the online daters were more honest to the interviewer about their lies, or maybe they are more likely to lie than people writing personal ads). These fabrications were often gender-defined and predictable according to evolutionary theory. For example, women lied about looks or used outdated photos more than men. Slightly more men exaggerated or lied about their social status, as illustrated in the following extract:

B: I was a bit fed up with no return, so I just made up something that I'm very wealthy, I'm some entrepreneur and used my friend's Porsche and pictures and stuff like that. I'm standing next to a Porsche 911 turbo and made it sound really exciting ... I basically wrote down the profile of me of what I'd like to be in 10 years because I was getting no return. I was being very sincere with a lot of people, so I put that profile in and guess what? I get returns, absolutely everywhere. I'm telling you it is coming, like, I don't even have to approach people. People just come and I renamed myself as entrepreneur 23.

If we were to consider the above gender differences in light of exchange and equity theory, it seems that, to some extent, each gender is expecting some qualities over others in another. However, it also seemed apparent (as mentioned above) that these online daters were setting the hurdle higher—hoping perhaps for an "unfair trade." With so many choices, why not aim a little higher?

Comparing online dating with other ways of "meeting" online

Research on internet relationships has stressed how individuals gradually get to know one another online. Researchers have argued that cyberspace is a safe space to flirt and learn about potential romantic mates (e.g., Whitty, 2003). These studies have, in the main, focused on individuals who meet in chat rooms (e.g., Whitty & Gavin, 2001) and newsgroups (e.g., Bargh et al., 2002). For example, Whitty and Gavin (2001) found that individuals in chat rooms gradually develop romantic relationships by progressing through levels of trust through different mediums until they decide to meet face-to-face. Bargh et al. (2002) and McKenna et al. (2002) have argued that individuals in newsgroups feel more comfortable in revealing their "true" selves. Moreover, those who do are more likely to develop romantic relationships online that move successfully offline.

Screening not dating

In previous work I have argued that a different process takes place for individuals who meet in online dating sites compared to other online spaces (see Whitty & Carr, 2006; Whitty, 2007(a)). Online daters are not as concerned as others in other online spaces to get to know one another in cyberspace. This is demonstrated in the following extracts:

J: I had learnt from a few very early test runs that too many emails and phone calls before actually meeting over coffee or whatever can be a big mistake. Well, at least for me, because although you start to develop a sort of friendship and a certain intimacy, if there is no chemistry and you don't want to retain them as a friend, it feels very awkward. So I make it a rule that ... I don't sort of become emotionally close to someone I don't actually—I haven't seen in the flesh—because it is disappointing for both parties and it can feel quite strange.

(Jenny)

I: So did you email each other?
A: Not for very long. I don't use email for very long because I don't think it works very well. Some people like it; I just find you can email someone for weeks and then find that they are quite a different person in real life. Email gives you time to respond and compose your responses, and I don't have that sort of time. I don't want to sit there typing—I do it all day. I get on the PC all day for work, so I don't want to do it all night. So, I basically say to people that unless they are prepared to meet quickly then don't worry about it.

(Ann)

Online daters interviewed for this study talked about their keenness to discover if the profile they had identified online matched with the "actual" person. Moreover, they talked about the importance of testing for "chemistry" with that person—which they believed can only be determined face-to-face. They say this for two reasons: (a) because they believe that physical attraction can only really be judged when with a three-dimensional person in the flesh, face-to-face; and (b) because people can communicate differently face-to-face than in cyberspace. To give some examples:

A: I could use the word "chemistry" and I think is more apparent and longer lasting and of a greater foundation when it is a person face-to-face, than it is when it is telephone or email. There is the ground work, but it is obviously cemented when you met personally, and if there is an affinity from the word go, then you are going to get further quicker.

(Alan)

P: I sort of had a thing back then where I wasn't going to email for months on end and then meet this person to find out there is no chemistry at all, because people actually write differently than they speak— and I found that so much—so I actually try to make a point to write how I speak.

(Patricia)

Online daters typically sought out others who lived in their vicinity— again this contrasts with other spaces online where individuals are likely to know others within a range of distances and often great distances (Baker, 2005). This allowed them to meet their dates face-to-face quickly. In fact, 65 percent of the sample stated that they typically met their date within a week of first making contact online, and 11 percent said they typically met within a month of initial contact. One online dater aptly described the population of online daters as "kids in a lolly shop." Given the plenitude of perceived options on the site, individuals wanted to wade through the sea of choices—testing the waters with as many as possible as quickly as possible. This is again different from other spaces online where not everyone in a newsgroup or chat room is there with the intention (or at least the obvious intention) of moving toward an offline romantic and/or sexual relationship.

The science of finding the perfect match

The BAR approach

In previous work I have developed a theory about how individuals might more successfully find an appropriate match on an online dating site (Whitty, 2004; 2005; 2007(a); Whitty & Carr, 2006). From interviews conducted with online daters it has become apparent that a more successful approach is the *BAR approach*. That is, the more successful strategy that online daters need to adopt is to create a profile that presents both an "attractive" and a "real" self. This approach I have compared with Bargh *et al.*'s (2002) and McKenna *et al.*'s (2002) work on presentation on self in online newsgroups. These theorists drew on Higgins and Rogers' work of self and considered what they referred to as two forms of self, the "true" self and the "actual" self. The "true" self they define as traits or characteristics that individuals possess and would like to but are not typically able to express. The "actual" self they refer to as traits or characteristics that individuals do typically display in their everyday lives. They argued and found evidence to support their theory that individuals who participate in newsgroups who display their "true" selves are more likely to develop romantic relationships online that move successfully offline. I have found that their theory does not hold when one considers online daters (see Whitty, 2004, 2005, 2007(a); Whitty & Carr, 2006). This is because online daters claimed to be more attracted to honest and genuine people—determined by the profile and the first date. Profiles that appeared too outrageous or clichéd (e.g., described candlelit dinners and strolls on the beach) were deemed dishonest or unreal. Moreover, if the person did not match up to all the claims made in their profile on the first date they were judged as dishonest and people who could not be trusted (hence, not worthy of any further time in getting to know). In saying this, however, it was nonetheless important for online daters to present themselves in the best possible light so that they could attract possible dates. Hence, a more effective profile was one that achieved a good balance between an attractive and real self.

Leaving it in the hands of the "experts"

The art of successfully finding one's perfect match might not, however, be just down to constructing the perfect profile. Online dating sites are now developing matching tools to help match up individuals so that online daters do not have to do as much of the work. Various sites have developed compatibility tests for mate selection that claim to be scientifically based. For example, eHarmony (cited in Houran *et al.*, 2004: 509) makes the claim on their website that:

> Harmony's service is underpinned by its highly accurate, patented scientific model for matching. It is squarely built upon research conducted with more than 5,000 married persons. From careful statistical analyses of this data, a team of Ph.D. psychologists led by eHarmony founder Dr. Neil Clark Warren extrapolated a series of insights and understandings about relationships.

Some sites allow individuals to select profiles of their own choice, but also offer to match people on the site for compatibility and provide a list of appropriate matches. Other sites solely match people using their compatibility scales. Some of these sites claim to match on similarity of personality traits. Houran *et al.* (2004) challenge such tests, arguing that complementarity might be just as important to consider. In addition to personality tests, however, some sites are trying to match people on sexual compatibility. How successful these tests are in finding the perfect matches is yet to be determined; however, online dating companies do appear to be embracing these so-called scientific tools.

Conclusions

Online dating seems to have lost its social stigma and is becoming a popular dating arena worldwide (Whitty & Carr, 2006). These sites, however, will continue to be modified to suit people's needs. Moreover, individuals will no doubt become savvier in their presentations of self on these sites, as well as in their selections of appropriate partners. This chapter has demonstrated that while presentations of self on online dating sites are similar in some ways to personal ads and video dating, there are also some important differences. Theories, such as evolutionary theory, and exchange and equity theories, have been applied throughout the chapter to explain the dating processes involved across these different media. A new theory, named the BAR approach, was outlined to show how online dating is unique, not only when compared to older and more traditional forms of dating but also when compared to meeting romantic partners in other online spaces. Such a difference is important for social scientists, as well as designers of online dating sites, to consider.

References

Ahuvia, A. C., & Adelman, M. B. (1992) "Formal intermediaries in the marriage market: A typology and review." *Journal of Marriage and the Family, 54*, 452–463.

Albright, J. M. (2007) "How do I love thee and thee and thee: Self-presentation, deception, and multiple relationships online." In M. T. Whitty, A. J. Baker, & J. A. Inman. (eds.), *Online Matchmaking*. Palgrave Macmillan. pp. 81–93.

Baker, A. J. (2005) *Double Click: Romance and Commitment Among Online Couples*. (R. Rice, Editor). Cresskill, NJ: Hampton Press.

Bargh, J. A., McKenna, K. Y. A., & Fitzsimons, G. M. (2002) "Can you see the real me? Activation and expression of the 'true self' on the internet." *Journal of Social Issues, 58*, 33–48.

Brym, R. J., & Lenton, R. L. (2003) "Love at first byte: internet dating in Canada." Retrieved March 25, 2005, from http://www.societyinquestion4e.nelson.com/Chapter33Online.pdf.

Buss, D. M. (1987) "Sex differences in human mate selection criteria: an evolutionary perspective." In C. Crawford, M. Smith, & D. Krebs. (eds.), *Sociobiology and Psychology: Ideas, Issues and Perspectives*. London: Lawrence Erlbaum, pp. 335–352.

Buss, D. M., & Barnes, M. (1986) "Preferences in human mate selection." *Journal of Personality and Social Psychology, 50*, 559–570.

Cameron, C., Oskamp, S., & Sparks, W. (1977) "Courtship american style: Newspaper ads." *Family Coordinator, 26*(1), 27–30.

Gonzales, M. H., & Meyers, S. A. (1993) "Your mother would like me: Self-presentation in the personal ads of heterosexual and homosexual men and women." *Personality and Social Psychology Bulletin, 19*(2), 131–142.

Green, S. K., Buchanan, D., & Heuer, S. (1984) "Winners, losers, and choosers: A field investigation of dating initiation." *Personality and Social Psychology Bulletin, 10*, 502–511.

Greenless, I. A., & McGrew, W. C. (1994) "Sex and age differences in preferences and tactics of mate attraction: analysis of published advertisements." *Ethology and Sociobiology, 15*, 59–72.

Harrison, A., & Saeed, L. (1977) "Let's make a deal: an analysis of revelations and stipulations in lonely hearts advertisements." *Journal of Personality and Social Psychology, 35*,

257–264.

Houran, J., Lange, R., Rentfrow, P. J., & Bruckner, K. H. (2004) "Do online matchmaking tests work? An assessment of preliminary evidence for a publicized 'predictive model of marital success'." *North American Journal of Psychology, 6*(3), 507–526.

Kenrick, D. T., Sadalla, E. K., Groth, G., & Trost, M. R. (1990) "Evolution, traits, and the stages of human courtship: qualifying the parental investment model." *Journal of Personality, 58*, 97–116.

Koestner, R., & Wheeler, L. (1988) "Self-presentation in personal advertisements: the influence of implicit notions of attraction and role expectations." *Journal of Social and Personal Relationships, 5*, 149–160.

McKenna, K. Y. A., Green, A. S., & Gleason, M. E. J. (2002) "Relationship formation on the Internet: What's the big attraction?" *Journal of Social Issues, 58*, 9–31.

Riggio, R. E., & Woll, S. B. (1984) "The role of nonverbal cues and physical attractiveness in the selection of dating partners." *Journal of Social and Personal Relationships, 1*, 347–357.

Scharlott, B. W., & Christ, W. G. (1995) "Overcoming relationship-initiation barriers: the impact of a computer-dating system on sex role, shyness, and appearance inhibitions." *Computers in Human Behavior, 11* (2), 191–204.

Smith, J. E., Waldorf, V. A., & Trembath, D. L. (1990) "Single white male looking for thin, very attractive …" *Sex Roles, 23*(11/12), 675–685.

Thibaut, J. W., & Kelley, H. H. (1959). *The Social Psychology of Groups.* New York: Wiley.

Townsend, J., & Wasserman, T. (1997) "The perception of sexual attractiveness: Sex differences in variability." *Archives of Sexual Behavior, 26*, 243–268.

Whitty, M. T. (2003) "Cyber-flirting: playing at love on the internet." *Theory and Psychology, 13*, 339–357.

Whitty, M. T. (2004) "Shopping for love on the Internet: men and women's experiences of using an Australian Internet dating site." *Communication Research in the Public Interest.* New Orleans LA: *ICA, May 27–31, 2004.*

Whitty, M. T. (2005) "Searching for love on the net." *BPS Quinquennial Conference, University of Manchester, Manchester, U.K., March 30–April 2, 2005.*

Whitty, M. T. (2007(a)) "The art of selling one's 'self' on an online dating site: the BAR approach." In M. T. Whitty, A. J. Baker, & J. A. Inman. (eds). *Online Matchmaking.* Palgrave Macmillan. pp. 57–69.

Whitty, M. T. (2007(b)) "Introduction." In M. T. Whitty, A. J. Baker, & J. A. Inman. (eds.), *Online Matchmaking.* Basingstoke: Palgrave Macmillan. pp.1–14

Whitty, M. T., & Buchanan, T. (in press) Looking for love in so many places: characteristics of online daters and speed daters. *Interpersona.*

Whitty, M. T., & Carr, A. N. (2006) *Cyberspace Romance: the Psychology of Online Relationships.* Basingstoke: Palgrave Macmillan.

Whitty, M., & Gavin, J. (2001) "Age/sex/location: uncovering the social cues in the development of online relationships." *CyberPsychology & Behaviour, 4*, 623–630.

Woll, S. B., & Young, P. (1989) "Looking for Mr. or Ms. Right: self-presentation in video-dating." *Journal of Marriage and the Family, 51*(2), 483–488.

Chapter 13

Social identification with virtual communities

Sonja Utz

Interpersonal communication often takes place in groups: groups of friends, family members, sport teams, or work teams. The same holds true for mediated interpersonal communication—a great deal of it takes place in virtual groups or virtual communities. Horrigan *et al.* (2001) report that 84 percent of American internet users have contacted an online group at least once. This chapter focuses on virtual communities—on the well-established ones as well as on new trends.

Virtual communities have been studied since the early 1990s. In the beginning, the central research questions were: (a) whether virtual communities were indeed communities; and (b) what the societal consequences of participation in virtual communities were. Some authors saw mediated relationships as inferior to face-to-face (ftf) relationships, and virtual communities were consequently seen as pseudo-communities (Beniger, 1987). Skeptics worried that virtual communities destroyed "real" communities—that is, they assumed that engagement in virtual communities would lead to disengagement in offline communities (Fox, 1995; Kraut *et al.*, 1998; Slouka, 1995). Other people were overly enthusiastic and thought that virtual communities would create new forms of communities which would unite people across different races and classes (Barlow, 1995; Rheingold, 1993).

Research has meanwhile shown that virtual communities can be real communities rather than pseudo-communities (e.g., Baym, 1995; Bruckman, 1992; Utz, 1999). Neither skeptics nor enthusiasts turned out to be entirely right. People continue to meet each other ftf; and although some forms of social capital have declined (Putnam, 1995), new forms have emerged (for example bottom-up internet projects; Horrigan, 2001). Therefore, the current chapter does not focus on the question *whether* virtual communities can be "real" communities. Instead, it will focus on *how* group formation takes place in virtual communities. According to the social identity approach (Haslam, 2001; Tajfel, 1978; Tajfel & Turner, 1986), group identity formation can occur via a top-down process, categorization, or a bottom-up process, interpersonal communication. A social psychological rather than a socio-logical (e.g., social network analysis; Wellman & Gulia, 1999) approach is chosen because it avoids reducing groups to interpersonal relation-ships or ties. Instead, group behavior and group identity are explained on a more abstract level than interpersonal behavior (Postmes & Baym, 2005). Before talking about the processes underlying group behavior in more detail, a definition of virtual communities will be worked out and an overview of the various venues in which virtual communities can arise will be given. The chapter will also discuss the consequences of participation in virtual communities, and raise open questions to show directions for further research.

Virtual communities—a definition

The term "virtual communities" became popular in 1993 when the book *Virtual Communities* by Howard Rheingold appeared. He defined them as "social aggregations that emerge from the [internet] when enough people carry on those public discussions long enough, with sufficient human feeling, to form webs of personal relationships in cyberspace" (Rheingold, 1993: 5). A more specific definition is given by Fernback and Thompson (1995), who define virtual communities as "social relationships forged in cyberspace through repeated contact within a specific boundary or place (e.g., a conference or a chat line) that is symbolically delineated by topic of interest." These definitions were appropriate for the computer-mediated communities like the WELL (Rheingold, 1993), or the ones that arose in newsgroups (Baym, 1995), chats (Reid, 1991), or multi-user-dungeons (MUDs; Bruckman, 1992; Curtis, 1992; Utz, 1999). However, they have been challenged by the rise of commercial communities, the blurring between media and the development of new forms of mobile communi-ties.

Porter (2004) gives a definition which also captures these new forms; she sees virtual communities as "an aggregation of individuals or business partners who interact around a shared interest, where the interaction is at least partially supported and/or mediated by technology and guided by some protocols or norms." This definition does not insist on computer-mediated communication, but on mediation by technology in general. Additionally, it does not exclude ftf interactions—the communication can be mediated by technology only partially as well. Indeed, most commu-nities are not exclusively virtual; members start to meet each other ftf (Parks & Roberts, 1998; Utz, 1999). The definition also explicitly includes commercial communities. Porter regards the existence of norms or proto-cols as a defining characteristic, concurring with anthropologists and soci-ologists. However, in the current chapter a social psychological approach is taken and the existence of social relationships is seen as the essential element: "Without the personal investment, intimacy, and commitment that characterizes our ideal sense of community, some on-line discussion groups and chat rooms are nothing more than a means of communication among people with common interest" (Fernback, 1999: 216).

In social psychology, two types of relationships are distinguished: attachment to other persons or group members (interpersonal attraction) and attachment to a group as a whole (social identification; Hogg & Turner, 1985; Utz, 2003). Social identification with a (virtual) group explains the emergence of group norms and other forms of (inter)group behavior and is therefore regarded as more important than the existence of interpersonal attraction between individual community members. Thus, social identification is considered as the factor that turns an aggregation of individuals whose interaction around a shared interest is at least partially supported and/or mediated by technology into a virtual community. However, before providing the arguments for this statement, I will provide an overview over the various virtual settlements in which virtual communities can develop. The differentiation between virtual settlements and virtual communities was introduced by Jones (1997) to distinguish between online venues which have the *potential* to become a virtual community and *actual* virtual communities. Virtual settlements are virtual places in which people interact; in virtual communities social relationships have emerged.

A short history of virtual settlements

The early days of the internet—separated services

In the early days of the internet, several separate services existed. Starting in 1979 discussions took place in the *newsgroups* of the Usenet. Newsgroups are virtual bulletin boards; and discussion in newsgroups is usually topic-centered. The Usenet is hierarchically organized. Originally, there were seven main hierarchies, such as *comp* (discussions about computer science), *soc* (discussions about societal topics), or *talk* (general discussions). Under these parent hierarchies, the newsgroups have become more and more specific. Under the *alt.sports* hierarchy, several discussion groups about various sports can be found, and *alt.sports.baseball.ny-yankees* focuses specifically on the baseball team the New York Yankees. Within a newsgroup, the discussion is organized around so-called threads—the discussion is sorted around topics, not in a temporal order. Communication in newsgroups is asynchronous—as in the case of a traditional bulletin board, one does not have to be present at the moment the message is posted. To be able to read the postings of others or to post your own messages, you had to install a specific program, a so-called newsreader. Nowadays, it is also possible to read newsgroups in a web browser, for example via groups.google.com.

Whereas news servers used to list about 2,500 groups in the early 1990s (Krol, 1995), Google listed more than 53,000 newsgroups in January 2006.

Chats were also developed in the early days of the internet. In the late 1980s, Internet Relay Chat (IRC), a multiuser chat system, was very popular. Again, one needed to install a specific chat-client to be able to communicate with other chatters. Chats are an example of synchronous CMC: that is, one can only chat with people who are logged in at the same time. Synchronous CMC can bridge geographic boundaries, but it is not free from temporal restrictions. The IRC has several thousands of channels; most of them are topic-centered. Nowadays, many chats are webchats—the installation of a chat-client is no longer necessary and not much technological knowledge is required. There are also graphical or 3D-chats in which participants are represented by avatars. Chats are also no longer necessarily topic-centered, general small talk and flirt-lines have become more and more popular. Webchat.de lists more than 2,000 chats in Germany and reports more than half a million visitors per month.

Although they have existed since 1978, MUDs are less well-known online venues. MUDs are text-based role-playing adventure games. That is, people choose the name, gender, and race (e.g., elf, fairy, dwarf) of their character. The goal of the game is to solve quests and to kill monsters, improving skills and advancing in levels. There are also more socially oriented MUDs that focus on socializing and interacting with other players rather than on killing monsters. By the early 1980s MUDs had already integrated various forms of communication and are therefore an example of complex virtual communities. In principle, communication in MUDs is synchronous, but they have also an internal mail and newsgroup system. After a certain level one can become a wizard and develop the MUD further by programming new areas or quests. Although many players see MUDs mainly as recreational games, the wizards view them as a joint programming project (Utz, 1996). MUDs are close mirrors of society—they are complete virtual *worlds*. There are small bars, shops, and churches; small villages and big cities; different races and classes; differences in status and power. MUDs are therefore especially suited for studying issues of power, hierarchy, and norm violation (Duval Smith, 1999; Reid, 1999). Originally, MUDs were entirely text-based. Such MUDs still exist, www.mudconnector.com lists about 1,600 of them worldwide. Nowadays, graphical and three-dimensional multiuser games such as World of Warcraft or Second Life are much more popular. Second Life is more like a social MUD, with the difference that the Linden dollars earned in the virtual world can be exchanged into real currencies. This makes Second Life attractive for companies which open branch offices in the virtual world (e.g., Philips, ABN Amro, Adidas). World of Warcraft alone has more than 7.5 million subscribers (Blizzard, November 2006), Second Life has more than 1.7 million inhabitants (www. secondlife.com, December 2006).

The rise of web browsers—integration of the various services

Since web browsers became established, the various forms of synchronous and asynchronous communication have been integrated in web communities and their user-friendliness has grown. Web communities are one of the fastest growing types of website. Most web communities have web forums—discussion boards similar to newsgroups, but with the difference that messages can be easily posted via a web form. Additionally, they often contain webchats and allow the sending of community internal mails. Members can create user profiles containing a picture and/or personal information, they may have a weblog, or can leave messages in another member's guestbook.

One of the reasons for the exponential growth of web communities in the late 1990s is the idea of using them commercially to increase customer loyalty. This idea was promoted by Hagel and Armstrong in their book, *Net Gain* (1997). This book created a hype—and many companies tried to make money by building virtual communities. However, it turned out that putting a chat room or a discussion board on a website is not sufficient to create a virtual community; and many of those virtual settlements never reached a break-even point (Bughin & Zeisser, 2001). Nevertheless, web communities are currently the most well-known and popular online venues among average internet users. However, newer technologies, which have already been developed and are being used by innovators and early adopters, will be described in the next section.

Current trends

Mobile communities

More recently, mobile communities have been developed—virtual settlements in which the communication is mediated via cell phones. Whereas the advantage of the internet has long been seen as its capacity to connect people from all over the world, mobile communities use global positioning systems (GPS) to connect people locally. One example is dodgeball (www.dodgeball.com)—a service available in 22 American cities (January, 2006) with about 15,000 users. Playtxt (www.playtxt.net) is the U.K. equivalent. Founded in 2004, it had 6,000 users in March 2005 and covers 200 countries (November, 2006). These services might inform people that a friend, or a friend of a friend, is sitting in the cafe around the corner, or that someone they have a crush on is out walking two blocks further on. Such technologies are also used to connect people with similar interests—for example, with similar research interests at a conference (Eagle & Pentland, 2005). The internet can globally connect people with similar interests, but the combination of cell phones and geographical positioning techniques enables people to connect with one another within a defined local distance. Whereas globalization was one of the catch phrases used to describe the rise of the internet, there is now a trend away from globalization toward localization, as predicted by Castells as early as 1997 (p. 65): "When networks dissolve time and space, people anchor themselves in places."

Web 2.0—the social web

An entire group of new developments is captured by the term *Web 2.0*. This term became a buzzword after it was used at a conference brainstorming session between the media company O'Reilly and MediaLive International (O'Reilly, 2005). As in software development, where small changes are indicated by, for example, a change from version 1.6 to 1.7, a change from version 1.0 to version 2.0 indicates a fundamental change. Instead of a formal definition, contrasts were provided to explain the distinction: such as Britannica Online is Web 1.0, Wikipedia is Web 2.0; personal websites are Web 1.0, blogging is Web 2.0; publishing is Web 1.0, participation is Web 2.0; directories (taxonomies) are Web 1.0, tagging ("folksonomies") is Web 2.0. A common characteristic is the social nature of these technologies; and the term *social software* is often used to describe them. Social software connects people *bottom-up*.

One example is social network sites. Whereas newsgroups or mailings lists have been primarily dedicated to a *topic*, and contacts and relationships evolved as a by-product, social network sites such as friendster (www. friendster.com), linkedIn (www.linkedin.com), MySpace (www.myspace. com), passado (www.passado.com), or hyves (www.hyves.net) aim to connect *people*. They allow the users to make profiles describing their interests and hobbies and to find old friends or classmates, people with similar interests, or possible business partners.

Another new trend is social sharing technologies—people share their pictures with other users on sites such as flick.r (www.flickr.com), they share their bookmarks on sites such as del.icio.us (http://del.icio.us), or they share their goals on sites such as 43things (http://www.43things. com). In these *tagging* plays a central role. Tagging is a new collaborative form of organizing content. Users can assign freely chosen keywords to their pictures, bookmarks, or other pieces of information they want to share. Thus, users are no longer forced to use the categories and taxonomies imposed top-down from authoritative systems. Instead, they can create the classification systems bottom-up, so-called folksonomies, that best suit their personal needs. The software makes it possible to look at pieces of information other users connect with the same tag.

Wikis are another example of a Web 2.0 technology. The most famous one is the Wikipedia encyclopedia, but wikis are used in many other contexts as well (see http://en.wikipedia.org/wiki/List_of_wikis). Wikis are websites which contain an additional "edit this page" option. Websites are built and developed by the users themselves, not provided by an institution. Although the co-authoring technology is often used by virtual teams in teaching, or other small groups, and access is sometimes restricted to a specific group of users, there are very large wikis in which thousand of authors contribute (http://meta.wikimedia.org/wiki/List_of_largest_wikis).

Another popular example of active content creation by users is the *weblog*. Walker (2003) defines a weblog (shortened name: blog) as "a frequently updated website consisting of dated entries arranged in reverse chronological order so the most recent post appears first." The first weblogs appeared in the mid-1990s; they became popular as simple and free publishing tools became available. Most blogs are published by individuals, but there are also weblogs maintained by groups (e.g., www.dutchcowboys.nl). Many blogs allow other users to comment on them or have links to other blogs. Interblog-conversations appear, and search machines such as *technorati* keep track of what is happening in the blogosphere.

The integration of media

The two trends described above are still based on a distinction between mobile communities and internet-based communities. However, a third trend is the blurring of this distinction. Nowadays, many virtual environments integrate various media. In many web communities, it is possible to send short messages to the cell phones of other members via the website. Instant message programs such as ICQ also include options for sending SMS, email, or for sending links to websites. People use their phones to access the internet, and use the internet to make phone calls (e.g., Skype).

A classification of virtual communities

As we have seen, there is a wide variety of virtual communities, and although the older forms still continue to exist, virtual communities are constantly developing and new forms are evolving. First, asynchronous and synchronous forms of CMC have been integrated in web communities. Now, the boundaries between media, as well as that between mediated communication and ftf communication, are blurring. Instead of distinguishing underlying technologies (newsgroups, chat) in terms of the integration of media, it makes more sense to classify virtual communities around other criteria.

Porter's (2004) typology is one of the most comprehensive and exhaustive ones. It starts with a very general distinction between member-initiated vs. organization-sponsored communities. As the name implies, member-initiated communities have been established by and are maintained by the members, whereas organization-sponsored communities are run by commercial or non-commercial organizations. Member-initiated communities are further subdivided into communities with a social relationship orientation and communities with a professional relationship orientation. The former focus on nonprofessional topics such as hobbies and leisure activities, whereas the latter are formed around shared professional interests: for example, a mailing list of internet researchers. Similarly, organization-sponsored communities are subdivided into commercial communities, nonprofit communities, and government-sponsored communities. Porter states that each community can be described by taking account of five attributes (the five Ps of virtual communities): purpose, place, platform, population interaction structure, and profit model.

Thus, "virtual community" is an umbrella term describing a wide variety of different *online* groups. However, there is also a wide variety of *offline* groups—work teams, sport teams, friends, school classes, and so on. Social psychology has identified general principles and processes which underlie group behavior in *all* groups.

From virtual settlement to virtual community

As stated above, the existence of social relationships is necessary to turn a virtual settlement into a virtual community. Sociologists often use the social network approach to analyze (virtual) communities (e.g., Haythornthwaite, 2002; Wellman, 1988; Wellman & Gulia, 1999). Community is no longer defined in terms of space—neighborhoods or villages (e.g., Tönnies 1887/1963)—but in terms of social networks. A network consists of members (the "knots" of the network) and the ties between these members. Social network analysis examines, for example, the density, strength, or heterogeneity of ties within a network. This often leads to interesting and important results (e.g., Hampton & Wellman, 2001; Wellman & Gulia, 1999), but overlooks the point that groups are more than the sum of interpersonal ties (Postmes & Baym, 2005).

The *social identity approach* (Haslam, 2001; Tajfel, 1978; Tajfel & Turner, 1986) views group behavior as different from individual behavior: group processes take place on a different level of abstraction. Behavior in groups is not guided solely by personal motives and goals, but by the group goals and other group-level considerations. Group goals might even be in conflict with individual goals, as is the case in social dilemmas. Social identification with a group can then overrule the individual's own goals (De Cremer & Van Vugt, 1999). The social network approach can describe the structure of networks, but it cannot explain these transformations of motivation.

The social identity approach considers social identity as "the causal basis of group processes" (Turner & Oakes, 1989: 240), or the social glue that fosters group loyalty (Van Vugt & Hart, 2004). It can explain a wide variety of group behaviors, such as conformity to group norms, group influence, cohesion and solidarity, or stereotyping. Social identity is "that part of an individual's self-concept which derives from his knowledge of his membership of a social group (or groups) together with the value and emotional significance attached to that membership" (Tajfel, 1978: 63). Thus, knowledge of membership is sufficient; and (self) categorization as group member does not require ftf contact with other group members. Indeed, studies in the minimal group paradigm have shown that interaction between group members is not necessary to produce ingroup-favoring behavior (Tajfel et al., 1971). The social identity theory can therefore be applied to a wide variety of groups, for example large-scale groups such as nations. In these groups, members do not know all other members personally. This holds also true for many virtual communities.

However, social identity is more than the cognitive categorization as a group member; it also includes affective attachment to the group. Categorization refers to the cognitive aspect of social identity; identification refers to the affective aspects of social identity. Social identity research has for a long time mainly focused on the question of how the top-down processes of categorization and identity salience influence group behavior; more recently, it turned to the question of how group norms emerge bottom-up through interpersonal communication and interaction (e.g., Postmes et al., 2005). As will be outlined below, both processes are important for virtual communities.

The social identity approach makes a distinction between personal and social identity (Haslam, 2001; Tajfel, 1978; Tajfel & Turner, 1986). The self-concept of a person comprises their personal identity and their social identities. In a given situation, one type of identity is salient, "switched on." Categorization divides people into members of in- and outgroups, based on similarities with ingroup members and differences from outgroup members. When personal identity is salient, people perceive themselves as unique individuals with an idiosyncratic combination of interests and characteristics—no or few similarities with other people are perceived. When a social identity is salient, people perceive themselves in terms of similarities with other ingroup members and dissimilarities with outgroup members. Which identity becomes salient in a given moment is determined by the accessibility and the fit of the various possible identities (Oakes, 1987).

Can virtual settlements provide a basis for a salient social identity? In many online venues, the members are relatively anonymous, only represented by a nick-name. Skeptics therefore worried whether group behavior could occur in text-based CMC in which all nonverbal cues are filtered out. The Social Identity and DEindividuation (SIDE-)model deals exactly with that question (Reicher et al., 1995). The model consists of a cognitive and a strategic aspect. The cognitive aspect determines which type of identity is salient, whereas the strategic aspect determines to what extent behavior is guided by group norms. The latter is not directly relevant for the current chapter (see Chapter 10, this volume). For the cognitive aspect, anonymity is the key variable. SIDE argues that anonymity can even foster group identities. In a nutshell, anonymity—that is, not knowing (much about) the other interaction partners—further strengthens the salience of an already salient identity. If personal identity is salient when one enters a virtual community, anonymity hinders the perception of similarities between oneself and the other members of the community. As a consequence the perception of one's own person as a unique individual is further stressed, and potential bases for categorization are not perceived as such. However, when a social identity is salient, anonymity results in an overestimation of similarities between oneself and the other members of the community. Differences are not perceived, categorization is exaggerated.

People often choose the virtual community which best fits their current goals and interests; therefore, it can be assumed that they often enter a virtual community with a salient social identity. Thus, categorization processes can be enhanced in CMC, and social identification with a virtual community can be high from the very beginning. Indeed, Utz (2003) found in a study of MUD users that social identification was unrelated to duration of membership in the virtual community, whereas interpersonal relationships became stronger with duration of membership. This confirms the top-down process of group identity formation via categorization—social identification can be strong from the first moment. Interpersonal relationships on the other hand need time to develop (Walther, 1992). Social identification and interpersonal attraction were only moderately correlated at $r(206) = .23, p < .01$, indicating that group identity formation is relatively independent from interpersonal communication in relatively anonymous topic-centered communities. Remember that MUDs are purely text-based role-playing adventure games; there are no member profiles with pictures; and the character profiles describe a role-playing character but not the person who plays the character.

Further evidence for the SIDE-model comes from Rogers and Lea (2005), who found that subtle cues that stressed the belonging to a common social identity enhanced levels of social identification with virtual groups in *anonymous* CMC. Thus, the cognitive representation of a group and self-categorization as a group member is more important for social identification than actual affective bonds between group members in anonymous CMC.

However, communication in many web communities is not as anonymous as early CMC used to be and as CMC in laboratory experiments (e.g., Rogers & Lea, 2005) often is. Members can often create profiles containing a picture and personal information. The blurring of media allows the addition of additional channels such as audio and video. Often, the communities are not so much centered around a shared interest, but around people (e.g., social network sites). Postmes *et al.* (2005) found that in individuated and interpersonal settings, group identity is developed bottom-up through the interpersonal communication among community members. These characteristics apply to many of the new virtual settlements, in particular for social network sites and mobile communities. Utz (2005) conducted a study in such an environment, more specifically, a consumer community. In consumer communities, people write reviews about products. The idea is to provide other consumers with more unbiased information about the quality of products than company websites usually do. In this particular community, members had profiles which could contain their picture, information about age, gender, occupation, hobbies and interests, or additional contact information. Social identification with the community was clearly correlated with interpersonal attraction, $r(303) = .55, p < .001$, indicating that group identity formation is related to interpersonal communication and interaction in these communities.

Consequences of social identification with a virtual community

Consequences within the virtual community

Social identification with a virtual group has consequences within the community as well as for real life outside of the community. Within the community, social identification or self-categorization as a group member leads to depersonalization: that is, people perceive themselves as interchangeable group members and ascribe the group's typical characteristics to themselves. In the study on MUDders, Utz (2003) found a correlation, of $r(205) = .56, p < .001$, between social identification and perceived prototypicality, i.e. agreement with the statement "I am a typical MUDder." Perceived fit of the categorization, measured as the difference between the statement "In many respects, I am different from non-MUDders" and "In many respects, I am different from other MUDders," was also positively correlated with social identification, $r(202) = .32, p < .001$.

The salient social identity also determines which norms are relevant in a specific situation. If personal identity is salient, people orient their behavior on their own personal standards. However, if a social identity is salient, the group's norms start to guide the behavior. A norm within a virtual community can be to contribute actively to the community by posting messages. The idea behind virtual communities is that the community is maintained by the community members itself; they create the content which can be found in the web forum and chat boxes (Hagel & Armstrong, 1997). In a study of the community of a large Dutch music provider, positive correlations between social identification with the community and active contribution to the chat, $r(330) = .36$, $p < .001$, to the forum, $r(330) = .36$, $p < .001$, and to the weblog, $r(330) = .26$, $p < .001$, emerged (Utz & Bijleveld, 2006).

Consequences outside the virtual community

Social identification does not only affect behavior within the virtual community; it can also affect intergroup behavior. MUDders who identified highly with their virtual community also showed more ingroup favoring behavior; they showed higher levels of ingroup bias than low identifiers did (Utz, 2003). In a commercial context, Utz and van Bijleveld (2006) found that individuals who showed high levels of social identification with the virtual community of a music television channel not only produced more content within the virtual community, but also showed higher levels of loyalty toward the TV channel.

McKenna and Bargh (1998) focused on the consequences of (active) participation in virtual communities. They focused on people with marginalized identities who participated in newsgroups, for example gays or people with extreme political opinions. McKenna and Bargh (1998) conducted an online survey of active and passive members of these newsgroups. Active members judged the importance of this social identity as a higher priority, and participation in the newsgroup led to greater self-acceptance as well as to a "coming out." A significant percentage of the active members revealed their embarrassing and socially sanctioned aspect to family members and friends. Active community members also showed less estrangement from society in general. Rodgers and Chen (2005) studied the effects of participating in a virtual community by women with breast cancer and found a positive correlation between the amount of participation and psychosocial wellbeing.

Whether virtual communities have negative or positive consequences for society as a whole cannot be answered generally; it depends on the norms of the specific virtual community. By introducing the concept of various social identities and corresponding ingroup norms, the social identity approach can also explain behavior that seems at first glance to be anti-normative. In early CMC research, incidents of flaming were reported and the conclusion that the internet is a hostile, unfriendly medium was reached (Kiesler et al., 1984). However, this behavior can be normative within a specific group, even though it violates societal norms (Reicher et al., 1995). For example, militant Muslims also use newsgroups, chats, or web forums to communicate with each other, but within these subgroups radical statements are appreciated. This phenomenon could also be seen in the riots in Paris in 2005. Gang members used the internet to call others to arms (Moore & Williams, 2005; see Chapter 10, this volume, for more examples of anti-normative behavior). Thus, there are cases in which participation in virtual communities has negative consequences for society.

However, virtual communities can also be used to organize collective action and to produce collective goods. People who contribute to Wikipedia create a public good which can be accessed by everybody, not only active contributors. Blanchard and Horan (2000) showed that social capital increases when opportunities for civic engagement are facilitated by physically based virtual communities. Some virtual communities are explicitly dedicated to collective action. Postmes and Brunsting (2002) showed that collective action is possible via the internet and, more importantly, that the internet changes collective action. This is attributed to the mobilizing power of a mass medium like the internet. Again, social identity is supposed to play a central role in this process. A shared social identity can motivate people who are physically isolated to engage in collective action.

Where are we heading? An agenda for future research

Although some authors think that virtual community research suffers from novelty fatigue (Feenberg & Bakardjieva, 2004: 41), there are still a lot of unsolved questions. There are several promising new technologies, such as mobile communities and social software. Web 2.0 is supposed to fundamentally alter the internet by strengthening participation and interaction (folksonomies, social network sites). Where are these developments leading to?

The first unanswered question is directed at specific virtual settlements. Will virtual communities develop in all these new venues? We do not want to repeat the old doubts about whether community is possible—but does tagging one's photos or writing one's personal journal in a public weblog already make a community? This question has barely been studied. Many blogs are not virtual communities; according to Lampa (2005) two-thirds of them are not updated within two months, and 80 percent are abandoned after a few months. However, many newsgroups, chat rooms, or web communities also fail to become lively communities. Blanchard (2004) reports a case study about the Julie/Julia project. In this blog the author Julie Powell described for one year how she tried to cook the recipes in the cookbook by Julia Child, *Mastering the Art of French Cooking*. This blog used to be very popular, receiving more than 7,000 hits per day (Blanchard, 2004). For some of the participants in the survey, the blog clearly was a community. These were the active participants who commented on Julie's entries. They developed emotional bonds with Julie and other active commentators. However, for many—especially lurkers who only read the blog but never added a comment—it was not a community. Whereas lurkers in other contexts such as newsgroups usually consider the virtual settlement as a virtual community in which they define themselves as rather peripheral and low-identified members (Blanchard & Markus, 2004), they did not do so in the case of this weblog. Blanchard (2004) argues that lurkers in newsgroups usually follow the interactions of the other group members (reading questions and answers), whereas lurkers on blogs often only read the blog, but not the comments. Despite the undisputed popularity of weblogs (60 million tracked by Technorati, November 2006), the question of their community-forming potential still remains open. The results of Blanchard (2004) suggest that the bottom-up process of group identity formation via interpersonal communication is more important than the top-down process via categorization in blogs. Further research should test this hypothesis.

The same questions arise for social network sites. Do people see these services just as additional means to keep in touch with friends, former classmates, and work colleagues, or do they really categorize themselves as a member of the respective community and perceive similarities between themselves and other—not (yet) personally known—users? In a similar vein, most mobile communities mainly provide information about the location of friends one already has. Thus, existent interactions are simply extended to another medium. The question arises as to how far communication via these new media influences group identity (formation).

The community forming potential might be higher for wikis or other communities in which collaboration takes place. At least, the top-down process of categorization should be more important than in social networking sites or mobile communities because the common goals are clearer and also more important than the maintenance of relationships. Communication is also much more task-focused and less interpersonal. However, the decision about whether a virtual settlement is a community or not can often not be made from outside—it resides in the minds of the members. If a significant percentage perceives the virtual settlement as a community and identifies with it, it *is* a virtual community. More studies are needed to find out to what extent the social web actually creates communities.

However, research should also look at the bigger picture—how do people integrate virtual communities into their everyday lives? We know that there are virtual communities, and we also know that many people are members of virtual communities—or have contacted them at least once (Horrigan *et al.*, 2001). However, most of the studies have focused on one specific virtual community and the processes occurring there (e.g., Baym, 1995; Bruckman, 1992, Curtis, 1992; Utz, 1999, 2000). Less is known about what types or combination of virtual communities people prefer—worldwide groups or mobile communities which bring them in contact with people in their neighborhood? Discussion groups or groups which require collaboration and lead to collective action? And how do their virtual communities relate to their offline group memberships? Some studies have examined both the online and offline relationships of individuals. Baym *et al.* (2004) assessed the interpersonal interactions of college students across several media. However, they focused on interactions with acquaintances, friends, family members, and partners, and did not explicitly address interactions with virtual group members in their analysis. The Netville project focuses on the impact of new media on a community. Netville is a newly built neighborhood in a suburb of Toronto. All of the homes are equipped with a broadband high-speed local network and several advanced communication technologies which are not yet publicly available (Hampton & Wellman, 2001). The project started in 1997, and for three years the inhabitants of Netville have been the subject of many scientific studies employing a variety of research methods and research questions. These studies take a social network approach: that is, they focus on the strong and weak ties of individuals, but do not assess social identification with various communities. Nevertheless, the papers from this project give interesting insights into people's networking, how the networks are maintained via ftf contact and multiple media, and how the new communication technologies change this pattern. More such detailed longitudinal studies are necessary to examine the short- and long-term consequences of participation in virtual communities. How many virtual and traditional groups do people belong to, and how stable is this pattern over time? Do people abandon a virtual community more easily than a traditional one? Are individuals who are active in one community also very active in others, or do most individuals have communities in which they are central members and others in which they are more peripheral members? Studies across communities and media are needed to answer these questions.

On a broader, more sociological level, the rise of mobile communities and Web 2.0 raises the question of how all this will impact on society. Bakardjieva (2003: 291) argues that over the internet a cultural trend of *immobile socialization* has occurred—"socialization of private experience through the invention of new forms of intersubjectivity and social organization online". She thereby reverses Williams's (1974) concept of *mobile privatization*. Williams (1974) argued that technologies such as radio and television led to a withdrawal of middle-class families from public spaces into private suburban homes, whereas at the same time the automobile made them more mobile. Bakardjieva (2003) states that the internet reversed this trend. People start to engage in collective action while staying at home. With regard to the blurring of media and the rise of mobile-social software, I would argue that we are now entering a stage of *mobile socialization*—people associate with others or engage in collective action from wherever they are. However, the questions of whether the social and collaborative technologies of Web 2.0 increase collaboration and collective action remain open to future research.

Conclusion

Being a member of groups is an important aspect in people's lives, and virtual communities extend the possibilities of finding others with similar interests. Whether interpersonal communication is ftf or mediated by technology is not the decisive criterion for the formation of group identity. More important is whether individuals categorize themselves as members of a group and exhibit social identification with that group. Social identity is the social glue that holds groups together and explains a variety of group behaviors (Van Vugt & Hart, 2004). Although the fundamental principles underlying virtual communities do not differ from those underlying ftf interacting groups, virtual communities differ in some aspects: They make it easier to connect people from all over the world as well as to bring them together locally (e.g., dodgeball). They facilitate large-scale collaboration and the coordination of collective action. They provide access to information otherwise not available in such an organized way and on such a large scale (e.g., consumer communities). Virtual communities are already a part of many people's everyday lives; and with the development of social software and mobile communities, this development will go on. Instead of worrying whether virtual communities are equivalent to traditional ones, research should turn to the question of how people integrate various forms of (virtual) communities and whether the social Web 2.0 indeed makes the world a more social place.

References

Bakardjieva, M. (2003) "Virtual togetherness: an everyday-life perspective." *Media, Culture & Society, 25*, 291–313.

Barlow, J.P. (1995, March-April) "Is there a there in cyberspace?" *Utne Reader, 50*–56.

Baym, N.K. (1995) "The emergence of community in computer-mediated communication." In S.G. Jones (ed.), *CyberSociety: Computer-Mediated Communication and Community.* Thousand Oaks: Sage, pp. 138–163.

Baym, N.K., Zhang, Y.B., & Lin, M. (2004) "Social interactions across media. Interpersonal communication on the internet, telephone and face-to-face." *News Media & Society, 6,* 299–318.

Beniger, J.R. (1987) „Personalization of mass media and the growth of pseudo-community." *Communication Research, 14,* 353–371.

Blanchard, A. (2004) "Blogs as virtual communities: identifying a sense of community in the Julie/Julia project." Retrieved January 7, 2006, from http://blog.lib.umn.edu/blogo-sphere/blogs_as_virtual.html

Blanchard, A., & Horan, T. (2000) "Virtual communities and social capital." In: G. David Garson (ed.), *Social Dimensions of Information Technology: Issues for the New Millennium.* Hershey, Pa.: Ideas Group, pp. 5–20.

Blanchard, A.L., & Markus, M.L. (2004) "The experienced 'sense' of a virtual community: characteristics and processes." *Database for Advances in Information Systems, 35,* 65–79.

Blizzard press release. World of Warcraft®: "The burning crusade™ in stores January, 2006." Retrieved November 29, 2006 from http://www.blizzard.com/press/061109.shtml

Bruckman, A. (1992) "Identity workshop: Emergent social and psychological phenomena in text-based virtual reality." Retrieved January 8, 2001, from http://www.cc.gatech.edu/fac/Amy.Bruckman/papers/index.html#IW.

Bughin, J., & Zeisser, M. (2001) "The marketing scale effectiveness of virtual communities." *EM–Electronic Markets, 11,* 258–262.

Castells, M. (1997) *The Information Age: Economy, Society and Culture. Vol. 2. the Power of Identity.* Oxford: Blackwell.

Curtis, P. (1992) "MUDding: social phenomenon in text-based virtual realities." *Intertrek, 3*, 26-34.

De Cremer, D., & Van Vugt, M. (1999) "Social identification effects in social dilemmas: A transformation of motives." *European Journal of Social Psychology, 29*, 871–893.

Duval Smith, A. (1999) "Problems of conflict management in virtual communities." In M.A. Smith & P. Kollock (eds.), *Communities in Cyberspace*. London: Routledge, pp. 134–163.

Eagle, N., & Pentland, A. (2005) "Social serendipity: mobilizing social software." Retrieved January, 10, 2006, from http://reality.media.mit.edu/pdfs/serendipity.pdf.

Feenberg, A., & Bakardjieva, M. (2004) "Virtual community: no 'killer implication'." *New Media & Society, 6*, 37–43.

Fernback, J. (1999) "There is a there there. Notes toward a definition of cybercommunity." In S.G. Jones (eds.), *Doing Internet Research*. Thousand Oaks: Sage, pp. 203–220.

Fernback, J., & Thompson, B. (1995) "Virtual communities: abort, retry, failure? Computer-mediated communication and the American collectivity: the dimensions of community within cyberspace." Retrieved March 24, 1997, from http://www.well.com/user/hlr/texts/Vccivil.html.

Fox, R. (1995) "Newstrack." *Communications of the ACM, 38*, 11–12.

Hagel, J. III & Armstrong, A.G. (1997) *Net Gain. Expanding Markets through Virtual Communities*. Boston, Mass: Harvard Business School Press.

Hampton, K., & Wellman, B. (2001) "Long distance community in the network society. Contact and support beyond Netville." *The American Behavioral Scientist, 45*, 476–495.

Haslam, S.A. (2001) *Psychology in Organizations: the Social Identity Approach*. London: Sage.

Haythornthwaite, C. (2002) "Strong, weak, and latent ties and the impact of new media." *Information Society, 18*, 385–401.

Hogg, M.A., & Turner, J.C. (1985) "Interpersonal attraction, social identification and psychological group formation." *European Journal of Social Psychology, 15*, 51–66.

Horrigan, J.B., (2001) "Online communities: Urban development and the Internet." Retrieved January, 10, 2006, from http://www.pewinternet.org/PPF/r/50/report_display.asp.

Horrigan, J.B., Rainie, L., & Fox, S. (2001) "Online communities: Networks that nurture long-distance relationships and local ties." Retrieved November, 3, 2001, from www.pewinternet.org.

Jones, Q. (1997) "Virtual communities, virtual settlements, and cyber-archaeology: A theoretical outline." *Journal of Computer-Mediated Communication, 3*. Retrieved October 21, 2002, from http://jcmc.indiana.edu/vol3/issue3/jones.html

Kiesler, S., Siegel, J., & McGuire, T. (1984) "Social psychological aspects of computer-mediated communication." *American Psychologist, 39*, 1123–1134.

Kraut, R., Lundmark, V., Patterson, M., Kiesler, S., Mukopadhyay, T., & Scherlis, W. (1998) "Internet paradox. A social technology that reduces social involvement and psychological well-being?" *American Psychologist, 53*, 1017–1031.

Krol, E. (1995) *Die Welt des Internet: Handbuch & Übersicht*. Bonn: OReilly.

Lampa, G. (2005) "Imagining the blogosphere: An introduction to the imagined community of instant publishing." Retrieved January 10, 2006, from http://blog.lib.umn.edu/blogosphere/imagining_the_blogosphere.html.

McKenna, K.Y.A., & Bargh, J.A. (1998) "Coming out in the age of the Internet: Identity 'demarginalization' through virtual group participation." *Journal of Personality and Social Psychology, 75*, 681–694.

Moore, M., & Williams, D. (2005, November 10) "France's youth battles also waged on the web." *Washington Post*. Retrieved January 10, 2006, from http://www.washingtonpost.com/wp-dyn/content/article/2005/11/09/AR2005110902134_pf.html.

Oakes, P.J. (1987) "The salience of social categories." In J.C. Turner, M.A. Hogg, P.J. Oakes,

S.D. Reicher & M.S. Wetherell (eds.), *Rediscovering the Social Group: a Self-Categorization Theory*. Oxford: Blackwell, pp. 117–141.

O'Reilly, T. (2005) "What is Web 2.0? Design patterns and business models for the next generation of software." Retrieved January 10, 2006, from http://www.oreillynet.com/lpt/a/6228.

Parks, M.R., & Roberts, L.D. (1998) "'Making MOOsic': The development of personal relationships on-line and a comparison to their off-line counterparts." *Journal of Social and Personal Relationships, 15*, 517–537.

Porter, C.E. (2004) "A typology of virtual communities: A multi-disciplinary foundation for future research." *Journal of Computer-Mediated Communication, 10*. Retrieved November, 3, 2005, from http://jcmc.indiana.edu/vol10/issue1/porter.html.

Postmes, T., & Baym, N. (2005) "Intergroup dimensions of Internet." In J. Harwood & H. Giles (eds.), *Intergroup Communication: Multiple Perspectives*. New York: Peter Lang Publishers, pp. 213–238.

Postmes, T., & Brunsting, S. (2002) "Collective action in the age of internet: Mass communication and online mobilization." *Social Science Computer Review, 20*, 290–301.

Postmes, T., Spears, R., Lee, A.T., & Novak, R.J. (2005) "Individuality and social influence in groups: Inductive and deductive routes to group identity." *Journal of Personality and Social Psychology, 89*, 747–763.

Putnam, R. (1995) "Bowling alone: America's declining social capital." *Journal of Democracy, 6*, 65–78.

Reicher, S.D., Spears, R., & Postmes, T. (1995) "A social identity model of deindividuation phenomena." In W. Stroebe & M. Hewstone (eds.), *European Review of Social Psychology*, vol. 6. Chichester: Wiley, pp. 161–197.

Reid, E. (1991) "Electropolis—communication and community on internet relay chat." Retrieved January 7, 2000, from http://www.aluluei.com/

Reid, E. (1999) "Hierarchy and power: Social control in cyberspace." In M.A. Smith & P. Kollock (eds.), *Communities in Cyberspace*. London: Routledge, pp. 107–133.

Rheingold, H. (1993) *Virtual Communities. Homesteading on the Electronic Frontier*. New York: Addison-Wesley.

Rodgers, R., & Chen, Q. (2005) "Internet community group participation: Psychosocial benefits for women with breast cancer." *Journal of Computer-Mediated Communication, 10*. Retrieved January 9, 2006, from http://jcmc.indiana.edu/vol10/issue4/rodgers.html

Rogers, P., & Lea, M. (2005) "Social presence in distributed group environments: The role of social identity." *Behaviour & Information Technology, 24*, 151–158.

Slouka, M. (1995). *War of the Worlds: Cyberspace and the High-Tech Assault on Reality*. New York. Basic Books.

Tajfel, H. (1978) *Differentiation between Social Groups*. London: Academic Press.

Tajfel, H., Billig, M., Bundy, R., & Flament, C. (1971) "Social categorization and intergroup behavior." *European Journal of Social Psychology, 1*, 149–178.

Tajfel, H., & Turner, J. C. (1986) "The social identity theory of inter-group behavior." In S. Worchel & L. W. Austin (eds.), *Psychology of Intergroup Relations*. Chicago: Nelson-Hall, pp. 2–24.

Tönnies, F. (1887/1963) *Gemeinschaft und Gesellschaft*. [Community and society] Darmstadt: Wissenschaftliche Buchgesellschaft.

Turner, J.C., & Oakes, P.J. (1989) "Self-categorisation theory and social influence." In P.B. Paulus (ed.), *The Psychology of Group Influence*, second edition, Hillsdale, NJ: Erlbaum. pp. 233–279.

Utz, S. (1996) Kommunikationsstrukturen und Persönlichkeitsaspekte bei MUD-Nutzern. [Communication structures and personality aspects of MUD users]. Unpublished diploma thesis. Retrieved December 1, 2006, from http://www.mediensprache.net/archiv/pubs/3032.htm.

Utz, S. (1999) *Soziale Identifikation mit virtuellen Gemeinschaften—Bedingungen und Konsequenzen*. [Social identification with virtual communities—causes and consequences]. Lengerich: Pabst.

Utz, S. (2000) "Social information processing in MUDs: the development of friendships in virtual worlds." *Journal of Online Behavior, 1*(1). Retrieved November 15, 2000, from http://www.behavior.net/JOB/v1n1/utz.html

Utz, S. (2003) "Social identification and interpersonal attraction in MUDs." *Swiss Journal of Psychology, 62*, 91–101.

Utz, S. (2005) Participation in online consumer communities. Unpublished data.

Utz, S., & Bijleveld, L. (2006) "Community rules?!—building brand loyalty with virtual communities." Paper presented at the GOR conference, 21–22 March, Bielefeld.

Van Vugt, M., & Hart, C. M. (2004) "Social identity as social glue: the origins of group loyalty." *Journal of Personality and Social Psychology, 86*, 585–598.

Walker, J. (2003) "Final version of weblog definition." Retrieved December 13, 2005, from http://huminf.uib.no/~jill/archives/blog_theorising/final_version_of_weblog_definition.html.

Walther, J.B. (1992) "Interpersonal effects in computer-mediated interaction: a relational perspective" *Communication Research, 1*(9), 52–90.

Wellman, B. (1988) "The community question re-evaluated." In M.P. Smith (ed.), *Power, Community, and the City*. New Brunswick, NJ: Transaction Books, pp. 81–107.

Wellman, B., & Gulia, M. (1999) "Virtual communities as communities. Net surfers don't ride alone." In M.A. Smith & P. Kollock (eds.), *Communities in Cyberspace*. London: Routledge, pp. 167–194.

Williams, R. (1974) *Television: Technology and Cultural Form*. London: Fontana.

Chapter 14

Problems and interventions in computer-mediated virtual groups

Joseph B. Walther

Virtual teams are composed of group members who collaborate from different locations using communication technology. Virtual teams can offer flexibility, responsiveness, and diversity of perspectives in ways that differ from traditional groups (see for review Hinds & Kiesler, 2002; Walther & Bunz, 2005). By connecting people situated in different places, they can bring together a variety of diverse perspectives and experiences that traditional, face-to-face, geographically co-located groups are often unable to achieve. Virtual groups are composed to capitalize on different perspectives, abilities, and local knowledge so that a distributed virtual group should, in principle, offer immense benefits to the organizational and educational purposes to which they are put.

At the same time, virtual groups face several challenges that local groups do not face, or they experience old challenges in different ways. These include not only the affordances and constraints of the technological media they must use, but also the temporal adjustments and alterations in communication frequency and kind that they must make. Unfortunately these challenges are often out of the range of cognizance of virtual group members; they do not conceive of them, or do not quickly appreciate their importance, or respond to them. Quite possibly, because the patterns and processes of face-to-face group behaviors are so wellingrained (see Gersick, 1988), even explicit instruction in the adaptations required for virtual groups' best practices are often ignored in the behavioral routines of virtual partners.

When virtual groups do not adapt to the mechanical, symbolic, and temporal adjustments necessitated by mediated, distributed interaction, the consequences often manifest themselves not in a focus on technology's demands but rather in interpersonal attributions and evaluations—quite negative ones. Characterizations of remote partners may be disparaging, and participants point to their remote colleagues as a source of the blame for poorly performed processes and inferior task accomplishments. Not only is such blame an illusion—after all, if people at several locations all blame the others, someone or everyone cannot be right—but patterns of blaming others incur a consequence more serious than the assignment of fault. When faulty processes are blamed on others, the individual agent has no motivation to examine his or her own behavior, behavior which may itself have failed to accommodate virtual communication's requisites. Without recognizing that oneself may be to blame, there can be no introspection and no learning. This is to say that the failures to adapt to virtual group communication can lead to a self-fulfilling prophecy of skepticism and commensurate poor performance in virtual group arrangements. In other words, computer-mediated group communication requires sociotechnical adaptations: that is, adaptation to characteristics of the channel and the sociometric nature of distributed groups. Failure to deal effectively with the mechanically imposed differences between mediated and face-to-face interaction affects interpersonal judgments, and these in turn raise the specter of interpersonal attributions that are affected by sociometric factors—who is with whom, where, and therefore like or unlike oneself. These inter-personal evaluations affect further motivation, group effectiveness, and individual improvement. This being so, as research has demonstrated, interventions that facilitate adaptations to computer-mediated commu-nication (CMC) and foster rewarding interpersonal relations online can, and do, instigate greater success and individual improvements in virtual interactions.

As onerous as these patterns may be, they also suggest that the way out of such self-sealing syndromes may be to motivate alternative behav-iors and/or motivations that enhance interpersonal functioning. Doing so not only serves to remedy the ill will that often develops in such groups; interpersonally-oriented efforts can lead to extraordinary levels of trust, affinity, and accomplishment. The following material illuminates these pitfalls and remedies, as documented in numerous studies about virtual interaction, for bad and for good.

Mediated communication and distributed members

Concerns over virtual groups center on two factors and how they inter-relate: first, how communication media such as email, text-based discus-sion systems, and text-based chat alter basic communication dynamics in groups; second, how virtual group members deal with partners who are located remotely, who may be unknown to one another, and are embedded in different local, cultural, and/or institutional landscapes. The limitations of communication media are often thought to inhibit the ability to over-come the strangeness that is bestowed as a result of geographic distribu-tion. Thus, longstanding concerns about virtual groups typically include questions about how their members can develop familiarity, trust, and liking for partners with whom they do not share proximity, nor see and hear, nor easily share implicit knowledge about one another's local circumstances.

Communication media, and the limitations of CMC so common to virtual teams, are often characterized as inherently problematic. Several prominent approaches to the effects of CMC have argued that since relational cues are normally conveyed nonverbally in traditional communication, the relative absence of nonverbal cues in such systems as email and computer conferencing occlude the expression of inter-personal dynamics. As a result, it has been argued, electronic communication systems make it difficult, if not impossible, for the development and detection of relational aspects critical to the social dimensions of group work (see for review Walther, 2006). Indeed, a sizable amount of research has accumulated attesting to the task-orientation, impersonality, and occasional hostility attributed to working via CMC compared to face-to-face (see for review Walther & Parks, 2002). Online groups in early research reached decisions less frequently than face-to-face groups did, within limited time periods. Generally, when online groups have relatively short time periods they tend to exhibit impersonal relations, low rates of consensus, and other performance detriments (see Hiltz *et al.*, 1986; Siegel *et al.*, 1986). The quality and productivity of distributed groups' output has been found to be suboptimal compared to their face-to-face counterparts' in various tests. These effects may be due to dynamics related to the relational aspects discussed above, or, in the case of asynchronous communication media, due to discretionary participation, free-riding, difficulty integrating information, or other information-processing aspects of virtual work (see e.g. Smith & Vanacek, 1990).

Despite the fact that subsequent research has found that these effects are generally limited to certain contexts, such as unfamiliar groups with no history or expected longevity (see Walther, 2006), arguments about the inherent deficiency of CMC for collaborative work still arise. Nardi and Whittaker (2002), for example, argue that proximity and face-to-face interaction are critical for establishing collaborative interpersonal relationships. Such relationships, they argue, must be built on non-task communication early in working partners' interactions. In subsequent interactions, Nardi and Whittaker argue, collaborators need full-cue communication in order to detect when partners are paying attention, listening, and exhibiting backchanneling behavior—and computer-based communication systems do not readily provide this (see also Galagher & Kraut, 1994). Since virtual groups do not have such affordances, they are not expected, by some theorists, to have much of a chance to succeed.

Trust is another relational dimension that has significant import for virtual groups, one that has received particular attention in the literature. Handy (1995) projected that, as a presumed consequence of using CMC, virtual teams simply cannot develop trust. Jarvenpaa and Leidner (1998) countered that traditional definitions of trust are misleading when it comes to virtual groups. Traditionally, trust is assumed to derive from personal knowledge about particular individuals, and/or past or future memberships in common social groups that have norms for obligation and responsibility among members. In the realm of virtual groups, however, trust is more akin to the expectation that an individual's stated inclinations will develop as promised, and this expectation develops over time if it is reinforced. This contractual, interpersonal nature of trust may indeed be a more potent approach to trusting relations in online groups than approaches to trust based on a feeling that one member knows another's personality or social groups: Trust is the assessment one has for colleagues who come through rather than fail to complete agreements. In the online communication literature, greater levels of trust have been positively related to a number of outcomes, including group performance (Cascio, 2000; Jarvenpaa et al., 1998), problem and uncertainty resolution, as well as social information exchange (Jarvenpaa & Leidner, 1998), and liking (Greene, 2002). As with other relational dynamics, ratings of trust are lower when group members use media with fewer visual and vocal cue systems to do their work (Bos et al., 2002; Rocco, 1998).

Whether as a cause or consequence of lack of trust, dysfunctional behavioral routines often emerge in virtual groups. It is not uncommon that such teams engage in last-minute efforts. Although offline teams may also procrastinate until the end, offline groups still have rapid-fire, multi-cue communication at their disposal; virtual groups' communication systems are slower and, aside from real-time chat systems, generally more intermittent. Even if they are conducted using real-time conferencing systems, computer-based chat conveys less information per exchange than face-to-face communication does. Virtual group members often fail to realize this. Thus, when their last-minute communications still do not get them moving toward task completion as well or as quickly as they expected, virtual groups experience hostility and suboptimal performance (see e.g. Jarvenpaa & Leidner, 1998; Jarvenpaa et al., 1998).

The characteristics of CMC over distance are further exacerbated by the geographic dispersion of virtual group members among a variety of disparate locations. Because virtual group members may reside in different places, ranging from different offices to different states or countries, there may be numerous differences among their situations of which partners are not aware. These include incongruities between work environments and social structures, dissimilar organizational cultures, and time zone differences associated with different locations. Any or all of these can create disparities in working contexts for team members and disrupt the work flow, shared work interpretation, and experiences of such groups (Hinds & Bailey, 2003).

When some of these factors escape the attention of distributed group members, these factors may lead to pernicious interpersonal problems. Cramton (2001) outlines how the placement of team members in different locations and institutions leads to disruptions in common knowledge. Specifically, members are often unaware of the situational and contextual factors that impact remote subsets of team members but not their own. These factors may be as simple as different vacation or holiday schedules, leading to differences in participation and contribution cycles. Or they may be as fundamental as different incentives for group projects, leading some partners to experience greater motivation than other partners to work— how often, and how hard. It is difficult enough when these differences are known to all. In many cases, however, group members assume that what is salient for themselves is also salient elsewhere. As a result, natural conflicts arise that lead to misunderstandings, blame, and inappropriate attributions for behaviors that are in actuality situationally-based and normal for local actors but personality-based and disruptive to remote partners.

Cramton (2001) suggested that the dynamic underlying such negative perceptions is the "fundamental attribution error" (Ross, 1977): the tendency to focus blame on another person's disposition, or personality, for events and behaviors that are in reality due to external, situationally-driven factors. Because virtual group members lacked common knowledge about one another's locally situational circumstances and frames of reference, they attributed incongruous behavior by others as reflections of those partners' willfulness and undesirable personality traits. This characterization fit well with other extant findings on virtual groups. Burke, Aytes, Chidambaram and Johnson, (1999) found that when some partners are geographically distributed from others, frustration tends to be directed at remote colleagues. When conflict arises in such situations, it may involve reciprocal denigration by virtual group members of their collective remote partners (i.e., "what's wrong with those people?"), including aspersions about personal characteristics such as laziness, irresponsibility, and lack of commitment (Walther et al., 2002).

As insightful as Cramton's (2001) suggestion was, empirical research on attributions in virtual groups found a different, more complex, yet equally disturbing pattern of attributions in virtual groups. Walther and Bazarova (2007) reported a field experiment using virtual groups, some of whose members were completely distributed, whereas other groups' members were geographically co-located yet entirely online. In this manner, the researchers were able to isolate what the effects were due to differences in location on top of, but not confounded with, the use of mediated communication. None of the group members knew each other before this experiment, even those from the same institutional location, although the results seemed to indicate, as Cramton suggested, that people from the same place seem to relate to one another as similars. Participants addressed a decision-making problem using information provided to them, adequate enough to reach an optimal decision if sufficient communication took place. They used an asynchronous discussion board system over the internet, available to them 24 hours a day for two weeks, for all their communication.

After the group decisions were submitted, the researchers inquired who participants blamed for their *own* poorest behaviors. Members were asked what their best and worst behaviors had been in their groups, and why they thought they had behaved as they did. Most responses indicated that participants had not participated frequently enough, argued strongly enough, or debated their partners adequately. In the completely distributed groups, more so than in the co-located groups, members blamed their remote partners significantly more often for having influenced their misbehavior. They cited others' lack of participation (an empirically false judgment) or others' foolishness, for example, as having frustrated them into recalcitrance. In co-located groups, where members seemed to recognize that everyone faced the same constraints, they were more liable to admit personal responsibility for their inaction. Although interpersonal, dispositional attributions might be deleterious, as Cramton (2001) speculated, these empirical findings about people's denial of personal responsibility in distributed virtual groups, more so than in co-located ones, establishes a social cognitive basis for discomfort and suboptimal performance in distributed teams.

Research has not yet established just why CMC users who believe that their partners are proximal versus distant respond to those partners differently. Although some researchers have speculated that such effects might reflect intergroup dynamics (i.e., behaviors reflecting assumptions about ingroup/outgroup differences; Fiol & O'Connor, 2005), such conclusions do not seem adequate under a variety of virtual interaction conditions. For one thing, it is not unreasonable for people to assume that people who are somewhere other than themselves are somehow different than they themselves are, and that people who are nearby are more similar, ingroup/outgroup perceptions notwithstanding (see for review Latané *et al.*, 1995). For instance, Tanis and Postmes (2003) found that virtual dyad partners from two universities in the same city behaved more like colleagues than rivals. In contrast, Bradner and Mark (2002) found that a member of experimental CMC dyads acted less trustingly and familiarly when they believed the partner was in a city across the country rather than in the same town (even though the partner was always in the same town). Although virtual group members perceived greater dominance by distant than by proximal members in another virtual group study, these perceptions did not occur when there were geographically collocated subgroups—the condition most likely to engender ingroup and outgroup perceptions—than when everyone was actually remote from one another (Peña *et al.*, 2007).

In sum, a number of problems associated with distance and restricted communication media have been alleged to impact the ability of distributed groups to function as effectively as nonmediated groups. From one perspective these disparities may seem insurmountable, given that the constraints of distance and media are relatively impervious when groups truly operate under these conditions. However, other research has indicated that the bases for the presumably deleterious effects of distance and media are more permeable. Accommodations may emerge or be derived by which participants adjust to the alternative environment, and/or the bases of the relational dynamics themselves may change.

Adaptations to virtuality

Other research has harnessed different perspectives on the effects of CMC and its impacts on interpersonal interaction and, in so doing, has charted very different prognoses about the potential of virtual groups to perform and cohere. These studies challenge the conclusion that virtual groups must suffer decrements regarding relational dynamics, trust, attributional errors, and poor performance. Moreover, their findings include theoretically derived strategies for intervening in virtual groups' conduct so as to remediate problems and improve the functioning of such groups.

Although interpersonal liking can be expressed in a variety of ways through nonverbal cues offline, it can be expressed equivalently well through language and symbols online (Walther *et al.*, 2005). Thus it is not the case that liking cannot be expressed online. Rather, it appears that the initial basis for liking is different in virtual groups than in traditional ones. Weisband and Atwater (1999) experimented with mediated and traditional groups, quantifying group communication behaviors and measuring members' degree of liking for one another. They found a significant correlation in virtual groups involving the number of members' verbal, task-related statements related to the group task and the amount that other members liked the contributor. In traditional groups there was no relationship between task contributions and liking. In offline groups, Weisband and Atwater concluded, liking comes from idiosyncratic, possibly nonverbally based nontask characteristics, whereas in virtual task-oriented groups, people like others more to the extent that others contribute to the group's work.

It is very important to note that the majority of all the experimental findings in virtual groups research come from relatively short-term, ad hoc groups. It is in these settings that deleterious effects of media on interpersonal relations seem to accrue most often. In longer-term online groups, research finds fairly consistently that groups function more effectively, with greater interpersonal effectiveness and greater task effort and quality (see for review Walther, 2006). There are two explanations for this pattern: a mechanical one and an adaptational one.

At the mechanical level, virtual groups need time to adapt to the specific software or groupware applications they employ. Lebie *et al.* (1995) examined synchronous virtual groups and face-to-face groups over multiple, time-limited tasks. Virtual groups made fewer comments over time, but, more revealing, content analysis indicated that they devoted a greater proportion of initial comments to the mechanics of the technology, detracting from the proportion of communication they could dedicate to the group task. As the number of mechanical comments reduced over time, online groups' decision-making quality also improved. It appears that, in the short term, virtual team members need time to adapt to technology, and, until they do so, their attention to task or relationship issues is sacrificed.

In terms of adaptation, it is now well established that group members accommodate to the medium and exhibit interpersonal behavior through language online, when motivated to do so, in ways that facilitate the development of effective interpersonal relations. The social information processing theory (Walther, 1992) describes how virtual group members adapt to the paucity of nonverbal cues in mediated communication by imbuing their text-based messages with both task and social information. Due to the differential capacity of CMC to convey a great deal of information within a typical message exchange, computer-mediated exchanges require more frequent interactions and more time in order for users to reach the level of relational development that offline group partners accomplish more quickly. Given enough time, however, virtual groups achieve liking, trust, and sociable states, often as well as offline groups (Walther & Burgoon, 1992; see for review Walther & Parks, 2002).

Following this framework, whereas liking in short-term groups may be based on task-related behavior (Weisband & Atwater, 1999), long-term groups do accrue interpersonal relations as a result of the exchange of both work-related and sociable messages over time, despite the fact that their sociable relations develop via mediated channels. Indeed, in one experiment, short-term virtual group members benefited from seeing pictures of one another before a decision-making task. Seeing pictures before chatting, in short-term groups, raised social attraction ratings after discussion. However, in longer-term online groups, who had exchanged a large number of messages over many weeks, with no photos to help them, members liked each other more if they did not see one another's photographs than if they did (Walther *et al.*, 2001). Such is the power of relational development over time, online, to overcome the deficits of the medium and to foster online working relations of robust quality.

Several studies support the assertion that when virtual groups have extended periods of time to develop, they often can relate more positively and perform more successfully (e.g. Iacono & Weisband, 1997; Jarvenpaa & Leidner, 1998). Levels of trust and liking are higher in long-term than short-term virtual teams (Chidambaram, 1996; Walther, 1995; see for review Walther, 2002) and long-term virtual groups lend more effort to their group tasks (Walther, 1997; Walther *et al.*, 2001). Moreover, the extent to which virtual partners anticipate future interaction, rather than a one-shot assignment, triggers more favorable interpersonal orientations as well (Walther, 1994).

As suggested above, trust is also an important variable in virtual groups. Like the effects of time and message accrual on group liking, trust develops over time in longer-term virtual groups consistent with social information processing theory (Walther & Burgoon, 1992; Wilson *et al.*, 2006). In other approaches, Jarvenpaa and Leidner (1998) distinguished between (1) swift trust, and (2) an alternative, developmental trust that may develop in online groups. Swift trust is conceived as a depersonalized action based on categorically derived information and stereotypical assumptions about virtual partners and their behavior. It resembles enduring trust, but it is interpersonally untested (Meyerson *et al.*, 1996). In other words, before having interpersonal knowledge with which to make a decision about the trustworthiness of colleagues, partners act as though they trust one another based on a presumption of trustworthiness, at least until shown they should not.

Jarvenpaa and Leidner (1998) argue that online trust is not as depersonalized or categorically stereotypical as swift trust. Rather, it may be more behaviorally based. That is, group members infer trust from observations about other members' electronic communication. In their research, students from different universities participated in global, virtual groups teams of six to eight members over six weeks' duration. Measurements of members' trust levels were collected, and the researchers compared the communication behaviors among high-trust and low-trust groups. Findings indicated that the virtual groups who had experienced great trust had exhibited sociability, exchanged intensely frequent messages, showed interest in other members' responses, showed initiative, provided substantive feedback to one another, and notified others of their expected participation periods or absences. Those with low levels of trust showed little initiative. They had meager social content in their messages. The researchers concluded that in online groups, trust is a function of members' consistency of performance rather than due to the categorical or affective perceptions typical of offline groups.

Interventions that improve virtual groups

The previous discussion has offered the general conclusions that virtual groups may, but need not necessarily, suffer decrements in relationship and performance levels relative to traditional groups. These decrements appear to result from faulty adaptations to the nature of CMC. Computer-mediated communication in virtual groups affects the rate and nature of the social and instrumental information group members exchange. When groups fail to take these factors into account, there is less information traversing the group, limiting in turn the members' abilities to become familiar with one another, to address their task thoroughly, and to develop sufficient cycles of vulnerability and fulfillment of commitments to develop trust for one another (see Walther & Bunz, 2005). When virtual groups experience conflict or perform poorly as a result of these factors, a group member tends not to examine his or her own adaptations to virtual work, but, rather, to blame remote colleagues—sometimes in derisive, personality-centered ways—for the failures of the group and as the cause of the individual's own performance. These patterns are more likely to appear in short-term groups—groups in which members have no prior familiarity, and in which there is no expectation of a continuing commitment. When groups anticipate longer-term relations, members tend to take greater interest in one another (Walther, 1994). Despite the limitations of CMC channels, groups that anticipate greater longevity exchange more personal information and get to know and like one another better than do short-term groups.

Two significant implications are apparent from these conclusions. First, the prospects are not particularly good for participants in short-term virtual groups. Even if an individual participates in several short-term virtual groups in succession, they may not experience the interpersonal dynamics that are aroused in a single long-term virtual group experience, and may repeat instead the interpersonal disinterest and blame that occurs in limited groups. Second, the theoretically derived understanding of these problems offers two potential remedies. In one, we take the lessons of faulty patterns attributing blame to remote unknown partners, and develop attribution-based remedies. In another, we capitalize on the communication patterns that develop naturally in longer-term groups and implement them in the shorter durations of a less lengthy group experience. The following discussions explain and illustrate these interventions.

Redirecting attributions

Short-term virtual groups often experience weak performance, a tendency to blame remote and otherwise unknown partners for the groups' experiences and, as a result, generate negative interpersonal evaluations. Walther *et al.* (2002) conducted a three-part study investigating whether attributions of responsibility can become unbiased when virtual group members are familiar with one another, and whether the unbiased attribution patterns can then transfer from one virtual group experience to another. The premise of this study was that, when a virtual group contains no unknown partners on which to scapegoat the poor performance of the group, members are impelled to refocus their attention on their own behaviors that did not contribute to the group's adaptation. By refocusing the explanation for failure on oneself, individuals can then recognize their failings and learn not to repeat them. Such awareness is occluded when there is a remote, unknown partner on which to focus blame, as Walther and Bazarova (2007) demonstrated, as explained previously. If self-focus can be made salient, however, learning and subsequent improvement are potentially enabled.

In order to test these premises, Walther *et al.*, (2002) utilized three rounds of short-term virtual groups. In the first, baseline panel, virtual groups of three or four members, composed of students from two U.S. universities, worked via the internet on two two-week problem-solving projects in succession, with different partners each time. These groups operated in the most onerous conditions for virtual groups: short-term teams with no history and no anticipated future interaction, membership mixed across locations spanning geographical fault lines. They were provided with explicit guidelines to help them adapt to the communication timing, rate, and explicitness issues that have been discovered in virtual groups research, such as that reviewed above. Despite this overt instruction, the timing and coordination efforts of these groups were subjectively poor, and questionnaire data gathered at the end of each task showed low scores on various measures of affection and liking, impression development, and task-related effort expenditure. Some participants at both respective sites made comments blaming the people at the other institution. This panel, composed of short-term virtual groups with no specific intercession, was the baseline for subsequent comparison conditions.

A second panel of online groups was developed to see whether the absence of a remote, unknown partner could redirect attributions, enable learning, and improve subsequent virtual group behavior. This panel involved students from a university in the United States and one in Germany, where participants also met in classes several times a week. Three- or four-member short-term groups were compiled that contained only *co-located* partners (in each respective location), but who were assigned to communicate exclusively via the internet on their group task despite seeing their partners offline for other activities. The groups were offered the same recommendations about adaptation to messaging and rate that were provided in the previous panel. Like the previous panel, their group projects were poorly done, and exhibited the typical difficulty and frustration, procrastination, and initially infrequent communication that typify short-term virtual groups. However, in this case there was no unknown and unseen scapegoat on whom to blame the group's poor performance. Group members were guided to reflect on their adaptation problems, which they appeared to recognize, and many expressed an inclination to approach things differently next time.

Subsequent rounds involved participants from both Germany and the United States together in each group of three or four for two more short-term virtual group projects via the internet. In each group none of the members had worked together previously. In contrast to the previous round, these groups performed well, used time effectively, and communicated frequently. They enjoyed their projects and many made friends with their remote colleagues. The same measures from the first panel were administered after each international round of group projects, collapsed across rounds, and compared to the results of the first panel. Analyses demonstrated significantly superior outcomes for the teams who had the initial, co-located sensitization session compared to those in the previous panel who had not, on the same measures of affection and liking, impression development, project effort, and even on measures of perceived physical attractiveness.

Although these results were promising, the two panels begged comparability. Whereas students from the United States participated in each panel, their counterparts (other U.S. students versus German students) differed culturally. In neither panel were the conditions experimentally crossed (i.e. no local practice in Panel 1 and no initially distributed group in Panel 2). Therefore, Walther *et al.* (2002) conducted a third panel with two rounds, employing a more deliberate cross of experimental treatments, albeit nested within a single institutional location. For the first round groups of four were either composed of students who were all in the same class section (familiars), or were in different classes (strangers). Groups engaged in a two-week project using the internet exclusively. In the second round, all groups were composed of strangers. Groups whose members had been in the same class during the first round were expected to realize their individual need for adaptation to virtuality, since they had no strangers on whom to deflect responsibility; they were expected to perform better during the second round than those who had been in initial virtual groups with strangers. After the second round (where all four members were unfamiliar), member ratings were compared on the basis of whether the target had previously been in a group of familiars or strangers. As predicted, those members who were familiar with any others in round 1 performed in more interpersonally positive ways in round 2.

The results of these studies offer further support for the effects of distributed versus collocated partners on the tendency for virtual group members to deflect or accept responsibility for dysfunctional behaviors in virtual groups. However, these studies also demonstrate the potential to intervene in the self-serving attribution bias that blinds distributed groups' members to their own adaptation failures. Although improvement over successive virtual group experiences might reflect a maturation effect, the first panel (which included two episodes) suggests that experience alone was not sufficient to overcome the myopia that seems to occur in repeated, short-term distributed group encounters. The implications are that adequate training on adaptation to virtual groups might play an effective role in improving individual and group adaptation to the difficulties that short-term virtual groups often encounter. Repeated experience in short-term virtual groups does not in and of itself provide such training. Nor does explicit instruction on a recommended set of behaviors go far enough without additional motivation to attend to these lessons. A poor experience with a local virtual group may provide the impetus for such reflection.

Time, messages, and incentivization

Another method with which to promote adaptation to the demands of virtual collaboration involves providing explicit, external incentives for at least some of the behaviors associated with effectiveness. Compelling certain adaptation behaviors in short-term virtual groups can overcome the problems and dysfunctions that mediated communication imparts. To do so requires that groups enact communication behaviors, willfully and deliberately—long-term groups seem to do so more spontaneously and fluidly – behaviors that accommodate for the reduced rate, specificity, and information density that is part of mediated interaction. Recent research has demonstrated that the deliberate adoption of strategies to counter the relative losses in frequency and nuance in mediated communication could promote significant increases in trust, liking, and performance quality in short-term virtual groups (Walther & Bunz, 2005).

These strategies were presented to student virtual group members as a set of rules to follow. For some groups, adherence to one or another of these rules was tied to explicit reward/punishment incentives. For others, they were free to adopt or ignore these rules as they chose; but all groups, incentivized or not, were encouraged to follow all the rules regardless. The rules included: (1) to communicate frequently [to accommodate for the slower rate of information exchanged in mediated interactions]; (2) to confirm others' messages explicitly [to translate what might otherwise be signified using head nodding into explicit verbal messages]; (3) to begin a project early [to get a head start on the differential rate of progress that mediated communication is likely to impose]; (4) to combine both organizing and substantive contributions to the group's project [since it is common, offline, to delay doing substantive work until allocations and assignments have been made, a process which consumes an inordinate amount of time online]; (5) to express intention explicitly [to facilitate interpersonal commitments and the evaluation of their remission]; and (6) to adhere to deadlines [in order to maintain the group's pace despite the medium's degradation in information-per-message].

These guidelines represent many of the successful ad hoc adaptations to virtual group communication noted in the literature (see for review Walther & Bunz, 2005). For instance, Iacono and Weisband (1997) argued that various forms of interpersonal exchange promote trust in virtual groups. These researchers focused specifically on a particular exchange of messages in which the first expression initiated work processes (asking a specific question or proposing action, essentially expressing vulnerability to getting a response from others), and a reply that responded directly to, and thereby confirmed, the prior work process initiation. These pairs, when fulfilled, equate to trust, according to Iacono and Weisband. The researchers established a number of virtual teams among students at several universities for three weeks, and they analyzed messages from these groups for initiations and responses, as well as several other communication types (including work process, work content, technical aspects, contact regulation, and fun). They also evaluated the quality of the groups' work. Results showed that initiations and responses were significantly associated with the quality of team performance. While fun messages were not as frequent, they appeared most frequently in the higher-performing teams. Additional analyses indicated that the better-performing teams formed quickly, and multi-tasked several activities at once. Poor performing teams procrastinated and struggled to meet deadlines; they interacted less frequently overall.

Returning to the Walther and Bunz's (2005) research, these experimental virtual groups worked together for two weeks on collaborative research papers. Some groups were assigned to follow one of the rules, and others were not. Participants indicated the extent to which they had followed the various rules. Other measures included assessments of trust and liking for other group members, a self-assessed estimation of the quality of the group project, and an objective assessment by outside judges of the group projects' quality.

Results of the study revealed that those groups who were assigned to follow one rule were significantly higher in their adherence to all rules, compared to the groups who had no rule assigned. Moreover, there were strong, significant correlations between the extent to which each of the rules was followed and the amount of trust participants developed for one another. Each rule also correlated strongly with liking for others, and for the groups' assessment of how good their work was. The effects of the rules were self-administered data illusion: Each rule, except for the rule on multi-tasking organizing and substantive comments, also correlated significantly with the outside evaluations of the quality of the group projects. Walther and Bunz concluded:

> Virtual groups sometimes do overcome geographic dispersion and channel constraints, and/or they possibly could do so when we recognize different behavioral bases for judgments important to group work, and foster them. ... (T)here are several viable behavioral routines

available to virtual groups and the more these behavioral routines are adopted, the better the experience and the better the results of virtual teams efforts.

Conclusions

Virtual groups have become a popular topic in academic research, just as more groups, formal or informal, adopt the internet to coordinate their work. Our understanding of the dynamics of these groups has grown considerably, from initial skepticism about their ability to function effectively or affectively whatsoever, to understanding many of the contingencies that moderate their likelihood to work. In the near future we must learn more about virtual international and intercultural groups. Some previous research that has employed international groups has done little to examine how culture-specific or intercultural influences may generate predictable and/or solvable problems among online partners. Limited work that has considered global or international groups has considered attribution issues and intergroup issues rather generically. For instance, whereas Fiol and O'Connor (2005) predict considerable intergroup interference within dramatically distributed groups, Hinds and Mortensen (2005) empirically determined that frequency of communication moderates group identification among international virtual colleagues. Much more research is needed that explores the micro-relational and communicative nuances that different cultural backdrops imbue on the manner in which criticism is offered and received, explicitness is valued, deference is shown, and other dynamics come into play that can become disturbances or sources of delight whenever individuals from different backgrounds work together, as virtual groups allow people to do.

Despite the increased sophistication of our understanding, many naysayers—both amateur and academic—conclude that virtual groups are prone to failure, and that at least some face-to-face contact is needed to establish trust (e. g., Rocco, 1998). Given the growing collection of research on the mechanisms, manner, and methods by which virtual groups can work well, as reviewed in this chapter, it is worthwhile asking why there is not greater agreement about the desirability of using and participating in virtual groups. The answer to this paradox may lie in a basic assessment of the nature of communication and media, in terms of affordances and effort, across settings, such as that articulated as the efficiency threshold principle by Walther (in press) and colleagues (Nowak et al., 2005).

There can be no question that using telecommunication media of any kind incurs more effort than having a face-to-face conversation does. We develop our abilities to detect and use voice and body cues innately. We are adept at the astounding efficiency that comes from conveying and inferring meaning at multiple levels using simultaneous and multiple systems of expressive behaviors. As frustrating as it often is, face-to-face communication is easier than its alternatives that require the translation of meanings into alternative symbol systems (such as conveying affect through writing; do-able but less automatic) and deploying mechanical interfaces in order to do so (such as typing). When efficiency is the goal of communication, face-to-face communication is a clear winner. Anything other than face-to-face incurs greater effort, and when there is no additional gain from doing so, alternative media are employed with reluctance and disfavor. People do not like greater effort unless there is a benefit from its application. When compelled to expend it, their evaluations of the activity are negative.

Virtual groups are difficult. Adapting to the mechanics of CMC is not automatic, and further adaptation to the rate and time requirements that allow online interaction to function well incurs extraordinary dedication and effort. Learning who our partners are and remembering their local constraints adds difficulty. To the extent that we have other communication tools in our lives that get our questions answered faster, are easier to use, and more intuitive, or grounded in visual representations of the things we communicate about (see Gergle *et al.*, 2004), virtual groups can be a chore. There is little surprise, from this perspective, why people would denigrate or avoid them, or why some research might fairly conclude they are poor alternatives. It is no surprise that, unless one clearly understands the potency of various contribution patterns in online interaction, one may be inclined to decline participation. Indeed, the history of research on media richness theory, which proposes efficient and satisfying outcomes from matching the right kinds of media with the complexity of the communication task (Daft & Lengel, 1986) can be seen as a contest between users' *evaluations* of CMC, as opposed to users' effective *use* of CMC (see for review Walther & Parks, 2002).

The tipping point, at which the detriments and benefits come closer to equivalence, comes when there is some benefit to working virtually, and/ or less difficulty in doing so. New technologies with notification systems such as RSS feeds, or email or cell phone alerts of postings to a discussion, can take a lot of uncertainty out of wondering if colleagues have made contributions to a project. But social engineering is the factor more likely to motivate colleagues to make those contributions. In other words, when there is no easier-to-use alternative to virtual group technology, then the extra effort required to collaborate distributedly becomes less relevant to users. In that case (which has been overlooked by media richness theory), extra effort is essential rather than a superfluous encumbrance. When such effort is applied, users reap the interpersonal and instrumental rewards. In this sense, the more we know about harnessing motivations to contribute, the more groups may be likely to avoid the sporadic aspects, and the dysfunctional, conflict-producing, attribution-biasing effects of distributed virtual groups. And then, despite getting no easier, the interpersonal and instrumental payoffs may accrue more dramatically. Future research exploring social and technical features that ease and motivate participation will help virtual groups achieve the benefits for which their promises of diverse perspectives and expanded information resources were originally conceived.

References

Bos, N., Olson, J., Gergle, D., Olson, G., & Wright, Z. (2002) "Effects of four computer-mediated communications channels on trust development." *Proceedings of the SIGCHI Conference on Human Factors in Computing Systems: Changing Our World, Changing Ourselves.* New York: ACM Press, April, pp. 135–140.

Bradner, E., & Mark, G. (2002) "Why distance matters: Effects on cooperation, persuasion and deception." Paper presented at the ACM Conference on Computer-Supported Cooperative Work, New Orleans, LA, November.

Burke, K., Aytes, K., Chidambaram, L., & Johnson, J. J. (1999) "A study of partially distributed work groups: The impact of media, location, and time perceptions on performance." *Small Group Research, 30,* 453–490.

Cascio, W. F. (2000) "Managing a virtual workplace." *The Academy of Management Executive, 14*(3), 81–90.

Chidambaram, L. (1996) "Relational development in computer-supported groups." *MIS Quarterly, 20,* 143–163.

Cramton, C. D. (2001) "The mutual knowledge problem and its consequences for dispersed collaboration." *Organization Science, 12,* 346–371.

Daft, R. L., & Lengel, R. H. (1986) "Organizational information requirements, media richness, and structural determinants." *Management Science, 32,* 554–571.

Fiol, C. M., & O'Connor, E. J. (2005) "Identification in face-to-face, hybrid, and pure virtual teams: untangling the contradictions." *Organization Science, 16,* 19–32.

Galagher, J., & Kraut, R. E. (1994) "Computer-mediated communication for intellectual teamwork: an experiment in group writing." *Information Systems Research, 5,* 110–138.

Gergle, D., Kraut, R. E., & Fussell, S. R. (2004) "Language efficiency and visual technology: minimizing collaborative effort with visual information." *Journal of Language and Social Psychology, 23,* 491–517.

Gersick, C. J. G. (1988) "Time and transition in work teams: toward a new model of group development." *Academy of Management Journal, 31,* 9–41.

Greene, M. C. (2002, April) "Development of trust in on-line social relationships." Paper presented at the Conference on Computer-Supported Social Interaction, Oxford, OH.

Handy, C. (1995) "Trust and the virtual organization." *Harvard Business Review, 73*(3), 40–50.

Hiltz, S. R., Johnson, K., & Turoff, M. (1986) "Experiments in group decision making: Communication process and outcome in face-to-face versus computerized conferences." *Human Communication Research, 13,* 225–252.

Hinds, P. J., & Bailey, D. E. (2003). "Out of sight, out of sync: Understanding conflict in distributed teams." *Organization Science, 14,* 615–632.

Hinds, P. J., & Kiesler, S. (eds.), (2002) *Distributed work: New research on working across distance using technology.* Cambridge, MA: MIT Press.

Hinds, P. J., & Mortensen, M. (2005) "Understanding conflict in geographically distributed teams: The moderating effects of shared identity, shared context, and spontaneous communication." *Organization Science, 16,* 290–307.

Iacono, C. S., & Weisband, S. (1997, January) "Developing trust in virtual teams." Paper presented at the 30th Hawaii International Conference on System Sciences, Maui, HI.

Jarvenpaa, S. L., Knoll, K., & Leidner, D. (1998) "Is anybody out there?: The implications of trust in global virtual teams." *Journal of Management Information Systems, 14*, 29–64.

Jarvenpaa, S. L., & Leidner, D. E. (1998) "Communication and trust in global virtual teams." *Journal of Computer-Mediated Communication, 3*(4). Retrieved March 16, 2004, from http://www.ascusc.org/jcmc/vol3/issue4/jarvenpaa.html

Latané, B., Liu, J. H., Nowak, A., Benevento, M., & Zheng, L. (1995) "Distance matters: Physical space and social impact." *Personality and Social Psychology Bulletin, 21*, 795–805.

Lebie, L., Rhoades, J. A., & McGrath, J. E. (1995) "Interaction process in computer-mediated and face-to-face groups." *Computer Supported Cooperative Work, 4*, 127–152.

Meyerson, D., Weick, K. E., & Kramer, R. M. (1996) "Swift trust and temporary groups." In R. M. Kramer & T. R. Tyler (eds.), *Trust in Organizations*, Thousand Oaks, CA: Sage, pp. 166–195.

Nardi, B., & Whittaker, S. (2002) "The place of face to face communication in distributed work." In P. J. Hinds & S. Kiesler (eds.), *Distributed Work: New Research on Working Across Distance Using Technology*. Cambridge: MIT Press, pp. 83–110.

Nowak, K. L., Watt, J., and Walther, J. B. (2005) "The influence of synchrony and sensory modality on the person perception process in computer-mediated groups." *Journal of Computer-Mediated Communication, 10*(3), article 3. Retrieved December 9, 2006, from http://jcmc.indiana.edu/vol10/issue3/nowak.html

Peña, J., Walther, J. B., & Hancock, J. T. (2007) "Effects of geographic distribution on dominance perceptions in computer-mediated groups." *Communication Research, 34*, 313–331.

Rocco, E. (1998) "Trust breaks down in electronic contexts but can be repaired by some initial face-to-face contact." *Proceedings of ACM CHI Conference on Human Factors in Computing Systems*. New York: ACM Press, pp. 496–502.

Ross, L. (1977) "The intuitive psychologist and his shortcomings: Distortions in the attribution process." In L. Berkowitz (ed.), *Advances in Experimental Social Psychology*. New York: Academic Press, pp. 173–220.

Siegel, J., Dubrovsky, V., Kiesler, S., & McGuire, T. W. (1986) "Group processes in computer-mediated communication." *Organizational Behavior and Human Decision Processes, 37*, 157–187.

Smith, J. Y., & Vanacek, M. T. (1990) "Dispersed group decision making using nonsimultaneous computer conferencing: A report of research." *Journal of Management Information Systems, 7*, 71–92.

Tanis, M., & Postmes, T. (2003) "Social cues and impression formation in CMC." *Journal of Communication, 53*, 676–693.

Walther, J. B. (1992) "Interpersonal effects in computer-mediated interaction: A relational perspective." *Communication Research, 19*, 52–90.

Walther, J. B. (1994) "Anticipated ongoing interaction versus channel effects on relational communication in computer mediated interaction." *Human Communication Research, 20*, 473–501.

Walther, J. B. (1995) "Relational aspects of computer-mediated communication: Experimental observations over time." *Organization Science, 6*, 186–203.

Walther, J. B. (1997) "Group and interpersonal effects in international computer-mediated collaboration." *Human Communication Research, 23*, 342–369.

Walther, J. B. (2002) "Time effects in computer-mediated groups: Past, present, and future." In P. Hinds & S. Kiesler (eds.), *Distributed work: New research on working across distance using technology*. Cambridge, MA: MIT Press, pp. 235–257.

Walther, J. B. (2006) "Nonverbal dynamics in computer-mediated communication, or : (and the net : (' s with you, :) and you :) alone." In V. Manusov & M. L. Patterson (eds.), *Handbook of Nonverbal Communication*.Thousand Oaks, CA: Sage, pp. 461–479.

Walther, J. B. (in press) "Visual cues in computer-mediated communication: Sometimes less is more." In A. Kappas (ed.), *Face-to-Face Communication over the Internet: Issues, Research,*

Challenges. Cambridge, UK: Cambridge University Press.

Walther, J. B., & Bazarova, N. (2007) "Misattribution in virtual groups." *Human Communication Research, 33*, 1–26.

Walther, J. B., & Bunz, U. (2005) "The rules of virtual groups: Trust, liking, and performance in computer-mediated communication." *Journal of Communication, 55*, 828–846.

Walther, J. B., & Burgoon, J. K. (1992) "Relational communication in computer-mediated interaction." *Human Communication Research, 19*, 50–88.

Walther, J. B., & Parks, M. R. (2002) "Cues filtered out, cues filtered in: Computer-mediated communication and relationships." In M. L. Knapp & J. A. Daly (eds.), *Handbook of Interpersonal Communication,* third edition. Thousand Oaks, CA: Sage, pp. 529–563.

Walther, J. B., Boos, M., & Jonas, K. J. (2002) "Misattribution and attributional redirection in distributed virtual groups." *Proceedings of the 35th Hawaii International Conference on System Sciences.*

Walther, J. B., Loh, T., & Granka, L. (2005) "Let me count the ways: The interchange of verbal and nonverbal cues in computer-mediated and face-to-face affinity." *Journal of Language and Social Psychology, 24*, 36–65.

Walther, J. B., Slovacek, C., & Tidwell, L. C. (2001) "Is a picture worth a thousand words? Photographic images in long term and short term virtual teams." *Communication Research, 28*, 105–134.

Weisband, S., & Atwater, L. (1999) "Evaluating self and others in electronic and face-to-face groups." *Journal of Applied Psychology, 84*, 632–639.

Wilson, J. M., Straus, S. G., & McEvily, W. J. (2006) "All in due time: The development of trust in computer-mediated and face-to-face teams." *Organizational Behavior and Human Decision Processes, 99*, 16–33.

Chapter 15

What makes the internet a place to seek social support?

Martin Tanis

> Thank you so much! I can't begin to express how I feel with so much encouragement, love and support that everyone is giving me. Already I feel so much better knowing I have friends to help me get through this. I feel very blessed to have found you all. Thank you so much for your support and friendship, you'll never know what it means to me!
>
> Judith

This message was posted on an online social support group (OSSG) and clearly illustrates that people can find support and encouragement in times when they need it. (This and the other examples in this chapter serve merely as illustrations; for reasons of privacy names are fictional.) This chapter will focus on why people seek support in f OSSGs by looking at characteristics of computer-mediated communication (CMC) in general and online *communities* in particular, and examining how these characteristics may facilitate people who seek social support. More specifically, this chapter will address how the relative anonymity that CMC affords, the text-based character, and the possibilities for extending social networks may be reasons that people go online to seek support. These characteristics can influence not only *with whom* one interacts (due to the possibilities for extending one's network), but also have an impact on *how* one interacts (due to the impact of the text-based, anonymous character that can influence interpersonal communication).

Social support plays an important role in everyday life and it may contribute to mental as well as physical wellbeing (Albrecht & Goldsmith, 2003; Burleson *et al.*, 1994; Heany & Israel, 1995; Uchino *et al.*, 1996). Social support is found to be beneficial for people who go through a period of uncertainty or anxiety caused by a traumatic experience (Leffler & Dembert, 1998; Pennebaker & Harber, 1993), feel lonely or isolated because of a stigmatized personal characteristic (such as a deviant sexual preference, an extreme political or religious opinion, a history of imprisonment, etc., see: Davison *et al.*, 2000; McKenna & Bargh, 1998) and may help people who suffer from disorders such as depression, anxiety, obesity, cancer, HIV, etc (see: Cohen & Syme, 1985). Social support, consisting of a range of assistances that people can provide to one another in order to improve the quality of life, is found to be important because it can reduce feelings of stress, loneliness, or isolation; can provide people with useful knowledge and information; and may teach people strategies that help them to cope with the situation they are facing (Albrecht & Adelman, 1987; Buunk & Hoorens, 1992; Cohen & Wills, 1985; Colvin *et al.*, 2004; House & Kahn, 1985; Thoits, 1995).

Traditionally, social support was primarily provided by family, friends or colleagues; professionals such as family doctors, psychologists, or other healthcare professionals; or locally organized groups that meet on a regular basis to talk about a shared topic (with probably Alcoholics Anonymous the most well known). However, following the large increase in those who have access to the internet, people are able to interact with others who would otherwise be less easy or even impossible to reach, and in a manner that can be quite different from the more "traditional" face-to-face (FtF) forms of support, as will be elaborated on in this chapter. This may explain the exponential growth of social support groups online in the last decade (Burleson *et al.*, 1994; McKenna & Bargh, 1998; Rice, 2006; Wright & Bell, 2003).

OSSGs can take many forms, but the most common form in which people meet each other to exchange support online is via so-called *bulletin boards* or *discussion forums*. In these usenet or web-based discussion forums members can contribute by posting messages that others can read and respond to messages posted by others. The discussions have the form of *threads* that consist of reactions to previous postings, and members are free to start a new thread whenever they wish. Contributions are retained for a period of time and most forums offer the possibility of searching through the list for a specific topic of interest.

On these forums, active participation is not required and people can visit the forums without contributing to the discussion. People who do not contribute but only read postings are called *lurkers* (on some forums newcomers are even advised not to contribute if they have nothing to say, but first get acquainted with the mode of conduct of the group). By lurking, people can follow discussions by others and pick up information that is relevant to them. Web forums are generally not under supervision of healthcare professionals and are accessible to all visitors (even though registration is sometimes required). Some forums are not moderated at all, and others have members (or administrators) that monitor the contributions and take action when inappropriate or irrelevant messages are posted.

Web forums are thereby easily accessible locations where people can give and receive support and where people who are interested can browse through the postings in an attempt to find the information they need. This makes them a good place not only for people who suffer from some kind of condition themselves, but also for their close relatives or caregivers: They can very easily visit web forums in order to increase their level of understanding and knowledge about the specific situation another is facing. Before going into more detail about how characteristics of these online groups may facilitate support seekers, I will first discuss what social support entails, and how different types of social support can be distinguished.

Online social support

Social support is a very broad concept that comprises many supportive functions such as instrumental, informational, or emotional assistance (House & Kahn, 1985). For the purpose of this chapter social support is defined as the "communication between recipients and providers that reduces uncertainty about the situation, the self, the other or the relationship and functions to enhance a perception of personal control in one's life experience" (Albrecht & Adelman, 1987: 19). Thus, next to *instrumental support*, consisting of providing goods or services and giving practical assistance with daily living, social support can be seen as a communication process through which people can exchange *informational* and *emotional* support (House & Kahn, 1985)—forms of support that are found to be most common in online health-related communities (Braithwaite *et al.*, 1999; Finn, 1999; Preece & Ghozati, 2001).

Informational support concerns the exchange of practical information such as tips on new types of medication, relevant addresses of institutes, knowledge about medical or psychological treatments, legal issues, but also stories of firsthand experiences of members. So, the primary function of this type of support is to expand the knowledge a person has (Reeves, 2000). This type of support is important because it gives people more control over the situation and can reduce uncertainty about the self in such a way that better decisions can be made (Albrecht & Adelman, 1987; Wright, 2002). The next fragment illustrates how firsthand experiences can be used for informational support:

> Hi. Just wondering ... if any other restrictors have experienced dimmed eyesight. Definitely NOT "blacking out" (I've had that too, and this is completely different). This just feels like I can't quite see right, like the lights (indoors or out) need to be turned up a couple of notches. This could be nothing—or a touch of the flu, or maybe need a new eyeglass prescription, but I thought I'd check in with you and see if this sounded familiar to anyone. Thanks, Mike

> Reaction: Mike, I don't know if this would count as dimmed eyesight but I have on occasion experienced visual disturbances somewhat akin

to a sunspot before the eyes and all I get is peripheral vision. In my case I can always connect it to dehydration. I think the first move might be to get your eyes checked out. Perhaps it is just a matter of a prescription adjustment. It's just whenever I hear anyone describing vision problems I always think DRINK, DRINK, and DRINK some more but that is just the particular problem that I experience (and my doctor always "harps" at me to make sure that some of the fluid at least be something containing isotonic salts). [...]

Andy

Emotional support on the other hand, refers to the display of understanding what the other person goes through and involves showing compassion and commitment (Albrecht & Adelman, 1987; Albrecht & Goldsmith, 2003). The next fragment from a forum devoted to cancer is an example of this emotional support:

Hospice has told us that my father in law has at the longest 48 hours. Andrew and I are heartbroken. I think the hardest part is seeing him deteriorate. I know you guys care so much about us and my father in law so I wanted to write and let everyone know. I think in some way, death will be merciful for him. I want him to stay, but that is selfish of me. His entire backside is covered in open sores on top of all his other sufferings. I will let you guys know when the end comes, I can't write any more through all the tears. Sadly, Kirsty

Reaction: Sending you lots of hugs Kirsty, and to your family also. You will be in my prayers over the coming days. Hugs, Emily

So, in emotional support, empathy plays a vital role: Knowing what the other feels, feeling what the other feels, and responding to these feelings in an appropriate manner is a very important form of supporting someone (Levenson & Ruef, 1992: 234). This more affective type of support is characterized by comforting and encouraging and can be highly important for people's self-esteem (Reeves, 2000). Emotional support is found to be especially relevant in situations where people feel they cannot change the situation they are in, but have to adapt to it (Albrecht & Adelman, 1987; Wright, 2000a). Providing emotional support can also imply giving people the opportunity to tell their story. Talking about painful or traumatic experiences, or disclosing personal information can have a therapeutic effect (Pennebaker, 1997), and being there to listen can be a relatively passive but relevant form of social support. In particular in times of stress or misery, it can be comforting to be accompanied by others who are in the same or a similar situation (Davison *et al.*, 2000), because part of the social and emotional problems that people endure stem from feelings of being misunderstood or cut off from society. These feelings may very well result in depression, loneliness, and alienation (Braithwaite *et al.*, 1999) as is illustrated by the following fragment from a forum on dissociative disorder.

> hi there, feeling lonely. dunno what to say. just feeling lonely. not fitting anywhere. like shit. wanna hide, wanna run, maybe would even rather wanna have somebody hold me but that's totally impossible cuz it means I'd have to ask and I wouldnt do that, no way, never. So what am I whinin abot here?Dunno. Prolly it's simply my f*cking fault. better shut up, XX

And the reaction was:

> hiya there, just wanting to say i hear you and i see you, i know how it feels so much about not fitting anywhere... shut up is maybe something that has been done too long and too often, i think more and more that it is ok and even good to not shut up anymore, it' s not wrong or bad to speak or be visible imho even if it is often so hard.. you can email if you like or find me on msn under the name of [name removed] i am here for a while this evening

Thus, social support is important for people who find themselves confronted with distress, (inter)personal problems or unwanted life situations (House *et al,.* 1988; Pennebaker & Harber, 1993; Taylor *et al.*, 1986; Thoits, 1995; Wills, 1985; Wright & Bell, 2003) and a lot of this support can be provided by people who have similar experiences or at least feel empathic with the situation someone is facing. In the next part, I will elaborate on why online social support groups can be beneficial in providing this support. This is done by discussing a number of characteristics of CMC in general, and OSSGs in particular, that may prove to have an impact on social support seeking. First, I will discuss how the anonymity that online communication can provide may affect interactions, then I will focus on the possible consequences of the text-based and a-synchronous character of conversation, and, finally, the consequence of expanding one's social network will be discussed.

Anonymous interactions

An important characteristic of OSSGs is that it can provide a sense of anonymity (Bordia, 1997; Rice & Gattiker, 2001; Sproull & Kiesler, 1991). In most forums or chat rooms, people do not have to reveal their name or other personal information, and visitors are free to make use of pseudonyms or nicknames (Finn, 1999). Not only do people not have to disclose their names, the absence of cues that reveal information about one's identity (such as first name, gender, age, appearance) is also believed to enhance feelings of anonymity (Sproull & Kiesler, 1986; Tanis & Postmes, 2003; Wallace, 1999). This (perception of) anonymity can result in strong feelings of shared identity and higher degrees of self-disclosure, as will be elaborated on in the next part.

Social identification

Being more or less anonymous to one another may result in strong feelings of "groupiness" or cohesion (Lea *et al.*, 2001; Postmes *et al.*, 1998; Postmes *et al.*, 2001): Based on the Social Identity model of Deindividuation Effects, or SIDE model (Reicher *et al.*, 1995; Spears & Lea, 1992), it can be argued that in online support groups where people recognize themselves and others as sharing similarities on the basis of the situation they are facing, the absence of cues that might draw the attention to potential differences (such as differences in age, gender, appearance, cultural background, etc.) may even increase perceptions of similarity and a shared social identity (cf. Sassenberg & Postmes, 2002, and Utz, this volume). These feelings of shared identity may result in more interpersonal trust (Tanis & Postmes, 2005) and a stronger focus on the social norms of the group (Postmes *et al.*, 2001).

Self-disclosure

Anonymity (or at least the perception of being anonymous) can also have consequences for the way people express themselves, and could partly explain why online groups are characterized by such high levels of self-disclosure (Joinson, 2001; Parks & Floyd, 1996; Rheingold, 1993; Swickert *et al.*, 2002; Wallace, 1999; Wright, 2000b): "Under the protective cloak of anonymity users can express the way they truly feel and think" (McKenna & Bargh, 2000: 62) as is illustrated in the following fragment of someone planning to leave her abusive husband:

> Hi, I don't know where to start. I guess I just want to say that I'm glad there is a place to talk and watch anonymously. Right now I'm having such a difficult time.[...] I just feel so guilty about leaving because he's trying so hard right now and he's being so nice. But I've had this planned for a month. [...] I just wanted to talk... I needed to get this out in a place that felt safe. Thank you...

Joinson (2001) found that people disclose more information about themselves in CMC compared to FtF interactions. A possible explanation for this is that the anonymity causes a reduction of public self-awareness and lowered feelings of accountability (Joinson, 2001). The anonymity can provide the freedom to express oneself with less shame and without the feeling that one's privacy is violated, and allows people to ask intimate or potentially embarrassing questions that they would not ask as easily in an *offline* context (Braithwaite *et al.*, 1999; Wallace, 1999). In this way OSSGs may open up possibilities for people to discuss topics that they feel embarrassed or ashamed to talk about face-to-face.

Text-based conversations

CMC differs from FtF interactions in that it is primarily text-based and a-synchronous. Even though the visual and auditory options of the internet increase (a number of forums offer possibilities for web cams and audio), the lion's share of the online interactions are in written form. Much of the early theorizing on mediated communication has predicted that this form of communication would be relatively cold, impersonal, and primarily task-focused because it is not capable of conveying nonverbal, social cues. This would make all forms of mediated communication inherently less suited for intimate interactions when compared to FtF communication (Connolly, *et al.*, 1990; Hiltz *et al.*, 1986; Kiesler *et al.*, 1984). However, this does not sit comfortably with the high number of individuals who voluntarily choose to open their heart, or engage in highly personal interactions by means of written text (from old-fashioned correspondence by letter to personal disclosures on the internet, or even via the technically limited form of text messaging).

In OSSGs, the text-based character has a number of benefits that may be highly relevant for exchanging informational or emotional support. There are cognitive benefits in writing, it is a-synchronous, there is an emphasis on the contribution, and it allows for selective self-presentation.

Cognitive benefits of writing

Research by Pennebaker and colleagues has shown that writing about personal or emotional issues can positively affect mental and physical health (Pennebaker, 1997; Pennebaker & Harber, 1993; Pennebaker *et al.*, 1997). Their findings suggest that the act of writing about emotional feelings or experiences causes cognitive changes which can work therapeutically: When disclosing personal feelings or traumatic experiences to others, individuals must narrate an understandable account of the situation. By doing so, they must formulate a coherent and insightful explanation of what they go through which provides them with more understanding of the situation they are in (Pennebaker *et al.*, 1997). Translating emotional experiences (such as traumas) into language seems more effective for the healing process than to express them in a different manner (Miller & Gergen, 1998; Pennebaker, 1997; Pennebaker & Harber, 1993; Pennebaker *et al.*, 1997).

A-synchronous interactions

A-synchronous interactions afford people the opportunity to carefully compose and formulate their messages without having to worry about interruptions or immediate responses by others. This gives people the chance to reflect upon messages before sending them to the group. Taking your time can be especially valuable when the topic of discussion is one that concerns sensitive or emotional issues (Braithwaite *et al.*, 1999; Walther, 1996; Weinberg *et al.*, 1995).

A more practical advantage of the way interactions are organized in online forums is that they are automatically stored on the website. This enables people to catch up with the discussion when unable to visit the forum on a regular basis, but also allows people to search for information in discussion threads that are no longer active but are still archived on the site. In this way, OSSGs have an important role in informational support, and can provide people with relevant information and knowledge.

Emphasis on contribution

Another potential advantage of the text-based contribution is that people are valued for their contribution instead of on the basis of their physical appearance (Weinberg *et al.*, 1995). This can be liberating, especially for people who see themselves confronted with prejudices based on age, sex or ethnicity in their offline life, but also for people who suffer from stigmatized physical characteristics such as obesity, mutilation, skin problems, etc. (Erwin *et al.*, 2004; Wallace, 1999). Also for people whose ability to speak or hear is affected, or who have cognitive disabilities or other handicaps that cause them to take more time to express themselves, text-based interactions can be highly constructive: The problems these people face in FtF interactions can lead to a restriction in their opportunities to engage in social interaction. Text-based online interaction enables them to participate in the same manner as the other members, and it provides them with equal opportunities to partake in the discussion (Braithwaite *et al.*, 1999; Nelson, 1995).

Selective self-presentation

A different though related reason why people may choose to participate in OSSGs is that it provides them with the opportunity for selective self-presentation. According to the Social Information Processing perspective (SIP: Walther, 1992, 1996), people will adapt their linguistic and textual behaviors when using CMC. They do this in an attempt to overcome the nonverbal limitations of CMC in such a way that the presentation of socially revealing and relational signals that would normally be conveyed through a variety of channels will now be communicated via text only. This factor, however, also allows people to present themselves in a more friendly, knowledgeable, empathic way, because it gives them the opportunity to carefully shape their appearance, and enables selective self-presentation—often called *hyperpersonal* interaction (for detailed discussion of hyperpersonal interaction, see: Walther, 1996; Walther & Boyd, 2002). Selective self-presentation is believed to be very common in online communities, dating sites, online games, etc., and some research on hyperpersonality and social support exists (Walther & Boyd, 2002; Wright & Bell, 2003; Whitty, this volume). However, more research is needed as to how this might affect the process of social support and the perceptions that are formed of support seekers and providers.

Expanding social networks

Probably the most important reason why people seek social support on the internet is because it provides them with easy access to others who face a similar situation. Sitting in front of the computer, individuals can engage in social interactions with others all over the world who potentially have an understanding of their specific situation (Braithwaite *et al.*, 1999; Finn & Lavitt, 1994; Rice & Katz, 2001). The only restriction is that people need to have access to the internet, and must not feel too uncomfortable in reading and writing in the common language of the group. Online forums are not troubled by geographical barriers and the a-synchronicity of the interaction provides the members with flexibility in when they want to interact. Members can post and read messages at times that suit them best, which can be beneficial for people that have conflicting time schedules caused by work, different time zones, or other obligations. This might be why these groups are more easily found, chosen, or started online (Madara, 1997: 23).

So, these online groups can be a valuable extension to one's *offline* social network and increase the possibilities for finding support. This might be especially beneficial for people who live in isolated parts of the world, have disabilities that restrict their mobility, or have anxieties that cause them not to dare to leave their homes, but also for people who feel lonely, unique, or misunderstood and live in a social environment in which social support is not easily found (for example homosexuality in an orthodox religious community). However, OSSGs may provide people who just want to tell their story, seek information, or are looking for social interaction with a social network. Not only do they provide a network of others who are, at least to a certain degree, similar, but the online network may contain more diverse information and the type of relationship with people who provide support may vary to a greater extent than often found offline.

Networks of perceived similarity

The ease of access to a large number of people, unrestricted by time or place barriers, can provide a sense of universality and communality in online groups (Braithwaite *et al.*, 1999; Madara, 1997; Preece & Ghozati, 2001; Wright & Bell, 2003). Despite the fact that members of online communities can (and probably will) differ on a lot of dimensions, they may all find themselves in a similar situation, may be faced with the same mental or physical condition, or have gone through a similar traumatic experience. Contrary to one's offline environment, people voluntarily choose to participate in the online community because of an interest in the topic of concern. It is therefore not surprising that members perceive the others on the forum as more similar as compared to others in their offline networks (Wright, 2000b). This perceived similarity can even be increased by the absence of cues that may signal individual differences: As mentioned earlier when discussing the anonymity that OSSGs afford, the anonymity may result in increased attention to what all members in the group share, and thereby contribute to feelings of belonging and social identification (Lea *et al.*, 2001; Postmes *et al.*, 1998; Postmes *et al.*, 2001).

The need to belong

Finding similar others can be an important motivation for joining an online community because perceived similarity and the feeling that one is part of a larger group is part of the basic *need to belong* (Brewer, 1991; Deaux, 1993; McKenna & Bargh, 1998). For people who feel isolated or cut off in their offline environment because they feel unique, being surrounded by similar others can be especially important. The following fragment from a discussion forum about mood swings illustrates the need for being among others who recognize what someone is going through:

> This has been an interesting week—I feel like I'm on the verge of a crying jag, but ready to snap at any given second. I can feel tears in the back of my throat, but it doesn't stop me from saying or thinking really mean things about people. My patience has gotten to be virtually nill and I'm not sure where I'm at emotionally. Does anyone else feel like this?

Research has shown that in online support groups where people are surrounded by others who understand, very little suspicion exists, and interactions are characterized by low levels of negative emotional remarks and high levels of empathic communication (Finn, 1999; Preece & Ghozati, 2001; Wallace, 1999). People who find themselves in a similar situation tend to be more empathic and show more understanding: "the more similar we are the less we have to go outside of ourselves to gather cues and the more we can respond as we ourselves would naturally to the circumstances" (Hodge & Wegner, 1997, in Preece & Ghozati, 2001).

Being among similar others might be especially important for people who suffer from a stigmatized physical or mental condition (such as obesity, stuttering, schizophrenia, or manic depression), or who feel that an important part of their identity is not accepted by society (such as a deviant sexual preferences, or extreme religious or political beliefs). People who perceive themselves outsiders or outliers because they differ from others in an important part of their identity—i.e. that have a *marginalized identity* (Frable, 1993)—can have difficulties because they feel being unique or deviant from the people in their social circle.

Frable (1993) distinguishes between two forms of marginal identities: those that are conspicuous, and those that are concealable. OSSGs may prove beneficial for both of these groups. People with visible or *conspicuous marginal identities* (for example people who suffer from obesity, skin conditions, mutilation, or physical disabilities) can have a feeling that the first thing that others note about them is the part that is deviant. As a result, people can realize that those in their social environment act uncertainly and awkwardly when they are present, which can ultimately lead to feelings of isolation and social exclusion (see: Braithwaite *et al.*, 1999). In online interaction (i.e. in the absence of visual cues) people can feel liberated from this burden, and feel valued on the basis of their written contributions and not on the basis of their more or less unique physical appearance (Weinberg *et al.*, 1995).

The sense of being unique can even feel of greater importance to people who have *concealable marginal identities* (Frable, 1993; McKenna & Bargh, 1998) because for people with concealable marginal identity (such as a venereal disease, multiple personality syndrome, or a deviant sexual preference) the chance of recognizing someone with a similar condition is very small: "those with hidden conditions are not able to see similar others in their environment, so there is no visible sign of others who share the stigmatized feature"(McKenna & Bargh, 1998: 682). Especially when it concerns a stigmatized identity, it can be difficult to find support or understanding: It is not easy to take the first step in revealing stigmatized information about an important part of your identity, without knowing whether you can count on recognition or understanding. Therefore, members of this group run the risk of social exclusion and loneliness without the possibility of finding people to interact with on the internet (McKenna & Bargh, 1998).

Through participation in online social support communities, people can attain more self-esteem and confidence. According to McKenna and Bargh (1998), this can reduce the inner conflict between the marginalized part of the identity and the socially accepted standards, and result in more openness to discuss this aspect of identity with significant others such as friends and family.

Source for social comparison

As mentioned in the beginning of this chapter, informational support not only consists of *hard* information such as advice about medication, addresses of health-related institutes, etc. but also of stories about experiences and accounts of how others cope with a specific situation. People can use these accounts for social comparison (Davison *et al.*, 2000). Social comparison theory (Festinger, 1954) posits that people will compare themselves with others in times of uncertainty or anxiety. Therefore, the need for social comparison is inherent to a physical or mental healthcare setting, because of its high level of ambiguity and anxiety (Davison *et al.*, 2000). However, people can only compare themselves with others who are relatively similar to each other, which makes online support groups a good place for social comparison purposes.

There is, however, another reason why OSSGs may benefit social comparison. Research has shown that when the situation is humiliating or embarrassing, people do not want to be in the presence of others out of shame or loss of self-esteem (Sarnoff & Zimbardo, in Davison *et al.*, 2000). However, Davison *et al.* (2000) show that people who have illnesses that are perceived embarrassing, socially stigmatized, or disfiguring, seek support from similar others but prefer to do this online. Attentative conclusion would therefore be that because of the anonymity and the perception of privacy that online communities afford, partaking in online communities can be helpful for social comparison, even when the situation is embarrassing or socially stigmatized.

Weak-tie networks

The accessibility of the OSSGs, unrestricted by time and place barriers may result in users who differ a lot in their backgrounds, and have a large diversity in their relations to one another (from complete strangers to close friends). So, as a side-effect of looking for others who are similar—to the extent that an interest in the topic of discussion is shared—the people in these online networks may vary more compared to one's offline network, potentially making these groups more heterogeneous. Individuals become a member of an OSSG of their own accord, and often visit the community on a regular basis. but the only thing that binds the individuals together is the topic of interest of the group. When the personal situation (and the reason for attending the group) changes, the online community can become irrelevant, and people will most likely stop attending the group. As a result, at least some of the relationships will be of relatively short duration and be based on the shared interest only. Unlike one's offline social network, that largely consists of family, friends and colleagues with whom strong and usually long-lasting relationships exist, relations in online support communities often take the form of *weak ties* (Adelman *et al.*, 1987; Wright & Bell, 2003). *Weak ties* are relations between people who communicate on a regular basis, but who are not necessarily close to one another (Granovetter, 1973).

Even though strong social ties with relevant others are very important for social support (Cummings *et al.*, 2002; House *et al.*, 1988; Thoits, 1995; Wills, 1985), weak ties can play an important part in the wellbeing of people who seek support as well (Adelman *et al.*, 1987; Granovetter, 1973; Wright & Bell, 2003). Research has shown that an extended network may offer a large diversity of information (Granovetter, 1973; Rice & Katz, 2001; Wellman, 1997), and weak ties may be able to provide support that strong ties can not (Albrecht & Adelman, 1987; Thoits, 1995). These potential benefits will be discussed in the next section.

Networks of varied information

One of the characteristics of weak-tie networks is that they consist of people who vary in background, and come from different groups, communities, or cultures. Because members in a weak-tie network are themselves embedded in other social communities, they can open up totally different sources of knowledge and information, and thereby offer more variety than offline networks often do (Wellman, 1997). Therefore, one of the potential advantages of these online groups is that through these relations, information can be gathered that would otherwise be inaccessible. Members in online groups may especially benefit from this variety of information because of the layout of most web forums. In most forums, postings are archived for a period of time, which allows members to search for information about the topic of their interest, by which OSSGs have the potential to make a large amount of diverse information available for a large number of individuals.

Networks with various strengths of relations

Weak-tie networks might also be beneficial in that they provide an opportunity for members to seek support and to talk about their situation without the risks that sometimes accompany talking to people who are close by (Thoits, 1995; Wright & Bell, 2003). In an offline situation support is most often provided by significant others that are close to the individual, such as parents, partners, family, friends, and colleagues (Wills, 1985). Even though these people have an important function in supporting (House & Kahn, 1985; Thoits, 1995), these more or less obligatory relations can have negative consequences in that they may lead to expectations and demands that can cause stress by themselves (Thoits, 1995).

People who are close by can push too hard, or anticipate seeing too swift improvements in the situation. Strong-tied others can also be so overprotective, causing the individual to suffer under the perception of complete dependency. Another potential downside of receiving support from significant others may be that they can be inclined to rule a verdict about the behavior that is responsible for causing the situation: Even though friends and family are close and bonds are strong, and despite the good intentions, they can sometimes be the first to judge (Wright & Bell, 2003), especially when people find themselves in a situation they can be held responsible for (for example HIV in relation to unsafe sex or intravenous use of drugs, cardiac disease in relation to not being able to give up smoking or drinking, financial problems in relation to a gambling addiction, etc.). Additionally, friends and family can have stronger role obligations that can result in listening to the problems not because they want to, but because they feel it is their duty to do so, which can be felt as a burden by the support seeker (Albrecht & Adelman, 1987).

So, it can be a relief to tell one's story to a relative stranger on the internet where relations tend to be looser, chosen voluntarily and have no reciprocal expectations (Thoits, 1995), just as it can be comforting to spill one's heart to a stranger on the train (Bargh & McKenna, 2004). Another advantage of asking support from weak ties has to do with the low risk in asking potentially embarrassing questions. According to Adelman *et al.* (1987) weak ties "allow people to seek information and support without having to deal with the uncertainty of how those in primary [strong-tie] relationships might respond" (p. 131), thereby facilitating "low-risk discussions about high-risk topics" (p. 133).

Conclusion

Online social support groups may form a valuable supplement to one's social network, and may be beneficial in providing people with social support. The anonymity can enhance feelings of cohesion and social identification (Lea *et al.*, 2001; Postmes *et al.*, 1998; Postmes *et al.*, 2001), and may stimulate self-disclosure (Joinson, 2001; Parks & Floyd, 1996) which enables people to talk more easily about sensitive topics (Braithwaite *et al.*, 1999; Wallace, 1999). The text-based character may have a therapeutic effect in itself because it forces individuals to formulate a coherent story that can improve their understanding of the situation (Miller & Gergen, 1998; Pennebaker *et al.*, 1997). The a-synchronous form allows people to carefully reflect on messages and compose reactions without having to worry about interruptions, and enables people to browse through interactions looking for relevant postings. Because of the written form, there can be more attention for the actual message instead of how one looks, which might be liberating for people that see themselves confronted with prejudices or who suffer from stigmatized physical characteristics (Erwin *et al.*, 2004; Wallace, 1999), and may provide opportunities for selective self-presentation (Walther, 1996; Walther & Boyd, 2002). Finally, online interactions are not restricted by geographical or time constraints and thereby enable people to get into contact with others that would otherwise never have been reached (Braithwaite *et al.*, 1999; Finn & Lavitt, 1994; Rice & Katz, 2001). This might make these weak-tie networks a good source of diverse information (Granovetter, 1973; Wellman, 1997), and the other users can offer support in a freer and less obligatory manner than often found offline (Albrecht & Adelman, 1987; Thoits, 1995).

So in general, online social support groups have a number of features that can make them a fruitful supplement for people who seek social support. However, there are also potential downsides to online support: Whereas close ties can provide assistance with adhering to health regimes, weak ties have less obligatory norms (Albrecht & Goldsmith, 2003). This makes online relations probably less suited for "forcing" people to take their medication, do their daily exercises, or restraining people from taking drugs or alcohol. The anonymity that online support groups offer to their members can also have some downsides. In these anonymous groups, people can be confronted with disinhibited behavior (Kiesler *et al.*, 1984; Sproull & Kiesler, 1986), people run the risk of being harassed or stalked online (Finn & Banach, 2000), and the information or advice people provide may be inaccurate or even harmful. However, these negative outcomes are only rarely reported in empirical studies (even though these potential dangers are almost always addressed in introductions or discussions), and more research is necessary that specifically focuses on these potentially negative consequences of online social support groups.

Future research should also address who it is that makes use of these groups, and how personal characteristics determine whether or not participation in OSSGs has positive effects on mental as well as physical well-being. Do OSSGs have a different effect on users that are socially isolated or introvert, which see the OSSG as their main platform for social interaction because of the safety they may provide, or extravert people that use the internet as an extension of their online network? Is there a difference between people that primarily use the groups to gather information, or people that mainly come to the groups to get emotional support? These and other questions would be interesting to answer for they would provide us with more understanding of how computer-mediated communication in general has become an integrated part of everyday life, and how online social support groups in particular may benefit the wellbeing of people that seek support.

References

Adelman, M. B., Parks, M. R., & Albrecht, T. L. (1987) "Beyond close relationships: Support in weak ties." In T. L. Albrecht & M. B. Adelman (eds.), *Communicating Social Support*. Newbury Park: Sage, pp. 126–147.

Albrecht, T. L., & Adelman, M. B. (1987) "Communicating social support: A theoretical perspective." In T. L. Albrecht & M. B. Adelman (eds.), *Communicating Social Support*. Newbury Park, CA: Sage, pp. 18–39.

Albrecht, T. L., & Goldsmith, D. J. (2003) "Social support, social networks, and health." In T. L. Thompson, A. M. Dorsey, K. I. Miller & R. Parrott (eds.), *Handbook of Health Communication*. Hillsdale, NK: Erlbaum, pp. 263–284.

Bargh, J. A., & McKenna, K. Y. A. (2004) "The Internet and social life." *Annual Review of Psychology, 55*, 573–590.

Bordia, P. (1997) "Face-to-face versus computer-mediated communication: A synthesis of the experimental literature." *Journal of Business Communication, 34*(1), 99–120.

Braithwaite, D. O., Waldron, V. R., & Finn, J. (1999) "Communication of social support in computer-mediated groups for people with disabilities." *Health Communication, 11*(2), 123–151.

Brewer, M. B. (1991) "The social self: On being the same and different at the same time." *Personality and Social Psychology Bulletin, 17*(5), 475–482.

Burleson, B. R., Albrecht, T. L., & Sarason, I. (1994) *Communication of Social Support: Messages, Interactions, Relationships and Community*. Newbury Park, CA: Sage.

Buunk, B. P., & Hoorens, V. (1992) "Social support and stress: The role of social comparison and social exchange processes." *British Journal of Clinical Psychology, 31*(4), 445–457.

Cohen, S., & Syme, S. L. (1985) *Social Support and Health*. Orlando, FL: Academic press, Inc.

Cohen, S., & Wills, T. A. (1985) "Stress, social support, and the buffering hypothesis." *Psychological Bulletin, 98*(2), 310–357.

Colvin, J., Chenoweth, L., Bold, M., & Harding, C. (2004) "Caregivers of older adults: Advantages and disadvantages of Internet-based social support." *Family Relations, 53*(1), 49–57.

Connolly, T., Jessup, L. M., & Valacich, J. S. (1990) "Effects of anonymity and evaluative tone on idea generation in computer-mediated groups." *Management Science, 36*(6), 689–703.

Cummings, J. N., Sproull, L., & Kiesler, S. B. (2002) "Beyond hearing: Where real-world and online support meet." *Group Dynamics-Theory Research and Practice, 6*(1), 78–88.

Davison, K. P., Pennebaker, J. W., & Dickerson, S. S. (2000) "Who talks: The social psychology of illness support groups." *American Psychologist, 55*(2), 205–217.

Deaux, K. (1993) "Reconstructing social identity." *Personality and Social Psychology Bulletin, 19*(1), 4–12.

Erwin, B. A., Turk, C. L., Heimberg, R. G., Fresco, D. M., & Hantula, D. A. (2004) "The Internet: Home to a severe population of individuals with social anxiety disorder?" *Journal of Anxiety Disorders, 18*(5), 629–646.

Festinger, L. A. (1954) "A theory of social comparison processes." *Human Relations, 7*, 117–140.

Finn, J. (1999) "An exploration of helping processes in an online self-help group focusing on issues of disability." *Health & Social Work, 24*(3), 220–231.

Finn, J., & Banach, M. (2000) "Victimization online: The down side of seeking human services for women on the Internet." *Cyberpsychology & Behavior, 3*(2), 243–254.

Finn, J., & Lavitt, M. (1994) "Computer-based self-help groups for sexual abuse survivors." *Social Work With Groups, 24*, 220–240.

Fox, S. (2005) *Health Information Online: Pew Internet and American Life Project*. Pew Internet and American Life Project. Retrieved May 2006 from the World Wide Web: http://www.pewinternet.org

Frable, D. E. S. (1993) "Being and feeling unique: Statistical deviance and psychological marginality." *Journal of Personality, 61*(1), 85–110.

Granovetter, M. (1973) "The strength of weak ties." *American Journal of Sociology, 78,* 1360–1380.

Heany, C. A., & Israel, B. A. (1995) "Social networks and social support." In K. Glanz & F. M. Lewis & B. K. Rimer (eds.), *Health Behavior and Health Education: Theory, Research and Practice,* second edition. San Francisco: Jossey-Bass, pp. 179–205.

Hiltz, S. R., Johnson, K., & Turoff, M. (1986) "Experiments in group decision-making: Communication process and outcome in face-to-face versus computerized conferences." *Human Communication Research, 13,* 225–252.

Hodges, S. D., & Wegner, D. M. (1997) "Automatic and controlled empathy." In W. Ickes (ed.), *Empathic Accuracy.* New York: Guilford, pp. 311–339.

House, J. S., & Kahn, R. L. (1985) "Measures and concepts of social support." In S. Cohen & S. L. Syme (eds.), *Social Support and Health.* Orlando, FL: Academic Press, pp. 83–108.

House, J. S., Landis, K. R., & Umberson, D. (1988) "Social relationships and health." *Science, 241*(4865), 540–545.

Joinson, A. N. (2001) "Self-disclosure in computer-mediated communication: The role of self-awareness and visual anonymity." *European Journal of Social Psychology, 31,* 177–192.

Kiesler, S., Siegel, J., & McGuire, T. W. (1984) "Social psychological aspects of computer-mediated communication." *American Psychologist, 39,* 1123–1134.

Lea, M., Spears, R., & de Groot, D. (2001) "Knowing me, knowing you: Anonymity effects on social identity processes within groups." *Personality and Social Psychology Bulletin, 27*(5), 526–537.

Leffler, C., & Dembert, M. (1998) "Posttraumatic stress symptoms among U.S. Navy divers recovering TWA flight 800." *Journal of Nervous and Mental Disorders, 186,* 574–577.

Leimeister, J. M., & Krcmar, H. (2005) "Evaluation of a systematic design for a virtual patient community." *Journal of Computer-Mediated Communication, 10*(4).

Levenson, R. W., & Ruef, A. M. (1992) "Empathy: A physiological substrate." *Journal of Personality and Social Psychology, 63*(2), 234–246.

Madara, E. J. (1997) "The mutual-aid self-help online revolution." *Social Policy, 97*(3), 20–26.

McKenna, K. Y. A., & Bargh, J. A. (1998) "Coming out in the age of the Internet: Identity 'demarginalization' through virtual group participation." *Journal of Personality and Social Psychology, 75*(3), 681–694.

McKenna, K. Y. A., & Bargh, J. A. (2000) "Plan 9 from cyberspace: The implications of the internet for personality and social psychology." *Personality and Social Psychology Review, 4,* 57–75.

Miller, J. K., & Gergen, K. J. (1998) "Life on the line: The therapeutic potentials of computer-mediated conversation." *Journal of Marital & Family Therapy, 24*(2), 189–202.

Nelson, J. A. (1995) "The internet, the virtual community and those with disabilities." *Disability Quarterly, 15*(2), 15–20.

Parks, R. M., & Floyd, K. (1996) "Making friends in cyberspace." *Journal of Communication, 46*(1), 80–97.

Pennebaker, J. W. (1997) "Writing about emotional experiences as a therapeutic process." *Psychological Science, 8*(3), 162–166.

Pennebaker, J. W., & Harber, K. D. (1993) "A social stage model of collective coping: The Loma Prieta earthquake and the Persian Gulf War." *Journal of Social Issues, 49*(4), 125–145.

Pennebaker, J. W., Mayne, T. J., & Francis, M. E. (1997) "Linguistic predictors of adaptive bereavement." *Journal of Personality and Social Psychology, 72*(4), 863–871.

Postmes, T., Spears, R., & Lea, M. (1998) "Breaching or building social boundaries? SIDE-effect of computer-mediated communication." *Communication Research, 25*(6), 689–715.

Postmes, T., Spears, R., Sakhel, K., & de Groot, D. (2001) "Social influence in computer-mediated communication: The effects of anonymity on group behavior." *Personality and Social Psychology Bulletin, 27*, 1243–1254.

Preece, J. J., & Ghozati, K. (2001) "Experiencing empathy online." In R. E. Rice & J. E. Katz (eds.), *The Internet and Health Communication* .Thousand Oaks, CA: Sage, pp. 237–260.

Reeves, P. M. (2000) "Coping in cyberspace: The impact of Internet use on the ability of HIV-positive individuals to deal with their illness." *Journal of Health Communication, 5*, 47–59.

Reicher, S., Spears, R., & Postmes, T. (1995) "A social identity model of deindividuation phenomena." In W. Stroebe & M. Hewstone (eds.), *European Review of Social Psychology* Vol. 6. Chichester, England: Wiley, pp. 161–198.

Rheingold, H. (1993) *The Virtual Community: Homesteading on the Electronic Frontier.* Reading, MA: Addison-Wesley.

Rice, R. E. (2006) "Influences, usage, and outcomes of Internet health information searching: Multivariate results from the Pew surveys." *International Journal of Medical Informatics, 75*(1), 8–28.

Rice, R. E., & Gattiker, U. E. (2001) "New media and organizational structuring." In F. M. Jablin & L. L. Putnam (eds.), *The New Handbook of Organizational Communication.* Thousand Oaks, CA: Sage, pp. 544–581.

Rice, R. E., & Katz, J. E. (2001). *The Internet and Health Communication: Experiences and Expectations.* Thousand Oaks, CA: Sage.

Sarnoff, I., & Zimbardo, P. (1961) "Anxiety, fear, and social affiliation." *Journal of Abnormal and Social Psychology, 62*, 356–363.

Sassenberg, K., & Postmes, T. (2002) "Cognitive and strategic processes in small groups: Effects of anonymity of the self and anonymity of the group on social influence." *British Journal of Social Psychology, 41*, 463–480.

Spears, R., & Lea, M. (1992) "Social influence and the influence of the 'social' in computer-mediated communication." In M. Lea (ed.), *Contexts of Computer-Mediated Communication.* Hemel Hempstead: Harvester Wheatsheaf, pp. 30–65.

Sproull, L., & Kiesler, S. (1986) "Reducing social context cues: Electronic mail in organizational communication." *Management Science, 32*(11), 1492–1512.

Sproull, L., & Kiesler, S. (1991) *Connections: New Ways of Working in the Networked Organization.* Cambridge, MA: The MIT Press.

Swickert, R. J., Hittner, J. B., Harris, J. L., & Herring, J. A. (2002) "Relationships among Internet use, personality, and social support." *Computers in Human Behavior, 18*(4), 437–451.

Tanis, M., & Postmes, T. (2003) "Social cues and impression formation in CMC." *Journal of Communication, 53*(4), 676–693.

Tanis, M., & Postmes, T. (2005) A social identity approach to trust: Interpersonal perception, group membership and trusting behaviour." *European Journal of Social Psychology, 35*, 413–424.

Taylor, S. E., Falke, R. L., Shoptaw, S. J., & Lichtman, R. R. (1986) "Social support, support groups, and the cancer patient." *Journal of Consulting and Clinical Psychology, 54*(5), 608–615.

Thoits, P. A. (1995) "Stress, coping, and social support: Where are we? What next?" *Journal of Health and Social Behavior, 35*, 53–79.

Uchino, B. N., Cacioppo, J. T., & Kiecolt-Glaser, J. K. (1996) "The relationship between social support and psychological processes: A review with emphasis on underlying mechanisms and implications for health." *Psychological Bulletin, 119*(3), 488–531.

Wallace, P. (1999). *The Psychology of the Internet.* Cambridge: Cambridge University Press.

Walther, J. B. (1992) "Interpersonal effects in computer-mediated interaction: A relational perspective." *Communication Research, 19*(1), 52–90.

Walther, J. B. (1996) "Computer-mediated communication: Impersonal, interpersonal, and hyperpersonal interaction." *Communication Research, 23*(1), 3–43.

Walther, J. B., & Boyd, S. (2002) "Attraction to computer-mediated social support." In C. A. Lin & D. J. Atkin (eds.), *Communication Technology and Society: Audience Adoption and Use.* Cresskill, NJ: Hampton Press, pp. 153–188.

Weinberg, N., Schmale, J., Uken, J., & Wessel, K. (1995) "Computer-mediated support groups." *Social Work With Groups, 17*, 43–54.

Wellman, B. (1997) "An electronic group is virtually a social network." In S. Kiesler (ed.), *Culture of the Internet.* Mahwah, NJ: Lawrence Erlbaum, pp. 179–205.

Wills, T. A. (1985) "Supportive functions of interpersonal relationships." In S. Cohen & S. L. Syme (eds.), *Social Support and Health.* New York: Academic, pp. 61–82.

Wright, K. B. (2000a) "Computer-mediated social support, older adults, and coping." *Journal of Communication, 50*(3), 100–118.

Wright, K. B. (2000b) "Perceptions of on-line support providers: An examination of perceived homophily, source credibility, communication and social support within on-line support groups." *Communication Quarterly, 48*, 44–59.

Wright, K. B. (2002) "Social support within an on-line cancer community: An assessment of emotional support, perceptions of advantages and disadvantages, and motives for using the community from a communication perspective." *Journal of Applied Communication Research, 30*(3), 195–209.

Wright, K. B., & Bell, S. B. (2003) "Health-related support groups on the Internet: Linking empirical findings to social support and computer-mediated communication theory." *Journal of Health Psychology, 8*(1), 39–54.

Chapter 16

Mediated interpersonal communication in multiplayer video games

Implications for entertainment and relationship management

Christoph Klimmt and Tilo Hartmann

The investigation of mediated interpersonal communication is typically concerned with "serious" contexts, such as organizational communication and group processes (Walther, this volume) or health communication (Tanis, this volume). Online dating (Whitty, this volume) is an exception in this respect, since it features some playful and enjoyable dimensions. In general, however, *entertainment* contexts have received far less attention from mediated interpersonal communication scholars than work-related or other "serious" domains (e.g., Blythe *et al.*, 2003). Therefore, little is known about the importance of mediated interpersonal communication for users of interactive video games although these games have conquered a key position in today's landscape of media entertainment (Copier & Raessens, 2003; Raessens & Goldstein, 2005; Vorderer & Bryant, 2006). Until recently, this lack of research was not problematic, because interpersonal communication was simply not a (relevant) feature of video games. With the increase in affordable computing power and the advent of broadband internet connections, however, more and more video games adopted modes of interpersonal communication between users as a part of their "multiplayer gaming" functionality (Chan & Vorderer, 2006; Jansz & Martens, 2005). Today, a significant variety of "multiplayer games" is available and very popular. For instance, World of Warcraft, an internet-based multiplayer fantasy universe, was used by more than five million people worldwide in December 2005 (Blizzard Entertainment, 2005). For these types of video game, interaction and communication among human players (e.g., in competitive settings) is an important characteristic that distinguishes them from conventional single-player games and raises new questions about the enjoyment of playing as well as the social consequences of (prolonged) game consumption.

From the perspective of mediated interpersonal communication, multiplayer video gaming is a special case (Pena & Hancock, 2006) that is bound to new context variables such as enjoyment but also features similarities with better-known cases such as impression formation in

CMC (Tanis & Postmes, 2003) or group communication (Walther, this volume). In this chapter, we review the existing research on communication among "multiplayer gamers" and present some initial theory-based considerations on the role of mediated interpersonal communication in (1) video game *enjoyment* and (2) the *social impact* of video gaming. These two dimensions have been understudied (Vorderer & Bryant, 2006) although especially relevant: Enjoyment is the conceptual key for understanding the motivation to play, the experience of playing, the economic importance of games, as well as a variety of game effects (e.g., Ritterfeld & Weber, 2006; Slater *et al.*, 2003). The social impact of video games has been discussed extensively, and various concerns about social issues such as aggression, social isolation, or decline of social relationships circulate in the public discourse (e.g., Bruner & Bruner, 2006). Given the growing popularity of multiplayer games, an indepth discussion of the role of interpersonal (interplayer) communication in video game enjoyment and video game effects is relevant and can help to identify directions for more systematic research in this domain; this would open up new conceptual connections to entertainment and media effects issues for interpersonal communication researchers.

Manifestations of mediated interpersonal communication in multiplayer video games

An analysis of today's multiplayer games reveals a great diversity in the form and content of mediated interpersonal communication that is built into game properties and recognized by players (e.g., Steinkuehler, 2006). To structure our discussion, we distinguish three prototypical forms: (1) encounters with (mostly) unknown other human players in large-scale gaming environments; (2) inner-group communication among players organized as stable and task-oriented teams ("clans"); and (3) communication among members of social units created and existing within a virtual-narrative world, such as "guilds" in fantasy game environments. We describe each form in detail in order to derive conclusions about their implications for game enjoyment and the social effects of heavy gaming.

Encounters with (mostly) unknown other human players in large-scale game environments

Persistent virtual worlds that enable large numbers of players to explore huge environments and interact with other users represent one important innovation in video gaming that attracts millions of people worldwide. While these games are highly diverse in terms of narrative context (see Klimmt, 2006), for instance science-fiction (Star Wars Galaxies) versus medieval-fantastic (World of Warcraft) and in terms of the rules and regulations that apply to all users, these "massively multiplayer online role playing games" (MMORPG, or for short: MMO, cf. Chan & Vorderer, 2006) share the basic principle that each player is represented by one character or "avatar" (McDonald & Kim, 2001). Players direct their avatar through a game world that is usually displayed as a 3D environment. Avatars of other players that are within one's own avatar's visibility range are displayed on the screen. All games allow the individualization of the physical properties and appearance of avatars (e.g., creature type, gender, skin color, clothing, armory, and equipment) which is the (nonverbal) foundation for a game-specific form of impression formation. Processes of social perception (e.g., categorization, activation of stereotypes; cf. Kalyanaraman & Sundar, this volume) are therefore likely to occur in such MMOs before actual mediated interpersonal communication begins.

MMO players can decide to initiate explicit communication with one or more players whose avatars are in the immediate surroundings. Contemporary games offer written text communication that is comparable to instant messaging (see Leung, 2001) as a channel for interaction among avatars or players, respectively. Messages written by one player temporarily appear on the screens of all players whose avatars can "hear" the "speaking" avatar. Explicit selection of one target person who is to be addressed for secret communication is also facilitated by most MMOs. Some games also provide standardized procedures for common types of player-to-player communication such as trading goods. Overall, the opportunities to communicate with other players through the avatars that occupy the game universe try to imitate real-world interpersonal communication in terms of social settings (e.g., only avatars in the vicinity can be communication partners; private communication to selected avatars is an equivalent to whispering in real settings). In most cases, such interplayer communication is bound to text messaging, although this technical requirement will certainly change with technological progress towards more natural oral contact among players (e.g., through VoIP technology, see below). Thus, complex matters are difficult to negotiate, because players would have to type and/or read long messages. The dynamic progress of game events (e.g., discoveries, increase of character skills etc., see Taylor, 2003) would suffer from lengthy text communication with individual players. Not surprisingly, unsystematic observation of mediated interpersonal communication in large-scale multiplayer games suggests that most players limit their communication to the exchange of short messages and have adopted a repertoire of codes and abbreviations that allows them to compress message content (Thon, 2006; Wright et al., 2002). Pena and Hancock (2006) studied the communication among players of Jedi Knight II, which includes an internet-based multiplayer environment that could best be described as a "light saber dueling club", but does not feature the rich and complex universe of an MMO (Chan & Vorderer, 2006: 103). Their findings suggest that indeed players tend to exchange only short messages, like a "running report ... that depicts their current [states and] activities, with little requests for more elaborated opinions and suggestions." In accordance with Social Information Processing theory (Walther, 1996), however, communication between players was socio-emotionally rich and focused more on positive than on negative feedback (e.g., "Good fight!"). The use of abbreviations (such as "lol" for "laugh out loud") increased with the experience of players. Task-oriented instructions (e.g., "attack the enemy!" or "show me the way to xy") were less frequent than socio-emotional expressions.

The findings in part resemble the results of earlier studies that analyzed interplayer communication in MUDs (Multi-User Dungeons, i.e., text-based online multi-user games; cf., Curtis, 1996; Utz, 2000, 1999). The studies found that MUD users strongly engage in relationship building by communicating extensively with each other. Primarily, both feelings and symbolic behavior are expressed, whereas communication related to the actual game task was less frequent. The gameplay of MUDs, however, creates no or only low time pressure (in contrast to other online games like ego-shooters or real-time strategy games). In MMOs only some episodes exist that establish a similar pressure-free context: for example, when the users are strolling around in a city where they cannot be attacked by any opponents. From this perspective, both MMOs and MUDS provide an opportunity to engage in extensive unhurried communication. Such deeper methods of communication are only likely, however, if the effort to chat with others is perceived as reasonably easy and if players are motivated to engage in social bonding (instead of, for example, focusing on the tasks posed by the game; cf. Williams *et al.*, 2006).

The results obtained by Pena and Hancock (2006) suggest that most players focus on the gameplay and seek challenges that will exert time pressure. They use interplayer communication to comment on the ongoing gameplay and to share their immediate feelings and opinions via short messages. Therefore, although the opportunities for unhurried "private" (one-to-one) communication certainly also enable longer conversations, patterns of mediated interpersonal communication seem to emerge in large-scale multiplayer games that are similar to other interface-bound modes of interpersonal communication such as SMS (Döring, 2002; Grinter & Eldridge, 2003) or chat (Merchant, 2001): Messages are mostly short, utilize specialized codes and abbreviations, and serve only narrowly defined purposes.

Innergroup communication among members of formalized player groups ("clans")

Two other types of multiplayer video game provide the setting for a different type of mediated interpersonal communication among players

(Wright *et al.*, 2002). One is commonly referred to as "first-person shooters" (FPS; cf. Schneider *et al.*, 2004; Thon, 2006); the other genre is classifed as "real-time strategy games" (RTS games). FPS online gaming, such as Counterstrike or Battlefield, and RTS games, such as Lord of the Rings or Starcraft, allow the establishment formalized teams or alliances of various players ("clans"; cf. Pena & Hancock, 2006). Most often, such teams are joined by frequent players and exist over long periods of time, which facilitates strong social bonds among members and improvement of coordinated game play (e.g., assault tactics). Clans compete in organized leagues or tournaments, sometimes even for prize money, and thus train in group play frequently. An integral part of the coordinated game play of clan members is constant interpersonal communication (see, for "performance talk", Thon, 2006; Wright *et al.*, 2002). Message exchange between players is: (1) based on text typed using the keyboard; (2) performed through selecting prewritten options from a list (e.g., tactical commands); (3) channeled by specific devices such as a "tactical plot" onto which arrows and lines can be drawn to indicate movement directions to other clan members (e.g., in Guild Wars); or (4) facilitated as voice communication (VoIP): Players wear earphones and a microphone that allows permanent "radio contact" with other clan members. Just as real soldiers or generals organize their tactics, this type of group communication among clan members relies on audio messages. This possibility of synchronous interpersonal communication adds substantially to the complexity and experiential richness of multiplayer FPS and RTS games, since it allows for effective group coordination under strong time pressure. Through audio messaging among players, both genres combine highly dense within-team interaction with dynamic and intense competition (Manninen & Kujanpää, 2005). Consequently, team battles that feature radio messaging within teams belong to the most challenging and demanding forms of video game play today.

Nonsystematic observation of interpersonal communication among clan members indicates that the use of specific (tactical) language is the object of the group training. In many FPS clans, individual players occupy distinct roles (e.g., sniper, engineer, machine gunner), so role-specific actions must be coordinated and synchronized. In a similar fashion, in RTS clans, players often specialize in different "cultures." In turn, they demand a coordinated strategy when playing together. Shared, information-rich vocabulary is also required to distribute warnings about dangers within the team effectively (see Thon, 2006). As a consequence, the interpersonal communication among clan members seems to be dominated by short, formulaic, partly group-specific messages that enable quick coordination and fast team action within the dynamic game environment. Only through repeated training, can this kind of message production facilitate successful team game play.

Communication in established virtual communities within large-scale multiplayer environments

The third type of mediated interpersonal communication among multi-player gamers that we believe to be relevant is a mixture of the types portrayed above. In virtually all large-scale multiplayer environments, players can establish new or join already founded "organizations" that operate within the game world. For instance, in most fantasy game universes, players can create "guilds" or religious "orders" and try to gain new members from among other players (Utz, 2000; Williams *et al.*, 2006). Such organizations serve multiple functions for players. They

- offer sources of game-related information,
- support individual players in improving the properties of their game character (e.g., through "training sessions" or by exchanging powerful weapons or items), and
- provide a social and geographic environment for socializing and networking that allows for more depth and complexity of communi-cation than the typical encounters of players unknown to each other as described above (Kolo & Baur, 2004).

Interpersonal communication within virtual groups of this kind also relies on instant messaging through typed text. Most players maintain their membership of such virtual groups within the game worlds for long periods and return to their group's virtual headquarters frequently. As a consequence, most members experience repeated contact with a limited number of players – that is, the other group members, and most impor-tantly, the very active core members of the group such as "guild masters" who typically hold formally defined hierarchic positions within the group. These core members display strong involvement with the group and spend much time at the group's virtual headquarters. By bringing individual players together repeatedly, virtual groups within MMOs serve as platforms for establishing comparatively strong social bonds among players that can even extend to offline contacts and turn into "real-life" friendships (Kolo & Baur, 2004): The virtual group allows for the development of long and rich interaction histories with other players and for addressing complex issues in interpersonal messages that may relate to the game world but also to the world outside of the game (e.g., talking about romantic partnerships and even dating; see Whitty, this volume; Steinkuehler & Williams, 2006).

Nonsystematic observation and initial empirical findings about commu-nication in such established virtual groups suggests that interplayer message exchange does indeed occur more frequently, is longer, and addresses more complex issues than typical communication among players who meet each other outside of group contexts (Steinkuehler, 2006; Steinkuehler &

Williams, 2006). The goal of keeping the group "running" for instance, by ensuring the availability of skilled "healers" who can provide assistance to severely "injured" group members, seems to consume significant efforts in interpersonal communication. Other examples of "group management" that are resolved through mediated interpersonal communication are information exchange about competing, collaborating with other groups, or the discussion of the future of group strategy within the game world.

Commonalities across types of interplayer communication and mixed forms

The three described manifestations of mediated interpersonal communication among video game players are of course only prototypes. Pena and Hancock (2006), for instance, report communication patterns among players who presumably do not know each other well that differ at least on the dimension of task orientation versus socio-emotional orientation of message content from what has been portrayed here. Similarly, the excerpts from MMO player communication presented by Steinkuehler and Williams (2006) indicate mixtures of our prototypes of task-oriented and primarily "social" conversation. However, the three types we have discussed so far are still useful for deriving specific assumptions about game enjoyment and game effects which can be hypothesized to be distinct for each type. Thus, our three-modes structure holds some theoretical-heuristic value for our further discussion.

There are some issues that are common to all three modes and that are potentially relevant for the discussion about the implications of interplayer communication for game enjoyment and the social consequences of games. One is the distinction between "in-character" and "out-of-character" communication. In-character communication refers to the game world and its internal logic: Players communicate from within their role in the game, use a communication style appropriate for their character, and contextualize their messages within the overall game narrative. Out-of-character communication, in contrast, ignores the game-based setting of the conversation and addresses real-life issues, just as in conventional mediated interpersonal communication (e.g., instant messaging or chats, cf. Leung, 2001; see also "game technical/external talk", Wright, 2002, which might be regarded as a subdimension of out-of-character communication). All three modes of interplayer communication described here allow both in-character and out-of-character communication; however, it is reasonable to assume that full out-of-character communication (i.e., one that goes beyond mere technical talk) is mostly prevalent in the third mode (communication among members of established groups within MMOs), for only in this kind of setting do players develop the social bonds and have the time to address issues outside the game world with sufficient depth. Communication among clan members is—at least during competitive game play, not necessarily during training games—strictly focused on task resolution, which requires in-character communication. Communication among MMO players who meet occasionally and do not share a long interaction history is also less likely to refer to out-of-game contexts (although Steinkuehler and Williams, 2006, report some examples that may fall into this category).

A second and related commonality of all modes of interplayer communication is that different qualities of anonymity can be kept or revealed by players (e.g., Joinson, 2001). Players can choose to hide or to disclose parts of their real-life personal identity (name, gender, home location, etc.); they can also "manage" the anonymity of their avatar: for instance, by hiding which avatar they are controlling from other players they know from real-life settings. Such techniques of separation or integration of real-world and in-game identity are common among video game players (especially in MMO contexts, cf. Turkle, 1995) and are potentially relevant both to game enjoyment and to social consequences of game play.

The third important commonality is the dominance of text-based and verbal modes of interplayer communication. Technical restrictions limit players' possibilities for communicating nonverbally (e.g., through gestures) in virtually all video games; so interpersonal communication is mostly text-oriented and uses the "channels" offered by the game software such as chat or VoIP. Many experienced players have adopted textual replacements for nonverbal communication, such as emoticons, from conventional CMC (Thon, 2006; Utz, 2000; Walther & D'Addario, 2001).

Table 16.1 summarizes our description of mediated interpersonal communication and compares the three introduced forms along the dimensions of modality (voice versus text), anonymity, message length and complexity, specific message styles and forms, message content, and, finally, message purpose. Our subsequent analysis of the role of mediated interpersonal communication in video games for game enjoyment and social game effects will refer to these categories as well as the commonalities addressed above.

Implications of interplayer-communication for video game enjoyment

Game enjoyment theory

Significant theoretical advances in the explication and explanation of video game enjoyment have been achieved only recently (Raessens & Goldstein, 2005; Grodal, 2000; Jansz, 2005; Schneider *et al.*, 2004; Vorderer & Bryant, 2006). Klimmt (2003) has proposed a model that argues for a multidimensional structure of the entertainment experience derived from video game play and a multifactor explanation of game enjoyment. In short, the model proposes the following mechanisms of game enjoyment:

Table 16.1 Overview of typical modes of mediated interpersonal communication in multiplayer video games

	Encounter among players unknown to each other in MMOs	Within-team communication in multiplayer FPS or RTS games	Within-group communication in MMOs
Modality	Text/instant messaging	Voice ("radio transmissions") or text/instant messaging	Text/instant messaging
Anonymity (of players' real-life identity)	High	Very low	Low
Typical length and complexity	Short messages, low complexity	Short messages, low complexity	Longer messages, high complexity
Specific communication styles and forms	Common / widely used abbreviations and symbols (e.g., AFK for "away from keyboard")	Specific codes and abbreviations shared by clan members	Both common and group-specific codes
Typical content orientation	Socio-emotional and task	Task only	Socio-emotional and task
Typical main purpose	"Running report," instant comments	Facilitate group performance (e.g., synchronization of players' actions for team battle)	Support group goals and/or individual goals within or outside of game world

- As video games respond immediately to player inputs, they constantly evoke the perception of causal agency ("effectance", cf. Klimmt & Hartmann, 2006). Players find the experience of being the most important causal agent in the game world highly enjoyable.
- Video games create numerous situations of *suspense* (Zillmann, 1996) that arise from challenges and threats to the players imposed by autonomous game elements such as attacking opponents. In such situations, players are insecure about the outcome but desire a favorable end (namely their own victory over the opposing forces). This mixture of uncertainty about the outcome and desire for one specific outcome is the prototypical precondition of suspense.
- "If players manage to resolve a challenge or threat in the desired way, positive experience (e.g., euphoria) results due to physiological *excitation transfer* (sensu Zillmann, cf. Bryant & Miron, 2003) and increased self-esteem (*pride*), which strongly improves overall enjoyment.
- *Exploration* of environments, actions, characters, and narratives further adds to game enjoyment in situations without immediate pressures (e.g., Berlyne, 1960).
- Finally, *simulated life experiences* through identification (Cohen, 2001) contribute to video game enjoyment. Most video games invite players

to occupy a defined role, for instance to "be" a soldier, sorcerer, or policeman. Because such roles are often highly attractive to players for developmental reasons (Jansz, 2005), their experience in video games is enjoyable (e.g., Durkin, 2006).

Some empirical evidence has been reported that supports these assumptions about video game enjoyment (Klimmt, 2006; Klimmt *et al.*, submitted for publication), and the model has been designed to converge with recent advances in general entertainment theory (Bryant & Vorderer, 2006; Vorderer, 2001; 2003). But like most other explications of video game enjoyment available so far, it neglects issues of multiplayer gaming and interplayer communication.

The added entertainment value of interplayer communication

Research on video game motivations has revealed that communicating with other players is an enjoyable activity during game play. Findings from various survey studies support this contention in the context of LAN parties (Jansz & Martens, 2005), online gaming in general (Griffiths *et al.*, 2003; Pena & Hancock, 2006), and MMOs (Griffiths *et al.*, 2004; Yee, 2006).

It is therefore necessary to integrate interplayer communication as a key variable into multidimensional models of video game enjoyment. In this regard, the question emerges whether interplayer communication merely functions as a manifestation or "amplifier" of already established enjoyment mechanisms, or if interplayer communication creates completely new pathways to game enjoyment that should be modeled separately from the existing concepts. We suggest that both lines of argumentation are theoretically relevant. Using our three prototypical modes of interplayer communication to structure our discussion, we shall briefly refer to interplayer communication's impact on the established mechanisms of game enjoyment and then address the new and unique mechanisms of game enjoyment resulting from interplayer communication.

Encounters with unknown other players in MMOs (type 1 in the description section of this chapter) are likely to reinforce already modeled processes of game enjoyment. Specifically, receiving information from other players that is helpful to resolve a "quest" or task within the game world increases the likelihood of success and consequently contributes to an increase in self-esteem and related pleasurable feelings. Because players typically do not know each other when they "meet" in the game world, however, the anonymity increases uncertainty about how the other player will act in the communication episode. Thus, curiosity and suspense can also be increased through this kind of interplayer communication. Moreover, players may also regard the messages they produce as part of their influence on the game world (e.g., by helping another player to complete a task or by impressing other players with their own knowledge), which would also render this type of player-to-player communication as a facilitator of effectance experiences. As the empirical results suggest, next to task-bound communication most short messages that players construct are used to signal positive comments of the ongoing gameplay (e.g., "Good hit!"). It seems plausible that in this way players underline and mutually reassure their effectiveness, thereby enhancing their experiences. Communication with other players or their avatars may also serve to identifiy with one's own role or character, for instance if other players recognize a player's character as a war hero or as an altruistic helper (see Yee, 2006, for examples). Consequently, mediated interpersonal communication of that described as type 1 is assumed to contribute to all established enjoyment dimensions presented earlier (effectance, suspense, curiosity, increase in self-esteem, and identification processes). In contrast, we do not argue that this kind of interplayer communication adds a unique new mode of game enjoyment to the model, because the properties of this communication pattern are similar to interaction between the player and so-called "nonplayer character" in single-player gaming. Rather, unique experiences resulting from interplayer communication are more likely if the pattern shifts from this type to the second or third type of our list (see below).

Communication within clans (type 2 from our list), which is even more task-focused, is obviously related to performance issues. Sending and receiving radio messages helps the group to survive and succeed in the game environment, and thus facilitates the occurrence of enjoyment dimensions related to winning (i.e., increase in self-esteem, excitation transfer). Especially voice contact among team members should also intensify suspense experiences because of the more direct and immediate impression of the game situation. For instance, a danger communicated by one player should "alert" all team members and thus fuel the suspenseful state for each as soon as they receive the warning. In turn, sending messages and seeing the other team members respond to them should also add to the experience of effectance. In this sense, communication among game team members is not a structurally new feature to video games and to game enjoyment, but rather—similar to our discussion of the first prototypical case of interplayer communication—an amplifier of already known processes of game enjoyment.

Nevertheless, within-clan communication is probably more than a mere tool to improve the already known mechanics of game enjoyment. As clan members build long interaction histories, they get to know each other very well, which renders communication with each other socially (as opposed to tactically) meaningful. Identity processes such as actualization of perceived group membership and sense of belonging ("I am part of the team") are certainly an important by-product of the continuous message exchange among players (see Utz, this volume). Moreover, through competent communications (e.g., effective warnings about dangers), radio contact with the clan may be used by individual players to negotiate their status within the group: for instance, to distinguish themselves as a skilled scout or team leader.

It is therefore likely that within-clan communication also serves identity-related issues of video game enjoyment: that is, the fun of negotiating, acquiring, and maintaining a group identity and the definition of one's own position within an important peer group (i.e., the clan). Brewer (1991) argues that people prefer to identify with groups that enable both a sense of belonging (in our context: to feel as part of the team) and to fill a distinct position within the group (in our context: to perceive one's unique role in and contribution to the team). Within-clan communication can foster exactly such kinds of group identification and should therefore— as the realization of social and self-related motives—establish a unique pathway to video game enjoyment that has not been accounted for by conventional models of game enjoyment.

Communication among members of stable groups within virtual worlds (type 3 of our list), finally, is quite similar to meeting old friends (long interaction histories between communication partners, long and complex messages enabled, a broad range of topics addressed). As long as communication is "in-character," such conversation among "old friends" would evoke a peak-level experience of identification with the avatar/player role, as a very complex and deep interaction with other characters and about game-related issues is conducted. Within-character communication should be expected to address similar identity processes (perceived integration into a social group and perceived position of oneself within the group) as within-clan communication does (see above). Through interaction with other group members, players can attain formalized hierarchical positions (e.g., "chief alchemist of the guild") which are the most visible mani-festations of one's relationship with the group. Enjoyable processes of social identity (see Trepte, 2006) are therefore also likely to occur through (repeated, intense) interplayer communication within established in-game groups. As mentioned earlier, communication within such groups can also serve task-oriented goals and thus also facilitate already known dimen-sions of game enjoyment (e.g., boost of self-esteem evoked by success). This renders type 3 interplayer communication a powerful facilitator of established mechanisms of game enjoyment, especially in regard to iden-tification processes.

However, since this type of interplayer communication frequently reaches out to issues unrelated to the game world (out-of-character communica-tion, see above and Steinkuehler & Williams, 2006), it is reasonable to look for unique "social" aspects of game enjoyment related to type 3 interplayer communication. Chatting with well-known members of one's "guild," for instance, provides the enjoyable experience of a benevolent atmosphere, mutual trust, and the opportunity to construe idiosyncratic messages that are comprehensive and/or funny only within the group of friends sitting together next to the guild headquarter's fireplace. This kind of interplayer communication is video games' best approximation to the experience of friendship and entails the possibility of receiving substantial social support from others (see Utz, 2000; social support is an important motivator of interpersonal communication in general and is directly linked to psychological well-being, cf. Turner, 1981). Therefore, the new and unique dimension of game enjoyment that is determined by communication among members of stable groups within the game world is the pleasure of receiving and giving social support. There are, of course, differences and potential limitations to the depth and sustainability of the social benefits players gain from communication within virtual in-game groups compared to real-life networks, but, in general, this kind of interplayer communication is likely to open up a "sense of community" (Bromberg, 1996) or "friendship"(Parks & Floyd, 1996) dimension of game enjoyment that is completely new to the single-player model of game enjoyment discussed above.

Summary

The theoretical discussion of how mediated interpersonal communication among players relates to video game enjoyment suggests that there are similarities but also substantial differences that should be expected among the identified types of communication. Occasional encounters between players unknown to each other are proposed to primarily serve instrumental goals that closely relate to existing concepts of video game enjoyment. While clan communication also displays such instrumental value (specifically for securing successful game play that is enjoyable for reasons of increased self-esteem and positive excitation transfer), its specific "enjoyment value" can also refer to identity processes in the sense of social identity theory (Trepte, 2006). Communication within established in-game groups such as guilds, finally, seems to provide primarily new social forms of game enjoyment, such as the joys of (active and passive) social support. In addition, it is related to conventional game enjoyment, specifically to identification processes but also to task-oriented enjoyment dimensions. Overall, the discussion has revealed that significant parts of the existing conceptualizations of video game enjoyment (see Klimmt, 2003; 2006) are also valid in the context of multiplayer gaming and that interplayer communication can serve those already elaborated dimensions of enjoyment. However, the conceptually new "added value" of interplayer communication to the entertainment experience of playing video games has now also been related to pleasures of identity elaboration and social support issues. Consequently, this analysis could be helpful in determining new dimensions of the enjoyment concept (Vorderer, *et al.*, 2004) that should be considered in further research about the experience of playing video games.

Implications of interplayer communication for the social effects of frequent gaming

In addition to the importance of mediated interpersonal communication for video game enjoyment, the inclusion of this communication feature in interactive entertainment is also relevant for media effects research. Investigations of video game effects have primarily addressed issues of game violence and aggression (Anderson, 2004; Sherry, 2001). While mediated interpersonal communication can certainly be aggressive and antisocial (Douglas, this volume), the dimensions that can be expected to be affected by this communication in video game contexts are rather of a social nature. Multiplayer gaming extends the universe of people one can get to know and "meet" regularly as well as the repertoire for communicating with members of one's individual social network. Therefore, this section speculates on the social impact of mediated interpersonal communication in video games on frequent players. We use the conceptual framework for internet communication proposed by McKenna and Bargh (1999, Bargh & McKenna, 2004) to structure our analysis. Their matrix of analysis combines self-related versus social-related dimensions of: (1) motives; (2) processes (being online); and (3) consequences of internet interactions. For our purpose, the consequences are especially relevant (as we have discussed manifestations of interplayer communication extensively above). McKenna and Bargh (1999: 252) focus on the following consequences of internet communication.

- self-acceptance (self-related)
- coming out (self-related)
- decreased estrangement and isolation (self-related)
- decreased loneliness (social-related)
- decreased depression (social-related)
- greater liking and acceptance by others (social-related)
- widened social circle (social-related)
- meeting and knowing internet friends face-to-face (social-related).

In this section, we will review the prototypical modes of interplayer communication in respect of these consequences and thus speculate systematically on the social functions and effects of multiplayer video gaming in general.

Because of its great anonymity and the short, noncommittal quality of the message exchange, *encounters with unknown other players in MMO environments* (type 1 from our list) should not be expected to resonate with many of the above-mentioned consequences of internet social interaction, especially those consequences that relate to sustained, rich relationship qualities such as meeting online friends face-to-face. However, encounters with new people in MMOs certainly *widens the social circle* and increases the number of "weak ties" whenever conversation lasts longer than extremely brief messages such as "Out of my way!" A broader social network of people "one has met before" is therefore postulated as the main effect of this type of interplayer communication. Some of these new "contacts" may turn into more relevant relationship partners (as communication shifts toward type 2 or 3 from our list; see below). To the extent that communication with "new"' players leaves the in-character dimension and also addresses out-of-character issues (see above), the broadened social network resulting from such MMO encounters would also reach out into players' portfolio of non-game-specific online ties and, in the long run, into players' integrated online and offline social network. It remains to be examined empirically, however, which portion of newly established contacts with other MMO players can effectively turn into in-game weak ties, into general online contacts (beyond the actual game environment), and/or integrated online/offline social network members (see for example Utz, 2000).

A secondary social consequence of type 1 interplayer communication may be a contiunous perception of reduced *loneliness*. Since encounters with other players in MMOs occur frequently, the activity of playing MMOs is characterized by many social interactions that should diminish players' sense of being alone, at least for the time of playing. Whether this sense is sustained after game play (e.g., through the many acquired memories of interaction episodes available for fighting loneliness when not playing) is an empirical question, however.

Within-clan communication (type 2 from our list) is suggested to facilitate two primary types of social consequences from McKenna and Bargh's (1999) list: One refers to the great social cohesion within clans that should typically *establish new or enrich existing real-life friendships*. In-clan communication represents an additional channel through which the social bonds among members can be built, continued, and fortified. As ambitious clans spend much time with group training ("power gamers" cf. Taylor, 2003), mediated communication within the game setting may even displace other forms of interpersonal message exchange and advance to the dominant channel through which group members interact with each other. In this sense, interplayer communication can potentially "virtualize" social relationships (see Nass & Robles, this volume; Utz, this volume), which would be a profound social impact of in-game communication. For less ambitious teams, however, within-clan communication should be considered as an addition to the activity repertoire that the peer group relies on for their social activities, which suggests considering type 2 of our list of interplayer communication modes as serving positive functions for players' social network and relationship management (see also Jansz & Martens, 2005).

The other primary consequence (out of McKenna and Bargh's (1999) matrix) of within-clan communication that we propose is *"greater liking and acceptance by others."* Our argument is that clan communication and inter-action establishes a group setting in which individual players serve the group. They present their skills and characteristics in a social environment that heavily depends on each participant's contribution and performance. Thus, clans should be considered as groups that are ready to acknowledge individual properties and contributions (and, at the same time, demand contributions such as team support very explicitly), which renders posi-tive social effects such as increased acceptance of clan members very likely—if players manage to meet the requirements of the group—but this should be the case for most members of most clans that have evolved over time. The issue of performance orientation in clans deserves more empirical attention in the future. CMC research should illuminate whether clans are indeed—as we speculate—both ready to acknowledge and gratify individual self-presentations as group contributions and intolerant of members who fail to meet group criteria of achievement and success. If our assumption is corrrect, in-clan communication would have interesting positive social effects on players as well as a risk component of social rejection and increased depression or loneliness.

Communication among members of stable groups within virtual worlds (type 3 of our list). This type of mediated interpersonal communication among video game players holds the largest potential to become a key element in frequent players' social life. We assume that virtually all self- and social-related consequences of internet interaction that McKenna and Bargh (1999) discuss are linked to such interplayer communication. Players can search for and find communication partners (actually whole virtual groups of partners) who share their characteristics, world views, attitudes, etc. The diverse world of MMOs should thus offer social environments that help to *decrease estrangement and isolation.* The opportunity to return to a virtual community place and meet "old friends" there should also *decrease loneliness* sustainably, even beyond the actual gaming time (Yee, 2006). Giving and receiving social support within in-game networks such as guilds should also improve players' well-being and in turn *decrease depression.* Furthermore, continuous participation in in-game communities can facilitate *greater liking and acceptance by others,* in this case, by the other group members. In addition to such positive relationship development, the organizational dynamics—new players joining, others leaving the group—the number of relationships will also rise over time (*"widened social circle"*), albeit not as fast as with interplayer communication type 1 (see above), as guilds and other groups produce fewer new contacts per time unit than interplayer conversation outside of group contexts. Finally, communication among members of virtual in-game organizations is very likely to facilitate a transformation of online-relationships into offline relationships (*"meeting and knowing internet friends face-to-face"*), because players learn much about one other, which reduces uncertainty and facilitates liking (Zajonc, 1968). Some aspects related to McKenna and Bargh's (1999) analysis are also relevant for type 3 inter-player communication. Real-life relationships that cannot really be main-tained due to geographic distances may benefit from intense within-game contact. The deep-level exchange with other players that comes along with increased control over impression formation may also help individuals with low communication-related self-efficacy (Bandura, 1997; Lee, 2000), social anxieties, or other difficulties in managing social relationships successfully to improve their social life sustainably (e.g., Stritzke *et al.*, 2004).

The consequences of type 3 interplayer communication do not neces-sarily have to be benign for (heavy) players. Caplan (2005) argues that to the extent that people reduce their social life to online communication, the risk for communication-related impulse control problems ("problematic internet use") increases, indicating that the social impact of intense inter-player communication may imply risks for psychological health and nega-tively affect some of McKenna and Bargh's (1999) dimensions of analysis.

Overall, in-game groups mark a turning point where multiplayer video gaming shifts from mere media entertainment to a computer-based social experience that has profound consequences for the players' social life. In the case of displacement of real-life social interaction through in-game communication, these consequences are likely to emerge as a social problem; in the case of enrichment and complementarity to other forms of (mediated and nonmediated) interpersonal communication, these consequences may contribute to the players' well-being and satisfaction with their social lives.

As the phenomenon of interplayer communication is still limited to comparatively small numbers of individuals (only a few million people around the globe), the time is ripe to investigate these sets of assumptions systematically and empirically. Research in interpersonal communication and social psychology can provide powerful conceptual frameworks and methods for this endeavor, and we call explicitly for theory-driven research based on the established lines of CMC (e.g., McKenna & Bargh, 1999; Tanis & Postmes, 2003) to explore interplayer communication in more detail in order to disclose its social implications before multiplayer video gaming will have advanced to a real mass (media) activity.

Conclusion

The purpose of this chapter is to open up a comparatively new manifes-tation of mediated interpersonal communication that is bound to multi-player video gaming to research in communication and social psychology.

We have offered a descriptive account of the phenomenon and discussed its implications both from a game-oriented perspective on entertainment and from a life-oriented perspective on social relationships. We conclude that (certain types) of mediated interpersonal communication between players should be expected to have a potentially profound impact on video game enjoyment that warrants further and more systematic examination of the phenomenon in entertainment research. We also suggest that at least within-clan communication in multiplayer combat games and within-group communication in large-scale MMOs could have social impacts beyond the actual game contexts (e.g., Bargh & McKenna, 2004; Caplan, 2005), also implying the need for further investigation into interpersonal communication and social psychology. While the overall importance of the phenomenon is still comparatively small (in terms of involved individuals, for instance), there are good reasons to expect a rapid increase in the social and scientific relevance of mediated interpersonal communication among video game players: the already impressive and still growing popularity of multiplayer video games; the continuous technological progress towards ever-more natural modes of contact among players; the closer ties between the game industry and other entertainment industries such as Hollywood (which result, for instance, in the MMO Star Wars Galaxies; cf. Yee, 2006) that will attract more and more users; and, overall, multiplayer games' transition to a mainstream leisure activity. Just as with other forms of internet-based communication, interplayer contact will become more and more of a typical cornerstone in (young) people's relationship management and channel repertoire for interpersonal communication. In fact, research on interplayer communication may turn out to be a key approach for assessing the (presumably increasing) effects of video gaming on people's social lives.

Our conclusion, and the expected increase in relevance of the phenomenon, calls for a research agenda that can answer the many questions and find out which of our assumptions (and speculations) can be empirically justified. With respect to the social impact of the phenomenon, rich theoretical frameworks are already available, and many of them are well represented in this volume (e.g., chapters by Biocca *et al.*, Tanis, Walther, and Utz,) and/or widely used in media psychology and communication (McKenna & Bargh, 1999). For a perspective on enjoyment, the general lack of substantial theory on interactive entertainment (e.g., Vorderer, 2003) is a constraint that has to be resolved before significant progress can be made with respect to interplayer communication. In terms of methodologies, systematic analyses of communication among game players are required as starting point for developing hypotheses for both the entertainment and the social-impact domains. Some initial studies (Pena & Hancock, 2006; Wright *et al.*, 2002) and theoretical elaborations (Thon, 2006) have been reported, but further descriptive content analyses will be required to identify genre- or game-specific patterns that might converge with our description of three forms of interplayer-communication. Starting from such a (more) systematic account of the phenomenon, studies on the relevance of mediated interpersonal communication for both entertainment and social life should proceed experimentally (e.g., McKenna *et al.*, 2002), and especially with longitudinal designs, because the implications of inter-player communication should become best visible in people with high levels of habitualization (LaRose & Eastin, 2004) and experience, which should be reflected in diachronic data. Our chapter should therefore be considered as an invitation to entertainment researchers and investigators of interpersonal communication alike to dedicate some attention to interplayer communication, which seems to be a niche case of application in both fields today, but could soon turn into a major issue that allows us to keep track of (young) people's communicative and social-emotional adoption of interactive media technologies.

References

Anderson, C. A. (2004) "An update on the effects of playing violent video games." *Journal of Adolescence, 27*(1), 113–122.

Bandura, A. (1986) *Social Foundations of Thought and Action: a Social Cognitive Theory.* Englewood Cliffs, NJ: Prentice Hall.

Bandura, A. (1997) *Self-Efficacy: the Exercise of Control.* New York: Freeman.

Bargh, J. A., & McKenna, K. Y. A. (2004) "The internet and social life." *Annual Review of Psychology, 55*, 573–590.

Berlyne, D. E. (1960) *Conflict, Arousal, and Curiosity.* New York: McGraw-Hill.

Blizzard Entertainment (2005) "World of Warcraft surpasses five million customers worldwide," Available: http://www.blizzard.com/press/051219.shtml.

Blythe, M. A., Monk, A. F., Overbeeke, K., & Wright, P. C. (2003) *Funology: From Usability to Enjoyment.* Lancaster, UK: Kluwer Academic Publishers.

Brewer, M. B. (1991) "The social self: On being the same and different at the same time." *Personality and Social Psychology Bulletin, 17*(5), 475–482.

Bromberg, H. (1996) "Are MUDs communities? Identity, belonging and consciousness in virtual worlds." In R. Shields (ed.), *Cultures of Internet: Virtual Spaces, Real Histories, Living Bodies.* London: Sage, pp. 143–152.

Bruner, O., & Bruner, K. (2006) *Playstation Nation: Protect Your Child from Video Game Addiction.* New York: Center Street.

Bryant, J., & Miron, D. (2003) "Excitation-Transfer theory and three-factor theory of emotion." In J. Bryant, D. R. Roskos-Ewoldsen & J. Cantor, (eds.), *Communication and Emotion: Essays in Honor of Dolf Zillmann.* Mahwah, NJ: Lawrence Erlbaum Associates, pp. 31–60.

Caplan, S. E. (2005) "A social skill account of problematic internet use." *Journal of Communication, 55*(4), 721–736.

Chan, E., & Vorderer, P. (2006) "Massively multiplayer online games." In P. Vorderer & J. Bryant (eds.), *Playing Video Games: Motives, Responses, and Consequences.* Mahwah, NJ: Lawrence Erlbaum Associates.

Cohen, J. (2001) "Defining identification: A theoretical look at the identification of audiences with media characters." *Mass Communication and Society, 4*(3), 245–264.

Cohen, J. (2006) "Identification." In J. Bryant & P. Vorderer (eds.), *Psychology of Entertainment.* Mahwah, NJ: Lawrence Erlbaum Associates.

Copier, M., & Raessens, J. (eds.), (2003) *Level Up: Digital Games Research Conference*. Utrecht: Faculty of Arts, Utrecht University

Curtis, P. (1996) "Mudding: Social phenomena in text-based virtual realities." In S. Kiesler, (eds.), *Culture of the Internet*. Mahwah, N.J.: Lawrence Erlbaum, pp. 121–142.

Deci, R. M., & Ryan, E. L. (2000) "Self-determination theory and the facilitation of intrinsic motivation, social development, and well-being." *American Psychologist, 55* (1), 68–78.

Döring, N. (2002) "' x Brot, Wurst, 5 Sack Äpfel I.L.D.'—Kommunikative Funktionen von Kurzmitteilungen (SMS)" [1 bread, sausage, 5 sacks apples, I.L.Y. – communication functions of short messages (SMS)]. *Zeitschrift für Medienpsychologie, 14*(3), 118–128.

Durkin, K. (2006) "Game playing and adolescents' development." In P. Vorderer & J. Bryant (eds.), *Playing Video Games: Motives, Responses, and Consequences*. Mahwah, NJ: Lawrence Erlbaum Associates.

Griffiths, M. D., Davies, M. N., & Chappel, D. (2003) "Breaking the stereotype: The case of online gaming." *CyberPsychology & Behavior, 6*(1), 81–91.

Griffiths, M. D., Davies, M. N., & Chappel, D. (2004) "Online computer gaming: a comparison of adolescent and adult gamers." *Journal of Adolescence, 27*(1), 87–96.

Grinter, R., & Eldridge, M. (2003) "Wan2tlk?: everyday text messaging." In G. Cockton & P. Korhunen (eds.), *Proceedings of the SIGCHI Conference on Human Factors in Computing Systems*. New York: ACM Press, pp. 441–448.

Grodal, T. (2000) "Video games and the pleasures of control." In D. Zillmann & P. Vorderer (eds.), *Media Entertainment. The Psychology of its Appeal*. Mahwah, NJ: Lawrence Erlbaum Associates, pp. 197–212.

Harter, S. (1978) "Effectance motivation reconsidered: Toward a developmental model." *Human Development, 21*, 34–64.

Jansz, J. (2005) "The emotional appeal of violent video games for adolescent males." *Communication Theory, 15*(3), 219–241.

Jansz, J., & Martens, L. (2005) "Gaming at a LAN event: The social context of playing video games." *New Media & Society, 7*(3), 333–355.

Joinson, A. N. (2001) "Self-disclosure in computer-mediated communication: The role of self-awareness and visual anonymity." *European Journal of Social Psychology, 31*(2), 177–192.

Kirsh, S. J. (2003) "The effects of violent video games on adolescents: The overlooked influence of development." *Aggression and Violent Behavior, 8*, 377–389.

Klimmt, C. (2003) "Dimensions and determinants of the enjoyment of playing digital games: A three-level model." In M. Copier & J. Raessens (eds.), *Level Up: Digital Games Research Conference*. Utrecht: Faculty of Arts, Utrecht University, pp. 246–257.

Klimmt, C. (2006) *Computerspielen als Handlung: Dimensionen und Determinanten des Erlebens interaktiver Unterhaltungsangebote* [Playing computer games as action: Dimensions and determinants of the experience of interactive entertainment]. Köln: von Halem.

Klimmt, C., & Hartmann, T. (2006) "Effectance, self-efficacy, and the motivation to play computer games." In P. Vorderer & J. Bryant (eds.), *Playing Video Games: Motives, Responses, and Consequences*. Mahwah, NJ: Lawrence Erlbaum Associates.

Klimmt, C., & Vorderer, P. (2003) "Media psychology 'is not yet there': Introducing theories on media entertainment to the presence debate." *Presence: Teleoperators and Virtual Environments, 12*(4), 346–359.

Kolo, C., & Baur, T. (2004) "Living a virtual life: Social dynamics of online gaming." *Game Studies, 4* (1), Article 3 (Available: http://www.gamestudies.org/0401/kolo).

LaRose, R., & Eastin, M. S. (2004) "A social cognitive theory of internet uses and gratifications: Toward a new model of media attendance." *Journal of Broadcasting and Electronic Media, 48*(3), 358–377.

Lee, K. M. (2000) "MUDs and self-efficacy." *Educational Media International, 37*(3), 177–183.

Lee, K. M. (2004) "Presence, explicated." *Communication Theory, 14*(1), 27–50.

Leung, L. (2001) "College student motives to chat on ICQ." *New Media and Society, 3*(4), 483–500.

Manninen, T., & Kujanpää, T. (2005) "The hunt for collaborative war gaming—Case: Battlefield 1942." *Game Studies, 5*(1), Article 2. (Available: http://gamestudies.org/0501/manninen_kujanpaa).

McDonald, D. G., & Kim, H. (2001) "When I die, I feel small: Electronic game characters and the social self." *Journal of Broadcasting and Electronic Media, 45*(2), 241–258.

McKenna, K. Y. A., & Bargh, J. A. (1999) "Causes and consequences of social interaction on the Internet: A conceptual framework." *Media Psychology, 1*, 249–269.

McKenna K.Y.A, Green A.S., & Gleason M.J. (2002) "Relationship formation on the Internet: What's the big attraction?" *Journal of Social Issues, 58*, 9–31.

Merchant, G. (2001) "Teenagers in cyberspace: An investigation of language use and language change in internet chatrooms." *Journal of Research in Reading, 24*(3), 293–306.

Parks, M. R., & Floyd, C. (1996) "Making friends in cyberspace." *Journal of Communication, 46*, 80–97.

Pena, J., & Hancock, J. T. (2006) "An analysis of socioemotional and task communication in online multiplayer video games." *Communication Research, 33*(1), 92–109.

Raessens, J., & Goldstein, J. (eds.), (2005) *Handbook of Computer Game Studies.* Cambridge, MA: MIT Press.

Ritterfeld, U., & Weber, R. (2006) "Video games for entertainment and education." In P. Vorderer & J. Bryant (eds.), *Playing Video Games: Motives, Responses, Consequences.* Mahwah, NJ: Lawrence Erlbaum Associates, pp. 399–414.

Schneider, E. F., Lang, A., Shin, M., & Bradley, S. D. (2004) "Death with a story: How story impacts emotional, motivational, and physiological responses to first-person shooter video games." *Human Communication Research, 30* (3), 361–375.

Sherry, J. L. (2001) "The effects of violent video games on aggression. A meta-analysis." *Human Communication Research, 27*(3), 409–431.

Slater, M., Henry, K. L., Swaim, R. C., & Anderson, L. L. (2003) "Violent media content and aggressiveness in adolescents: A downward spiral model." *Communication Research, 30*(6), 713–736.

Steinkuehler, C. (2006) "Massively multiplayer online video gaming as participation in a discourse." *Mind, Culture, and Activity, 13*(1), 38–52.

Steinkuehler, C., and Williams, D. (2006) "Where everybody knows your (screen) name: Online games as 'third places.'" *Journal of Computer-Mediated Communication, 11*(4), article 1. http://jcmc.indiana.edu/vol11/issue4/steinkuehler.html.

Stritzke, W. G. K., Nguyen, A., & Durkin K. (2004) "Shyness and computer-mediated communication: A self-presentational theory perspective." *Media Psychology, 6*, 1–22.

Tanis, M., & Postmes, T. (2003) "Social cues and impression formation in CMC." *Journal of Communication, 53*, 676–693.

Taylor, T. L. (2003) "Power gamers just want to have fun? Instrumental play in a MMOG." In M. Copier & J. Raessens (eds.), *Level Up: Digital Games Research Conference.* Utrecht: Utrecht University, pp. 300–311.

Thon, J.-N. (2006) "Communication and interaction in multiplayer first-person-shooter games." In G. Riva, M. T. Anguera, B. K. Wiederhold & F. Mantovani (eds.), *From Communication to Presence: Cognition, Emotions and Culture Towards the Ultimate Communicative Experience.* Amsterdam: IOS Press, pp. 243–265.

Trepte, S. (2006) "Social identity theory." In J. Bryant & P. Vorderer (eds.), *Psychology of Entertainment.* Mahwah, NJ: Lawrence Erlbaum Associates.

Turkle, S. (1995) *Life on the Screen: Identity in the Age of the Internet.* New York: Simon and Schuster.

Turner, R. J. (1981) "Social support as a contingency in psychological well-being." *Journal of Health and Social Behavior, 22*(4), 357–367.

Utz, S. (1999) Soziale Identifikation mit virtuellen Gemeinschaften—Bedingungen und Konsequenzen [Social identification with virtual communities—causes and consequences]. Unpublished doctoral thesis, Katholische Universität, Eichstätt.

Utz, S. (2000) "Social Information Processing in MUDs: The development of friendships in virtual worlds." *Journal of Online Behavior, 1*(1). Available: http://www.behavior.net/JOB/v1n1/utz.html retrieved November 15, 2000.

Vorderer, P. (2001) "It´s all entertainment, sure. But what exactly is entertainment? Communication research, media psychology, and the explanation of entertainment experiences." *Poetics, 29,* 247–261.

Vorderer, P. (2003) "Entertainment theory." In J. Bryant, D. R. Roskos-Ewoldsen & J. Cantor, (eds.), *Communication and Emotion: Essays in Honor of Dolf Zillmann.* Mahwah, NJ: Lawrence Erlbaum Associates, pp. 131–154.

Vorderer, P., & Bryant, J. (eds.), (2006) *Playing Video Games: Motives, Responses, Consequences.* Mahwah, NJ: Lawrence Erlbaum Associates.

Vorderer, P., Klimmt, C., & Ritterfeld, U. (2004) "Enjoyment: At the heart of media entertainment." *Communication Theory, 14*(4), 388–408.

Vorderer, P., Hartmann, T., & Klimmt, C. (2006) "Explaining the enjoyment of playing video games: The role of competition." In D. Marinelli (ed.), *ICEC Conference Proceedings 2003: Essays on the Future of Interactive Entertainment.* Pittsburgh: Carnegie Mellon University Press, pp. 107–120.

Walther, J. B. (1996) "Computer-mediated communication: Impersonal, interpersonal, and hyperpersonal interaction." *Communication Research, 23,* 3–43.

Walther, J. B., & D'Addario, K. P. (2001) "The impacts of emoticons on message interpretation in computer-mediated communication." *Social Science Computer Review, 19*(3), 324–347.

White, R. W. (1959) "Motivation reconsidered: The concept of competence." *Psychological Review, 66*(5), 297–333.

Williams, R. B., & Clippinger, C. A. (2002) "Aggression, competition and computer games: Computer and human opponents." *Computers in Human Behavior, 18,* 495–506.

Williams, D., N. Ducheneaut, L. Xiong, Y. Zhang, N. Yee & E. Nickell (2006) "From tree house to barracks: The social life of guilds in World of Warcraft." *Games & Culture, 1*(4), 338–361.

Wright, T., Boria, E., & Breidenbach, P. (2002) "Creative player action in FPS online video games." *Games Studies, 2* (2), Article 4 (Available: http://gamestudies.org/0202/wright).

Yee, N. (2006) "The psychology of massively multiplayer online role playing games: Motivations, emotional investment, relationships, and problematic use." In R. Schroeder & A. Axelson (eds.), *Avatars at Work and Play: Collaboration and Interaction in Shared Virtual Environments.* London: Springer, pp. 187–207.

Zajonc, R. (1968) "Attitudinal effects of mere exposure." *Journal of Personality and Social Psychology Monographs, 9*(2, pt. 2), 1–27.

Zillmann, D. (1983) "Transfer of excitation in emotional behavior." In J. T. Cacioppo & R. E. Petty (eds.), *Social Psychophysiology: A Sourcebook.* New York: Guilford Press, pp. 215–240.

Zillmann, D. (1996) "The psychology of suspense in dramatic exposition." In P. Vorderer, H. J. Wulff & M. Friedrichsen (eds.), *Suspense: Conceptualizations, Theoretical Analyses, and Empirical Explorations.* Mahwah, NJ: Lawrence Erlbaum Associates, pp. 199–231.

Chapter 17

Flaming and blaming

The influence of mass media content on interactions in online discussions

Dirk Oegema, Jan Kleinnijenhuis,
Koos Anderson, and Anita van Hoof

Discussion forums on the internet are one of the fascinating new possibilities for examination in mediated interpersonal communication. Public access is a defining feature of discussion forums. Everyone who wishes to participate in a discussion forum is entitled to do so. Discussion groups enable their participants to articulate their thoughts and feelings, regardless of whether the subject is politics, music, products, partner relations or any other subject.

Because of their public access, discussion forums may play an interesting role in a democracy. They may overcome one of the weaknesses of the traditional mass media: namely, their inability to articulate the concerns of their audience. In an influential book from the 1950s, Frederick Siebert, Theodore Peterson, and Wilbur Schramm developed their normative theory of the "social responsibility of the press," which maintained that the press should not only facilitate a top-down stream of information, but also a *bottom-up* stream. The press ought to articulate public concerns. The press should also raise latent and manifest societal conflicts to the plane of discussion (cf. Siebert *et al.*, 1956). Rudolf Wildenmann and Werner Kaltefleiter (1965) elaborated on this idea by distinguishing three functions of the press that were at the heart of the German research tradition on press functions. The *transparency function (Transparenz)* entails that both citizens and authorities should know what happens in the outside world. The *information function (Mitteilung)* entails that the media should inform the citizens top-down about policies and policy plans of public authorities such as parties and the government. The *articulation function (Artikulation)* entails that the media should create a platform for the expression of public concerns. The ability of the media to provide a swift and *transparent* outlook on all types of foreign and domestic real world developments has improved as a result of advances in ICT (information and communicatons technology), such as satellite television, and the Blackberry. The mass media provide an abundance of *top-down information* due to the enormous growth in public relations and governmental information services, to the extent that journalists are actually losing autonomy because of their dependency on these services (Cook, 1998). But the likelihood that newspapers, radio and television *will articulate* public concerns has not increased. Few letters to the editor are published, and those selected are mostly cleaned up, sometimes to the degree of being censored. Selecting "original" letters obscures which issues are raising most public concern. Street interviews on radio and television are stylized according to the taste of program makers. Opinion polls by the mass media are a new attempt to fulfill their articulation function, but the media themselves provide the topics, the questions, and the predefined possible answers. Discussion forums on the internet may therefore supplement the mass media by enabling citizens to articulate their thoughts and feelings freely, thereby countervailing the "colonization" of the private sphere (*Lebenswelt*) by the traditional mass media (Habermas, 1981, part II: 571–575).

Doubts have been raised, however, as to whether discussion forums do yield an unbiased articulation of public concerns. In computer-mediated communication "the dominant voices are those who have developed online authority, and these again tend to be educated, white, English-speaking and male," at least according to Dahlberg (2001), who does not present research results to back up his broad statement that discussion forums reflect the status quo. Participation in political discussion forums takes precious time. Both the empirical literature and the game-theoretical literature on political participation state that anti-status-quo extremists particularly have incentives to pay the costs of political action (Lohman, 1993). In addition to anti-status-quo motivations, a supportive personal network is required to transpose anti-status-quo motivations into political action (Klandermans & Oegema, 1987). Shah *et al.* (2005) show that online discussions form an intermediating variable between being informed (via mass media) and mobilized for political action. On the basis of the political participation literature one would expect that anti-status-quo extremists rather than status-quo fans would participate in discussion forums. Discussion forums simply reduce the costs of articulating anti-status-quo feelings and shape nationwide, and even worldwide, personal networks to support these feelings.

The prediction from the participation literature that anti-status-quo extremists rather than dominant voices develop online authority appears to be plausible, at least in the Netherlands. The voices of the mainstream political parties—Christian-Democrats, Liberals, and Social Democrats—are underrepresented in discussion forums. Until the mid-1990s these parties treated immigration as a taboo issue. Only in the aftermath of 9/11 did Pim Fortuyn—who was assassinated shortly before the 2002 elections—bring the issue of Islamic immigrants to the center of the political debate. The second generation of Moroccans, the sons of guest workers who came to the Netherlands in the late 1960s and 1970s, attracted most attention because of their involvement in street crime and in urban riots. Right-wing persons, who want to kick out the immigrants, and fairly fundamentalist Moroccan youngsters, who propagate

Islam, appear to have been especially successful in the establishment of vivid discussion groups on the internet.

The empirical part of this chapter is based on a comparison of five large national daily newspapers in the Netherlands, the largest discussion group of right-wing persons in the Netherlands (the Usenet group NL.politiek), and the largest discussion group of Moroccan youngsters (the website forum www.marokko.nl, shortened to Marokko.NL). All editorials and postings between 1 October 2003 and 31 July 2005 relevant to the immigration issue were collected. Using automated content analysis, the content from these three media sources relating to immigration issues, relevant actors, emotions, polarization, and flaming will be compared. Time series analysis will be used to estimate the pattern of influence among newspapers and the two discussion forums.

Two research questions interest us here. The first question is whether the forums display a more negative tone than newspapers and, if so, what is the reason for this negativity? The assumption is that the typical style used in discussion forums gives rise to the selective expression of negative emotions, polarization, and flaming. Needless to say, discussion forums dominated by negative emotions, polarization and flaming fulfill their articulation function poorly. Eventually this verbal negativity could lead to intergroup aggression. The second question deals with agenda setting and asks how these old and new media influence each other. The broader context of this second research question is whether the mass media fulfill their functions adequately by setting not only the agenda for traditional public discussions (information and transparency function), but also by feeding the agenda of the newer discussion forums and by picking up public concerns via the online discussions (articulation function).

Theory

A style of flaming and blaming

On the axis from formal written language to informal conversational language, postings to discussion forums come closer to conversational language than news items in newspapers. Conversational language is characterized not only by obvious stylistic marks such as relatively short sentences, little subordination, incomplete sentences, colloquial or slang vocabulary, and the avoidance of the passive voice (Brown & Yule, 1991: 15–17), but also by linguistic choices that seem to indicate a focus on human interaction rather than on objective description. Typically an animated agent rather than an abstract noun will be the subject. Relatively few nouns are used. Many words indicate personal involvement and a drive to persuade others (Steen, 2003). The written language of newspaper journalists is usually more polite. The news genre still rests on objective descriptions rather than on personal evaluations, although during the last decades the formal written language has become slightly more conversational, as indicated by a greater use of involved and persuasive style markers in the British newspaper *The Times* (Steen, 2003). Journalists still attribute rabidly negative evaluations to quoted sources. During the last decades these sources learned that more negative statements guaranteed more news (Kepplinger, 2002).

H1   (Negative Emotions hypothesis:) Postings to discussion forums hold more linguistic markers of negative emotions towards others than newspaper articles.

Negative emotions towards others are defined as emotions that often precede negative acts *towards others*, which means that emotions are viewed from the perspective of social relations (Parkinson *et al.*, 2004). Hate is an example of a negative emotion towards others, since hate often precedes aggression. Because of the focus on a negative action tendency, fear is *not* an example of a negative emotion towards others. Being afraid feels very negative and disturbing, but fear often results in positive acts towards others, such as the acceptance of recommendations (Das *et al.*, 2003) or in compromising with aggressors (Huddy *et al.*, 2005).

It is to be expected that the discussion groups on the internet of anti-status-quo Moroccans on the one hand and anti-status-quo right-wing persons on the other are very aware of each other's existence. Negative emotions towards others combined with awareness of opponents will easily end up in polarization. Polarization is defined as the dogmatic emphasizing of us-them antagonisms.

H2   (Polarization hypothesis:) Postings to discussion forums will show more linguistic markers of polarization than newspaper articles.

Polarization is based on the feeling that one's own group is threatened with losses by its enemies. When such a danger is signaled but still far away a *societal loss-frame* dominates, which means that shouting to mobilize one's own group and to deter the enemy appears to be most effective. It is to be expected that in discussion groups of anti-status-quo groups a *societal loss-frame* dominates. Research results indicate that such a frame does not give rise to elaborated, cognitively complex thoughts (Shah *et al.*, 2004) of the type that should underlie democratic decision making. The precise reasons and motives of opponents become noteworthy only when danger comes near to an individual person. A genuine interest in the reasons and motives of others should be expected with an *individual loss-frame*. Since anti-status-quo discussion groups of Moroccans and right-wing persons must be very aware of each other, because they use the same search engines to browse the internet, one could expect also that their negative emotions will be transposed easily to outrageous insults of opponents that surpass the usual 'region-of-acceptability' in a parliamentary democracy (Rabinowitz & McDonald, 1989).

> H3   (Flaming hypothesis:) Postings to discussion forums hold more outrageous insults towards opponents ("flaming") than newspaper articles.

Flaming can be defined "as an uninhibited expression of hostility, such as swearing, calling names, ridiculing, and hurling insults towards another person, his/her character, religion, race, intelligence, and physical or mental ability" (Kayany, 1998). Condemnations of flaming have become a familiar element of Netiquette.

Agenda setting

What structures online discussions? This is a very basic question, not only for forums about political themes but also for any other theme (e.g. music, partner relations, health, sport or products) and not only for online forums but also for any form of interpersonal communication on the internet. Are online discussions a creative product of emerging interactions between participants in the discussion, as is suggested by romantic ideas about anarchy on the web? Will the absence of authority on the web facilitate profound deliberations between open and fearless minds, of the type that Jürgen Habermas (1981) labeled "basic communication" or "herrschaftsfreie Kommunikation"? Will discussants articulate freely what worries them without being stirred by the authorities, thereby shaping bottom-up influence processes?

In general, the analysis of influence is a tough problem in social science. Agenda-setting research however offers a surprising simple way to find answers to these questions. For example, the influence of Parliament on newspapers and vice versa is assessed by simply counting how often a specific theme is mentioned in Parliament and in newspaper articles. With statistical procedures, like time series analysis, one can assess how strong variations in one agenda precede variations in the other agenda. This research technique is mostly applied to political communication with a strong focus on the role of mass media. We think it is also an ideal tool for analyzing influence processes with regard to (interpersonal) communication on the internet.

The empirical work on agenda setting suggests that what worries free citizens is affected by the media agenda. The vast number of agenda-setting studies (Dearing & Rogers, 1996; McCombs, 2004; McCombs & Shaw, 1972) maintain that the amount of attention for an issue in the media affects the salience of an issue for citizens. This influence of the media on the public is in general rather strong. In a meta-analysis on the basis of 90 empirical studies Wanta and Ghanem (2006) found a mean

correlation of +0.53 between these two agendas. We expect that participants in discussion forums will still be dependent on the mass media for
new information, even when it comes to their favorite issues. Most of
them do not have direct access to sources and events as do journalists.
So, participants in online discussions are expected to resemble ordinary
citizens when it comes to their dependence on the mass media.

> H4   (First-order agenda-setting hypothesis:) Changes in mass media
> attention for an issue result in corresponding changes in discussion
> forums.

The relationship between the old mass media and the newer discussion
forums on the internet has received little scholarly attention as yet, but the
available evidence on the effect of the media agenda on the online agenda
supports hypothesis H4 (Roberts *et al.*, 2002). Internet use is somewhat to
the detriment of television watching, but not to the detriment of newspaper reading, neither in Europe (Huysmans *et al.*, 2004), nor abroad (Lee
et al., 2005). Related research found that participants in online discussions
participated more often in their local community (Dutta-Bergman, 2006),
which suggests also that users of discussion forums are also relatively
often attuned to traditional information sources.

Agenda-setting theory has been extended with second-order agenda-
setting theory (McCombs *et al.*, 1997). Second-order agenda-setting theory
maintains that attributions in the mass media will have a contagious effect
on associations made by the audience: for example, when the media characterize a certain politician as competent or honest, the public is inclined
to copy these attributes. Here we will pay attention to one particular type
of attributes, namely relations of objects towards other objects.

> H5   (Second-order agenda-setting hypothesis:) Changes in mass
> media attention for specific relations between objects result in corre-
> sponding associations between these objects in discussion forums.

First-order agenda setting deals with the frequency of *occurrences* of objects,
whereas second-order agenda setting deals with the frequency of their
being together in a text, thus with *co-occurrences*.

Method

Data

With regard to the broad domain of immigration we analyzed 38,212 postings of NL.politiek and 28,671 postings of Marokko.NL from October 1
2003 until July 31 2005 (see Table 17. 1). For the same issue, 40,429 arti-

cles from the five biggest Dutch national newspapers were retrieved from the LexisNexis archive. The selected national newspapers (*Telegraaf, NRC Handelsblad, Algemeen Dagblad, de Volkskrant* and *Trouw*) represent mainstream politics in the Netherlands and these newspapers reach one-third of the Dutch population (official figures in 2004, http://www.cebuco.nl). Unfortunately, the two excluded big national newspapers, *Metro* and *Spits*, are especially popular among the younger public, but these are not digitally available. Although most Moroccans in the Netherlands do not read the selected newspapers (Bakker & Scholten, 2003), the inclusion of television news programs (and more newspapers) would not make much difference because of similarities between the agendas of Dutch newspapers and television programs (Kleinnijenhuis *et al.*, 2003). Articles from regional newspapers were not included, because the agenda of the national newspapers is a closer approximation of the television news agenda.

For the national newspapers all articles were collected. In the case of the postings a random sample was taken of 30 percent of all relevant postings. NL.politiek counted more than 40,000 participants. Since extreme rightist groups act as a coherent network on the internet (Tateo, 2005), the inclusion of more related discussion groups would probably not change our results much.

According to a marketing report Marokko.NL has been growing strongly over the last few years, especially after the murder of Theo van Gogh. The forum counted 89,000 participants, and was especially popular among young Dutch Moroccan students (Marokko Media, 2004). In numbers, 90 percent of the registered participants are between 15 to 30 years of age. The fact that 68 percent of this group are considered to be "student," means that they belong to the intellectual elite both as compared to their parents, who usually did not have much education when they came to the Netherlands, as well as compared to the vast majority of their own ethnic age group, who attend a vocational school (the percentage of Moroccan students in higher education is still low). For Marokko.NL, postings were retrieved only from the subdivision "Current affairs and youngsters" on this site. This subdivision is similar in its political focus to NL.politiek. The other subdivisions are devoted to topics like romantic relations, dating, Islam, and poetry.

Table 17.1 Number of analyzed documents and words, October 1 2003–July 31 2005

	Documents (units of measurement)	Number of words	Average document length
Newspapers articles (complete set)	40,429	19,148,036	474
NL.politiek postings (sample 30%)	38,212	3,137,655	82
Marokko.NL postings (sample 30%)	28,671	4,013,452	140
Total	107,312	26,299,143	232

Documents were collected for all media for as long a period as possible. Because Usenet groups are stored on Usenet providers for no longer than about two years, and postings seemed to be incomplete for the first months, October 1 2003 was chosen as the starting point. July 31 2005 (shortly after terrorist attacks on the London metro) was chosen as the end of the research period. A posting or a newspaper article was relevant for the issue of immigration when a relevant actor (minister of immigration, involved pressure groups or one its spokesmen) or a relevant issue (related to immigration, Islam, the position of women, and terror) was mentioned. From now on this domain will be labeled as "immigration." The measurement units for the automatic content analysis were separate postings and news articles. To ensure that a keyword was relevant for an object, disambiguation criteria were used that take into account the surrounding paragraph (e.g., the presence of other words within 10 words of a keyword), or the complete article, or posting. A small percentage of articles contained more than 1,500 words and some postings had over 500. Because of the risk of database failures and the risk of long copied texts in postings, these items were removed, a normal procedure in automated content analyses. The average length of newspaper articles (474 words) exceeds the average length of a discussion group posting. The postings of NL.politiek are shorter than those of Marokko.NL (respectively 82 and 140 words).

Operationalization

Negative emotions, polarization, and flaming

Emotions not only have an effect on the beholder but also on social relations, since others infer one's state of mind and the direction of one's acts partly from the emotions one expresses (Parkinson *et al.*, 2004). The hypothesis on negative emotions (H1) deals with emotions that often precede negative acts toward others. We will operationalize *disgust, hatred,* and *shame* as examples of such emotions. Humans tend to root out what disgusts them, to attack what they hate, and to take revenge when shame is brought upon them. Disgust, hatred, and shame (hypothesis H1) are expected to go hand in hand with *polarization* (hypothesis H2), which is defined as a dogmatic emphasis on us-them antagonisms, and *flaming* (hypothesis H3), which was defined earlier as an uninhibited expression of hostility towards others (Kayany, 1998).

To highlight the test results regarding negative emotions towards others (H1), we will also operationalize emotions that often precede positive acts towards others, namely *love, eagerness,* and *pleasure*. Humans tend to cherish those whom they love, to approach what makes them eager, and to protect those who give them pleasure. Moreover a comparison will be made with seesaw emotions that often result in a delayed response, either in a positive or a negative direction, such as *detachment, strain,* and *fear.* One is inclined to keep a distance, at least for a while, when one feels detached, which may be due to apathy or amazement, or strained, which may be due to tensions and conflicts. Being afraid suppresses direct aggressive acts that would normally result from negative feelings toward others that after a while may even bring about a tendency to compromise with aggressors (Huddy *et al.,* 2005).

Disgust, hatred, shame (H1), polarization (H2), flaming (H3), as well as the positive emotions of love, eagerness, and pleasure and the seesaw emotions of detachment, strain, and fear were measured using an automated content analysis procedure with typical words as their indicators. To get a full account of such words and expressions, an electronically available thesaurus for the Dutch language with positive and negative words and expressions (Brouwers & Claes, 1922 (1997), comparable to Roget's thesaurus for the English language (Roget & Kilpatrick, 1852 (2000)), served as the point of departure. Words were selected, regardless of whether they were verbs, adverbs, adverbials, or nouns. To get rid of ambiguous words with many different meanings in different contexts, the Brouwers and Claes list was heavily curtailed. For the remaining words conditions were formulated to ensure that they occurred in an emotional context. In contrast to an available operationalization of emotions by means of an automatic content analysis (Pennebaker & Francis, 1999), the procedure applied in this chapter excludes potential antecedents of emotions and potential behavioral consequences of emotions. Thus words like "murder" and "rape" (as cause or consequence of hatred) were excluded as indicators of emotions.

Agenda setting

To test the agenda-setting hypotheses (H3 and H4), the units of analysis must be specified for which attention in the media will be compared with attention in the discussion forums. Table 17.2 gives an overview of the relevant clusters of issues and actors that underlie the choice of the units of analysis. Each cluster of issues or actors consists of several objects. Table 17.2 gives also an overview of the number of clusters and the number of objects per cluster.

Automated content analysis software can handle a long list of objects quite efficiently. In this case a list was constructed of 522 objects that were joined into 42 clusters. These objects consist of 256 different actors (17 clusters) and 266 issues (25 clusters). The list of actors for the government includes all the members of the government, the list for the political parties all parties in Parliament (9), and the names of all the Members of Parliament who were mentioned in the texts. The list for the public administration covers the police, the secret service, the immigration office etc. In order to cover all perspectives that can come up in the immigration

Table 17.2 Operationalization of and attention paid to actors and issues

	Name cluster	Example keywords	n-clusters	n-objects	news papers	NL. politiek	Marokko. NL
Actors	Government	Prime Minister, Queen, ministers, ministries, advisory boards, government	1	56	27.8	12.8	10.6
	Rightist ideologues	Ayaan Hirsi, Van Gogh, Wilders	1	12	20.1	36.6	37.9
	Three coalition parties	Party leaders, MPs, well known party members	1	54	15.4	8.3	5.7
	Public administration	Provinces, municipalities, police, army, public administration	3	12	12.2	5.5	8.5
	Six opposition parties	Party leaders, MPs, well known party members	6	73	10.4	13.4	5.6
	Judicial power	Supreme Court, judges, prosecutors, judicial power	1	10	6.6	3.7	6.0
	Islamite extremists	Dutch Islamite extremists: Mohammed B. etc.	1	14	3.8	3.2	7.9
	Rightist extremists	Rightist extremist organizations	1	7	1.7	14.3	12.6
	Immigrant pressure groups	Immigrant interest groups and organizations and their spokesmen	1	15	1.5	0.8	0.8
	Islamite ideologues	Arabic European Liga and spokesmen	1	3	0.6	1.4	4.4
	Subtotal actors		17	256	157033	39006	17058
Issues	Terror	Terror, terrorist attacks, bombings, attack New York, attack Madrid, attack Van Gogh, Al-Qaeda, terrorist networks	2	20	33.4	26.3	18.2
	Crime	Crime, murder, rape, arson, domestic violence, child abuse, molesting, possession of firearms, criminals	8	105	19.8	17.3	11.5
	Islam	Islam, Koran, mosque, jihad, holy war, Muslim	1	14	14.0	19.7	40.6
	Remigration	Asylum seekers, refugees, asylum policy, expulsion, deportation	1	25	6.5	4.1	0.9

Name cluster	Example keywords	n-clusters	n-objects	news papers	NL. politiek	Marokko. NL
Demands on immigrants	Residence permit, language course, naturalization duty, vignette method, equal rights	1	18	5.7	14.8	7.0
Conflict Iraq, EU enlargement	Enlargement EU, Schengen convention, foreign conflicts, peace mission, war in Iraq	1	24	5.2	1.4	0.7
Muslim women rights	Equal rights women, headscarf, chador, shariah	1	7	4.1	8.0	13.8
Christianity	Christian religion, ministers, churches	1	2	3.6	2.9	2.8
Immigration	Immigration, tolerance, integration	1	3	3.2	2.2	1.4
Black neighbourhoods	Culture, origin, multicultural society, segregation, preservation of identity, nationality	3	19	2.4	2.2	2.4
Freedom education	Freedom of education, problems in education	1	4	0.8	0.3	0.2
Social security	Child allowance, (law for) disablement insurance act, unemployment benefit, fraud with benefits, reform social security	1	15	0.3	0.2	0.1
Employment	(Un)employment, stimulate employment, unemployed immigrants	1	3	0.3	0.2	0.1
Immigration policy	Immigration policy, integration debate, Islamic debate	1	3	0.3	0.1	0.1
Immigration by marriage	Reunification of families, naturalization (courses), marry off, import brides	1	4	0.2	0.1	0.1
Subtotal issues		25	266	245723	49229	54502
Total actors and issues		42	522	402757	88235	71560

debate, a rather long list of issues has been applied. All core issues are represented (ranging from immigration, demands on immigrants, education, and remigration to Islam and terror), as well as a set of issues that were often associated in the news with immigrants (employment, crime, social security fraud, EU enlargement, and peace missions).

To test the first-order agenda-setting hypothesis (H4), the 522 objects in each of the 22 months of the research period will be the units of analysis. This guarantees a large number of units of analysis (n = 522*22 = 11,484), and therefore a strong test of first-order agenda setting. To test the second-order agenda-setting hypothesis (H5), relationships between each possible pair of object clusters per month will be the units of analysis. Again this results in a strong test of the hypothesis (n = ½ * 42 * (42-1) = 861 distinct pairs of clusters, starting from 34 clusters). The relationship or co-occurrence between two clusters is operationalized as the degree to which two objects occur simultaneously in the same document, which is dependent only on the amount of attention given to each of the objects (in formula: co-occurrence = (a*b)/(a+b), where a and b represent the number of occurrences in one document of object a and object b respectively).

Analyses

To test the hypotheses on linguistic style differences between the formal written language of national newspapers and the conversational informal language of discussion forums, the frequency of the linguistic style markers for negative emotions (H1), polarization (H2), and flaming (H2) per 10,000 words will be used.

To test the hypotheses on agenda setting, correlations between the attention paid in the media and the discussion forums to actors and issues will be used. Pooled correlations will be computed per month to see whether the same issues are discussed at the same time. Furthermore, a structural equation model will be estimated to assess the causal order of the agendas of the newspapers and the two discussion groups. The assumption underlying such a model is that each of the three agendas is determined autoregressively by its own recent past (i.e., the agenda of last month) as well as by the current editions of the two other agendas.

Results

A longitudinal exploration

Figure 17.1 presents a longitudinal overview of the total amount of attention paid to immigration issues in the national newspapers and in the two discussion forums.

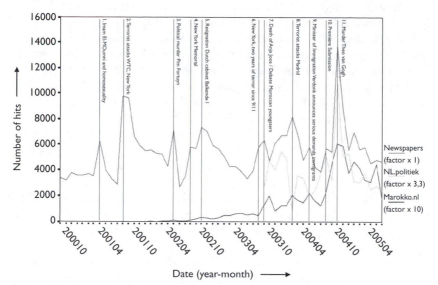

Figure 17.1 Total attention for immigration issues per month, for newspapers and forums

The eleven flags in Figure 17.1 represent key events that gave rise to peaks or even enduring higher levels of attention paid to immigration issues, both in the national Dutch newspapers and in the two discussion groups.

In May 2001 the Dutch imam Khalil el-Moumni stated that "homosexuality is a disease," which was considered in the politically correct liberal Dutch press as a violation of the constitutional prohibition of discrimination based on sexual orientation

Of course, the ultimate key event during the study period is 9/11. The obliteration of the Twin Towers in New York prompted an association in editorials between Islam and terror, and increased the attention paid to the immigration issue for the rest of this study. During many weeks in the election campaigns that followed, a flamboyant, gay, and charismatically gifted newcomer to the political scene, Pim Fortuyn, attracted more media attention than any other politician. This attraction was acquired via statements that had thus far been regarded as taboo in the liberal press. Examples of Fortuyn's "radical" slogans are "no Islamite will come in," "Islam is a backward culture," or "I want to get rid of the constitutional prohibition of discrimination." Attention paid to immigration issues rose to a climax in May 2002, the election month during which Pim Fortuyn was assassinated by a left-wing animal rights extremist. Apparently now the constitutional rights of free speech and press were deemed more important than the other constitutional rights, despite the fact that one year earlier these rights were almost refused to El-Moumni. 9/11 and Pim Fortuyn broke the taboo against negative statements, or even against flaming about immigrants.

In September 2002, one year after 9/11, its commemoration gave rise to a new peak in attention given to immigration issues. In October 2002, within only a hundred days of the May elections, the Dutch cabinet resigned. The vested parties got rid of Pim Fortuyn's former party, the LPF, which had dropped in the polls due to internal squabbles. Once more the immigration theme attracted attention, but in the election campaign that followed other issues were raised to the fore by the vested parties. However, terror and Islam remained important, because of the Dutch military mission to Afghanistan. The 9/11 commemoration of September 2003 placed the connection between Islam and terror once more on the agenda.

In October 2003 a homeless woman, Anja Joos, was kicked to death by two young Moroccan employees of a supermarket who presumed that she was stealing. January and February 2004 centered around the news that a trifle was enough to motivate a Moroccan youngster, Murat D., to shoot his teacher to death, and around the plans of Minister Verdonk to send asylum seekers without residence permits back to their home countries. In March 2004 the Madrid attacks brought terror to Europe. Until June 2004 the Dutch Minister of Immigration, Verdonk, received considerable attention for his new plans for placing serious demands on immigrants.

From September 2004 until November 2004 the attention given to immigration issues started climbing again. Geert Wilders, a politician with strong anti-Islamic sound bites, was kicked out of the liberal party (VVD). In September 2004 the film *Submission* was launched by Ayaan Hirsi Ali, a liberal MP (another VVD MP) of Somalian descent, and by Theo van Gogh, a filmmaker and television star who regularly insulted Muslims (e.g. "goat fuckers"). Verses from the Koran were depicted on the tortured body of a naked woman. By this time many hate postings regarding Wilders, van Gogh, and especially Hirsi Ali, were circulating on the web.

In November 2004 an Islamic fundamentalist, Mohammed B., slit Van Gogh's throat in broad daylight. A moral panic, or at least moral confusion, appeared to grip Holland. This incident led to an even higher peak in Figure 17.1 than 9/11. "Yes, it is war," declared Vice-Prime Minister Zalm. As with Fortuyn, Van Gogh was praised posthumously as a champion of the constitutionally guaranteed freedom of expression, but at the same time many voices were saying that fundamentalists and terrorists like Imam El-Moumni or Mohammed B. should be deprived of the freedom to express their ideas.

A few took justice into their own hands by burning several mosques. In a police attempt to eliminate a terrorist network, television viewers were provided with lengthy news reports and images of the police and Islamic terrorists on top of the roofs of buildings in The Hague. The July 2005 London metro attacks brought together elements that had thus far still been separated: terror, on the one hand, and second-generation Islamic immigrants on the other.

Thus peaks in the attention curves reflect attention given to the danger of terrorism and crime perpetrated by Islamic immigrants. The shocking nature of the events may be one explanation for an ascending spiral of negative emotions, polarization, and flaming (H1, H2, H3). The events may have given rise to moral indignation on both sides. Reference to the same Dutch constitution is used to admonish Muslims not to publicly utter their beliefs about societal issues such as homosexuality, and to dismantle the taboo on expressing negative opinions about immigrants.

A glance at the figure shows that the newspapers and the forums follow more or less the same attention curves. Remarkably enough, relatively unsupervised discussion forums produce the same attention patterns as hierarchically organized newspapers. Agenda setting by the media (H4, H5) provides a plausible explanation for this parallelism.

Negative emotion, polarization, and flaming hypotheses

The use of a negative tone became more common both in politics and in the press, especially in statements attributed to the news sources (Kepplinger, 2002), but became even more so in discussion forums. A few examples of negativity in discussion forums may be illuminating before the presentation of test results.

Postings in NL.politiek dealt with daily annoyances (rise in taxes, impertinent youngsters, traffic jams, crime). Many of them ask for a tougher policy on crime and immigrants, which sometimes ends up in flaming. The tone can be very aggressive, as the following examples demonstrate.

> It's all right with me if they shoot to bits all of Islam and all the cancerous dogs who belong to it. ROTTEN BASTARDS, death to all of you, filthy headscarf bitches and stinking blokes. Fuck the goats in your own rotten country. AND NOW BUGGER OFF, ALL OF YOU. PHEW!

A first analytical grip on such a flaming posting can be obtained by distinguishing between the assumed cause of the problems, and their supposed solution (Iyengar, 1991). In the posting above the immigrants are clearly the problem, but anonymous actors, called "they." provide a violent solution. In the last sentence the author himself gives a command, apparently hoping that "they" (albeit this time a different, Muslim one) will act upon it.

> Now we are really fed up. Butchering all Muslims is the ONLY solution And they fired the starting shot themselves.
>
> [MohammedIsGay]

Again the Muslims are the problem, and again the solution should be provided by a vague category ("we" in the first sentence). A vague delineation of the subject who could deal with the problems is apparent in most postings. It's not *I, you* or a *concrete actor* who is named to deal with the problems.

The postings from Marokko.NL appear to have somewhat more specific problems and solutions. The two postings below from Marokko.NL have fairly concrete problems, although still fairly general solutions.

> Filthy whorish Soussian glutton, may your gullet be given an acute shits-virus and your ra3ker ra3ker make a somersault through your cellulites thing as far as your bulging eye.
>
> […]

> I think Mr. Wilders is in the right nowhere. :angry: :angry: :angry: That filthy dog simply must keep his mouth and not engage himself with things that have nothing to do with him …:angry: :angry: :angry: : angry: and everything has its own limits thus FREEDOM OF SPEECH also …:angry: :angry:
>
> […]

The diagnosis in these postings is that individual politicians, namely MP Ayaan Hirsi Ali—who is denoted as a "filthy whorish Soussian [Somalian] glutton"—and MP Geert Wilders—"a filthy dog"—pose the problem. In the postings above the hoped for outcome for Hirsi Ali and Geert Wilders is expected from a prayer to heaven and an appeal to Wilders' reason respectively. Both politicians were put under continuous surveillance by personal bodyguards because of the large number of flamings and threats that were taken seriously by the Dutch Information Agency, AIVD.

Postings to Marokko.NL may also be directed at other participants in the forum, especially to the fairly large proportion (roughly 30 perent) of Dutch contributors who want to discuss issues with Moroccans or just scold them.

> Shut your cancerous muzzle stupid phthisis **** **** you. What do you think not now? You are now indeed delighted hey that those foreigners piss off in the end. Don't think that that you'll easily get rid of us Moroccans, and neither the Turks and the Antilleans. We will still make your lives very difficult.
>
> […]

Jews, Zionists, Israel, and the United States are other popular targets of flaming. In sum, these citations illustrate that specific persons are the targets of flaming in Marokko.NL, whereas all immigrants are the targets in NL.politiek. Discussants on Marokko.NL pray for a solution from above, whereas discussants on NL.politiek hope for a solution from a very vague in-group. Of course, a few citations do not provide definitive conclusions regarding the nature of flaming.

Table 17.3 gives a comparison based on the complete dataset over 22 months among newspapers, the right-wing Usenet group NL.politiek, and the Moroccan web forum Marokko.NL with respect to the number of linguistic markers of negative emotions, polarization, and flaming per 10.000 words. Negative emotions were divided into the categories of shame, disgust, and hatred.

Due to the large numbers, the difference between each of the two forums and the newspapers is significant for each variable (T-test, p < .001). Table 17.3 shows that the three emotions with a negative action tendency towards others—disgust, shame, and hate—are much more prominent in discussion forums than in newspapers, as was expected on the basis of the negative emotion hypothesis (H1). The hypothesis with regard to polarization (H3) is accepted for NL.politiek, but rejected for Marokko.NL. Flaming (H3) is much more prominent in the discussion forums. Thus, participants in discussion forums do indeed show negative emotions toward each other (negative emotions, H1), which go hand in hand with vulgar insults (flaming, H3). Although the big distinction is between newspapers and the two discussion forums, the latter two are not precisely identical. Disgust and hatred are even more prominent in Marokko.NL than in the right-wing discussion forum NL.politiek. Polarization and flaming are most prominent, however, on NL.politiek. In only one case are the first three hypotheses rejected: The level of polarization in Marokko.NL is lower than that of the newspapers, but the general pattern for this forum is also one of negativity.

Table 17.3 also presents results for three emotions with a positive action tendency—love, eagerness, and pleasure—and for three seesaw emotions that often give rise to a delayed reaction, either positive or negative—detachment, strain, and fear. The surprising result is that the national newspapers and NL.politiek resemble each other closely with respect to positive emotions and seesaw emotions. Discussants at Marokko.NL appear to express positive emotions less often than the Dutch newspapers or the discussants at NL.politiek. They speak less often in terms of love and eagerness.

Discussants at Marokko.NL are also less detached, less strained, and less fearful than their counterparts. One interpretation is that the debate on Islamic immigrants in the Netherlands since 9/11 threatens the identity of the discussants at Marokko.NL to such a degree that seesaw emotions, which would result in delayed reactions, are almost absent. Apparently they rarely behave as *detached* spectators who feel *strained* because of the many

Table 17.3 Number of linguistic stylistic markers of various types per 10,000 words

Hypotheses	Emotions	Examples	Newspapers	NL.politiek	Marokko.NL
Control: positive emotions	Love	Love, sympathy, tenderness, happiness	2.9	3.0	2.5
	Eagerness	Eager, passionate	0.7	0.6	0.4
	Pleasure	Pleasure, sensuality	2.5	3.6	2.6
Control: seesaw emotions	Detachment	Apathy, tired, cool, stunned	3.8	4.6	2.5
	Strain	Tension, conflict, nervous, arousal	1.8	1.0	0.6
	Fear	Fear, fearful	7.9	7.2	5.6
H1: negative emotions	Shame	Ashamed, embarrassed, faulty	2.5	4.2	4.2
	Disgust	Distaste, aversion, nauseating, being fed up	5.5	6.4	7.2
	Hatred	Hate, absolute disdain, revenge	3.4	5.3	5.8
H2: polarization	Polarization	Crazy, lunatic, total, enormous, extraordinary, unbelievable, extreme	5.6	8.7	5.0
H3: flaming	Flaming	Racial, religious, blasphemous, bestial, inhuman insults, e.g. Berber, Zionist, goat fucker, pig, Mongol	4.1	21.5	17.5
N			40,429	38,212	28,671

tensions and conflicts in the outer world and who are *afraid* because of the aggression of others. Islamic fundamentalists and Islamic terror give rise to expressions of fear in newspapers and NL.politiek, as was seen from the chronology above. Research findings indicate that fearful people will see aggression as a good response to an external threat less often than those who simply perceive a large threat at a far distance, or in the future (Huddy *et al.*, 2005), which raises the question of why the fearful discussants at NL.politiek nevertheless exhibit the highest level of flaming. One might speculate that flaming participants in discussion forums do not see their insults as aggression towards others, but rather as shouting to mobilize one's own group on the basis of a *societal loss-frame*. This may also explain the remarkable lack of elaborated, cognitively complex thoughts (Shah *et al.*, 2004) that is apparent from the majority of postings on these discussion forums, despite the fairly high educational level of the participants.

Agenda setting

The similarities as well as the differences among the three agendas are clearly visible in the attention scores in Table 17.2. Marokko.NL devotes more attention to issues than NL.politiek and the newspapers, not only because of its extra attention given to the position of women (14 percent) as a reaction to the fierce criticisms made by MP Hirsi Ali, but especially because of its massive attention given to Islam (41 percent). The profiles of the newspapers and NL.politiek resemble each other. In the newspapers terror is at the top of the agenda, followed by crime, and here Islam is found in third position. NL.politiek stands out in its demands for the integration of immigrants.

Both forums differ most strikingly from the newspapers in their preoccupation with extreme actors (Lohman, 1993): in the very first place with those with an extreme Western ideology (the rightist ideologues Theo van Gogh, Ayaan Hirsi Ali, Geert Wilders, and Pim Fortuyn), and to a much lesser extent with political Islamic extremists and with rightist extremists. This focus on extreme actors offers an initial explanation for their relatively high levels of negativity as shown in Table 17.3. As previously noted, the newspapers give more attention to the actors in power, such as the government and the political parties.

Table 17.4 gives an overview of the magnitude of agenda setting of

Table 17.4 Agenda setting as indicated by correlations for newspapers and discussions groups

	variables to correlate (measured in the same way for newspapers, NL.politiek and Marokko.NL)	correlations between		
		newspapers NL.politiek	newspapers Marokko.NL	NL.politiek Marokko.NL
First order	– actors and issues (attention for 522 objects in 22 months, n=522*22=11484)	0.77	0.60	0.68
	– actors (attention for 256 actors in 22 months; n=256*22=5632)	0.83	0.85	0.86
	– issues (attention for 266 issues in 22 months; n=266*22=5852)	0.72	0.55	0.67
Second order	– actors and issues (symmetric relations 42 clusters for complete research period; n=1/2 * 42 * (42 – 1) = 861)	0.69	0.82	0.82
	– actors and issues versus negative evaluations (relations between 42 clusters of actors and issues and 5 clusters of negative evaluations, complete research period; n= 42 * 5 = 210)	0.63	0.66	0.78

the first- and second-order. With regard to first-order agenda setting, the correspondence between the agendas of the media and the discussion forums within one month is expressed by correlation coefficients. In a first step the relevant actors and issues are selected, resulting in a list of 522 objects. In a second step the attention given to each of these objects is assessed in each of the three agendas for each of the 22 months in this study, resulting in 11,484 units of analysis (522 objects times 22 months). For each unit of analysis there are, just as in Table 17.2, three attention scores: the attention in the newspapers, in NL.politiek, and in Marokko. NL. The three correlation coefficients between these three scores are used as indicators for the connections between the agendas. These correlation coefficients reflect the correspondence between two agendas during the same month on a scale ranging from −1 to +1. A high correlation is, of course, not a proof of causality, but the absence of correlation between the agendas would also exclude a causal flow of influence.

With respect to this first-order agenda setting, the strongest correspondence arises between newspapers and NL.politiek (+0.77), the second largest one between the two discussion forums NL.politiek and Marokko. NL (+0.68), whereas the correspondence between the newspapers and Marokko.NL is slightly lower (+0.60). This rank order applies both to the agenda of actors and to the agenda of issues, as is shown by the figures in the second and third rows respectively in Table 17.4. All these correlations, which range from +0.55 to +0.86, offer clear support for first-order agenda setting (H4). As mentioned before, Wanta and Ghanem (2000) reported in a meta-analysis a mean correlation for first-order agenda setting of +0.53 between the agenda of the mass media and the public agenda. Such strong results are surprising, because many ascribe a high autonomy to online forums and accentuate the differences from the mainstream public debate as found in the news media. Online discussion groups are notorious for their autonomy, extremeness, and negativity, but these figures show, even for the Moroccan forum, a relative high level of integration with the public debate in the mass media.

The results for second-order agenda offer a further confirmation of this integration. Second-order agenda setting maintains that the attention given to associations between specific objects in forums follows attention given to the same associations in the newspapers. Two types of association are analyzed here: all possible associations within the 42 clusters of actors and issues and all associations between these 42 clusters and the negative evaluations from H1, H2 and H3 (shame, disgust, hatred, polarization, and flaming).

With regard to issues and actors, the second-order correlation coefficients are based on all possible relationships between all possible pairings among the 42 selected clusters of actors and issues. The type of relationship is not analyzed here; it can comprise causal relationships between issue developments, conflict or cooperation between actors, issue positions of actors, and consequences of issue developments for actors. Strong correlation coefficients, ranging from +0.69 to +0.82, underscore the power of second-order agenda setting (H5). Whereas the resemblance between Marokko.NL and the national newspapers was relatively low with respect to the attention given to specific actors and issues (+0.60), this resemblance is high when the *associations* between these actors and issues are considered (+0.82). An interpretation is that discussants at Marokko. NL decide for themselves which actors and issues they find important, but that newspapers still have a large impact on the associations that are made between these actors and issues. Users of Marokko.NL appear to reproduce the newspapers in their judgments about the importance of specific issue positions of salient actors and of specific coalitions or conflicts between the salient actors. It's interesting that a lower magnitude of first-order agenda setting does not exclude a strong effect of second-order agenda setting.

The power of second-order agenda setting is only slightly weaker with regard to the associations between the 42 clusters of issues and actors and negative emotions. Here the correlations range from 0.63 to 0.78. Old and new media tend to converge with respect to the nature of their negative emotions, notwithstanding the clear differences, especially between the old and the new media as shown in Table 17.3.

It should be noted that the precise magnitude of the correlation coefficients depends on the precise choice of objects, clusters of objects, and periods. With regard to the combination of actors and issues, the average correlation coefficients for second-order agenda setting appear to be higher than those for first-order agenda setting, but this could have been caused also by differences in operationalization. For example a choice for objects (first order) rather than for clusters of objects (second order) or a choice for the complete research period rather than for a month as the research period. However, computations based on various other choices of period and object clusters revealed essentially the same results. One interesting last result with regard to the correlations between the agendas is that the level of attention for objects has a rather strong effect on the correlations. First- and second-order agenda-setting effects are substantially stronger for the most newsworthy objects.

Since correlations do not prove causality, a Structural Equations Model was used to split up each of the three correlations between the agendas in two directions of influence. Our model starts from the assumption that each agenda is influenced also by its own past, whereas influences from the past of other agendas were already incorporated in an agenda's own past. Exclusion of a direct influence of one agenda's past on another agenda does not preclude an indirect influence of the first on the latter. To put it differently, the model assumes that if a newsgroup currently discusses a specific issue, whereas nobody else discusses this issue now but this issue was highly prominent in the newspapers one month ago, it may well be the case that this newsgroup had already come to consider this issue as important one month earlier.

The three equations below give a restrained overview of the simultaneous estimates of the parameters for the three resulting structural equations.

$$\text{Newspapers} = 0.33 \text{ NL.politiek} + 0.12 \text{ Marokko.NL} \\ + 0.37 \text{ newspapers-past}, R^2 = 0.65$$

$$\text{NL.politiek} = 0.37 \text{ Newspapers} + 0.22 \text{ Marokko.NL} \\ + 0.28 \text{ NL.politiek-past}, R^2 = 0.69$$

$$\text{Marokko.NL} = 0.16 \text{ Newspapers} + 0.20 \text{ NL.politiek} \\ + 0.62 \text{ Marokko.NL-past}, R^2 = 0.75$$

Figure 17.2 gives a visualization of the equations. To understand Figure 17.2, it is worthwhile bearing in mind that the unexplained variance (or, to put it more precisely, the error variance) in reciprocal agenda-setting models can be labeled as news that is added to the circulation. The autoregressive influence of an agenda's past on the present agenda is represented in Figure 17.2 as a boomerang arrow.

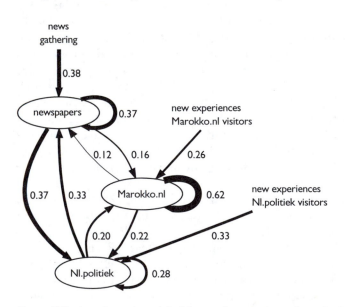

Figure 17.2 A reciprocal model of first order agenda setting: who influences whom?

Each of the estimated parameters is highly significant and the fit of the model is acceptable (CFI=0.91, df=3). From a statistical viewpoint this fit can be improved by assuming in addition that news sometimes produces not only effects within the same month, but also in the next month. The simpler model is presented, because it fits the data sufficiently, and more complex models would not lead to substantially different interpretations.

As was expected on the basis of earlier research on agenda setting, top-down agenda setting (from newspapers to the discussion forums) is stronger than bottom-up agenda setting (from discussion forums to newspapers). The striking fact is that agenda-setting influences are not unidirectional from press to public. Journalists are reported to have felt a need to express the feelings of the people in the street after the shock of the entrance of Pim Fortuyn on the political stage. Certainly, newspapers exert a slightly stronger influence on the right-wing discussion forum NL.politiek than vice versa (0.37 as compared to 0.33), but Marokko.NL is anything but a simple derivative of newspapers (0.16 as compared to 0.12). Apparently visitors to Marokko.NL do not pay close attention to the mass media, whereas journalists may get some of their content from sites such as Marokko.NL.

The equations show that Marokko.NL and NL.politiek have a similar agenda-setting effect on each other (0.20 and 0.22), with NL.politiek getting more input every month from the media than Marokko.NL (0.37 as compared to 0.16), but Marokko.NL getting far more regeneration from its own past (0.62 as compared to 0.28).

It should be noted that indirect effect paths in the model have an infinite length, due to the cyclic loops resulting from the reciprocal influence coefficients between the three agendas. These coefficients are in the range between -1 and $+1$, implying that in the absence of further exogenous shocks the agendas of the discussion forums would return gradually to an equilibrium state in which they are perfectly identical. The model predicts that without new external shocks, the distinctive features of the right-wing agenda of NL.politiek will fade away soon, since the national newspapers, and especially Marokko.NL, are more strongly revitalized by their own past. In fact this is what happened in the year after the murder of Van Gogh, when the newspapers gradually came to diminish their interest in the immigration issue. This resulted in a virtual disappearance of outrage on NL.politiek. The estimated model indicates also that huge exogenous shocks on the news agenda are more likely than exogenous shocks on the other two agendas. The latter implies that a future news hype with respect to immigration and Islam will be sufficient to spark off the right-wing agenda once more.

A concern of both a methodological and a substantial nature is whether the three agendas are just proxies for broader discussion arenas. In all likelihood, the newspaper agenda is just a proxy for the media agenda, since high correlations between attention paid to various issues in newspapers, radio, and television is the rule rather than the exception. The right-wing discussion forum NL.politiek is just one of the possible outlets for right-wing discussants, with similar forums and ordinary public discussions as alternatives. The same holds true for Marokko.NL. From a methodological point of view, the agendas of these alternative outlets may also interact with each other, thereby rendering the relationships between the three agendas partly spurious. From a substantial point of view, this means that one should interpret the coefficients as indicators of influence relationships between three broad arenas rather than as a precise assessment of the influence between the three agendas included here. For example, it is likely that the estimated influence of the media agenda on the agenda of Marokko.NL refers to television influence rather than to the precise influence of the newspapers investigated here. Including only the specific media that are used should increase the coefficients.

Discussion

Discussion forums on the internet were the topic of this chapter. These forums enable the public articulation of thoughts and feelings of citizens on a scale that was hitherto unknown and technically impossible. Therefore they may be a worthwhile complement to the traditional mass media, who may fulfill their transparency and information provision function properly but are less likely to articulate the concerns of their audience (Siebert et al., 1956; Wildenmann & Kaltefleiter, 1965), thereby contributing to a "colonization" of the "Lebenswelt"or "private sphere" (Habermas, 1981). Discussion forums appear to be ideally suited to enable bottom-up communication, free from authority intervention.

To see whether discussion forums live up to these high expectations, this chapter presented a large-scale automatic content analysis of the postings in two discussion forums and of newspaper articles dealing with (especially Islamic) immigration in the Netherlands after 9/11. NL.politiek was analyzed because it is the largest Dutch political discussion forum: with many right-wing postings expressing the view that immigrants should leave or at least should integrate. Marokko.NL was analyzed because large numbers of Moroccan youngsters in the Netherlands, who (rightly or wrongly) face an image as Islamic extremists and criminals, use this site to express their thoughts and feelings.

The events of 9/11 and the series of subsequent newsworthy events in the years thereafter allowed Hollanders to associate immigration with worrying issues such as Islam, crime, and terror. Public reactions to these events incorporate an opportunistic usage of constitutional rights in the Netherlands, such as the freedom of speech. On the one hand the newspapers and NL.politiek proclaimed that freedom of speech should be curtailed for imams who wanted to express Islamic beliefs, e.g. that homosexuals should be punished. On the other hand, numerous cited sources also praised the assassinated charismatic politician Pim Fortuyn and the assassinated filmmaker Theo van Gogh, because they had dared to use their freedom of speech to slight Muslims. Because offending is at the core of this debate and because of the high levels of involvement, this is a good place to study *in vivo* the role of negative emotions, polarization, and flaming on the internet.

Three hypotheses were developed to test whether feelings expressed in discussion forums facilitate mutual understanding. Since discussion forums belong to the realm of informal language, we expected a greater use of emotional language. The results showed that discussion forums quite often exhibit negative emotions that justify negative acts towards others (H1), polarization to emphasize us-them antagonisms (H2), and flaming to insult others ruthlessly (H3). Discussion forums exhibit a strong negativity bias—negative emotions, polarization, flaming—in the fulfillment of their articulation function. They appear to be a breeding ground for the articulation of feelings—negative emotions, polarization, flaming—that are at odds with mutual respect, mutual understanding, and democratic problem solving. One interpretation would be that a societal loss-frame is dominant (Shah *et al.*, 2004). Such a frame explains that the discussants may shout to warn each other to prepare for an approaching danger at a great distance that is still too far away to have detailed thoughts about.

The three agendas showed a surprisingly high level of integration. Starting from agenda-setting theory (McCombs *et al.*, 1997; McCombs & Shaw, 1972), we tested whether discussion forums shape bottom-up communication, or whether the discussants in discussion forums are influenced in a top-down fashion by the mass media, just like ordinary citizens. Two varieties of agenda setting, first-order agenda setting (hypothesis H4) and second-order agenda setting (hypothesis H5) were tested. First-order agenda setting entails that citizens obtain from the media their thoughts about which issues and actors make a difference. Second-order agenda setting adds that citizens also obtain their beliefs about the attributes of these actors and issues from the media, for example beliefs about the precise relationships between actors and issues and the relationship between these actors and issues and negative evaluations. The assessed predominance of first- and second-order top-down agenda setting contradicted the assumed autonomy of web forums. But the results also showed a strong sensibility on the part of the traditional newspapers for the themes being jointly debated in discussion forums. From an agenda-setting perspective, one may conclude that discussants in discussion forums react in the usual way to themes provided by the mass media. However, more often than expected, the mass media use the topics and feelings of discussion forums to adjust the media agenda.

The negativity of these online discussions is not just an interaction pattern typical of the internet, but appears to be directly and indirectly linked to ordinary agenda setting by the news media. The indirect link is established by the selection of topics for a forum discussion. The more extreme segments of the public are especially mobilized to participate in the online discussions (Lohman, 1993). They predictably pick out the most extreme and controversial actors from the actors who gained high attention on the agenda of the mass media. A direct link is found in the power of second-order agenda setting with regard to negative evaluations. Evaluations of the extreme actors on the forums differ in absolute terms from the news media, but they do not differ in relative terms.

To put it briefly: Blaming in the news turns into flaming on the forums. There is empirical evidence that discussions on the internet form a link between being informed and becoming politically active. The negativity of these discussions suggests that these create a political participation that will not be very friendly. Although discussion forums on the web exert a significant bottom-up influence on the mass media, they do not live up to the high expectation that they create an articulation function for citizens that would stop the top-down colonization of the private sphere ("Lebenswelt"). Following earlier studies (Kayany, 1998) this study found a strong negativity bias in discussion forums which is at odds with the ideals of mutual understanding and open discussions aimed at democratic problem solving. Moreover, bottom-up effects are still overruled by reverse effects, which enable a further colonization of the private sphere.

With regard to the methodology used in this study, some improvements are desirable. As mentioned before, mass media with a stronger reach among the participants in the discussion groups should be selected. The ideal is a set of agendas directly linked to each other. Such a dataset should produce stronger effects, which means that the reported effects are a conservative estimation. A second improvement would be the inclusion of real world cues, e.g. the number of attacks on immigrants or on natives. With these kinds of figures one could control for direct effects of events in the real-world on all three agendas. Theoretically, it is possible that all covariations between the agendas are a product of a correlation between each agenda and these developments in the real word. However, the coefficients found are not based on a small list of events (e.g. the murder of Van Gogh, etc.), but on a list of 522 different objects. Also, the effects found for first-order agenda setting are supplemented with even stronger effects for second-order agenda setting, and these second-order effects are not related to events. So, these suggested improvements are desirable but will probably consolidate our conclusions.

This study shows that agenda-setting research also applies to personal communication on the internet. Agenda-setting theory is used traditionally to explain communication effects in the political domain on an aggregated, macro level with a central role for the mass media. But it is also possible to analyze the flows of influence in the building of agendas in personal inter-action, as is illustrated in this study of the interaction within and between discussion forums on the internet. This type of research can be done for online discussion groups, but also for chat rooms, msn-sessions, etc.; it can be done for any subject: for support groups, for political subjects, marketing, or romantic relationships. "What do we talk about?" is one of the first questions in any research on interpersonal communication effects. Recent advances in automatic content analysis enable fast analyses of flexible arrays of features of vast amounts of intermediated commu-nication. In the current study automated content analysis was used not only to obtain detailed measures of agendas but also to measure classical concepts in CMC research such as emotions and flaming.

Future research could link personality features such as self-disclosure, attraction, self-presentation and trust, or features of the social context—for example, the role of gender or of social networks—to the analysis. In the study of CMC these data may be used to broaden the perspective from the beliefs of the communicators as expressed in experiments or surveys toward the thoughts and feelings that were actually communicated, both for descriptive and explanatory purposes. In time, vast amounts of quasi-experimental data on communicative interactions may become available to assess the effects of linguistic, stylistic, psychological, social, and political aspects of communication messages *in vivo*.

References

Bakker, P., & Scholten, O. (2003) *Communicatiekaart van Nederland: Overzicht van media en communicatie*, third edition. Alphen aan den Rijn / Diegem: Kluwer.

Brouwers, L., & Claes, F. (1997 (1922)) *Het juiste woord: betekeniswoordenboek der Nederlandse taal*. Antwerpen: Standaard.

Brown, G., & Yule, G. (1991) *Discourse Analysis*. Cambridge: Cambridge University Press.

Cook, T. (1998). *Governing with the News*. Chicago: University of Chicago Press.

Dahlberg, L. (2001) "Computer-mediated communication and the public sphere: A crit-ical analysis." *Journal of Computer-Mediated Communication, 7*(1), http://jcmc.indiana.edu/vol7/issue1/dahlberg.html.

Das, E. H. H. J., de Wit, J. B. F., & Stroebe, W. (2003) "Fear appeals motivate accept-ance of recommendations: Evidence for a positive bias in the processing of persuasive messages." *Personality and Social Psychology Bulletin, 29*(5), 650–664.

Dearing, J. W., & Rogers, E. M. (1996) *Agenda Setting*. Thousand Oaks: Sage.

Dutta-Bergman, M. J. (2006) "Community participation and Internet use after September 11: Complementarity in channel consumption." *Journal of Computer-Mediated Communica-tion, 11*(2), article 4. http://jcmc.indiana.edu/vol11/issue12/dutta-bergman.html.

Habermas, J. (1981) *Theorie des kommunikativen Handelns*. Frankfurt am Main: Suhrkamp Verlag.

Huddy, L., Feldman, S., Taber, C., & Lahav, G. (2005) "Threat, anxiety, and support of antiterrorism policies." *American Journal of Political Science, 49*(3), 593.

Huysmans, F., de Haan, J., & van den Broek, A. (2004) *Achter de schermen: een kwart eeuw lezen, luisteren en internetten*. Den Haag: SCP.

Iyengar, S. (1991). *Is Anyone Responsible? How Television Frames Political Issues*. Chicago: University of Chicago Press.

Kayany, J. M. (1998) "Context of uninhibited online behavior: Flaming in social newsgroups on Usenet." *Journal of the American Society for Information Science, 49*(12), 1135–1141.

Kepplinger, H. M. (2002) "Mediatization of politics: Theory and data." *Journal of Communication, 52,* 972–986.

Klandermans, B., & Oegema, D. (1987) "Potentials, networks, motivations and barriers: Steps towards participation in social movements." *American Sociological Review, 49,* 583–600.

Kleinnijenhuis, J., Oegema, D., de Ridder, J. A., van Hoof, A. M. J., & Vliegenthart, R. (2003) *De puinhopen in het nieuws*. Alphen aan de Rijn: Kluwer.

Lee, W., Tan, T. M. K., & Hameed, S. S. (2005) "Polychronicity, the internet, and the mass media: A Singapore study." *Journal of Computer-Mediated Communication, 11*(1), article 14. http://jcmc.indiana.edu/vol11/issue11/wplee.html.

Lohman, S. (1993) "A signaling model of informative and manipulative political action." *American Political Science Review, 87*(2), 319–333.

Marokko media (2004) *Internet tariefkaart*. Marketing report ordered by Marokko. NL.

McCombs, M. E. (2004) *Setting the Agenda: The Mass Media and Public Opinion*. Cambridge: Polity Press.

McCombs, M. E., & Shaw, D. L. (1972). "The agenda-setting function of mass media." *Public Opinion Quarterly, 36,* 176–187.

McCombs, M. E., Pablo Llamas, J.-P., Lopez-Escobar, E., & Rey, F. (1997) "Candidate images in Spanish elections: Second-level agenda-setting effects." *Journalism & Mass Communication Quarterly, 74*(4), 703–717.

Parkinson, B., Fischer, A. H., & Manstead, A. S. R. (2004) *Emotion in Social Relations: Cultural, Group and Interpersonal Processes*. Manchester: Baker & Taylor.

Pennebaker, J. W., & Francis, M. E. (1999). *Linguistic Inquiry and Word Count*. Mahwah: Erlbaum.

Rabinowitz, G., & McDonald, S. E. (1989) "A directional theory of issue voting." *American Political Science Review, 83,* 93–122.

Roberts, M., Wanta, W., & Dzwo, T.-H. (2002) "Agenda setting and issue salience online." *Communication Research, 29*(4), 452–465.

Roget, P. M., & Kilpatrick, B. E. (1852 (2000)) *Roget's Thesaurus of English Words and Phrases*. London: Penguin Books.

Shah, D. V., Cho, J., Eveland, W. P., Jr., & Kwak, N. (2005) "Information and expression in a digital age, modeling internet effects on civic participation." *Communication Research 32*(5), 531–565.

Shah, D. V., Kwak, N., Schmierbach, M., & Zubric, J. (2004) "The interplay of news frames on cognitive complexity." *Human Communication Research, 30*(1), 102–120.

Siebert, F. S., Peterson, T., & Schramm, W. (1956) *Four Theories of the Press*. Urbana: University of Illinois Press.

Steen, G. (2003) "Conversationalization in discourse. Stylistic changes in editorials of The Times between 1950 and 2000." In L. Lagerwerf, W. Spooren & L. Degand (eds.), *Determination of Information and Tenor in Texts*. Münster: Nodus.

Tateo, L. (2005) "The Italian extreme right on-line network: An exploratory study using an integrated social network analysis and content analysis approach." *Journal of Computer-Mediated Communication, 10*(2), article 10. http://jcmc.indiana.edu/vol10/issue12/tateo.html.

Wanta, W. and Ghanem, S.I. (2006) "Effects of agenda-setting." In R. W. Preiss, B. M. Gayle, N. Burell, M. Allen, & J. Bryant, (eds.), *Meta-Analyses of Media Effects*. Mahwah, NJ: Lawrence Erlbaum Associates.

Wildenmann, R., & Kaltefleiter, W. (1965) *Funktionen der Massenmedien*. Frankfurt am Main, Bonn: Athenäum Verlag.

Chapter 18

Leisure boredom, sensation seeking, self-esteem, and addiction

Symptoms and patterns of cell phone use

Louis Leung

According to a study by the Pew Internet and American Life Project, 45 percent of 12–17-year-olds in the U.S.A. have cell phones, and 33 percent have used a cell phone to send text messages (Lenhart *et al.*, 2005). Of those who often do texting on their cell phone, almost one in three (29 percent) teenagers use it to communicate with their parents. In another cell phone use study by Pew (Rainie & Keeter, 2006), it was reported that teenagers often use their cell phone to take still pictures (28 percent), play electronic games (22 percent), surf the internet (14 percent), and send/receive emails (8 percent). Playing with features on the cell phone (including reading online news and downloading songs, wallpaper, and ring tones) appears to have become the adolescent leisure phenomenon in recent years. As the phones have become cheaper and more sophisticated, sales of cell phones to teenagers have become more common. However, as the cell phones become more compact, concerns about problem use are growing. To date, there has been almost no study of whether cell phone use is addictive or dependence-forming.

This study was established to center upon the people directly involved with a modern syndrome—adolescents and young adults whose cell phones had come to dominate their lives and interests. The investigation aims to examine whether certain factors could be isolated as instrumental in the development of such a syndrome. Past research has found that the heaviest substance users or addicts tended to be those who scored high on sensation seeking and leisure boredom and low on self-esteem (Gordon & Caltabiano 1996; Iso-Ahola & Crowley, 1991; Iso-Ahola & Weissinger, 1990). As a result, theoretical constructs, such as leisure boredom, sensation seeking, and self-esteem, will be used as the basis from which to explain addiction symptoms and cell phone use.

Theoretical frameworks

Cell phone addiction

This research was initiated based upon previous studies (Beard, 2002; Beard & Wolf, 2001; Chak & Leung, 2004; Griffiths, 1998, 2000; Katz & Akhus, 2002; Leung, 2004; Ling, 2004; Scherer, 1997; Young, 1996, 1998, 1999) which indicated that some online users were becoming addicted to the internet in much the same way that others became addicted to gambling, drugs, and alcohol. Traditionally, the concept of "addiction" was based on a medical model and is properly reserved for bodily and psychological dependence on a physical substance—and not a behavioral pattern. Recent research has argued that addiction should be widened to cover a broader range of behaviors (Lemon, 2002; Orford, 2001; Shaffer, 1996). As a subset of behavioral addiction, Griffiths (1996) proposed the concept of technological addiction, which is operationally defined as human-machine interaction and is non-chemical in nature. Despite whether the excessive use of various technologies, such as internet surfing, TV watching, and computer gaming, can be or should be called an "addiction," scholars have argued that excessive use of technology can be considered problematic (Griffiths, 1998; Griffiths & Hunt, 1998; Shotton, 1989). Today, as the capability of the cell phone becomes more and more sophisticated and multifunctional, adolescents and young users are becoming increasingly dependent or "addicted" to this technology, not only for mediated inter-personal communication through voice or text (such as SMS) but also as a tool for seeking information online, for entertainment, relaxation, passing time, picture and video taking and other yet-to-be invented applications, and as an expression of status and identity.

To clinically define addictive use of the cell phone, it is necessary to compare it against criteria for other established addictions. The American Psychiatric Association's *Diagnostic and Statistical Manual of Mental Disorders* (known as DSM) has established objective and measurable criteria for assessing "substance dependence" (American Psychiatric Association, 1994). The main diagnostic criterion is a maladaptive pattern of substance use, leading to significant psychological impairment. This impairment is manifested by *seven* symptoms from a list of conditions including withdrawal, tolerance, preoccupation with the substance, loss of control over the substance, more use of the substance than intended, continued consumption of the substance despite adverse consequences, and loss of interest in other social, occupational, and recreational activities.

Addictive cell phone use can be regarded as an impulse control disorder that does not involve an intoxicant and is similar to pathological gambling. Bianchi & Phillips (2005) identified a number of signs that cell phone addicts would exhibit and developed the cell phone problem-use scale. It was found that dependents of cell phones preoccupy themselves with the cell phone (e.g., when out of range for some time, users become worried with the thought of missing a call); use the cell phone for an increasing amount of time in order to achieve satisfaction; repeat unsuccessful efforts to control, cut back, or stop cell phone use; feel lost, restless, moody, depressed, or irritable when attempting to cut down cell phone use; stay on the cell phone longer than originally intended; hide from family and friends or others to conceal the extent of involvement with the cell phone; and use the cell phone as a way of escape from problems or to relieve a dysphoric mood (e.g., feeling of isolation, anxiety, loneliness, and depression).

Given the lack of similar research in this area, this study expands the work by Bianchi and Phillips (2005) and seeks predictors from the addiction literature and other psychological theories about topics such as leisure boredom, sensation seeking, and self-esteem in order to differentiate the addicts and the nonaddicts and to explain usage patterns of cell phones. Therefore, this study asked:

RQ$_1$: What cell phone addiction symptoms can be identified among a group of adolescents and young adults?

RQ$_2$: Who are the cell phone addicts and to what extent are adolescents and young adults addicted to cell phone use?

Leisure boredom

Research suggests that unless leisure is optimally arousing, it is experienced as boredom (Iso-Ahola, 1980), and that individuals who experience high levels of leisure boredom may engage in deviant activities such as substance use (Iso-Ahola & Crowley, 1991). Perceptions of leisure as boredom are associated with negative affect, and can be manifested as beliefs that available leisure experiences are not sufficiently frequent, involving, exciting, varied, or novel (Iso-Ahola & Weissinger, 1990). Iso-Ahola and Weissinger argue that leisure behavior is optimally arousing for it to be psychologically rewarding, especially when individuals perceive that they have just the right amount of time for leisure activities; not too much or too little. Thus, leisure boredom is a likely consequence of conflicting perceptions of having too much time available with too little to do (Hill & Perkins, 1985). In fact, Phillips (1993) has suggested that having an abundance of time is central to boredom.

Leisure boredom is related to other forms of addiction and has been implicated in deviant activity involvement, particularly drug use and delinquency (Iso-Ahola & Crowley, 1991). Frequency and quantity of alcohol use among female college students has been found to be positively correlated with boredom susceptibility, and adolescents who smoke report being more bored and less challenged than nonsmokers (Orcutt, 1984). In addition, young smokers perceive their leisure time as qualitatively less fulfilling (Smith & Caldwell, 1989). Mattick and Baillie (1992) also found that adolescent smokers cite relaxation and relief from boredom as reasons for smoking. Furthermore, leisure boredom may also be correlated with adolescent participation in crime (Mukherjee & Dagger, 1990).

Despite increased attention to adolescent leisure pursuits over the past decades, researchers have generally overlooked leisure-related factors as correlates and causes of addictive use, and other deviant behaviors, with the cell phone. Increasingly, the cell phone allows adolescents, while having not much to do, to be engaged in a number of activities, such as texting in SMS, gaming, accessing the internet, reading online news, shooting and viewing pictures or video, among others. This is surprising considering that such activities probably occur most often during leisure time and in leisure settings. In this study, relationships between leisure boredom and cell phone dependency, phone use, and use of special features in the cell phone will be examined. Accordingly, the following hypotheses are posed:

$H_{1.1}$: The higher the level of leisure boredom one experiences, the higher the likelihood one will be addicted to the cell phone.

$H_{1.2}$: Subjects who score high on the level of leisure boredom will report a higher frequency of phone calls on the cell phone.

$H_{1.3}$: Subjects who score high on leisure boredom will report a higher amount of cell phone features use.

According to an optimal arousal perspective, individuals' motivation to seek out leisure activities and the activities they choose, vary according to their arousal levels. The psychological construct used to conceptualize this notion is Zuckerman et al.'s (1964) sensation-seeking motive.

Sensation-seeking behavior

Past research suggested that sensation seeking has emerged as being capable of explaining a variety of behaviors, such as drug use, aggression, sex, skydiving, bungee jumping, body-contact sports, hiking and camping, or playing computer and video games (Zuckerman, 1979; 1994). Zuckerman's sensation-seeking scale (1979) measures individual differences in sensation seeking along four dimensions: thrill and adventure seeking, experience seeking, disinhibition, and susceptibility to boredom. While the adventure-seeking dimension can be defined as a desire to engage in sports or other activities involving speed or danger (Zuckerman et al., 1978), the experience-seeking dimension measures behaviors involving the pursuit of new experiences through travel, music, art, and drug usage. The disinhibition dimension features behaviors that ignore social constraints, such as fighting, seeking social stimulation through parties, social drinking, and a variety of sex partners. The susceptibility to boredom subscale measures the level to avoid boredom produced by unchanging circumstances.

Adolescence is a time for experimentation with rules, roles, and relationships. According to Jessor and Jessor (1977), adolescents purposely seek out risks. They suggest that such behaviors permit adolescents to: (1) deal with anxiety, frustration, and failure; (2) gain admission to peer groups and demonstrate identification with a youth subculture; (3) confirm personal identity; (4) express opposition to adult authority and conventional society; (5) take control of their lives; and (6) affirm maturity and mark a development transition into young adulthood. Further, Jessor and Jessor also explain the need for sensation seeking as a function of pleasure- or fun-seeking behaviors. The need for change, variety, and intensity of stimulation manifests itself in sensory, social, and thrill-seeking behaviors.

Just as there are inappropriate times to seek out leisure activities to maintain the optimal arousal level, there will also be times to use the cell phone features for entertainment, or to contact someone to escape from boredom. This study analyzed whether sensation seeking is related to adolescents' and young adults' phone calls and features use of the cell phone. As a result, the following hypotheses are formulated:

$H_{2.1}$: Subjects who score high on sensation seeking will exhibit a higher tendency to be addicted to cell phone use.

$H_{2.2}$: Subjects who score high on sensation seeking will have a higher frequency of phone calls on the cell phone.

$H_{2.3}$: Subjects who score high on sensation seeking will report a higher amount of cell phone features use.

Self-esteem

Self-esteem is a part of the "unwillingness to communicate syndrome" since individuals who have low self-esteem expect others to react negatively because they have an unfavorable concept of self (Infante, 1976). When individuals have low self-esteem, they lack self-confidence in general, and they have little faith that their stance on controversial issues is valid. As a result, they are less motivated to communicate because they expect to fail. Adolescence is marked by a growing sense of self-identity. Adolescents' self-perceptions of their capabilities could be expected to impinge on activity choices. Such perceptions and expectations have been conceptualized as the self-concept, a construct which has been regarded by psychological theorists as a major motivating factor in the control and direction of human behavior (Burns, 1979). Satisfaction with one's current activities, appearance, and friendships contributes to a positive self-concept, while deficits in such areas lower the self-concept (Deaux & Wrightsman, 1988). Negative self-concept has been used to explain a wide array of deviant behaviors and has become an important feature in many explanations of delinquency (Oyserman & Markus, 1990). Past research has also found that perceptions of boredom in leisure activities increased with a corresponding decrease in perceived self-esteem, social competence, and leisure satisfaction (Iso-Ahola & Weissinger, 1990). Gordon and Caltabiano (1996) found that adolescents who were the heaviest substance users, and may even develop addictive behavior, were those who scored low on self-esteem and high on sensation seeking. As a result, we propose:

$H_{3.1}$: Subjects who score low on self-esteem (who perceive themselves as not being in control) will demonstrate a higher tendency toward cell phone addiction.

$H_{3.2}$: Subjects who score high on self-esteem will report a higher frequency of phone calls on the cell phone.

$H_{3.3}$: Subjects who score low on self-esteem will report a higher amount of cell phone features use.

In discussing media use from the uses and gratifications perspective, Rubin (2002) argued that individual life-position attributes—such as personality or psychological health (e.g., leisure boredom, sensation seeking, loneliness, and depression) and situational variables (e.g., social interaction or size of social capital)—will affect our motives to communicate, our strategies for seeking information and diversion, and our dependency on a medium. Here, social capital refers to the amount of communication that takes place among its members within their social network (Putnam, 1995). In general, the relationship between social capital and information and communication technologies (ICTs) seems to be an ambivalent one. High levels of social capital or strong, preexisting networks, for example, are seen to be a success factor in establishing an electronic-based network (Fukuyama, 2001). At the same time, the existence of ICT creates networking infrastructure that encourages the formation of social capital (Calabrese & Borchert, 1996). Thus, the relationship between social capital and ICTs seems to be reciprocal. Since social capital is about connections among people, one obvious question is whether social capital affects the need for ICT (e.g., the cell phone) in order to maintain their level of social engagement. In examining the addictive nature of the internet, Wallace (1999) suggested that some psychological spaces of the internet might be so attractive, so absorbing, that they may lead people into very heavy use, even compulsive overuse. A similar question could also be asked: What is it about the psychological spaces created by the cell phone that draws out behavior that in extreme cases looks like an addiction? Grounded in the cell phone addiction construct, together with leisure boredom, sensation seeking, self-esteem, and social capital, this study examined their influences on addictive use of the cell phone. Therefore, this study seeks to expand previous research by addressing a two-part research question:

RQ$_3$: How can demographics, leisure boredom, sensation seeking, self-esteem, cell phone dependency symptoms, and social capital predict: (a) cell phone use in general and (b) features use of the cell phone in particular?

Methodology

Sample and sampling procedure

Data were gathered from a probability sample of 624 teenagers and young adults ranging in age from 14 to 28 (M = 19.4) who responded to a telephone survey in August 2005. The 14–28-year-olds were targeted because they were the heaviest users of the cell phone in Hong Kong (Leung & Wei, 1999). Telephone numbers were randomly drawn from the most recent edition of the territory telephone directory. All of the calls were made from a central location using a Computer-Assisted Telephone Interviewing (CATI) system. Noneligible respondents (i.e., younger than 14 and older than 28), numbers that were unobtainable, and numbers that were not answered after five attempts were excluded. In addition, eligible respondents had to be cell phone users. The sample consisted of 51.8 percent male respondents. The response rate was 62.1 percent.

Measurement

Cell phone addiction

The 27-item Mobile Phone Problem Use Scale (MPPUS) developed by Bianchi and Phillips (2005) was adapted to measure cell phone addiction in this study. However, only 17 items from MPPUS, which contained eight revised items from the *Diagnostic and Statistical Manual of Mental Disorders* (DSM-IV) for screening gambling problems, were used to create the composite *cell phone addiction index* (MPAI). The eight items adapted from DSM-IV were also used by Young (1996) to develop her screening instrument for addictive internet use. A 5-point Likert scale was used on the 17-item MPAI scale with 1 = not at all, 2 = rarely, 3 = occasionally, 4 = often, and 5 = always. The Cronbach's alpha was remarkably high at .89.

Leisure boredom

To assess perceptions of boredom in leisure, the Leisure Boredom Scale (LBS: Iso-Ahola & Weissinger, 1990), containing 16 items that ask people to indicate how they feel about their leisure time (i.e., nonwork hours), was used. LBS is potentially usable in clinical and applied research involving the examination of leisure dysfunctions such as lethargy, substance abuse, and vandalism. The scale items (e.g., "For me, leisure time just drags on and on; leisure time activities do not excite me") were used on a 5-point scale ranging from strongly disagree (1) to strongly agree (5), with high scores indicating greater leisure boredom. The factor structure of the LBS was examined and the results indicated the existence of a single factor with a high internal consistency reliability of .78.

Sensation seeking

The adventure-seeking subscale, consisting of 4 items from the 4-dimension sensation-seeking scale, was adapted from Zuckerman *et al.* (1978) to assess desire to engage in sports-related and other activities involving speed or danger (Cronbach's alpha = .78). Other subscales were excluded because they deal with behaviors such as drinking, sex, and drugs. Respondents were asked if they would participate in the following activities: flying an airplane, sky diving, downhill skiing, and bungee jumping. A 5-point scale was used with 1 = would never try and 5 = often do.

Self-esteem

The 10-item Rosenberg Self-esteem Scale was used to assess this construct. It is a brief measure with high test-retest internal reliability and validity of .80 – .84 (Kivimaki & Kalimo, 1996). In the current study, Cronbach's alpha was .80.

Cell phone call usage patterns

Respondents were asked three questions regarding the cell phone call usage pattern: (1) How much time each day (in minutes) do you find yourself communicating with someone on the cell phone? (2) How many minutes on average do you spend on each call? (3) How many people do you talk to on the cell phone on a regular basis?

Features use

Three most common features in the cell phone are for texting, entertainment, and information seeking. To assess texting, respondents were asked: "How often do you send/receive SMS/MMS/e-mail messages?" For entertainment, respondents were asked: "How often do you take/send/receive pictures, play electronic games, record video/audio, or download ring tones on your cell phone?" And for information seeking, they were asked: "How often do you read online news?" A 5-point scale was used with 1 = never and 5 = very often on all the feature questions.

Social capital

To measure social capital, respondents were asked to report the estimated active time in minutes the previous day that they met face-to-face with (a) family and relatives and (b) friends and schoolmates.

Findings

Cell phone addiction symptoms

The cell phone addiction index (MPAI) scale was developed to collect responses from 624 adolescents and young adults to identify cell phone addiction symptoms and, as a composite, to assess their level of cell phone addiction. As shown in Table 18.1, the principal components factor procedure yielded a four-factor cell phone addiction symptoms structure and accounted for 57.73 percent of total variance. The first factor was "*inability to control craving,*" which consisted of seven items reflecting the inabilities of adolescents and young adults to hide from others the amount of time they spent on the cell phone, to avoid complaints they received from friends and family on their compulsive cell phone use, and to evade loss of sleep due to excessive use. This factor had an eigenvalue of 6.2 and explained 36.48 percent of the total variance. The reliability of these seven items as indicated by Cronbach's alpha was high at .83 (M = 2.00, s.d. = .78). "*Anxiety and feeling lost*" was the second factor (eigenvalue = 1.47, 8.62 percent of variance, α = .76, M = 2.66, s.d. = 1.01). It included four items characterizing that young adults and adolescents felt anxious, lost, preoccupied, and had difficulty switching off their cell phone. "*Withdrawal and escape*" was the third factor (eigenvalue = 1.12, 6.56 percent of variance, α = .81, M = 2.97, s.d. = 1.15). It consisted of 3 items illustrating how adolescents and young adults used the cell phone to escape from loneliness and feeling down and isolated. The fourth factor, "*productivity loss*" (eigenvalue = 1.03, 6.07 percent of variance, α = .60, M = 2.22, s.d. = .79) contained 3 items indicating that adolescents and young adults found that excessive use of

Table 18.1 Factor analysis of cell phone addiction

	Mean	SD	Factors			
			1	*2*	*3*	*4*
Inability to Control Craving						
1 You have been told that you spend too much time on your cell phone	1.85	1.11	0.790			
2 Your friends and family complained about your use of the cell phone	1.98	1.20	0.774			
3 You have tried to hide from others how much time you spend on your cell phone (7)*	1.84	1.00	0.640			
4 You find yourself engaged on the cell phone for longer period of time than intended (5)*	2.46	1.17	0.583			
5 You can never spend enough time on your cell phone (2)*	2.03	1.04	0.576			
6 You have attempted to spend less time on your cell phone but are unable to (3)*	2.02	1.09	0.520			
7 You lose sleep due to the time you spend on your cell phone	1.85	1.12	0.517			
Feeling Anxious & Lost						
8 When out of range for some time, you become pre-occupied with the thought of missing a call (1)*	2.70	1.26		0.728		
9 You feel anxious if you have not checked for messages or turned on your cell phone for some time (4)*	2.55	1.27		0.723		
10 You find it difficult to turn off your cell phone	2.60	1.42		0.6901		
11 You feel lost without your cell phone	2.80	1.36		0.648		
Withdrawal/Escape						
12 You have used your cell phone to talk to others when you were feeling isolated	3.10	1.29			0.839	
13 You have used your cell phone to talk to others when you were feeling lonely	3.18	1.29			0.824	
14 You have used your cell phone to make yourself feel better when you were feeling down (8)*	2.62	1.24			0.705	
Productivity Loss						
15 You find yourself occupied on your cell phone when you should be doing other things, and it causes problems (6)*	2.46	1.17				0.807
16 Your productivity has decreased as a direct result of the time you spend on the cell phone	2.02	1.05				0.741
17 There are times when you would rather use the cell phone than deal with other more pressing issues	2.18	1.21				0.424
Eigenvalue			6.20	1.47	1.12	1.03
Variance explained (percent)			36.48	8.62	6.56	6.07
Cronbach's Alpha			0.83	0.76	0.81	0.60

Notes
Scale used: 1 = Not at all; 2 = Rarely; 3 = Occasionally; 4 = Often; and 5 = Always; N = 624
* Items marked with '*' resemble or are equivalent to the 8-item Young's internet addiction diagnostic scale.

the cell phone has caused problems in their lives, decreased productivity, and diverted attention from pressing issues that they should be facing. The mean score for the 17-item cell phone addiction index (MPAI) was 39.73 with s.d. = 12.12.

As a whole, this study identified four cell phone addiction symptoms which were conceptually consistent with the theoretical origins described in the diagnostic criteria for pathological gambling in DSM-IV. The original DSM measure for pathological gambling was based on eight items; however, this study employed 17.

Profiles of the cell phone addicts

To assess the extent to which adolescents and young adults are addicted to the cell phone, Young's classic definition of internet addiction was adopted; in this, a total of eight items from the 17 that are most conceptually equivalent to Young's (1996) screening instrument on internet addiction were employed. According to this classical measure, 28.7 percent in our sample can be classified as cell phone addicts. This means that over a quarter of the 624 adolescents and young adults were cell phone dependents. To further distinguish the cell phone addicts and nonaddicts, a canonical discriminant analysis procedure was ordered. Results in Table 18.2 suggest that adolescents and young adults addicted to the cell phone were distinguished (in the order of the strength in the structure coefficients) by scoring higher in leisure boredom and sensation seeking, more general use (i.e., higher overall use of the cell phone in minutes per day and staying longer on each call in minutes), and more features use of the cell phone (e.g., sending/receiving e-mail/SMS/MMS; taking/sending/receiving pictures; recording video and audio; reading news; downloading ring tones and games; and keeping their cell phone on at bed time) when compared to the nonaddicted users. More specifically, the cell phone addicts spent about 54.5 minutes a day more on the cell phone ($t = -3.71$, $p < .001$) than the nonaddicted. On average, addicted cell phone users spend 108.82 minutes a day on the cell phone, while the nonaddicted spend 54.41 minutes. The function correctly classified 71.7 percent of the cases.

As a whole, irrespective of whether they are cell phone addicts or not, the average time on the cell phone for the sample was 84 minutes per day. This figure was about 4.77 times more than Bianchi and Phillips' (2005) study at 17.62 minutes per day. This is probably due to the age difference, as the present study focused on adolescents and young adults (ages from 14 to 28 with M = 19), while the Bianchi and Phillips (2005) study was from ages 18 to 85 with the mean age equaling 36. Unlike any other, a cell phone is the medium of choice for mediated interpersonal communication for adolescents and young adults. This new generation is at the heart

Table 18.2 Discriminant analysis of cell phone addicts with psychological variables, cell phone usage pattern, features used, and demographics as predictors[a] (N = 545)

Predictors	Structure Coefficients
Psychological Variables	
Leisure boredom	0.30***
Sensation seeking	0.30***
Self-esteem	0.29
Cell phone Usage Pattern	
Amount of use (in minutes per day)	0.54***
Average length of each call (in minutes)	0.39***
Number of people talked to regularly	0.17
Features Used[b]	
Send SMS/MMS/email	0.57***
Receive SMS/MMS/email	0.50***
Take pictures	0.36***
Send/receive pictures	0.36***
Record video/audio	0.38***
Read news/surf the internet	0.56***
Play electronic games	0.25
Download ring tones/games	0.45***
Turn it off when you go to bed	−0.35***
Demographics	
Age	0.12
Gender	−0.02
Education	0.05
Eigenvalue	0.23
Canonical correlation	0.43
Degree of freedom	15.00
Wilks' Lambda	0.81
Significance	p<.001
Group Centroids	
Addicts	0.71
Nonaddicts	0.33
Cases correctly classified	71.7 percent

Notes

a   The classification of subjects into being addicts or nonaddicts was carried out according to the classical definition of Young's (1996) internet addiction scale, which consists of 8 items (from the 17) conceptually similar to the classical measure. Items were dichotomized and the data used ranged from 0 to 8. Respondents were considered "addicted" to the cell phone when answering "yes = 1" to five (or more) of the eight "yes" or "no" questions for addictive cell phone use. Addicts were dummy coded as 1 and nonaddicts as 0.

b   Scale used on these items: 1 = Never; 5 = Very often.

of a new youth culture treating the cell phone as a companion, where in profound and fundamental ways they play, communicate, shop, and spend their leisure time very differently than their parents.

Hypotheses testing

$H_{1.1}$ predicted that the higher the level of leisure boredom one experiences, the higher the likelihood one will be dependent on the cell phone. As expected, bivariate results in Table 18.3 show that leisure boredom was significantly related to the composite of the 17-item MPAI (r = .13, p<.01). Further analyses of the relationships between leisure boredom and cell phone addiction symptoms, such as inability to control craving (r = .18, p < .001) and productivity loss (r = .17, p<.001), were also found to be significantly linked. Thus, $H_{1.1}$ received strong support. $H_{1.2}$ proposed that the higher the level of leisure boredom one experiences, the more phone calls will be reported in using the cell phone. Results shown in Table 18.4 show that relationships between leisure boredom and amount of use in minutes per day, length of call in minutes per call, as well as number of people talked to regularly were all insignificant. Therefore, $H_{1.2}$ failed to receive any support. Similarly, $H_{1.3}$ hypothesized that the higher the level of leisure boredom one experiences, the more cell phone features one will use on a typical day. However, no significant relationships were found (see Table 18.5) between leisure boredom and use of cell phone features such as texting in SMS/MMS for interpersonal communication, taking/sending/receiving pictures, playing electronic games and downloading ring tones for entertainment, and reading online news for information. As a result, $H_{1.3}$ was not supported.

Table 18.3 Correlation of demographics, leisure boredom, sensation seeking, self-esteem, and cell phone addiction

	Cell phone Addiction Index (MPAI)[a]	Cell phone Addiction Symptoms			
		Inability to Control Craving	Feeling Anxious & Lost	Withdrawal/ Escape	Produc- tivity Loss
Demographics					
Age		−0.08*	0.11**		
Gender (male=1)	−0.11**	0.11**			
Household monthly income					
Education		−0.10**			
Psychological Variables					
Leisure boredom	0.13**	0.18***			0.17***
Sensation Seeking	0.17***	0.18***	0.08*	0.16***	0.11**
Self-esteem	−0.19***	−0.22***	−0.14**		−0.15**

Notes
a   This is a composite measure of all 17 cell phone addiction symptom items; the higher the score, the higher the tendency to have the symptoms.
*   Figures are Pearson coefficients.
*   #p<=.1; *p<=.05; **p<=.01; ***p<=.001

Table 18.4 Regression of demographics, leisure boredom, sensation seeking, self-esteem, cell phone dependency symptoms, and social capital on patterns of cell phone use

Predictors	Patterns of cell phone calls					
	Minute of use per day		Minute of use per call		Number of people talk to regularly	
	r	ß	r	ß	r	ß
Demographics						
Age		0.10*			0.27***	0.26***
Gender (male = 1)			−0.13**	−0.10*	0.11**	
Household monthly income					0.11**	
Education	−0.09*	−0.11**	−0.08*		0.10*	
Psychological Variables						
Leisure boredom						
Sensation seeking	0.15***	0.18*				
Self-esteem		0.07#		−0.09*	0.15***	0.14**
Cell phone addiction symptoms						
Inability to control craving	0.36***	0.21***	0.27***	0.22***		
Feeling anxious & lost	0.29***	0.10*	0.16***			
Withdrawal/escape			0.16***		0.11**	
Productivity loss			0.14***		0.08*	
Social Capital						
Time spent with family/relative yesterday		0.13***				
Time spent with friends/classmates yesterday		0.23***		0.09*		
R^2		0.23		0.10		0.11
Final adjusted R^2		0.21		0.08		0.09

Notes
* Figures are Pearson's r and standardized beta coefficients.
* #p< = .1; *p< = .05; **p< = .01; ***p< = .001; N = 624

H$_{2.1}$ hypothesized that subjects who score high on sensation seeking will exhibit a higher tendency to be addicted to the cell phone. As shown in Table 18.3, the relationship between sensation seeking and MPAI was significant (r = .17, p<.001). Further bivariate analyses between sensation seeking and addiction symptoms also show significant results. Thus, H$_{2.1}$ was also supported. Contrary to an insignificant relationship existing between leisure boredom and usage pattern of cell phone, results in Table 18.4 show that sensation seeking and overall phone call usage patterns of the cell phone in minutes per day were found to be significantly related (r = .15, p<.001). The higher in sensation seeking one scores, the more the cell phone will be used. Therefore, $H_{2.2}$ was supported. $H_{2.3}$ predicted that subjects who score high on sensation seeking will report a higher amount of cell phone features use. As shown in Table 18.5, correlation relationships between sensation seeking and use of cell phone features for entertainment ($r = .22$, $p<.001$) and for information ($r = .12$, $p<.01$) were significant. Thus, these results supported $H_{2.3}$.

$H_{3.1}$ predicted that subjects who score high on self-esteem will demon-

Table 18.5 Regression of demographics, leisure boredom, sensation seeking, self-esteem, cell phone dependency, and social capital on features use

Predictors	Features Use					
	Interpersonal communication[a] (SMS)		Entertainment[b]		Information[c]	
	r	ß	r	ß	r	ß
Demographics						
Age		−0.19***	−0.14***	−0.12*		
Gender (male = 1)	−0.20***	−0.14***				
Household monthly income				0.07#		
Education	0.10*	0.20***	−0.12**		0.09*	0.10*
Psychological Variables						
Leisure boredom						
Sensation seeking			0.22***	0.17***	0.12**	
Self-esteem				−0.13**		
Cell phone addiction symptoms						
Inability to control craving	0.39***	0.21***	0.34***	0.20***	0.28***	0.23***
Feeling anxious & lost	0.40***	0.26***	0.24***		0.16***	
Withdrawal/escape	0.32***	0.12**	0.25***	0.09*	0.14***	
Productivity loss	0.17***	−0.09*	0.18***		0.22***	0.11*
Social Capital						
Time spent with family/ relative yesterday						
Time spent with friends/ classmates yesterday	0.17***	0.11**	0.18***	0.12**	0.13**	0.09*
R^2		0.29		0.20		0.11
Final adjusted R^2		0.27		0.18		0.09

Notes

a How often do they send/receive SMS/MMS/email messages? Scale: 1 = Never and 5 =Very often.
b How often do they send/receive pictures, play electronic games, or download ring tones on their cellular phones? Scale: 1 = Never and 5 =Very often.
c How often do they read online news? Scale: 1 = Never and 5 =Very often.
* Figures are Pearson's r and standardized beta coefficients.
* #$p<$ = .1; *$p<$ = .05; **$p<$ = .01; ***$p<$ = .001; N = 624

strate less tendency toward cell phone addiction than those who are dependent. Results in Table 18.3 indicate that self-esteem and MPAI were negatively and significantly linked (r = −.19, p<.001). This suggests that people who perceive themselves as being in control will be less likely to be a cell phone addict. As a result, $H_{3.1}$ was confirmed. Furthermore, $H_{3.2}$ proposed that subjects who score high on self-esteem will report higher frequency in cell phone calls. Data in Table 18.4 show that self-esteem was significantly related to the number of people who talk regularly via the cell phone (r = .15, p<.001), but the average length of each call was significantly shorter (r = −.09, p<.05). This suggests that confident people with a high self-esteem generally enjoy a large social circle, but they only spend a short time on the cell phone—just sufficient to achieve their ends. However, the amount of cell phone use (in minutes per day) was not linked to self-esteem. Thus, $H_{3.2}$ was only partially supported. According to $H_{3.3}$, it was proposed that subjects who score low on self-esteem will report a higher amount of cell phone features use. Results in Table 18.5 seem to provide partial support for this hypothesis because self-esteem was found only significantly and negatively related to entertainment (r = −.13, p<.01; e.g., taking/sending pictures, electronic games, and ring tone downloads).

Predicting cell phone use

To assess how demographics, leisure boredom, sensation seeking, self-esteem, cell phone addiction symptoms, and social capital can predict patterns of phone calls using the cell phone, three regression analyses were conducted. Results in Table 18.4 show that heavy use of cell phone calls in minutes per day was significantly linked to addiction symptoms, especially in the inability to control craving (β = .21, p<.001) and having anxiety and feeling lost (β = .10, p<.05). Scoring high in sensation seeking (β = .18, p<.05) was also predictive of the amount of cell phone calls. Being older (β = .10, p<.05), less educated (β = −.11, p<.05), and often got together with family/relatives (β = .13, p<.001) and friends/classmates (β = .23, p<.001) indicated those who used the cell phone calls for more minutes per day. These seven predictors explained 21 percent of the total variance. Data also show that exhibiting greater inability to control craving (β = .22, p<.001) in the use of the cell phone, being female (β = −.10, p<.05), and spending a lot of time with friends/classmates face-to-face (β = .09, p<.05) were also those who spent more minutes on each call. Finally, findings also reveal that adolescents and young adults who talked regularly to a large number of people on the cell phone tended to be older (β = .26, p<.001) and scored high in self-esteem (β = .14, p<.01). The last two regression equations explained 8 percent and 9 percent of the variance respectively.

Predicting features use

In predicting features use, three separate regression analyses were conducted, examining the predictive power of demographics, psychological variables, and addiction symptoms on three dependent measures—use of the cell phone for texting, for entertainment, and for information seeking. Results in Table 18.5 show that heavy users of texting features (such as SMS/MMS/e-mail) were those who exhibited more addictive symptoms such as feeling anxious and feeling lost without the cell phone and the thought of missing a call ($\beta = .26$, p<.001), having trouble controlling craving ($\beta = .21$, p<.001), and withdrawal and escape ($\beta = .12$, p<.01), but did not feel they had productivity loss due to excessive texting ($\beta = -.09$, p<.05). Demographically, heavy texters seemed to be younger, educated, and often females. However, no psychological predictors such as leisure boredom, sensation seeking, and self-esteem were found significant. Similar to SMS texting, having addiction symptoms such as inability to control craving ($\beta = .20$, p<.001) and use of the cell phone to withdraw and escape when feeling lonely and isolated ($\beta = .09$, p<.05) appeared to be significantly related to heavy use of entertainment features of the cell phone. High sensation seekers ($\beta = .17$, p<.001) seemed to use the cell phone for entertainment more so than others. In terms of age and social capital, they tended to be young ($\beta = -.12$, p<.05) and often got together with friends and classmates ($\beta = .12$, p<.01). Furthermore, highly educated ($\beta = .10$, p<.05) and being socially active ($\beta = .09$, p<.05) users who often used the cell phone for information seeking, such as reading news online, tended to be those who experienced great trouble in controlling craving ($\beta = .23$, p<.001) and experienced a significant decrease in productivity ($\beta = .11$, p<.05) as a direct result of the time spent on the cell phone for information. The three regression equations explained 27 percent, 18 percent, and 9 percent of the variance, respectively, for SMS use, for entertainment, and for information seeking.

Conclusions and discussion

Psychometric properties of the MPAS

One of the major aims of this study was to identify the underlying structure of adolescent cell phone addiction symptoms. Specifically, our data yield four clearly identifiable factors: inability to control craving, feeling anxious and lost, withdrawal and escape, and productivity loss. Principal components factor analysis results appear to provide adequate construct validity of the cell phone Addiction Scale (MPAS) and accounted for 57.7 percent of the variance. Moreover, not only is the 17-item MPAS able to provide a wealth of contextual information relating to adolescent cell phone addiction, but the data also yielded clear evidence for the multi-factorial nature of cell phone addiction symptoms—four distinct factors representing an array of domains of adolescents' behavioral consequences from cell phone addiction.

As a whole, MPAS (both the index MPAI and the four-symptom subscales) correlated mostly in the hypothesized manner with measures of psychologically meaningful constructs such as leisure boredom, sensation seeking, and self-esteem. These constructs cover a wide array of theoretically and practically important factors relevant for influencing cell phone addiction in general.

Effects of psychological attributes on cell phone addiction

In line with our hypotheses, the cell phone addiction index (MPAI) and addiction symptom subscales were inversely related to self-esteem and directly related to sensation seeking and leisure boredom. This means that the higher one scored on sensation seeking and leisure boredom, the higher the likelihood one would be addicted to the cell phone. Conversely, subjects who scored high on self-esteem—who perceived themselves as being in control—demonstrated less of a tendency to be addicted. While high sensation seekers (HSS) reported more addiction symptoms, those who scored high on leisure boredom experienced only inability to control craving and loss in productivity. Past research suggests that unless leisure is optimally arousing, it is experienced as boredom especially when having too much time available with too little to do (Iso-Ahola, 1980). According to Iso-Aloha and Weissinger (1991), limited leisure opportunities have been major contributing factors to leisure boredom. This seems logical because, as it was found in the study, the longer the leisure boredom state the individual experiences, the higher the likelihood of the person being addicted to the cell phone.

It is also interesting to note that sensation seeking and self-esteem played the largest role in cell phone addiction, while gender and leisure boredom appeared to have a lesser but significant influence. In particular, those who were female and had low self-esteem were the most vulnerable. These results seem to support the notion that adolescents and young adults like to experiment with rules, roles, and risks—often to deal with anxiety and boredom they purposely seek pleasure, variety, and stimulation through the use of the cell phone. Furthermore, this result is also in line with Gordon and Caltabiano's (1996) finding that adolescents who were the heaviest substance abusers and may have developed addictive behavior were those scoring low on self-esteem and high on sensation seeking.

Effects of psychological attributes on cell phone calls usage patterns

In terms of use, this study found that the more time one spent with family and friends, the more one would use the cell phone. This indicates that there is no decline or displacement of face-to-face interaction despite the increased use of the cell phone. Cell phone use may, in fact, facilitate or coordinate face-to-face interaction. As expected, regression results also show that those who used the cell phone more in minutes per day were those who scored high on sensation seeking, were older, less educated, and tended to exhibit more addiction symptoms (such as losing control, receiving complaints, and experiencing anxiety or craving). The relatively strong relationship between sensation seeking and daily cell phone use is consistent with the argument made by Donohew and his colleagues that high sensation seekers seek out arousal in mediated stimuli as well as in their real-world experience (Donohew *et al.*, 1991; Palmgreen *et al.*, 1995).

However, a comparison of the correlations and the regression analyses in Table 18.4 shows that the beta coefficients are often lower than the correlations or not significant at all between cell phone addiction symptoms and cell phone use variables. Given that psychological variables such as sensation seeking correlate significantly with addiction, this relationship suggests mediation. Therefore, the links between the psychological variables and cell phone use seem to be mediated by cell phone addiction. According to Baron and Kenny (1986), the necessary conditions for partial or full mediation are: direct relationships between (1) the proposed mediator and the exogenous variable; (2) the proposed mediator and the dependent variable; and (3) the exogenous and dependent variable. Further, the sufficient condition for partial mediation is that including the mediator variable or variables weakens the relationship between the exogenous and dependent variables. To test the possible mediation effect of addiction on cell phone use, a series of bivariate regressions using sensation seeking (the exogenous), the composite cell phone addiction index (the mediator), and the amount of cell phone use in minutes per day (the dependent variable) were conducted. Leisure boredom and self-esteem were excluded from the test since they were not significant predictors in minutes of use per day (as shown in Table 18.4). In this study, reductions in the standardized beta of 10 percent were accepted as representing substantively nontrivial evidence for partial mediation. Results show that inclusion of addiction (MPAI) as a mediator variable reduced the relationship of sensation seeking with cell phone use (in minutes per day) by 46.6 percent. Thus, it appears that cell phone addiction does partially mediate the effects of sensation seeking on cell phone use.

Consistent with the literature, low self-esteem did not predict the level of cell phone use (Bianchi & Phillips, 2005). Therefore, the present study supports our initial prediction that differential use of the cell phone depends on personality tendencies. Furthermore, it is also worthy to note that females tended to spend longer on each call, while those who were older and high on self-esteem talked to a larger pool of people on a regular basis using their cell phones. This suggests that, as a social technology, the cell phone has become a popular communication utility and a relationship facilitator.

Effects of psychological attributes on cell phone features use

Addiction symptoms were found to be the most powerful predictors for features use of the cell phone. Heavy feature users of the cell phone tended to be those who often felt anxious and even lost, experienced a higher sense of losing control without their cell phones, and often received complaints from family and friends.

Contrary to what was hypothesized, psychological attributes, such as leisure boredom, sensation seeking, and self-esteem, were not significantly linked to features used except for entertainment. Specifically, HSS tended to spend more time on the cell phone, especially on playing electronic games, downloading ring tones, and sending/receiving pictures. This finding may be explained by the fact that high sensation seekers gravitate toward the cell phones that offer more opportunities to satisfy their need for stimulation. In doing so, HSS can maintain their optimal arousal levels, especially through the varied, novel, and risky behaviors in their leisure by engaging in the entertainment functions of the cell phone (Gordon & Caltabiano, 1996). This is especially true and provides strong support for Arnett's (1992) proposal that adolescence is marked by higher levels of sensation seeking. The insignificant relationship between the use of SMS and psychological attributes indicates that SMS has become a preferred method of communication for young adults regardless of what psychological state they are in. Demographically, young and educated females tended to use SMS more, while the entertainment features attracted the young and the information functions for online news captivated the educated.

Limitation and suggestions for future studies

First, it is important to note that since the addiction questionnaire may contain some questions that were embarrassing or not applicable to respondents, particularly the younger adolescents or girls (e.g., learn to fly an airplane and parachute jumping), the overall result may have been affected. Second, spending time with friends face-to-face may be considered a normal developmental step among adolescents and young adults—important for their identity development. The heavy use of the cell phones may in fact be a natural developmental behavior. In light of this, interpretation of these findings should be conducted with caution. Future research should widen the scope of this study by comparing results of different age groups. Furthermore, the significant links between patterns of cell phone usage and sensation seeking, an inability to control craving, and feeling anxious and lost have clear implications for treatment and intervention. Intervention strategies need to focus on helping addicts slow down their decision-making processes so that they can appreciate the potential risks of their behavior. Treatment also needs to assist addicts in developing coping skills that will allow for more effective control of impulsivity. Future studies should focus on adaptive versus maladaptive patterns of adolescent cell phone use and, as such, would provide some directions for educators and parents with regard to the focus of intervention on strategies aimed at reducing addictive use of cell phones in adolescents.

References

American Psychiatric Association (1994) *The Diagnostic and Statistical Manual of Mental Disorders*, fourth edition. Washington, D.C.: American Psychiatric Association.

Arnett, J. (1992) "Reckless behavior in adolescence: A developmental perspective." *Developmental Review*, *12*, 339–373.

Baron, R. M., & Kenny, D.A. (1986) "The moderator-mediator distinction in social-psychological research: Conceptual, strategic, and statistical considerations." *Journal of Personality and Social Psychology*, *51*, 1173–1182.

Beard, K. W. (2002) "Internet addiction: Current status and implications for employees." *Journal of Employment Counseling*, *39*, 2–11.

Beard, K. W., & Wolf, E. M. (2001) "Modification in proposed diagnostic criteria for Internet addiction." *CyberPsychology and Behavior*, *4*(3), 377–383.

Bianchi, A., & Phillips, J. G. (2005) "Psychological predictors of problem cell phone use." *CyberPsychology & Behavior*, *8*(1), 39–51.

Burns, R. B. (1979) *The Self-Concept in Theory, Measurement, Development and Behavior*. London: Longman Group.

Calabrese, A., & Borchert, M. (1996) "Prospects for electronic democracy in the United States: Rethinking communications and social policy." *Media, Culture, and Society*, *18*, 249–268.

Chak, K., & Leung, L. (2004) "Shyness and locus of control as predictors of internet addiction and internet use." *CyberPsychology and Behavior*, *7*(5), 559–570.

Costa, P. T., & McCrae, R. R. (1985) *The NEO Personality Inventory Manual*. Odessa, FL: Psychology Assessment Resources, Inc.

Deaux, K., & Wrightsman, L. S. (1988) *Social Psychology*, fifth edition. Pacific Grove, CA: Brook/Cole.

Donohew, L., Lorch, E. P., & Palmgreen, P. (1991) "Sensation seeking and the targeting of televised anti-drug PSAs." In L. Donohew, H. E. Sypher, & W. J. Bukoski (eds.), *Persuasive Communication and Drug Abuse Prevention*. Hillsdale, NJ: Erlbaum, pp. 209–226.

Fukuyama, F. (2001) "Social capital, civil society and development." *Third World Quarterly*, *22*(1), 7–20.

Gordon, W. R., & Caltabiano, M. L. (1996) "Urban-urban differences in adolescents' self-esteem, leisure boredom, and sensation seeking as predictors of leisure-time usage and satisfaction." *Adolescence*, *31*(124), 883–901.

Griffiths, M. D. (1996) "Gambling on the Internet: A brief note." *Journal of Gambling Studies*, *12*, 471–473.

Griffiths, M. D. (1998) "Internet addiction: does it really exist?" In J. Gackenbach (ed.), *Psychology and the Internet: Intrapersonal, Interpersonal, and Transpersonal Applications*. New York: Academic Press, pp. 61–75.

Griffiths, M. D. (2000) "Does Internet and 'addiction' exist? Some case study evidence." *CyberPsychology and Behavior, 3*, 211–218.

Griffiths, M. D., & Hunt, N. (1998) "Dependence on computer games by adolescents." *Psychological Reports, 82*, 475–480.

Hill, A. B., & Perkins, R. E. (1985) "Towards a model of boredom." *British Journal of Psychology, 76*, 235–240.

Infante, D. A. (1976) "Persuasion as a function of the receiver's prior success or failure as a message source." *Communication Quarterly, 24*, 21–26.

Iso-Ahola, S. E. (1980) *Social Psychological Perspectives on Leisure and Recreation*. Dubuque, Iowa: Brown.

Iso-Ahola, S. E., & Crowley, E. D. (1991) "Adolescent substance abuse and leisure boredom." *Journal of Leisure Research, 23*(3), 260–271.

Iso-Ahola, S. E., & Weissinger, E. (1990) "Perceptions of boredom in leisure: Conceptualization, reliability and validity of the leisure boredom scale." *Journal of Leisure Research, 22*(1), 1–17.

Jessor, R., & Jessor, S. L. (1977) *Problem Behavior and Psychological Development: a Longitudinal Study of Youth*. New York: Academic Press.

Katz, J. E., & Akhus, M. (eds.), (2002) *Perceptual Contact: Mobile Communication, Private Talk, Public Performance*. Cambridge: Cambridge University Press.

Kivimaki, M., & Kalimo, R. (1996) "Self-esteem and the occupational stress process testing two alternative models in a sample of blue-collar workers." *Journal of Occupational Health Psychology, 1*, 187–196.

Lemon, J. (2002) "Can we call behaviors addictive?" *Clinical Psychologist, 6*, 44–49.

Lenhart, A., Madden, M., & Hitlin, P. (2005) "Teen and yechnology: Youth are leading the transition to a fully wired and mobile nation." Retrieved April 17, 2007, from http://www.pewinternet.org/pdfs/PIP_Teens_Tech_July2005web.pdf.

Leung, L. (2004) "Net-generation attributes and seductive properties of the Internet as predictors of online activities and Internet addiction." *CyberPsychology & Behavior, 7*(3), 333–348.

Leung, L., & Wei, R. (1999) "Who are the cell phone have-nots? Influences and consequences." *New Media and Society, 1*(2), 209–226.

Ling, R. (2004) *The Mobile Connection: the Cell Phone's Impact on Society*. San Francisco, CA: Morgan Kaufmann Publishers.

Mattick, R. P., & Baillie, A. (eds.), (1992. *National Campaign Against Drug Abuse: an Outlet for Approaches to Smoking Cessation (Monograph No. 19)*. Canberra: Australian Government Publishing Service.

Mukherjee, S. K., & Dagger, D. (1990) *The Size of the Crime Problem in Australia*, second edition. Canberra: Australian Institute of Criminology.

O'Malley, S. S., Jaffe, A., Chang, G., Schottenfeld, R. S., & Rounsaville, B. J. (1991) *Naltrexone in the Treatment of Alcohol Dependence: Preliminary Findings. Novel Pharmacological Interventions for Alcoholism*. New York: Springer-Verlag, pp. 148–157.

Orcutt, J. D. (1984) "Contrasting effects of two kinds of boredom on alcohol use." *Journal of Drug Issues, 14*, 161–173.

Orford, J. (2001) *Excessive Appetites: a Psychological View of Addictions*, second edition. Chichester, UK: Wiley.

Oyserman, D., & Markus, H. R. (1990) "Possible selves and delinquency." *Journal of Personality and Social Psychology, 59*(1), 112–125.

Palmgreen, P., Lorch, E. P., Donohew, L., Harrington, N., D'Silva, M., & Helm, D. (1995) "Reaching at-risk populations in a mass media drug abuse prevention campaign:

Sensation seeking, message sensation value, and drug use as mediators of PSA effectiveness." *Drugs and Society, 8*, 29–45.

Phillips, A. (1993) *On Kissing, Tickling, and Being Bored: Psychoanalytic Essays on the Unexamined Life*. Cambridge, MA: Harvard University Press.

Putnam, R. (1995) "Bowling alone: America's declining social capital." *Journal of Democracy, 6*(1), 65–78.

Rainie, L., & Keeter, S. (2006) "How Americans use their cell phones." Retrieved April 17, 2007, from http://www.pewinternet.org/pdfs/PIP_Cell_phone_study.pdf.

Rubin, A. M. (2002) "The uses-and-gratifications perspectives of media effects." In J. Bryant, & D. Zillmann, (eds.), *Media Effects: Advances in Theory and Research*, second edition. Mahwah, NJ: Lawrence Erlbaum.

Scherer, K. (1997) "College life on-line. Healthy and unhealthy Internet use." *Journal of College Student Development, 38*, 655–665.

Shaffer, H. J. (1996) "Understanding the means and objects of addiction: Technology, the Internet and gambling." *Journal of Gambling Studies, 12*, 461–469.

Shotton, M. A. (1989) *Computer Addiction?: a Study of Computer Dependency*. London: Taylor & Francis.

Smith, E. A., & Caldwell, L. L. (1989) "The perceived quality of leisure experiences among smoking and nonsmoking adolescents." *Journal of Early Adolescence, 9*, 153–162.

Volpicelli, J. R., Alterman, A. I., Hayashida, M., & O'Brien, P. (1992) "Naltrexone in the treatment of alcohol dependence." *Archives of General Psychiatry, 49*: 876–880.

Wallace, P. (1999) *The Psychology of the Internet*. New York: Cambridge University Press.

Young, K. S. (1996) *Caught in the Net: How to Recognize the Signs of Internet Addiction—and a Winning Strategy for Recovery*. New York: John Wiley & Sons.

Young, K. S. (1998) "Internet addiction: the emergence of a new clinical disorder." *CyberPsychology & Behavior, 1*(3), 237–244.

Young, K. S. (1999) "Internet addiction: Symptoms, evaluation, and treatment." In L., VandeCreek, & T. Jackson, (eds.), *Innovations in Clinical Practice: A Source Book*, Vol. 17. Sarasota, FL: Professional Resource Press, pp. 19–31.

Zuckerman, M. (1979) *Sensation Seeking: Beyond the Optimal Level of Arousal*. Hillsdale, NJ: Lawrence Erlbaum Associates.

Zuckerman, M. (1994) *Behavioral Expressions and Biosocial Bases of Sensation Seeking*. New York: Cambridge University Press.

Zuckerman, M., Eysenck, S., & Eysenck, H. J. (1978) "Sensation-seeking in England and America: Cross-cultural, age, and sex comparisons." *Journal of Consulting and Clinical Psychology, 46*(1), 139–149.

Zuckerman, M., Kolin, E. A., Price, L., & Zoob, I. (1964) "Development of a sensation-seeking scale." *Journal of Consulting Psychology, 28*, 477–482.

Index